RESEARCH IN ORGANIZATIONAL BEHAVIOR

Volume 6 • 1984

RESEARCH IN ORGANIZATIONAL BEHAVIOR

An Annual Series of Analytical Essays and Critical Reviews

Editors: **BARRY M. STAW**
School of Business Administration
University of California, Berkeley

L. L. CUMMINGS
Kellogg Graduate School of Management
Northwestern University

VOLUME 6 • 1984

 JAI PRESS INC.

Greenwich, Connecticut   *London, England*

CONTENTS

LIST OF CONTRIBUTORS

Seymour Adler

Applied Psychology Program
Management Science Department
Stevens Institute of Technology

Stephen R. Barley

Sloan School of Management
Massachusetts Institute of
    Technology

Nakiye A. Boyacigiller

School of Business Administration
University of California, Berkeley

Kim Cameron

Director of Organization Studies
National Center for Higher
    Education Management Systems
Colorado

Faye Crosby

Department of Psychology
Yale University

Thomas G. Cummings

Department of Organizational
    Behavior
University of Southern California

Richard L. Daft

Department of Management
Texas A & M University

Robert H. Lengel

Department of Management and
    Marketing
University of Texas at San Antonio

Daniel R. Ilgen

Department of Psychological
    Sciences
Purdue University

James C. Naylor

Department of Psychological
    Sciences
Purdue University

Karlene Roberts

School of Business Administration
University of California, Berkeley

Blair Sheppard

Fugua School of Business
Duke University

John Van Maanen

Sloan School of Management
Massachusetts Institute of
    Technology

Howard Weiss

Department of Psychological
    Sciences
Purdue University

EDITORIAL STATEMENT

This volume of Research in Organizational Behavior is perhaps the broadest we have published in the Series. The chapters span from topics in individual behavior to questions of interorganizational and crosscultural behavior, and the approach of the essays ranges from critical analyses of established topics to the mapping of relatively new territory in the field.

The volume begins with three micro level chapters that reformulate some older issues in individual behavior. Howard Weiss and Seymour Adler review the application of personality constructs in the field, arguing that the concept of individual differences has been seriously misused, and suggesting several conceptual and methodological improvements. Faye Crosby provides a historical review of relative deprivation theory, illustrating how deprivation research can be conducted in organizations, and posing many provocative questions that should stimulate research on job attitudes. Finally, Naylor and Ilgen offer a conceptual model for understanding the effects of goal-setting, using a set of deductive theoretical statements that is much more precise and elegant than we usually see in organizational behavior.

The second set of chapters in this volume are both more macroscopic in focus and normative in tone. Blair Sheppard reviews the diverse literature on conflict resolution and presents a framework which specifies gaps in the type of research which has been conducted on third party interventions. Richard Daft and Robert Lengal present an analysis of information processing in organizations, concentrating on how organizations can simultaneously retain the richness inherent in environmental stimuli as well as the simplicity and clarity needed to conduct organizational business. Finally, Kim Cameron provides a fresh look at organizational effectiveness through a Fault Tree Analysis that specifies in a rather straightforward fashion the sources of ineffectiveness within an organization.

The third group of chapters in this volume goes beyond the analysis of individuals, groups, or social structures within organizations. John Van Maanen and Stephen Barley present a detailed analysis of occupational communities that span organizations and show how occupational norms, loyalties and commitments can exert as much influence on behavior as more traditional organizational socialization. Tom Cummings then examines the emerging subarea of transorganizational development, the practice of creating, changing and improving multi-organizational systems. Finally, Karlene Roberts and Nakiye Boyacigiller critique current cross-national research on organizational behavior, specifying those substantive and methodological changes that are needed for future research.

As with past volumes of the series, the chapters were written by an invited group of scholars who wished to develop their ideas more fully than is typically possible in journal publications. We feel that the essays in the present volume, while diverse in nature, all represent useful advances for the field and deserve the serious attention of organizational researchers.

Barry M. Staw
Berkeley, California

L. L. Cummings
Evanston, Illinois

PERSONALITY AND ORGANIZATIONAL BEHAVIOR

Howard M. Weiss and Seymour Adler

ABSTRACT

In this paper traditional and potential roles for personality constructs in explanations of work behavior are discussed. The paper begins with an overview of the way personality has been treated in organizational research, arguing that current negative evaluations about the contributions of personality are based upon research that is conceptually and methodologically limited. It follows with a discussion of three general topics—situation strength, dependent variable analysis and interactions—to illustrate issues relevant to a more appropriate examination of personality and organizational behavior. It concludes with a discussion of the nature of personality constructs and the efficient use of personality to advance theories of individual behavior in organizations.

Research in Organizational Behavior, vol. 6, pages 1–50
ISBN: 0-89232-351-5

INTRODUCTION

Researchers in Organizational Psychology have not had much regard for personality constructs in recent years. Personality differences, once fundamental to the study of work motivation, attitudes, and leadership are now assigned only secondary roles in most theories of organizational behavior, if they are given any role at all. The current situation is typified by Mitchell's statement in his 1979 Annual Review of Organizational Behavior:

> We will find throughout this review that personality traits appear as predictors of attitudes (e.g. involvement) motivation (e.g. expectancies) and leadership (e.g. behavioral styles), but the central focus of that research is usually motivation, attitudes, or leadership and not personality.
>
> *This secondary role seems justified and necessary.* If Mischel's arguments are correct than we will be better served by continuing in the direction we are heading. Personality variables probably control only a minor percentage of variance in behavior when compared to situational factors (Mitchell, 1979, p. 247) (Italics added)

It is possible that Mitchell's statement may be seen as too extreme by many or even most organizational researchers. Yet there is no real evidence to suggest anything but implicit acceptance of the position. While it is true that many current models of various sorts of organizational behaviors have obligatory boxes designed to contain "individual differences," in most cases these boxes play no fundamental theoretical role and the empirical research on the models tends to focus on other issues. Some theories are even quite explicit in stating their avoidance of personality constructs. Van Maanen and Schein (1979) for example in presenting their theory of organizational socialization state "a theory of organizational socialization must not allow itself to become too preoccupied with individual characteristics . . ." (p. 216).

We disagree with those who advocate relegating personality to minor or nonexistant positions in theories of individual behavior in organizations. We are inclined to agree with their assessment of the contribution of personality to current understanding of organizational behavior. On the whole that contribution has been disappointing. We disagree however with the conclusions about personality which can be drawn from that research. Historically, personality research on organizational behavior has suffered from inadequate conceptual development and poor methodology and these factors have conspired to give personality a bad name. It is simply premature and unproductive to make any general normative statements about restricting the role of personality in organizational research. Adequate tests of the usefulness of personality must be conducted with theory based, operationally precise efforts, and past and current research on personality and OB has failed to do this.

This paper presents an overview of the way personality has been used in organizational research and suggests issues of theory and design which must be addressed if personality is to be given a fair hearing as an explanatory construct. We should state early on that we do not intend to defend, a priori, the usefulness of personality. Such a defense can only come from the outcome of adequate research. Nor do we presume to prescribe the nature of that research. Our objective is simply to raise and discuss certain issues of theory and method which bear on studying personality and work behavior.

Many readers are probably aware that the explanatory usefulness of personality constructs has once again become a popular topic in psychology. Strong attacks (Mischel, 1968; 1973) have stimulated creative responses. Clearly we have been influenced by this recent work and our discussion will rely heavily on this literature. However, this paper will not be a tutorial on current research and thinking in the field of social and personality psychology. Our objective will be the integration of relevant aspects of this work with organizational behavior.

We should also say that our discussion will focus almost totally on the use of trait conceptions of personality within a nomothetic framework. We recognize that a number of interesting nontrait approaches to personality are being examined (see Helson & Mitchell, 1978; Rychlak, 1981). However, our field has been and continues to be dominated by trait conceptions of personality and there is much of relevance being done with this approach. The limitation to traits is therefore based primarily on interest, ours and what we see as the field's. We believe that this limitation in no way inhibits the usefulness of the discussion.

Our preference for a nomothetic viewpoint is less arbitrary. We have been aware of a number of recent papers advocating idiographic approaches to organizational analyses of various sorts (e.g. Luthans & Davis, 1982). Our position is simply that in the area of personality, recurrent attempts to resurrect Allport's (1937) often referenced and often misunderstood statement about idiographic analyses have simply not been, nor will be, productive for advancing the science of individual behavior.

Frank (1982) has traced the development of idiography from the Scottish philosopher Duns Scotus through existentialist positions on scientific knowledge. He notes that the core of an idiographic position is that every individual, indeed every object, has a certain essence or "thisness" and that there can be no real understanding of the object without understanding its essence. Additionally, since each essence is unique and cannot be resolved into class concepts, the search for scientific laws and generalizations is an impediment to real knowledge. A true idiographic position precludes as meaningful knowledge the acceptance of lawful relationships which generalize across individuals. We do not take this position nor do we think that it characterizes any but a minority of organizational researchers.

We should point out that Allport's position was never so extreme. He did not reject the meaningfulness of scientific generalizations and envisioned nomothetic and idiographic "sciences" coexisting in the study of personality. For example, in discussing the differences between the two approaches Allport (1937) stated "the dichotomy is too sharp: it requires a psychology divided against itself . . . It is more helpful to regard the two methods as overlapping and contributing to each other" (p. 22). More importantly for our position, the issues which prompted Allport to call for an idiographic approach are easily resolved within a nomothetic framework (Frank, 1982). Allport argued that the "idiographic sciences . . . endeavor to understand some particular event in nature or society" (Allport, 1937, p. 22). Clearly, as Frank (1982) points out, there is nothing contradictory about explanation of particular events within the framework of nomothetic generalizations. In fact, nomothetic science is based upon the deduction from the general to the particular through laws and singular observations. Finally, Frank argues that most so-called idiographic analyses are based upon hidden nomothetic principles. He cites history which is often taken as a prototypic idiographic approach and notes that the historian bases his analysis on unstated generalizations and assumed regularities. Similarly therapists are described as taking an idiographic approach, but essentially depend on nomothetic generalizations.

In arguing for a nomothetic viewpoint we are not denying the practical or scientific importance of analyzing particular cases. However, we believe that this is accomplishable within a nomothetic framework. To us it seems clear that idiographic approaches are nomothetic at heart. The difference between the two lies in whether the matrix of generalizations and set of categories are theory based and public or implicit and private to the observer. Based upon these considerations we see no reason to abandon the nomothetic approach to studying personality and work behavior.

Finally, we should note that this is not a review of personality influences on organizational behavior. In fact we have taken great pains to avoid discussing such findings. Extensive reviews on specific topics have been presented elsewhere (see, for example, White, 1978, on job design or Bass, 1981, on leadership) and we have therefore seen our task as one of extracting underlying issues of theory and method which bear on examining personality influences. Certainly some key findings will be noted.

However, these notations will be made primarily to illustrate more general arguments.

Our paper has three major segments. The first step toward advancing new approaches and issues is an understanding of current approaches and we therefore begin with a general overview of the way personality is studied in OB research. We do this by reviewing four areas of organizational activity and drawing some common themes from these representative literatures. Our second section discusses three general issues—interactionism, dependent variable analysis and situation strength—which need to be addressed if our understanding of personality influences on organizational behavior is going to advance. Finally, we conclude with a general discussion of the explanatory nature of personality constructs and the efficient use of such constructs in theories of individual behavior in organizations.

PERSONALITY IN ORGANIZATIONAL BEHAVIOR RESEARCH

We have structured our discussion of the way personality constructs have been and are now being used in organizational research around three non–orthogonal issues; their role in theory, the types of research designs used, and the types of personality variables examined. Although these issues obviously do not capture the myriad ways in which personality has been integrated into OB research, differences in these areas struck us as particularly meaningful as we examined the nature of personality research in organizations.

Role in Theory

When personality constructs are incorporated into theories of individual behavior in organizations, the nature of that incorporation varies on two dimensions; centrality and specification of mediating processes.

1. Centrality. Theories that utilize personality variables differ in the extent to which personality is an integral component of the explanatory framework being advanced. A test of centrality would be to ask whether the theory would still exist coherently if the personality variable were removed. Theories used in OB research have clearly differed in this regard. For example, self–esteem lies at the core of Korman's (1970; 1976) theory of work motivation. Since, in his view, people are motivated to perform in a manner consistent with their self–esteem, removing self–esteem from the theory would destroy its usefulness. By contrast, in Lawler's (1971) revision of expectancy theory, self–esteem is seen as only one influence on effort—performance expectancies. While the introduction of this personality variable into the model may help enhance its comprehensiveness, removing self–esteem would basically leave the central components of the theory unaffected. Unlike Korman's self–consistency theory, the validity of Lawler's expectancy theory does not rest on the inclusion of self–esteem. We should add that centrality does not imply that the personality construct is seen as the sole influence on behavior, nor is it equivalent to a theory based upon direct as opposed to interactive effects. For example, need for Achievement and Fear of Failure are both central to the theory of achievement motivation (Atkinson, 1964), but without additional knowledge about the probability and incentive values of success and failure, specific predictions about motivation and behavior cannot be derived.

   2. *Specification of Mediating Processes.*   Theories also differ in the extent to which the links between personality and criteria are specified. Obviously much of the personality research in our field is not systematically derived from theory, personnel selection research for example, and in such research, personality–criteria links are rarely elaborated on. While this is certainly more likely to occur in research that is not theory driven, theoretical perspectives which incorporate personality also vary on this dimension. For example, the mediating processes linking LPC and group performance are not specified in Fiedler's (1967) contingency theory of leadership. By contrast, other theories systematically work through the linkages between personality and the other variables being studied. To return to Lawler's (1971) revised expectancy theory, self esteem is hypothesized specifically to affect effort—performance expectancies, which in turn interact with performance—outcome beliefs and valences to influence motivation. While one might expect centrality to be positively associated with specification of mediating processes, it is clear by looking at these two examples that this is not always the case. LPC is central to Fiedler's theory while self esteem is peripheral to Lawler's.

Role in Design

   We have drawn on Magnusson and Endler (1977), Howard (1979), Terborg (1981) and others to identify four ways that personality can be treated in the design of research. These different design treatments correspond to differences in expected personality-behavior relationships.

   1. *Direct Effects.*   Here the direct effect of a personality variable on some relevant dependent variable is examined. In such research, the effects of other personality and situational variables are seen as irrelevant to interpretation of the effects of the personality variable in question and

are either ignored, controlled or reported separately. While much of the OB research fitting this design is cross–sectional, the research generally is interpreted in terms of the personality variable having a direct causal influence on levels of the criterion in question.

2. *Mechanistic Interaction.* In mechanistic interaction designs, the effects of a personality variable on a criterion are considered at least partially dependent on other situational and/or personal factors. Included in this category would be those studies in the analysis of variance tradition, in which main effects of personality and situational variables, as well as their interactive effects, are isolated. Also included would be those studies in the correlational tradition, in which personality is seen to moderate the relationship between a situational variable and the criterion, or in which the situation is seen to moderate the relationship between personality and the criterion. The mechanistic interaction design, like the direct design, implies a clear distinction between independent and dependent variables (Magnusson & Endler, 1977; Olweus, 1977). While most mechanistic interactions in OB examine the interactive effects of persons and situations, interactive effects of multiple personality constructs can and have been studied in the same way (see for example, McClelland & Boyatzis, 1982). In contrast with the direct design which examines single bivariate relationships (what Mischel, 1968, calls "personality coefficients"), mechanistic interaction designs are used to investigate more complex multivariate relationships.

3. *Reciprocal Effects.* In both the direct and interaction designs described above, personality is studied as an independent variable. Studies which look at reciprocal effects are those in which personality is treated as the dependent variable. Personality has been conceptualized as the dependent variable in studies on the effects of job ambiguity (Brousseau & Prince, 1981), rural and urban upbringing on adult work needs (Adler, Aranya & Amernic, 1981), and job mobility on locus of control (Hammer & Vardi, 1981). As with studies using the designs described above, most of the studies of reciprocal effects in the OB literature have, in fact, relied on data collected cross-sectionally.

4. *Dynamic Interaction.* While the direct effects design conceptualizes personality as the independent variable, and the reciprocal effect design treats personality as the dependent variable, the dynamic interaction design "stresses an interaction process in which persons and situations form an inextricably interwoven structure (Magnusson & Endler, 1977, p. 18)." In this view, personality, situations and behavior are continuously influencing each other in a process that Bandura (1978) calls reciprocal determinism. Examples of research examining dynamic interactions include

the work of Duncan and Fiske (1978) on verbal interaction, Bales and Cohen (1979) on the development of Symlog to analyze group interactions, and the 10 year longitudinal study on the mutual influences of job conditions and personality reported by Kohn and Schooler (1982). While the conceptual emphasis in these designs is on the ongoing reciprocal influences of personality and on personality (Endler & Magnusson, 1976; Schneider, 1983), statistically, in any given analysis, personality is temporarily treated as the dependent or independent variable.

Type of Personality Variable

Personality constructs employed in OB research can be grouped into two broad categories, although some constructs have components of both of these categories.

1. *Cognitive.* These refer to characteristic properties of the individual's perceptual and thought processes, how the individual processes information. Such cognitive style variables (Goldstein & Blackman, 1978) as cognitive complexity, reflectivity–impulsivity, dogmatism, and locus of control would be included in this category. Also included would be stable differences in the manner in which people perceive the world around them. Well known examples of such perceptual personality constructs would be field articulation or field dependence-independence (Witkin & Goodenough, 1977), cognitive complexity (Goldstein and Blackman, 1978) and self–monitoring (Snyder, 1974).

2. *Motivational.* Those stable individual differences in the why, when, where and how behavior is energized and maintained comprise the motivational personality variables. Needs, motives, and values all fall into this category. Stable affective or drive–related variables, like trait anxiety, would be included here as well.

Overview of Literature

In order to capture a sense of how personality constructs have been employed, research in four representative areas will be described within a framework of the descriptive categories just discussed.

Job Scope

The extensive use of individual difference variables in the job scope literature has its roots in the classic studies by Turner and Lawrence (1965) and Hulin and Blood (1968). These early studies utilized the sociological constructs of urban–rural upbringing and alienation from middle class norms to explain different worker reactions to jobs. Since the important research of Hackman and Lawler (1971), the subsequent development of the Job Characteristics Model by Hackman and Oldham (1975; 1980) and the construction of the Job Diagnostic Survey (Hackman & Oldham, 1976), personality variables have been included in most studies of job scope. This extensive use of personality makes the job scope literature instructive for examining how personality has been studied when it is considered important and its importance follows from theory. As stated previously, our review will describe how personality is treated rather than the nature and extent of personality effects. Reviews of this latter issue are available in Hackman and Oldham (1980), Roberts and Glick (1981), and White (1978).

Although personality constructs have been widely used in research on job scope, personality typically plays a peripheral role in the theories being tested. The best–developed and most frequently employed theory of job scope, the Job Characteristics Model (Hackman & Oldham, 1975), has as its prime focus a description of the influence of core job characteristics on the psychological states and subsequent behavioral reactions of workers. Personality is introduced into the theory to specify the type of person for whom the model is more or less likely to be predictive. The function of personality, then, is to establish some boundary conditions for the effectiveness of the model, to "fine–tune" (Mitchell, 1979) the model. It is assumed that for people in general, the model will be valid. Were personality to be removed, the Job Characteristic Model would still stand as a coherent theory of job scope.

The Job Characteristics Model says relatively little about the linkages between the aspect of personality considered and the other components of the theory. In Hackman and Lawlers' (1971) original paper, they did provide a brief discussion of the nature of the linkage. Their initial position was that enriched jobs provide intrinsic rewards related to higher order need fulfillment and therefore enrichment should work only for those for whom these needs are salient. Essentially, in trying to use an expectancy framework to understand the effects of task characteristics, they imply that higher order need strength affects the valences of outcomes provided by working on enriched jobs. This was a reasonable starting point. However, it should be noted that neither instrumentalities nor valences are presented as specific components of the model and no discussion of how HONS might effect, in a unique way, any of the three key psychological states is provided. As research on the model has progressed, the linkages have become, if anything, less precise. Recent statements of the theory (Hackman & Oldham, 1980) make no systematic use of expectancy theory to derive a role for Growth Need Strength and GNS is now hypothesized to moderate a number of relationships less predictable from valence differences within an expectancy framework (Hackman & Oldham, 1980). No research has been conducted which tries to explicate the way moderator or main effects of GNS on perceptions, psychological states or outcomes might occur and linkages to antecedent or consequent components are left unclear.

In the job scope literature, personality is almost always studied using mechanistic interaction designs, with personality variables analyzed as moderators of task characteristics—criteria relationships. The mechanistic interaction design so dominates the thinking of researchers that many often neglect to report the direct zero order correlations of personality and the dependent variables or the job scope measures. Historically, the rigid use of the mechanistic interaction framework can be traced directly to Turner and Lawrence's (1965) study of moderating influences on reactions to task characteristics. The use of the approach was solidified by the work of Hackman and Lawler (1971) which has served as a model for subsequent research on job scope. So influential was Hackman's and Lawler's original design that through much of the 1970s, research continued to use their subgrouping approach to moderator analysis, with many researchers going as far as using the same arbitrary top–third, bottom–third split (Roberts & Glick, 1981). Although we now see more use of the moderated regression approach (Abdel-Halim, 1979; Arnold & House, 1980; Champoux & Peters, 1980), this is simply a more appropriate way of examining mechanistic interactions and does not represent a change in thinking about the nature of personality effects.

A peripheral role for personality in a mechanistic interaction framework was logical as an initial approach to studying personality and job scope. Peripheral was logical because the essential issue was the general effect of some property of the environment (tasks). Mechanistic interaction was logical within the context of an experimental tradition which, because of the direct manipulation of stimuli and the random assignment of subjects to conditions, directed thinking towards persons and situations as separate causal variables [B = f(P, E)] that, while independent, could have interactive effects on some dependent measure [B = f(P, E, P × E)].

Strict adherence to this conceptualization of persons and situations as independent now seems limiting with the recognition that people can choose the situations they encounter, they can modify their tasks to fit their needs, their behavior is a function of their perceptions and their perceptions are only partly determined by objective task properties, etc. As a result, we see more attempts to move away from the traditional approach. Examples include Salancik and Pfeffer's (1977, 1978) work, the research by Stone (1979) and Jones and Butler (1980) on the direct effects of personality on perceptions of job characteristics and the interesting work on dynamic interactions by James and Jones (1980) and Kohn and Schooler (1982).

Personality constructs used in job scope research are almost exclusively motivational. The reason for this is best understood by again examining the historical context of personality research in this area. Turner and Lawrence's (1965) original moderator results were based on demographic analyses and explained by the authors using sociological constructs. There soon ensued a concerted effort to provide a more psychological explanation of these original results and that effort focused primarily on motivational variables in the form of needs or values.

Blood and Hulin (1968) offered an explanation in terms of individual differences in a constellation of variables they labeled as "middle class norms." Although their empirical research was conducted at a community level of analysis and many of their construct labels had a sociological ring, their explanation was primarily psychological, focusing on differences at the individual level, and motivational, referring to variations in work values and needs. Research stimulated by this work has been more explicit in examining individual differences in motivational personality constructs (see for example, Stone 1976).

The explanation provided by Hackman and Lawler (1971), the next influential attempt to translate the Turner and Lawrence (1965) findings into psychological constructs, was fundamentally quite similar to Hulin and Blood (1968). To be sure, the Hackman and Lawler position was substantially better grounded in psychological theory, derived essentially from a combination of expectancy theory and Maslow's hierarchy of needs. It also was initially more thorough in explicating the mediating processes. Yet their construct of Higher Order Need Strength was and remains, in the more recent form of Growth Need Strength (Hackman & Oldham, 1975), motivational in character. The development of operationalizations of the Hackman and Oldham constructs has contributed to the domination of motivational personality constructs, specifically Growth Need Strength, in research on personality effects. Not only has much of the job scope research conceptualized personality in terms of this specific variable, measurement of GNS has been almost exclusively limited to the GNS scales included in the Job Diagnostic Survey (Hackman & Oldham, 1975) or close variants of these scales (e.g., the measure of self-actualization need strength used by Sims & Szilagyi, 1976). As a result, findings in this area may not only be construct-bound (motivational variables), they are to a large extent measure-bound, with an instrument whose construct validity has been seriously questioned (Aldag & Brief, 1975; Stone, Ganster, Woodman & Fusilier, 1979) and whose personality construct is drawn from a theory (Maslow's) which has been appropriately

criticized both for its conceptual fuzziness and its lack of empirical support (Wahba & Bridwell, 1976).

While recent work in the area has begun to pay attention to more cognitive personality variables (Sims & Szilagyi, 1976; Stone, 1979; Weiss
& Shaw, 1979), motivational approaches continue to be dominant. As a
result, it is fair to say that discussions of research on personality and job
scope are limited to the effects of motivational variables of a very circumscribed type.

After reviewing personality–job scope findings, White (1978) concluded
that this whole line of research would best be abandoned. Our review of
the way personality has been treated would suggest that White's conclusion is premature. We have seen that designs other than mechanistic interaction and personality variables that are non–motivational have
scarcely been employed. Too often the use of personality has been based
not on theory but on the availability of the Job Diagnostic Survey, a clear
manifestation of what Kaplan (1964) calls the Law of the Instrument.

Our conclusions about the effects of the original research by Hulin and
Blood or Hackman, Lawler and Oldham should not be read as a criticism
of these early efforts. That work was, in a way, too stimulating. Particularly in the case of the Job Characteristics Model, the comparative comprehensiveness of the theory, the development of theory–based instru-
mentation and the initial empirical payoffs created a compelling paradigm
for studying job characteristics. Unfortunately, the initial success of that
paradigm restricted thinking about alternative ways of incorporating personality into job scope theory. We are now seeing some movement in
other directions. For example, Salancik's and Pfeffer's (1978) Social Information Processing approach suggests alternative ways in which personality might influence perceptions and evaluations of task characteristics. Activation Arousal Theory reference might be useful in suggesting
more complex and well defined roles for personality variables related to
characteristic arousal or anxiety levels. In any case, our examination of
the limited way in which personality has been studied in job scope research to date makes it clear that contrary to White's (1978) assessment,
the potential contribution of personality in this area has scarcely been
explored.

Leadership

In contrast with the job scope area, leadership research has not been
dominated by any one approach. Yet, by and large, when personality has
been introduced into leadership theory, it has played a central role. Trait
theories of leadership (i.e., Ghiselli, 1971), explicitly argue that leaders
can be distinguished from followers, and successful leaders from unsuc-

cessful leaders, on the basis of specific personality traits. While, it is often the case that theory is not employed to make specific a priori predictions about which trait will be important, trait approaches clearly place personality, along with demographic and ability variables, at the core of leadership theory.

The centrality of personality constructs is also exhibited in the leadership research out of the Ohio State tradition (Fleishman, 1953; Halpin & Winer, 1957). This work is often seen as a major break from the trait approach which characterized the area before 1950. Indeed in his 1973 retrospective Fleishman quite explicitly talks of the sense of excitement felt in moving away from traits and focusing on leader behaviors. Yet actual analysis of the nature of the constructs and measures indicates that this movement was more apparent than real. Consideration and Initiating Structure are nothing if they are not dispositional constructs. The LBDQ, SBDQ and LOQ clearly are meant to assess broad cross–situational behavioral tendencies. That the Ohio State researchers were reluctant to use these labels to refer to supposed internal entities or personal characteristics does not alter the fact that the constructs are operationalized and utilized in the same way as are other trait variables. The absence, until recently, of any significant research on the determinants of these "behaviors" further indicates that their development was less of a break from the personality tradition than is usually believed.

The centrality of personality traits in leadership research is not limited to main–effect conceptualizations. In Fielder's (1967) Contingency Model of leadership, the effects of LPC, which is often conceptualized as a stable personality trait (Fiedler, 1967; Rice, 1978; Strube & Garcia, 1981), can only be predicted with knowledge of the situation. Yet LPC is, of course, a central rather than peripheral component of Fiedler's theory of leadership.

This tendency for personality to play a more central role in leadership research is not, however, manifested in more recent work on perceptions of leader behavior (Lord, Foti & Phillips, 1981), the symbolic nature of leadership (Pfeffer, 1981) or leader attributions (Mitchell, Green & Wood, 1981). Yet, these would appear to be areas where differences in perceptual and processing variables could make a contribution (see, for example, Weiss & Adler, 1981).

While research and theory on leadership frequently consider personality as central to understanding leader behavior and effectiveness, too often the linkages between personality and other components of the theory remain unexplicated. Even the contingency model, which made a significant contribution by advocating the importance of the interaction between persons and situations, has very little to say about the links between LPC and group outcomes. In fact, the history of the model is partially a story of attempts to derive a meaningful mediating process to explain inductively derived LPC-situation interactions, with the explanations offered over the years being less than satisfying. This lack of attention to mediation is also generally true for leadership style research, although path–goal theory (Evans, 1970; House, 1971) has attempted to specify some of the links between Consideration and Initiating Structure on the one hand and follower motivation and satisfaction on the other.

While most of the Industrial/Organizational research on leader traits has left linkages unspecified, there are noteworthy exceptions in small group work. Here, for instance, researchers have offered models that link specific traits (e.g., extroversion or energy) to behaviors (e.g., rate of talking), leader behavior to group acceptance, and acceptance, in turn, to group performance (e.g., see Bass, 1981, Chapter 6).

Classic research on personality and leadership was clearly dominated by direct effects designs (see Bass, 1981, for a review). Much research using the direct effect design is still being conducted (for example, Anderson & Schneier, 1978, on locus of control and leader effectiveness and Miner's, 1978, work on managerial motivation) particularly when the focus is on managerial selection and training. However, generally the main effect design has given way to the mechanistic interaction design. Fiedler's (1967) Contingency Model is, of course, specifically structured to reflect the mechanistic interaction of persons and situations and research on the model typically analyzes the pattern of personality outcome correlations across varying situational conditions. In fact, Fielder explicitly dismisses the possibility of any meaningful reciprocal effects of the situation on leader personality. Path goal theory (House, 1971) and work on substitutes for leadership (Kerr & Jermier, 1978) are additional examples of this design. Mechanistic interaction in leadership research is not limited to person–situation effects as some work has focused on multiple trait effects as well. Examples include Fleishman and Harris (1962), O'Reilly and Roberts (1978) and Larson, Hunt and Osborne (1976) in the Ohio State tradition and McClelland's work on the Leadership Motive Pattern (McClelland & Boyatzis, 1982).

Recently, leadership research has begun to examine reciprocal effects on leader behavior (Podsakoff, 1982), but only a few studies have addressed whether these reciprocal effects generalize to leader personality. One such study is Bons, Bass and Komorita's (1970) longitudinal examination of how years and type of military experience affect the LPC of military leaders. Overall though, while reciprocal effects on leadership have begun to receive well–deserved attention, systematic exploration has yet to be made on reciprocal effects on leader personality, or on dynamic interactions between leader personality and the leadership situation.

Research following the trait model has often used the "shotgun" approach in the choice of personality variables. While generally this research has neither been guided by nor contributed to leadership theory, it has generated data over a broad array of motivational, cognitive, and perceptual constructs. New personality measures are quickly incorporated into leadership trait research. At the same time, it is interesting to note the difficulty in classifying the traits used in some of the more systematic research on leader characteristics. LPC, for instance, has alternatively been understood as a motivational variable reflecting differences in primary or secondary needs, a cognitive variable reflecting differences in cognitive complexity and an attitudinal variable, simply reflecting beliefs about one's least preferred co–worker (Rice, 1978). This has contributed to the inability to find a reasonable theoretical explanation for the pattern of data described by the model. Consideration and Initiating Structure are similarly difficult to classify. While, operationalized as overt behavioral dispositions, it is possible that these dispositions may result from latent cognitive or motivational constructs (or their interaction), although the use of these variables suggests that they are generally considered more motivational than cognitive.

Research on personality and leadership generally has shown personality to have statistically significant, though not strong, direct and interactive effects (Bass, 1981). Reactions to Stodgill's famous 1948 review article (Stogdill, 1948), as Stogdill himself later pointed out, disproportionally "over-emphasized the situational, and underemphasized the personal, nature of leadership (Stogdill, 1974, p. 72)." While personality effects have been found, understanding of leadership processes has not advanced as a result. Our belief is that this is because not enough attention has been paid to building theories that systematically examine the mediating links between leader behavior and relevant outcome variables. At the simplest level we assume that some traits have their effect by influencing leader behaviors that influence, in turn, follower goal–directed behavior. However, leader behaviors are not the only links between leader traits and subordinate reactions. Research by Lord and his associates on leader categorization (Lord, Foti and Phillips, 1981) suggests that leader traits may affect subordinate reactions in ways apart from the mediating influence of leader behavior. So, for example, a particular characteristic may be one element of a perceptual category whose other elements are relevant to the acceptance of influence (i.e., perceived competence, reward power). Perception of the initial characteristic may lead to classification of the leader in this category and the inference of the existence of these other elements. This research only highlights the importance of specifying the mediating processes between traits and leader effectiveness if the study of personality and leadership is to progress.

Employee Withdrawal

Until recently there has been little theory in the area of withdrawal behavior (turnover, absenteeism, and lateness). However, models of various forms of withdrawal are now being presented (Steers & Rhodes, 1978; Mobley, 1977; Mowday, Porter & Steers, 1982). These models all include a role for personality, suggesting that personality research in this area may soon be conducted more systematically than in the past. Steers and Rhodes (1978) specifically talk about a person's work ethic as an influence on attendance pressures. Both Steers and Rhodes and Mobley (1977) see individual values as key influences in employee dissatisfaction which in turn may lead to absenteeism or quitting. Further, the Mobley model includes such factors as the tendency to seek immediate versus delayed reinforcement, impulsive behavior and work centrality as influences on turnover. It is, however, unclear whether these later factors are being conceptualized as personality constructs. The consideration of personality in these areas could potentially be productive as there are well-developed literatures on a number of constructs relevant to these issues (see, for example, the work on reflexivity–impulsivity, Messer, 1976). Interestingly, while personality is included in these models, its role is quite peripheral. In both the Steers model of turnover and the Mobley model of absenteeism, the removal of personality variables would not substantially alter the processes postulated.

Given that so much research on withdrawal was until recently non-theoretical and stimulated mostly by applied problems, it is not surprising that direct effects studies are most often encountered. In their review of the turnover literature, Porter and Steers (1973) found weak–to–moderate correlations for such factors as achievement orientation, anxiety, independence and self-confidence. Muchinsky and Tuttle (1979), after surveying the available data, concluded that the effect of personality on turnover is marginal. Very few studies exist that examine the influence of personality on other forms of withdrawal behavior (Muchinsky, 1977).

In an interesting departure, Porter and Steers (1973) suggested that direct effects of personality might be manifested as curvilinear rather than linear relationships. In the one study testing this idea, however, Bernardin (1977) found little evidence of higher turnover or absenteeism from those at either end of the continuum of several personality traits when compared with those not at the extremes.

A recent exception to studies using direct effects designs was reported by Mowday and Spencer (1981) in which moderated regression was used to test both the direct and interactive effects of autonomy and achievement needs on turnover and absenteeism. Personality and job scope interacted significantly in determining absenteeism, but not turnover. However, the pattern of those interactions was not consistently in line with predictions.

Though little actually has been done on personality and withdrawal, the recent development of more theoretical approaches which include personality suggest that more research will be forthcoming. Analysis of the role of personality in these models suggests, however, that future work is likely to concentrate on direct effects and mechanistic interactions and focus primarily on a few motivational variables, presumed to influence values. Perhaps some of the recent attention given to the consequences of absenteeism and turnover (Mowday, Porter & Steers, 1982) will stimulate research on reciprocal and dynamic interactions. As yet, discussions of these consequences have not contained effects on personality.

Goal-Setting

Locke's (1968) major statement of goal-setting theory makes little mention of personality as a determinant of goal-setting behavior. Locke (1968) does imply that an individual's conscious desires (p. 183) or preferences (p. 185) could mediate the effects of incentives on the choice of goals. Beyond this, however, no specific role for personality is discussed. The absence of any integration of personality constructs into the theory is surprising since goal setting has its conceptual roots in Lewin's work on level of aspiration. In that original research, the choice of task difficulty levels was seen as partly a reflection of stable personality dispositions (Campbell, 1982). After reviewing the empirical literature on level of aspiration, much of which appeared over 40 years ago, Campbell concludes that "the evidence suggesting that level of aspiration (i.e., level of goal difficulty) is partially a personality characteristic is quite impressive." (p. 89). Relating these findings to contemporary goal setting research, Campbell speculates about personality influences in goal setting. None the less, in spite of relevant existing literature, a systematic role of personality, either central or peripheral, within contemporary goal setting theory has yet to be worked out.

Consistent with this lack of theoretical consideration, the research on personality reported in the goal setting literature has been somewhat haphazard. Almost universally, personality is treated as a moderator within a mechanistic interaction design. The predominance of the mechanistic moderator design is in keeping with the emphasis on goal setting as an external intervention rather than an internal self regulatory process. While much has been done on examining the effects of externally set goals, less attention has been paid to self-set-goals. (Rakestraw & Weiss, 1981).

Attention to this later issue would necessitate a broader approach to examining personality effects—emphasizing research on direct and particularly reciprocal effects.

Even within the mechanistic framework, the role of personality is of marginal interest in studies on goal setting. When personality is examined, measures are typically "tacked on" to research on other issues. Locke, Shaw, Saari and Latham (1981) describe how severe weaknesses in these studies with respect to the treatment of personality make it impossible to draw any conclusions about personality and goal setting. Among the weaknesses they cite are inconsistencies in the measures used for a given construct, administration of personality scales after experimental manipulation of goals, performance or both, reported interactions that are not subjected to appropriate statistical tests, and the assignment of goals which inhibits the emergence of individual differences.

Why include a discussion of personality and goal setting when relatively little has been done and the results have been discouraging? Our answer involves more than the fact that this is an important area of current organizational research. In significant ways, the use of personality in this area is more widely generalizable. The study of personality in goal setting has been of secondary importance with personality hypotheses much less firmly grounded in theory than other aspects of the research. The choices of personality variables seem very haphazard with little written about the reasons for choosing the particular variables or measures. The research is almost always conducted in the context of attempting to find effects for goal setting interventions, creating very "strong" situations likely to overwhelm individual differences. When goals are assigned, researchers have not considered the reciprocal effects this manipulation might have on personality. Yet in spite of these restricted uses of personality, researchers in the area are beginning to conclude that personality is unimportant here. This may in fact be true, but certainly we should reserve judgment until more systematic work is conducted.

Conclusions

A number of themes emerge from this review. First, it is obvious that few of the available ways of conceptualizing and studying personality effects on organizational behavior have been used in empirical research. Few studies of reciprocal or dynamic interaction effects have been reported. Research has been very mechanistic, assuming a clear distinction between independent and dependent variables. Few studies have employed longitudinal designs, emphasizing correlational studies or relatively short term experimentation. Scholars in our field have long been aware that the prevalence of cross-sectional research generally limits the construction of strong causal models of work behavior. It is sometimes assumed, however, that this problem is less critical for personality research, given the presumption of causal precedence for fixed personality traits. Our recent awareness of organizational influences on personality traits and values (see, for example, Weiss, 1978) and of attributional processes in which personality is inferred from outcomes, suggests that our early complacency about interpreting cross–sectional personality research is no longer justified. Movement away from main effects and mechanistic interaction will require longitudinal analyses. In addition, as will be discussed later, personality effects may vary over time indicating that even studies still focusing on main or interactive effects will have to become more cognizant of processes that occur and change over time. Further illustrating the limitations of previous work is the fact that the personality variables we have used are overwhelmingly motivational. This may reflect an earlier emphasis on motivational traits among personality researchers, an emphasis that was a legacy of psychodynamic roots in the development of personality theory. This emphasis is becoming less and less true of personality research outside of OB.

A second theme which emerges concerns the general homogeneity of approach within areas. While we have pointed out that diversity certainly does not characterize the field as a whole, we are particularly struck by the homogeneity of constructs, designs and instruments within each area. It is interesting to note that against this backdrop of similarity, modest changes in measurement, design or theory in any one area are seen as quite innovative. Substituting Growth Need Strength for Protestant Ethic or moderated regression for subgroup analyses within the job scope area are examples. From outside the job scope area, these changes seem more like minor variations. Job scope research remains limited to motivational variables studied from a mechanistic interaction perspective. Similarly, the change from focusing on traits to focusing on behavioral dispositions in the leadership area was really less of a change than the researchers believed it to be at the time. It seems that as a field develops, the range of alternatives explored often begins to narrow. This is no doubt due to the influence of one or a few key studies which excite the field (e.g., Turner & Lawrence, 1965, and Hackman & Lawler, 1971, in job scope, the Ohio State work in leadership).

A final theme which emerges is the superficial thought given to personality in our theory and research. This is manifested in a number of ways. First, linkages between personality and the other components of our theories are given substantially less theoretical specification than are those related to situational variables. Second, much of the data collected on personality effects is collected as part of larger studies where other issues are given theoretical procedence. This is particularly true in those areas where there is an important applied issue being analyzed. In such research, the creation of effective interventions is of primary importance and dominates the researcher's attention. Third, we tend to draw on personality variables in isolation, lifting them out of their nomological networks, neither building upon nor feeding back to their theoretical underpinnings. Indeed we too frequently ignore the nature and extent of those construct–relevant data. This point goes beyond our frequently choosing measures with little construct validity (which is, unfortunately, true). It means that even where good construct validity evidence exists, we rarely use it to enlighten us on the issue at hand. Our use of personality measures is too often intended to account for a little more variance and too seldom intended to extend explanation.

ISSUES OF PERSONALITY ANALYSIS

If the usefulness of personality is going to be adequately evaluated, organizational researchers will need to give greater thought to the nature of personality effects. In this section we discuss three important topics for consideration in personality—OB research, situational strength, dependent variable analysis and interactionism.

Situational Strength

Mischel (1977) has suggested that situations can be characterized by their relative "strength" and he and other personality researchers (Monson, Hesley & Chernick, 1982; Snyder & Ickes, in press; Stagner, 1977); have argued that situational strength moderates trait-behavior relationships. Essentially their position is that certain situations have well recognized and widely accepted rules of conduct which constrain and direct behavior. In such situations interindividual variability in behavior is low and personality differences are likely to have little predictive power. Other situations are more ambiguously structured, allowing for variation in meaning and behavior and better prediction from personality constructs.

Mischel (1977) has provided the clearest specification of differences between the two types of situations. For Mischel strong (powerful) situations:

1. Lead everyone to construe the situation the same way.
2. Induce uniform expectancies regarding appropriate response patterns.
3. Provide adequate incentives for the performance of that response pattern.
4. Require skills that everyone has.

In contrast, weak situations:

1. Are not uniformly encoded.
2. Do not generate uniform expectancies.
3. Do not offer incentives for performance.
4. Fail to provide the learning conditions necessary for successful genesis of the behavior.

To illustrate the effects of situational strength, Monson et al. (1982) have examined the relationship between extroversion and talkativeness in strong and weak situations they created in the laboratory. In two strong situation conditions, confederates conversing with a volunteer subject directed their conversation toward or away from topics which were known, by prior assessment, to interest the subject. In a weak situation condition, confederates neither encouraged nor discouraged conversation. As predicted, the correlation between extroversion and talkativeness was r = .56 in the weak situation but averaged only r = .24 in the two strong situations.

Differences between strong and weak situations raise a number of issues relevant to analyzing personality effects on organizational behavior. Perhaps most obvious is the problem of interpreting personality findings generated in typical laboratory studies. The laboratory is a place for testing theory–derived predictions under controlled conditions. As such, it can be and has been a useful setting for studying personality and work behavior. However, that usefulness is often attenuated by failure to consider the strength of the laboratory situation and the importance of representative design.

It is easy to recognize that in any experiment, the variance attributable to persons, situations, and interactions is as much a function of the researcher's ingenuity as it is the validity of theoretical propositions. Yet, laboratory research on personality and organizational behavior has frequently ignored the implications of this basic point. In the experimental tradition, as Cronbach noted some years ago (Cronbach, 1957), individual differences are an annoyance and substantial effort is devoted to the maximization of variance due to experimental conditions. Essentially, the aim of the typical laboratory experiment is the creation of strong situations guided by theoretical propositions, and success is gauged by whether the situations are as strong as theory would suggest they should be. As a result, the typical laboratory experiment is a situation where personality effects are going to be minimized. This is clearly appropriate for certain types of hypotheses. Frequently however, researchers interested in studying personality and personality-situation interactions have unthinkingly tried to graft personality hypotheses onto typical experimental procedures, creating artificially strong manipulations and using homogeneous samples with restricted variance on the individual difference variable. The potential for misrepresentation of personality effects in such experimental situations is obvious. This is not to say that laboratory settings are inappropriate for testing general theoretical propositions about personality effects. Ickes' (in press) weak situation paradigm in which spontaneous behavior among interactants is assessed and predicted with good success in an unstructured laboratory situation well illustrates that point.

We have so far limited our discussion to problems associated with examining general theoretical propositions. However, frequently our laboratory studies are implicitly intended to describe the effects of personality in some target situation, even if that target is more conceptual than real. Under these conditions, our research becomes more particularistic than universalistic (Kruglanski, 1975) and we must be careful to create settings which are representative (Brunswick, 1956) of the target. This obviously does not imply the inappropriateness of laboratory abstractions. It does imply that those abstractions must be operationalized with manipulations which approximate differences manifested in the situation to which we wish to generalize. Similar considerations of representativeness must be applied to the personality variable (not necessarily the persons) as well.

Organizational settings are characterized by neither Ickes' "weak situation" nor the strong conditions of typical laboratory experiments. Organizational settings do, however, differ in situational strength and laboratory researchers should pay more attention to the parameters of "real world" strength in designing their experimental conditions. Failure to do so can easily lead to misinterpretation of results.

A clear illustration of this point is provided by Ganster's (1980) laboratory experiment investigating the moderating influences of various personality dimensions on perceptions of, and reactions to, task characteristics. Using a between–groups design, subjects were assigned to either a "fairly complex electronic assembly operation" (high scope task) or a parts identification and sorting task (low scope task). Protestant Ethic, Growth Need Strength, Need for Achievement and Sensation Seeking Tendency were examined as predictors of task satisfaction and perceptions of task characteristics and as moderators of the relationships among task manipulations, perceptions and satisfaction. The results of the study showed weak and generally inconsistent personality effects. Across experimental conditions, very small main effects on satisfaction and perception were found. Only one moderating influence was shown and this was in the direction opposite to what was predicted.

Ganster's findings suggest the relative unimportance of personality for predicting reactions to task design interventions. However, this conclusion must be tempered in light of the extremely strong, nonrepresentative manipulations. The difference between an electronic assembly task and a parts sorting task seems particularly nonrepresentative of probable job changes in organizations. Indeed, Ganster notes that the extremely strong manipulations were created to deliberately represent a wide range of core dimensions. The strength of the manipulations is seen by their accounting for between 45% and 74% of the variance in task perceptions and 58% of the variance in satisfaction. Using perceptions of the four core dimensions as predictors of satisfaction resulted in a multiple correlation of $R = .84$.

Clearly, Ganster produced an extremely strong manipulation of task differences which could easily eliminate the possibility for more than trivial personality main or moderator effects. While his attempt to break away from the correlational design which has characterized the job scope literature is laudable, his failure to consider the impact of the strength or the representativeness of his manipulations reduces the meaningfulness of his results. This seems particularly unfortunate and unnecessary in the task design area where so much parametric data is available to the researcher. JDS scores are available for many different jobs. It should be possible to examine the representativeness of laboratory manipulations by comparing the JDS scores of experimental tasks, or at least JDS differences between tasks, with scores from actual jobs or reported score changes after real redesign interventions. Group differences in the laboratory would then represent the changes likely to occur as a result of typical task redesign efforts. Such representative designs would take advantage of experimental control while, at the same time, providing more meaningful information about the importance of personality effects outside the laboratory.

Although the topic of situational strength quite naturally leads to a discussion of appropriate experimental design, it should not be forgotten that this is more than a methodological issue. It is also a conceptual issue of the extent of behavioral constraint in organizations and the relative importance of personality differences in organizational situations characterized by more or less constraint. Theoretically, it should be possible to scale work situations in terms of underlying strength and thereby predict personality-behavior relationships. The ability to do this will help us learn about the way both personality and situations influence behavior. However, operationalizing the theoretical construct of situational strength in an organizationally relevant way seems to us to be a particularly difficult task, one which will require extensive work on three distinct problems.

First, a clear specification of the differences between strong and weak situations at the theoretical level is needed. While Mischel's delineation is a useful beginning, it is ambiguous and uninformative in places. For example, Mischel states that strong situations provide adequate incentives. Yet, how are we to gauge the "adequacy" of incentives independently from the uniformity of displayed behavior? Mischel gives no advice here. Similarly, Mischel argues that strong situations lead everyone to construe the situation in the same way and induce uniform expectancies. Here we need to ask what aspects of the situation induce these expectancies (adequacy of incentives?) and lead to similarity in construal. Mischel's focus on the nature of incentives and the implied importance of social norms and cue salience seems relevant. However, we still must be able to understand and assess strong and weak situations in ways apart from the uniformity of behavior they are meant to explain.

A second problem for adequate operationalization concerns the identification of relevant situational units. What "situations" in organizations are to be assessed? What constitutes a relevant "situation" in work experience? Clearly we cannot think in terms of jobs as situational units since jobs are clusters of tasks constituted for organizational efficiency. Nor does it help to break jobs down to tasks, since tasks are only one component of work situations. The analysis of situational strength requires a situational unit based upon a classification procedure relevant to the display of behavior. While the general issue of situational analysis is complex and beyond the scope of this discussion, we can say that we believe that jobs can be broken down to discrete behavior settings which can vary in strength. These behavior settings are perceptually discriminable by participants and observers and tend to be repeatedly encountered by job incumbents. For a college professor, for example, interaction with the department head, teaching a seminar and meeting with one's graduate students might all represent frequently encountered behavior settings that can be assessed in terms of strength and also analyzed in terms of the personality traits they activate.

Finally, once a clearer theoretical definition is obtained and adequate situational units conceptualized, procedures for measuring strength must be developed. An interesting attempt at measurement is provided by Price and Bouffard (1974). Their method involves the creation of a matrix of social situations and behaviors. Respondents provide ratings of the appropriateness of each behavior in each of the different situations. Situational constraint or strength is assessed by averaging behaviors for each situation. High averages suggest that multiple behaviors are appropriate to the situation. Alternatively, as suggested by Mischel (1977), variance in respondents' ratings within situations might also be used as an index of strength. Personality would then manifest itself in situations with low constraint. While this seems promising for application to organizational analysis, it still requires the delineation of appropriate situational units as components of the matrix.

Dependent Variables Analysis

Any attempt to integrate personality constructs into theories of organizational behavior must pay particular attention to certain critical dimensions of the dependent variables. Generally organizational researchers are only superficially aware of the way differences in their dependent variables influence differences in the types of explanatory constructs which will be useful. Obviously certain behaviors are likely to be predictable by some personality constructs and not others. However this simply scratches the surface of the dependent variable issue. We will illustrate by discussing the relevance of three general dimensions of dependent variable analysis—aggregation, differences between means and variance in behavior and time of collection. The first issue has generated the most research in the personality literature and will therefore be discussed at length. The latter two will be more briefly presented in the hope of stimulating work on the general problem of dependent variable analysis.

Aggregation.   Implicit in the definition of traits is consistency. It is therefore not suprising that the most persuasive argument against the usefulness of traits has centered on the prevalence of cross-situational variability in behavior (Mischel, 1968; 1973). It is also not surprising that defenders of traits have expended much effort in analyzing the issue of consistency and trying to demonstrate the logical and empirical weaknesses of Mischel's position.

Mischel argued that personality traits are thought of as broad underlying dispositions that exert a generalized influence on behavior. As a result, "data that demonstrate strong generality in the behavior of the same person across many situations are critical for trait and state personality theories; the construct of personality itself rests on the belief that individual behavior consistencies exist widely and account for much of variance in behavior" (Mischel, 1968, p. 13). However, Mischel argued, existing evidence for consistency in behavior, particularly across situations and measurement modes, is weak, indicating the lack of explanatory and predictive utility of trait constructs.

Responses to Mischel's critique have taken many forms. The most cogent logical arguments have revolved around the multiple meanings of "consistency" and the restrictive nature of Mischel's use of the term. So, for example, a number of researchers have drawn distinctions between absolute consistency (low within person variance in behavior across situations) and relative consistency (stable rank orderings among people across situations) suggesting that it is the latter rather than the former which is implied by trait concepts. Still others have pointed to the distinction between constructs and the behaviors they are meant to explain. According to this position, the utility of traits is not assessed by the degree of behavioral consistency but rather by the explanatory power of theoretical systems in which these constructs are embedded. Traits at the mediating level can be stable yet interact with other traits and situational factors to produce behavioral diversity (Endler & Magnusson, 1977).

In a series of influential papers, Epstein (1977, 1979, 1980) has empirically examined the issue of consistency in a manner which he believes to be more appropriate to a dispositional conception of personality than that used in studies cited by Mischel. Epstein points out that traits are aggregate concepts. They focus on consistent patterns or tendencies in behavior. However, consistency has typically been inappropriately evaluated by correlating data (behaviors, personality measures, etc.) at two points in time. The resulting correlation, usually no higher than r = .30, has then been unjustifiably taken to indicate behavioral inconsistency. For Epstein, a more appropriate test of consistency is to examine correlations between behavior indices aggregated across multiple occasions. Such aggregations have greater reliability and better operationalize the dispositional quality of traits. Epstein (1977) supports his argument with data showing that when behavioral measures are collected over several occasions and aggregated into composite scores, their stability increases and so do their correlations with personality predictors.

Jaccard (1977), building on work by Fishbein and Ajzen (1974), has advanced a taxonomy of behavioral measures that extends Epstein's aggregation concepts and specifies the types of criteria most likely to be predictable from personality variables. Jaccard begins by presenting a matrix of behaviors (rows) and occasions (columns) and uses it to distinguish among a number of different behavioral criteria. The simplist type in Jaccard's taxonomy consists of single–act, single observation criteria. As Epstein (1979) notes, personality variables are unlikely to predict criteria of this sort. Jaccard's second type of criterion involves aggregation of observations of the same behavior repeated over multiple occasions (single–act repeated observation). These multiple occasions can be homogeneous, the same behavior in the same replicated situation, or heterogeneous, the same behavior in different situations. Epstein's operations use this approach to criterion measurement—aggregating observations collected over a period of several days. Jaccard then extends single–act/repeated–observation measures to describe multiple act criteria. In his matrix, the rows represent separate behaviors that are viewed as being different manifestations of the same trait. Multiple–act criteria are aggregated across these different behaviors and thereby operationalize "behavioral patterns" consistent with the underlying trait. Again, these multiple–act criteria can be aggregated across homogeneous and heterogeneous occasions, producing multiple–act/repeated–observation criteria. Jaccard argues that multiple act criteria are operationalizations most compatable with the definition of traits as broad underlying dispositions. He suggests therefore that multiple–act/repeated–observation criteria would be most appropriate for personality research.

The logic of Epstein's and Jaccard's position clearly suggests that personality should be a better predictor of aggregated behavioral indices than of measurement of single behaviors or behaviors over a short period of time. Data supporting the increased predictability of aggregated indices by personality is provided by McGowan and Gormly (1976) and Jaccard (1974). McGowan and Gormly obtained peer ratings of students' energy levels and then collected observations on five energy–related behaviors (i.e. walking speed, posture adjustments during class). The energy ratings correlated r = .70 with the multiple–act criterion aggregated over the five behaviors but averaged only r = .43 with the five components. Jaccard (1974) created a "dominance" relevant multiple-act criterion by asking undergraduates to generate a list of behaviors they thought "dominant" and "non dominant" females would perform. A second group of undergraduates filled out the resulting 40 behavior checklist and three different measures of dominance. For each of these measures the correlation with the multiple-act criterion was substantially greater than the average correlation with the individual behaviors. So, for example, one measure of dominance correlated r = .64 with the multiple-act criterion but averaged r = .20 with the individual behaviors.

The relevance of this work on criterion aggregation to organizational behavior is clear. Criteria of interest to organizations vary in their degree of aggregation over time and situations. For example, one can think of a dimension anchored by task performance at a single time or day and career performance or progress. The latter aggregated criteria are likely to be more predictable from personality than the former criteria. Yet often only short term criteria are used to examine personality effects on organizational behavior.

Research on goal setting and individual differences well illustrates this point. In this area, as in others, studies of personality effects have typically relied on single act measures. One can distinguish, however, between the goal an individual might set for a specific task versus the general level of goals he has set for the many tasks he has performed on his job over an extended period, a year, for example, or a career. Often organizations are interested in the latter while research on personality and goal setting typically uses the former. The results of that research might therefore provide a distorted picture of the role of personality.

We have recently examined this issue with regard to self esteem and goal setting (Adler & Weiss, Note 1). Subjects set goals for each of three trials on anagram and creativity tasks. Single–act/single–observation criteria of goals set and performance on single trials were assessed. Single–act/repeated–observation criteria in homogeneous situations were operationalized by averaging goals over trials and performance over trials for each task. Single–act/repeated–observation criteria in heterogeneous situations were measured by aggregating across trials and tasks for both goals and performance. The effects of aggregation can be seen in the correlations presented in Table 1. Interestingly, aggregation over repeated wrials of the same task (homogeneous situations) had only a negligible effect on the correlations with self esteem. On the other hand, aggregation across different tasks (heterogeneous situations) produced substantially stronger correlations (r = .46 for self esteem and goals and r = .50 for self esteem and performance). We note that these correlations are much higher than those usually found in laboratory studies of goal setting and personality.

For conceptual as well as psychometric (see Ghiselli, Campbell & Zedeck, 1981) reasons, organizational researchers should pay particular attention to the level of aggregation in their dependent variable. However, we caution that researchers not treat aggregation as a gimmick designed to improve prediction from personality. They should instead remain cognizant of the meaning and the importance of criteria created by different types of aggregation. Certainly our operationalizations must be understood as simply "slices" from an ongoing stream of behavior. Different researchers create units of varying size depending on needs and objectives (Turner, 1965). For the experimental psychologist, a blink of the eye is a unit of relevance. For the organizational researcher, career progress may be the cut of greatest interest. However, the fact that our criterion

Table 1. Correlations of Self Esteem with Goals
and Performance as a Function of Criterion
Aggregation

Criteria	Goals	Performance
Single Observation		
Anagram	.30[1]	.16[1]
Creativity	.24[1]	.27[1]
Multiple Observation—Homogenous Situations		
Anagram	.34	.18
Creativity	.30	.34
Multiple Observation—Heterogeneous Situations		
Anagram and Creativity	.46	.50

[1] Average Correlations.

units are creations of the researcher does not in any sense suggest that these units are arbitrary. We can aggregate behaviors and increase reliability and predictability but we should not do this if there is a cost in meaningfulness.

We believe that personality researchers who have studied the issue of aggregation have been deficient in this regard, often implicitly inverting the typical research problem. That is, the appropriate question of whether personality predicts a particular criterion chosen on the basis of practical or theoretical importance is often reversed to become "how can we operationalize behavior so that it is predictable from personality?" While advocating aggregation, they have ignored the key issue of the conceptual importance of the newly created dependent variable.

Jaccard's (1977) typology is illustrative. Jaccard argues that multiple–act/repeated–observation criteria come closest to operationalizing the dispositional quality of traits and they should therefore be used in evaluating the usefulness of personality. Jaccard is probably right when he suggests that multiple–act criteria are more closely related to personality than other criteria. Yet this is exactly the wrong reason for choosing dependent variables. We would argue that for most (but not all) organizational problems, single–act/repeated–observations across heterogeneous situations are more likely to be theoretically relevant aggregations. Goal setting, conformity and information search may all be organizational manifestations of self esteem, yet an aggregate of all these behaviors would be less than meaningful for most organizational problems. More meaningful would be goal setting over time and situations or conformity over time and situations.

Additionally, even when we focus on single behaviors we must be vigilant in questioning the relevance of aggregation. Sometimes we are interested in operationalizing longer term trends, patterns or averages. Our example of career performance is relevant here. In other cases we are less interested in understanding response trends than we are in predicting single instances. So, for example, aggregating responses to emergencies would make little sense since we are more interested in knowing how a person will respond in each instance. Analysis of this issue suggests to us that legitimately aggregated variables are typically ones where higher values at one time can compensate for lower values of at another. Variables which do not lend themselves to aggregation do not allow for compensation across instances. This, as well as other ways of distinguishing between legitimate and nonlegitimate aggregation, should be explored.

A final point regarding aggregation needs to be made. Often, ratings are used as dependent variables in organizational research involving personality. Since raters implicitly average performance observations collected over time and occasions one might argue that these operationalizations are aggregations and should therefore be more predictable from personality than other types of criteria. We would submit that while ratings are aggregations, they are haphazard aggregations produced by unequal weighting of poorly sampled observations (Ilgen & Feldman, 1983). In these aggregations, the independence of observations is questionable and the effect of time (recency, primacy) is uncontrolled. Equating performance ratings with the type of aggregation implied by this discussion would be inappropriate given current appraisal procedures.

Performance Distributions. The assessment of inconsistency in performance has recently been advocated by Kane and Lawler (1979). While their discussion focuses on subjective appraisals, much of what they say applies to any type of performance measurement system. Essentially their point is that most appraisal systems require that a distribution of performance relevant behavioral instances be summarized with a single index representing average or typical performance, much as a mean is used to represent the central tendency of an array of scores. However, just as score arrays have other parameters, so too do distributions of performance instances. Kane and Lawler argue that organizations should expand their performance measurement systems to include characteristics of performance distributions in addition to central tendencies. Specifically, they argue that for many situations, the variation in performance—signaling unpredictability—is a relevant performance parameter. Presumably meaningful differences exist among employees in the distribution of their performances across instances in addition to differences in average performance levels. In many cases, organizations would be well advised to pay attention to these differences in performance variance.

The debate among personality researchers over behavioral consistency has generated a great deal of research on individual differences in consistency that has relevance for understanding variations in performance distributions. This research has taken two distinct paths. One path begins with the work reported by Bem and Allen (1974). They argue that the lack of consistency among supposed trait indicators may result from a fallacious assumption that each trait dimension is equally relevant for describing all assessees. They argue that not all traits are relevant to all individuals and therefore the utility of any particular trait is limited to that subgroup to whom the trait applies. For those individuals, and only for those individuals, consistency among trait indicators is expected. Bem and Allen provided empirical support for their position by simply asking people how consistently friendly they were from situation to situation. Answers to this simple question were used to form subgroups of consistent and nonconsistent respondents, presumably reflecting differences in trait relevance. Subgroup analyses indicated that reports of friendliness from various observers (mother, father, peers, etc.) showed higher correlations among those who described themselves as consistent than among those who did not. Similarly for the group characterized as consistent, friendliness behavior was substantially more predictable from standardized measures of friendliness and extroversion.

Bem and Allen are often mistakenly understood as suggesting that there are individual differences in consistency. In fact, they do not suggest that people differ in their level of behavioral consistency but rather that what appears to be inconsistency reflects instead a difference between the researcher's and respondent's definition of consistency. The Bem and Allen position rests on a constructual nature of traits, regarding traits as researcher–created constructs formed by an "investigator's partitioning of behaviors into the same equivalence class" (p. 509). According to Bem and Allen, individuals can be quite consistent "within themselves" but be inconsistent in terms of the investigator's construct. This latter inconsistency neither invalidates the concept of personality nor the usefulness of the investigator's trait. It does however limit that trait's usefulness to certain individuals.

In contrast to the Bem and Allen position, a number of researchers have suggested the existence of stable, predictable differences in behavioral consistency. In their view, some people are more dispositional; more influenced by internal personality factors and others are more situational; responsive to demands and differences among situations. Dispositional individuals are more likely to demonstrate cross–situational consistency and their behavior is more likely to be predictable from standard trait measures than situational individuals. In effect, what is being suggested is a personality trait of the most general kind—individual differences in the degree of dispositional behavior. Some researchers, in fact, have had a fair amount of success classifying people into these two types. The most extensive and successful work in this area has been done by Snyder and his colleagues using the personality dimension of self–monitoring (Snyder, 1974). High self–monitors are guided more by situational cues than low self–monitors and their behaviors are generally less consistent across situations and less predictable from personality traits than low self–monitors. A similar pattern of results has been found using the personality dimension of private self–consciousness (Fenigstein, Scheier, & Buss, 1975). (A recent review of the work on both dimensions as moderators of personality behavior relationships is found in Snyder & Ickes, in press.)

While theoretical differences exist between the Bem and Allen position and the consistency–as–trait position, the results of the research guided by both positions has demonstrated the same thing—individual differences in cross situational consistency exist and can be predicted. In the Bem and Allen case, these differences are quite trait–specific. In the cases of self–monitoring and self–consciousness, the differences at least are presented as being quite general.

The recognition of performance variability as an important criterion of work behavior quite naturally leads to an appreciation of the personality research on differences in behavioral consistency. However, the translation of that research to the study of performance distributions is substantially more complex than any surface similarity would suggest. The major complicating factor is, of course, the difference between performance and behavior. Performance results from the interaction of behavior and task demands. If task demands or behavioral requirements were constant over all potential performance instances, behavioral variability might translate into performance variability. Obviously such is not the case, and therefore the extent to which predictors of behavioral consistency also predict performance variability will depend upon the variance in behavioral requirements across the potential performance instances of a job. In certain jobs, behavioral consistency will produce wide variations in performance as individuals respond with a characteristic behavior pattern in both appropriate and inappropriate situations. For other jobs, the behavioral requirements for efficient performance may be similar across seemingly disparate situations. Here, behavioral consistency might directly translate to performance consistency. On the first job, we might expect self–monitoring or self–consciousness to be negatively correlated with performance variance. On the second job, our expectation would be for a positive correlation.

To summarize: in our opinion, performance consistency is a potentially important dependent variable for organizational research. As researchers begin to analyze differences in this type of criterion, they might profitably look to the personality research on behavioral consistency. However, in doing so they would be advised to remember the distinction between behavior and performance and not expect simple predictability of performance consistency paralleling the predictions of behavioral consistency in the personality research. Analyses of task requirements, situational variability and expected intercorrelations among trait indicators will be necessary and, as with other personality effects, interactions are more likely than main effects.

Time.   Finally, the time at which the dependent variable is collected is a critical issue for the explanatory usefulness of personality. An old, generally ignored, but insightful paper by Weitz (1966) first raised this issue in the context of selection and criterion evaluation. It has relevance to organizational phenomena as well. Weitz' major point was that different types of predictors will be more or less valid (predictive of the criterion) depending upon when the criterion is measured. If measured early in the workers' tenure, aptitude differences will be more predictive and personality less predictive. If measured later, aptitude differences will account for less variance (job experience will wash out meaningful initial aptitude differences) and personality, as an influence on motivation in Weitz's discussion, will explain more variance.

Recent papers by Katz (1980) and Organ (1981) have raised this issue again in the context of individual and situational influences at different career points. Both discussions suggest that situational factors have a greater influence on the behavior of new workers than do individual difference variables such as personality. This proposition follows from the idea (expressed also by Louis, 1980; Weiss, 1977, 1978) that the new work situation generates a good deal of uncertainty with prior experience providing insufficient cues for behavioral guidance. Under such conditions, individuals become particularly attentive to external sources of information, making them susceptible to what Katz refers to as "situational control."

We believe that this description of the psychological state and behavioral requirements of new workers, along with the contrasting views of the states and requirements of more advanced workers, is essentially correct and has important implications for personality research and the likelihood of discovering personality effects. However, we think that the implications of career stage differences for personality research lie less with expected differences in the global role of "personality" than with the relevance of different types of personality variables at different points in the worker's job tenure. It would be a mistake to assume that the conceptual distinction between strong and weak situations can easily be mapped onto career stages. While Katz' description might suggest that "strength" is greatest earlier in one's career, decreases in the ambiguity of reward structures and greater acceptance of norms over time might suggest the opposite (Note 2). Forcing an artificial correspondence between tenure and situational strength will close our thinking to important personality and situational effects at all career stages.

For example, Katz's discussion about the prevalence of uncertainty and the search for informational cues among new workers suggests not so much the absence of important personality effects as that those effects might be found among variables assessing differences in uncertainty (self-esteem, for example,) or reflecting differences in the weight given to various types of information likely to be encountered during search. In this vein, Weiss (1977, 1978) has found that self-esteem predicts the degree of imitation of role models among workers and has suggested that this effect results from differences in uncertainty and uncertainty inspired search (Weiss & Knight, 1980). In addition, Weiss and Shaw (1979) have shown that field independence predicts the weight given to social information in judgments of task characteristics. Katz' own work (Katz, 1978) on the different issues which concern workers at different career points also suggests the relevance of career stages to understanding the importance of different aspects of personality. We therefore agree with Katz that the combining of respondents at different career points may well mask important differences in individual and situational influences on behavior. We believe, however, that the problem is which personality variables are operating not whether personality is operating.

Adequate evaluation of personality influences on reactions to organizational interventions also requires awareness of temporal effects. Manipulation strength may dissipate over time, turning initially strong situations into weaker ones and allowing both main and interactive effects of personality to emerge.

Finally, time is a critical issue for any analysis of dynamic interaction. If individuals to any extent modify and influence the situations they encounter, that process must be studied longitudinally. Cross–sectional analyses will not capture the dynamic interaction process. In addition, if one suspects that interventions are likely to be modified as a result of individual dispositions, not an unreasonable suspicion, research must be conducted with appropriate time intervals built into the design. Similar sensitivity to appropriate intervals must characterize those studies which examine long-term personality changes that occur as a result of organizational experiences. We must admit that we have no guidelines to offer about appropriate time frames for studying these issues. We would simply advise researchers to be cognizant and active on this issue.

Personality—Situation Interactionism

Much of the creativity in personality theory over the past decade and a half was stimulated by Mischel's (1968) critique of personality research. The ensuing controversy over whether personality or situation is the more important determinant of behavior is now generally recognized as a pseudoissue. This controversy revolved around the percentage of criterion variance accounted for by personality and situational factors. However, we have seen that in any given study these percentages may be affected by restrictions of range in the personality variable, level of criterion aggregation, situationally imposed constraints on behavior and other factors unrelated to the relative importance of personality or situation as a determinant of behavior.

The personality-situation debate has been an important stimulus to the development of a new model of personality: interactionism (Endler & Magnusson, 1976). Interactional psychology sees behavior as being determined by "a complex interplay of situations and persons" (Magnusson

& Endler, 1977). In a previous volume of this series, Schneider (1983) has noted some important implications of interactionism for the field of organizational behavior. Rather than restating the basic propositions of interactional psychology, the reader is referred to Schneider's (1983) summary or to more extensive discussions in Endler and Magnusson (1976), Magnusson and Endler (1977) or Pervin and Lewis (1978). Our purpose here is to focus on two key aspects of interactionism and discuss their implications for the study of personality and organizational behavior.

Person and Situation Inextrixably Linked in Determining Behavior. As we have seen, OB theory and research generally treat personality and situational variables as independent from one another. Personality-situation interaction, when studied at all, is defined as mechanistic interaction, the nonadditive joint contribution of a personality-situation interaction term within the general least squares (ANOVA or moderated regression) model (Terborg, 1981). The assumption is that the distinct contributions of personality and situations can be individually identified. In contrast, interactionists argue that personality and situation are inherently inseparable. This is true in two important senses.

For one, as Weick (1979) has argued, situations are enacted: that is they are our cognitive constructions of the environment. The actor brackets the ongoing stream of experience, imposes structure, and attaches meaning to the components of that structure. For each individual, his construal of the environment is the situation. In this way of thinking it makes little sense to speak of the situation as being apart from personality. A basic element of interactionism then is that "on the situation side, the psychological meaning of situations for the individual is the important determining factor (Magnusson & Endler, 1977, p. 4)."

A second sense of personality-situation linkage relates to the dynamic interaction designs that we have been discussing all along, the notion of continuous reciprocal influence. In Weick's (1979) words, "the actor does something that produces an ecological change, which change then constrains what he does next, which in turn produces a further ecological change, and so on (p. 130)." Green's (1976) analysis of role-making and Porter, Lawler and Hackman's (1975) discussion of the complementary processes of organizational socialization and individualism capture this sense of dynamic interactionism. In these approaches, the organizational environment is seen to exert pressures toward change on the new member while the new member in turn seeks to place his stamp on the organizational environment. As opposed to person-job matching which is conceived as a one-time fit, the interactionist view is of ongoing change, mutual influence and person-situation accomodation (Schneider, 1983). Although the importance of dynamic interactionism has been recognized in theory, we have seen little use of the dynamic interaction design in research, as our earlier review indicated. To move ahead in this area, we need to see more programatic longitudinal research. Programatic because, while our theory may speak of bidirectional influence, any one study might choose to focus on specific, directional effects. It is only through the systemic accumulation of studies of this sort that the dynamic interplay of personality, situation, and behavior can be fully captured (Magnusson & Endler, 1977). Longitudinal, since personality is by definition relatively stable and will be affected only gradually. Sudden enduring changes in personality traits are not to be expected.

Recent developments in statistical analysis may help us better examine such dynamic interactive phenomena. Wolfle and Robertshaw (1982), for example, used LISREL to investigate the interplay of personality and environment in a recent longitudinal study of the effects of college attendance on locus of control. The correlation between college attendance and locus of control measured at a later point was shown to be significant. However, LISREL analysis demonstrated that only 20% of this relation was due to the effects of the college experience on locus of control. Some 80% of the correlation was attributable to the influences of an earlier locus of control score and to ability—both on the decision to attend college and on later locus of control. Kohn and Schooler (1982) used a similar analytic approach called MILS, to estimate the relative influences of personality and job conditions on each other over a ten year period. Through their analysis, the authors were able to identify contemporaneous and lagged effects of personality on job conditions, and job conditions on personality, as well as lagged effects of some personality traits on other traits. These analytical tools may become invaluable to us in our study of such interactions in organizational behavior.

Coherence of Behavior.   One argument against the usefulness of personality traits rests, as we have noted, on the lack of consistency in behavior from situation to situation. According to the interactionist response (Magnusson and Endler, 1977) this argument confuses two classes of variables, mediating variables and reaction variables. Personality dispositions are hypothetical contructs that are seen to act as mediating variables in explaining overt reactions or behavior. The interactionists argue that a lack of consistency at the behavioral level may not reflect a lack of consistency at the mediating level. Inconsistencies in an employee's level of effort from task to task, for example, do not necessarily mean that behavior is wholly determined by situational factors. Nor do Magnusson and Endler (1977), in developing this argument, imply that there is always consistency at the mediating level; merely that there is no simple correspondence between these two levels. Rather than focus on consistency in behavior, we should focus on coherence. Coherence in behavior means that "behavior is inherently lawful and hence predictable without necessarily being stable in either relative or absolute terms. We are referring to patterns of behavior that may vary across situations of various kinds but in which the behavior is coherent and lawful all the same (Magnusson & Endler, 1977, p. 7)." This, then, is a key message of interactionism for the study of personality in organizational behavior. We need to search for coherence of behavior at the mediating level and should not be deterred by inconsistency at the reaction level.

Nygard (1981) gives us a good illustration of the critical role of personality in understanding behavioral coherence in his analysis of Atkinsons's (Atkinson & Raynor, 1978) theory of achievement motivation. The components of this theory include two motivational personality variables: the need for achievement and the motive to avoid failure. Another crucial variable, from which the remaining components of the theory can be derived, is the individual's perception of his probability of succeeding in a particular situation. As Nygard (1981) points out, Atkinson's theory is interactionist par excellence; strong need for achievement does not mean strong effort for all tasks. Rather, the theory specifically predicts little difference in effort between those high and low in need achievement when the perceived probability of task success is close to either 0 or 1. The difference in effort between those with different need for achievement grows as the probability of task success moves toward the .5 level of difficulty. What is important for this discussion, then, is that achievement behavior is lawful, specific behavioral predictions can be made and tested, and that this behavior cannot be understood without considering personality. We believe that this is the role we should be building for personality in our theories of organizational behavior.

EFFICIENT USE OF PERSONALITY CONSTRUCTS

Analysis of the literature on personality and organizational behavior suggests to us that efficient use of personality constructs will require more than a consideration of aggregation or situational strength or dynamic interactionism. Efficient use of personality, in the sense of enhancing theory, will require systematic understanding of the nature of personality constructs and the role these constructs play in explanatory systems. We have neither the space nor the expertise to fully discuss all the relevant philosophical details. The reader is directed toward Alston (1975) and Ryle (1949) for discussions of dispositional concepts and to Beck (1953), Messick (1981), and of course MacCorquodale and Meehl (1948), for discussions on the nature of psychological constructs. However, we do believe that a few issues are worth mentioning in the context of the objectives of this paper.

Personality traits are frequently defined as dispositions to behave in certain ways. That is, as Alston (1975) notes, they are seen as probabilistic "if-then" relationships with the then component referring to a class of multiple, co-varying responses. "To say that X has a certain disposition is to assert a hypothetical proposition, a proposition that if X is in a certain type of situation (S) X will emit a certain type of response (R)." (Alston, 1975, p. 19) Often, to move personality traits beyond being solely inductive summaries of stimulus–response relationships, the concep of "underlying state" is added to the definition.

Mischel (1968, 1973) uses this type of definition in formulating his attack on traits. He states:

> Personality comprises broad underlying dispositions which pervasively influence the individual's behavior across many situations and lead to consistency in his behavior.
>
> Mischel, 1973, p. 253

Aside from the problem of operationally defining "broad' or "consistency" such a dispositional definition is misleading because it does not capture how personality concepts are actually used by personality theorists, it confuses the explanatory construct (trait) with the phenomenon being explained (behavior patterns) and, in so doing, restricts the nature of confirming and disconfirming evidence. So, for example, by including cross–situational consistency in his definition of traits, Mischel is able to argue against their validity by reporting evidence of inconsistency. We might respond by arguing that Mischel's data regarding consistency was inappropriate (following Epstein, 1977, or Jaccard, 1977). However, such a response would not be necessary because, as we have seen in our discussion of interactionism, trait concepts do not necessarily imply cross–situational consistency.

Personality traits are theoretical constructs. These constructs are used to refer to attributes of people. They are presumed to be stable but not necessarily unchangeable. Like all theoretical constructs, they are inferred from observables or sets of observables but are not equivalent to these operationalizations (MacCorquodale & Meehl, 1948). They derive their meaning from their position in larger theoretical systems.

Obviously, if these constructs are to be of any value they must enter into lawful functional relationships with other theoretical and observable variables. But to say that they have lawful relations with observable behavior is not to say that the relationships are of the cross–situational consistency variety outlined by Mischel. It is to say that from operational assessments of the theoretical construct and from knowledge of the functional relationships of that construct to other constructs in the system and from operationalizations of those other constructs, one can derive behavioral predictions for specific settings. The predictions can be used to test the theoretical propositions, including those related to the personality construct, and the explanatory usefulness of the system and its components can be assessed.

We should note that organizational researchers use many types of theoretical constructs that have no greater logical claim to usefulness than do personality constructs. Skills, abilities and aptitudes are notable examples. These are also unobservable hypothetical constructs inferred from overt behavior and deriving their meaning from their position in theoretical systems. Yet we have rarely questioned the legitimacy of these constructs in explanatory systems. Why? To us, the answer lies more in the current empirical rather than logical superiority of ability constructs.

In thinking about appropriate constructs, it is useful to remember that it makes little sense to worry about the "reality" of personality traits. Reality is, of course, impossible to determine and a personality trait, like any theoretical construct, can be judged only in terms of the explanatory usefulness of the theoretical system of which it is a part. This is not to say that a presumption of reality cannot sometimes be helpful. Such a presumption can result in the discovery of more basic processes. Additionally, thinking in terms of analogous "real" structures can help us cognitively by allowing us to think about personality in the same way we like to think about environments. However, such thinking can just as easily be disruptive when it restricts theory to mechanistic process orientations or leads to extensive unproductive searches for microstructures. We should note, parenthetically, that the environmental characteristics we include in our theories—such things as skill variety, role conflict, and reward structure—have no better claim to reality than personality traits. Essentially, both personal and situational characteristics are constructs that are understandable only in terms of theory (Turner, 1965). This is not to argue for or against the ultimate reality of some constructs but simply to say that reality is not a criterion of scientific explanation. As Einstein (1938) stated:

> In our endeavor to understand reality we are somewhat like a man trying to understand the mechanism of a closed watch. He sees the face and the moving hands, even hears the ticking, but he has no way of opening the case. (p. 31)

If theoretical constructs derive their meaning from the interlocking set of theoretical and empirical laws in which they play a part, then a "necessary condition for a construct to be scientifically admissable is that it occur in a nomological net at least some of whose laws involve observables" (Cronbach & Meehl, 1955). While personality constructs all have the same theoretical status, clearly there are differences in the extensiveness of the networks and therefore the meaningfulness of the constructs.

To us, recognition of the importance of theoretical systems in the meaning of constructs is the critical issue for the productive use of personality in organizational behavior. Specifically, we see three critical implications. Obviously, we need to use personality indices that have good construct validity. This is so well understood by the field that it is simply astounding how frequently it is ignored. Even a cursory examination of the literature indicates that the choice of measures is less a function of its construct validity than its use in previous studies, reported coefficient alpha levels, or the availability of enough copies of the instrument.

However, the issue of adequate theoretical systems suggests more than choosing measures with adequate construct validity. It means we have to stop treating construct validity as if it were a property of the measure only and use the construct validity evidence, the whole network, as an aid to our thinking about organizational phenomena. Every time we find a personality effect, we tie two sets of laws together: those that relate to the organizational problem and those that relate to the personality construct. The nomological network that is provided to us by the personality construct can become an invaluable tool in helping derive an appropriate explanatory system for our organizational problem. An empirical finding of a relationship between a personality construct and an organizational behavior (be it main effect or interactive) puts that behavior into the nomological network of the personality construct, suggesting new potential relationships and ways of expanding the explanatory system for the organizational phenomenon of interest. Similarly, although less efficiently, the absence of an effect suggests areas where explanation is less likely to be found. It makes sense therefore in developing our theories and choosing our personality variables to focus on constructs and measures with well worked out nomological nets and use those nets to our advantage.

In our opinion, this use of personality constructs is rarely done in organizational research. Too often, a personality variable is created solely for use within a particular theory of work behavior (Growth Need Strength for job scope or LPC for leadership) and its network therefore contains only relationships within the theory. In such a case, the personality variable may help account for more variance but it will not provide additional heuristic information. Other times, an external personality variable, often with reasonably extensive construct validity evidence, is brought into a theoretical system, either conceptually or empirically, but the construct validity evidence is only superficially alluded to or ignored. Examples are the use of self-esteem and need achievement in goal-setting research. Treating the variable in isolation of its theoretical context expands neither the network of the personality construct nor the organizational behavior.

Finally, a third implication for efficient use of personality in OB is derived from analysis of the constructual nature of personality. Theoretical constructs are unobservables that are inferred from observable indicants. For any theoretical system, a set of correspondence rules exists by which a theoretical term is translated to an observable or set of observables so that theoretical laws can be used to derive empirical relationships. We know that our measures obviously are not equivalent to our constructs and we also know that as signs of the constructs, they are often flawed. Recognition of this should, but rarely does, lead to the use of multiple indicants. As we have already discussed, much of our personality research in OB is instrument–bound. Progress will require using multiple operationalizations within and across studies.

Our reading of the OB literature suggests that the most critical need in creating a more productive role for personality is to begin thinking more deeply and creatively about where personality fits in our individual theories of organizational behavior and about the personality constructs we use. We are not arguing that personality must always occupy a central role. We are arguing against the continued treatment of personality as ad hoc, scattered, shotgun attempts to predict behavior or as appendages to existing research designs.

Part of the discipline of thinking through the role assigned to personality involves the specification of the linkages between the personality construct and other theoretical constructs. Even when the ultimate purpose of our research is pure prediction, as in the selection context, our efforts will be more efficient if we analyze the steps by which personality ultimately influences performance in a particular job over a given period of time. We suspect that had researchers invested in such thought more often, many of the negative or inconsistent findings that have emerged from personality research would have been avoided. How can we do a better job of thinking through the role of personality in our theories of work behavior? Obviously, all of the issues we have discussed are relevant. However, two additional points need to be made:

1. Theory before Design. We should not commit ourselves to a particular design for the study of personality until we have first developed our preliminary conceptual ideas about the influence of personality constructs. For a long while, the direct–effects design dominated research. Disappointment with the results of simple bivariate research, an increasing appreciation for the complexity of factors determining work behavior and advances in computer technology that have facilitated application of multivariate analyses have led to an increased commitment to the mechanistic interaction design. The inclusion of more independent variables, however, does not inevitably lead to more careful thinking about the role played by personality factors. Once we have freed ourselves from a commitment to a particular design, we can think creatively about where personality should fit within a useful explanatory system, (e.g., centrally, peripherally, direct effect, interactive effect). Theory before design also means that we cannot productively study personality effects in contexts designed to examine other issues. Research settings must be appropriate for personality manifestations as suggested by our theories.

   2. *Theory before Measurement.*   As we have seen in our review, personality research in specific areas is often dominated by particular types of constructs and specific measures. Clearly, personality constructs are of various sorts with different expected effects on behavior. It might be useful to think first in terms of types of constructs before focusing on any particular construct. In any case, as discussed earlier, we should be attracted to personality constructs with well developed nomological nets. Drawing from such constructs will improve our chances of attaining meaningful findings and, in turn, our research will extend existing nomological nets to include work related behaviors. Obviously the choice of constructs must precede the choice of personality measures. As we stated before, researchers in OB are often guilty of grasping available popular personality measures, measures that presumably come with reliable short forms or which assess many different constructs simultaneously, and include them in research because of convenience. Our choice of measures, as well as design, must be more carefully considered.

CONCLUSIONS

We began our paper by noting the tarnished reputation of personality constructs among organizational researchers. This reputation has developed from years of research which has produced comparatively little insight into organizational behavior. It has also developed from the awareness among OB researchers of the criticisms being leveled at personality in more basic areas of psychology.

   These criticisms have been based upon both empirical data and logical analysis. We have noted, however, that reasonable objections come more from empirical rather than logical considerations. In fact, most of the criticisms offered by personally researchers place greater emphasis on the inability of personality constructs to predict behavior patterns then from the question of construct legitimacy. Even Mischel (1973), who provides logical arguments against the explanatory usefulness of personality, suggests we examine a set of cognitive individual difference variables which are similar to the kinds of mediating traits discussed by Endler and Magnusson (1977).

   Organizational researchers also have based their criticisms of personality more on empirical than logical problems. As we have stated, we do not disagree with those who argue that the contribution of personality to organizational behavior has been disappointing. We do, however, disagree with the conclusions about the usefulness of personality that can be drawn from this data. The reasons for this disagreement, which should now be apparent, center on two general issues.

First, once we accept the legitimate, logical status of personality constructs, it no longer makes any sense to discuss the usefulness of "personality" in global terms. Personality traits come in all sizes and shapes. Some relate to cognitive styles, some relate to motivational principles. Some constructs in use are well developed. Others are poorly conceptualized. Some have reasonable measurement procedures. Others do not. It is simply inappropriate to think in terms of the overall utility of "personality." We must instead recognize that usefulness relates to particular constructs, particular situations and particular issues. We have no right to make inductive statements about the whole class of constructs when we have not sampled systematically from that class or from a class of problems where personality might be useful theoretically.

Our second general point relates to this last statement. Our review suggests that OB researchers have barely scratched the surface of the ways in which personality constructs may enter into theoretical systems. It is interesting to note that the large number of empirical studies of organizational behavior incorporating personality variables does not translate into a wide variety of designs, constructs, or conceptualizations. Reasonable inference always involves the ruling out of plausible alternative hypotheses. Before we use the existing data to infer that personality research is not likely to be productive, we must entertain the plausible rival hypothesis that we have not adequately studied the issues.

In this paper we have tried to offer suggestions on how research examining personality effects might be more adequately conducted. These suggestions were not designed to serve as a shopping list of do's and don'ts. Rather they were offered in the hope of encouraging OB researchers to study personality in a more systematic way. The results of more systematic attention may, in fact, lead to the same conclusions which are now being entertained. We think not. However, if they do, these conclusions will be based upon a substantially sounder set of evidence.

NOTES

1. Adler, S., and Weiss, H. M. Criterion aggregation in personality research: Self esteem and goal setting. Paper presented at the 90th annual convention of the American Psychological Association, Washington, D.C., August, 1982.
2. We wish to thank Larry Cummings for suggesting this alternative.

REFERENCES

Abdel-Halim, A. A. Individual and interpersonal moderators of employee reactions to job characteristics: A reexamination. *Personnel Psychology*, 1979, *32*, 121–137.

Adler, S., Aranya, N., & Amernic, J. Community size, socialization, and the work needs of professionals. *Academy of Management Journal*, 1981, *24*, 504–511.

Adler, S., & Coolan, J. Lateness as a withdrawal behavioral. *Journal of Applied Psychology*, 1981, *61*, 544–554.

Aldag, R. J., & Brief, A. P. Some correlates of work values. *Journal of Applied Psychology*, 1975, *60*, 757–760.

Allport, G. W. *Personality: A Psychological Interpretation*. N.Y.: Holt, Rinehart and Winston, 1937.

Alston, W. P. Traits, consistency and conceptual alternatives for personality theory. *Journal for the Theory of Social Behavior*, 1975, *5*, 17–47.

Anderson, C. R., & Schneier, C. E. Locus of control, leader behavior and leader performance among management students. *Academy of Management Journal*, 1978, *21*, 690–698.

Andrisani, P., & Nestel, G. Internal-external control as a contribution to and outcome of work experience. *Journal of Applied Psychology*, 1976, *61*, 156–165.

Arnold, H. J., & House, R. J. Methodological and substantive extensions to the job characteristics model of motivation. *Organizational Behavior and Human Performance*, 1980, *25*, 161–183.

Ashour, A. S. The contingency model of leadership effectiveness: An evaluation. *Organizational Behavior and Human Performance*, 1973, *9*, 339–355.

Atkinson, J. W. *An Introduction to Motivation*. Princeton, NJ: Van Nostrand, 1964.

Atkinson, J. W., & Raynor, J. O. (Eds.), *Personality, Motivation and Achievement*. New York: Wiley & Sons, 1978.

Bales, R. F., & Cohen, S. P. *SYMLOG: A System for the Multiple Level Observation of Groups*, N.Y.: Free Press, 1979.

Bandura, A. The self system in reciprocal determinism. *American Psychologist*, 1978, *33*, 344–358.

Bass, B. M. Leadership opinions as forecasts of supervisory success. *Journal of Applied Psychology*, 1956, *40*, 345–346.

Bass, B. M. *Stogdill's Handbook of Leadership*. New York: The Free Press, 1981.

Beck, L. W. Constructions and inferred entities. In H. Feigl and M. Brodbeck (Eds.), *Readings in the Philosophy of Science*. New York: Appleton-Century-Crofts, 1953.

Bem, D. J., & Allen, A. On predicting some of the people some of the time: The search for cross-situational consistencies in behavior. *Psychological Review*, 1974, *81*, 506–520.

Bernardin, H. J. The relationship of personality variables to organizational withdrawal. *Personnel Psychology*, 1977, *30*, 17–27.

Blood, M. R. Work values and job satisfaction. *Journal of Applied Psychology*, 1969, *53*, 456–459.

Blood, M. R., & Hulin, C. L. Alienation, environmental characteristics, and worker responses. *Journal of Applied Psychology*, 1967, *51*, 284–290.

Bons, P. M., Bass, A. R., & Komorita, S. S. Changes in leadership style as a function of military experience and type of command. *Personnel Psychology*, 1970, *23*, 551–561.

Brousseau, K. R., & Prince, J. B. Job-person dynamics: An extension of longitudinal research. *Journal of Applied Psychology*, 1981, *66*, 59–62.

Brunswick, E. *Perception and the Representative Design of Psychological Experiments*. Berkeley, CA: University of California Press, 1956.

Caldwell, D. F., & O'Reilly, C. A. Boundary spanning and individual performance: The impact of self-monitoring. *Journal of Applied Psychology*, 1982, *67*, 124–127.

Campbell, D. J. Determinants of choice of goal difficulty level: A review of situational and personality influences. *Journal of Occupational Psychology*, 1982, *55*, 79–95.

Champoux, J. E., & Peters, W. S. Applications of moderated regression in job design research. *Personnel Psychology*, 1980, *33*, 759–783.

Cronbach, L. J. The two disciplines of scientific psychology. *American Psychologist*, 1957, *12*, 671–684.

Cronbach, L. J., & Meehl, P. E. Construct validation in psychological tests. *Psychological Bulletin*, 1955, *52*, 281–302.

Dossett, D. L., Latham, G. P., & Mitchell, T. R. The effects of assigned versus participatively set goals, KR, and individual differences when goal difficulty is held constant. *Journal of Applied Psychology*, 1979, *64*, 291–298.

Duncan, S., & Fiske, D. W. *Face-to-Face Interaction: Research, Methods, and Theory.* Hillsdale, NJ: Lawrence Erlbaum Associates, 1976.

Einstein, A., & Infeld, L. *The Evolution of Physics.* N.Y.: Simon and Schuster, 1938.

Endler, N. S., & Magnusson, D. Toward an interactional psychology of personality. *Psychological Bulletin*, 1976, *83*, 956–974.

Epstein, S. Traits are alive and well. In D. Magnusson and S. Endler (Eds.) *Personality at the Crossroads: Current Issues in Interactional Psychology.* Hillsdale, N.J.: Erlbaum, 1977.

Epstein, S. The stability of behavior: I. On predicting most of the people much of the time. *Journal of Personality and Social Psychology*, 1979, *37*, 1097–1126.

Epstein, S. The stability of behavior: II. Implications for psychological research. *American Psychologist*, 1980, *35*, 790–806.

Evans, M. G. The effects of supervisory behavior on the path goal relationship. *Organizational Behavior and Human Performance*, 1970, *5*, 277–298.

Fenigstein, A., Scheier, M. F., & Buss, A. H. Public and private self-consciousness: Assessment and theory. *Journal of Consulting and Clinical Psychology*, 1975, *43*, 522–527.

Fiedler, F. E. *A Theory of Leadership Effectiveness.* New York: McGraw-Hill, 1967.

Fiedler, F. E., & Chemers, M. M. Leadership and Effective Management. Glenview, Ill.: Scott, Foresman, 1974.

Fishbein, M., & Ajzen, I. Attitudes toward objects as predictors of single and multiple behavioral criteria. *Psychological Review*, 1974, *81*, 59–74.

Fleishman, E. A. The measurement of leadership attitudes in industry. *Journal of Applied Psychology*, 1953, *37*, 153–158.

Fleishman, E. A. Twenty years of consideration and structure. In E. A. Fleishman and J. G. Hunt (Eds.) *Current Developments in the Study of Leadership*, Carbondale, IL.: SIU Press, 1973.

Fleishman, E. A., & Harris, E. F. Patterns of leadership behavior related to employee grievances and turnover. *Personnel Psychology*, 1962, *15*, 43–56.

Frank, I. Psychology as a science: Resolving the idiographic-nomothetic controversy. *Journal for the Theory of Social Behavior*, 1982, *12*, 1–20.

Ganster, D. C. Individual differences and task design: A laboratory experiment. *Organizational Behavior and Human Performance*, 1980, *26*, 131–148.

Ghiselli, E. E. The prediction of predictability. *Educational and Psychological Measurement*, 1960, *20*, 3–8.

Ghiselli, E. E. *Explorations in Managerial Talent.* Pacific Palisades, CA: Goodyear, 1971.

Ghiselli, E. E., Campbell, J. P., & Zedeck, S. *Measurement Theory for the Behavioral Sciences.* San Francisco: W. H. Freeman, 1981.

Goldstein, K. M., & Blackman, S. *Cognitive Style: Five Approaches and Relevant Research*. New York: Wiley, 1978.

Graen, G. Role making processes within complex organizations. In M. D. Dunnette (Ed.) *Handbook of Industrial and Organizational Psychology*. Chicago: Rand-McNally, 1976.

Gruenfeld, L. W. Field dependence and field independence in a framework for the study of task and social orientations in organizational leadership. In D. Graues (Ed.), *Management Research: A Cross-Cultural Perspective*. Amsterdam, The Netherlands: Elsevien-North Holland Biomedical Press, 1973.

Gruenfeld, L. W., & MacEachron, A. E. A cross-national study of cognitive style among managers and technicians. *International Journal of Psychology*, 1975, *10*, 27–55.

Guion, R. M., & Gottier, R. F. Validity of personality measures in personnel selection. *Personnel Psychology*, 1965, *18*, 135–164.

Hackman, J. R., & Lawler, E. E. Employee reactions to job characteristics. *Journal of Applied Psychology*, 1971, *55*, 259–286.

Hackman, J. R., & Oldham, G. R. Development of the Job Diagnostic Survey. *Journal of Applied Psychology*, 1975, *60*, 159–170.

Hackman, J. R., & Oldham, G. R. Motivation through the design of work: Test of a theory. *Organizational Behavior of Human Performance*, 1976, *16*, 250–279.

Hackman, J. R., & Oldham, G. R. *Work Redesign*. Reading, Mass.: Addison-Wesley, 1980.

Halpin, A. W., & Winer, B. J. A factorial study of the leader behavior descriptions. In R. M. Stogdill & A. E. Coons (Eds.) *Leader Behavior: Its Description and Measurement*. Columbus: Ohio State University, Bureau of Business Researchers, 1957.

Hammer, T. H., & Vardi, Y. Locus of control and career self-management among nonsupervisory employees in industrial settings. *Journal of Vocational Behavior*, 1981, *18*, 13–29.

Helson, R., & Mitchell, V. Personality. In M. R. Rosenzweig and L. W. Porter (Eds.) *Annual Review of Psychology*, Vol. 29, Palo Alto, CA: Annual Reviews, Inc., 1978.

Hemphill, J. K., & Coons, A. E. Development of the leader behavior description questionnaire. In R. M. Stogdill & A. E. Coons (Eds.), *Leader Behavior: Its Description and Measurement*. Columbus: Ohio State University, Bureau of Business Research, 1957.

House, R. J. A path-goal theory of leader effectiveness. *Administrative Science Quarterly*, 1971, *16*, 321–338.

Howard, J. A. Person-situation interaction models. *Personality and Social Psychology Bulletin*, 1979, *5*, 191–195.

Hulin, C. L., & Blood, M. R. Job enlargement, individual differences, and worker responses. *Psychological Bulletin*, 1968, *69*, 41–55.

Ickes, W. A basic paradigm for the study of personality roles and social behavior. In W. Ickes and S. Knowles (Eds.) *Personality, Roles and Social Behavior*. N.Y.: Springer-Verlay, in press.

Ilgen, D. R. & Feldman, J. M. Performance appraisal: A process focus. In B. M. Staw & L. L. Cummings (Eds.) *Research in Organizational Behavior*, (*Vol. 5*). Greenwich, CT: JAI Press, 1983.

Jaccard, J. J. Predicting social behavior from personality traits. *Journal of Research in Personality*, 1974, *7*, 358–367.

Jaccard, J. J. Personality and behavioral predictions. An analysis of behavioral criterion measures. In L. Kahle and D. Fiske (Eds.) *Methods for Studying Person-Situation Interactions*. San Francisco: Jossey-Bass, 1977.

James, L. R., & Jones, A. P. Perceived job characteristics and job satisfaction: An examination of reciprocal causation. *Personnel Psychology*, 1980, *33*, 97–135.

Jones, A. P., & Butler, M. L. Influences of cognitive complexity on the dimensions underlying perceptions of the work environment. *Motivation and Emotion*, 1980, *4*, 1–19.

Kane, J. S., & Lawler, E. E. III. Performance appraisal effectiveness: Its assessment and determinants. In B. M. Staw (Ed.) *Research in Organizational Behavior*, Vol. *1*. Greenwich, CT: JAI Press, 1979.

Kaplan, A. *The Conduct of Inquiry*. San Francisco: Crowell, 1964.

Katz, R. The influence of job longevity on employee reactions to task characteristics. *Human Relations*, 1978, *31*, 703–725.

Katz, R. Time and work: Toward an integrative perspective. In B. M. Staw and L. L. Cummings (Eds.) *Research in Organizational Behavior*, Vol. 2. Greenwich, CT: JAI Press, 1980.

Kerr, S., & Jermier, J. M. Substitutes for leadership: Their meaning and measurement. *Organizational Behavior and Human Performance*, 1978, *22*, 375–403.

Kerr, S., Schriesheim, C. A., Murphy, C. J., & Stogdill, R. M. Toward a contingency theory of leadership based upon the consideration and initiating structure literature. *Organizational Behavior and Human Performance*, 1974, *12*, 62–82.

Kerr, S., & Schriesheim, C. Consideration, initiating structure, and organizational criteria: An update of Korman's 1966 review. *Personnel Psychology*, 1974, *27*, 555–568.

Kohn, M. L., & Schooler, C. Job conditions and personality: A longitudinal assessment of their reciprocal effects. *American Journal of Sociology*, 1982, *87*, 1257–1286.

Korman, A. K. "Consideration," "Initiating Structure," and organizational criteria. *Personnel Psychology*, 1966, *18*, 349–360.

Korman, A. K. The prediction of managerial performance: A review. *Personnel Psychology*, 1968, *21*, 295–322.

Korman, A. K. Toward an hypothesis of work behavior. *Journal of Applied Psychology*, 1970, *54*, 31–41.

Korman, A. K. Hypothesis of work behavior revisited and an extension. *Academy of Management Review*, 1976, *1*, 50–63.

Kruglanski, A. W. The human subject in the psychology experiment: Fact and artifact. In L. Berkowitz (Ed.) *Advances in Experimental Social Psychology*, Vol. 8. N.Y.: Academic Press, 1975.

Larson, L. L., Hunt, J. G., & Osborn, R. N. The great hi-hi leader behavior myth: A lesson from Occam's razor. *Academy of Management Journal*, 1976, *19*, 628–641.

Lawler, E. E. *Pay and Organizational Effectiveness*. New York: McGraw-Hill, 1971.

Locke, E. A. Toward a theory of task motivation and incentives. *Organizational Behavior and Human Performance*, 1968, *3*, 157–189.

Locke, E. A., Shaw, K. N., Saari, L. M., & Latham, G. Goal setting and task performance: 1969–1980. *Psychological Bulletin*, 1981, *90*, 125–152.

Lord, R. G., Foti, R. J., & Phillips, J. S. A theory of leadership categorization. In J. G. Hunt, U. Sekaran & C. Schriesheim (Eds.), *Leadership: Beyond Establishment Views*. Carbondale, Ill.: Southern Illinois University Press, 1981.

Louis, M. R. Surprise and sense making: What newcomers experience in entering unfamiliar organizational settings. *Administrative Science Quarterly*, 1980, *35*, 226–251.

Luthans, F. & Davis, T. R. V. An idiographic approach to organizational behavior research: The use of single case experimental designs and direct measures. *Academy of Management Review*, 1982, *7*, 380–391.

MacCorquodale, K., & Meehl, P. E. On a distinction between hypothetical constructs and intervening variables. *Psychological Review*, 1948, *55*, 95–107.

McGowan, J., & Gormly, J. Validation of personality traits: A multi-criteria approach. *Journal of Personality and Social Psychology*, 1976, *34*, 791–795.

Magnusson, D., & Ekehammer, B. Similar situations—similar behaviors? A study of the intraindividual congruence between situation perceptions and situation reaction. *Journal of Research in Personality*, 1978, *12*, 41–48.

Magnusson, D., & Endler, N. S. Interactional psychology: Present status and future prospects. In D. Magnusson & N. N. S. Endler (Eds.) *Personality at the Crossroads: Current Issues in Interactional Psychology.* Hillsdale, NJ: Lawrence Erlbaum, 1977.

Maslow, A. H. *Motivation and Personality.* New York: Harper, 1954.

McClelland, D. C. & Boyatzis, R. E. Leadership motive pattern and long term success in management. *Journal of Applied Psychology,* 1982, *67,* 737–743.

Messer, S. B. Reflection–impulsivity: A review, *Psychological Bulletin,* 1976, *83,* 1026–1052.

Messick, S. Constructs and their vicissitudes. *Psychological Bulletin,* 1981, *89,* 575–588.

Middleton, W. L. Personality qualities predominant in campus leaders. *Journal of Social Psychology,* 1941, *13,* 199–201.

Miller, D., De Vries, M. F. R., & Toulouse, J. M. Top executive locus of control and its relationship to strategy-making, structure, and environment. *Academy of Management Review,* 1982, *25,* 237–253.

Miner, J. B. Twenty years of research on role-motivation theory of managerial effectiveness. *Personnel Psychology,* 1978, *31,* 739–760.

Mischel, W. *Personality and Assessment,* N.Y.: Wiley, 1968.

Mischel, W. Toward a cognitive social learning reconceptualization of personality. *Psychological Review,* 1973, *80,* 252–283.

Mischel, W. The interaction of person and situation. In D. Magnusson and N. S. Endler (Eds.), *Personality at the Crossroads: Current Issues in Interactional Psychology.* Hillsdale, N.J.: Erlbaum, 1977.

Mitchell, T. R. Organizational Behavior in M. R. Rosenzweig and L. W. Porter (eds.) *Annual Review of Psychology* Vol. *30* Palo Alto, CA: Annual Reviews Inc., 1979

Mitchell, T. R., Green, S. G., & Wood, R. An attributional model of leadership and the poor performing subordinate. In L. L. Cummings and B. M. Staw, *Research in Organizational Behavior,* Vol. *3,* Greenwich, CT: JAI Press, 1981.

Mobley, W. H. Intermediate linkages in the relationship between job satisfaction and employee turnover. *Journal of Applied Psychology,* 1977, *62,* 237–240.

Mobley, W. H., Griffeth, R. W., Hand, H. H., & Meglino, B. M. Review and conceptual analyses of the employee turnover process. *Psychological Bulletin,* 1979, *86,* 493–522.

Monson, T. C., Hesley, J. W., & Chernick, L. Specifying when personality traits can and cannot predict behavior: An alternative to abandoning the attempt to predict single act criteria. *Journal of Personality and Social Psychology,* 1982, *43,* 385–399.

Moskowitz, D. S. Coherence and cross-situational generality in personality: A new analysis of old problems. *Journal of Personality and Social Psychology,* 1982, *43,* 754–768.

Mowday, R. T., Porter, L. W., & Steers, R. M. *Employee Organization Linkages. The Psychology of Commitment, Absenteeism and Turnover.* N.Y.: Academic Press, 1982.

Mowday, R. T., & Spencer, D. G. The influence of task and personality characteristics on employee turnover and absenteeism incidents. *Academy of Management Journal,* 1981, *24,* 634–642.

Muchinsky, P. M., & Tuttle, M. L. Employee turnover: An empirical and methodological assessment. *Journal of Vocational Behavior,* 1979, *14,* 43–77.

Muchinsky, P. M. Employee absenteeism: A review of the literature. *Journal of Vocational Behavior,* 1977, *10,* 316–340.

Nygard, R. Toward an interactional psychology: Models from achievement research. *Journal of Personality,* 1981, *49,* 363–387.

Olweus, D. Aggression and peer acceptance in preadolescent boys: Two short term longitudinal studies of ratings. *Child Development,* 1977, *48,* 1301–1313.

O'Reilly, C. Personality–job fit: Implications for individual attitudes and performance. *Organizational Behavior and Human Performance,* 1977, *18,* 36–46.

Organ, D. W. Direct, indirect, and trace effects of personality variables on role adjustment. *Human Relations,* 1981, *34,* 573–587.

Payne, R. L., Fineman, S., & Jackson, P. R. An interactionist approach to measuring anxiety at work. *Journal of Occupational Psychology*, 1982, *55*, 13–25.

Pervin, L. A., & Lewis, M. *Perspectives in Interactional Psychology*. N.Y.: Plenum, 1978.

Pfeffer, J. Management as symbolic action: The creation and maintenance of organizational paradigms. In L. L. Cummings and B. M. Staw (Eds.) *Research in Organizational Behavior*, Vol. *3*. Greenwich, CT: JAI Press, 1981.

Podsakoff, P. M. Determinants of a supervisor's use of rewards and punishments: A literature review and suggestions for further research. *Organizational Behavior and Human Performance*, 1982, *29*, 58–83.

Porter, L. W., & Steers, R. M. Organizational, work and personal factors in employee turnover and absenteeism. *Psychological Bulletin*, 1973, *80*, 151–176.

Porter, L. W., Lawler, E. E. III & Hackman, J. R. *Behavior in Organizations*, N.Y.: McGraw-Hill, 1975.

Price, R. H., & Bouffard, D. L. Behavioral appropriateness and situational constraint as dimensions of social behavior. *Journal of Personality and Social Psychology*, 1974, *30*, 579–586.

Rabinowitz, S., Hall, D. T., & Goodale, J. G. Job scope and individual differences as predictors of job involvement: Independent or interactive? *Academy of Management Journal*, 1977, *20*, 273–281.

Rakestraw, T. L., Jr. & Weiss, H. M. The interaction of social influences and task experience on goals, performance, and performance satisfaction. *Organizational Behavior & Human Performance*, 1981, *27*, 326–344.

Rice, R. W. Construct validity of the least preferred coworker score. *Psychological Bulletin*, 1978, *85*, 1199–1237.

Roberts, K. H., & Glick, W. The job characteristics approach to task design: A critical review. *Journal of Applied Psychology*, 1981, *66*, 193–217.

Rotter, J. B. Generalized expectancies for internal versus external control of reinforcement. *Psychological Monographs*, 1966, *80* (1, Whole No. 609).

Rychlak, J. F. *Introduction to Personality and Psychotherapy*. Boston: Houghton-Mifflin, 1981.

Ryle, G. *The Concept of Mind*. N.Y.: Barnes and Noble, 1949.

Salancik, G. R., & Pfeffer, J. An examination of need satisfaction models of job attitudes. *Administrative Science Quarterly*, 1977, *22*, 427–456.

Salancik, G. R., & Pfeffer, J. A social information processing approach to job attitudes and task design. *Administrative Science Quarterly*, 1978, *23*, 224–253.

Schneider, B. An interactionist perspective on organizational effectiveness. In K. Cameron & D. Whetten (Eds.) *Organizational Effectiveness*. New York: Academic Press, 1982.

Schneider, B. Interactional psychology and organizational behavior. In L. L. Cummings & B. M. Staw (Eds.) *Research in Organizational Behavior*, Vol. *5*. Greenwich, CT: JAI Press, 1983.

Sims, H. P., & Szilagyi, A. D. Job characteristic relationships: Individual and structural moderators. *Organizational Behavior and Human Performance*, 1976, *17*, 211–230.

Snyder, M. The self-monitoring of expressive behavior. *Journal of Personality and Social Psychology*, 1974, *30*, 526–537.

Spector, P. E. Behavior in organizations as a function of employee's locus of control. *Psychological Bulletin*, 1982, *91*, 482–497.

Stagner, R. On the reality and relevance of traits. *Journal of General Psychology*, 1977, *96*, 185–207.

Steers, R. M., & Rhodes, S. R. Major influences on employee attendance: A process model. *Journal of Applied Psychology*, 1978, *63*, 391–407.

Stogdill, R. M. Personal factors associated with leadership: A survey of the literature. *Journal of Psychology*, 1948, *25*, 35–71.

Stogdill, R. M. *Handbook of Leadership*. N.Y.: Free Press, 1974.

Stone, E. F. The moderating effect of work related values on the job scope-job satisfaction relationship. *Organizational Behavior and Human Performance*, 1976, *15*, 147–167.

Stone, E. F. Field independence and perceptions of task characteristics: A laboratory investigation. *Journal of Applied Psychology*, 1979, *64*, 305–310.

Stone, E. F., Ganster, D. L., Woodman, R. W., & Fusilier, M. R. Relationships between Growth Need Strength and selected individual differences measures employed in job design research. *Journal of Vocational Behavior*, 1979, *14*, 329–340.

Strube, J. J., & Garcia, J. E. A meta-analytic investigation of Fiedler's model of leadership effectiveness. *Psychological Bulletin*, 1981, *90*, 307–321.

Snyder, M., & Ickes, W. J. Personality and social behavior. In G. Lindzey and E. Aronson (Eds.) *Handbook of Social Psychology (3rd Edition)*. Reading, MA: Addison-Wesley, in press.

Terborg, J. R. Interactional psychology and research on human behavior in organizations. *Academy of Management Review*, 1981, *6*, 569–576.

Turner, A. N., & Lawrence, P. R. *Industrial Jobs and The Worker*. Cambridge, MA: Harvard Graduate School of Business Administration, 1965.

Turner, M. B. *Philosophy and the Science of Behavior*. N.Y.: Appleton-Century-Crofts, 1965.

Van Maanen, J., & Schein, E. H. Toward a theory of organizational socialization. In B. M. Staw (Eds.) *Research in Organizational Behavior*, Vol. *1*. Greenwich, CT: JAI Press, 1979.

Wahba, M. A., & Bridwell, L. G. Maslow reconsidered: A review of research on the need hierarchy theory. *Organizational Behavior and Human Performance*, 1976, *15*, 212–240.

Weick, K. E. *The Social Psychology of Organizing (2nd ed.)*. Reading, Mass.: Addison-Wesley, 1979.

Weiss, H. M. Subordinate imitation of supervisor behavior: The role of modeling in organizational socialization. *Organizational Behavior and Human Performance*, 1977, *19*, 89–105.

Weiss, H. M. Social learning of work values in organizations. *Journal of Applied Psychology*, 1978, *63*, 711–718.

Weiss, H. M., & Adler, S. Cognitive complexity and the structure of implicit leadership theories. *Journal of Applied Psychology*, 1981, *66*, 69–78.

Weiss, H. M., & Knight, P. A. The utility of humility: Self esteem, information search and problem solving efficiency. *Organizational Behavior and Human Performance*, 1980, *25*, 216–223.

Weiss, H. M., & Shaw, J. B. Social influences on judgments about tasks. *Organizational Behavior and Human Performance*, 1979, *24*, 126–140.

Weissenberg, P., & Kavanagh, M. J. The independence of initiating structure and consideration: A review of the evidence. *Personnel Psychology*, 1972, *25*, 119–1961.

Weitz, J. Criteria and transfer of training. *Psychological Reports* 1966, *19*, 195–210.

White, J. K. Individual differences in the job quality-worker response relationship: Review, integration and comments. *Academy of Management Review*, 1978, *3*, 267–280.

Witkin, H. A., & Goodenough, D. R. Field dependence and interpersonal behavior. *Psychological Bulletin*, 1977, *84*, 661–689.

Wolfle, L. M., & Shaw, R. D. Effects of college attendance on locus of control. *Journal of Personality and Social Psychology*, 1982, *43*, 802–810.

Zedeck, S. Problems with the use of "moderator" variable. *Psychological Bulletin*, 1971, *76*, 295–310.

RELATIVE DEPRIVATION IN
ORGANIZATIONAL SETTINGS

Faye Crosby

ABSTRACT

The chapter narrates the history of relative deprivation theory and outlines
some ways in which to study the theoretical questions in organizational
settings. Relative deprivation theory has traditionally attempted to account
for the lack of correspondence between objective and subjective reality by
noting that deprivation or grievances are experienced relative to some psychological standard. The exact nature of that standard has been a matter
of scholarly debate.

Two trends in the current research may be discerned. First, both survey
and laboratory data suggest that feelings of deprivation depend on the joint
occurrence of frustrated wants and of violated entitlements. People feel
aggrieved, in other words, when their present condition is not as good as
they want and not as good as they think it ought to be. The second important
finding in the contemporary work on relative deprivation is the lack of
connection between personal and group deprivation. Disadvantaged people
appear much more prone to recognize that their group suffers than to recognize that they personally suffer.

The challenge now is to study relative deprivation in organizational settings. How, for example, do the nature and structure of an organization
influence the development of personal grievance and the development of
group grievance? To better meet the challenge, researchers ought to consider three issues. First comes focus: when do disadvantaged people evaluate
themselves and when do they evaluate their situation? Second comes the
distinction between procedural and distributive justice. Finally there is the
issue of evaluations. Reactions to positive events or outcomes may have
little to do with reactions to negative events or outcomes.

The chapter closes with the hope that a full understanding of the past
and present problems in relative deprivation research will clear the way for
a brighter future.

Research in Organizational Behavior, vol. 6, pages 51–93
Copyright © 1984 by JAI Press Inc.
All rights of reproduction in any form reserved.
ISBN: 0-89232-351-5

Scholars and administrators both display an abiding interest in the question of how the circumstances of work life affect the cognitions and emotions of individuals at work. No less fascinating is the sister question: how do cognitions and emotions relate to performance in organizational settings? Among the numerous considerations of how the objective realities of work life affect and are affected by the subjective realities of workers, one concept has gained prominence, if only sporadically. That is the concept of relative deprivation, which acknowledges that people's feelings of deprivation, discontent, grievance, or resentment often do not relate in a simple, direct, or isomorphic way to their objective situations.

This chapter tells the story of relative deprivation. It boasts of a beginning, a middle, and an end. The first part of the chapter chronicles the history of relative deprivation from its status as a conceptual seedling during World War II to its theoretical flowering three decades later. In full bloom, the theory of relative deprivation has identified no less than a half dozen psychological factors—such as the awareness that someone else is better-off than oneself—which could mediate the relationship between objective and subjective reality within a given context. The first part of the chapter may appear unconventional both in the amount of detail it offers and in its narrative quality. Both are mandated by the conviction that ignorance of our past mistakes tends to condemn us to repeat them.

The middle of the story brings a summary of current work. One major portion of the current research in relative deprivation consists of pruning. From six hypothesized mediators between objective and subjective reality, we move to two. Feelings of deprivation, resentment or grievance are currently thought to depend on the discrepancy between the actual situation and the desired situation *and* between the actual situation and the deserved situation. If one portion of current research involves cutting away distinctions which have not proved useful, another aspect centers around developing and clarifying a distinction which has, off and on, intrigued theorists. It is the distinction between resentments felt about one's own situation (personal deprivations) and resentments felt about the situation of a given group (group deprivations). Current research underscores the prevalence of group deprivations, especially as compared to the rarity of personal deprivations.

In the final stretch of the chapter, the focus shifts to future research. The chapter admonishes researchers to document the occurence of different types of resentment within organizations; to study how the natures and structures of organizations influence the development of various types of deprivation; and to outline the ways in which feelings of personal and group deprivation could be harnessed for the good of the organizations themselves. Despite their persistent interest in discontented workers, social scientists have failed to consider systematically the importance of organizational factors in the creation and consequences of discontent. Since some of the failure appears to spring from an indifference to three specific issues which enjoy some attention throughout the social sciences, the story draws to a close with an examination of the issues and a word about the practical and the theoretical benefits of studying felt deprivation in organizational settings.

DEVELOPMENT OF A THEORY

People's feelings of resentment, grievance, deprivation or dissatisfaction do not depend, in a direct, simple and obvious way on their objective situation. Sometimes the people who are well-off objectively feel more satisfied with their outcomes than do their poorer cousins. Sometimes the opposite is true. Sometimes the people with a six-digit salary feel more contented with their pay than do the people with a four-digit or a five-digit salary. Quite often—if anecdotal evidence and journalistic accounts are to be believed—they do not. Many successful business people attest to the relative nature of monetary gains: even after allowing for inflation, the bonus which represented an astronomical sum at the beginning of one's career quickly becomes less celestial. Nor is one promotion equal to another. A promotion to Vice-President gives less satisfaction when all the District Managers are given the title than when the hierarchical pyramid retains its steep slopes. That the satisfactions and dissatisfactions are relative to some psychological standard and are not in any sense absolute is a matter of common sense. The phenomenon has not escaped the notice of either ancient or modern sages. Marx, for example, expressed the idea neatly when he said:

> A house may be large or small; as long as the surrounding houses are equally small, it satisfies all social demands for a dwelling. But let a palace arise beside the little house, and it shrinks from a little house to a hut. (Quoted in Useem, 1975, p. 53)

Foundations

Although philosophers and social observers throughout the ages have remarked on the relative nature of human pleasure and displeasure, it was not until World War II that someone gave a label to the observation. At that time, Samuel Stouffer and his colleagues in the Research Branch of the Army, created the term "relative deprivation" to help convey the paradoxical character of some of their findings (Stouffer, Star, deVinney & Williams, 1949). They never defined the term explicitly but its meaning was clear from the context in which they used it. The most famous of their findings concerned the satisfaction with the promotion system. Quite to their surprise, Stouffer and his co-workers found satisfaction with the promotion system to be greater in the military police, where promotions were infrequent, than in the air corps. where most survivors could anticipate rapid promotions. Another paradox to which Stouffer et al. alluded with the term relative deprivation was the attitude of black soldiers. Black soldiers who were stationed at training camps in the South appeared more contented with army life than did those stationed in the North. Stouffer et al. explained this puzzle by speculating that black soldiers in the South must have felt privileged relative to black civilians in the South, while black soldiers in the North did not experience the same sense of relative privilege.

Soon after Stouffer's creation of the term as a convenient label for some paradoxical findings, the construct of relative deprivation was doubly promoted in the social sciences. First, Robert Merton and Alice Kitt Rossi (1957) bathed the term in a scholarly glow by linking it with the concept of reference groups. Although reference group theory has itself become multi-faceted over the years (Hyman & Singer, 1968), the critical link between feelings of deprivation and reference group has remained the 'referent other' or 'comparison other'. Briefly, the idea is that people's expectations about what they would like to possess and should possess derive from explicit or implicit comparisons to other people. Usually the other people are friends, neighbors, or colleagues with whom they have face-to-face interactions. Sometimes the 'reference group' consists of a nominal group like political science professors, employed women or admirals in the Navy. When a person feels himself or herself to belong to a group and believes that the other group members enjoy certain advantages or outcomes, the person becomes discontented if he or she does not enjoy those same outcomes. This much Merton and Rossi, elaborating on Stouffer et al., suggest.

While Merton and Rossi's paper made relative deprivation a household term among social scientists, James A. Davis (1959) presented a formal theory of relative deprivation. The theory advances beyond the simple heuristic concept of relative deprivation and, indeed, beyond what we know by common sense, by specifying the conditions under which discontents occur. Davis builds his model on two fundamental distinctions: a) the distinction between ingroups and outgroups and b) the distinction between those who are objectively nondeprived (i.e., the 'haves') and those who are objectively deprived (i.e., the 'have-nots'). When an individual compares his own lot to someone who is outside his own group, he experiences social distance if the other person's outcomes differ from his own. If the other person lacks desired outcomes which the person possesses, he feels relative superiority. If the other person possesses desired outcomes, which the person lacks, the person experiences relative subordination. In one organization, for example, the many windows and mahogany desk of the executive suite may contrast starkly with the windowless pine-and-linoleum station of the clerk. The contrast may reinforce status differences and may contribute to the conviction, by boss and clerk alike, that the executive ought to receive much greater compensation for his efforts than does the clerk.

The perception of cross group differences reinforces the status quo, but the perception of differences within a group threatens it. In Davis' model, when a have-not compares his lot to a better-off member of his own ingroup, he experiences relative deprivation. If he himself is the have, and the other group member is the have-not, relative gratification follows from the comparison. The blue-collar worker who sees that his mate's paycheck exceeds his own will experience relative deprivation, while his mate will feel relative gratification, according to Davis' system.

Davis does not specify how people decide group membership. Nevertheless, his model does allow for the fact that characteristics which impress one person as a legitimate basis of distinction, may not so impress another. Thus one person may experience social distance while another in the same situation experiences relative deprivation. The clerk who believes that upper management constitutes a separate breed should experience subordination at the sight of the boss' office, while the contrast between the well–appointed management milieu and the drab workers' offices may simply enrage the worker who disputes the distinction between managers and workers. One likely case occurs when the privileged party imagines distinctions are justified while the disadvantaged party does not.

Davis assumes that people make comparisons in a random fashion. From this assumption and from the two fundamental distinctions, Davis derives a formal statement concerning the frequency of perceived unfairness and of social distance within social groups. He tests his postulates against the materials presented in Stouffer et al. *The American Soldier* and finds his interpretation to be confirmed in 10 out of 11 cases.

Davis also develops a set of propositions about sub-group formation. He specifies that the possibility of sub-group formation is greatest when the ingroup distribution of outcomes is perceived to be fair and when social distance between groups is great. Ingroup fairness, in turn, is greatest when all members of the ingroup are treated in the same way. When half of the ingroup members are objectively deprived and half are objectively nondeprived, fairness is at its lowest point.

If we assume that the disequilibrium of any group is greatest when subgroup formation is greatest, Davis' theory of relative deprivation allows us to predict social unrest. But the system seems rudimentary. The individuals in the system behave like rather simple machines—comparing themselves to other ingroup individuals and other outgroup individuals without preference or bias. Not only must we assume that the individuals act in a simple fashion; we must also assume that the context produces no modifications in emotions or behaviors. We must assume, in other words, that everyone who perceives unfairness acts in the same way about that unfairness and that everyone who experiences social distance acts in the same way on the basis of that experience. We must also assume that all acts of discontent affect the system identically.

A more sophisticated account of unrest comes from T. R. Gurr's theory of relative deprivation. Unlike Davis, Gurr (1970) restricts his model building to political systems. In a complex set of theorems and hypotheses, Gurr proposes that the amount of political unrest depends on feelings of discontent; the extent of the regimes' institutional support; the dissidents' institutional support; the regimes' coercive control; and the dissidents' coercive control.

Deprivation is defined by Gurr as a tension state that exists in someone who perceives a discrepancy between the way things are and the way things ought to be. People experience deprivation when they desire to and feel entitled to possess certain objects or opportunities and when they perceive that possession is or very soon will be impossible. If possession is seen to be impossible today but quite likely tomorrow, the person does not experience deprivation. Comparison with others, central to Merton and Rossi and to Davis, figures into Gurr's theory indirectly. One important way that people come to feel entitled to enjoy certain privileges, Gurr maintains, is by noticing that others, especially others who are similar to themselves, enjoy these desired privileges.

Gurr bills his theory as a dynamic rather than a static one. He recognizes the importance of time and notes that the way in which discontent develops over time affects the expression of that discontent. He identifies three major types of deprivation. Aspirational deprivation is thought to occur when people's expectations about legitimate or deserved outcomes accelerate more rapidly than do their capabilities for meeting their expectations. Decremental deprivation occurs when people's expectations remain constant over time while their actual capabilities decline. In progressive deprivation, capabilities decline while expectations accelerate.

To test his theory, Gurr (1968a, 1968c, 1969) performs a series of elaborate statistical maneuvers. Prior to analysis, newspaper stories and other records are coded for evidence of unrest. All told, 114 polities were coded for signs of unrest during a five year period. Each polity is also scored for the degree of deprivation, coercive force size, and so on. Gurr finds that his measures of deprivation account for a sizable proportion of the variance in unrest.

On the basis of such results, Gurr and like-minded researchers (Feierabend & Feierabend, 1966; Feierabend, Feierabend & Nesvold, 1969) draw happy conclusions about the theory of relative deprivation, but others (e.g., Spilerman, 1970, 1971) declare themselves less persuaded. Two problems make it particularly hard to draw strong inferences from Gurr's work. First, several critics (e.g., Kramnick, 1972) have noted the circumstantial nature of Gurr's evidence. On the basis of observed relationships between antecedent conditions and resultant behaviors, he draws conclusions about the thoughts and emotions which intervene. Worse still, the antecedents and resultants are measured with aggregate data while the intervening emotional state is said to occur in individuals, that is, at an individual level. The second reason why Gurr's results may be unconvincing is that his operational measures correspond rather poorly to his theoretical variables. He formally defines deprivation for example, by the formula:

$$RD = \frac{V_e - V_c}{V_e}$$

In the formula, RD stands for relative deprivation; V_e stands for value expectations, i.e., the goods to which people feel entitled; and V_c stands for value capabilities, i.e., the goods which people feel they can attain. Yet Gurr's standard operational measure of deprivation, for example, is obtained by calculating the weighted sum of six measures. These include: (a) economic discrimination; (b) political discrimination; (c) potential separatism; (d) dependence on private foreign capital; (e) religious cleavages; and (f) lack of educational opportunity. Whether economic discrimination or political discrimination affect value expectations or value capabilities seems arbitrary, to say the least.

Less subject to criticism perhaps than Gurr's work is the work of W. G. Runciman (1966). While Gurr seeks to explain the occurence of unrest, Runciman expresses wonder at the lack of unrest. "All societies are inegalitarian," says Runciman in the first sentence of his book *Relative Deprivation and Social Justice*. But the unequal distribution of goods and opportunities rarely elicits discontent, either in the overprivileged or in the underprivileged. This paradox makes Runciman ask: "What is the relation between the inequalities in a society and the feelings of acquiescence or resentment to which they give rise? People's attitudes to social inequalities seldom correlate strictly with the facts of their own position."

The inequality which particularly intrigues Runciman is the case of working class conservatives in twentieth century England. Runciman marvels at the fact that many working class men and women support a conservative political party, a party pledged to preserve the advantages of the middle and the upper classes at the expense of the working class. Part of the reason for the phenomenon is that some working class individuals actually consider themselves to be part of the middle class. Even those working class people who label themselves as working class, furthermore, do not feel unjustly deprived of many goods and opportunities. In fact, most members of the underprivileged classes do not compare their own outcomes with the outcomes of middle and upper class people. Historical reflections such as these lead Runciman to propose that an individual who is objectively deprived of something (X) will not feel deprived unless he:

> sees some other person or persons, which may include himself at some previous or expected time, as having X (whether or not this is or will be in fact the case), . . . he wants X, and . . . he sees it as feasible that he should have X (Runciman, 1966, p. 10).

An additional distinction concerns egoistical, fraternal and double deprivation. An individual can feel deprived because of his or her own position within a group. For example, a female executive can feel that she earns less than most other female executives. This type of deprivation Runciman entitles egoistic. Alternately, an individual can feel dissatisfied because of the position of his or her group is society. A female executive, for example, may feel that she is paid less than a male executive would be paid. This type of deprivation Runciman calls fraternal deprivation. Finally, an individual can experience both egoistic and fraternal deprivation according to Runciman.

Some of Runciman's theoretical notions imbue his survey of approximately 1600 British voters interviewed in the early 1960s. Although the connections between the theory of relative deprivation and the survey seem tenuous at times, the survey does show that people rarely imagine others to be better off than themselves. Rarer still is the idea that they lack goods which they want and to which they are entitled. People who are disadvanted, in short, tend to underestimate the extent of their disadvantage. In other words, people who appear to the social scientist to be poorly off tend not to share the view. Other researchers have found the same basic phenomenon among Scandinavian (Scase, 1974) and American (Patchen, 1958, 1961) workers.

Theoretical Elaborations

Building on the work of Davis, Runciman and Gurr and inspired by Pettigrew's (1967) comparison of the different theories, I have attempted an integration of theory and empirical research. In 1976, my article "A model of egoistical relative deprivation" appeared. One unambitious goal of the article has been to clarify terminology. After two decades, several meanings seem to have attached themselves to the words relative deprivation. More particularly, social scientists appear to employ the words in two distinct senses. Sometimes relative deprivation refers to an emotion. This is the way in which Stouffer and his co-workers use the term. In the first usage, 'relative deprivation' stands for 'felt deprivation'. Other times—as in some of the work of Davis, Runciman and Gurr—the term refers to a theory which makes propositions about the antecedents, concomitants and results of the emotion of discontent.

While the first usage of the term provides social scientists with a colorful and evocative phrase of convenience, the second makes a real advance over common sense. Common sense, as we have seen, informs us that feelings of discontent do not vary simply as a function of one's objective situation, but instead are relative to some psychological standard. The parameters of that standard remain unclear. Comparison to a better-off other seems important, but the vision of a better-off another cannot tell the full story. Most people can easily name others who are more advantaged than they themselves, but they do not exist in a continual state of discontent. Common sense, in other words, tells us that felt deprivations are relative but leaves us asking relative to what? Relative to what one wants? Relative to what one expects? To what one feels one deserves? When social scientists use the term relative deprivation in its second sense, that is, as part of a theory, these are the questions they seek to answer.

Having resolved some terminological ambiguities, I then march in the 1976 article toward the more ambitious goal of articulating and corroborating a theory of relative deprivation. The theory features the emotion of deprivation, which I equate with grievance or resentment, and which I see as one type of anger. Ranged around the emotion of felt deprivation are four other segments of the model. The distant precursors of felt deprivation (antecedent conditions) and the proximal 'preconditions' of felt deprivation precede the felt deprivation. Some mediating variables and four classes of resultant behaviors follow the emotion of deprivation. Table 1 shows an overview of the model.

The 1976 model subdivides the antecedent conditions into factors concerning: (a) people's personality; (b) their personal past; (c) their immediate environment; (d) societal dictates; (e) survival needs. The tendency to blame oneself or to blame the system exemplifies a personality factor. Whether or not an individual formerly possessed a desired object and how many of his or her friends currently possess the desired object illustrate antecedent conditions having to do with personal past

Table 1. Overview of 1976 Model

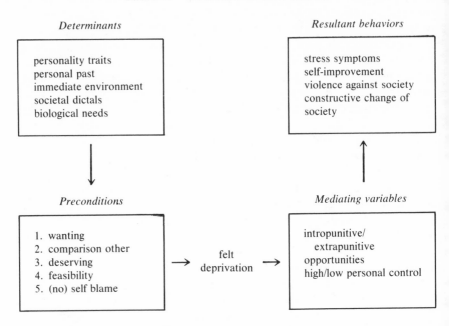

and with immediate environment. Societal norms about which behaviors and characteristics ought to be rewarded and punished represent the antecedents listed under societal dictates. Survival needs are included (without further division) in the model because it seems intuitively obvious that the starving person feels aggrieved about his lack of food in a different way or to a different degree than does the dandy feel aggrieved about his inability to attain a new silk shirt.

Each of the twenty antecedents in the model affects one or more of what I call the preconditions of felt deprivation. The preconditions are five cognitive or emotional factors identified by at least one prior theorist and supported by at least some empirical work. In the 1976 article, I assert that the five factors, taken together, represent the sufficient and the necessary preconditions of feelings of resentment, grievance or deprivation. More specifically, the model claims that people who lack some object or opportunity (X) must: (a) want X; (b) feel entitled to X; (c) perceive that someone possesses X; (d) think it feasible to attain X; (e) refuse personal responsibility for their current failure to possess X themselves.

The core propositions are easy to illustrate with an example from life at work. Imagine that there is a European meeting of executives in the airline industry and that company Y does not send executive A, who is a woman, to the meeting. What will make executive A feel upset with the situation? According to the model, she must want to attend the meeting. If she hates to travel or dislikes the location of the meeting, for example, it seems unlikely that the executive will feel aggrieved. Simply wanting to attend is not enough. Suppose that the executive wants to attend but believes that her lack of seniority means that she is not automatically entitled to European trips. The element of comparison figures in also. If the executive in our example wants to attend and feels entitled to attend, she may nonetheless feel cool and calm if no one else from her company attends the meeting. But imagine her anger if some other person, and especially someone less deserving than she, is sent to represent the company at the meeting! Only two conditions, according to the 1976 model, will stem her outrage. If the woman thinks it infeasible or impossible to be sent, no matter how deserving of the trip she personally is, the thought of privileged colleagues would not excite her anger. The executive might, for instance, be an old-fashioned wife who accepts without question the company's pre-liberation policy that married women are not to be sent to conventions or meetings. Finally, if the woman thinks that something she has done, something like scheduling another meeting at the same time as the European meeting, has caused her disappointing situation, then feelings of deprivation will not develop.

As the example illustrates, the system proposed in 1976 makes strong demands: five preconditions are a lot. Nor are the various preconditions separate from each other. They are sometimes affected by the same determinants. The executive's previous experience with traveling, to continue with our example, would affect her wants, her feelings of entitlement, and the degree to which the trip seems feasible. The preconditions also interact. It may, for instance, be hard to want something over a period of time without coming to feel entitled to it. Feeling that one is somehow to blame for one's lack of a desired outcome also tends to erode one's conviction about deserving it.

Although I have been less interested in the consequences of felt deprivation than in the preconditions of deprivation, the 1976 model does specify some potential outcomes of feelings of resentment. J. S. Mill (Mill in Fogarty, Rapoport, & Rapoport, 1971, p. 277) has observed that it is better to be a dissatisfied person than to be a satisfied pig. In a similar vein, I argue that resentment or discontent are not in and of themselves bad emotions. Resentment can result in negative behavior or in positive behavior. Whether positive or negative behaviors eventuate from a sense of grievance depends, in the model, on some mediating variables. More specifically, we must know whether the system allows for change and whether the individuals believe that they can effect change. Figure 1 presents the proposed relationship among the different variables.

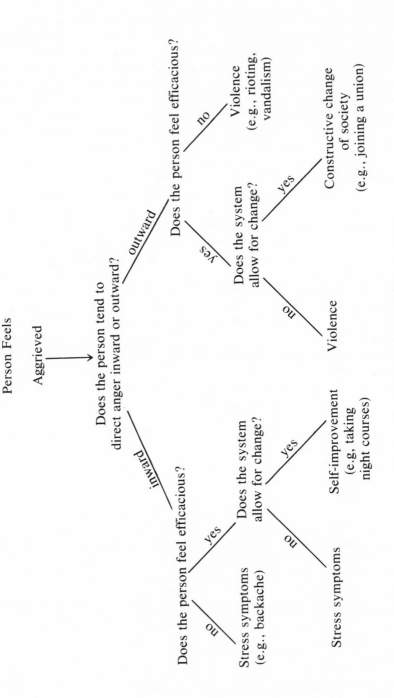

Figure 1. Consequences of Resentment

CURRENT DIRECTIONS

The 1976 article has functioned as a sort of spring cleaning for relative deprivation enthusiasts (Appelgryn & Plug, 1981; de Carafel, 1981; Folger, in press; Grajek & Scarr, Note 1; Guimond & Dubé-Simard, 1983; Martin, 1979) and as often happens, one result of tidying things up has been to make obvious problems previously hidden. Some problems involve conceptual distinctions which are overly refined and are likely to prove unproductive. Other problems occur, on the contrary, because some important distinctions are given insufficient attention. In this section we discuss two issues which receive a great deal of research attention at present. One issue concerns the reduction in the number of hypothesized preconditions of felt deprivation; the other is the importance of group deprivation, especially in contrast with personal deprivation.

Eliminating Some Distinctions: The Overabundance of Preconditions

The first obvious issue concerns the overabundance of hypothesized preconditions of felt deprivation. My own 1976 model of relative deprivation, coming after all the others, specifies five separate but interconnecting preconditions of feelings of grievance. Complex as it was in 1976, the model became more complex still the following year. In an attempt to reconcile Gurr's statement that deprivation is not experienced until one's expectations are dashed, with Runciman's and my own statements that hope for better conditions constitutes an essential ingredient of discontent, Tom Cook, Karen Hennigan and I have distinguished between past expectations and expectations for the future. We argue that people become aggrieved, given the other necessary factors, when expectations in the past were high but expectations about the future are low. The employee who had expected his supervisor to prove sympathetic and intelligent but who now sees his supervisor to be pigheaded and who, furthermore, sees no escape from his boss ought to be quite discontented, assuming the other preconditions of deprivation have been fulfilled. The distinction between past and future expectations brings to six the number of hypothesized preconditions of deprivation and increases the number of models of deprivation, with each model possessing a distinct constellation of preconditions.

To complicate matters further, the various models of relative deprivation overlap considerably with other social psychological theories of discontent. The frustration-aggression hypothesis, for example, could be construed as claiming that anger occurs when people who are deprived of some object or opportunity (X): (a) want X; and (b) had high past expectations of receiving X. Even more striking is the overlap between equity theory and relative deprivation theory. Adams' and Walster's versions of equity theory can be rewritten to state that people feel upset about their lack of X if they: (a) want X; (b) believe another person or people possess X; and (c) feel entitled to X themselves. To these factors, Patchen (1961) adds another in his rendition of equity theory. Patchen specifies that the people must feel no personal responsibility for their plight. When people do feel responsibility, says Patchen, discrepant comparisons to better-off others produce no feeling of dissatifaction.

With six hypothesized preconditions and even more proposed grievance-producing constellations of preconditions, relative deprivation research finds itself in a peculiar position. One may call it an embarassment of riches; but, riches or no, the situation is embarassing. We would claim that relative deprivation theory adds most to our common sense understanding of grievance by specifying the factors which produce resentment, but it is precisely in terms of the theory's greatest potential addition to our understanding, that the theorists have been most negligent. Until very recently, no one has attempted to discover which of the hypothesized preconditions of deprivation *do actually function* to produce feelings of deprivation or grievance. Reviewing the pertinent empirical literature, Cook et al. find evidence consistent with the claim that each of the hypothesized preconditions, considered individually, affects discontent. They discover, however, no study which examines all of the preconditions simultaneously, and hence they can draw no conclusions about any particular constellation of preconditions.

Eliminating some of the hypothesized preconditions and producing a new, slimmed down version of relative deprivation theory has been one of the central aims of a recent simulation experiment and of an interview survey. In the experiment (Bernstein & Crosby, 1980), each subject read a vignette about a character who did not obtain a desired outcome such as a high grade or a certain promotion. The stories systematically differed in terms of the hypothesized preconditions of felt deprivation, and the subjects indicated how discontented they would feel in the various situations. The results of the experiment revealed problems with the hypothesized precondition of 'self-blame'. Contrary to Patchen's (1961) equity model and to my own model of relative deprivation, it does *not* seem that people must absolve themselves from personal responsibility for a misfortune in order to resent the misfortune. The vision of someone else who is better-off predicted resentment *per se* in the experiment but did not predict a more generalized indicator of discontent. High past expectations predicted the generalized indicator (discontent) but did not predict resentment. In sum, the vignette experiment allows us to exclude (no) self blame from the list of preconditions of deprivation and suggests that the factors of comparison other and past expectations are not crucial and direct antecedents of felt deprivation.

More substantial evidence comes from a survey of over 400 residents of Newton, Massachusetts.[2] We questioned each of the 345 employed respondents in the survey about his or her own job, his or her own home life, and his or her views of the job situation of American women. Each of the 60 housewives in the survey was interviewed about her home life and her views of the job situation of American women. For all three attitude domains (own job, own home life, women's jobs), we created a scale for every hypothesized precondition of deprivation and a scale for deprivation itself. Table 2 lists samples of the questions asked about one's

Table 2. Operational Measures of Deprivation and the Hypothesized Preconditions (Attitudes Toward One's Job)

Variable	*Sample Question*
Deprivation	Within this last year, how often have you felt some sense of grievance concerning each of these aspects of your job: pay and fringe benefits number of hours chances for advancement challenge respect and prestige job security general working conditions (Response options: always; frequently; occasionally; seldom; never; not applicable)
Discrepancy between what one has and what one *wants*	During the last month how often have you felt that you wanted more from your job than you are getting from it now? (Response options: constantly; at least once a day; a couple of times a week; not very often; never)
Perception that *others* are doing better.	[Concerning work around the job] would you say that you are better off, worse off, or about the same as [three people named by participant.]
Discrepancy between what one has and what one *deserves*.	In view of your training and abilities, is your present job as good as it ought to be? (Response options: definitely, probably; I'm not sure; probably not; definitely not)

Table 2. (Continued)

Variable	Sample Question
Discrepancy between what one has and what one's *past expectations* were.	Could you think back now for a minute to the expectations you had when you first started working. How does your present job compare with those expectations?
	(Response options: It's much better than I expected; It's slightly better than I expected; It's about what I expected; It's slightly worse than I expected; It's much worse than I expected)
Pessimism about the *future*.	How do you feel about the kind of salary you'll be earning in the next five or so years?
	(Response options: Very optimistic; fairly optimistic; uncertain; fairly pessimistic; very pessimistic)
No feelings of *self-blame* for undesirable outcomes.	Did you select your present job as a matter of choice or not?
	(Response options: it was entirely my own choice; It was mostly my own choice; It was not really my own choice; It was not at all my own choice)

own job. Analogous questions exist for attitudes about one's own home life and for attitudes about the job situation of American women.

The complex analyses of the various clusters of data collected in the Newton survey are presented in detail elsewhere (Crosby, 1982). Of special interest here are two types of analyses, both of which were performed for the three attitude domains. First, we performed regression analyses in which the extent of grievance and resentment served as the criterion variable and the six cognitive emotional factors plus various demographic factors (e.g., gender, job level) were the predictor variables. Concerning attitudes towards one's own job situation, the regression analyses show that the extent of resentment is predicted by the variables wanting and future expectations. The greater the discrepancy between what one has and what one wants, the greater the discontent. The more pessimistic one is, the more one is discontented. Concerning attitudes towards the division of labor in the home, discontent is predicted by the variables wanting and deserving. The greater the discrepancy between what one has and what one wants, the more one is resentful. The greater the discrepancy between what one has and what one feels one deserves, the greater is the resentment. When it comes to attitudes towards the position of working women, gender and the variables comparison other and deserving all predict variation in the extent of resentment. Women express more resentment than men. People who think that women are not as well off as men express more resentment. And people who think that the discrepancy is great between what women have and what they deserve to have express more deprivation.[3]

Complementing the regression analyses were tests on the extreme scorers. For each attitude domain we selected the respondents who feel most aggrieved and those who feel least aggrieved. These are not, of course, necessarily the same people in all three instances. We then contrasted the two groups in terms of each of the six hypothesized preconditions of deprivation. For attitudes towards one's own job, the most deprived people and the least deprived people differ from each other in terms of five of the hypothesized preconditions. Only when it comes to personal responsibility (self-blame) are the two groups the same. In the contrast between the most resentful and the least resentful respondents concerning the division of labor at home, the two groups differ in terms of what they want and what they feel they deserve. Finally, the contrast for extreme scorers concerning attitudes towards working women look virtually identical to the contrast concerning one's own job.

On the basis of the experiment and of the Newton survey, I have proposed a new model of deprivation (Crosby, 1982). It features *wanting* and *deserving* as the two preconditions of resentment, grievance or deprivation. Comparisons and expectations can augment or decrease feelings of resentment once those feelings exist. They also help a person decide what he or she deserves to obtain. But comparisons and expectations are no longer essential parts of the model. Self-blame is excluded from the model altogether.

The validity of the core of the new model has been demonstrated. In some secondary analyses of the data collected in Newton, Peter Muehrer (Note 2) has tested the proposition that resentment or deprivation varies as a function of wanting and deserving, in concert. In each attitude domain, Muehrer created four constellation groups by dichotomizing scores on the variables of wanting and of deserving and by dividing people into those who felt they were doing: (1) less well than they wanted and deserved; (2) less well than they wanted but as well as they deserved; (3) less well than they deserved but as well as they wanted; and (4) as well as they deserved and wanted. Muehrer assessed the level of grievance in each group and tested for statistical significance with one-way analyses of variance. A strict test of the new model required that the first constellation group differ from the other three groups and that none of the other groups differ from each other.

The tests confirmed the revised model. In all three attitude domains, there is a significant main effect, and resentment is highest among the respondents in the first group. That is, people who feel that they are doing less well than they both want and deserve express significantly more resentment than do others. Neither wanting nor deserving, in isolation, produces the same effect consistently. Concerning their own job situation, the average deprivation score among the first constellation group was 11.2 while the deprivation score among the other three groups averaged 8.5. For reactions to the job situation of women (group deprivation), the scores were 3.3 and 2.0 and for feelings about one's own domestic situation they were 12.4 and 8.7 respectively.

In sum, one aspect of the current research in relative deprivation has been to reduce the model. From a complex model with many hypothesized preconditions, I have moved to a model which contains only two preconditions. The new model, which appears to be valid, asserts that people experience deprivation when they perceive: (1) a discrepancy between actual outcomes and desired outcomes and (2) a discrepancy between actual outcomes and the outcomes they deserve.

Types of Deprivation

Runciman, as we have seen, distinguishes between egoistical deprivation, fraternal deprivation, and double deprivation. He originally draws the distinction in the early, conceptual part of his book and he returns to it at points in his description of the empirical data. Runciman alludes to 'fraternalistic' deprivation, for example, when he reports some findings concerning reference groups and the inequalities of class (1966, ch. 10). More specifically, he found that slightly under half of the manual workers who describe themselves as working class agree with the statement that "manual workers are doing much better nowadays than white-collar workers." Over three-quarters of those describing themselves as middle class endorse the same statement. Runciman implies that the latter group suffers from a mild case of false-consciousness while the former displays a proper sense of fraternal deprivation.

Runciman's theoretical definitions are brief, and his empirical contrasts between egoistical and fraternal deprivation occur in passing. It may not be entirely by accident, furthermore, that his concept of fraternal deprivation contains some ambiguity. In one meaning of the term, deprivation occurs whenever someone compares his situation unfavorably with that of a dissimilar comparison person. The working class person who feels resentful because middle class people are better off than he is experiences fraternal deprivation in this first sense. So does the employed woman who feels aggrieved at her own wage when she compares it to the average male wage. So too does the secretary who experiences discontent when she contrasts her own working conditions and perquisites with the working conditions or perquisites of a senior vice-president. The first meaning of fraternal deprivation does not imply that the individual has a conscious and well articulated sense of his or her group nor of some "contrast" group. All that is required is that the better-off other be somehow different from the self.

Fraternal deprivation in Runciman's first meaning of the term has been examined experimentally. In some carefully controlled studies of pay comparisons, Joanne Martin (1981) has investigated within group (egoistical) and across group (fraternal) comparisons. Typical of her line of research is her first experiment. In it, secretaries from a large organization viewed a tape and slide show picturing executives and secretaries in a company alleged to be similar to their own. The secretaries were told that they would be paid the average secretarial salary in the alleged company. When asked whose pay they would like to know, the subjects almost always chose the highest paid secretary and rarely chose an executive. This finding supports Festinger's (1954) assertion that people tend to make similar upward comparisons and it is one of the reasons why Martin (1981) suggests that egoistical deprivation may occur more frequently than fraternal deprivation. After collecting the data on comparison choices, Martin presented subjects with figures on the supposed salaries of executives and secretaries in the fictitious company. The average expected dissatisfaction with the pay situation was greater, Martin found, when the executives pictured were three males than when the slides showed two male and one female executive. In subsequent experiments Martin discovered that people who are "externally controlled"—people, that is, who tend to disclaim responsibility for their own fates—tend to express more dissatisfaction with large intergroup pay differences than do their more internally controlled counterparts.

Although encouraged by her experimental findings, Martin is critical of the concept of fraternal deprivation in the first sense of the word. It sounds fine in the abstract to distinguish between comparisons to dissimilar others and comparisons to similar others. In practice, however, a problem arises as soon as we realize that people are multi-dimensional. Only if the people who serve as referents are either similar or dissimilar on all the relevant dimensions, says Martin, can one easily operationalize the concept. But referents are usually similar on some dimensions and dissimilar on others. Take the case of the employed woman who compares herself to an employed man. This may sound like fraternal deprivation. If the woman earns less it may well be, however, that she feels dissatisfied precisely because she believes herself and the man to be similar in all pay-relevant respects. Her deprivation is, thus, personal and not fraternal. Indeed, if a person believes that she has nothing in common with her referent, if she makes an out-group comparison, then she probably only experiences social distance, in Davis' terms, when she notices a difference in salaries.

A second meaning of Runciman's term fraternal deprivation avoids some of the problems of the first meaning. In the second meaning, fraternal deprivation occurs whenever a person feels resentful about the situation of his or her group relative to the situation of some other group or groups. The woman who deplores sex discrimination in general, the worker who feels that the working classes are mistreated, the black who resents racism are all examples of people experiencing fraternal deprivation in the second interpretation of the term. How these people feel about their individual situations is moot.

Ronald Abeles (1976), who like Martin has been a student of Pettigrew, defines fraternal deprivation in the second way. In some secondary analyses of survey data collected in the late 1960s in Cleveland, Abeles examined militancy among blacks as a function of several factors including fraternal deprivation. From the Cleveland data, he extracted two measures of fraternal deprivation. The first measured whether the respondent believed that whites, white-collar workers, professionals, or blue-collar workers, had made economic gains to which they are not entitled. The second measure was derived from ratings on a modified Cantril (1965) Ladder Scale. Respondents were shown a picture of a ladder with eleven rungs and were asked to imagine that the top rung represented the highest rank in American society and that the bottom rung represented the lowest rank. They placed on the ladder various groups including blacks in general, whites in general, white-collar workers, professionals and blue-collar workers. Measures of fraternal deprivation were derived by subtracting the rung-rating for whites and other groups from the rung-rating for blacks and by summing across the various resulting scores. Analogous measures of egoistical deprivation were derived by comparing ratings for the self with ratings for others.

The results of Abeles' study underscore the importance of fraternal deprivation and give force to Pettigrew's (1978) claim that fraternal deprivations, unlike personal deprivation, tend to have societal consequences. In all instances, the fraternal measures correlate more highly with militancy than do the egoistic measures, but while confirming the role of group comparisons, the analyses by Abeles also illustrate how important it is to define one's group. Militancy was predicted by the perceived discrepancy between well-educated blacks and other groups. The perceived discrepancy between poorly educated blacks and (a) whites in general, (b) white-collar workers and (c) professionals did not statistically predict militancy. Just as well-educated blacks constituted a more psychologically salient in-group than did blacks in general, so too did white-collar workers make a more meaningful point of reference than did whites in general. To predict militancy, it was important to know how blacks compared the situation of well-educated blacks to white-collar workers and not just to white people in general.

Given the ambiguities of Runciman's terminology, a recent conceptual paper by Laurie Rhodebeck (1981) comes as a welcome addition. Rhodebeck replaces Runciman's fraternal and double deprivations with the term 'group deprivations'. She defines it as "the negative feeling that group members have about the situation of their group as a whole, regardless of their own situation within the group" (Rhodebeck, 1981, p. 245). Patterning her piece closely after my 1976 article on egoistical relative deprivation, Rhodebeck specifies five necessary conditions for group deprivation. In order for someone to find that his or her group is unjustly deprived of some object or opportunity (X), the person must

1. acknowledge membership in the group
2. see that others possess X
3. want X for the group
4. feel the group deserves X
5. feel the group can attain X (p. 246).

The major thrust of Rhodebeck's paper concerns the consequences of group deprivation. She identifies 12 variables which may affect how the emotion of deprivation becomes translated into action and she places them within three rubrics. Under the rubric 'variables affecting aggregation' are: (1) the proportion of group members who feel deprived; the degree of (2) interaction and (3) communication among group members; (4) the organizational resources (e.g., existing leadership); (5) currency of belief that collective action will ameliorate matters. Three variables are listed as affecting politicization of the emotion: (6) questioning of the legitimacy of the regime; (7) perceptions that authorities have been unsuccessful in alleviating deprivation and (8) intervention of the authorities. Finally, Rhodebeck maintains that the likelihood of violence increases if (9) few opportunities for peaceful change exist; (10) the group possesses some resources; (11) people condone violence; and (12) an incident occurs.

Although of primary interest to political scientists, Rhodebeck's model of group deprivation contains several nuggets for organizational psychologists seeking to understand the dynamics of discontent (cf, Zald & Berger, 1978). Especially interesting is her assertion that when authorities intervene in a situation, they help to politicize the emotion of deprivation. In an organizational setting, if Rhodebeck is correct, whenever the authorities intervene, they increase the likelihood of polarization. Thus, for example, whenever upper management becomes involved in a situation where they were not previously involved, they increase the likelihood of polarization.

As a hypothetical case, consider a boot manufacturing plant in which the zipper seamstresses tumble to the fact that they earn less than other workers. Imagine that group deprivation is pervasive among the seamstresses; that one of the older women emerges as a natural leader; and that in the course of their daily coffee breaks (in the zipper seamstresses' canteen), the group comes to believe that they could improve conditions by approaching senior management. Imagine further that the seamstresses take a rather belligerent approach in which they vastly overstate their case. Senior management has several options for reacting. At one extreme, they could refuse even to recognize the group. At the other extreme, senior management could accede immediately to all the demands of the zipper seamstresses. Note that, if Rhodebeck is correct, senior management in such a situation must be extremely careful to avoid any sudden moves. A sudden move would make it appear that management is intervening in the situation and thus could further inflame passions. The potential for harm in any sudden move—and this is really the kicker— is virtually as great if the move favors the seamstresses as if it moves against the seamstresses.

What is the moral of this tale? The moral is that organizations may suffer unless they have institutionalized grievance and bargaining procedures. To the degree that procedures are codified, to the degree that options are prescribed, management reactions in cases such as the zipper seamstress example run little risk of appearing to be interventions. The regularization of collective bargaining, with the contract being renegotiated periodically, typifies a procedure which ironically helps to preserve the status quo. Riot, revolution, sabotage, and severe strikes are no doubt less frequent in environments where the various interest groups, such as management and labor, benefit more from prescribed and systematic modes of communication than in environments where such procedural rules are lacking.

Rhodebeck's model holds interest for other psychologists as well. My own recent survey profits from the conceptual crispness of Rhodebeck's model. In the interview study of Newton residents, mentioned earlier, we measured feelings of resentment, feelings of dissatisfaction and the six (formerly) hypothesized preconditions of deprivation concerning; (a) one's own job; (b) one's own home life and (c) the job situation of women in America today. The first two attitude domains concern personal deprivation while the last concerns what we call group deprivation. Note that our use of the word group deprivation differs slightly from that of Rhodebeck: We consider group deprivation to cover feelings of grievance about any group, whether or not one feels part of the group in question.

The Newton study aimed to contribute to relative deprivation theory in several ways. One way was by eliminating non-essential factors from the list of hypothesized preconditions of grievance. The results of that quest, in which wanting and deserving carried the day, have already been described above. Another way in which the survey aimed to contribute to relative deprivation theory was by examining the relationship between different types of deprivation. Here the central question was: how does group deprivation relate to personal deprivation? That is, how do resentments about the situation of working women relate to resentments about one's own job situation among women and men? We also wondered how personal deprivation at work related to personal deprivation at home.

The final aim of the Newton study was to document the distribution of grievances among various groups. The sample contained three major subsamples: working men, working women and housewives. Each of these groups was further subdivided into high and low prestige on the basis of the person's own occupation (for the employed women and men) or on the basis of the husband's occupation (for housewives). All housewives were married and had children. The four employed groups (high prestige employed women, low prestige women, high prestige men, low prestige men) were further subdivided according to their family status. Approximately one-third of each group was single; one-third was married but childless; and one-third was married with children. All respondents were between 25 and 40 years old and were white. The sampling design of the study is shown in Table 3. The sample was a modified random stratified sample.

The survey produced some unexpected results. The first concerns group deprivation. In 1971 only 4% of a national sample expressed concern about sex discrimination (Schwartz & Schwartz, 1976). This contrasted, for example, with about 50% of the sample who at that time thought drug addiction was a major problem. By 1978, when my survey was conducted, times had changed. The majority of respondents in my study claimed to be interested in women's issues. Only 3% of the sample, furthermore, believed that women and men receive equal compensation for equal work; the other 97% know that women tend to be undercompensated.

Not only were the Newton respondents aware of sex discrimination, they are also upset about it. In fact, the people in Newton expressed considerably more dissatisfaction and grievance about the situation of women than about their own job and home situations. Considering 100 to be the most deprived score possible and 0 to be the least, the average scores for

Table 3. Sample of the Newton Study

Family Status	Employed Men	*Grouping* Employed Women	Housewives
High NORC prestige (above 60)			
Single	n = 30	n = 31	
Married	n = 31	n = 31	
Parents	n = 31	n = 28	n = 30
Low NORC prestige (40 and below)			
Single	n = 30	n = 30	
Married	n = 30	n = 22	
Parents	n = 30	n = 21	n = 30

group deprivation, personal deprivation about one's job, and personal deprivation about one's home life were 52, 30 and 32 respectively.

Some people in Newton were more aggrieved than others about the situation of working women. Table 4 presents the average group deprivation scores of the samples of high and low prestige employed women, employed men and housewives. Deprivation was assessed by asking re-

Table 4. Group Deprivation Scores Among High and Low Prestige Employed Men, Employed Women, and Housewives

		Employment Group			
		Employed Men	Employed Women	Housewives	
NORC Prestige Rating	High Prestige	x̄ = 2.80 (n = 90)	x̄ = 3.96 (n = 90)	x̄ = 3.75 (n = 30)	x̄ = 3.42
	Low Prestige	x̄ = 2.24 (n = 90)	x̄ = 3.73 (n = 72)	x̄ = 3.23 (n = 30)	x̄ = 2.95
		2.52	3.86	3.49	

Note: Scores can range from 1 to 6. The higher the score, the greater is the grievance felt about the situation of working women in America.

spondents:

> Would you say that you feel bitter or resentful about any of the following aspects of women's employment situation? In particular, are you bitter or resentful about: pay and fringe benefits, number of hours, chances for advancement, challenge, respect and prestige, job security, general working conditions?

Response options ranged from "not at all", scored as 1, to "very", scored as 6. An average score was obtained by looking across the different factors. A 2 × 3 analysis of variance of the data presented in Table 4, treating job prestige and employment category as independent variables, resulted in two highly significant main effects and no interaction. High prestige people were more aggrieved than low. Employed women were more aggrieved than employed men and housewives.

The distribution of dissatisfaction scores mimicked the distribution of group deprivation scores. With a 1 to 4 scale, where 1 translated to "very satisfied about the condition of working women" and 4 translated to "very dissatisfied", the high prestige people averaged a score of 3.0 and the low prestige people a score of 2.5. Among employed women, employed men and housewives these scores were 2.9, 2.7, and 2.6 respectively. These differences were statistically significant. The pattern also repeated itself for the preconditions of group deprivation. High prestige respondents were more certain than were low prestige respondents that women receive less than they want from employment and less than they deserve. Employed women, as a group, expressed more conviction about these facts than employed men or housewives.

Although the degree of awareness of sex discrimination among working women and, indeed, among the entire sample seems surprisingly high in view of earlier studies, the discovery that employed women are most aware about and most aggrieved about sex discrimination does not, perhaps, shake the earth under every reader. Who, after all, should know better than the employed woman about sex discrimination? Nor, perhaps, is it astonishing to find, as I did in the Newton survey, strong objective indications of sex discrimination. We had taken elaborate sampling precautions and managed to obtain a sample of employed women and employed men who were perfectly matched in terms of their age, education, and most importantly, job prestige ratings. In spite of their absolute comparability, the two samples differed in terms of annual earnings: the employed women in our study earned significantly less than the (strictly comparable) employed men.

Here then comes a jolt: the employed women in the study had virtually no sense of personal grievance. When it came to attitudes about one's job, not for personal deprivation, for dissatisfaction, nor for any of the hypothesized preconditions were there any gender effects. The employed women in Newton—who were discriminated against and who resented sex discrimination in general—seemed as contented with their job as the men. It was as if each working women knew of oppression in general but imagined herself to be the exception.

Other patterns of results in the survey also illustrated the separation between group (fraternal) and personal (egotistical) deprivation. The correlation between group deprivation and personal deprivation was low among employed men. It was equally low among employed women. The factors which predicted the level of group deprivation in a hierarchical multiple regression analysis were the same among women and men.

How can we explain the separation between group deprivation and personal deprivation? Why doesn't group deprivation among employed women lead to personal deprivation, especially in view of their objective situation? As indicated elsewhere (Crosby, 1982), three aspects of the explanation seem especially important. First, in the apt words of Robert Lane (1962), people tend to morselize their lives. Support for or opposition to political issues, for example, cannot be accounted for primarily in terms of people's self interest or the events of their individual lives (Kinder & Kiewiet, 1979; Kinder & Sears, 1981).

Some patterns of results in my survey suggest that Newtonites are no less prone to morselize their lives than are other people. Many of the men in the survey showed a great deal of sympathy with women's issues. They were interested in the progress of working women and they deplored sex discrimination. Other men showed less concern. Curiously, male sympathy with women in the survey was not predicted by whether the men had a working wife or a working mother. Respondents also seemed to compartmentalize their personal lives and work lives. Work and home remained separate domains for most of the people in the study. Perhaps as a result of this compartmentalization, work seemed to provide a refuge from the cares of home and home provided a refuge from the traumas of work.

The tendency to morselize life is not the only reason for the separation of group and personal deprivation. Another reason has to do with the ease of judging how fairly people are compensated. When two groups are equated on all relevant dimensions except gender, and when the two groups are large enough—and working women in America or working men in America certainly constitute large groups—averages can be obtained. When the comparison involves individuals, however, it seems impossible to "average out" irrelevancies. Comparisons between individuals usually defy strict comparability. The woman who notices that she, as an individual, receives less pay than do the men in her office may have many explanations at hand. She may think she is younger, that her career line has been more non-traditional, that her manner is less polished. In performing her equity calculations, she may forget the dimensions in which she excels.

Finally, there seems to be something quite protective about not noticing that one is being mistreated. The cognition that we, as individuals, are being mistreated often leads to the hunt for a malefactor or villain. Human beings can quite readily comprehend that a group may suffer through no one's fault, but a primitive non-logical cause–and–effect bias appears to operate in the case of personal suffering. People tend to believe that if one *individual* suffers, it is because another *individual* caused the suffering. The tendency to deny one's own victimization may, therefore, spring from a disinclination to hunt for villains. The lack of a sense of personal grievance among the employed women of Newton, despite their objective situation, may reflect a strategy for protecting smooth interactions at work.

The lack of connection between group deprivation and personal deprivation among the employed women of Newton is only one of the surprises in the study. Another set of unexpected findings has to do with reactions to the over-benefits of others (Crosby & Gonzalez-Intal, 1982). One question in the survey asked working people if they know of anyone at work who received things to which he or she is unentitled. The 160 people who replied in the affirmative were then asked to indicate how they felt about the perception. Contrary to what we would expect on the basis of relative deprivation theory, many individuals admitted that they resented the others' over-benefit even though they did not feel deprived themselves. Contrary to equity theory, furthermore, some people viewed the over-rewards of others at work with equanimity. Nine percent of the respondents who perceived someone else as over-benefited claimed that they themselves "don't think about" the over-benefit. Another 18% said that they felt nothing about the perception or, even more altruistically, that they felt good for the over-benefited person. The other 73% expressed some form of discontent.

Such findings, coupled with the findings about the presence of group deprivation and the absence of personal deprivation, suggest a modification in relative deprivation theory. More specifically, it seems wise to distinguish between four categories of resentment about the distribution of outcomes. First, an individual can feel upset because he or she is personally deprived of an outcome which he or she desires and to which he or she feels entitled. This type of deprivation we call personal deprivation. Identifying a malefactor or agent of harm seems to be critically important in personal deprivation. An individual can also feel upset that a group lacks something. When the group is one to which he belongs, the resentment may be termed in-group deprivation. When it is a group with which the person sympathizes but to which he does not belong, we may call the feeling ideological deprivation (Hennigan, 1977). Finally, backlash refers to the case where an individual feels resentful about the fact that others possess positive outcomes.

The four types of resentment differ in frequency and in stability. Backlash is probably more common than ideological deprivation. Because it is easier to notice what people do have than what they do not have, it is easier to feel upset about what others do possess than about what they do not possess. In-group deprivation may be more common than ideological deprivation and personal deprivation because part of the process of group identification is to delineate one's group from other groups. In the process of delineation unequal outcomes gain salience. Of course, in-group deprivation is also more frequent than personal deprivation: the necessity of choosing a harm agent for personal deprivation—of finding a villain who violates personal entitlements—makes people reluctant to express discontent about their own situation. Given the difficulty of feeling personally deprived, when feelings of personal deprivation do exist, they tend to be unstable. In fact, they are often quite explosive. The view that one has been unfairly treated tends to come about in lurches. Radical changes in one's Gestalten are often involved. Outcomes to which one felt unentitled before are now accepted and expected; an erstwhile friend now becomes an enemy. Personal deprivations can also disappear rapidly. Edward Albee's play *Who's Afraid of Virginia Wolf?* gives brilliant testimony to the instability of feelings of personal deprivation. At any one moment the husband or wife in the drama may express a towering rage; at the next, he or she repents and expresses shame at having felt entitled to certain things the moment before.

Less dramatic than personal deprivation is group deprivation. Perhaps because it involves comparatively little emotional violence, group deprivation has received less than its fair share of scholarly attention. If Pettigrew (1978) and Rhodebeck (1981) are correct, feelings of in-group deprivation ought to incur greater societal consequences than do feelings of personal deprivation. The observation certainly seems appropriate to work organizations. How do people in organizations come to recognize unfair deprivation of themselves personally, their own group, or some other group? How do they come to feel that some other person or group is over-rewarded? What becomes of feelings of resentment or deprivation? These questions have not yet been addressed. When we want to consider relative deprivation in organizational settings, we leave the ghosts of Christmas past and present and follow the ghost of Christmas to come.

FUTURE PROGRAMS

Historically, studies of worker satisfaction have formed one of the legs on which relative deprivation theory has stood, with archival studies of political events and survey studies of black attitudes and behaviors forming the other two legs of the empirical tripod. Current research in relative deprivation—as we have just seen—continues to feature worker attitudes and focuses especially on the contrast between a worker's contentment with his own situation and his discontent with the situation of his group. Given the centrality of job issues in relative deprivation research, it comes as a shock to realize that hardly any studies have looked at the occurence, development or consequences of resentments as a function of organizational setting or structure. To state the case differently: researchers have studied the resentments or grievances of workers, most of whom work in organizations, but they have not examined how resentments depend on or are influenced by any aspect of the organization. One potentially fruitful line of research, in broad terms, is to understand the *role of various organizational factors in the dynamics of discontent.*

As a point of departure, one might ask whether the quantity or the quality of felt deprivation is different when one works in an organization than when one works alone or in anarchy. Or one might ask whether work organizations differ from other types of associations (e.g., clubs, churches, play groups) in the number or kind of deprivations occuring within them. In other words, researchers ought to give some thought to the deceptively simple question: how does the very fact of being within a work organization affect the manifestation of discontent?

Researchers ought not simply to trace the development of grievance within the work setting as opposed to other life situations. They ought also to investigate the role of various aspects of organizational structure and of organizational climate. The degree of specialization in an organization that affects the genesis, development, and consequences of personal deprivation and of group deprivation could be examined. One could see how the linkage between personal deprivation and group deprivation depends on the hierarchical structure of the organization. One could also determine how organizational norms concerning participation and commitment influence the positive and negative outcomes of felt deprivation. These are, of course, but a few examples of relationships which may prove interesting to academic analysts and practitioners alike.

Recommendations

Future research on resentments in organizational settings may profit from three specific recommendations. First, particular attention ought to be given to the relationship between personal grievance and group griev-ance. As we have seen, Martin (1981) believes egoistical deprivations occur more frequently than group deprivations, while the data from New-ton and elsewhere (Guimond & Dubé-Simard, 1983) suggest the op-posite pattern. It may be interesting to document the incidence and in-tensity of both types of deprivation in a variety of settings. It ought to be even more interesting to learn about the circumstances in which group deprivation triggers personal deprivation and vice versa. The link between personal deprivation and group deprivation may be more visible within organizations than outside organizations because of the cognitive avail-ability of villains in bureaucracies. Bosses—and especially the big brass whom they never see—can be blamed by the workers and the staff for many ills; the workers furnish a similar scapegoat for the bosses. The accuracy of their perceptions may not really matter. What matters is the potential for saying "I am suffering because of the characteristics or ac-tions of this person or people". The manager who feels foiled by the stupidity of his staff and the staff who feel frustrated by the malice of the manager are both more susceptible to feelings of violated entitlements than are people who lack a ready scapegoat. Given the importance of a putative malefactor in the creation of personal deprivation, personal dep-rivations occur rarely but they may occur somewhat less rarely *in* work organizations than *outside* them.

Many of the factors which indirectly influence personal deprivation also affect feelings of group deprivation. In highly articulated organizations, the potential for group deprivation may be especially great: the division of organizational members into various categories (even on the basis of their function or duties) invites comparison between categories and can lead to an "us-them" mentality. Of course, a multitude of small divisions may contain the scope of one's comparisons while a few large divisions may not. Surely it would profit organizational administrators as well as benefit researchers to understand group deprivation and personal depri-vation and to manage the dynamic links between the two.

The second strategic suggestion is that researchers devote their efforts to the issue of deservingness. One of the two critical preconditions for deprivation, according to current wisdom, is the violated sense of enti-tlement. We know little about the dynamics of deserving in any context. The modern organizational setting may provide an excellent specimen for dissection because issues of deservingness may operate more neatly or more visibly there than elsewhere. The hallmark of modern bureaucratic work organizations is standardization. Functions are standardized; re-wards are standardized. The work one ought to do is made explicit; so are the rewards one ought to receive. The perception that someone's actual situation is not aligned with what he or she deserves may occur more readily or may be more solid in an organizational setting than else-where.

Devoting one's attention to deservingness will spell a change in how we examine comparison processes at work. For years researchers have tried to decompose work grievances almost exclusively through the prism of comparison processes. Comparison processes are important at work; of that there is no question. In one survey that asked managers about how they decided if they were satisfied with their pay, about 70% of the managers compared their own pay with that of another (Goodman, 1974). When asked if they ever compare themselves with someone else to de-termine how good their own job is, about 80% of the employed respond-ents in the Newton survey said yes. While comparison to a better-off individual or to a category of people may be a common element in dis-content, however, researchers need to subordinate the examination of comparison processes to the examination of deservingness issues. Rather than ask how discordant comparisons affect worker satisfaction, for ex-ample, researchers should ask how discordant comparisons affect feelings of unfairness or the perception of violated entitlements.

The third strategic suggestion is that researchers ought to investigate how one can capitalize on discontent within organizational contexts. So-cial psychologists and others have, by and large, assumed that discontent is a negative occurrence under any circumstance. They have directed their efforts at finding ways to avoid discontent. Social philosophers have not agreed. We have already referred to J. S. Mill's assertion that he would prefer to be a dissatisfied person than a satisfied pig. It is, of course, no easy matter to engineer a situation so that the dissatisfaction and re-sentments of workers benefit the organization rather than harm the organization, but efforts to channel anger may often prove more effective and rewarding than the effort to prevent anger. At present, there is little systematic research from which to draw guidelines about utilizing griev-ance. From some of the current work on organizational and vocational commitment, however, we can guess that commitment will prove a critical factor in the ways discontent may lead to constructive change within organizations. Perhaps in work settings, as in romances, anger can mo-tivate improvements among those commited to the adventure and per-haps, too, a little anger can sometimes help keep alive and solid a sense of commitment to the endeavor.

In sum, the clearest mandate for future researchers is to take a very serious look at the origins, development, and outcomes of feelings of deprivation within organizational contexts. Three interrelated questions grow out of the current work on relative deprivation. Addressing any one of the three questions would probably prove a good strategy for those who wish to see how resentments depend on organizational setting. The first question asks: what are the connections between personal grievance and group grievance within various types of organizations? Second, in what ways do organizational factors affect feelings of deservingness? Finally, what positive outcomes can organizations reap from discontent and in what ways can they do so?

New Issues

Looking at resentments as a function of organizational realities may bring practical payoffs to administrators. The effort may enrich our general understanding of organizational life. It should also improve our understanding of the dynamics of grievance. When it comes to resentments and kindred forms of distress, some organizations may be like frogs: their anatomy is simple and yet closely related to more complex organisms so a clean dissection tends to instruct us about more than the mere inside of a frog.

Although it promises substantial positive outcomes, the effort to study grievances as a function of organizational structure and climate contains costs. The clearly articulated organization may rival the frog for its usefulness as a laboratory device, but entry into an organization is certainly a great deal more costly than entry into a frog. To help insure a high return on their research investment, future researchers would be well advised to reflect about three conceptual issues before designing their research programs. These issues have been virtually ignored in the traditional research on relative deprivation, but they are currently receiving some attention elsewhere in social psychology. The present chapter closes with a look at these three issues and how they may affect organizational life.

Focus. Typically, relative deprivation researchers, equity researchers and justice researchers in general ask: how do disadvantaged people react to or evaluate their outcomes? They do not ask: how do they evaluate themselves? The inattention to issues of self-evaluation strikes me as curious because of the close link between relative deprivation, equity, and social comparison theory (Pettigrew, 1967). Since Festinger's (1954) articulation of social comparison theory, psychologists have noted that people use others as standards for judging their own opinions and abilities, as well as their own outcomes. The vast majority of the work in social comparison has focused on how people judge their own abilities (Gruder, 1977), and a substantial portion has dealt with judgments of one's own opinions (Castore & deNinno, 1977). Virtually no social comparison experiments look at people's judgments of outcomes (Suls & Miller, 1977).

The difference between the social comparison approach and the justice approach to unequal outcomes has gone unrecognized until recently. Pettigrew (1978) posed the issue in terms of intergroup relations and noted that disadvantaged minorities can interpret their inferior status as a statement about themselves or as a statement about the system. Carver (1979) claims that individuals may focus on themselves or on the system in which they operate and that it is virtually impossible to focus inward and outward at the same time. (See also Carver & Scheier, 1981) Finally, in an extremely clever experiment, Janice Steil (1979) created an inequality in the reward system of children performing a task. She asked the children both about their own abilities and about the fairness of the system under different conditions. Her results show that when the disadvantaged children evaluate the system as a fair one, they tend to denigrate their own abilities. Conditions which allow the children to label the system as unfair, on the other hand, do not lead to self-deprecation among the disadvantaged children.

When do disadvantaged people focus on themselves, and assume that the system is just and when do they assume that they themselves are competent and focus on the system? Recent analyses of attributional processes (Bradley, 1978; Miller & Ross, 1975; Nisbett & Ross, 1980), the results of a few experiments such as that of Steil, and anecdotal information suggest some answers. When people are newcomers to an established organization or system, they tend to focus on their own performance. Successes are taken as indications of competence; failures as indications of incompetence. The fairness of the system itself is rarely evaluated. Also, the more static the status quo, the more likely is the system to remain a perceptual ground. A questioning of the system by those in authority (Milgram, 1974) and the possibility of change in the system (Steil, 1979) both tend to produce changes in the Gestalt so that ground becomes figure. Some personality factors probably influence focus as much as situational factors do. We could expect an introvert to question his own capabilities before questioning the system while we would expect an extrovert to question the system first. Perhaps the critical variable is a sense of security. The characterologically secure person may resolve his or her doubts and not question him or herself.

The issue of focus ought to improve especially important for understanding the link between personal and group deprivation. Perhaps the absence of personal deprivation can be explained in part by focus: when one observes an individual, there may be a cognitive and perceptual pull toward an evaluation of the individual and away from an evaluation of the negative or difficult circumstances in his or her environment. It would be difficult to see that the individual deserves better treatment than he or she has if we tend to see the individual as responsible for his or her own situation. Observations about groups, on the other hand, involve little cognitive pull away from the group's circumstances. It may thus be harder to blame a group than to blame an individual victim (cf. Ryan, 1971). Finally, some thought about focus may give researchers and administrators clues about the techniques for optimizing the effects of discontent. Organizational policies ought to differentiate between the source of a problem and the remedy for a problem. No doubt many people function best if they locate the blame for their work problems outside themselves while, simultaneously, identifying themselves as the ones responsible for rectifying the situation.

Procedural and Distributive Justice. The second distinction comes from studies of the law (e.g., Hart, 1961; Rawls, 1971) and from psychological studies of justice (Folger, 1977; Lerner & Whitehead, 1980; Thibaut & Walker, 1975). It is the difference between distributive justice and procedural justice. Distributive justice concerns the allocation of goods and privileges among members of a legal community or other group. As Brickman, Folger, Goode, and Schul (1981) point out in their thought–provoking essay, the allocation of goods and privileges can be considered just because it gives to individuals what they as individuals are thought to deserve and it can be considered just because it conforms with certain system-wide rules. A rule that says that the richest person should not be more than twice as rich as the poorest person, is an example of a system-wide rule. When a distribution seems fair or unfair because individuals receive what they deserve to receive, we are—in the Aristotelian tradition—judging by a system of micro-justice. When a distribution seems fair or unfair because it results in the whole system attaining a certain state, we employ a more Platonic system of macro-justice. Whether we use the rules of micro-justice or macro-justice, as long as we focus on the allocation of items among group members, the issues concern distributive justice.

More basic than distributive justice, claim some scholars, is procedural justice. As the name implies, procedural justice concerns the rightness or fairness of the ways in which we go about making and implementing decisions. According to John Rawls (1971), a legal philosopher who is currently popular in political science and allied disciplines, distributive justice can be attained only if procedural justice obtains. An allocation of rewards among a group of people, for instance, is deemed fair only if the procedures for deciding the allocation are themselves fair.

How are we to know if procedures are fair? From Rawls' writings and from some of the trenchant criticisms of Rawls (e.g., Wolff, 1977), a simple and elegant answer can be extrapolated. It is this: procedures are fair if the participants agree to the rules before learning whether they would be benefited or hurt by them. When expectations about the outcomes under the existing set of rules cause a change in procedures, we suspect cheating.

Hart (1961) implies that among the diverse sets of 'fair' procedures devised by different societies some invariant factors can be found. Fair practices prohibit anyone (including the state) from using violence or from restricting the liberty of people without strong justification and they enjoin everyone to tell the truth and to honor pledges (Hart, 1963).

The distinction between distributive and procedural justice, it seems to me, has important implications for the study of grievance in organizational settings. Both relative deprivation and equity theorists have trained their sights on the distribution of rewards and punishments and have ignored procedural issues. Yet, as Morton Deutsch (1975, 1979) reminds us, anger and discontent with the rules by which decisions are made and with the implementation of those rules probably occurs as frequently as anger with the decisions themselves. A student may feel unhappy with a "C" grade, but his disappointment often does not solidify into grievance or resentment unless he questions the teacher's means of arriving at the grade.

Our disregard of procedural issues had made us blind to one limiting condition of relative deprivation. No doubt, when one considers the allocation of outcomes, everything is relative. What is rich in one context, is poor in another; the princely salary in Oasis, Arkansas seems a tinker's fee on Park Avenue. Yet, when it comes to procedures, to certain basic rules of conduct, absolutes appear. Lying is wrong. Even if person B lies more than person A, person A commits a wrong or an injustice if he or she lies too. Of course, what constitutes a lie may vary from one context to another, but the distance between the strict code of a religious person and the flexible code of a politician, a pimp, or a used car salesman seems more finite than infinite. When one considers the enormous variability in the subjective value of *things,* in other words, variations in the evaluation of *deeds* become trivial.

The importance of procedural justice for the study of deservingness within organizations cannot be overemphasized. One very interesting specific question illustrates how the conceptual distinction between distributive injustice and procedural injustice can enrich empirical approaches to deservingness. People in an organization may feel upset because they have experienced the loss of a positively valued outcome that they feel they deserved or because they received more of a negatively valued outcome than they feel they deserved. Salaried employees may, for example, feel they have received too little pay or too many weekend assignments. Alternately, people may feel upset because they have been denied due process (e.g., have not been not properly reviewed) or have been actively mistreated (e.g., unfairly singled out for blame or punishment). On the basis of past and present theories, I would predict that procedural resentments often masquerade as distributive resentments and that, if they go undiagnosed, resentments about procedures can prove very harmful to organizations. The validity of my hypotheses must be left for future researchers to demonstrate, but the line of inquiry appears now, in any event, to have merit.

Evaluations. The final distinction which seems to be worthy of notice concerns positive and negative outcomes. Almost all of the pertinent literature blurs the distinction. Equity theory treats positive and negative outcomes as inverse equivalents. Runcimam states: "Possession of X may, of course, mean avoidance of or exception from Y" (1966, p. 11) where X is a positive outcome and Y a negative one. In my own 1976 article, I state that the lack of a positive outcome or reward is the equivalent of the possession of a negative outcome or a punishment. I consider the dynamics of resentment to be the same in the case where a worker receives less salary than he would like and in the case where the worker is fired from his job.

Upon reflection, treating positive and negative outcomes as equivalent appears to be a mistake (cf. Keeley, 1978). A basic human distinction, one which begins to operate in our earliest years, is the distinction between good and bad. If our models seek to mimic the attitudinal processes of real people in real situations, then they ought to make distinctions which appear to be important to the people themselves. Several other observations also suggest that the distinction between positive and negative outcomes will prove interesting for future researchers. One suggestive observation concerns 'set points' or 'zero points' or 'comparison levels' (Thibaut & Kelley, 1959). People—within and without organizational settings—appear to use set points or zero points when performing the type of calculation that interests equity theorists and relative deprivation theorists. Outcomes below the set point are experienced as losses or punishments; outcomes above the set point, as gains or rewards. An individual's satisfaction with an outcome, relative to another person's outcome, depends not only on the size of the gap between the two outcomes, but also on whether one or both of the outcomes are above or below the set point. My dissatisfaction will be greater, in other words, if my opponent has a score of 15 and I have a score of negative 5, than if my opponent has a score of 35 and I of 15.

A simple game demonstrates the importance of set points. Tell an individual that he may win up to ten dollars in a short game with a series of bets. Tell him further that he starts with ten points to his credit and that at the end of the game any credit that he has may be exchanged for a dollar. If, after five minutes, the player has won four points, you give him four dollars. He feels quite happy. Now engage a second individual in the game with one modification: instead of giving the player ten points to begin the game, give him ten dollars. Tell him that the money is his and that he is to use it in the game. Tell him that whatever is left after five minutes of play plus whatever additional winnings he has will be his to take home. If at the end of play, the player has four dollars, he feels quite frustrated! Why? The reason is that the second player changed his set point the minute he received the money so that every dollar gone feels like a loss (Parducci, 1968).

Judgments about whether one has more or less of an outcome are usually made relative to the outcomes of others, but dichotomous judgments—judgments in which we pronounce ourselves winners or losers—are always made with reference to a set point. Of course, the set point itself can be mercurial and can sometimes be governed totally by the outcome of another. In a competitive zero-sum game like baseball, the dividing line between win and lose wiggles about as the opponents' score varies. But set points, as the game described above illustrates, are not always just a matter of comparison. Both theorists and practitioners ignore, at their peril, the distinction between positive, above–set–point outcomes and negative, below–set–point outcomes.

Another observation causes us to ring the alarm even louder. By erasing the dividing line between good and bad and by treating all units as fungible, equity and relative deprivation theorists have forgotten that some outcomes are so bad in one person's mind or in another's that no good can outweigh them. To the woman who suffered a Depression Childhood, an empty larder may be a negative outcome of such consequence that virtually no positive outcome equals it. Such a person would forego considerable opportunities rather than risk loss. To a man whose parents, long ago, were delivered into a concentration camp through falsehood, the telling of a small lie may be a wrong so great that no positive outcome nor opportunity can justify it. Indeed, I would go so far as to claim that for everyone save the sociopath, and in all circumstances except insanity (including war), some consequences are felt to be incalculably bad. Death of a member of one's family, friends, or self constitute the type of outcomes which defy an input-outcome ratio. Other less dramatic examples, no doubt, also exist.

Are there also positive outcomes that are so good that they justify any price? At a societal level, perhaps there are. Certaintly, Niccolo Machiavelli thought wise and stable government so important that the ruler could justify virtually any infringement on civil liberty in order to achieve it. More recently some scholars have maintained that personal liberty is so important that it justifies almost any ill including, for example, anarchy. Other philosophers (Hart, 1963) take a more moderate position. If we extrapolate from Hart, it would appear that while there are some wrongs which are so grave that they must be avoided at all costs, there are no rights which are so important that they must be achieved at any cost.

At an individual level the issue becomes even foggier. It is instructive to consider the opposite of negative consequences. Many people will say that dishonesty is an activity which they seek to avoid at all costs, but few will say that honesty is an activity in which they must engage at all costs. Most people maintain that killing is to be avoided whenever possible and only the certain hope of saving more lives justifies the taking of some lives. It seems nonsensical to maintain that life must be maintained at all costs, even death. Perhaps the nontransitive relationship here springs from our ability to differentiate between the mere fact of life and the quality of life and our simultaneous inability to differentiate between the fact of death and the quality of death. Whatever the source, the consequence remains that theorists (including myself) have been wrong. Being deprived of a valued outcome and being given an aversive outcome are not the same experience, either in their extreme forms or in less extreme forms.

These reflections bear on life in organizations. One implication is that the system of annual or bi-yearly bonuses may offer psychological advantages as well as monetary advantages to individuals and organizations. As long as the bonus is not so regular that it becomes part of the set figure of rewards, failure to receive a bonus may result in the type of discontent that one experiences when one is deprived of a valued outcome rather than in the type of discontent that one experiences when one is subjected to a punishment. Another implication is that rotational duty makes good sense when workers must withstand debilitating conditions. High wages or salaries and extensive fringe benefits may compensate for extremely difficult conditions in the short run. In the long run, however, it is probably a mistake to think in terms of tradeoffs. Over the long run, some conditions simply cannot be borne. The situation of air traffic controllers and combat soldiers comes to mind readily in this context. Higher wages are not be the best solution to discontent among air traffic controllers. Only a decrease in hours with the attendant decrease in stress would—according to their own rhetoric—satisfy most air traffic controllers. The statement "I wouldn't work there if you paid me a million dollars" expresses at an intuitive level the same notion—that there are some negative outcomes which one will not, under any circumstance, support.

At a more general level, and one which applies to the research strategies proposed for future work on relative deprivation in organizational settings, the issues of negative outcome bears on the question of organizational commitment. If organizations are to prosper, and more specifically if they are to reap positive benefits from discontent, they require commitment (Dittrich & Carrell, 1979; Farrel & Rusbalt, 1981; Porter, Crampon, & Smith, 1976; Porter, Steers, Mowday, & Boulian, 1974). Commitment can be built in many ways, no doubt. But while commitment seems to grow through the cumulative effect of a number of small positive incidents, it seems to take only one clear or dramatic negative incident to undercut that commitment. Researchers would probably be well advised to mind the distinction between positive and negative outcomes when they study resentments or deprivations sharp enough to result in defections, betrayals, and perhaps even, in some cases, strikes.

CONCLUSION

To study feelings of deprivation as a function of organizational contexts is no easy task. It ought to prove worthwhile both in terms of our knowledge of life in organizations and in terms of our understanding of the dynamics of grievance. Whether the outcomes of our research will be as good as they ought to be will, of course, depend in part on the procedures. This chapter has attempted to contribute to the endeavor in several ways. Perhaps because relative deprivation research occurs in many disciplines, researchers have sometimes displayed an ignorance of each other's work. This chapter has chronicled the history of relative deprivation and described current work in great detail so that future researchers may avoid re-plowing old fields and has tried to turn a discontent with the present state of affairs to advantage. It is hoped that some of the strategies proposed here will bear fruit.

NOTES

1. Some of the conceptual groundwork for the present chapter has been laid with the help of a grant from the Program on Non-Profit Organizations at Yale University. I would also like to express my gratitude to Larry Cummings, Andrée Newman, Robert Newman, Carol Schreiber, Barry Staw and Janice Steil for their helpful comments on earlier versions of the chapter.

2. The Newton survey was supported by a three year grant from the National Institute of Mental Health, grant RO1-MH31595.

3. For each of the regression analyses, the results were virtually identical whether we used raw scores or standardized scores. More importantly, the results remained the same when we repeated the tests using the LISREL IV structural equation program. Since the LISREL program is designed to compensate for variations in the reliability of different scales, we feel safe in concluding that our results are not primarily an artifact of how we measured our variable.

REFERENCE NOTES

1. Grajek, S., & Scarr, S. *Psychological and structural determinants of sibling rivalry.* Unpublished manuscript, Yale University, 1982. (Available from Susan Grajek, Department of Psychology, Yale University, Box 11A Yale Station, New Haven, CT 06520).

2. Muehrer, P. *Wanting and deserving: the crucial preconditions of felt deprivation?* Unpublished manuscript, Yale University, 1982. (Available from Peter Muehrer, Silliman College, Yale University, New Haven, CT 06520).

REFERENCES

Abeles, R. D. Relative deprivation, rising expectations and black militancy. *Journal of Social Issues,* 1976, *32*(2), 119–137.

Appelgryn, A. E. M., & Plug, C. Application of the theory of relative deprivation to occupational discrimination against women. *South African Journal of Psychology,* 1981, *11*, 143–147.

Bernstein, M., & Crosby, F. An empirical examination of relative deprivation theory. *Journal of Experimental Social Psychology,* 1980, *16*, 442–456.

Bradley, G. W. Self-serving biases in the attribution process: A re-examination of the fact or fiction question. *Journal of Personality and Social Psychology,* 1978, *36*, 56–71.

Brickman, P., Folger, R., Goode, E., & Schul, Y. Micro and macro justice. In M. J. Lerner & S. C. Lerner (Eds.), *The justice motive in social behavior. Adapting to times of scarcity and change.* New York: Plenum Press, 1981.

Cantril, H. *The patterns of human concerns.* New Brunswick, N.J.: Rutgers University Press, 1965.

Carver, C. S. A cybernetic model of self-attention processes. *Journal of Personality and Social Psychology,* 1979, *37*, 1251–1281.

Carver, C. S., & Scheier, M. F. *Attention and self-regulation: A control-theory approach to human behavior.* New York: Springer-Verlag, 1981.

Castore, C. H., & De Ninno, J. A. Investigations in the social comparison of attitudes. In J. M. Suls & R. L. Miller (Eds.), *Social comparison processes.* New York: John Wiley, 1977.

Cook, T. D., Crosby, F., & Hennigan, K. M. The construct validity of relative deprivation. In J. Suls and R. Miller (Eds.), *Social comparison processes.* New York: John Wiley, 1977.

Crosby, F. A model of egotistical relative deprivation. *Psychological Review,* 1976, *83*, 85–113.

Crosby, F. *Relative deprivation and working women.* New York: Oxford University Press, 1982.

Crosby, F., & Gonzalez-Intal, M. Relative deprivation and equity theories: Felt injustice and the underserved benefits of others. In R. Folger (Ed.), *The sense of injustice: Social psychological perspectives.* New York: Plenum Press, in press.

Davis, J. A. A formal interpretation of the theory of relative deprivation. *Sociometry,* 1959, *22*, 280–296.

de Carufel, A. The allocation and acquisition of resources in times of scarcity. In M. J. Lerner & S. C. Lerner (Eds.), *The justice motive in social behavior. Adapting to times of scarcity and change.* New York: Plenum Press, 1981.

Deutsch, M. Equity, equality and need: What determines which value will be used as the basis of distributive justice? *Journal of Social Issues,* 1975, *31*(3), 137–149.

Deutsch, M. Education and distributive justice. *American Psychologist,* 1979, *34*, 391–401.

Dittrich, J. E., & Carrell, M. R. Organizational equity perceptions, employee job satisfaction, and departmental absence and turnover rates. *Organizational Behavior and Human Performance,* 1979, *24*, 29–40.

Farrell, D., & Rusbult, C. E. Exchange variables as predictors of job satisfaction, job commitment, and turnover: The impact of rewards, costs, alternatives, and investments. *Organizational Behavior and Human Performance*, 1981, *28*, 78–95.

Feierabend, I. K., & Feierabend, R. L. Aggressive behaviors within polities, 1949–1962: A cross-national study. *Journal of Conflict Resolution*, 1966, *10*, 249–271.

Feierabend, I. K., Feierabend, R. L., & Nesbold, B. A. Social and political violence: Cross-national patterns. In H. D. Graham & T. R. Gurr (Eds.), *Violence in America*. New York: Signet Books, 1969.

Festinger, L. A. A theory of social comparison processes. *Human Relations*, 1954, *7*, 117–140.

Fogarty, M. P., Rapoport, R., & Rapoport, R. N. *Sex, career and family*. London: George Allen and Unwin, 1971.

Folger, R. Distributive and procedural justice: Combined impact of 'voice' and improvement on experienced inequity. *Journal of Personality and Social Psychology*, 1977, *35*, 108–119.

Folger, R., Rosenfield, D., & Robinson, T. Relative deprivation and procedural justifications. *Journal of Personality and Social Psychology*, in press.

Goodman, P. S. An examination of referents used in the evaluation of pay. *Organizational Behavior and Human Performance*, 1974, *12*, 170–195.

Gruder, C. L. Choice of comparison persons in evaluating oneself. In J. M. Suls & R. L. Miller (Eds.), *Social comparison processes*. New York: John Wiley, 1977.

Guimond, S., & Dubé-Simard, L. Relative deprivation theory and the Québec Nationalist Movement: On the cognition-emotion distinction and the personal-group deprivation issue. *Journal of Personality and Social Psychology*, 1983, *44*, 526–535.

Gurr, T. R. A causal model of civil strife: A comparative analysis using new indices. *American Political Science Review*, 1968, *62*, 1104–1124. (a)

Gurr, T. R. Psychological factors in civil violence. *World Politics*, 1968, *20*, 245–278. (b)

Gurr, T. R. Urban disorder, perspectives from the comparative study of civil strife. In L. H. Masotti & D. R. Bowen (Eds.), *Riots and rebellion: Civil violence in the urban community*. Beverly Hills, California: Sage, 1968. (c)

Gurr, T. R. A comparative study of civil strife. In H. D. Graham & T. R. Gurr (Eds.), *Violence in America*. New York: Signet Books, 1969.

Gurr, T. R. *Why men rebel*. Princeton, N.J.: Princeton University Press, 1970.

Hart, H. L. A. *The concept of law*. Oxford: The Clarendon Press, 1961.

Hart, H. L. A. *Law, liberty, and morality*. Stanford, CA: Stanford University Press, 1963.

Hennigan, K. *The construct validity of relative deprivation: conceptual and empirical analyses*. Unpublished doctoral dissertation, Northwestern University, 1977.

Hyman, H. H., & Singer, E. (Eds.), *Readings in reference group theory and research*. New York: Free Press, 1968.

Keeley, M. A social-justice approach to organizational evaluation. *Administrative Science Quarterly*, 1978, *23*, 272–292.

Kinder, D. R., & Kiewiet, R. D. Economic grievances and political behavior: The role of personal discontents and collective judgments in Congressional voting. *American Journal of Political Science*, 1979, *23*, 495–527.

Kinder, D. R., & Sears, D. O. Prejudice and politics: Symbolic racism versus racial threats to the good life. *Journal of Personality and Social Psychology*, 1981, *40*, 414–431.

Kramnick, I. Reflections on revolution: Definition and Explanation in recent scholarship. *History and Theory*, 1972, *11*, 26–63.

Lane, R. E. *Political ideology: Why the American common man believes what he does*. New York: Free Press, 1962.

Lerner, M. & Whitehead, L. Procedural justice viewed in the context of justice motive theory. In G. Mikula (Ed.), *Justice and social interaction*. New York: Springer-Verlag, 1980.

Martin, J. *When prosperity fails: Distributional determinants of the perception of justice.* Unpublished doctoral dissertation, Harvard University, 1979.

Martin, J. Relative deprivation: A theory of distributive injustice for an era of shrinking resources. In L. L. Cummings & B. M. Staw (Eds.), *Research in organizational behavior. An annual series of analytic essays and critical reviews.* (Vol. 3). Greenwich, CT: JAI Press, 1981.

Merton, R., & Rossi, A. S. Contributions to the theory of reference group behavior. In R. Merton (Ed.), *Social theory and social structure.* New York: Free Press, 1957.

Milgram, S. *Obedience to authority: An experimental view.* New York: Harper & Row, 1974.

Miller, D. T., & Ross, M. Self-serving biases in the attribution of causality. Fact or fiction? *Psychological Bulletin,* 1975, *82,* 213–225.

Nisbett, R., & Ross, L. *Human inference: Strategies and shortcomings of social judgment.* Englewood Cliffs: Prentice Hall, 1980.

Parducci, A. The relativism of absolute judgments. *Scientific American,* 1968, *219*(6), 84–90.

Patchen, M. The effect of reference group standards on job satisfaction. *Human Relations,* 1958, *11,* 304–314.

Patchen, M. *The choice of wage comparisons.* Englewood Cliffs, N.J.: Prentice-Hall, 1961.

Pettigrew, T. Social evaluation theory. In D. Levine (Ed.), *Nebraska Symposium on Motivation* (Vol. 15). Lincoln: University of Nebraska Press, 1967.

Pettigrew, T. Three issues in ethnicity: Boundaries, deprivations, and perceptions. In J. M. Yinger & S. J. Cutler (Eds.), *Major Social Issues: A Multidisciplinary View.* New York: Free Press, 1978.

Porter, L. W., Crampon, W. J., & Smith, F. J. Organizational commitment and managerial turnover: A longitudinal study. *Organizational Behavior and Human Performance,* 1976, *15,* 87–98.

Porter, L. W., Steers, R. M., Mowday, R. T., & Boulian, P. V. Organizational commitment, job satisfaction, and turnover among psychiatric technicians. *Journal of Applied Psychology,* 1974, *59,* 603–609.

Rawls, J. *A theory of justice.* Cambridge, MA: Harvard University Press, 1971.

Rhodebeck, L. Group deprivation: An alternative model for explaining collective political action. *Micropolitics,* 1981, *1,* 239–267.

Runciman, W. G. *Relative deprivation and social justice: A study of attitudes to social inequality in twentieth-century England.* Berkeley, CA: University of California Press, 1966.

Ryan, W. *Blaming the victim.* New York: Random House, 1971.

Scase, R. Relative deprivation: A comparison of English and Swedish manual workers. In D. Wedderburn (Ed.), *Poverty, inequality, and class structure.* Cambridge, England: Cambridge University Press, 1974.

Schwartz, S. K., & Schwartz, D. C. Convergence and divergence in political orientations between Blacks and Whites: 1960–1973. *Journal of Social Issues,* 1975, *32*(2), 153–168.

Spilerman, S. The causes of racial disturbances: A comparison of alternate explanations. *American Sociological Review,* 1970, *35,* 627–649.

Spilerman, S. The causes of racial disturbances: Tests of explanations. *American Sociological Review,* 1971, *36,* 427–442.

Steil, J. M. Efficacy and the response to injustice by relatively advantaged and disadvantaged persons. Unpublished doctoral dissertation, Columbia University, 1979.

Stouffer, S. A., Suchman, E. A., DeVinney, L. C., Star, S. A., & Williams, R. M. *The American soldier: Adjustment during Army life* (Vol. 1). Princeton, NJ: Princeton University Press, 1949.

Suls, J. M., & Miller, R. L. (Eds.), *Social comparison processes*. New York: John Wiley, 1977.

Thibaut, J., & Walker, L. *Procedural justice: A psychological analysis*. Hillsdale, NJ: Lawrence Erlbaum, 1975.

Thibaut, J., & Kelley, H. H. *Social psychology of groups*. New York: Wiley, 1959.

Useem, M. *Protest movements in America*. New York: Bobbs-Merrill, 1975.

Wolff, R. P. *Understanding Rawls: A reconstruction and critique of A Theory of Justice*. Princeton, NJ: Princeton University Press, 1977.

Zald, M. N., & Berger, M. A. Social movements in organizations: Coup d'Etat, insurgency and mass movements. *American Journal of Sociology*, 1978, *4*, 823–861.

GOAL SETTING:

A THEORETICAL ANALYSIS OF A MOTIVATIONAL TECHNOLOGY

James C. Naylor and Daniel R. Ilgen

ABSTRACT

The recent theoretical explanation for complex behavior proposed by Naylor, Pritchard, and Ilgen (1980b) is suggested as a conceptual framework for understanding the effects of goal setting. The motivational component of the theory is first elaborated upon and then applied to an analysis of goal setting. It is argued that the goal setting intervention has its major influence upon motivation (and thus behavior) by affecting a task performer's perceptions of the shape of the product-to-evaluation contingency function. This results in changes in the motivational force to commit resources to acts. Also examined and redefined within the theory are the traditional goal setting terms of goal difficulty, specificity and acceptability. Numerous analytical arguments are suggested as ways of viewing how these traditional goal setting constructs may be operating in a goal setting situation.

Research in Organizational Behavior, vol. 6, pages 95–140
Copyright © 1984 by JAI Press Inc.
All rights of reproduction in any form reserved.
ISBN: 0-89232-351-5

INTRODUCTION

An extensive review of the goal setting literature from 1969 through 1980 led Locke, Shaw, Saari, and Latham (1981) to conclude that the positive effect of goals on performance is one of the most robust and replicable findings in the psychological literature. They found over 90% of the studies reviewed reported at least some beneficial effects on performance. Clearly, goals can strongly influence performance, and therefore, the process of setting goals is an important technology with respect to work motivation.

In spite of the success of goal setting, adequate explanations concerning why goals work are fewer than would be expected from such a widely used and acclaimed procedure. For some years, researchers and practioners alike either focused only on the performance effects (ignoring the causes of the performance) or they accepted without question Locke's early model of the goal setting process (Locke, 1968). Only recently has the actual process of goal setting been explored in more detail (e.g. Locke, et al., 1981; Terborg, 1976; Umstot, Bell, & Mitchell, 1976).

Our purpose here is to continue this trend. We will treat goals from a psychological perspective. We shall explore what we believe are the major parameters of interest in the goal setting process. Next, we shall address their affects upon individuals' beliefs and actions. To do this, we shall first review and comment upon critical features of goal setting that have been identified in the literature. This will be followed by our theoretical interpretations of goal setting effects as described by Locke et al. (1981) and then by our development of an alternative framework for addressing goal setting effects. The framework developed for goal setting is a deductive one following directly from positions of Naylor et al. regarding behavior in organizations. As such, the deductive statements are more precise (and tedious) than those frequently available in the organizational behavior literature. Yet, we feel the advantages of precision more than justify the effort required to understand the material. The result of the deductive logic is a clear exposition of assumptions followed by precise definitions and constructs that can be tested and either supported or not supported. To date the field of organizational behavior has tended to survive on brute empiricism and informal theory comprised of loosely defined constructs often represented in boxes and connected by lines. We feel there is a need to attempt to go beyond this; we hope the reader will share our view.

THE GOAL SETTING PROCESS

Elements

A performance goal is "what an individual is trying to accomplish; it is the object or aim of an action." (Locke, et al., 1981). This simple definition captures the essence of goals, but its simplicity is deceiving. In order to describe goals with any degree of precision, much more must be addressed beyond definition. Additional considerations for expanding upon the definition can be classified into issues or factors that describe the attributes of the goals and those that are relevant conditions affecting the impact of goals on performance. Each of these will be considered in turn.

Goal Attributes. Two attributes or dimensions of goals are necessarily present in every goal. The first of these is *goal specificity.* Specificity refers to the extent to which the performance level to be accomplished is explicit as to its content and its clarity (Locke, et al., 1981). Content refers to the nature of the performance units used to describe the goal and clarity to the quantity or amounts of these units to be performed. In the latter case, these quantity units are usually banded in time—e.g. words per minute, publications per year, etc. Specificity decreases when the goal is expressed either in (1) less precise content units (e.g. instead of publications per year the goal could be scientific contributions per year with the definition of scientific contribution unspecified) or (2) in less objective quantitative units (a "substantial number" of publications). Typically, goal setting research studying the effects of non-specific goals uses the imprecise, "Do your best," as a goal (Locke, et al., 1981). We will examine this particular manipulation in detail later in the paper and argue that it is actually not a specificity manipulation at all.

The second attribute of a goal is its *difficulty.* Whenever a goal is expressed, it defines a level of performance and reflects the costs to the performer of meeting the goal. The costs may be in units of ability, time and effort, number of skills required, amount of experience or any other terms needed to accomplish the goal. In goal setting research, the nature of these costs is frequently ignored when describing difficulty in terms of the probability of success. Easy goals are those with a high probability of accomplishment and hard goals are those with a low probability of accomplishment—regardless of what kinds of units must be expended to reach the "easy" or "hard" goals.

Using probability–of–task–accomplishment as an index of goal difficulty, Terborg (1976) pointed out that goal difficulty can be construed from two perspectives. The first perspective is from the point of view of all of those who perform the task. From this point of view, the difficulty of a goal is the probability of accomplishment or the ratio of the number of individuals who reach the goal to the number who attempt to reach it. On the other hand, for any given individual, goal difficulty can be referenced against a self standard. In this case, difficulty is the probability of the individual reaching the goal on any given attempt, or the ratio of the number of successes to number of attempts. Obviously, goals that may be seen as relatively difficult for most people may be quite easy for any one particular individual or vice versa. Therefore, it is important to keep in mind the frame-of-reference being used when goal difficulty is described. Our treatment of goal setting in later sections will be based upon perceptions of the second of these two types of goal difficulties.

Relevant Conditions.   Often confused with the attributes of goals are the conditions under which goals develop and operate in performance settings. These conditions differ from attributes in that they are not inherent dimensions of goals per se; they are simply conditions surrounding goals that affect the effectiveness of them. The conditions themselves cluster into three sets: *sources of goals, conditions within the task performer,* and *conditions within the task environment.*

Goals may originate from two *sources,* either from the actual task performer or from some external source (person, group, organization, etc.). Although several popular organization theories urge the use of goals set by the performer rather than by outside sources, the empirical literature is not too convincing. One major review on participation in decision making (Locke, & Schweickert, 1980) and another discussion of participation specifically in goal setting (Latham, et al., 1978) lead to the same conclusion—participation by performers in setting goals for their own performance only infrequently has led to improved performance. We will present arguments for these results later in the paper.

From the performer's point of view, the two conditions of goal *acceptance* and goal *commitment* have been shown to have a major impact on goal effectiveness. These two conditions differ in their temporal association with the goal itself. Goal acceptance, as typically defined, refers to the extent to which the task performer believes that the goal is a reasonable one for him or her when that goal is assigned to the person by someone else. Ignoring for a moment all the ambiguity in what is meant by "reasonable", it can be seen that the notion of goal acceptance is a complex set of beliefs in which the individual must take into account his or her own ability to accomplish the goal, the legitimacy of the source to prescribe the goal, and many other factors in order to decide whether the goal is one that he or she accepts as the level of performance for which to strive. Goal commitment, on the other hand, is manifested after the goal has been accepted, although the literature is not very clear on this timing notion. Nevertheless, we feel that the distinction between acceptance and commitment is logical. If construed in this fashion, commitment refers to the degree to which an individual is willing to commit resources toward accomplishing a goal. We shall later explicitly define these resources as time and effort.

The final set of conditions for goal development exists in the environment of the task performer. One element of this set is the feedback the performer receives with respect to goal accomplishment. It is widely accepted that performance is highest in the presence of both goals and feedback (Locke, et al., 1981). Erez (1977) took a more extreme position and stated that goals are *only* effective if the performer receives sufficient feedback to be able to ascertain his or her progress with respect to the goal. This conclusion has rarely, if ever, been violated when well constructed designs of feedback and goals have been used. It should be pointed out that the joint occurance of feedback and goal setting does not imply that supervisors or some other specific source must provide feedback in all goal setting situations. It may be that the task performer has developed enough personal expertise to be able to judge quite accurately how well he or she is doing. The point with respect to feedback is only that it must be possible for the performer to form such beliefs, and these beliefs must be relatively accurate.

A second condition of the external environment is the performance-outcome (reward) contingencies. These contingencies refer to the extent outcomes of some value to the task performer are associated with task performance and, more importantly, goal accomplishment. The nature of these outcomes varies widely from very explicit factors such as pay or selection for a promotion to less obvious conditions such as the friendliness of co-workers. The exact nature of these associations is critical to our treatment of motivation (Naylor, Pritchard, & Ilgen, 1980b), and they will be dealt with at length in this paper. At this point, it suffices to say that the number of outcomes associated with task accomplishment, the attractiveness of these outcomes, and the strength of association between goal accomplishment and outcome obtainment are important conditions affecting the influence of goals on performance.

The importance of these external factors is due to their demonstrated influence upon the level of performance defined as necessary for goal accomplishment. Either implicitly or explicitly, goals are typically viewed from a cognitive framework (Locke, et al., 1981) which assumes that (a) the performer takes into consideration the attractiveness of performing at several levels of performance then (b) attempts to reach those levels of performance that are seen as most attractive. We believe that through the association of valued outcomes with goal accomplishment, the attractiveness of a goal is established and that individuals respond to goals, at least in part, on the basis of their perceived attractiveness.

Psychological Processes

The psychological processes invoked through the use of goals have received only modest attention when one considers the widespread use and acceptance of goal setting. The most complete explication appeared only recently in Locke, et al. (1981) updated review of the literature. In that review, four mechanisms are offered as explanations for the goal setting process. The first of these is *directing attention*. This refers to the fact that goals indicate what needs to be done in the work setting. Thus, if sales goals are stated in terms of establishing new accounts, salespersons are made aware of valued behaviors and will tend to direct their attention toward those behaviors most likely, in their opinion, to lead to the establishment of new accounts—perhaps at the expense of behaviors needed to maintain old accounts.

A second proposed mechanism is that of *mobilizing effort*. Assuming that an individual knows what behaviors to display to accomplish a goal, having a stated goal also carries an implication of the effort needed to accomplish that goal. In manifesting the required amount of effort over an extended period of time, the goal serves to influence the *persistance* of the individual at the task. Persistance for Locke, et al. (1981) represents the mechanism through which goals influence performance. This mechanism is seen as a combination of the first two mechanisms with the introduction of a time dimension.

Finally goals are said to influence performance through *strategy development*. This more complex cognitive mechanism involves the individual's active attempt to consider the task carefully and decide on the best way to accomplish the goal. The implication in strategy development is that the individual considers a set of alternative courses of action and selects that course best able to lead to task accomplishment. In the absence of goals, individuals may give less consideration to the types of things they should be doing to do the task well. Goals are assumed to trigger a more problem-solving mode in the individual which, in turn, should lead to more efficatious procedures or strategies for working on the task.

We find the introduction of the conceptual framework offered by Locke, et al. (1981) laudible. It meets a need unmet in most of the previous literature. Yet, we also must recognize some of its weaknesses. Most apparent are the lack of precision and the lack of independance of the constructs used. The more apparent but less serious of these problems is the latter. For example, the authors themselves acknowledge that the notion of persistence is little more than a combination of directing attention and mobilizing effort. While we see no utility in insisting on totally independent constructs in theory development, there is a point where too much redundancy among constructs becomes burdensome and even confusing.

Less apparent but more serious is the lack of precision associated with the constructs used by Locke, et al. At first glance, all four of these constructs seem to make perfectly good sense. They are expressed in common everyday language, and their definitions are very reasonable and straightforward. Yet with closer scrutiny, it is apparent that each of these constructs is really very complex requiring the use of several other constructs only vaguely implied from the descriptions. Consider, for example, directing attention. The notion that goals lead the individual to select a subset of relevant behaviors to perform requires that we understand the nature of the set of behaviors related to the task, those subsets that are attended to if goals are not used (in some sense, the "base rate" for invoked sets), the individual's actual ability to do the behaviors, the individual's ability to accurately perceive his or her ability to perform the "appropriate" behavior, and several other factors that we have overlooked. Likewise, for the other explanatory mechanisms, we would argue that there is considerable imprecision which, in turn, makes it difficult to understand the clear implications of the mechanisms for effective use of goal setting.

In the remainder of this paper, we shall provide what we believe is a framework that does allow for a more precise conceptualization of the goal setting process. In this, the reader will recognize many of the notions suggested by Locke, et al. (1981) and by many of the authors they cite. That is, much of what we will have to say is not totally new. What we offer is primarily a frame-of-reference that provides more precision to our ability to conceptualize goal setting. In doing so, we also hope to suggest directions to go in the future with respect to the design of systems using goal setting technology.

MOTIVATION MECHANISMS OF NPI THEORY

To aid the discussion of goal setting manipulation, we first must examine the theoretical context which will be used. Not surprisingly, we propose that the theory recently developed by Naylor, Pritchard and Ilgen (1980b) provides a powerful conceptual framework for goal setting. For convenience we shall refer to this framework as NPI theory in subsequent discussions.

NPI theory is a theory of cognitive choice behavior based upon a set of cognitive constructs and their proposed interrelationships which are in turn postulated as forming the necessary logical components for rational behavior. Rational behavior itself is defined as the process of attempting to maximize one's anticipated influence under a set of constraints. (Note: Satisficing behavior *is* a maximization strategy to the individual). Like nearly all cognitive theories, NPI theory views the motivational process as a procedure in which the individual combines feelings of positive or negative affect about future outcomes with self perceptions of contingency relationships between behavioral choices and the amount or likelihood of these outcomes. Thus, in the general sense, NPI theory is based upon classical subjective expected utility assumptions.

However, its treatment of uncertainty in the choice process is quite different than that of classical SEU theory in general and Expectancy theory in particular. In NPI theory, utilities are not weighted by their respective subjective probabilities to obtain optimality. Instead, subjective uncertainty is treated as a bivariate density function expressing the relationships between values of two variables. The theory assumes that individuals will conceptually derive best fitting functions to such probability relationships and then base their subsequent behaviors on the shape of these subjective functions. That is, behavior will be based upon the individual's intuitive conception of the expected value of Y for any value of X, regardless of the conditional variance ($s_y^2 \mid X$). More explicitly, behavior is assumed to be a result of perceived differences in the expected value of Y for various levels of X, i.e., $(Y \mid X_i - Y \mid X_j)$. The degree of uncertainty associated with these expected values, as represented by the conditional variances $s_y^2 \mid X_i$, is not assumed to be a choice parameter in the theory. An individual's perception of the conditional mean $(\bar{Y} \mid X)$ is assumed to be independent of the conditional variance. The reasonableness of this assumption has been demonstrated in numerous studies (Naylor & Clark, 1968; Naylor & Domini, 1981).

A second, but less fundamental, distinction between NPI theory and traditional expectancy theory lies in the addition of several contingency relationships. Expectancy theory has historically utilized two basic contingency relationships in dealing with work motivation (Ilgen, Nebeker & Pritchard, 1981). These are the effort-to-performance relationship (called the $E \rightarrow P$ contingency) and the performance–to–outcomes relationship (called the $P \rightarrow O$ instrumentality). Thus traditional expectancy theory can be crudely diagrammed as a process involving the sequences $E \rightarrow P \rightarrow O$. NPI theory has broadened this sequence to one which can be written $A \rightarrow P \rightarrow E \rightarrow O$, where A = commitment to an act, P = the product produced by the act (behavior), E = the evaluation by an observer of what has been produced, and O = the outcomes resulting from the evaluation. This sequence results in two additional contingency relationships not present in expectancy theory. The traditional performance-to-outcomes contingency relationship is seen as actually being comprised of two, more specific relationships—the relationship between what the person produces and how that output is evaluated and the relationship between the evaluation and the administration of rewards (outcomes) to the worker.

The theory presents the motivational process as a sequence consisting of three cognitive processing stages. Each of the three stages involves the conversion of a prior utility function into a new utility function as a result of an individual's perception or belief about one of three different contingency relationships. These three perceived contingency functions are contingencies between acts and products ($C_{A \to P}$), products and evaluations ($C_{P \to E}$), and evaluations and outcomes ($C_{E \to O}$). All the major elements of the motivational sequence are future oriented, and the separate stages of cognitive processing in the sequence are best described as predictive evaluative judgment processes (Naylor, Pritchard, and Ilgen, 1980b). Figure 1 presents the complete sequence. It is composed of four utility functions and the three contingency functions which influence these utility functions. In describing the sequence, we will assume an artificially simple situation in which (a) an individual's motivational force to commit resources to a single act leads to (b) the creation of various amounts of a single product which (c) is subsequently evaluated by a single evaluator whose evaluation (d) results in the administering of various amounts of a single outcome (reward) to the focal individual.

The initial stage of the sequence is the utility function associated with

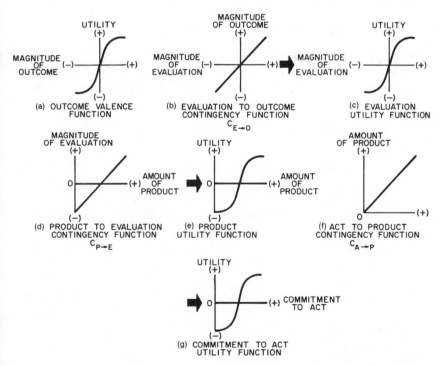

Figure 1. Components of the Motivational Sequences in NPI Theory

the outcome or reward variable (Figure 1a). We have chosen for our example a traditional utility function which has decreasing marginal utility for both increasing and decreasing amounts of the outcome. That is, outcome amounts are viewed as either gains or losses (+ or −) from a neutral reference outcome assigned a value of zero in the manner of Tversky and Kahneman (1981). Increasingly greater deviations from this zero point are associated with proportionally decreasing amounts of anticipated positive or negative affect (utility).

The energizing or drive level construct in NPI theory is called motivational force (MF). Motivational force is a derived construct defined in terms of a change ratio employing the two fundamental measures defining any utility function. For example, the utility function for any outcome O is based upon measures of the degree of utility associated with various amounts of the outcome. The MF for outcome level O_j is then defined as

$$MF_{O_j} = \frac{U_i - U_j}{O_i - O_j} = \frac{\Delta U}{\Delta O}$$

where O_i = present level of outcome being received
O_j = outcome to be received
U_i = utility for present outcome
U_j = utility of outcome to be received

Thus MF is defined as the slope of the utility function between any two outcome levels i and j. The steeper the slope, the greater the MF existing as an energizer to attain that outcome. This definition of MF is generalizable to any utility function, regardless of the dimension on the abscissa. This permits the tracing of the energizing component of motivation from its inception in the MF of outcomes to its culmination in the MF associated with basic acts.

Treating motivational force as the energizing component of motivation and keeping it conceptually distinct from the notion of goal attractiveness (utility) is an important characteristic of NPI Theory. It permits an analytic treatment of motivational issues which would be much more difficult otherwise. However, it should be recognized that the separateness of force and valence constructs in motivation theory is still a point of mild contention among motivational theorists (see Bolles, 1975, and Capaldi, 1979, for discussion of this issue).

Figure 1b depicts the second function in the motivational sequence— the evaluation-to-outcome contingency function. It represents the focal individual's belief about the relationships existing between the degree of favorableness of the evaluation as seen by some evaluator and the magnitude of the outcome the evaluator will then award, or give to, the individual (the focal) for producing products of varying amounts. For illustrative purposes we have assumed this function to be linear with a slope of 1.0, representing a belief by the focal that unit increases in outcomes are associated with corresponding unit increases in more positive evaluations by the evaluator.

Given the two belief functions represented in Figures 1a and 1b, it is then possible to postulate a cognitive process which involves combining these beliefs about a utility and a contingency into a new utility function representing the focal's perceived utility of evaluation as shown in Figure 1c. NPI theory assumes the new function to be a simple product of 1a and 1b. Since 1b is a linear with slope 1, this new utility function has the identical form of the prior utility in 1a, but the abscissa now becomes the magnitude of the evaluation made by the evaluator. Further, the MF for receiving evaluations of various magnitudes (the energizing component) is now expressable in terms of the slope of this function.

The second of the three critical contingency functions—the product-evaluation contingency ($C_{P \to E}$)—is shown in Figure 1d. This function represents the belief held by the focal concerning the relationship between the amount of the product produced and the magnitude of the evaluation (either positive or negative) of that output by the external evaluator. For simplicity, we show this function as being linear with slope 1.0, representing the belief by the focal that increasing units produced are associated with corresponding increases in units of positive evaluation.

A second cognitive processing stage can now be postulated which involves combining the beliefs represented by 1c and 1d into a composite belief which is the utility function of the focal's products (Figure 1e). This function represents the focal's perception of the functional relationship between levels of his or her own product and the amount of anticipated pleasure associated with those levels of the product. As before, the slope of this function for any ΔP represents the motivational force associated with the ΔP.

The third contingency ($C_{A \to P}$), shown in Figure 1f, represents the belief of the focal regarding the functional form of the relationship between the amount of personal resources committed to an act and the amount of the product created or produced.[1] The illustration shows a function for $C_{A \to P}$ which is linear with slope 1.0 indicating a belief by the focal that unit increases in amounts of commitment to the act will result in corresponding unit increases in the amount of the product being created by the act.

The third and last cognitive processing point in the sequence forms the final stage of utility formulation. Here the focal combines the utility–of–products function with the act-to-product contingency function to produce a utility function for commitment to the act itself. This function is shown in Figure 1g. This utility function expresses the degree of anticipated affect that the focal associates with various degrees of commitment to the act.

The slope of this utility function once again represents the amount of motivational force associated with a specified change in the amount of commitment to the act.

The entire basic motivational sequence can be represented in a more formal way. We have previously defined MF as the slope of a utility function. Specifically, the MF associated with a change in outcomes was defined as

$$MF_{\Delta O} = \frac{\Delta U}{\Delta O} = \text{Motivational force for a change} \qquad (1)$$
$$\text{in outcome level}$$

We can also define the slope of the $C_{E \to O}$, $C_{P \to E}$ and $C_{A \to P}$ contingencies respectively as $\Delta 0/\Delta E$, $\Delta E/\Delta P$, and $\Delta P/\Delta C$ ratios where ΔO represents a change in outcome, ΔE represents a change in evaluation, ΔP represents a change in the amount of the product, and ΔC represents a change in commitment to the act. From the above discussion we can thus express the following motivational force constructs:

$$MF_{\Delta E} = MF_{\Delta O} \cdot C_{E \to O} = \frac{\Delta U}{\Delta O} \cdot \frac{\Delta O}{\Delta E} = \frac{\Delta U}{\Delta E} = \begin{array}{l} \text{Motivational} \\ \text{Force for a} \\ \text{change in} \\ \text{Evaluation } \Delta E \end{array} \qquad (2)$$

$$MF_{\Delta P} = MF_{\Delta E} \cdot C_{P \to E} = \frac{\Delta U}{\Delta E} \cdot \frac{\Delta E}{\Delta P} = \frac{\Delta U}{\Delta P} = \begin{array}{l} \text{Motivational} \\ \text{Force for a} \\ \text{change in} \\ \text{Product } \Delta P \end{array} \qquad (3)$$

$$MF_{\Delta C} = MF_{\Delta P} \cdot C_{A \to P} = \frac{\Delta U}{\Delta P} \cdot \frac{\Delta P}{\Delta C} = \frac{\Delta U}{\Delta C} = \begin{array}{l} \text{Motivational} \\ \text{Force for a} \\ \text{change in} \\ \text{commitment } \Delta C. \end{array} \qquad (4)$$

The concept of the utility function for commitment to an act as a function which may be decomposed into a set of component functions is made even more clear if we express

$$MF_{\Delta C} = \frac{\Delta U}{\Delta C} = \frac{\Delta U}{\Delta O} \cdot \frac{\Delta 0}{\Delta E} \cdot \frac{\Delta E}{\Delta P} \cdot \frac{\Delta P}{\Delta C} \qquad (5)$$

In equation 5 we can see that the motivational force to commit an additional amount of resources to an act ($MF_{\Delta C}$) is determined by the MF associated with the utility of outcomes function $\Delta U/\Delta 0$ modified by the three intervening contingency functions $C_{E \to 0}$, $C_{P \to E}$, and $C_{A \to P}$.

With this brief review of the stages of the motivational sequence in NPI theory we are now in a position to examine several characteristics of the goal setting phenomenon and to propose a theoretical explanation for the motivating effects of goals. Recall that goals were defined as, "the object or aim of action" and that there are several conditions surrounding goals that must be specified. For our purpose here, we will assume that we are dealing with goals that have been set by an employee's supervisor. The supervisor was chosen only because the situation of a supervisor holding performance goals for his or her subordinate is a common one in organizations. From a theoretical standpoint, the position of the person setting the goal is of little or no importance; it is only of importance to distinguish between goals set by some person other than the performer from those set by the performer himself.

The Product to Evaluation Contingency

When an individual's supervisor informs the focal individual that a certain level of productivity is to be the behavioral goal, the goal is usually expressed in terms of the amount (or quality) of the focal person's measured work behavior. These measurements typically employ observable units of output which are created by the behavior of the focal individual. Such measured units are called products in NPI terminology, and therefore, for the supervisor to establish goals is to indicate to focal that a certain product level is to be the objective of the focal's behavior. Since the supervisor is an external evaluator of the focal's behavior, the setting of goals by the supervisor is an indication to the focal of the evaluation system the supervisor will be using to evaluate the amount of work produced by the focal. The obvious inference to be drawn by the focal is that the supervisor will be using an evaluation system which will look favorably on the focal's work behavior if he or she produces at or above the set goal and unfavorably if below.

The relationship the focal perceives as existing between his or her products and the magnitude of the external evaluation in NPI Theory is the product to evaluation contingency function ($C_{P \to E}$). Therefore, the goal setting intervention has its initial and primary effect upon both the motivation and the subsequent behavior of the individual by causing a modification, or distortion, in the individual's already existing $C_{P \to E}$ contingency function.

This effect upon the $C_{P \to E}$ contingency function is certainly apt to be most dramatic at the point of and in the region surrounding the announced goal. To illustrate, in Figure 2 a $C_{P \to E}$ function is presented for a hypothetical focal person. In the example, the individual is assumed to have an existing belief that the function relating the number of products created by her or his behavior and the evaluation of the supervisor is linear in form. That is, the more products created, the more positive the evaluation.

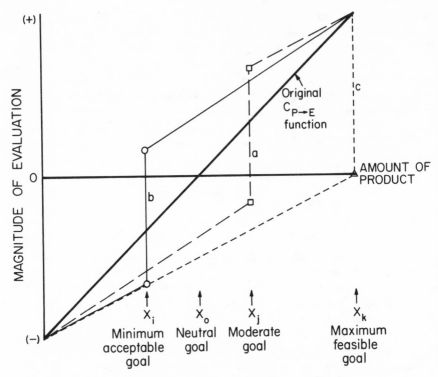

Figure 2. Hypothesized Displacement Effects in the $C_{P \to E}$ Function Caused by the Introduction of Goals of Differing Difficulty Level.

Further, the illustration assumes that the focal perceives some level of product creation (X_0) to be associated with a neutral evaluation and the creation of products in amounts less than X_0 are perceived as incurring displeasure, or a negative evaluation, on the part of the evaluator.

Figure 2 illustrates the possible distortion effects which might occur to the $C_{P \to E}$ contingency function as a result of three different assigned goal levels: (1) a minimum acceptable goal, (2) a moderate goal and (3) a maximum feasible goal. Several assumptions about the displacement effect of goal setting underly the three modified $C_{P \to E}$ functions shown in Figure 2. They are:

1. The displacement effect is assumed to be equal for equal positive and negative deviations from a neutral goal, X_0, defined by the point at which the magnitude of evaluation for the original $C_{P \to E}$ function is equal to zero.
2. The displacement effect produces a step function form of non-linearity into the $C_{P \to E}$ function.

3. Failure to reach an assigned goal is always perceived as being associated with a negative evaluation.
4. Reaching an assigned goal is always perceived as being associated with a positive evaluation.
5. The displacement effect at or above the point of the assigned goal "adds to" the prior $C_{P \to E}$ function (subject to the restrictions in 1 through 4), but the combination tends to be less than a simple sum toward the extremely high values of X. The negative displacement effect below the assigned goal also algebraically adds to the prior $C_{P \to E}$ function in the same manner.

Other assumptions about the displacement effect are certainly possible and we will examine these issues more completely in a subsequent section. For now, we shall restrict the discussion to the three functions in Figure 2 produced within the restrictions of assumptions 1–5. Using these three functions we can analyze how the distortions created by a goal setting intervention can affect subsequent utility functions and thus influence an individual's behavior. We can also analyze the way in which goal difficulty influences the obtained goal setting effect.

Modest Goal. The $C_{P \to E}$ function created by the introduction of a specific but modest goal X_j by the supervisor is shown in function (a) of Figure 2. The impact of the intervention is to distort the $C_{P \to E}$ function at the point of X_j into a step function.

Minimum Acceptable Goal. The $C_{P \to E}$ function created by the introduction by the supervisor of a minimum acceptable goal X_i is shown in function (b) of Figure 2. A minimum acceptable goal intervention by the supervisor might actually involve a level of X which the focal would normally believe to be associated with a mild negative evaluation by the supervisor (the case shown here).

Maximum Feasible Goal. The final modified $C_{P \to E}$ function in Figure 2 is function (c) which is a hypothetical function associated with the introduction of a goal X_k by the supervisor which represents a level of output by focal that lies at the upper extreme of his or her self–perceived capacity level. The point X_k is an amount of the product which, for the focal, represents the upper limit of his or her product creation under the constraints of the situation. (This point is associated with the form of the focal's perceived act–to–product contingency and it has relevance for the issue of "goal acceptance" which will be discussed later.) The effect of this intervention is to create a situation in which all X values less than X_k are perceived as receiving some degree of negative evaluation by the supervisor, and then, at point X_k, a massive change in perceived evaluation occurs, jumping from neutrality of evaluation to maximum perceived evaluation.

A word of caution is probably appropriate at this juncture. We must keep in mind that we have kept our illustration of the goal setting intervention as simple as possible at this stage. It deals only with its influence upon the perceptions the focal has about a single external evaluator (the supervisor). For example, we are ignoring, at this time, the possible effects which such an intervention may have on the focal's own internal evaluation system. This omission is particularly limiting with regard to function (c) since it is very likely that the introduction of very difficult goals will create less of a distortion effect on the individual's own self-evaluation system than on the shape of the $C_{P \to E}$ associated with the external evaluator.

Effects on Utility Functions

The hypothetical effect of the three goal setting interventions shown in Figure 2 may now be traced through the sequence previously presented in Figure 1 to assess the resulting effect upon the utility functions for products and for commitment to acts. The three modified utility functions for products resulting from the goal setting interventions X_i, X_j, and X_k are shown in Figure 3 as less heavy lines so they may be easily compared with the original utility–of–products function (solid line). The effects are clearly quite dramatic. The introduction of a minimum acceptable goal X_i shifts the utility for an $X \geq X_i$ from a very negative value to a fairly high positive value but has only a trivial effect upon the utility for X values less than X_i. Further, changes in product levels above X_i result in only small utility changes. The reverse of this pattern occurs with the modest goal X_j. Here, the utilities for values equal to or larger than X_j are affected very little, but the utilities for values less than the goal are shifted to substantially lower—and quite negative—utilities. For the maximum feasible goal of X_k the effect is to reduce the utility of an X just below X_k to slightly below the utility indifferent point. In addition, it leads to very little change in utility in the lower range of X values.

Since in Figure 1 we assumed the $C_{A \to P}$ function to be linear with slope 1.0, then the utility of commitment–to–acts functions produced by the three goal setting interventions will, in our example, be identical to the effects shown in the utility–of–products functions. These are shown in Figure 4 where, once again, the modified utility functions for X_i, X_j and X_k are lighter, while the original utility function is shown as a heavy solid line.

Commitment Predictions

While NPI Theory is intended to explain choices among acts as competing options for resource allocation (Naylor, et al., 1980a, 1980b), it

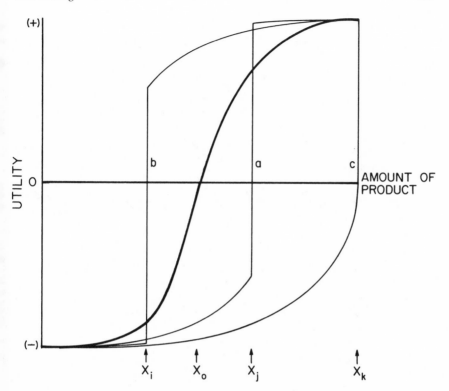

Figure 3.   Displacements in the Utility of Products Functions Caused
by the Hypothesized Changes in Figure 2.

can also be used to make predictions about behavior where only a single act is involved. To do so, we must consider both the attractiveness (utility) associated with resources to the act and the costs of those resources. There is always a utility associated with the expending of effort. This is an internally generated utility–of–commitment function which typically has a negative slope. For the illustration, we shall assume this internal cost of resources utility function to be linear with slope b throughout the range of C_{X_O} to C_{X_K} in Figure 4. If we make this assumption, and if we assume a person's original level of commitment to the act is 0, then we can use NPI Theory to predict the specific level of commitment to a given act, instead of predicting, for a fixed level of commitment, which act will be allocated the resources.[2] That is, normally we would determine the MF for several acts for a fixed level of commitment change and predict that the focal would select that act having the highest MF, thereby using the theory to predict direction but not amplitude of behavior. Here we will hold the act fixed and determine the MF for various levels of com- mitment change to that act, predicting that the individual will commit that

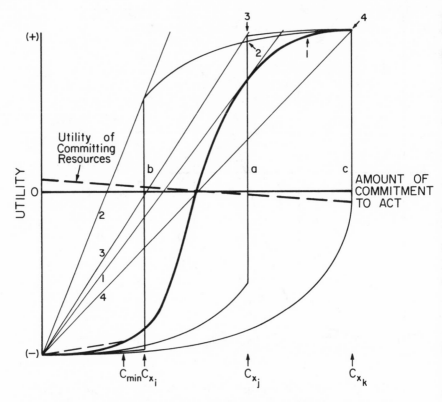

Figure 4. The Utility of Commitment to Acts Functions Produced by
Hypothesized Effects in Figure 2.

amount of resources which has the greatest MF. This approach uses the
theory to predict amplitude, rather than direction, of behavior.

Prediction of individual commitment levels under the different goal setting interventions may now be attempted from the curves in Figure 4. To
do so we will assume a multiple-stage model of commitment allocation.
The multiple-stage model may be stated as follows:

Let C_1 = present level of commitment to an act
        C_2 = some new level of commitment to an act
        $\Delta C = C_2 - C_1$
        ΔU = anticipated change in utility associated with ΔC

$$MF_{\Delta C} = \frac{\Delta U}{\Delta C}$$

Stage 1. Starting at C_1, the individual will select that value of C_2 which
maximizes $MF_{\Delta C}$.

Stage 2. Considering C_2 as the new C_1 starting point, a new C_2 will be selected which again maximizes $MF_{\Delta C}$ from this new starting point.[3]

In instances where the remaining portion of the utility function is negatively accelerated, small ΔC increases will maximize MF, which implies that the individual will make numerous and repeated mini-decisions about commiting additional resources in instances of decreasing marginal utility functions and that the more sharply the function decelerates the smaller the ΔC values apt to be used by people.

Stages 3-K. The process described in stages 1 and 2 will be repeated until the MF for the maximum possible marginal increase in utility becomes less than the negative slope of the cost–of–commitment utility curve. At this point no further resources will be committed to the set. Looking again at Figure 4 we can observe how the multiple-stage model would predict the final level of commitment of the individual under the four conditions represented by the utility functions for (1) no external goal, (2) a modest goal, (3) a minimum acceptable goal, and (4) a maximum feasible goal.

No External Goals. The theory would predict that the initial value of ΔC would be determined by line 1 of Figure 4 whose slope is maximum at the point where it is tangent to the utility curve for no goals. In the current illustration this occurs at a point about equal to C_{x_j} and thus C_{x_j} would represent a stage 1 prediction for focal's commitment. However, once the stage 1 commitment level is reached, we would expect the focal in subsequent stages to commit further increments of commitment until the positive MF for these small increments fell below the negative MF associated with the commitment expenditure function. The approximate point on the utility function where this occurs is given by the small arrow labeled with a 1.

Minimum Acceptable Goal. Utility function (b) represents a goal setting intervention in which the goal is quite low. The level of commitment chosen in stage 1 is given by the point on the function that maximizes stage 1 MF. This is shown by the point at which line 2 is touching (b) and it occurs exactly at level of commitment C_{x_j}, which is the amount of commitment to the act needed to achieve the goal as specified by the supervisor. But subsequent stages of the commitment model based upon C increments beyond C_{x_i} will still result in MF values greater than the negative slope of the cost function until the point is reached on the curve shown by the small arrow 2. Beyond this point further small C values will result in a net utility effect that is negative.

Moderate Goal. The effect of intervening with a goal of moderate difficulty is shown in function (a). The initial level of commitment predicted by Stage 1 of the multiple-stage model is the point on the function at which it contacts line 3. This is the point associated with the line of greatest slope and thus it defines the level of commitment possessing the greatest degree of MF. This level of commitment is C_{x_j}, and is the amount of commitment perceived as being needed by the focal to exactly meet the goal expectations of the supervisor. What differentiates the effect of the moderate goal from both the no goal and minimum goal condition is that no subsequent increments in commitment beyond C_{x_j} are predicted by the multiple-stage model. The slope of utility function (a) is less than the slope of the cost functions for all C's beyond C_{x_j}. Thus the focal person will not commit any additional resources, stopping at the point in the curve indicated by arrow 3.

Maximum Feasible Goal.   The final utility function is function (c) in Figure 4. It is the one associated with the setting of a goal so difficult that it is located at the extreme limits of the individual's capability. The level of commitment predicted under this type of intervention is determined by the point at which line 4 contacts the function, where line 4 is the line of maximum slope associated with function (c). Not unexpectedly, the amount of predicted commitment for Stage 1 is equal to C_{x_k}, the amount of commitment perceived by the focal as the amount necessary to obtain the goal. Also, no further increases in commitment would be predicted in this instance since C_{x_k} is at the focal's upper limit of capacity and therefore further increments are not possible.

Examining the predictions for the individual's final level of commitment in the four difficulty conditions, it is interesting to note that the effects of goal setting turn out to be similar for both the moderately difficult and the minimum acceptable goals. Further, both of the interventions produce predictions of commitment levels which actually fall somewhat below the level we would predict for the individual under the no goal condition. Only the extremely high goal produces a predicted commitment level greater than that which would be predicted in the total absence of external goals.[4] Given the set of assumptions which were used to define the set of utility functions given in Figure 4 it is possible, on the basis of the above examples, to draw some general conclusions:

1.   Any assigned goal which required a perceived level of commitment for its attainment that was less than the amount of commitment the individual would adopt in the absence of a goal reduced the amount of commitment to the act over what would have been the case in the absence of a goal.

2.   Any assigned goal which required a perceived level of commitment for its attainment that was greater than the amount of commitment the individual would adopt in the absence of a goal increased the amount of

commitment to the act over what would have been the case in the absence of a goal.

It is thus worth reviewing at this point the numerous assumptions which provided the parameters for the above example of the effects of goal setting interventions of various difficulty levels. First, the original form of the utility functions and contingency functions shown in Figure 1 were obtained by assuming (1) the utility outcome function was a decreasing monotonic function from the point of indifference and (2) all the contingency functions in the motivational sequence were linear with slope 1.0. To implement the example, we made further assumptions about (3) the type of model used to predict focal's level of commitment to the act (a multiple-stage model) and (4) the place and manner in which the goal setting intervention distorts the basic motivational process (by changing the product–to–evaluation contingency in a manner prescribed by the conditions listed in the explanation of Figure 2).

While all of these assumptions obviously play an important role in determining the exact nature of the prediction to be made concerning the effect of a goal setting intervention, the one most directly related to the intervention itself is assumption 4 which deals with the nature of the intervention distortion effect upon the process. Thus it is of some interest to discuss further other possibilities for the form of the distortion effect in the $C_{P \rightarrow E}$ function. Since we assume that the intervention has its primary locus of influence on the $C_{P \rightarrow E}$ function, the issue then becomes one of exploring alternative ways in which the $C_{P \rightarrow E}$ function might be influenced by a goal set by an external evaluator.

Some Possible Models for Influence

Figure 5 shows four different models (function forms) for the possible effects of goal-setting upon the $C_{P \rightarrow E}$ function. These are shown in the dashed line curves labeled a, b, c, and d. Each represents a $C_{P \rightarrow E}$ function produced by different goals set by an external evaluator. The two primary assumptions for Figure 5 are (1) the original $C_{P \rightarrow E}$ function is presented as being linear with slope 1.0 and (2) the level of goal difficulty is such that the magnitude of the goal in the example is originally perceived by the focal as being associated with a neutral evaluation by the evaluator.

The four different models in Figure 5 differ in terms of the way in which a pure change in perceived evaluation produced by the goal intervention combines with prior evaluation perceptions to produce a new $C_{P \rightarrow E}$ function. The pure effect of an intervention is defined as the amount of displacement observed at the point of intervention obtained by introducing a goal equal to that which would normally produce a neutral evaluation.

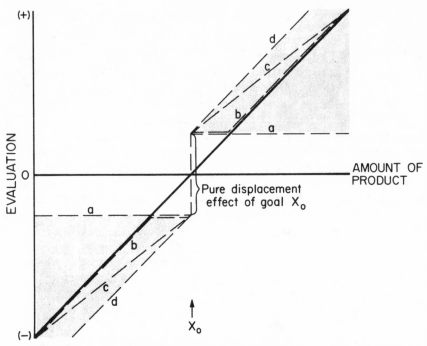

Figure 5. Four Different Models for the Manner in which a Goal
Setting Intervention Effects the Shape of the $C_{P \to E}$ Function
(see text for explanation).

Normally, the focal person would associate a neutral evaluation with the
productivity level X_0 shown in Figure 5. However, if the supervisor gives
the focal a goal of exactly X_0, we see that the result now is a step-function
at point X_0 where the size of the step, or amount of displacement, represents a pure assessment of the goal setting intervention effect. Models
a through d differ in terms of their assumptions about how this displacement effect combines with prior perceptions of positive and negative evaluations associated with values of work output (X) which are larger than
or smaller than X_0.

Model a. This model, seen in function (a) in Figure 5, represents the
extreme case in which the pure effect of the goal intervention entirely
replaces the prior $C_{P \to E}$ function. This is the case where all work output
above X_0 is perceived as being given the same positive evaluation, regardless of how far above, and all work output below X_0 is perceived as
being given the same negative evaluation, regardless of how far below.
(Again, the reader should remember that we are only considering how
the focal perceives the supervisor's evaluations of work output and are
not considering how the focal might evaluate his/her own output).

Model b. This model, seen in function (b) in Figure 5, also assumes that the pure effect of goal setting does not combine, or add to, the prior evaluation perception. It uses the simple assumption that the magnitude of the evaluation associated with a given output will be the greater of either (1) the amount of the pure displacement effect or (2) the amount normally associated with that output level without a goal intervention.

Model c. The third model is shown in Figure 5 as function (c). This function assumes that the pure displacement effect does combine with the original $C_{P \to E}$ function, but that the combining process results in a total that is less than the sum of the two parts. Further, the impact of the intervention is seen to diminish the further output levels are from X_0 (in either a positive or negative direction). This model was the one which was used to develop the original example of the goal setting mechanisms presented in Figure 2 and further explored in Figures 3 and 4.

Model d. The final possibility which might be postulated is given in function (d) of Figure 5. Here the pure effect of the goal setting intervention is assumed to be truly additive to the prior $C_{P \to E}$ function so that the intervention simply displaces the entire original $C_{P \to E}$ function by the size of the displacement observed at point X_0.

These four models would seem to represent the most likely possibilities from the entire set of models one might consider. Indeed, models a and d probably represent reasonable boundary models for the postulated intervention effect. It is not very reasonable to believe that the perceived overall evaluation effect would diminish for outputs successively farther above the goal. Such a model would be an inhibition model and only seems feasible in those instances in which the goal might represent some form of union or work group norm above whose level job encumbents would actually be discouraged from producing output. Thus for most settings, model a is probably a lower boundary for the goal setting effect. Similarly, it is also unlikely that the displacement effect would get larger at output levels farther away from X_0. This model would be an enhancement model postulating that the displacement effect increases the farther one's output is either above or below the goal. Therefore, we can probably consider function d as a reasonable upper limit model for the goal setting effect. This implies that the shaded area in Figure 5 contains the entire set of reasonable effect models associated with the introduction of a goal.

We can now examine each of these models separately to see how the problem of goal difficulty influences the perception of the $C_{P \to E}$ function. This should permit a more general assessment of the difficulty variable. We will examine difficulty for models a, b and d, since we previously examined the difficulty effect for model c in our original example. The first such representation is shown in Figure 6. It presents the four different $C_{P \to E}$ functions obtained under model a assumptions as goal difficulty is

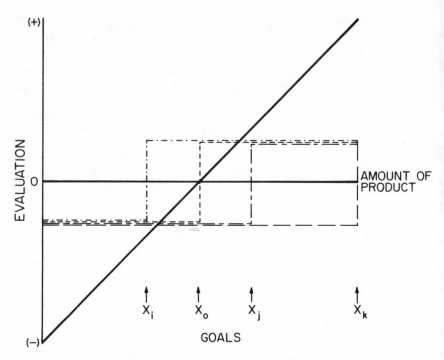

Figure 6.   The Effect on the $C_{P \to E}$ Function for Goals of Four
Different Difficulty Levels using Model a Assumptions.

manipulated across 4 levels—no goal (X_0), an easy goal (X_i), a moderately difficult goal (X_j), and a maximum feasible goal (X_k). Figure 7 presents $C_{P \to E}$ functions for the same four goal levels under the assumption of model b. Finally, Figure 8 presents functions for the same goal conditions under model d assumptions.

Model d, we might note, being a completely additive effect model, produces the rather interesting result that, for high goals, the failure to attain a goal can still result in a perception by the focal that her output will be positively evaluated. Earlier we assumed that such could never happen, but under a strictly additive model it can easily occur.

We can now examine the differential effects of the four influence models upon the predicted level of commitment to the act. Further, we can, at the same time, examine the effects of changing goal difficulty under each of the models. To do so, it is necessary to trace the influence of the distortions in the $C_{P \to E}$ functions under models a, b and d, shown in Figures 6, 7 and 8, upon the final commitment to act utility functions. (Since we previously did this for model c in Figure 4, we need only do it for models a, b and d here).

The effect of the distortions upon the commitment–to–act utilities produced under the model a assumptions shown in Figure 6 are presented in Figure 9. Four step-function utility curves, each a result of a goal of different difficulty level, are the result of the interventions assumed in Figure 6. The major, indeed the only, difference between the four step functions in Figure 9 is the levels of commitment at which the step functions occur. Arrows have been placed in Figure 9 to indicate the precise level of commitment for the focal which would be predicted given the previously proposed multiple-stage model. In the case of the four utility curves in Figure 9, the predicted level of commitment to the act is, in each instance, located exactly at the level associated with producing the goal of the supervisor. In the examples, three of the four goals (X_i, X_0, X_j) would thus result in predicted commitment less than that predicted in the absence of an external goal.

Model b predictions of commitment may be seen in Figure 10. Model b assumes that the perceived supervisory evaluation is the greater of either the pure displacement effect or the original evaluation under no goal conditions. The predicted amounts of commitment for goals X_i, X_0 and X_j

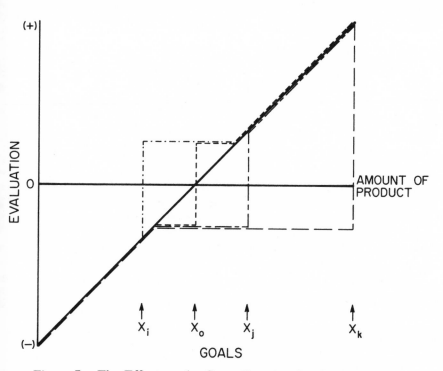

Figure 7. The Effect on the $C_{P \to E}$ Function for Goals of Four Different Difficulty Levels using Model b Assumptions.

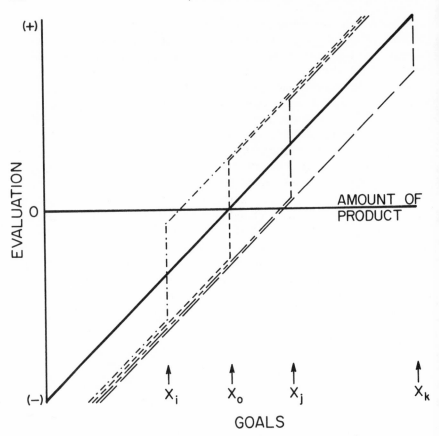

Figure 8.   The Effect on the $C_{P \to E}$ Function for Goals of Four
Different Difficulty Levels using Model d Assumptions.

are all equal in this situation and are themselves equal to the amount of
commitment predicted under the no goal condition. Only the very highest
goals result in increased levels of commitment being predicted. Thus,
under this model and this assumed cost function, the manipulation of goal
difficulty within normal ranges would have no apparent effect upon the
individual's actual level of commitment to the act in question.

   The final set of conditions is shown in Figure 11. Model d is used to
develop the four modified utility curves shown in Figure 11. Model d is
the other boundary condition model which represents a completely additive system in which the effect of the pure displacement to the $C_{P \to E}$
function is added to the original $C_{P \to E}$ function to obtain the new curves.
The result of these changes upon the utility of commitment to acts for
each of the four different goals show that predicted commitment levels

for goals X_i, X_0, and X_j are all equal but less than the level of commitment predicted under no goals, while once again the only goal to produce an increase in predicted level of commitment is X_k, the maximum feasible goal.

If we examine the total set of commitment predictions given by models a, b, c and d contained in Figures 4, 9, 10 and 11, certain regularities emerge. In one boundary model, model a, where the goal intervention displacement function completely replaces prior $C_{P \to E}$ function, we find that the predicted commitment levels correspond exactly to the level of goal difficulty. The more difficult the goal, the greater the predicted level of commitment. In model b, where the displacement effect is additive to the prior $C_{P \to E}$ function, the predicted commitment levels for all goals X_i, X_0, and X_j were all equal (although with a steeper cost slope, the less difficult goals X_i and X_0 would have had a lower predicted level of commitment than X_j). For the other two models, c and d, the less difficult goals were equal in amount of predicted commitment (although, again this

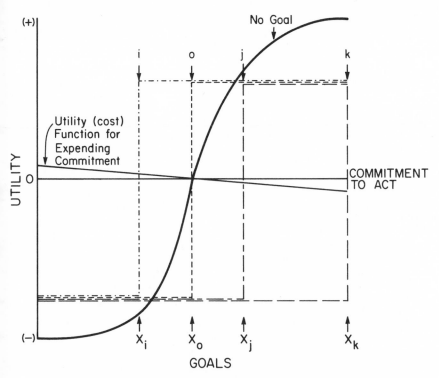

Figure 9. Utility of Commitment Functions for Goals of Four Different Difficulty Levels Under Model a.

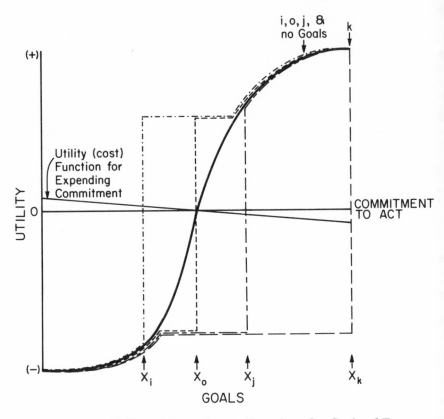

Figure 10. Utility of Commitment Functions for Goals of Four
Different Difficulty Levels Under Model b.

equality is due to the minimal steepness of the cost function and a steeper
cost function would produce greater predicted commitment for successively higher goals).

Another point of interest which emerges in the examples is that the
levels of predicted commitment for goals X_i, X_0 and X_j are always equal
to or less than the level of predicted commitment under the no-goal situation. This result is of course due primarily to the ogival shape of the
original commitment–to–act utility function. We have not yet explored
its generality with respect to other function forms. However, we do suspect that the pattern is a robust one that will generalize across a fairly
wide range of variations in the shape and slope of both the primary commitment to act utility function as well as across a fairly wide range of
reasonable shapes and slopes for the commitment cost function. This is
certainly still speculation at this juncture and meant for further discourse.

But, if true, it implies that goals generally must be rather high, or demanding, in order to motivate individuals to commit more resources than they would in the absence of these goals.

A final word is needed on the multi-stage model used to generate the point of predicted commitment. This model is based primarily upon the slope of the utility function. Recall that $MF = \Delta U/\Delta C$ and that (a) the individual chooses that ΔC which maximizes MF and then (b) compares that MF to the negative motivational force of the cost of commitment function, $(-MF = -\Delta U/\Delta C)$ for the same ΔC. If the algebraic sum of these two MF values is greater than zero, then the individual commits ΔC resources to the act and the process is repeated for the new base value of C.

There is another interesting model which might be postulated as being logical and worth further analytic development. We can define as MF

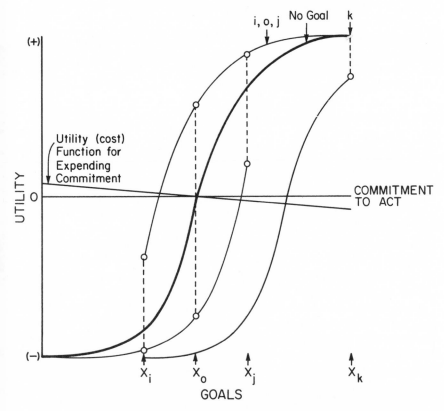

Figure 11. Utility of Commitment Functions for Goals of Four Different Difficulty Levels Under Model d.

benefits the motivational force resulting from the change in utility which occurs as a function of the outcomes obtained by commiting resources to an act. This is the MF which provides the foundation for the basic utility curves in the motivational sequence of NPI theory and is usually (although not always) a positive value. We can also define the negative motivational force resulting from a negative change in utility occurring as a function of expending resources on as act as MF_{Costs}. Then we have $MF_{Benefits} = \Delta U/\Delta C$ outcomes and $MF_{Costs} = \Delta U/\Delta C$ expenditures. A model for the individual might be to maximize the difference between these two MF values, choosing the value of C such that $MF_{Benefits} - MF_{Costs} = $ maximum. The predictions as to commitment level which might arise under this latter model are apt to be different than those obtained under the multi-stage model explored in the present article.

GENERAL VS SPECIFIC GOALS

In the preceding sections of the paper we examined the general mechanism of goal-setting and its predicted impact upon level of commitment using several different models of the ways goals change the $C_{P \to E}$ function. We also examined these predictions for several levels of goal difficulty—one of the two basic attributes of goals. We now turn to the second of the two goal attributes: Goal specificity.

Examination of the goal specificity dimension as it has been used in the goal setting literature presents certain problems that were not present in our examination of goal difficulty. Although studies which have manipulated goal difficulty have done so in a manner compatible with the dimension, the standard manipulation, in the case of goal specificity, does not conform as nicely to an intuitive expectation of a specificity manipulation.

A lack of specificity (or conversely, an increase in generality) in a goal given by a supervisor would imply an increased ambiguity, or diffuseness, in the exact level of performance desired by the supervisor. Thus, instead of saying "I want you to produce 20 units", if the supervisor said instead, "I expect you to produce anywhere from 15 to 25 units" we would have a more diffuse, or general, goal being given to the focal than in the first instance. The typical specificity manipulation has actually been quite different. The instruction given to the focal under the general, or diffuse goal condition is to "Do your best." We would argue strongly that a "Do your best" instruction from the supervisor is not a specificity manipulation except in the sense of distinguishing between the extremes of a presence of and an absence of a goal setting intervention. That is, "Do your best" instructions do not constitute a goal intervention by supervisor at all, at least not in the sense we have been using the term, since the setting of the goal is turned over to focal and abdicated by the supervisor. Thus this instruction should have no impact whatsoever on the form of the external $C_{P\to E}$ function. By telling the focal to do her or his best, the supervisor is not indicating a preference for any goal but is instead urging the focal to perform at a self-perceived maximum. If this intervention does affect the $C_{P\to E}$ function, it is more likely that the intervention would be perceived as the setting of a maximum possible goal (in the sense used in the prior discussion of goal difficulty) resulting in the distortion effect shown in Figure 12.

The effect shown in Figure 12 is not one that we find very compelling as an explanation, particularly since it would lead to a prediction that a "Do your best" instruction should result in a higher level of commitment

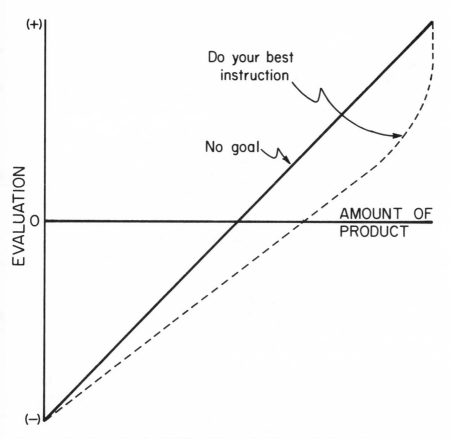

Figure 12. Hypothesized Effect Upon the External $C_{P\to E}$ Function of a "Do your best" Instruction.

than would be predicted for most, if not all, specific goals—a prediction which is certainly contrary to the available research findings that show this instruction as generally producing observed performance below that obtained with specific hard goals (Locke, et al. 1981).

We prefer to believe that the effect of such an inststruction is simply to shift the focal's attention more to his or her own intrinsic motivational system in such a way as to increase the relevance, or importance, of the intrinsic system as a determinant of commitment to the act in question. We would further suggest that this is accomplished by a change in slope of the internal utility of self-evaluation function.[5] The result of such a change in this utility function would mean that the total utility of commitment to the act (which is a combination of both the intrinsic and extrinsic motivational systems) will also be somewhat increased. This would lead to a prediction that an individual's commitment (and therefore performance) would be somewhat higher under such goal instructions than without any instruction at all, but whether it would be higher than for a particular specific goal would depend upon the difficulty level of the specific goal.

We further do not think that the shape of the intrinsic $C_{P \to E}$ function would be changed by a "Do your best" goal instruction. This issue would certainly appear to be empirically testable in a laboratory setting.

To briefly summarize the points of most importance, we are suggesting that the research which has attempted to examine the issue of goal specificity has not done so, since the typical instructional manipulation is more likely to have simply shifted the focal's attention to his or her intrinsic motivational system rather than manipulating the degrees of specificity of the external goal. As suggested earlier, a more relevant specificity manipulation would be to instruct the focal to perform within certain boundary conditions (e.g., produce 10 to 20 units). If such an instruction were given, we can then also make such predictions relative to the width of the boundaries.

Models for Non-Specific Goals

If we assume that non-specificity of a goal is best dealt with conceptually as a range of different goal values of apparently equal satisfactoriness to the supervisor, and if we further assume that the wider the range of equivalence, the lower the level of specificity, we can apply NPI theory to see what type of commitment predictions result from manipulations of specificity. To do this we need to first decide how the displacement effect should operate in applying the theory. In the case of a specific goal, we can again define a pure displacement effect as the increased amount of an anticipated evaluation associated with a set goal which normally would be perceived as leading to a neutral evaluation combined with the decreased amount of the anticipated evaluation associated with a product just below the set goal. When we are dealing with a range of equally evaluated and ambiguous goals, the question arises as to what evaluation level is used to describe the entire set of goals within the range. Does the focal treat all goals in the ambiguous set as having an anticipated evaluation equivalent to a specific goal at (a) the high end of the set, (b) the low end of the set, or (c) at an average or midpoint goal value of the set? While this issue is one which can be explored experimentally, intuition

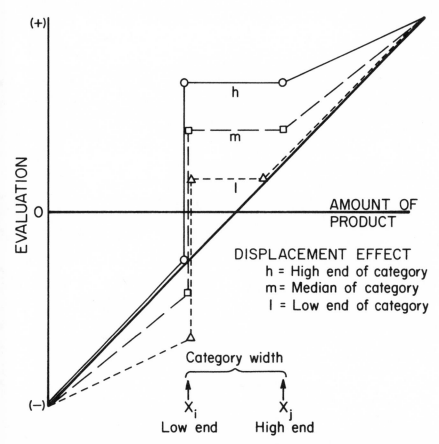

Figure 13. Different Effects on the $C_{P \to E}$ Function for an Ambiguous Goal Depending Upon Assumptions About the Displacement Effect (see text).

might argue that the displacement effect normally associated with the mean value of the ambiguous goal set might be the most sensible guess as to the focal's behavior. However, an equally compelling argument might be put forward for the displacement associated with the lowest goal in the acceptable set. Figure 13 illustrates these three different distortions in the goal $C_{P \to E}$ function for a general goal in which the instruction is to produce between X_i and X_j products. The step functions h, m and l are the displaced $C_{P \to E}$ functions associated with the evaluations for the high, middle and low goals, respectively, in the range of acceptable goals. Figure 14 then shows the three modified commitments to all utility functions associated with the displacements in Figure 13. As one would expect, the

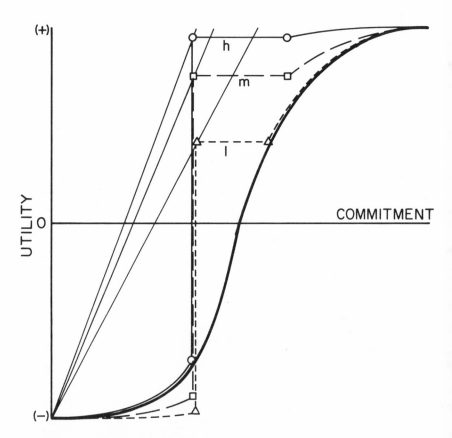

Figure 14.   Different MF Predictions Resulting from the Utility of Commitment Functions Resulting from the $C_{P \to E}$ Functions in Figure 13.

lower displacement values lead to lower amounts of first stage predicted task commitment.

Leaving the question as to the magnitude of the range of displacement effects to future empirical examination, let's turn to the issue of the potential effect of range size, or what might be best described as degree of goal ambiguity. We will examine the effect of ambiguity using several different sets of assumptions. The first set is presented in Figures 15 and 16.

The four $C_{P \rightarrow E}$ functions presented in Figure 15 represent different levels of goal specificity, a = no goal, b = specific goal, c = moderate

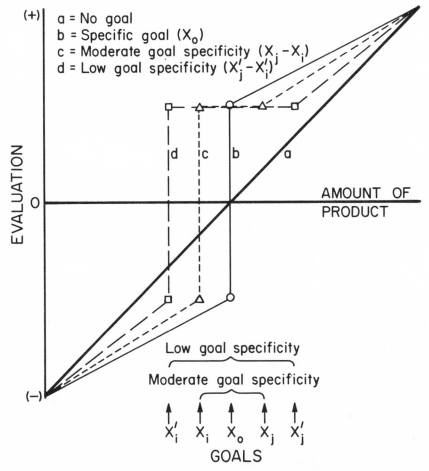

Figure 15. The Effect of Goal Instructions of Different Degrees of Specificity Upon the $C_{P \rightarrow E}$ Function. (For assumptions used see text).

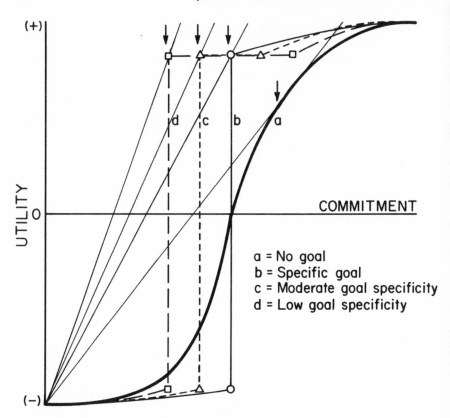

Figure 16.   MF Functions and Commitment Predictions Obtained from
the Utility of Commitment Functions Generated by the $C_{P \to E}$ Function
in Figure 15 (see text).

goal specificity and d = low goal specificity. The specific goal X_0 is a
goal of low difficulty in the sense it is a level of productivity normally
perceived as being associated with a neutral evaluation by the supervisor.
Both ranges of goals, X_i to X_j and X_i' to X_j' have X_0 as their midpoint.
We have further assumed that the focal perceives all goals in the range
to be equally evaluated by the supervisor.

   Figure 16 shows the four utility–of–commitment–to–act functions
which are associated with the four $C_{P \to E}$ functions just described. Since
the specific goal is a very low goal, we see that the predicted level of
original (stage 1) commitment to the act is lower for the specific goal than
for no goal at all. Further, we see that the level of predicted commitment
to the act continues to decrease as the degree of goal ambiguity increases,

leading to the prediction that greater specificity of goals should lead to increased performance.

In Figures 17 and 18, a slightly different set of assumptions are used to generate predictions about the effect of goal specificity. Here we assume that the focal person does not perceive the supervisor as evaluating equally all the productivity levels within the goal set. Higher product levels within the set are now assumed to be associated with higher evaluations. Further, it is assumed that the overall displacement effect diminishes substantially as the degree of goal ambiguity increases. This

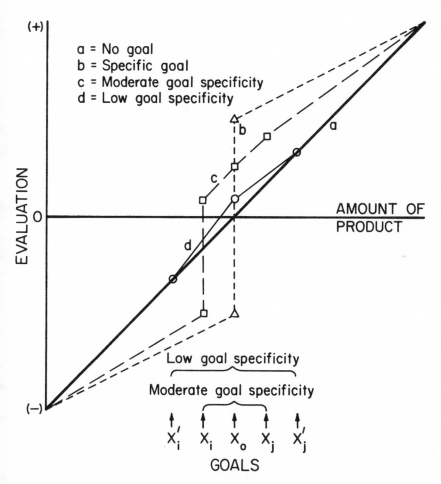

Figure 17. The Effect of Goal Instructions of Different Degrees of Specificity Upon the $C_{P \to E}$ Function. (For assumptions used see text).

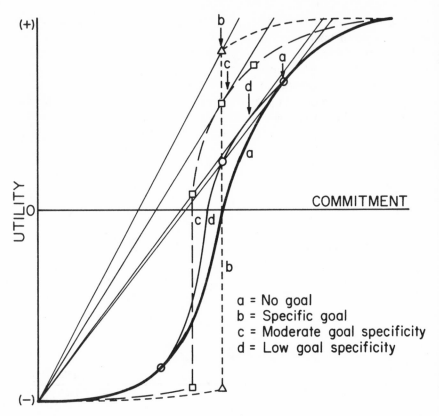

Figure 18. MF Functions and Commitment Predictions Obtained from
the Utility of Commitment Functions Generated by the $C_{P \to E}$
Functions in Figure 17 (see text).

diminishing process dilutes the effect on the original $C_{P \to E}$ to the point
that, when a great deal of goal ambiguity exists, it is as if no goals were
present. (This assumption is compatible with earlier comments made regarding the kind of instruction typically used in studies examining goal
specificity). The example once again uses a low difficulty specific goal
X_0 and the same range and midpoints of goals as in the prior example.

The four $C_{P \to E}$ functions in Figure 17 once again represent a = no goal,
b = specific goal, c = moderate goal specificity and d = low goal specificity. Figure 18 shows the subsequent result of these upon the stage 1
utility of commitment–to–act functions. Once again the easy specific goal
produces a stage 1 level of commitment prediction less than that which
would be predicted if no goal at all were present. But a quite different
effect upon predicted commitment is observed as the range of acceptable

goals is increased. We see that the level of predicted commitment goes up as the goal becomes more ambiguous, continuing to increase until, with a very ambiguous goal, it will become identical to the level of commitment predicted under the no goal conditions.

Both of the preceeding examples used a specific goal (X_0) which was easy—so easy that it would normally receive a neutral evaluation from the supervisor. In actual goal setting situations, it is unlikely that supervisors would use such easy goals. Goal setting, as a technology, has as its avowed purpose the objective of increasing productivity, and, therefore, goals, when they are used, are likely to represent levels of productivity which are very high. Our final example examines the specificity variable when the specific goal, X_+, is a level of productivity which is quite high. Indeed, X_+ is sufficiently high enough to result in a level of predicted commitment to the act which is greater than that which one would predict if no goal at all were present. All other parameters for the

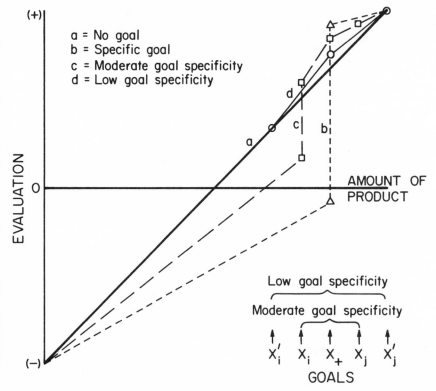

Figure 19. The Effect of Goal Instructions of Different Degrees of Specificity Upon the $C_{P\rightarrow E}$ Function. (For assumptions see text).

example are identical to those used in the previous example. Figures 19 and 20 show the assumed $C_{P \to E}$ functions and the resulting commitment–to–act utility functions, respectively.

The findings with respect to levels of predicted commitment now show a systematic decrease as the goal becomes more ambiguous. This decrease in predicted level of commitment continues until it reaches a level identical to that which would be predicted under a no goal condition. We therefore end up with the interesting pattern of increased goal specificity leading to a decrease in predicted performance when the goal range is very low (Figure 18) and to an increase in predicted performance when the goal range is very high (Figure 20). Initially, these predictions would seem intuitively acceptable, although the practical implication of the easy goal predictions are probably not very great, since we rarely want to decrease

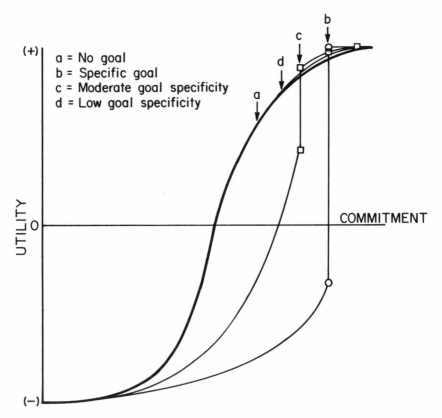

Figure 20. Commitment Predictions Obtained from the Utility of Commitment Functions Generated by the $C_{P \to E}$ Functions in Figure 19 (see text).

performance and even when we do, goal setting is probably not the most effective technology to achieve that desired end.

THE "ACCEPTABILITY" ISSUE

Locke et al. (1981); Latham (Latham, Mitchell, & Dossett, 1978; Latham & Saari, 1979a, 1979b; Yukl and Latham, 1978), and others (Dossett, Latham, & Mitchell, 1979) have suggested that an important component of goal setting technology is the idea of goal acceptability. It is argued that goals must be accepted by the focal before they can have any influence upon that focal's performance. Unfortunately, like the goal setting construct of goal specificity, goal acceptability has been a fuzzy concept which has suffered from a lack of any careful specification of its precise cognitive meaning. Its ambiguity has not been helped by the way in which it has been operationally used. For example, Latham et al. (1978) used a self report 5 point scale based upon the question "Your own personal determination to attain the goal." Such a question would seem much more likely to tap motivational force than to measure the degree to which the goal has been incorporated into the focal's cognitive system.

We suggest that the construct of goal acceptability has two distinct cognitive dimensions, both of which can be defined in terms of specific NPI theory constructs. In order for a goal to be accepted by a focal, two conditions need to be met. First, the focal must believe the goal to be a reality. This belief is represented in NPI theory in the distortion of the shape of the external $C_{P \to E}$ function and has been the focus of most of the discussion in this paper. Unless the goal has an impact upon the $C_{P \to E}$ function associated with the goal giver one cannot argue compellingly that goal acceptance has taken place since it has no apparent impact upon the focal's cognitive belief system about how his performance will be evaluated by the supervisor.

A second aspect of acceptability concerns the belief about attainability, or feasibility, of the goal. A goal might be clearly believable in the sense that the focal accepts its reality, yet be so high that it clearly falls beyond the capability limits of the worker. Such goals would be most likely to be "unacceptable" goals from the standpoint of the focal. In NPI theory, this belief function is represented by the Act to Product contingency function $C_{A \to P}$. The concept of feasibility is illustrated clearly in Figure 21, which presents the three different contingency beliefs for three hypothetical individuals, a, b and c. Also shown are two different goal levels, G_1 and G_2, which differ in terms of their difficulty with G_2 being a more difficult goal than G_1.

For person a, neither goal is perceived as being a realistic possibility

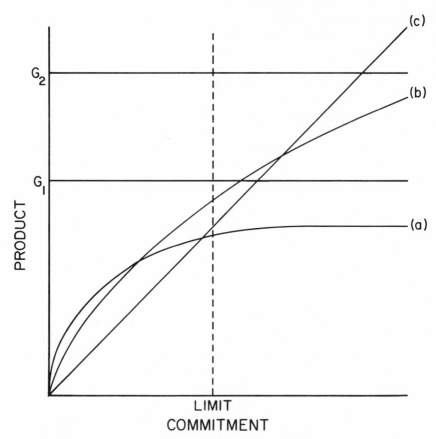

Figure 21. The Acceptability of Goals as Determined by the Shape of
the Individuals $C_{A \to P}$ Functions and by External Constraints or Limits.

in terms of personal accomplishment since no matter how much commitment she sees putting into the task, the maximum level of productivity
fails to reach even G_1, the lower of the two goals. Focal person b has a
perceived relationship between commitment and productivity which
makes G_1 feasible, but does not include the possibility of achieving G_2.
Finally, person c's $C_{A \to P}$ function is such that both goals are feasible.

Impossible goal perceptions can certainly occur in many work situations. One obvious set of constraints are those individual differences
(ID's) and work environment parameters which affect the shape, and/or
slope, of the perceived $C_{A \to P}$ function. A second way in which impossible
goals can occur is when the ID's and/or environmental parameters lead
to a limit of some sort on the amount of commitment which the focal

perceives as being possible to devote to the task. The dotted vertical line in Figure 21 shows how such a constraint operates to make a goal seem unattainable. Even though the function forms for both b and c do pass above G_1, this occurs for both individuals at a level of commitment above the level perceived as being possible due to the limit caused by the constraints. Perhaps the individual simply has exhausted his or her resources to the point that allocation of resources beyond the limit is not possible. Or perhaps the time constraints are such that no matter what the focal does it is impossible to exceed a commitment level beyond the limit in the time remaining. One could, of course, postulate conditions in which goals which are seen as not feasible are still effective. Goals which are unacceptable due to their lack of feasibility may be treated by the focal as goals at the extreme upper end of feasibility, i.e., as maximally feasible goals, if they are not too far beyond the feasibility limit.

Finally, a third aspect of goal acceptability resides in the degree to which the behavior required for attaining the goal is compatible with the focal's value system. This aspect has two components in NPI theory. First, it relates to the possible negative utility of secondary external outcomes which occur as a result of committing the necessary resources to the act required to achieve the goal. Second, it relates to the intrinsic product–to–evaluation contingency function which describes the focal's own self evaluation as associated with increasing amounts of output from the act in question.

The overall usefulness of a separate goal acceptability construct seems less compelling when viewed in terms of the motivational components of NPI theory since the implied cognitive processes involved in goal acceptance do appear to be easily dealt with in terms of the belief structure of the individual concerning act–to–product and product–to–evaluation contingencies.

DISCUSSION

As we pointed out in the introduction, our purpose was not to show that goal setting as a motivational technology has been misguided by previous research and theory building. Clearly it has not. On the other hand, the literature on goal setting has tended to focus on demonstration of the fact that it often works to increase performance. Why it works has received much less attention. It is our belief that a better understanding of why goals work is needed if the practice is to be refined and made more effective in more situations.

What we have offered here is theoretical framework, that of NPI theory, to construe the motivational effects of goal setting. Specifically, we have suggested that goal setting should be seen as a motivational process which first influences the anticipated evaluation of performance levels (product levels) and subsequently, the utility of commitment of effort to accomplish the performance at the level desired. The predictions made from the models presented here are generally substantiated by the empirical literature. In particular, difficult goals should lead to higher performance levels than easy goals and specific goals should be more beneficial than general goals. Likewise, it is first necessary that goals be accepted by task performers and then that these individuals should be committed to putting forth the effort necessary to accomplish the level of performance which meets the goal.

The presentation offered here does, however, make two unique contributions to the goal setting literature. First, it adds much needed precision to the conceptualization of goal setting. Of the two attributes of goals—difficulty and specificity—the latter needed this most. By removing specificity from the everyday common language in which general goals have been expressed as "Do your best", it was possible to capture the essence of specificity—the lack of precision about the performance level expected—and, at the same time, avoid the confounding effect of the degree to which goals are set by the performer from the definition of goal specificity. Equally important, through the use of the more precise definition, it was possible to hypothesize what the effects of specificity per se will be on performance through their effects on the utility of product and of commitment levels.

The second contribution of the motivational viewpoint of NPI theory to goal setting is the less obvious predictions it makes about the effects of goal attributes on performance (i.e. on production). Many of these nonobvious effects had to do with goal difficulty. On several occasions, it was demonstrated that if goals are set a level that is at the easier end of the continuum, the utility–of–product levels for the focal person is such that it was predicted that introduction of goals should lead to lower levels of performance. Exactly where that goal level that is likely to decrease performance is cannot be said without careful consideration of possible utility curves for targeted groups of individuals. However, the answer is potentially obtainable empirically. Our only point is that in one's zeal to recommend goal setting, the fact that, for many individuals, goals set by others may actually serve as a disincentive rather than an incentive cannot be overlooked. Only if more attention is paid to the psychological effects of goal setting, if theories and models are built to take these effects into account, and then if these theories and models are tested empirically are advances beyond the present knowledge of goal setting going to be made. In our opinion, the motivational aspects of NPI offer an excellent starting place for generating empirically testable hypotheses about goal setting phenomena.

NOTES

1. NPI Theory defines degree of commitment in terms of the two fundamental human resources of time and effort ($C = T \times E$). The specific act engaged in by an individual represents the direction of one's behavior while degree of commitment to the act represents the amplitude of behavior.

2. We must, of course, assume that the minimum level of commitment to be considered by the focal in Figure 4 is greater than C_{min} or the focal will never commit resources to the act. This is evident because the negative motivational force for any ΔC is given by the slope of the cost function. If we assume an initial C level of 0, then one must have ΔC values greater than C_{min} before the positive MF associated with external evaluator and reward system is larger than the negative MF associated with committing resources to the act.

3. We must recognize the remaining portion of the utility curves for the cost of resources function and the commitment to acts functions may change as a result of the individual having actually committed resources and experienced the results of that action.

4. The fact that only the extremely high goal level led to an increase over no goals should not imply that goals must always be at the highest level. The highest level was the only effective level in our example because only four discrete, and arbitrary, goal levels were examined. There is, within Figure 4, a range of possible goal levels above a line drawn from point 1 to the commitment line and below point 4 that would lead to increases in commitment. Nevertheless, all of these represent quite high levels of X.

5. In NPI Theory it is argued that with the internal system, the utility of evaluation and utility of outcome functions are essentially identical, since in most instances the evaluation itself is the outcome which produces the affective response (Naylor, Pritchard and Ilgen, 1980b). It should also be noted that while we have previously deliberately excluded the internal system for purposes of simplicity, we include it here because non-specific goals will increase its importance.

REFERENCES

Bolles, R. Theory of motivation (2nd ed.). New York: Harper and Row, 1975.

Capaldi, E. D., & Davidson, T. L. Control of instrumental behavior by deprivation stimuli. *Journal of Experimental Psychology: Animal Behavior Processes,* 1979, *5,* 355–367.

Dossett, D. L., Latham, G. R., & Mitchell, T. R. The effects of assigned versus particatively set goals, KR, and individual differences when goals are held constant. *Journal of Applied Psychology,* 1979, *64,* 291–298.

Erez, M. Feedback: A necessary condition for the goal setting performance relationship. *Journal of Applied Psychology,* 1977, *62,* 624–627.

Ilgen, D. R. *Goal setting research and practice: Where next?* Paper presented at Academy of Management, San Francisco, 1978.

Ilgen, D. R., Nebeker, D. M., & Pritchard, R. D. Expectancy theory measures: An empirical comparison in an experimental situation. *Organizational Behavior and Human Performance,* 1981, *28,* 189–223.

Latham, G. P., Mitchell, T. R., & Dossett, D. L. Importance of participative goal setting and anticipated rewards on goal difficulty and job performance. *Journal of Applied Psychology*, 1978, *63*, 163–171.

Latham, G. P., & Saari, L. M. The effects of holding goal difficulty constant on assigned and participatively set goals. *Academy of Management Journal*, 1979, *22*, 163–168. (a)

Latham, G. P., & Saari, L. M. The importance of supportive relationships in goal setting. *Journal of Applied Psychology*, 1979, *64*, 151–156. (b)

Locke, E. A. Toward a theory of task motivation and incentives. *Organizational Behavior and Human Performance*, 1968, *3*, 157–189.

Locke, E. A., & Schweiger, D. M. Participation in decision making: One more look. In B. M. Staw (Ed.), *Research in Organizational Behavior* (Vol. 1). Greenwich, CT: JAI Press, 1979.

Locke, E. A., Shaw, K. N., Saari, L. M., & Latham, G. P. Goal setting and task performance: 1969–1980. *Psychological Bulletin*, 1981, *90*, 125–152.

Naylor, J. C., & Clark, R. D. Intuitive inference strategies in interval learning tasks as a function of validity and sign. *Organizational Behavior and Human Performance*, 1968, *3*, 378–399.

Naylor, J. C., & Domine, R. K. Inferences based upon uncertain data: Some experiments on the role of slope magnitudes, instructions, and stimulus distribution shapes on the learning of contingency relationships. *Organizational Behavior and Human Performance*, 1981, *27*, 1–31.

Naylor, J. C., Pritchard, R. D., & Ilgen, D. R. A sequential view of behavior and motivation. In K. D. Duncan, M. M. Gruneberg & D. Wallis (Eds.), *Changes in working life*. New York: Wiley & Sons, 1980. (a)

Naylor, J. C., Pritchard, R. D., & Ilgen, D. R. *A theory of behavior in organizations*. New York: Academic Press, 1980. (b)

Terborg, J. R. The motivational components of goal setting. *Journal of Applied Psychology*, 1976, *61*, 613–621.

Tversky, A., & Kahneman, D. The framing of decisions and the psychology of choice. *Science*, 1981, *211*, 453–458.

Umstot, D. D., Bell, G. H., & Mitchell, T. R. Effects of job enrichment and goal setting on satisfaction and productivity: Implications for job design. *Journal of Applied Psychology*, 1976, *61*, 379–394.

Yukl, G. A., & Latham, G. P. Interrelationships among employee participation, individual differences, goal difficulty, goal acceptance, goal instrumentality, and performance. *Personnel Psychology*, 1978, *31*, 305–323.

THIRD PARTY CONFLICT
INTERVENTION:
A PROCEDURAL FRAMEWORK

Blair H. Sheppard

ABSTRACT

Conflict intervention happens almost everywhere—at home, at school, in
the neighborhood, at work, in society and between countries. This chapter
presents a framework for integrating the research and theory on the procedures used by third parties to manage conflict in these very diverse settings. In other words, the framework provides a generic basis for the study
of conflict intervention procedure. The framework was developed to promote several important recent trends in conflict intervention research, as
well as to provide a vehicle for expanding study of more informal conflict
intervention procedures, such as those used by managers within organizations. To identify the need for this framework, present research on conflict intervention is briefly reviewed, then the framework is presented. Finally, the framework is evaluated in terms of its suitability for fulfilling the
identified needs in conflict intervention research and some new directions
for organizational conflict research are included within this evaluation.

Research in Organizational Behavior, vol. 6, pages 141–190
Copyright © 1984 by JAI Press Inc.
All rights of reproduction in any form reserved.
ISBN: 0-89232-351-5

INTRODUCTION

Conflict is a phenomenon which is studied in many different fields: by sociologists, by psychologists, by psychiatrists, by economists, and by political scientists. It occurs in many different situations: among members of a family, between labor and management, between political parties and even within a single mind, as well as among nations. Many of the patterns and processes which characterize conflict in one area also characterize it in others. Negotiation and mediation go on in labor disputes as well as in international relations. Price wars and domestic quarrels have much the pattern of an arms race. Frustration breeds aggression both in the individual and in the state. The jurisdictional problems of labor unions and the territorial disputes of states are not dissimilar. It is not too much to claim that out of the contributions of many fields a general theory of conflict is emerging. The isolation of these various fields, however, has prevented the building of these contributions into an integrated whole.

Editorial, *Journal of Conflict Resolution* 1957, Volume 1, p.2.

As with conflict itself, in the quote above, the methods used by third parties for resolving conflict appear to be very similar across widely different conflict settings (e.g. Knowles, 1958; Rubin, 1980; Young, 1967). For example, parental intervention in sibling disputes and supervisory intervention in disputes between employees both involve intervention by an authority figure responsible for the two disputants. Labor arbitration seems similar to civil adjudication. Both involve hearings where a relatively passive third party listens to competing evidence and arguments and decides which disputant is correctly interpreting some law or contract clause. Similarly, mediation seems much like marital therapy and international conflict resolution has much in common with neighborhood conflict resolution. Surprisingly, no satisfactory representation of dispute resolution procedure has been developed for describing the various forms of dispute resolution used across this range of dispute settings. This chapter presents the rudiments of such a framework and discusses the implications of this framework for the study of conflict management within organizations. In order to lay the groundwork for this framework, the existing research on conflict intervention will first be reviewed.

Research and Theory on Conflict Intervention

Several authors suggested recently that conflict intervention is a "growth industry" (e.g. Rubin, 1980). Among other things, this growth has been stimulated by an increased awareness of the potentially devastating consequences of international conflict, combined with the dramatic success of Carter and Habib with earlier interventions in the Middle

East. Similarly, conflict in organizations seems to be increasing, thus necessitating the development of effective interventions for dealing with this increased conflict. Employees and consumers are more aware of their due process rights and are more willing to assert them (Ewing, 1977). Traditional lines of authority are blurring and increasingly leaving employees in the position of managing conflicting demands from several constituencies (Adams, 1976). Economic hard times have lead to conflict over decreasing resources and the need to identify mechanisms for better managing resulting budgetary, labor and policy conflicts. Possibly in response to these conditions of increasing conflict, the number of management courses, books, research articles and chapters of Organizational Behavior textbooks concerning conflict management are increasing (cf. Rahim, 1982). In addition to this growth, there are other recent trends emerging in research and thought about conflict intervention. Three such trends stand out in particular.

1. Recognition of the Multiple Aims of Conflict Intervention. The first recent trend in writing about conflict intervention concerns a long overdue recognition that conflict is not necessarily bad (Robbins, 1974). For example, Thomas (1976, p. 889) suggested, "Conflict itself is no evil, but rather a phenomenon which can have constructive or destructive effects depending upon its management". Conflict may, in fact, contribute to innovation (Robbins, 1974) and growth in the relationships of organizational members (Chesler, Crowfoot & Bryant, 1978). Therefore, much recent writing on conflict intervention has emphasized conflict management over conflict resolution (Strauss, 1978). As a result of this changing emphasis, many aims other than solving the conflict have surfaced recently in research and theory on conflict intervention. For example, some of the newly emerging aims of conflict intervention include improving decision-making, modifying existing relationships between the disputants, furthering organizational goals, and fairness (Brown, 1982; Thibaut & Walker, 1975; Thomas, 1982).

2. Innovative Approaches to Conflict Intervention. A second recent trend in conflict intervention has been a move to innovation and experimentation with the procedures utilized to manage conflict in the various dispute settings. Many states are experimenting with mediation or arbitration as alternatives to courtroom adjudication in both civil and criminal cases (Ford Foundation, 1978). In Industrial Relations, various new forms of arbitration are being tried as alternative ways for settling contract disputes (see Anderson, 1981 for a review). Additionally, interesting experiments are being conducted on the novel idea of utilizing mediation as a step in the grievance arbitration process (see especially Brett & Goldberg,

in press). Finally, marital researchers are seriously investigating mediation of divorce settlements or child custody questions (Ford Foundation,
1978). One side effect of this emergence of innovative ways of dealing
with conflict is the evolution of a plethora of terms describing the conflict
intervention process and the people who perform this function. Some of
these terms include process consultation, mediation, conciliation, facilitation, arbitration, Med/Arb, adjudication, factfinding, investigation, om-
budsman, justice boards, special masters, friends of the court, counsell-
ing, therapy, moot, inquisition, adversary intervention and Schriesman.

3. Recognition of Cross-situational Similarities. A final emergent
trend in recent work on conflict intervention is an increased appreciation
of the similarity of the techniques available for conflict intervention across
the very diverse realms in which conflict occurs. For example, two recent
books (Bazerman & Lewicki, in press; Bomers & Peterson, 1982) have
directly addressed the correspondence between conflict management in
Industrial Relations and Organizational Behavior. Similar comparisons
are being made between the law and Industrial Relations and the law and
conflict management practices in organizations (e.g., Erickson, Holmes,
Frey, Walker & Thibaut 1972; Sheppard, in press; Wall, in press;) as
well as marital therapy and both civil law procedure (e.g., application of
contracts to solve marital disputes), and Industrial Relations (e.g., divorce
mediation). This increased awareness of the applicability of conflict intervention approaches across the various dispute settings is probably due
to the expanded awareness of the multiple aims of intervention in these
various settings and the resulting willingness to experiment with new techniques. For example, the recent interest in labor relations among legal
writers is a direct result of the evolution of mediation as a technique to
solve legal conflict (Vidmar, Note 1; Wall, in press). This interest in mediation is, in turn, largely a result of a growing concern with the importance of timeliness in the resolution of legal disputes (Vidmar, Note 1).

   In summary, the quantity of research on conflict intervention is growing. In addition, the boundaries of this research are expanding to include
consideration of new techniques for intervention, new goals of conflict
intervention, as well as a comparison of the concerns and techniques
utilized in various conflict settings. Thus, the picture to be drawn of research on conflict intervention in general and in organizations in particular
is that of a healthy, growing field. However, there still exist clear limitations to this growth process. The next section of this chapter will review
these limitations. The section will conclude with the argument that a general framework of the form proposed in this chapter is needed to overcome
these limitations. This discussion of the limitations of the existing research
is best organized in terms of the three emergent trends just identified.

The Need for a General Framework

Expanding Goals. As indicated earlier, the range of goals (i.e., criteria for choosing or evaluating dispute intervention procedures) has been expanded in recent research. However, there are some limitations to the manner in which these many diverse goals of conflict intervention have been treated in the conflict literature. First, the principle goal(s) of concern to any particular writer is often imbedded in his or her discussion of intervention methods. As Pondy (1967) indicated, "Theorists have assumed goals rather than explicitly stating them". Thus, readers of this literature are often forced to infer the aims of the writer or assume the same theories apply to the achievement of multiple goals.

A second difficulty with the broad range of intervention goals is that they are widely scattered throughout the conflict literature. In other words, researchers and practitioners in any one conflict setting (e.g., international conflict, the law, marital conflict, management-labor conflict) tend to emphasize only a portion of the full range of criteria that exist for choosing or evaluating conflict intervention procedures (Lissak & Sheppard, 1983). Thus, although there are many such goals or criteria, few readers or even researchers, for that matter, are aware of them all.

Further, very different goals or criteria exist within sub-realms of the same general dispute arena. Conflict resolution within organizations illustrates this point well. Some of the most common processes of organizational conflict resolution include mediation and arbitration in management-labor negotiations, employee appeal processes, and inter-departmental or interpersonal conflict management. The criteria generally discussed in evaluating management-labor conflict resolution include avoiding strikes, controlling the number of issues resolved, minimizing impact on the pre–intervention negotiation process, avoiding systematic bias of the resolution outcome, protection of the public interest, protection of employee rights and assuring similar outcome to that which would have occurred without third party intervention (see Anderson, 1981; Feuille, 1979; Kochan, 1980). The literature on employee appeal processes, on the other hand, has tended to focus on issues such as fairness of the settlement, timeliness of the process, ease of utilization, freedom from recrimination, uniformity of treatment, individuality of treatment and level of utilization (see Aram & Salipante, 1981; Scott, 1965). Finally, writers principally concerned with interdepartmental or interpersonal conflict intervention have tended to focus on criteria such as the level of intensity of the conflict, impact of the intervention on normal office functioning, mutuality of benefit derived from the resolution, permanence of the settlement and impact of the intervention on the disputants' future conflict–handling behavior (see Filley, 1975; Likert & Likert, 1976; Walton, 1969).

A quick inspection of these divergent goals reveals that they are equally applicable in each of the above three conflict areas. Clearly, a single comprehensive list of criteria for choosing and evaluating conflict intervention procedures is needed. The presence of such a list should enlighten both conflict researchers, who tend to focus only on a limited subset of concerns in their work, and readers of the conflict literature who have difficulty disentangling the aims of conflict intervention from the forms such intervention can take (Lissak & Sheppard, 1983).

Increased Experimentation.   Recent attempts at increased innovation in applying conflict intervention procedure has also uncovered several limitations. One limitation relates to the plethora of terms previously alluded to in describing these various innovations. While this expanding terminology is a sign of healthy innovation, it is also diagnostic of a growing confusion about procedure. Thus, for example, very similar procedures are called by many different names (Sheppard, in press). Moreover, the same name is often being applied to quite different procedures. One example of this latter problem is the term "mediation", used to describe such diverse procedures as (a) an intervening party acting as an intermediary (Wall, 1981), (b) an intervening party dealing jointly with two (or more) disputants to confront a problem together (Fuller, 1971) and (c) a panel of outside persons making a non-binding decision about disposal of a particular dispute (Peach & Kuechle, 1975; p. 178). This last variant of mediation is identical to *non-binding arbitration* (Bigoness, 1976). The prevalance of such encompassing, overlapping and ill-defined procedural labels has led to confusion and difficulty in drawing reliable generalities from the research on the respective procedures. This confusion was evident at a recent session on dispute resolution attended by the author. Each participant began confidently presenting the conclusion of his/her own research on mediation effectiveness. However, it soon became clear that many of the conclusions drawn by the separate participants were contradictory. Moreover, each participant had been studying a different form of dispute intervention, all of which they called "mediation." By the end of the session, the discussion centered around the single question, "What is mediation?"

This confusion of terminology reflects a need for an all-encompassing grammar permitting researchers and practitioners to describe precisely the intervention they are using or evaluating. In other words, there is a strong need for a general toxonomy through which someone using an intervention procedure in a given setting can clearly communicate. Such a taxonomy may have the additional advantage of suggesting possible alternative intervention procedures.

One final limitation of this present growth in innovation concerns the misguided application of certain intervention procedures to unsuitable conflict settings. One of the most striking examples of such procedural overextension was the proliferation of T-groups in the late 1960s and 1970s. The expectation that this sort of sensitivity training technique would seriously aid in the resolution of the conflict in Northern Ireland (Doob & Foltz, 1973) was only one of many misapplications of a procedure useful within certain limited settings. An aid to improving our intuition about the generalizability of various procedures would be some treatment of the important dimensions differentiating conflict across various settings. (Deutsch, 1973). In other words, the ability to apply correct procedures to diverse conflict settings would probably improve if we (a) had a good procedural taxonomy and (b) better understood the dimensions of conflict that influence procedural effectiveness. As an example, Rubin (1980) has suggested that procedures in which the intervening party has a great deal of control (e.g., adjudication) are particularly appropriate to managing intense conflict, as opposed to conflict in which personal commitment and emotion are not very strong. A general list is needed of such procedurally relevant features of diverse conflict settings. Intensity is just one example.

Similarity of Procedures Across Settings. Finally, there is still only very limited recognition of the similarity between intervention procedures employed across the different areas of conflict management. Perhaps the most important limitation is the preoccupation with comparing only those procedures utilized in more formal (e.g., law or industrial relations) or professional (e.g., process consultation and psychotherapy) intervention settings rather than those used under more informal circumstances. For example, the comparability of formal legal intervention with informal managerial or parental conflict literature has been largely ignored (Sheppard, in press). This tendency to compare only the more formal or professional intervention procedures reflects a similar emphasis on such procedures in the conflict literature generally (Sheppard, in press). We know relatively little about how parents, managers, teachers, neighbors, colleagues or even the clergy intervene in conflict. One reason for the absence of research and theory on informal conflict intervention may be that we presently have no means of conceptualizing how to approach theory development or research in these more informal realms. Again there exists a clear need for a comprehensive taxonomy of conflict intervention procedure. In this case, a taxonomy is necessary as a guide to research describing informal conflict intervention.

One last limitation of the recent trend toward comparative procedure is that the comparisons are often incomplete. Such comparisons may focus on only limited aspects of the procedures used in several settings (e.g.,

Wall, in press) or some of the goals of intervention in two or more settings
(Thomas, 1982). Rarely is a thorough comparison of all aspects of intervention conducted between several settings. Aside from the difficulty of
such a comparison, the absence of a comprehensive framework as a guide
for comparison may be one cause of the present incomplete work.

Summary and Conclusion. In summary, while the recent growth of interest and the emerging trends in conflict intervention research are positive signs for the field, this growth is limited in several important ways.
What is necessary is a general framework to provide impetus and direction
to this growth. A general framework should be composed of three parts:
a comprehensive taxonomy of conflict intervention procedure, a complete
list of the criteria available for choosing or evaluating conflict intervention
procedures, and some discussion of the characteristics of conflict and
conflict settings relevant to the study of procedures. The next section of
this chapter presents the rudiments of such a framework. From the preceeding discussion, the following concerns motivated the development of
this framework and should be used in its evaluation.

1.   Constructs utilized in the framework need to be relatively explicit,
allowing the readers of the conflict literature to identify the exact goals
and procedures a given researcher is using. In this same vein, discussion
of the methods of conflict intervention and the aims of conflict intervention need to be clearly separated in this framework.
2.   The framework should be relatively comprehensive. In other
words, the elements of the framework should be derived from and applicable to a wide range of conflict settings. In particular, the framework
should relate to informal as well as more formal, professional intervention.
3.   The framework should show promise as an aid to identifying new
innovations in intervention procedure, facilitating procedural comparisons across various dispute realms and expanding the set of criteria utilized in conflict intervention research. In other words, the framework
should appear helpful to continuing development of the emerging trends
in the conflict intervention literature.
4.   The framework should be potentially useful as a guide to further
descriptive research as well as formal theory development, both of which
are important to sustained growth in the conflict intervention area.

A PROPOSED FRAMEWORK OF CONFLICT
INTERVENTION PROCEDURE

The development of the proposed framework is organized around the
three necessary elements of a framework cited above, i.e., a procedural
taxonomy, a list of goals or criteria and a list of conflict characteristics

relevant to procedure. However, it is useful first to define what is meant by conflict intervention procedure.

In its simplest form, conflict intervention can be conceived of as involving three parties—two disputants and a third or intervening party. The third party is less directly involved and intervenes in the dispute in order to facilitate the management or control of the conflict between the other two. Permanent resolution of the dispute is not necessarily the principal concern of a third party, since the existence of conflict is often functional (Litterer, 1966; March & Simon, 1958; Thomas, 1976; Walton, 1969), or unavoidable (Kerr, 1954; Marx, 1938; Young, 1967). However, the entrance of a third party suggests that some dysfunctional elements of the conflict exist or appear to exist, and that these require some attention or control.

In the context of conflict intervention, "procedure" can be defined as a set of pre-established implicit or explicit rules or norms governing the way a dispute is resolved. The term "norm" is included in this definition since the framework is intended to be applicable to informal conflict intervention, in which implicit understandings rather than formal rules govern behavior. It does appear that participants in these informal settings are aware of procedures governing the intervention, although often these are referred to as the style of the intervening party (see later discussion and Sheppard, in press).

Procedures can also be understood in contrast to process, or the actual sequence of events in a particular intervention and to outcome, or the result of an intervention. A football game is a useful analogy. The procedural aspects of a football game include such things as the formal rules of football, the setting (i.e., location and typical fan make-up), the players belonging to each team (since they are generally the same from week to week), and anticipated styles of the referees or coaches known to all parties. In other words, the procedure includes the formal and informal rules under which everyone expects the game to be played. Process concerns what transpires during the play of the game while outcome concerns the final score and any of its consequences.

Conflict intervention procedures exist at at least two levels of generality. At the most abstract level are procedures delineating the alternative modes of dispute resolution available to disputants and the ways they may access and proceed through these alternatives. Thus, the rules describing the types of courts in a state or country, the particular legal issues which can be heard in each, and the timing and processing of appeals through the stages of a court system are all at this level. Similarly, the description of the relationship between stages of a grievance process (and alternative mechanisms available to a disputant) including the sequencing, timing and choices for appeal at each stage is at this first level (for an interesting discussion of this topic in both profit and nonprofit organizations see

Scott, 1965). The second level of procedure involves the general processing of a dispute within any one segment of this larger process. Rules
at this level concern the issues of initiating the session, the range of topics
or questions, control of the proceedings, deciding who may be present and
appropriate times for speaking out. In this chapter, the term segment or
session refers not to one setting as in an hour with a therapist, but instead
to one complete try at resolution from initiation to conclusion. Thus, the
completion of an intervention segment is signaled by successful conclusion of some dispute issue or giving up on that issue.

The framework presented in this chapter principally concerns procedural questions relating to the second level of generality identified above,
i.e., those concerning the overall strategy to be adopted in a particular
session of dispute resolution. Thus, this framework is at the same level
of abstraction as procedures such as mediation, arbitration, adjudication,
or as a bargaining session, a therapy session or a consulting session. With
this introduction, we are now ready to consider the three elements of the
framework.

A Taxonomy of Conflict Intervention Procedure

The first necessary facet of a framework for research on conflict intervention is a procedural taxonomy. The taxonomy employed here bor-
rows heavily from the pioneering work of John Thibaut and Laurens
Walker (Thibaut & Walker, 1975) and their colleagues. Although the actual intention of their research was to develop a framework for analyzing
the psychological aspects of procedural justice, their elegantly simple
model of procedure was the first attempt to develop a universally applicable taxonomy of procedures to guide research.

The Thibaut and Walker Procedural Framework.   Thibaut and Walker have
conceived of dispute resolution as involving (a) three parties, including
the two disputants and the intervening or third party (e.g., a judge) and
(b) two stages, including a process stage in which conflicting evidence is
presented and a decision stage in which the facts are evaluated to determine which disputant has the weight of evidence in his/her favor. The
major distinction between dispute intervention procedures for Thibaut
and Walker is *the degree of third party control in each stage.* Third party
control can take the form of process control, much as football referee
controls the flow of the game but has no direct influence as to the outcome,
or decision control, the way a diving judge does not influence the dive
in progress but simply decides on the dive's quality. On this basis, Thibaut
and Walker have identified five dispute resolution procedures representing the possible ways in which these two forms of control could be as-

sumed by the intervening party. Table 1 outlines these five procedures which range from no third party control (bargaining) to complete process control and decision control (autocratic). According to Thibaut and Walker, these procedures are not simply theoretical possibilities, but in fact describe important forms of procedure presently used in resolving conflict. For example, the adversary legal procedure, utilized in North America and Great Britain, is similar to their arbitration procedure (see Table 1) and the inquisitorial legal procedure, found in Continental Europe, is similar to their autocratic procedure. In other words, following Thibaut and Walker's model, the major difference between the adversary (arbitration) and inquisitorial (autocratic) legal procedures is the presence of third party control in the process stage of the inquisitorial procedure. That is, the judge in the inquisitorial procedure directly controls the trial (determining what witnesses will be called, asking questions of the witnesses and disputants, etc.), whereas in North America the disputants' representatives (i.e., attorneys) control the trial process.

Finally, Thibaut and Walker have suggested two criteria for evaluating the effectiveness of any procedure. These include, (a) actual effectiveness, i.e., capacity to reveal the most evidence while maintaining the neutrality of the decision making party and (b) perceived fairness, i.e., the degree to which the involved parties feel that the procedure is fair.

In their own simulation research, Thibaut and Walker (1975) found overwhelming support for the arbitration (adversary) procedure on both these criteria. Arbitrators (as opposed to autocrats) appear to stay impartial longer. More evidence favoring an initially disadvantaged party surfaces in an arbitration process. Finally, the arbitration process is generally perceived by the parties as the most fair of the five procedures.

In summary, the Thibaut and Walker framework consists of two components, (a) a taxonomy of third party intervention procedures centering on the form of control available to the third party and (b) two criteria

Table 1. Five Dispute Intervention Procedures Identified by Thibaut and Walker (1975)

Type of Procedure	Type of Third Party Control Exhibited in Procedure	
	Process	Decision
Autocratic	Yes	Yes
Arbitration	No	Yes
Mediation	Yes	No
Moot	Shared	Shared
Bargaining	No	No

for evaluating the comparative effectiveness of these procedures. The model is extremely important because it represents the first attempt to develop a broad, generic framework describing conflict resolution procedures that permits empirical investigation of the comparative strengths of each procedure. However, there are two features of their taxonomy which merit modification and extension to meet this chapter's aim of building a more comprehensive framework.

Limitations of the Thibaut and Walker Model.   The first of these limitations concerns Thibaut and Walker's treatment of control. In their use of the terms process and decision control, Thibaut and Walker have combined two distinct and important elements of third party control. These are (a) the nature of the control assumed by the intervening party (e.g., control of the resolution process versus making a decision) and (b) the timing of that control (e.g., assuming control early versus late in the resolution process). This combination of the timing and the type of third party control is somewhat limiting. For example, it is possible for an intervening party to assume process control during the presentation of arguments, as does a chairperson in a debate, as well as when the final decision is being made, much as an electoral officer does in an election. Similarly, the judge in an adversary trial procedure is constantly being called upon to make decisions during the trial process itself, as well as when the disposition of the case is being determined, i.e., when a verdict is rendered. Thus, in a more general framework it should be possible to separate the type or form of control an intervening party assumes from the point at which the third party assumes control in the resolution process.

A second limitation of the Thibaut and Walker model is that it is too general for the purposes of this chapter. One problem with the simple differentiation provided in their model is that it does not permit identification of new innovative procedures. The techniques they identify are well established. In addition, the absence of greater detail is particularly troublesome for one audience being targeted in this framework. Telling a manager or a parent to mediate is somewhat analogous to telling a Tanzanian to play quarterback. In both instances, more detailed instructions would greatly increase the chances of successful accomplishment of the task. Finally, a model at this level of generality misses many important procedural nuances. For example, their model does not differentiate between factfinding, process consultation and mediation. Clearly, any taxonomy will not incorporate all existing procedural differences. However, a somewhat more detailed taxonomy is needed.

A Reformulated Taxonomy.   The conclusion of the preceding discussion is that a more comprehensive taxonomy can be achieved by elaborating the types and potential timing of third party control during the conflict management process. The Thibaut and Walker model can be reconceptualized in these terms as a 2 × 1 matrix. The rows of the matrix represent two stages in dispute resolution and the single column a general category encompassing any type of control exerted during a given stage. Each of the five procedures can be identified by entering an X (or a half X to represent moot) in the appropriate cell(s) of the matrix. It is clear from this representation that the Thibaut and Walker model is too simple for the purpose of this chapter, as certainly there exists more than two stages of dispute resolution and one form of third party control (cf. Filley, 1975; Walton, 1969). However, this representation suggests a means by which to expand their model to increase its comprehensiveness. Specifically, a more complete representation could be developed by elaborating upon the rows and the columns of this matrix.

To expand the rows of this matrix we need to answer the question, "*When* can a third party intervene in conflict?" or perhaps more simply, "What are the stages of conflict resolution?" To expand the columns we need to consider, "*How* can third parties intervene in conflict?" Note that this representation requires that types of control be identified that are, at least theoretically, applicable to any given stage of the dispute resolution process. While this requirement may seem extremely limiting, it is not so in fact. First, let us consider the stages of conflict resolution.

The Stages of Conflict Resolution. To flesh out the rows of this matrix, stage descriptions of conflict resolution were considered from the literature in most areas of dispute resolution. While some of the subtleties may vary from area to area, stage descriptions of dispute resolution look surprisingly similar to each other (see for example Filley, 1975; Douglas, 1957; Deutsch, 1973; Walton, 1969; Pondy, 1967; Young, 1967; Fisher, 1972; Gottman, 1978). This representation is also similar to more general models of problem-solving (Bruner, Goodnow & Austin, 1956; Janis & Mann, 1977, D'Zurilla & Goldfried, 1971). Table 2 presents one summary of these stage models. In this representation, dispute resolution is presumed to proceed through four stages: definition, discussion, alternative selection and reconciliation. Within each stage a number of events occur. For example, within the reconciliation stage the conflicting parties are reconciled with the final disposition of the conflict issue, required actions of the parties may be enforced and an appeal may be started, which would then initiate a new session. While the four stages occur in fixed sequence, the events or phases within a particular stage do not necessarily occur in any specific order. Thus, for example, deciding what is in dispute may or may not precede the choice of procedure(s) for resolving the dispute. All dispute resolution does not have to proceed explicitly through these four stages. However, it is a logical necessity that each stage be at least

Table 2.   Stages of Dispute Resolution

I.   *DEFINITION*:
- SELECT RESOLUTION PROCEDURE
- FEEL OUT PARTIES
- WHAT IS IN DISPUTE?
- WHAT RELEVANT INFORMATION EXISTS?
- WHAT ARE THE ALTERNATIVES FOR SETTLEMENT

II. *DISCUSSION*:
- PRESENT RELEVANT INFORMATION
- PRESENT ARGUMENTS FOR EACH ALTERNATIVE
- CLARIFY INFORMATION AND ARGUMENTS

III. *ALTERNATIVE SELECTION*:
- DECIDE VALIDITY OF INFORMATION AND ARGUMENTS
- SELECT AN ALTERNATIVE FOR SOLUTION

IV. *RECONCILIATION*:
- RECONCILE PARTIES WITH SOLUTION
- ENFORCE DECISION
- HEAR APPEALS

---

implicitly preceded by the earlier stages. For example, it is not possible to reconcile the disputants with a decision before a decision has been made, or to select an alternative for solving a dispute without identifying at least one such alternative.

Forms of Control.   To complete the matrix then, it is necessary to identify the types of control a third party can exhibit during the resolution process. Table 3 contains a relatively thorough and self-explanatory description of the various control forms evident throughout the literature. Table 3 however, only includes control forms centering around *what* a third party can actually do, rather than the aim of the third party's control attempt (e.g., to reduce the level of tension). The following references were the principal sources from which this list was derived: Deutsch (1973), Fisher (1972), Friedland (1970), Gottman (1980), Haley (1976), Schelling (1960), Kerr (1954), Thomas (1976), Wall (1981), Walton (1969), Walton & McKersie (1965), and Young (1967).

The types of control identified in Table 3 have been classified into four general categories which appear to summarize well the general sorts of control available to a third party. The first summary category is process control. Process control refers to any attempt by a third party to direct the manner in which the disputants and other parties interact during conflict management, but not what the topics or other substantive aspects of their interaction should be. For example, a manager intervening in a dis-

Table 3. Forms of Control Available to Third Parties in Conflict Intervention

I. *Process Control*

A. *General Controls*

1. Control location of disputants, e.g., separated or together.
2. Control general communication process: request written briefs, force disputants to talk, request eye contact, require reflective listening, establish an agenda, request role reversal, censure interruptions, encourage open discussion or close communication channels.
3. Act as an advocate of a position, devils advocate or sounding board.
4. Counsel one party.
5. Act as a go-between.
6. Control access to other parties or information.
7. Establish time limit on process.

B. *Specific Controls*

1. Suggest or require a specific process mechanism, e.g., require disputants to vote.
2. Limit or disallow particular process mechanism, e.g., disputants are not permitted to argue.
3. Audit process, e.g., look for process problems and flag them with disputants.
4. Establish particular rules of order.

II. *Content Control*

A. *General Controls*

1. Control general communication content: avoid sidetracking, limit discussion to a single item, expand discussion, censor "guilting" other party, censor affect statement, censor ultimatums, censor use of "always" or "never", censor use of trait names, encourage giving praise, encourage expressions of likes or dislikes, etc.
2. Establish an agenda.
3. Establish rules of evidence or content for consideration.

B. *Specific Controls*

1. Refute or attack particular point.
2. Present own content, e.g., state the nature of the dispute.
3. Disallow or discourage particular content.
4. Audit content.
5. Interpret of clarify content.
6. Edit content.
7. Withold content from some or all parties.

III. *Control by Request*

The use of any of the controls listed in sections I and II above after some party has explicitly requested such an intervention, e.g., a judge can decide on a rule of evidence after an objection by one of the attorneys.

IV. *Motivational Control*

1. Can provide incentive to perform desired action, e.g., a parent offers to take children to the fair only if they would settle their argument.
2. Can provide a disincentive to performing an undesired action, e.g., a boss threatens to fire an employee unwilling to negotiate with a fellow employee.

Table 3.   (Continued)

IV. *Motivational Control Continued*

3. Has legitimate authority over some facet of dispute resolution.
4. Voluntary agreement to control by some or all of the parties.
5. Can change the nature of the power distribution between disputants.
6. Has the ear of some figure having one of the controls described above, e.g., a mediator has access to the media and therefore public or stockholder opinion.
7. Has threat of control in later stage of the resolution process.
8. Persuasive capability.
9. Physical force.

---

pute between two employees may bring the two disputants together, disallow interruptions, place a time limit on discussion, require the disputants to paraphrase each other's point of view or even suggest that the employees let their peers decide what is right. These types of control mechanisms have been studied extensively, although not exclusively, in the realms of family therapy (Haley, 1976), process consultation (Walton, 1969) and organizational development (Beer, 1976).

The second summary category presented in Table 3—content control— concerns a third party's attempts to control the substance of the conflict management activity. When exercising this type of a control, a manager may, for instance, ask specific questions about the nature of the conflict, censor certain topics (e.g., particularly personal or embarrassing issues), define the employee's dispute for them, suggest solutions or arguments to the disputants and even choose the solution to the conflict. Thus, content control implies intervening in the *what* of conflict management while process control concerns intervention in the *how*. Writings on mediation (Wall, 1981), international conflict intervention (Young, 1967) and structural solutions to organizational conflict (Lawrence & Lorsch, 1968) have tended to focus on content control issues.

Unlike process and content control, a detailed treatment of control by request is not provided in Table 3. Such detail would be redundant, since control by request can take any of the forms of control listed under process or content intervention in Table 2, with the additional requirement that the intervention be at the direct request of one of the disputing parties. Thus, the exact nature of the control form taken in a particular intervention depends upon the issue raised by the party requesting intervention. For example, a judge may disallow certain content from discussion, a manager may establish an agenda, or a priest may suggest a solution to a problem, all at the request of one or more of the directly involved parties. The important features of control by request are that (a) a specific request for intervention be made and (b) after that particular request is dealt with, the third party resumes a relatively inactive stance.

The final form of control identified in Table 3 is labeled motivational control. This type of control is qualitatively different from the other three control forms. Process control, content control and control by request all involve an attempt by the third party to influence the conflict management activity of the disputing parties. In contrast, motivational control concerns the source of that influence, i.e., the source of power permitting the third party to direct the content or the process of conflict management. For example, what is it about the manager discussed above that made the disputants stop interrupting each other or accept his/her final decision? Threats, persuasive arguments, direct incentives and legitimate authority are all forms of motivational control that may be utilized to induce desired behavior on the part of the disputants or other involved parties. Since these forms of motivational controls are specifically related to conflict intervention, they are similar but not identical to more general categorization schemes of power or influence (e.g., French & Raven, 1958; Kipnis, Schmidt, & Wilkinson, 1980; Yukl, 1981).

It is further noteworthy that motivational controls will co-occur typically with at least one of the other forms of control. Thus, for example, motivational control could be linked with process control (e.g., an incentive could be provided for the disputants to meet), or content control (e.g., a disincentive could be provided for sidetracking the conversation). However, it is possible for the third party to impose motivational control for other reasons. A third party may wish to reinforce an agreement by the disputants themselves, e.g., a teacher could praise two students who reached a compromise. A third party may wish to keep the disputants working toward a settlement, e.g., a therapist could remind a couple of the cost of continued conflict. Finally, a third party may simply wish to influence the atmosphere during resolution, e.g., a judge could remind a disputant of the authority of the court to induce a serious demeanour during the trial or a mediator might take the negotiators to lunch to instill improved congeniality.

As with the various forms of motivational control, it is possible, but not necessary, for most of the specific control forms identified in Table 3 to co-occur with other specific forms of control. Thus, for example, it is possible for a third party to act as a go-between (process control) and to establish an agenda (content control) in the same phase or stage of dispute resolution. Clearly, some of these specific control mechanisms will co-occur more than others. For example, a third party is more likely to act as an intermediary with spearated disputants than when the disputants are together.

To summarize to this point then, four forms of control available to an intervening party during conflict intervention have been identified, specifically, process control, content control, control by request and motivational control. In addition, four separate stages of conflict management in which a third party may intervene have also been identified, specifically, definition, discussion, alternative selection and reconciliation stages. Both of these relatively simple schemes summarize more detailed representations of when and how a third party can intervene, that is, Table 2 presents thirteen phases of conflict management process and Table 3 identifies thirty-one specific forms of control available to the intervening party.

Combining the Timing and Form of Control.   When combined together, timing and form of control form a 4×4 matrix for representing conflict intervention procedure (see Figure 1). Alternatively, more detailed representations can be developed in the form of 13×4, 4×31 or 13×31 matrices. The simpler representation of the 4×4 matrix is useful for describing classes of procedure, whereas the more elaborate matrices are most useful for addressing detailed questions about a particular aspect of intervention (see example later) or for training and procedural development efforts, when explicit identification of what is to be done is necessary. In either case, a procedure would be identified by making an entry in those cells of the matrix in which the intervening party is permitted or exhibits a particular form of control in one of the stages of dispute resolution.

Exactly how this can be done is probably best illustrated with some examples. Figure 1 presents the author's representation of five intervention procedures drawn from several dispute resolution areas. These examples present one interpretation of procedures which often take very different forms. Thus, the purpose of these examples is not to provide an unquestionably accurate definition of each procedure, but simply to illustrate how to use this taxonomy.

Adversary Trial Procedure.   Figure 1(a) presents a representation of the adversary legal procedure. In an adversary legal system, the two disputants (or their representatives) are responsible for identifying what is in dispute, choosing their procedure and gathering their own evidence, including interviewing witnesses, and, to varing extents, actually preparing them for trial testimony. At the trial the party who calls each witness attempts to elicit, in a quasinarrative fashion, information favorable to his or her side ("examination-in-chief"). Thereafter, the witness is subjected to cross-examination by the opposing party. The judge remains an essentially passive listener to the evidence and arguments during the presentation of evidence. Thus, except for deciding whether or not to hear a case and settling disputes about procedure in response to an objection by one of the participants, the judge has no active control until the decision phase begins. Clearly, the accuracy of this description varies widely. For example, in small claims court the adversary judge often assumes process control over the presentation of information and arguments. One nice

Form of Third
Party Control

	Process	Content	Request	Motivational
Definition			X	X
Discussion			X	X
Alternative Selection	X	X		X
Reconciliation	X	X	X	X

Timing of Third Party Control

Adversary Legal Procedure
1a

Form of Third
Party Control

	Process	Content	Request	Motivational
Definition			X	X
Discussion	X	X		X
Alternative Selection	X	X		X
Reconciliation	X	X	X	X

Timing of Third Party Control

Inquisitorial Legal Procedure
1b

Form of Third
Party Control

	Process	Content	Request	Motivational
Definition	X	X	X	X
Discussion	X	X		X
Alternative Selection	X	X		X
Reconciliation	X	X	X	X

Timing of Third Party Control

Inquisitorial Legal Procedure
with Court Appointed Investigator
1c

Figure 1. A Model of Conflict Intervention Procedure with Some Examples

Form of Third
Party Control

		Process	Content	Request	Motivational
	Definition	X	X	X	X
Timing of Third Party Control	Discussion	X	X	X	X
	Alternative Selection	X	X	X	X
	Reconciliation				

Active Mediation
1d

Form of Third
Party Control

		Process	Content	Request	Motivational
	Definition	X	X		
Timing of Third Party Control	Discussion				
	Alternative Selection				
	Reconciliation				

Factfinding Procedure
1e

Figure 1.   Continued

aspect of this proposed framework, however, is that it allows specification of exactly how various versions of a given procedure differ from one another.

Inquisitorial Trial Procedure.   Two other legal examples are presented in Figures 1b and 1c, which depict two variants of the inquisitorial legal procedure. In an inquisitorial system, once one party files a suit, the judge may (Figure 1c) or may not (Figure 1b) seek out the evidence through a number of subordinates (court investigators). At the trial, there are no separate witnesses for the two parties. Rather, the witnesses testify for the court, and the parties are not allowed to prepare or influence the witnesses prior to the trial. The judge, equipped with a summary of the basic facts of the case, calls on the witnesses to give their testimony in narrative form. Following the judge's interrogation, the contending parties are permitted to ask clarifying questions or bring out omitted points favorable to their case. After final arguments from both sides, the judge renders a decision.

As can be seen from these three examples, the Thibaut and Walker model has ignored important differences between the adversary and inquisitorial legal procedures, as well as important variations within these two procedures (e.g., the presence or absence of a pre-trial investigator in inquisitorial procedure). In fact, even these 4 × 4 matrices ignore some important characteristics of these two systems. Figures 3a, 3b and 3c present this author's interpretation of these two systems in the form of a 13 × 4 matrix. (For a derivation of these representations, see Sheppard & Vidmar, Note 2).

Mediation. The two other examples provided in Figure 1 are more directly related to Organizational Behavior. Figure 1d is entitled Active Mediation. One defining characteristic of mediation is that in mediation the intervening party cannot make a decision binding the disputing parties (Kochan, 1980). Thus a representation of mediation would not include third party control over the enforcement of a decision, i.e., stage four of the conflict intervention. Additionally, most mediation will not involve the choice of an alternative for settlement by the intervening party (stage three), although the evaluation of disputant arguments (also within stage three) is often performed by mediators as a way to induce agreement. Given the wide range of intervention possibilities available to a third party prior to making and enforcing a decision, mediation is not so much one procedure, as it is an umbrella term for a whole range of intervention procedures that share the absence of enforceable decisions. Thus, it is not surprising that the symposium on mediation alluded to earlier ended with a futile search for the definition of the term "mediation."

The specific representation given in Figure 1d portrays an extremely active form of mediation, in which a mediator utilizes all forms of intervention available. This representation was given to illustrate the complete potential for intervention available to mediators, but may not reflect the most frequent form of mediation utilized. For example, mediators have generally been portrayed as emphasizing content–based interventions particularly when contrasted to Organizational Development techniques, (see Brett, Goldberg and Ury, Note 6) and the frequent use of separation of parties (Kochan, 1980). For the interested reader, one of the best discussions of the wide array of techniques utilized by mediators can be found in Wall (1981).

Factfinding. The second example taken from the labor relations area, is factfinding, presented in Figure 1e. Kagel and Kagel (1972) described an interesting alternative or complement to the grievance arbitration procedure. Briefly, two investigators, one recommended by the grievant and one by the employer, jointly search out evidence and attempt to agree on the facts of a case. This third party committee is directed to write a report summarizing the case, the facts, and the relevant arguments. If they cannot reach agreement, then each writes a separate report. Grievances are frequently settled following this report when one of the parties discovers the weakness of his/her case. This intervention is strikingly similar to that of the court-centered pre-trial investigator in many inquisitorial legal procedures (Kaufman, 1962), except that each disputant is represented by an investigator in factfinding.

Managerial Conflict Intervention.

All of the procedures illustrated above were formal procedures involving the intervention of professionals in conflict. Recall, that one of the primary purposes of developing the present framework was to permit better description of less formal non-professional interventions in conflict. A group of intervention procedures of particular interest to Organizational Behavior are those utilized by managers when they intervene in conflicts within their organizations. One of the strategies for validating the present framework involved interviewing managers involved in informal conflict interventions to determine whether or not the procedures utilized in organizational settings could be described by this taxonomy. (For a detailed description of the research methodology see Sheppard, in press; Sheppard, Lesser, Li & Mace, Note 3). The preliminary results of the research with managers are especially interesting for two reasons (Sheppard, in press). First, the taxonomy does appear to comprehensively describe the range of procedures utilized by managers. Second, managers most frequently appear to utilize one of three procedures which are quite different from those generally recommended in the Organizational Behavior literature. (Most textbooks referring to conflict resolution recommend conciliatory or mediational procedures such as those suggested by Filley, 1975; Robbins, 1976, Thomas, 1976; Walton, 1969; see for example Hampton, Summer & Webber, 1982; Hellriegal, Slocum & Woodman, 1983; Nadler, Hackman & Lawler, 1979; Wallace & Szilagyi, 1982). These three procedures will be presented to serve as a final illustration of how to utilize this taxonomy. The procedures are presented in the form of a 13×4 matrix, because the managers discussed their intervention in a manner permitting easy description in this more complicated form.

Procedure 1. The most frequently occurring procedure among managers was characterized by strong and active intervention in stages II, III and IV of the conflict management process (Procedure 1 is represented

Form of Third
Party Control

Timing of Third Party Control		Process	Content	Request	Motivational
	select resolution procedure	1	1	3	1
	feel out parties	2	2		2
Definition	what is in dispute?	3	3	1	1 3
	what information exists?				
	what are the alternatives?				
	present relevant information	3	1	3	1 3
Discussion	present arguments	3	1	3	1 3
	clarify information	3	3		1 3
Alternative Selection	decide validity of arguments	3	1 3		1 2 3
	select an alternative	3	1 3		1 2 3
	reconcile parties	3	1 3		1 3
Reconciliation	enforce decision	1 2 3	1 2 3		1 2 3
	hear appeals	1	1		1

This table is adapted with permission from Managers as inquisitors: some lessons from the law. In M. H. Bazerman and R. J. Lewicki (eds.) *Bargaining Inside Organizations*. Beverly Hills: Sage Publications, 1983.

1 — a cell entry of 1 indicates that the timing and form of control represented by that cell is exhibited by managers utilizing an Inquisitorial Intervention procedure.

2 — a cell entry of 2 indicates that the timing and form of control represented by that cell is exhibited by managers utilizing a Providing Impetus procedure.

3 — a cell entry of 3 indicates that the timing and form of control represented by that cell is exhibited by managers utilizing an Adversary Intervention procedure.

Figure 2. A Matrix Representation of Managerial Conflict Intervention Procedure

by cell entries of 1 in Figure 2). Managers who used this procedure actively guided the discussion, often censoring individual disputants, and made and enforced decisions much like benevolent parents or inquisitors. Thus, this procedure is very similar to inquistorial legal procedures. One example of this managerial intervention procedure described in the interviews concerned a dispute that took place in a brokerage firm. The dispute centered around a new broker who purportedly stole a client from an older broker. In this instance, the intervening manager, who supervised the two brokers, spoke with the client and confirmed that the client had in fact switched brokers. The manager then told the client that if the client were unwilling to return to the original broker then he should take his business elsewhere. In addition, the new broker was told that if a similar incident were to happen again, he would be fired. When the client and the junior broker attempted to explain their side of the story, the intervening manager indicated that he was not interested (thus, control over the presentation and clarification of arguments, in this instance was in the form of censorship). The manager indicated to us that it was necessary to be tough and consistent in such cases no matter what circumstances were involved.

Procedure 2.   In the second most frequently occurring procedure, managers initially contacted the disputants to determine the nature of the conflict then sent them away with a strong disincentive for not reaching agreement, such as threatened removal of one of the parties (Procedure 2 is represented by cell entries of 2 in Figure 2). Thus, this procedure could simply be called providing impetus (or as one manager said, a "kick in the pants."). An example of this sort of intervention, described in an interview, involved an intervention by the vice president of a retail store chain. The dispute was between the head of the data processing department, who needed to hire summer help immediately to fill shortages in staff, and the head of personnel, who wanted to avoid circumvention of normal hiring practices for summer interns. The vice president spoke briefly with both managers and then simply told them that they had "damn well better go back and work it out." Although no action was explicitly threatened if agreement was not reached, this manager indicated that both parties were aware of the likely uproar if their differences were not settled. In other interviews, this type of threat was coupled with active intervention in the definition stage of the resolution process. Also, positive incentives for reaching an agreement were sometimes provided, e.g., lunch out with the boss.

Procedure 3.   The third procedure, depicted in Figure 2, is similar to Procedure 1 in some respects. Like Procedure 1, managers using the procedure decided how the conflict was to be resolved and enforced the

decision if necessary. Unlike Procedure 1 however, the third party generally did not actively seek or restrict the content of particular evidence
and arguments of the disputing parties. Instead, the third party passively
listened to both (or several competing) sides of the dispute as presented
by the disputants. The intervener may, however, have specified how he/
she wanted the information presented, (e.g., who was to go first), how
rebuttals were to be dealt with, and may have actively sought clarifying
information and arguments. A second difference between this procedure
and Procedure 1 was that the third party often did not choose the procedure for resolving the dispute, but instead acceded to a request by the
disputants to listen to each side and suggest a solution. Thus, the choice
of procedure was generally in the form of "control by request". Because
the disputants argued their own cases and because they generally chose
the procedure, this procedure is surprisingly like adversary legal procedures (this procedure is represented by cell entries of 3 in Figure 2). An
example of this sort of intervention from the interviews concerned a dispute over the need for a new boiler for a school. The dispute was between
a member of the engineering department for a local school board who felt
a new boiler was needed and a consultant for the federal government
called in to evaluate this stated need, who felt that a new boiler was
unnecessary. The engineer and the consultant went together to the state
representative who listened at length to both sides of the case and then
accepted the school board's recommendation.

Summary of Taxonomy. In summary then, a matrix representation has
been developed to describe the range of procedures available for third
party conflict intervention. When and how a third party assumes control
are the two characteristics comprising this matrix. Therefore, at least at
the level of a single intervention session, all third party procedures can
be differentiated according to the cells of this matrix that contain entries.
A cell entry indicates that a particular form of control is available during
a particular phase of resolution.

For many purposes, a 4 × 4 matrix representation is inappropriate. It
may sometimes be desirable to further simplify this taxonomy to suit a
particular interest. In this case, procedures could be differentiated only
in terms of when a third party intervenes or by the types of control available to or assumed by a third party. However, these simplifications should
only be made with clear understanding that potentially important considerations have been collapsed. In addition, it is possible that for many
purposes the four categories of control and four stages of conflict management will require further elaboration, thus expanding the representation beyond 16 cells. Such elaboration is most useful when exact procedural description is desired, e.g., for training purposes or when
investigating modification of existing procedures. The full representation

(a 13 × 31 matrix) is intended to be a comprehensive and general taxonomy of procedure. Different pieces of this matrix will be useful to researchers with different interests.

Criteria for Choosing or Evaluating an Intervention Procedure

The second element of this framework concerns a list of criteria for
choosing and evaluating the alternative procedures identified by the preceding taxonomy. The terms choice and evaluation are used here to emphasize that such criteria can serve as either dependent or independent
variables in research on procedure. As dependent variables, they would
be used as a basis for contrasting various procedures or procedural variables identified in the previous section. For example, in a laboratory
simulation several alternative procedures could be contrasted in terms of
how quickly they resolve a negotiation problem or, in clinical research,
two modes of marital therapy could be evaluated along several criterial
dimensions. This is the typical manner in which criteria have been used
in the conflict literature. Research of this form is prescriptive in tone,
having the ultimate aim of identifying what is best done given a certain
aim or set of aims. As independent variables, these criteria would be used
to model participant choice processes. In this sort of research, variations
in the perceived importance of these criteria would be used to predict
disputant or third party procedural preferences. So, this research is more
descriptive in nature.

As indicated earlier, the full range of procedural effectiveness criteria
is generally widely scattered throughout the diverse conflict literatures.
Thomas (1982) has argued that the absence of a single complete list of
the goals of organizational conflict intervention has seriously impeded the
development of good theory. Without the broad perspective imposed by
such a list, individual conflict theorists have tended to limit their work
to just a portion of the conflict picture. Therefore Thomas has suggested
that too few of the important contingencies in conflict intervention have
been discerned. Recognizing the need for such a comprehensive list,
Thomas, Jamieson and Moore (1978) attempted to develop one for conflict
intervention within organizations. The strategy these authors employed
was to content–analyze the writings of four very diverse sets of organization conflict theorists (i.e., Chesler, Crowfoot & Bryant; Derr; Filley;
Robbins) to identify the criteria utilized by any of the set. Briefly, Thomas
et al. identified four general intervention criteria, including decision quality, effects upon individuals, effects upon relationships, and consumption
of organizational resources. A detailed discussion of these goals is provided in Thomas (1982).

Thomas' work is important largely because it represents the most concerted attempt to date to summarize the various, divergent goals of conflict intervention. However, there are several important limitations to the work. First, the list seems somewhat incomplete, since it is evident from the literature that more than four perspectives are important and since only the writings of organizational conflict theorists were utilized. For example, three of the four criteria relate to the outcome of the conflict after intervention. The single exception to this conflict outcome emphasis is consumption of organizational resources (i.e., efficiency) which is more directly a quality of the intervention procedure itself. (This distinction between procedure and outcome goals is similar to the distinction between behavioral and outcome goals in performance appraisal, Cummings & Schwab, 1973). However, there are many procedural criteria other than simple cost or efficiency, such as perceived fairness and timeliness (Thibaut & Walker, 1975; Sheppard & Vidmar, 1980) and Thomas himself acknowledged that his list was incomplete. Thomas' aim was not the development of a comprehensive list but instead a more restricted list emphasizing prescriptive criteria from the perspective of the organization in which the conflict occurred.

A second limitation of the Thomas et al. list is that the original sources of these goals were conflict theorists and not participants in conflict. Therefore, we cannot be sure that the criteria developed by Thomas et al. are important to the people who are most affected by conflict intervention attempts (e.g., employees, managers, parents, children, union representatives, etc.). In summary, an even more comprehensive list of criteria than that generated by Thomas is probably needed. Moreover, this list should more directly incorporate the actual concerns of the direct participants and other persons influenced by conflict intervention.

Development of a Comprehensive List of Intervention Criteria. In collaboration with several students, I have begun a series of studies across various realms of dispute intervention to identify empirically such a list (Lissak & Sheppard, 1983; Sheppard, Note 4; Sheppard, Lesser, Li & Mace, Note 3; Sheppard, Lissak & Palumbo, Note 5). To this point, the research has been completed with samples of managers and employees involved in conflict within organizations, police officers engaged in crisis intervention and parents engaged in conflict intervention in sibling disputes. Principally, the procedure has involved a critical incidents technique in which interviewees described a recent dispute in which they themselves were involved or had observed. After describing the dispute, interviewees were asked to identify the types of concerns they had (or would have had were they a principal in the conflict) for choosing or evaluating a procedure to resolve that dispute. The instructions provided to subjects were intentionally general in order to generate large lists of criteria. Interviewee responses were then content analyzed to identify a complete list of the concerns presented in any particular study. Finally, after the list of criteria had been identified, further research was conducted to develop a preliminary estimate of the perceived importance of these different criteria. Since only a small subset of the sorts of parties involved in dispute intervention has as yet been surveyed, this list is still considered incomplete. Therefore, Table 4 represents a combination of the criterial list developed to this point in the research and three other criteria which will probably be identified as important when a sufficiently broad range of disputants, intervening parties and conflict settings have been surveyed (i.e., outcome fairness, disputant commitment to the solution and cost of the solution). These additional criteria were included because they have been mentioned in the literatures of several dispute arenas.

The criteria listed in Table 4 appear to cluster well into a 2×4 classification scheme. The first dimension of this classification has two broad categories; those criteria that are directly related to procedure, such as implementability or cost and those that concern the outcome of the conflict, but that are probably influenced by the procedure used to resolve the conflict. An example of this last type of criteria is "reducing the likelihood of future similar conflict", which is clearly related to the outcome of the conflict but is probably better attained through some procedures than others. As mentioned above, direct procedural criteria have received relatively less emphasis in the conflict literature than criteria related to the outcome of the conflict after intervention.

One might ask why we should be concerned with the criteria directly related to procedure listed in Table 4 at all, since it is the outcome of the conflict itself that really matters? This view is extremely limited for several reasons (Thibaut & Walker, 1975; Leventhal, 1976). First, there are clear costs associated with the use of any conflict resolution procedure that need to be balanced against the potential or actual gain derived from settling the conflict. Some dispute resolution procedures require a great deal of participant time, some dispute resolution procedures cost a great deal (e.g., war) and in some instances, loss of privacy is especially costly no matter what the dispute outcome might be (e.g., a dispute between a man and woman involved in an extramarital affair). Second, recent research suggests the type of procedure utilized is often more important in determining disputant satisfaction with an outcome than is the outcome itself (Lind, Kurtz, Musante, Walker & Thibaut, 1980; Folger, 1977; Tyler & Caine, 1981). Finally, the outcome of a conflict is often not under anyone's control, whereas the procedure utilized to resolve that conflict can be highly influenced. This last point is a particular concern of third

Table 4. Procedural Effectiveness Criteria

Qualities of Procedures Themselves

I. Fairness

  1. perceived fairness[a]
  2. level of intervener process neutrality, e.g., a non-neutral third party may permit one party to speak but not the other[a]
  3. level of disputant control[a]
  4. protection of individual rights[a]

II. Participant Satisfaction

  5. level of privacy[a]
  6. level of participant involvement and seriousness[a]
  7. level on injury incurred by any party[a]

III. Effectiveness

  8. implementability of procedure[a]
  9. quantity and quality of facts, ideas or argument elicited[a]
  10. degree to which dispute surfaces or gets into the open[a]

IV. Efficency

  11. cost[a]
  12. timeliness and speed of resolution[a]
  13. disruptiveness of other events and everyday affairs[a]

Qualities of Outcome Related to Procedure

I. Fairness

  14. as defined by: equitability, consistency of results with similar conflicts, need, consistency with accepted rule or norm and perceived fairness.

II. Participant Satisfaction

  15. disputant commitment to solution
  16. benefit of outcome participants
  17. level of disputant animosity[a]

III. Effectiveness

  18. level of resolution achieved[a]
  19. permanence of solution[a]
  20. likelihood of future similar outcome[a]
  21. impact on indirectly involved parties[a]

IV. Efficiency

---

[a] Criteria repeatedly identified in our research.

parties who often have direct control over the choice of conflict resolution procedure, but only indirect control over the outcome of the conflict.

The second dimension of the classification scheme utilized in Table 4 has four categories and concerns the substantive issue of the criteria. The first category of this dimension is fairness. Fairness of the *procedure* has largely been emphasized by researchers concerned with legal and political procedure (e.g., Sheppard & Vidmar, 1980; Thibaut & Walker, 1975; Tyler & Caine, 1981). Procedural fairness can be thought of both in terms of the perceptions of participants, and by more objective indices of fairness, such as the neutrality of the intervening party and protection of individual rights. Recent research interest in the fairness of the conflict *outcome* has evolved from social exchange theory (Thibaut & Kelly, 1958; Homans, 1961) and its derivative equity theory (Adams, 1964). However, several alternative definitions of outcome fairness other than a given outcome's equitability have been developed (Leventhal, 1976). Some of the more important alternatives to equity are also listed in Table 4. Rationalizing these competing definitions of outcome fairness is a critical issue to most conflict intervention attempts. One proposed solution to this dilemma is to focus on the fairness of the procedure which is, after all, more under the third party's control (Lissak & Sheppard, in press).

The second of the four substantive categories is participant satisfaction. Concern for the participant has been emphasized in the literature on organizational development (Beer, 1976), interpersonal conflict management, (Walton, 1969) and family therapy (Haley, 1976). Satisfaction includes concern for the level of participant commitment to the procedure and the outcome as well as their participants' happiness with either the procedure or the outcome. Two dimensions clearly influencing participant satisfaction in our interviews were reduction in the level of felt animosity between the disputing parties and maintenance of privacy during intervention. Of course, the relative importance of the various influences on felt satisfaction depended upon which participant was being canvassed. For example, third parties have different interests than disputants.

The third substantive category is effectiveness. Concerning outcome of the conflict, at least, this has generally been the most researched criterial category. "Does the problem get resolved?" "How permanent is the resolution?" "Is there some learning so that future similar conflicts can be avoided?" "What is the impact on other members of the family, the organization, the country or the world?" These are all questions addressed in one way or another in conflict literatures. Again, procedural effectiveness has been less thoroughly considered, although the criterion, "quality and quantity of information or arguments", has been an emphasis in several diverse settings, including the law (Sheppard & Vidmar, 1981), interpersonal conflict management (Filley, 1975) and mediation within Industrial Relations (Wall, 1981). "Implementability or feasability of the procedure" appears infrequently in the conflict literature, but was a frequent concern of our sample of interviewees. This type of concern may arise more frequently in conflict literature in the future with increased emphasis on the development of new procedures and increased comparisons across settings. For example, one issue that has arisen in applying mediation to legal disputes concerns the set of legal cases for which mediation is feasible (Ford Foundation, 1978).

The final substantive category is efficiency. The trend for this category has been the reverse of that for the other three categories. Timeliness, cost of the procedure and disruptiveness of other functions are all highly emphasized procedural issues in the organizational (Thomas, 1982), industrial relations (Kochan, 1980), legal (Damaska, 1975), marital (Haley, 1976) and international (Young, 1967) conflict intervention literatures. On the other hand, the potential cost or inefficiency of the outcome has been less well emphasized.

Before concluding this discussion of the criteria for choosing and evaluating conflict intervention procedures, two more general points are in order. First, the labels for the eight sections of this 2×4 classification scheme should be treated only as labels. They are too general and simplistic to be used as criteria themselves. Each of the twenty-one criteria in Table 4 is independently important. Interviewees were quite capable of discriminating among them and considered each relatively important. (In a later study, with a managerial sample, the three criteria not elicited in the interviews were indicated to be similarly important to the other criteria.) Moreover, there has been too great a tendency to simplify our goals in the conflict intervention literature, with each author focusing on very few and fairly general aims. Conflict intervention is a complicated subject and our research and theory ought to reflect its complexity.

A second point is that it is not always clear whether it is best to be high or low on several of the listed criteria. Is it good or bad for a dispute to get out into the open? Do you always want many facts, ideas or arguments to be elicited? What is the proper level of disputant control? In these instances, the nature of the conflict and the setting in which it occurs influence what is best. Thus, for example, in a conflict in which accurate knowledge of the other's position would lead to permanent intransigence, *not* letting the dispute surface may be important. Clark Kerr (1954) graphically illustrated this possibility with respect to labor-management negotiations when he suggested, "mutual misunderstanding . . . and a barrier of imprecise language have often kept the parties from lunging at each other's throats" (p. 233).

In summary, a preliminary list of criteria for choosing and evaluating dispute intervention procedures was identified. Procedures can be evaluated either in terms of qualities of the procedures themselves or qualities of the resolution outcome potentially influenced by the type of procedure used to resolve the conflict. Finally, for some criteria whether its presence is good or bad depends on the type of conflict and the setting in which it occurs.

Characteristics of Conflict Important to the Study of Procedure

As this last point suggests, a complete framework of third party dispute intervention procedure needs to include a description of those features of conflict relevant to the study of conflict resolution procedure. Features of conflict are defined very broadly in this discussion to include such things as who is involved, the nature of the conflict and the setting in which the conflict occurs. Characteristics of conflict can be relevant to a procedural framework in two ways. First, they can influence the relative importance of the many criteria identified in Table 4 or the desirable direction and level of any single criterion. For example, in a conflict involving weapons, level of participant injury becomes an important concern. Second, certain procedures may be more or less effective on a given criterion across different types of conflict or conflict settings. For example, an adversary trial procedure may resolve some disputes quickly and permanently whereas other disputes would be solved faster and for a longer time period through certain kinds of mediation. Both of these ways in which dispute characteristics relate to a procedural framework suggest a contingency approach to the study of conflict resolution procedure. A given procedure may be the best choice in one setting, either because it is effective on those criteria of greatest concern in that setting or because it is especially effective in that setting, but that same procedure may be the worst choice in another setting. For example, the use of physical force during intervention may be highly desired when safety is an issue or in a brawl, but much less desirable in a dispute between a retired couple.

Identification of all of the features of conflict relevant to this model is an overwhelming task. Hundreds of books and articles have been written attempting to characterize conflict (e.g., Wright, 1942; Lewin, 1948; Kerr, 1954; Bernard, 1957; Mack & Snyder, 1957; Schelling, 1960; Evan, 1965; Druckman, 1971; Deutsch, 1973; Thomas, 1976; Billig, 1976; Strauss, 1978). Although not all of the variables differentiating conflict are relevant to the study of procedure, many are. Moreover, this segment of a complete framework has not yet been a focus of this author's research in developing a procedural model. Therefore, this section only includes a subset of the dispute characteristics from the general conflict literature that appear promising in terms of potential applicability to the study of procedure. Presented in Table 5 is this list. For each dispute characteristic, Table 5 also lists a few references where interested readers can see a more detailed treatment of that characteristic. The large number of variables in Table 5 should be taken to reflect the richness of research questions in this area rather than as a signal of an endless, unnavigable research journey.

Table 5. Characteristics of Conflict Potentially Relevant, to a General Framework of Dispute Intervention Procedure

Conflict Characteristics	*Selected References[a]*
1. Topic of the Conflict	Thomas & Schmidt, 1976 Lissak & Sheppard, 1983
2. Issue importance	Deutsch, 1973 Rubin, 1980
3. Issue rigidity	Deutsch, 1973 Lester, Beckham & Baucom, 1980
4. Centrality of issues	Deutsch, 1973 Pondy, 1967
5. Number and interdependence of issues	Deutsch, 1963 Strauss, 1978
6. Disputant consciousness of issues	Kerr, 1954 Walton, 1969
7. Potential mutality of interest vs. conflict of interest.	Axelrod, 1970 Walton & McKersie, 1965
8. Relevance of law or generally held norm	Aram & Salipante, 1981 Evan, 1965
9. Clarity of relevant evidence	Fuller, 1971 Burton, 1968
10. Polycentricity: no one answer	Fuller, 1971 Burton, 1968
11. Equality of disputant position or power	Fuller, 1971 Fisher, 1972
12. Clarity of issue(s)	Filley, 1975 Weiss, 1975
13. History of conflict	Walton, 1969 Haley, 1976
14. Basis of conflict in value; issue interpretation or conflict of interest	Brehmer, 1976 Filley, 1975
15. Presence of time pressure	Druckman, 1971 Thibaut & Walker, 1975

Disputants Characteristics	
1. Relative power	Fisher, 1972 Strauss, 1978
2. Personality variables	Terhune, 1970 Rubin & Brown, 1975
3. Estimations of success	Deutsch, 1973 Leff, 1970

173

Table 5. (Continued)

Disputants Characteristics	Selected References[a]
4. Stability of both disputants	Deutsch, 1973
5. Consensus on issue(s) and issue(s) importance	Deutsch, 1973 Filley, 1975
6. Consciousness of issue(s)	Wall, 1981 Haley, 1978
7. Perceptions of other party(ies): legitimacy, cooperativeness and anticipated tactics	Deutsch, 1973 Kelley & Stahelski, 1970
8. Desire for intervention	Haley, 1976 Fisher, 1972
9. Present strategy	Druckman, 1971 Wall, 1981
10. Experience	Druckman, 1971 Strauss, 1978
11. Interdependence	Brown, 1983 Kahn et al., 1964
12. Nature of contact: frequency, customer-company, business (personal), etc.	March & Simon, 1958 Friedman, 1975
13. Emotionality	Walton, 1969 Weiss, 1975
14. Awareness of transaction costs	Leff, 1970 Fischer, 1972

Characteristics of Conflict Setting	
1. Nature of constituency relationship and demands	Walton & McKersie, 1965 Adams, 1976
2. Nature of broader system in which embedded	Thomas, 1976 Megginson & Gullet, 1970
3. Involvement of other parties	Haley, 1976 Usery, 1975
4. Existence of a precedent	Aram & Salipante, 1981 Fuller, 1971
5. Characteristics and non-procedural tactics of third party	Wall, 1981 Landsberger, 1955
6. Presence of procedures or norms regarding dispute settlement	Weiss, 1975 Thomas, 1976

[a] Most of these references have been taken from literature relevant to Organizational Behavior. However, references from other areas have been included when they discuss a conflict characteristic particularly well.

EVALUATING THE FRAMEWORK

A comprehensive framework to guide research and theory on the procedural aspects of conflict resolution was presented. This framework includes a procedural taxonomy intended to permit identification of intervention procedures in any conflict setting, a list of criteria useful for choosing or evaluating dispute intervention procedures, and a preliminary list of conflict characteristics potentially useful to procedural research. Earlier, four reasons were given indicating a need for such a framework. The following section evaluates the proposed framework in terms of its potential for satisfying these four concerns. To evaluate this framework, its efficacy in terms of each of the motivations for developing such a framework will be considered in turn. This evaluation will emphasize the taxonomy and criterial list, since the list of conflict characteristics is not fully developed.

Comprehensiveness

The explicit purpose for developing this framework was to produce a generic model of conflict intervention procedure, i.e., a model which comprehensively applied across the entire range of dispute settings. Because they are largely ignored in much of the conflict literature, the applicability of the framework to informal conflict intervention settings is of particular importance. Clearly, a proper test of comprehensiveness would require testing the applicability of the framework in many diverse conflict settings. Preliminary results from a few settings, however, are very encouraging. Eighteen of the twenty-one listed criteria clearly apply to informal conflict settings since they were initially derived from interviews about informal conflict interventions. In addition, the complete list of twenty-one criteria were all indicated to be generally important by a new sample of managers in a later study. Concerning their more general applicability, the brief review of the relationship of the criteria to the writing in the various conflict literatures reveals that each criterion appears to have been of concern in more than one conflict area.

Similarly, the taxonomy appears to be useful for describing procedures in quite varied settings. Most promising are the results of research testing the usefulness of the taxonomy for describing informal interventions. Two different techniques were utilized in the research, described above, investigating the applicability of the taxonomy to managerial conflict intervention. In the first, managers were asked to describe how they intervened in the last dispute they handled. Two coders trained by the author then separately classified audiotapes of these descriptions in terms of the taxonomy. Validity was assessed in terms of how reliably they coded these descriptions. In the second procedure third parties and disputants were shown the taxonomy and asked to describe how the last dispute in which they were involved was handled vis a vis the taxonomy. Interviewees were then asked to identify aspects of their intervention procedure *not* in the taxonomy. In both instances, the results are initially very promising. Coding can be done very reliably and so far there have been no additions to the present taxonomy. These two techniques have also been applied to police descriptions of crisis intervention and parental descriptions of interventions in sibling disputes with similarly promising results (Sheppard, Lesser, Li, & Mace, Note 3).

Clearly, other techniques for testing the comprehensive validity of this framework need to be applied with new samples of people and conflicts. However, the present results provide very convincing preliminary evidence of the potential for the framework to serve as a generic representation of conflict intervention procedure.

Explicitness

The second aim in developing this framework was to provide sufficiently explicit and specific constructs to permit a clear description of the procedure and aims utilized in any given situation or research study. Clearly, there is an important tradeoff between the level of generality versus specificity in any theoretical endeavor. In this particular instance both are important, although specificity may be particularly important, since much of the work on conflict intervention has been too general and ambiguous. To satisfy both purposes of specificity and generality, the elements of the framework were developed at two levels of generality. Thus, for example, using the taxonomy it is possible to generate broad encompassing procedural descriptions via a 4×4 matrix or more detailed descriptions by means of a 13×31 matrix. Similarly, the goals of intervention can be identified in terms of eight broad criteria or twenty-one more specific criteria. The appropriate level of generality depends upon the aims of the project. My advice however, would be to be as precise as is reasonable for a given project, in order to minimize the level of ambiguity for consumers of the research.

It is, of course, possible to further refine the types of intervention procedures and goals of intervention. However, one has to stop somewhere. The particular level of detail provided in this framework represents this author's opinion of a reasonable compromise between the two concerns of explicitness and generality. Many readers will likely disagree with the choice. The ultimate test of the wisdom of this choice however, does not lie in opinion, but in the usefulness of the framework to future researchers and practitioners.

Complementarity to Present Research Trends

The third aim for developing this framework was to assist or promote continued development of the recent healthy trends in the conflict intervention literature. One way to illustrate the utility of the framework for this purpose is to present one example of how the framework has assisted in expanding the author's own research in the direction of each of the trends mentioned earlier.

Innovation in Procedure. One of the recent trends in the conflict literature is the identification of new, potentially useful intervention procedures. The following study, recently completed by the author, does illustrate the potential of the framework for furthering this trend. In essence, the framework was used to identify a procedure that appears initially to combine some of the strengths of both the adversary and inquisitorial legal systems identified by Thibaut and Walker.

Recall that Thibaut and Walker (1975) indicated that the adversary (arbitration) procedure was clearly superior to the inquisitorial procedure, largely because the adversary procedure is perceived to be more fair than the inquisitorial procedure. However, the clear superiority of the adversary procedure becomes somewhat less clear if criteria other than those utilized by Thibaut and Walker are considered. For example, research reported in Sheppard and Vidmar (1980) suggests that the adversary procedure results in the presentation of biased testimony and enhanced conflict when contrasted with the inquisitorial procedure. The purpose of the study described here was to determine the possibility of developing a hybrid of the adversary and inquisitorial procedures that maintained most of the features of the inquisitorial procedure, but was modified so as to be fair. Since the study is not reported elsewhere, it will be described in some detail.

This study conceptually replicated a series of studies reported by Thibaut and Walker (1975). From their studies, Thibaut and Walker concluded that an inquisitorial legal procedure which allowed the judge control over the trial (discussion stage), as well as the decision resulting from the trial (decision stage), was perceived as less fair than an adversary legal procedure in which the judge only had decision control. Six hundred and twenty undergraduates were asked to read descriptions and indicate their perceptions of four possible trial procedures. In the first two procedures, the judge was provided total control over the trial proceedings

(inquisitorial and inquisitorial with court appointed investigator procedures represented by cell entries B and C in Figure 3). In the third procedure, the judge was to render a decision after passively listening to the
evidence and arguments of the disputants (adversary legal procedure represented by cell entries of A in Figure 3). The fourth procedure attempted
to identify a possible hybrid of the adversary and inquisitorial procedure
that maintained most of the features of an inquisitoral procedure but was
modified so as to be perceived as fair. In this procedure the disputants
first presented their own arguments, after which the judge was allowed
to ask his own questions of witnesses, the disputants, or their representatives (new hybrid procedure represented by cell entries of D in Figure
3). The distinction between the third and fourth procedures then, was that
in the fourth procedure the judge was provided total control over the
clarification and information presentation phases of the trial (discussion
stage).

Subjects' perceptions of these procedures are reported in Table 6. As
expected, there is support for Thibaut and Walker's contention that a
procedure providing total judicial control over the trial is perceived as
less fair than one which provides total disputant control. However, and
more importantly for this discussion, the fourth procedure was most preferred by the subjects in this research.

Clearly, such questionnaire research has important validity limitations.
However, the results are suggestive in two ways. First, to be perceived
as fair, procedures may have to permit disputants unencumbered presentation of their 'side', especially if the third party is deciding the disposition of the conflict. Second, and most importantly, the results illustrate the potential of this framework for facilitating efforts to identify new
and useful intervention procedures. Similar identification of new procedures should be possible in many conflict settings.

Facilitation of Comparative Research. The second trend noted in recent
research on conflict intervention is a modest movement toward comparison of procedures utilized across various dispute realms. The framework
presented in this chapter should provide an increased capacity for such
comparison. The managerial research discussed earlier provides an example of how the framework can help.

In a chapter summarizing this work (Sheppard, in press), I noted that
managers do not utilize the sorts of procedures that Organizational Behavior theorists generally indicate they ought to (e.g., Filley, 1975). Managers are not mediators or conciliators, but instead they often act very
much like judges. A quick comparison of Figure 2 with Figure 3 will
illustrate this point. This detection of similarity between the procedures
utilized in two previously unassociated conflict settings (management and

Form of Third
Party Control

Timing of Third Party Control		Process	Content	Request	Motiva-tional
	select resolution procedure	C	C	A B C D	A B C D
Definition	feel out parties	C	C		C
	what is in dispute?	C	C	A B D	A B C D
	what information exists?	C	C		C
	what are the alternatives?	C	C	A B D	A B C D
Discussion	present relevant information	B C D	B C D	A	A B C D
	present arguments	B C	B C	A D	A B C
	clarify information	B C D	B C D	A	A B C D
Alternative Selection	decide validity of arguments	A B C D	A B C D		A B C D
	select an alternative	A B C D	A B C D		A B C D
Reconciliation	reconcile parties				
	enforce decision	A B C D	A B C D	A B C D	A B C D
	hear appeals		A B C D	A B C D	A B C D

Note: All precedures were described in narrative form.

A — cell entries of A represent the adversary legal procedure as presented to subjects

B — cell entries of B represent the inquistorial legal procedure as presented to subjects

C — cell entries of C represent the inquisitorial procedure with court appointed investigator as presented to subjects

D — cell entries of D represent the new hybrid legal procedure as presented to subjects

Figure 3. Versions of Four Legal Procedures used in Procedural Fairness Study

179

Table 6. Subject Perceptions of Four Trial Procedures

Measure	Pure Inquisitorial	Inquisitorial with Investigator	Pure Adversary	Hybrid Procedure	Test of Significance
1. Number of Respondents Preferring to Participate in Procedure	26	62	111	422	X^2 (3 d.f.) = 634.6 p .001
2. Number Preferring in Own Country	18	55	116	429	X^2 (3 d.f.) = 632.0 p .0001
3. Perceived Fairness (1 = Not at All 9 = Extremely)	3.05	4.21	6.18	7.16	F (3, 2197) = 648.57 p .0001

the law) was possible through the description of procedures used in each one on terms of the same taxonomic framework.

Identification of certain forms of managerial intervention with legal interventions is useful for several reasons. First, writing on comparative law may suggest hypotheses concerning the relative strengths and weaknesses of two of the three managerial conflict intervention strategies portrayed in Figure 2. In other words, Procedure 1 will likely have similar strengths and weaknesses as the inquisitorial legal procedure and Procedure 3 strengths and weaknesses similar to the adversary legal procedure. Second, modifications made to legal procedures to minimize the impact of their respective weaknesses may be similarly useful for lessening the adverse effects of comparable managerial intervention procedures. Specific suggestions concerning the potential applicability of legal writing to managerial conflict are presented in Sheppard (in press).

Clearly, wanton borrowing from the law and other fields may be as harmful as ignoring the correspondence between conflict intervention in organizations and other settings. Also, analogues other than the law should also be attended to, if only because not all managers act in a manner similar to judges (see Figure 2-2 for example). However, if done judiciously, communication between dispute arenas utilizing the proposed framework should improve everyone's understanding.

Expansion of Criteria.   The third trend in recent research on conflict intervention is toward increasing the range of criteria utilized in the research. In one sense this framework cannot aid further expansion of considered criteria, since all of the criteria listed in Table 4 have been mentioned somewhere in the conflict literature. However, all of these criteria are new to at least some specific conflict arenas. Moreover, many of the criteria have been largely underconsidered in most research arenas. Examples of this last point are the criteria relating to procedural strengths and weaknesses, as opposed to outcome dimensions. Except for recent interest in perceived procedural fairness initiated by Thibaut and Walker (1975) and a more general interest in the efficiency of dispute intervention, criteria listed within the procedural category in Table 4 have been greatly ignored across conflict settings. Hence, the presence of a relatively comprehensive list, such as the one developed here, may induce a more even treatment of the various criteria, and identify previously unconsidered criteria for researchers in the various specific conflict arenas.

An example of this last point in my own research is a study now underway to investigate why managers choose the sorts of intervention procedures they do for intervening in organizational conflict. Table 4 has suggested a number of possible reasons for their choices, several of which are relatively new to the organizational conflict literature. Some possible reasons include concern for indirectly involved parties whose interests are best protected by a powerful third party and concern for consistency across similar conflicts. Consistency may be jeopardized if potentially idiosyncratic disputants maintain control over alternative selection.

In summary, three examples of how the framework has guided my own research in the direction of recent research trends were provided. Similar utilization of this framework is possible for a variety of settings and research questions.

Encouragement of Further Research and Theory Development

There are, of course, other useful avenues to pursue than those trends noted in present conflict intervention research. Consequently, the final aim of this framework is to encourage other expansions in the conflict intervention research. Several such expansions relevant to Organizational Behavior suggest themselves from this model and the earlier discussion.

Micro-analytic Research. One potentially useful expansion of this research would be toward a more detailed micro-analytic orientation. Presently, research evaluating intervention procedures has been generally restricted to comparing entire procedures against one another along some criterion or criteria. For example, adversary and inquisitorial legal procedures are compared in terms of perceived fairness, quantity and quality of evidence and the level of conflict elicited by the procedure (Thibaut & Walker, 1975; Sheppard & Vidmar, 1980). While this approach has some ecological validity, since real procedures are compared, there are associated difficulties. One apparent difficulty with this 'macro' approach is the inability to determine what exactly is causing the results of the research, since whole procedures are being compared to each other. For example, it would seem difficult to determine whether adversary procedures are perceived to be more fair because (a) disputants are permitted to identify their own evidence, (b) disputants search out information before the trial, (c) disputants argue their own case, (d) the judge or his/her representative does not investigate the case before it comes to court, (e) the judge does not actively direct the trial process (f) the judge can only intervene at the invitation of a disputant or for other reasons.

Instead, of this "macro" research approach, it should be possible within the framework to perform more controlled research. That is, the impact of the forms of intervention represented by each cell of the matrix in Figure 2 (or an expanded version of the matrix) can be evaluated aong the criteria identified in Table 4. This way we can better understand the focus of any effects found in our research, since only one specific aspect of a procedure is being studied at a time. One example of this sort of approach to ferreting out procedural nuances is provided in the study described earlier in which a hybrid of the two legal procedures was identified. Disputant control over argument presentation appears possibly to be the critical element in the perceived fairness of procedures in which the third party controls the decision stage of conflict resolution. Clearly, this more "micro" research approach has a complimentary flaw to that of the literature's "macro" approach, in that different combinations of these cells will probably interact in various ways to enhance, reduce or otherwise change the effect of each facet alone. However, these interactions cannot properly be identified until the effects of each cell alone are understood. In addition, many of these interactions will still occur at a level less complex than a whole procedure and thus are best studied at a 'micro-macro' level. Clearly, neither a pure micro nor a pure macro approach is proper for the field to take. However, the present focus is largely imbalanced in the direction of more macro approaches and this framework provides a means of redressing this imbalance.

Procedural Emphasis. A second expansion suggested by the earlier discussion is toward a greater concern for the qualities of procedures in conflict research. Procedural fairness, procedural satisfaction and procedural effectiveness appear to be just as important to participants in conflict, as outcome fairness, satisfaction and effectiveness. These procedural goals, therefore, deserve greater attention than they are receiving in the conflict literature. For example, procedural variables influencing the level of participant privacy or perceived fairness of the procedure have been ignored in organizational research.

Descriptive Research. Another research need that clearly surfaces in this chapter is that of greater descriptive research. We know very little about what parents, managers, the police, the clergy or neighbors do in conflict intervention, or why they do it. This descriptive information is an important first step in developing theory applicable to these settings or more elaborate hypothetico-deductive research. Apparently, many of our hunches about what is or what ought to be done in these settings are wrong. Like the King with no clothes, we may have taken our prescriptions for proper managerial conflict intervention into the public unaware of their deficiency. A clear description of the setting to which the prescriptive notions were being applied may have avoided the embarassing observation that there was no conciliation (organizational theorists preferred procedures) present in most real world interventions. As evidenced above, this framework appears to be useful for guiding the necessary descriptive research efforts.

Contingency Perspective. Finally, as Thomas (1982) suggests, the com-

plexities of conflict settings, interventions and goals demand a more sophisticated theoretical approach to conflict intervention. There is no one
best way. Those procedures that are likely to be timely and inexpensive
are probably not those procedures likely to protect individual rights or
reduce the likelihood of future similar conflicts. An effective intervention
in a brawl is likely to be less effective in a boardroom disagreement. The
framework presented in this chapter hopefully contains most of the necessary elements of a comprehensive contingency approach to conflict
intervention.

Two very good models to follow in pursuing a contingency orientation
are Brown (1982) and Glasl (1982), both of whom make important suggestions about the comparative effectiveness of various procedures in
different types of conflict. It is also necessary to incorporate the third
element of this framework (i.e., criteria) into such formulations, however,
for any contingency orientation to be complete.

In summary, the framework appears to show promise for fulfilling the
motivations for which it was developed. However, there are some limitations to framework in its present form. These limitations also deserve
mention.

Limitations to the Framework

Perhaps the most important limitation to the framework is the absence
of a simpler scheme for representing conflict variables relevant to the
study of procedure. The development of this sort of scheme has not been
the focus of the author's research to this point. However, management
of this extremely difficult problem is necessary before the framework is
complete.

Another limitation concerns the entries into the cells of the taxonomic
matrix. For the moment a single entry is made in any cell where the third
party exhibits or is permitted to exhibit a particular form of control in a
particular stage of conflict resolution. It is likely however, that this simple
identification process will prove inadequate and that some value indicating
the degree of control will be required to be entered in the appropriate
cells. Exactly how this is best done requires further attention.

The last aspect of the framework requiring further clarification regards
exactly what constitutes an intervention "segment" or "session". Earlier, it was suggested that a segment incorporated a complete attempt at
intervention. This definition was used because any temporal bounds are
artificial and because the underlying stage model requires this "start-to-
finish" conception of a segment. However, some people may suggest that
identifying a session defined in this manner, would be very difficult in

complex multiple issue interventions, such as in marriage separation or contract negotiations. Because of their complexity these types of intervention are difficult to describe precisely. However, according to this representation, the difficulty is not unlike a difficult algebra problem in which simple mathematical operations are combined in complex ways. There is some evidence that such complications may be less troublesome than they seem, however. When participants in complicated conflicts were asked to describe the intervention procedure used to resolve their conflict, this apparently complex task appeared relatively simple for them to do (Sheppard, Lesser, Li & Mace, Note 3). When they discussed more than one procedure, each procedure tended to relate to the treatment of very different issues.

SUMMARY AND CONCLUSION

In summary, a need for a framework for enhancing and elaborating the growth and present trends in research on conflict intervention procedure was identified. Such a framework requires three elements: a procedural taxonomy, a comprehensive list of the goals of intervention, and a list of the characteristics of conflict and conflict settings relevant to the study of procedure. Two of these three elements (i.e., a taxonomy and criterial list) were provided in some detail. A fairly thorough list of the features of conflict potentially important to the study of procedure was also developed. Preliminary evaluation suggests that the proposed framework shows promise for enhancing the growth of research on conflict intervention procedure. Some modifications and elaborations of the framework appear necessary, but that is true of any theory.

Ultimately the value of the framework developed in this chapter lies in the research and theory generated by it. Hopefully, the framework will prove valuable in this way, since the organizations and the world in which we live demand a better understanding of conflict and how to manage conflict than we presently have.

ACKNOWLEDGMENTS

This chapter was completed with the support of the Business Associates fund of the Fuqua School of Business. The author wishes to thank Martha Putallaz and Roy Lewicki for their comments on an earlier version of this manuscript, and Robin Lissak for his participation in part of the research. Finally, the intellectual debt owed to John Thibaut, Laurens Walker, and Neil Vidmar cannot be overemphasized.

NOTES

1. Vidmar, N. *The resolution of small claims disputes in pre-trial hearings*: *The dynamics of success and failure*. Paper presented at the annual Law and Society Association meeting, Toronto, Canada, 1982.
2. Sheppard, B. H. & Vidmar, N. *Resolution of disputes: Some research and its implications for the legal process*. Invited address for Social Sciences Research Council Law and Psychology Conference, Trinity College, Oxford, England, 1981.
3. Sheppard, B. H., Lesser, S., Li, C. & Mace, M. *Preliminary validation of a comprehensive framework of third party intervention procedures*. Unpublished manuscript, Duke University, 1982.
4. Sheppard, B. H. *Procedural aspects of police crisis intervention*. Paper presented at the Law and Society Association annual meeting, Toronto, Canada, 1982.
5. Sheppard, B. H., Lissak, R. & Palumbo, P. *Criteria for evaluating police crisis intervention*. Paper presented at the Academy of Criminal Justice Sciences annual meeting, Louisville, Kentucky, 1982.
6. Brett, J. M., Goldberg, S. B. & Ury, W. *Mediation and organizational development*: *Models for conflict management*. Unpublished manuscript, Northwestern University, 1982.

REFERENCES

Adams, J. S. Inequity in social exchange. In L. Berkowitz (Ed.) *Advances in experimental social psychology, 2*, New York: Academic Press, 1965.

Adams, J. S. The structure and dynamics of behavior in organizational boundary roles. In M. D. Dunnette (Ed.), *Handbook of Industrial Organizational Psychology*. Chicago: Rand McNally, 1976.

Anderson, J. C. The impact of arbitration: A methodological assessment. *Industrial Relations*, 1981, *20*, 129–148.

Aram, J. D. & Salipante, P. F., Jr. An evaluation of organizational due process in the resolution of employee/employer conflict. *Academy of Management Review*, 1981, *6*, 197–204.

Axelrod, R. *Conflict of Interest*. Chicago: Markham, 1970.

Bazerman, M. & Lewicki, R. J. *Bargaining Inside Organizations*. Beverly Hills, CA: Sage, in press.

Beer, M. The technology of organizational development. In M. D. Dunnette, *Handbook of Industrial Organizational Psychology*, Chicago: Rand McNally, 1976.

Bernard, J. Parties and issues in conflict. *Journal of Conflict Resolution*. 1957, *1*, 111–121.

Bigonness, W. J. The impact of initial bargaining position and alternative modes of third party intervention in resolving bargaining impasses. *Organizational Behavior and Human Performance*, 1976, *17*, 185–198.

Billig, M. *Social Psychology and Intergroup Relations*. New York: Academic Press, 1976.

Blake, R. R., Sheppard, H. A. & Mouton, J. S. *Managing Intergroup Conflict in Industry*. Ann Arbor: Foundation for Research on Human Behavior, 1964.

Bomers, G. B. J. & Peterson, R. B. *Conflict Management and Industrial Relations*. Boston: Kluwer, Nijhoff Publications, 1982.

Brehmer, B. Social judgement theory and the analysis of interpersonal conflict. *Psychological Bulletin*, 1976, *83*, 985–1003.

Brett, J. M. & Goldberg, S. B. Mediator-advisors: A new third-party role in dispute resolution. In M. H. Bazerman & R. J. Lewicki (Eds.), *Bargaining Inside Organizations*. Beverly Hills, CA: Sage, in press.

Bruner, J. S., Goodnow, J. J. & Austin, G. A. *A Study of Thinking.* New York: Wiley, 1956.

Burton, J. W. *Systems, States, Diplomacy and Rules.* Cambridge, MA: Cambridge University Press, 1968.

Chester, M. E., Crowfoot, J. E. & Bryant, B. I. Power training: An alternative path to conflict management. *Califormia Management Review*, 1978, *21*, 84–90.

Damaska, M. Structures of authority and comparative criminal procedure. *Yale Law Journal*, 1975, *83*, 483–544.

Davis, J. H. Group decision and social interaction: A theory of social decision schemes. *Psychological Review*, 1973, *80*, 97–125.

Davis, J. H., Bray, R. M. & Holt, R. W. The empirical study of social decision processes in juries. In J. Tapp and F. Levine, (Eds.), *Law, Justice and the Individual in Society: Psychological and Legal Issues.* New York: Holt Rinehart & Winston, 1977.

Deutsch, M. *The Resolution of Conflict.* New Haven: Yale University Press, 1973.

Doob, L. W. & Foltz, W. J. The Belfast workshop: An application of group techniques to a destructive conflict. *Journal of Conflict Resolution*, 1973, 17, 489–512.

Douglas, A. The peaceful settlement of industrial and intergroup disputes. *Journal of Conflict Resolution*, 1957, *1*, 69–81.

Druckman, D. The influence of the situation in interparty conflict. *Journal of Conflict Resolution*, 1971, *15*, 523–555.

D'Zurilla, T. J. & Goldfried, M. R. Problem solving and behavior modification. *Journal of Abnormal Psychology*, 1971, *78*, 107–126.

Erickson, B.; Holmes, J. G.; Frey, R.; Walker, L. & Thibaut, J. W. Functions of a third party in the resolution of conflict. *Journal of Personality and Social Psychology*, 1974, *30*, 2, 293–306.

Evan, W. Superior-subordinate conflict in research organizations. *Administrative Science Quarterly*, 1965, *10*, 52–64.

Ewing, D. W. What business thinks about employees rights. *Harvard Business Review* (September/October), 1977, 81–94.

Feuille, P. The selected costs and benefits of compulsory arbitration. *Industrial and Labor Relations Review*, 1979, *33*, 64–76.

Filley, A. C. *Interpersonal Conflict Resolution.* Glenview, IL: Scott, Foresman, 1975.

Fisher, R. J. Third party consultation: A method for the study and resolution of conflict. *Journal of Conflict Resolution*, 1972, *16*, 67–95.

Folger, R. Distributive and procedural justice: Combined impact of voice and improvement on experienced inequity. *Journal of Personality and Social Psychology*, 1977, *35*, 108–119.

Ford Foundation, *New Approaches to Conflict Resolution.* New York: Ford Foundation, 1978.

Friedland, M. L. *Cases and Materials on Criminal Law and Procedure,* Toronto: University of Toronto Press, 1970.

Friedman, L. M. *The legal system: A social science perspective.* New York: Russel Sage Foundation, 1975.

French, J. R. P. Jr. & Raven, B. The bases of social power. In D. Cartwright (Ed.), *Studies in social power.* Ann Arbor, MI: Institute for Social Research, 1959.

Fuller, L. L. Mediation—its forms and functions. *Southern California Law Review*, 1971, *44*, 305–339.

Gandz, J. Resolving conflict: A guide for the industrial relations manager. *Personnel*, 1979, Vol. 22–32.

Gottman, J. M. *Marital Interaction: Experimental Investigations.* New York: Academic Press, 1978.

Haley, J. *Problem solving therapy: New strategies for effective family therapy.* San Francisco: Jossey-Bass, 1976.

Hampton, D. R., Summer, C. E. & Webber, R. A. *Organizational behavior and the practice of management.* Glenview, IL: Scott Foresman, 1982.

Hellriegel, D., Slocum, J. W., Jr. & Woodman, R. W. *Organizational behavior.* St. Paul, MN: West Publishing, 1983.

Homans, G. C. *Social behavior: Its elementary forms.* New York: Harcourt, Brace, 1961.

Janis, I. L. & Mann, L. *Decision making: A psychological analysis of conflict, choice and commitment,* New York: The Free Press, 1977.

Kagel, S. & Kagel, J. Using two new arbitration techniques. *Monthly Labor Review,* 1975, *95,* 11–14.

Kahn, R. L., Wolfe, D. M., Quinn, R. P., Snock, J. D. & Rosental, R. *Organizational stress.* New York: Wiley, 1964.

Kaufman, I. R. The philosophy of effective judicial supervision over litigation. *Federal Rules Decisions,* 1962, *29.*

Kelley, H. H. & Stahelski, A. J. Social interaction basis of cooperator's and competitor's beliefs about others. *Journal of Personality and Social Psychology,* 1970, *16,* 66–91.

Kerr, C. Industrial conflict and its mediation. *American Journal of Sociology,* 1954, *60,* 230–245.

Kipnis, D., Schmidt, S. M. & Wilkinson, I. Intraorganizational influence tactics: Explorations in getting one's way. *Journal of Applied Psychology,* 1980, *65,* 440–452.

Knowles, W. H. Mediation and the psychology of small groups. *Labor Law Journal,* 1958, *9,* 780–792.

Kochan, T. A. Collective bargaining and organizational behavior research. In B. M. Staw and L. L. Cummings (Eds.), *Research in Organizational Behavior* (Vol. 2). Greenwich, CT: JAI Press, 1980.

Kochan, T. A. & Jick, T. The public sector mediation process: A theory and empirical investigation. *Journal of Conflict Resolution,* 1978, *22,* 209–237.

Kuhn, J. W. *Bargaining and grievance settlement.* New York: Columbia Press, 1962.

Landsberger, H. A. Interaction process analysis of the mediation of labor–management disputes. *Journal of Abnormal Social Psychology,* 1955, *51,* 522–558.

Lawrence, P. R. & Lorsch, J. W. *New directions for organizations.* Boston: Graduate School of Business Administration, Harvard University, 1967.

Lester, G. W., Beckham, E. & Baucom, D. H. Implementation of behavioral marital therapy. *Journal of Marital and Family Therapy,* 1980, *6,* 189–199.

Leventhal, G. S. Fairness in social relationships. In J. W. Thibaut, J. T. Spence & R. C. Carson (Eds.) *Contemporary topics in social psychology.* Morristown, NJ: General Learning Press, 1976.

Lewin, K. *Resolving social conflicts.* New York: Harper & Bros., 1948.

Lind, E. A., Kurtz, S., Musante, L., Walker, L. & Thibaut, J. W. Procedure and outcome effects on reactions to adjudicated resolution of conflicts of interest. *Journal of Personality and Social Psychology,* 1980, *39,* 643–653.

Lind, E. A., Thibaut, J. W. & Walker, L. Discovery and presentation of evidence in adversary and nonadversary proceedings. *Michigan Law Review,* 1973, *71,* 1129–1144.

Likert, R. & Likert, J. E. *New Ways of Managing Conflict.* New York: McGraw-Hill, 1976.

Lissak, R. I. & Sheppard, B. H. Beyond fairness: The criterion problem in research on conflict intervention. *Journal of Applied Social Psychology,* 1983, *13,* 45–65.

Litterer, J. A. Conflict in organizations: A re-examination. *Academy of Management Journal,* 1966, *9,* 178–186.

Mack, R. W. & Snyder, R. L. The analysis of social conflict: Toward an overview and synthesis. *Journal of Conflict Resolution,* 1957, *1,* 212–248.

March, J. G. & Simon, H. A. *Organizations.* New York: Wiley, 1958.

Marshall, J., Marquis, D. & Oskamp, S. Effects of kind of question and atmosphere of interrogative on accurateness and completeness of testimony. *Harvard Law Review,* 1971, *84,* 1620–1642.

Marx, K. *Capital.* London: J. M. Dent & Sons, 1938.

McGrath, J. A. Social psychological approach to the study of negotiation. In R. V. Bowers (Ed.), *Studies on Behavior in Organizations: A Research Symposium.* Athens, GA: University of Georgia Press, 1966.

Megginson, L. C. & Gullett, C. R. A predictive model of union–management conflict. *Personnel Journal,* 1970, *49,* 495–503.

Miller, G. & Rosen, N. Members' attitude toward the shop steward. *Industrial and Labor Relations Review,* 1957, *10,* 516–531.

Morley, I. E. & Stephenson, J. M. *The Social Psychology of Bargaining.* London: Allen & Unwin, 1977.

Nadler, D. A., Hackman, J. R. & Lawler, E. E. III *Managing organizational behavior.* Boston: Little, Brown and Company, 1979.

Peach, D. A. & Kuechle, D. *The Practice of Industrial Relations.* Toronto: McGraw-Hill, 1975.

Pondy, L. R. Organizational conflict: Concepts and models. *Administrative Sciences Quarterly,* 1967, *12,* 296–320.

Rahim, A. & Bonoma, T. V. Managing organizational conflict: A model for diagnosis and intervention. *Psychological Reports,* 1979, *44,* 1323–1344.

Robbins, S. P. *Managing Organizational Conflict: A Non-traditional Approach.* Englewood Cliffs, NJ: Prentice Hall, 1974.

Rubin, J. Z. Experimental research on third-party intervention in conflict: Toward some generalizations. *Psychological Bulletin,* 1980, *87,* 379–391.

Rubin, J. Z. & Brown, B. R. *The Social Psychology of Bargaining and Negotiation.* New York: Academic Press, 1975.

Schelling, T. C. *The Strategy of Conflict.* Cambridge, MA: Harvard University Press, 1960.

Schmidt, W. H. & Tannenbaum, R. Management of differences. *Harvard Business Review,* November–December, 1960, *38,* 107–115.

Scott, W. *The Management of Conflict.* Homewood, IL: Irwin, 1965.

Selznick, P. *Law, Society and Industrial Justice.* New York: Russell Sage, 1969.

Sheppard, B. H. Managers as inquisitors: Some lessons from the law. In M. Bazerman & R. J. Lewicki (Eds.), *Negotiation in Organizational Settings.* Beverly Hills, CA: Sage Publications, in press.

Sheppard, B. H. & Vidmar, N. Adversary pre-trial procedures and testimonial evidence: Effects of lawyer's role and machiavellianism. *Journal of Personality and Social Psychology,* 1980, *39,* 320–332.

Strauss, A. *Negotiations.* San Francisco: Josey Bass, 1978.

Terhune, K. W. The effects of personality in cooperation and conflict. In P. Swingle (Ed.), *The structure of conflict.* New York: Academic Press, 1970.

Thibaut, J. W. & Kelley, H. H. *The social psychology of groups.* New York: Wiley, 1959.

Thibaut, J. W. & Walker, L. *Procedural Justice: A Psychological Analysis.* New York: Wiley, 1975.

Thomas, K. Conflict and conflict management. In M. D. Dunnette, *Handbook of Industrial Organizational Psychology.* Chicago: Rand McNally, 1976.

Thomas K. Manager and mediator: A comparison of third-party roles based upon conflict management goals. In Bomers, G. B. J. & Peterson, R. B. (Eds.), *Conflict Management and Industrial Relations.* Boston: Kluwer, Nijhoff Publications, 1982.

Thomas K.; Jamieson, D. W. & Moore, R. K. Conflict and collaboration: Some concluding observations. *California Management Review,* 1978, *21,* 91–95.

Thomas, K. & Schmidt, W. H. A survey of managerial interests with respect to conflict. *Academy of Management Journal,* 1976, *19,* 315–318.

Tyler, T. R. & Caine, A. The influence of outcomes and procedures on satisfaction with formal leaders. *Journal of Personality and Social Psychology,* 1981, *41,* 642–655.

Usery, W. J. Some attempts to reduce arbitration costs. *Monthly Labor Review,* 1975, *95,* 3–6.

Vollmer, H. M. *Employee Rights and the Employment Relationship.* Berkeley, CA: The University of California Press, 1960.

Wall, J. A. & Schiller, L. The judge off the bench: A mediator in civil settlement negotiations. In M. H. Bazerman & R. J. Lewicki (Eds.), *Bargaining Inside Organizations.* Beverly Hills, CA: Sage, in press.

Wall, J. A. Mediation: An analysis, review and proposed research. *Journal of Conflict Resolution,* 1981, *25,* 157–180.

Wallace, M. J. Jr. & Szilagyi, A. D. Jr. *Managing behavior in organizations.* Glenview, IL: Scott Foresman, 1982.

Walton, R. E. *Interpersonal peacemaking: Confrontations and third party consultation.* Reading, MA: Addison–Wesley, 1969.

Walton, R. E. & McKersie, R. B. *A behavioral theory of labor negotiations: An analysis of a social interaction system.* New York: McGraw-Hill, 1965.

Weiss, R. L. Contracts, cognition and change: A behavioral approach to marriage therapy. *The Counseling Psychologist,* 1975, *5,* 15–26.

Wigmore, J. *The science of judicial proof.* Boston: Little Brown, 1937.

Wright, Q. *A study of war.* Chicago: Chicago University Press, 1942.

Young, O. *The intermediaries: Third parties in international crises.* Princeton, NJ: Princeton University Press, 1967.

Yukl, G. A. *Leadership in organizations.* Englewood Cliffs, NJ: Prentice Hall, 1981.

Zacker, J. & Bard, M. Effects of conflict management training on police performance. *Journal of Applied Psychology,* 1973, *58,* 202–208.

INFORMATION RICHNESS:
A NEW APPROACH TO MANAGERIAL
BEHAVIOR AND ORGANIZATION DESIGN

Richard L. Daft and Robert H. Lengel

ABSTRACT

This chapter introduces the concept of information richness, and proposes three models of information processing. The models describe (1) managerial information behavior, (2) organizational mechanisms for coping with equivocality from the environment, and (3) organizational mechanisms for internal coordination. Concepts developed by Weick (1979) and Galbraith (1973) are integrated into two information tasks: equivocality reduction and the processing of a sufficient amount of information. The premise of this chapter is that the accomplishment of these information tasks as well as the ultimate success of the organization are both related to the balance of information richness used in the organization.

Research in Organizational Behavior, vol. 6, pages 191–233
Copyright © 1984 by JAI Press Inc.
All rights of reproduction in any form reserved.
ISBN: 0-89232-351-5

Organizations face a dilemma. They must interpret the confusing, complicated swarm of external events that intrude upon the organization. Organizations must try to make sense of ill-defined, complex problems about which they have little or unclear information (Weick & Daft, 1982). Inside the organization, more confusion arises. Departments pull against each other to attain diverse goals and to serve unique constituencies and technologies (Lawrence and Lorsch, 1967). Divergent frames of reference, values, and goals generate disagreement, ambiguity and uncertainty. In response to the confusion arising from both the environment and internal differences, organizations must create an acceptable level of order and certainty. Managers must impose structure and clarity upon ambiguous events, and thereby provide direction, procedures, adequate coupling, clear data, and decision guidelines for participants. Organizations must confront uncertain, disorderly events from within and without, yet provide a clear, workable, well defined conceptual scheme for participants.

How do organizations perform this miracle? Through information processing. The design of organizations—even the very act of organizing—reflects ways to handle information (Galbraith, 1977; Weick, 1979). Managers spend the vast majority of their time exchanging information (Mintzberg, 1973). Specific dimensions of organization structure, such as functional or product organizational forms, and the use of teams, task forces or vertical information systems, all reflect information processing needs within organizations (Galbraith, 1973; Tushman & Nadler, 1978). Several papers have appeared in recent years which focus on information processing requirements as the explanation for observed organizational performance (Arrow, 1974; Porter & Roberts, 1976; Weick, 1979; Galbraith, 1977; Tushman & Nadler, 1978). Consider, for example, the following information processing activities.[1]

City Government.   Late in the afternoon of March 13, 1980, a killer tornado bore down on the town of Elkhart, Oklahoma. The tornado cut a swath three blocks wide through the center of town. Everything in its path was destroyed. Several people were killed and scores were injured.

The city administration had prepared for the emergency. Four years earlier, the city council authorized development of an emergency plan. Working with a consultant, city department heads developed specific procedures to follow in the event of tornado, flood, explosion, or noxious gas. The procedures were similar to procedures that had solved emergencies in other towns. A national guard armory had been turned over to the city. Medical supplies were stored in the armory, along with food, water, sanitary facilities, and beds for people left homeless. A communication center to coordinate police, firemen, and utility departments was in one room. Equipment necessary for a temporary morgue was in another room. Space and personnel were allocated for counseling bereaved family members or others in a state of psychological disorientation. The city fathers had thought of everything . . . almost.

The armory was in the path of the tornado. The armory was destroyed. Thirty minutes after the tornado struck, the Mayor realized a new plan would have to be developed from scratch. City councilmen, department heads and the firechief were all called to police headquarters. Individuals toured the community and reported back. The group stayed up all night listening to reports of damage, discussing needs, setting priorities, developing alternatives, and assigning tasks. The administrators were emotionally distraught but by morning the injured had been found and delivered to hospitals, the damaged areas were secure, and a plan for the next week's activities was in place. City officials, working together, carved an excellent plan of action from an unpredicted emergency. They received high marks from townspeople and visiting officials for their effective response to the crisis.

Business College.   A new dean was hired to run a large school of business in a major university in the Southeast. The dean initiated a plan to hold aside a portion of the salary increase money to be allocated on top of normal raises—called super raises—for the ten best producers in the college. The department heads met with the dean to recommend top performers from each department and to discuss their relative merits. The purpose of this meeting was to establish a common criterion of performance across departments and to select top performers.

The dean quickly realized that assignment of super raises was going to be difficult. Each professor's record was unique. How did publication in a finance journal compare to publication in a marketing journal? What was the contribution to knowledge of an article, and how was journal quality to be weighted? What was the role of teaching and student learning in the evaluation? The dean simplified the problem by asking department heads to summarize in a single page the record of each individual they recommended for a raise. Seventeen names were submitted with a one page summary of activities. From these the dean had to select ten. He found the decision impossible so he returned the sheets to the department heads and asked them to rate all 17 people on a ten point scale. Professors with the highest average scores received the super raises. In essence, the complexity of each professor's record was first condensed onto a single page, and then into a single number. Several faculty members complained that the best performance in the college had not been rewarded. The following year, the dean and department heads devoted an entire day to discussion and analysis of performance records. Debate was lengthy and heated. Agreement was finally reached, and the outcome was acceptable to faculty members.

Retail Chain.   Matthew B. was chief executive of a high fashion retail chain. The chain had 36 stores in 13 cities. Matthew B. hated formal reports. He preferred to discuss matters face-to-face and to reach decisions through consensus and discussion. Staying in touch required extensive travel. He visited stores to see what was selling and to get a feel for store design and layout. He had weekly breakfast meetings with top executives for discussion and planning. He also visited the company's plants and went to fashion shows to stay abreast of new trends.

Following a serious heart attack, Matthew B. retired and James N. became chief executive. He immediately acted on his belief in strong financial controls and precise analysis. He requested detailed reports and analyses for every decision. He relied on paper work and computer printouts for information. He cancelled the breakfast meetings and trips to plants, stores, and fashion centers. Personal contact with others was limited to occasional telephone calls and quarterly meetings. James N. argued that managing a corporation was like flying an airplane. Watch the dials to see if the plane deviates from its course, and then nudge it back with financial controls. Within two years, a palace revolt led by a coalition of board members and vice-presidents ousted him as chief executive. They claimed that the chief executive had gotten hopelessly out of touch with the fast moving fashion environment.

The situations above illustrate ways organizations translate unexpected or complex problems into simpler, workable solutions. For the city of Elkhart, the ad hoc structure seemed to work well. Unclear events were interpreted and a workable course of action was developed. In the business college, the lengthy discussion used to evaluate faculty performance achieved a better outcome than the use of written descriptions or quantitative ratings. A similar thing happened in the retail chain. Management by discussion led to a more satisfactory outcome than managing by formal reports and paperwork.

Purpose of This Chapter

The purpose of this chapter is to propose new theoretical models that explain how organizations cope with the environment, coordinate activities, and solve problems through information processing, as illustrated in the above examples. The concept of information richness is introduced to explain how organizations meet the need for information amount and to reduce equivocality. *The premise of this chapter is that organizational success is based on the organization's ability to process information of appropriate richness to reduce uncertainty and clarify ambiguity.* The concept of information richness is combined with other information concepts to provide an integrated view of the organization as an information processing system. The chapter is divided into four parts.

1. The concept of information richness is presented in the next section and is used to integrate concepts from the information literature.
2. A model of manager behavior is then proposed, based upon the congruence between information richness and information needs.
3. Next, a model of organizations as information processing systems is proposed. Organizations have two information problems to solve: that of interpreting the environment and that of coordinating diverse internal activities. Models based on information richness explain how organizations such as the Elkhart city government and the business school described above resolve both interpretation and coordination needs.
4. Finally, traditional organization concepts, such as bureaucracy, politics, and organic structure are reinterpreted to show how they are associated with richness of information processing. Suggestions for future research are also explored.

DEFINITION OF INFORMATION RICHNESS

Daft and Wiginton (1979) proposed that human languages differ in their ability to convey information. The concept of language was used in the broadest sense to encompass various ways to transmit ideas, emotions, and concepts. High variety languages are those in which symbol use is not restricted and the language can communicate a wide range of ideas. Examples include art, music, and painting, which are subjective in interpretation. Low variety languages have symbols that are restrictive in their use, and the languages communicate a narrower range of ideas. Low variety languages include mathematics and statistics, which convey exact, unequivocal meaning to users. Daft and Wiginton argued that high variety languages were appropriate for communicating about difficult, ephemeral, social phenomena. Low variety languages communicate effectively about well understood, unambiguous topics.

The notion of language variety seems plausible, but it doesn't explain information processing in organizations. Managers typically don't use art, poetry, or mathematics to communicate about organizational phenomena. The range of language used within organizations is typically limited to natural language and simple numbers.

Lengel (1983) proposed a continuum of information richness to explain information processing behavior in organizations. Richness is defined as the potential information–carrying capacity of data. If the communication of an item of data, such as a wink, provides substantial new understanding, it would be considered rich. If the datum provides little understanding, it would be low in richness.

Lengel (1983), building upon the work of Bodensteiner (1970), argued that the communication media used in organizations determines the richness of information processed. He proposed that communication media vary in the richness of information processed. Moreover, communication media were proposed to fit along a 5-step continuum, as in Figure 1. Communication media include face-to-face discussion, phone calls, letters, written documents and numeric documents. The face-to-face medium conveys the richest information while formal numeric documents convey the least rich information.

The explanation for the hierarchy of media richness is contained in Figure 2. Each medium differs in (1) feedback capability, (2) communication channels utilized, (3) source and (4) language (Bodensteiner, 1970; Holland, Stead, & Leibrock, 1976).

Face-to-face is the richest form of information processing because it provides immediate feedback. With feedback, understanding can be checked and interpretations corrected. The face-to-face medium also al-

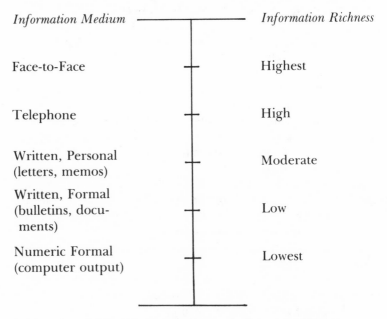

Figure 1. Communication Media and Information Richness.

Information Richness	Medium	Feedback	Channel	Source	Language
High	Face-to-Face	Immediate	Visual, Audio	Personal	Body, Natural
	Telephone	Fast	Audio	Personal	Natural
	Written, Personal	Slow	Limited Visual	Personal	Natural
	Written, Formal	Very Slow	Limited Visual	Impersonal	Natural
Low	Numeric, Formal	Very Slow	Limited Visual	Impersonal	Numeric

Figure 2. Characteristics of media that determine richness of information processed.

lows the simultaneous observation of multiple cues, including body language, facial expression and tone of voice, which convey information beyond the spoken message. Face-to-face information also is of a personal nature and utilizes natural language which is high in variety (Daft and Wiginton, 1979).

The telephone medium is somewhat less rich than face-to-face. Feedback capability is fast, but visual cues are not available. Individuals have to rely on language content and audio cues to reach understanding.

Written communications are less rich still. Feedback is slow. Only the information that is written down is conveyed so visual cues are limited to that which is on paper. Audio cues are absent, although natural language can be utilized. Addressed documents are of a personal nature and are somewhat richer than standard flyers and bulletins, which are anonymous and impersonal.

Formal numeric documents are lowest in information richness. An example would be quantitative reports from the computer. Numbers tend to be useful for communicating about simple, quantifiable aspects of organizations. Numbers do not have the information–carrying capacity of natural language. These reports provide no opportunity for visual observation, feedback, or personalization.

One value of the richness hierarchy in Figures 1 and 2 is that it organizes a diverse set of information concepts. For example, previous research has been concerned with information sources such as human versus documentary (Keegan, 1974), personal versus impersonal (Aguilar, 1967), and such things as files, formal reports, or group discussions (O'Reilly, 1982; Kefalas, 1975). The richness continuum makes sense of these differences, and may explain source utilization. Each medium is not just a source, but represents a difference in the act of information processing. Each medium utilizes differences in feedback, cues and language variety. Richness is a promising concept for understanding information behavior in organizations. In the next section, we show how information richness explains the information processing behavior of managers.

MODEL OF MANAGERIAL INFORMATION PROCESSING

Organizational phenomena confronting managers can vary from simple to complex. Simple phenomena tend to be mechanical, routine, predictable and well understood. Simple phenomena mean that managers typically can follow an objective, computational procedure to resolve problems. When phenomena are complex, however, no objective, computational procedure tells the manager how to respond. These issues are difficult, hard to analyze, perhaps emotion laden, and unpredictable. Managers have to spend time analyzing the situation and thinking about what to do. They will search for information and solutions outside normal procedures. Simple versus complex problems are similar to what Thompson (1967) called knowledge of cause-effect relationships and what Perrow (1967) called analyzability. Managers often experience difficulty seeing into complex tasks to analyze alternative courses of action, costs, benefits, and outcomes.

The proposed role of information media in managerial information processing is presented in the framework in Figure 3. Figure 3 illustrates that rich media are needed to process information about complex organizational topics. Media low in richness are suited to simple topics. The me-

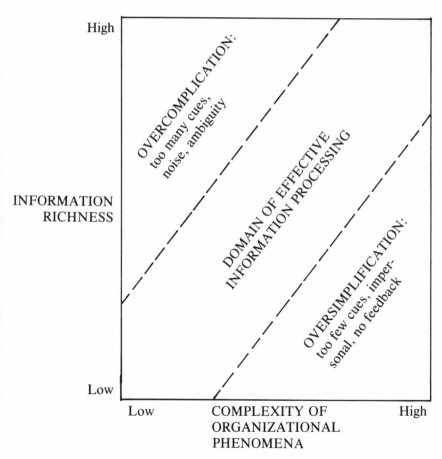

Figure 3. Model of managerial information processing.

chanical side of the organization is normally simple and measureable. Factors such as inventory control or employee attendance are not difficult to conceptualize. Managers can communicate about these phenomena through paperwork and quantitative reports. Other variables, such as organizational goals, strategies, managerial intentions or employee motivation, are intangible. These factors are not clear and discreet, and they can be difficult to interpret. Making sense of these factors requires a rich medium that provides multiple information cues, immediate feedback and a high variety language. Rich information enables managers to arrive at a more accurate interpretation in a short time.

The framework in Figure 3 hypothesizes a positive relationship between information richness and the complexity of organizational phenomena. Managers will turn to rich media when they deal with the difficult, changing, unpredictable human dimensions of organizations. Rich media enable them to communicate about and make sense of these processes. Face-to-face and telephone media enable managers to quickly update their mental maps of the organization. Rich media convey multiple cues and enable rapid feedback. Less rich media might oversimplify complex topics and may not enable the exchange of sufficient information to alter a manger's understanding. For routine problems, which are already understood, media of lower richness would provide sufficient information.

The Figure 3 framework is a significant departure from the assumption that precise, clear information is best for managers. Memos, reports and other written media can oversimplify complex problems. They do not provide a means to convey personal feelings or feedback. These media do not transmit the subtleties associated with the unpredictable, messy, emotional aspects of organizations. On the other hand, extensive face-to-face meetings for simple phenomena may also be inefficient. Face-to-face discussion sends a variety of cues, which may not always agree with one another. Facial expression may distract from spoken words. Multiple cues can distract the receiver's attention from the routine message.

This model, if correct, begins to explain why top managers make little use of formal information in organizations. Managers thrive on informal, personal communications (Mintzberg, 1973). The retail chain chief executives described earlier in this chapter illustrate the role of information media. The executive who used rich media such as store and plant visits, breakfast meetings and phone calls kept well informed on myriad environmental and company issues. The executive who relied on formal reports and financial data got behind and out of synchronization with events. Face-to-face and telephone media, with multiple cues and rapid feedback, are needed to help top managers deal with the complex issues confronting them.

Management scientists, operational researchers, and other staff specialists are frustrated when managers ignore formal reports, systematic studies, and standard procedures. The model in Figure 3 explains why. Those media only work for certain tasks. The reason managers often ignore these sources of information is not personal ignorance, lack of training, or personality defects. Informal, personal media simply are capable of providing richer information to managers about certain problems. Managerial behavior reflects an intuitive understanding of how to learn about things. Many management problems are difficult and complex; hence formal information is not rich enough to convey adequate insight and understanding. Personal sources are more insightful. Thus, managers' information processing behavior may make sense after all.

Research Evidence

Mintzberg's (1973) observation of top managers indicated that each manager is the nerve center for an information network. Managers have extensive contacts both within and outside the organization. They are plugged into channels for rumor and gossip, and are surrounded with formal information systems that provide periodic summaries and analyses of organizational activities. Managers spend over eighty percent of their time communicating. In this section we will review studies of information processing in organizations to determine whether previous research supports the Figure 3 relationship between media selection and problem complexity. This review is organized into three parts: (1) information sources, (2) mode of presentation, and (3) the use of management information systems.

Information Sources. Observations of managers indicate a strong preference for the verbal media. They prefer face-to-face meetings and the telephone. Mail and technical reports are used less frequently (Mintzberg, 1972, 1973). Managers prefer current information and move away from formal reports and quantitative documents.

The information sources observed by Mintzberg represent differences in media richness. Face-to-face and telephone are rich and enable managers to process information about intangible activities. Mail and formal reports are less rich, and usually pertain to well understood aspects of the organization. The majority of manager information is processed through rich media because organizations are often fast changing, and many of the manager's responsibilities pertain to the social, emotional and poorly understood aspects of organization. Our model is consistent with and explains manager behavior such as observed by Mintzberg (1973).

A study by Holland, Stead, and Leibrock (1976) comes closest to evaluating the Figure 3 model of manager information processing. They proposed that individuals working under high uncertainty would use richer media to transfer information than would individuals dealing with relative certainty. Holland, et al gathered questionnaire data from R&D units, and found that interpersonal channels of communication were important when perceived uncertainty was high. They also found a positive relationship between level of uncertainty and the reported usefulness of information sources. Holland, et al concluded that managers experiencing uncertainty should be encouraged to use rich sources of information, even if it meant making long distance telephone calls or traveling. High rich media enabled participants to learn about complex topics in a short time. Written information sources, such as the professional literature and technical manuals, were preferred when task assignments were well understood.

A study by Blandin and Brown (1977) looked at the search behavior of managers. They examined external, formal, and informal information sources and related these to environmental uncertainty. As the level of perceived uncertainty increased, managers relied more heavily on external and informal sources of information. The frequency and amount of time spent gathering information also increased. Thus, both the richness and amount of information increased with perceived uncertainty.

Although only a few studies have compared information source to topic complexity, the findings above do suggest that richer sources tend to be used when managers confront uncertain or complex topics. Less rich sources of information tend to be preferred when issues are well understood and routine. In general, the pattern of findings supports the positive relationship between media richness and task complexity proposed in the managerial information processing model.

Mode of Presentation.   Research into the mode of presentation typically presents data in two or more forms to learn how it is perceived and acted on. Nisbett and associates found that case illustrations have stronger impact on people's judgement than hard data (Borgada & Nisbett, 1977; McArthur, 1972, 1976; Nisbett & Ross, 1980). O'Reilly (1980) concluded that humans are more influenced by vivid, concrete examples than by dry statistics, even though statistics represent more systematic evidence from multiple observations. Other studies report that statistical data do have impact, but the case example gets more weight in decisions that appear to be objectively rational (Azien, 1977; Feldman, et al., 1976; Hansen and Donohue, 1977; Feldman & March, 1981; Manis et al., 1980). In a series of studies, Martin & Powers (1979, 1980a, 1980b) provided recipients with written statistical data and with a verbal story to assess which information swayed policy decisions. Stories tended to have more impact. They concluded that organizational reality is not objective, therefore statistical data pretends to report an objective reality which does not exist in the mental model of managers. Statistical data did tend to be influential when used to refute or overturn organizational policy. More precise evidence thus may be required to overturn a decision, while qualitative, story–based evidence is sufficient to support current policies.

Several studies show a strong preference for oral modes of information transfer. Mason and Mitroff (1973) argued that mode of presentation influences information preference. Landendorf (1970) found that interpersonal modes were preferred to written communication because interpersonal modes can be refined, adapted and evaluated to precisely fit the problem. Generally, oral information allows for rapid feedback and resolution of complex problems, and is often easier to gain access to. The importance of oral communication, especially face-to-face, is reflected in the impact of nonverbal signals. Eye contact, body movement, and facial expression communicate meaning beyond the verbal message. In one study of face-to-face communication, only seven percent of the content was transmitted by verbal language. The remaining ninety-three percent of information received was contained in the tone of voice and facial expression (Mehrabian, 1971). A sarcastic versus enthusiastic tone of voice conveys as much meaning as the specific statements processed between managers.

Management Information Systems.   Management information systems tend to be on the low end of the richness continuum presented in Figure 1. Most MIS's are formal and use quantitative or written reports.

Many studies designed to evaluate the usefulness of management information systems have attempted to operationalize economic value. Subjects purchase data and make simple decisions. These studies are not very helpful to understanding manager behavior because they employ naive assumptions about how managers use information. These studies are typically conducted in the laboratory, using sterile decision tasks and sterile information. The array of information cues typically available to managers are absent. The generality of these studies is extremely questionable (O'Reilly & Anderson, 1979).

Perhaps the most widely accepted conclusion is that computer-based management information systems are not very useful to managers. The efforts to implement and use these systems have fallen short of providing maximum effectiveness and efficiency (Ackoff, 1976; Deardin, 1972; Larson, 1974; Grayson, 1973; Leavitt, 1975). A number of factors have been cited to explain MIS failures. Management information systems provide data about stable, recurring, predictable events. MIS's provide data that skim over the nonquantifiable detail needed by managers. Management information systems supply quantifiable data. These data do not provide insight into the intangible, social dimensions of an organization.

Brown (1966) noted that information needs may depend upon level of decision. At the operational level in organizations, where decisions pertain to routine technical problems, decision support systems may have greater value. Several other studies support the conclusion that management information systems are most relevant to those managers who work with well defined operational and technical decisions (Dearden, 1972; Dickson, Senn, Cheway, 1977).

A survey of fifty-six organizations in England by Higgins and Finn (1977) examined attitudes toward management information systems. While computer reports could be useful, they found intuitive judgement was used more often than computer analysis in management's strategic decisions. Executives typically drew on a variety of sources of information, weighing each for importance, and then making a final decision. Computer based data could play a role in these decisions, but a small one.

The small role of management information systems is not completely understood, but the primary reason seems to be that they do not convey information that meets managers' needs. MIS's work under the assumption that managers need large amounts of precise data. As managers receive more and more data, they should be able to solve their problems, which is not the case (Ackoff, 1967).

Tushman and Nadler (1977) believe that information designers are more concerned with fitting data to their hardward than with understanding the overall information needs of managers. Information system designers lack a theory about manager needs and behavior. By limiting data to those things amenable to machine hardware, information designers miss the root causes of manager information processing. Most managerial tasks are too ill-defined for quantitative data, yet system designers assume that computer output is sufficient for management decisions. MIS systems are able to capture and communicate about the stable, predictable activities, but not about the important, subjective, ill-defined events relevant to decision making.

Summary.   The pattern of findings about managerial information processing tends to support the notion that information richness is a useful explanation for information behavior. Only a few studies have examined managers' utilization of various media, or have related media to specific tasks (Lengel, 1983). Available findings suggest that managerial behavior does reflect media choice based upon the uncertainty or complexity of management problems. When managers work in a highly uncertain context, they rely more heavily on rich media. These media provide a variety of information cues and immediate feedback to interpret and understand the situation. Managerial jobs are fast paced and fragmented, hence they often need to learn about a fuzzy situation quickly. Rich media serve this purpose.

Media of low richness, including formal information systems, seem best suited to well understood management issues. These media are used more often at the bottom of the organization and for problems that are considered objective and quantifiable. The evidence from the literature generally supports the theoretical model of managerial information processing presented in Figure 3. Managers use all media within the organization, and probably should be skilled with each one. Managers move toward rich media for information about difficult problems. They prefer rich media because it meets the information needs associated with the manager's job.

MODELS OF ORGANIZATIONAL INFORMATION PROCESSING

In this section we shift levels of analysis from the individual manager to the organization as a whole. Within organization theory, two theoretical perspectives have had significant impact on the conceptualization of information processing within organizations. These models pertain to what we call the vertical and horizontal information processing needs of organizations.

Two Perspectives

Vertical. The first theoretical view was developed by Karl Weick (1979). Weick focused on the concept of information equivocality. When managers observe or learn about an external event, the information cue is often ambiguous. Managers are unclear about what the event means or how to translate it into organizational action. Weick proposed that organizations are designed to reduce equivocality from the environment. Organizing is the construction of a consensually validated grammar for reducing equivocality (Weick, 1979, p. 3). This means that when managers are confronted with equivocal cues, they must discuss the issue among themselves and gradually arrive at a common interpretation and frame of reference. The equivocality is reduced to an acceptable level, and the common interpretation is then used within the organization and becomes the basis for future action.

Weick's notion of equivocality is intriguing because it demonstrates that organizations must do more than process large amounts of information. Organizational environments can be confusing, impenetrable, and changing. Organizations cannot tolerate too much ambiguity and must cope with equivocal cues in a way that reduces equivocality to an acceptable level so the organization can take action and get things done. The equivocal stimulus triggers information processing within the organization that leads to greater certainty and clarity for participants. Organizations, then, must interpret ambiguous stimuli and reduce them to sufficient clarity for action within the organization. Weick identified this as an important problem that organizing must solve. By processing equivocal information into an agreed upon interpretation, participants can decide what to do. The organization can be reasonably clear about what it is doing and where it is heading.

Horizontal.   The other view of information processing was developed by Jay Galbraith (1972; 1973). Galbraith proposed that as the level of uncertainty for managers increased, the amount of information processed should increase to reduce uncertainty. Galbraith argued that the uncertainty confronting an organization was influenced by factors such as diversity, task variability, and interdependence. Diverse products or goals means the organization must process a large amount of information to operationalize and monitor a number of activities. When task variability is high, managers confront unexpected events, so they must process additional information to learn about these events and thereby reduce uncertainty. Interdependence refers to the connectedness of departments. When the activities of one department influence other departments, information must be processed between them to provide the coordination needed for high performance.

The insight provided by Galbraith is that the amount of information processed within the organization explains why certain organizational forms are effective. By diagnosing points of uncertainty confronting the organization, a structure can be implemented that encourages appropriate information exchanges. When interdependence between departments is high, mechanisms can be designed to pass information between those departments. Likewise, when task variability is high, a structural design can be adopted to enable managers to acquire information in response to unexpected events. The selection of an overall structural form, such as product, function, or matrix, reflects the information processing needs of the organization. Each form directs the flow of information within the organization toward the points needed for effective performance. Galbraith provided a framework that explains the amount of information needed within an organization for effective performance. He also described how organizational design provides the correct amount of information where it is needed throughout the organization.

Interpretation vs. Coordination

Weick's theory of equivocality reduction pertains to the interpretation needs of organizations, which is the vertical dimension of information processing. Organizations interpret an ill-defined environment and define with some certainty a course of action for participants. Top managers are involved in the interpretation process. They read cues and then define goals, products, structure, strategy and technology. The vertical dimension of organizational information processing is top down. Upper level managers reduce equivocality to a level acceptable to others within the organization.

Galbraith's discussion of information amount pertains to information for internal coordination, the horizontal dimension of information processing. Horizontal information processing occurs within organizations to coordinate and execute organizational activities. Information is processed as needed for the organization to perform as a coordinated whole. Environmental interpretation is not the concern of people in the core of the organization. These people process large amounts of information when tasks are variable and activities are interdependent.

Figure 4 illustrates the two types of information requirements facing organizations. Organizations must both interpret the environment and coordinate tasks internally. As we will see, these two information needs are resolved in organizations through the use of rich information.

Information Tasks. Within the organization as a whole, a range of tasks are performed. Organizations use a technology to produce goods or services, and organizations work within an environment that is more or less uncertain. Organizational activities—in the broadest sense—impose specific information processing requirements associated with organizational technology, environment, and interdependencies (Poole, 1978). One information task is to reduce equivocality to the point where participants establish a shared view of events. The other task is to process sufficient amounts of information to enable internal coordination and task performance. These two information tasks represent the vertical and horizontal dimensions in Figure 4.

The importance of these two information processing tasks for human organizations can be seen in the comparison to other types of systems that also use information. Boulding (1956) proposed a hierarchy of system complexity that ranged from simple frameworks through control systems, cells, plants, animals, human beings and on to social systems (Pondy & Mitroff, 1979; Daft & Wiginton, 1979). Social systems are the most complex systems in the hierarchy. Figure 5 shows an abbreviated hierarchy of system complexity with 4 levels.

For machine systems at level one, the two information tasks are easy to resolve. Physical systems are usually closed off from the external environment, so little interpretation is necessary. Most knowledge required for performance is built into the physical structure of the system. In a machine system (e.g., clock, assembly line) internal elements are coor-

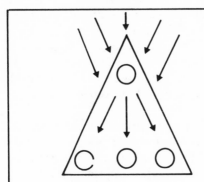

A. Vertical Information Processing: Purpose is to interpret the environment and reduce equivocality.

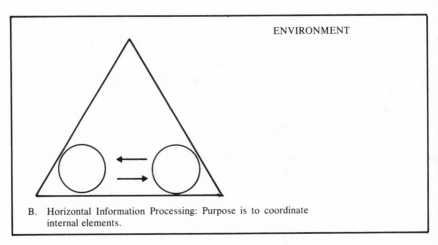

B. Horizontal Information Processing: Purpose is to coordinate internal elements.

Figure 4. Vertical and horizontal information processing in organizations.

dinated through physical linkages. In the case of the solar system, elements are linked by gravity, so that information processing is not required. For control type systems (e.g., thermostat), simple coordination data may be transmitted in response to predefined environmental stimuli (e.g. temperature). But this data is unequivocal and is processed in relatively small amounts compared to higher level systems.

Biological systems (level 2) require a greater amount of information processing than do physical systems. Biological organisms are differen-

System Type		INFORMATION TASK	
		Amount Processed	Equivocality Reduction
Social System	Interpretation:	High	High
	Coordination:	High	High
Human Being	Interpretation:	High	High
	Coordination:	High	Low
Biological System	Interpretation:	Mod	Low
	Coordination:	Mod	Low
Machine System	Interpretation:	Low	Low
	Coordination:	Low	Low

Complex ↑ ... Simple (left margin labels)

Figure 5. System complexity and information tasks.

tiated, so data must be communicated among cells, organs and life sustaining subsystems. For an advanced specie, a large amount of data would have to be processed on a continuous basis to enable physically differentiated subsystems to function congruently. Biological organisms also are open systems, so senses are used to interpret the environment. For the most part, however, environmental interpretation is unequivocal. Flowers sense and respond in a predictable way to sunlight. Birds and insects respond in an almost programmed way to environmental changes in weather, seasons, temperature, or location.

The internal information task for the human being (level 3) is similar to biological organisms at level 2. The human being is highly differentiated, so large amounts of data are transmitted among internal systems, although these data are typically unequivocal. Interpretation of the environment, however, is equivocal. In only a few instances, such as putting one's hand on a stove, is the stimulus unequivocal and the response predictable. The majority of stimuli contain ambiguity. The external environment is alive with sounds, observed behavior, music, language, and symbols of all types. Most of these phenomena have multiple interpretations. Knowledge on any single topic is incomplete. People act on scraps of information and form these scraps into coherent wholes (Weick & Daft, 1982). The ability to process and interpret equivocal stimuli from the environment is what distinguishes human beings from lower level systems.

The most complex system of all is the human social system (level 4). The human being is the building block of the social system. The information problem of interpreting the environment is similar to interpretation by individual human beings. Upper-level managers must respond to an uncertain, ill-defined environment, and define with some certainty a course of action for others within the organization.

Human organizations must also process information internally. Internal information must coordinate diverse activities as discussed by Galbraith, which may require enormous amounts of data, especially when the task is uncertain and the organization is complex. Internal coordination in a social system is also equivocal, a point not incorporated in Galbraith's framework. Organizational specialization and differentiation lead to autonomy among subgroups. Group participants have divergent frames of reference. They attend to their own tasks, use common jargon, and pursue group level goals. Information transmitted across departments often is not clear or easily understood. Ambiguities arise, especially when differences among departments is great. Disagreements will occur.

We propose in Figure 5 that critical information tasks in organizations are to meet the need for a large amount of information and to reduce equivocality. The need to process equivocal information both within the organization and from the environment is what distinguishes social systems from lower level systems. Unlike machine or biological systems, internal data can be fuzzy and ill-defined. Diverse goals and frames of reference influence information processing. The organization must be designed to reduce equivocality both from within and without. A model of organizational information processing that treats organizations as higher level social systems should explain the reduction of equivocality as well as the correct information amount. Concepts and models of organization design based on information richness that explain these two information tasks are developed in the remainder of this chapter.

VERTICAL INFORMATION MODEL

Hierarchical Level. The information task of reducing equivocality is a function of hierarchical level. At the top of the organization, the manager's world is subjective. Problems are fuzzy, complex, and poorly understood. Top managers shape reality for the rest of the organization. They decide goals and strategy, and influence internal culture (Pfeffer, 1981). Top managers create and maintain a shared belief andd interpretation system among themselves. They have few objective facts. They must confront uncertainty, make sense of it, and attempt to communicate order and meaning to the lower levels of the organization. Managers use symbols, metaphors, speeches, body language, and other forms of rich information to communicate values, goals and culture throughout the organization.

At lower organization levels, the need to reduce equivocality is minimal. The information task is objective. Employees and first-line supervisors can make use of policies, rules and regulations, formal authority, and the physical requirements of technology to govern their activities. The employees at lower levels work within the defined plans, goals, and technology of the organization. Interpretation is less equivocal. Information can be processed through less rich media and still convey relevant task information.

The equivocal information task along the hierarchy corresponds roughly to media usage, as illustrated in Figure 6. High rich media, such as face-to-face and telephone will dominate at the top management level. Issues here are complex and ill-defined, such as the relationship between the institution and the environment. Middle management works within a somewhat more well defined structure. High rich media will still be used, but paperwork, documentation and other forms of less rich data will also be processed. The lower levels are more objective. People within the technical core, for example, will make frequent use of numeric and written reports. To some extent, all media will be used at each level. But rich media will play a more prominent role in the interpretation of the environment and reduction of equivocality at the top level, while less rich media will play a more important role for lower level employees.

Richness Reduction. The information media used at each level is not random, but reflects the underlying process of organizing. Organizations must reduce subjectivity and equivocality (Weick, 1979). Organizations move from high rich media at the interface with the environment to low rich media within the technical core. Top managers use rich media to

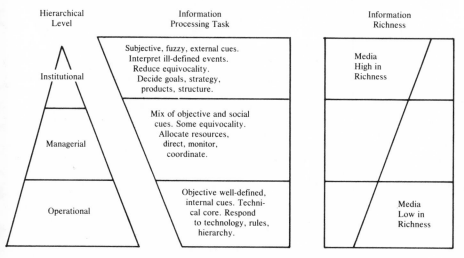

Figure 6. Hierarchical level and information richness.

discuss, analyze and interpret the external environment, and to develop goals and strategies. These interpretations can be translated into less rich policies, paperwork, rules and procedures for use at middle and lower organization levels. *Organizations reduce equivocality through the use of sequentially less rich media down through the hierarchy.* Reducing media richness is one way organizations reduce equivocality. Employees within the organization are thereby given a sense of specific roles, tasks, and purpose and are able to perform efficiently without having to interpret and define messy external issues. When organizations adapt to external changes, or when top managers develop new interpretations, the results work their way down through the organization in the form of new technologies, products, procedures, and reports.

The dynamic of richness reduction is illustrated in Figure 7. Media high in richness are used by top managers to cope with equivocal information processing tasks. Media low in richness are appropriate for the technical core. The diagonal in Figure 7 represents the extent to which the organizational context is objective or subjective. As top managers interpret the

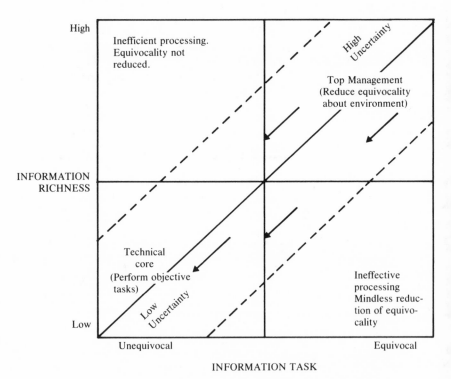

Figure 7. Process of equivocality reduction in organizations.

subjective environment and come to common definitions through the use of face-to-face discussions, they are able to reduce equivocality and provide greater objectivity for lower levels. Richness and equivocality are simultaneously reduced. Information processing inside the organization contains less equivocality and information tasks require less rich media.

The information processing that took place after the tornado in Elkhart, Oklahoma is a perfect example of the richness reduction process in Figure 7. City administrators were hit with an unexpected event that created a highly equivocal information task. They used rich media—continuous fact-to-face discussion and personal observation—to interpret and define the environmental situation. As they began to understand and reach a common definition of the situation, administrators provided a more well defined course of action for volunteers who were assigned objective tasks as the act of organizing progressed. As Weick argued, uncertainty triggers the act of organizing. People cluster around the equivocal event and pool ideas and perceptions. This information should be processed through media of high richness until equivocality is reduced to an acceptable level so that less rich media can be used to communicate specific goals and tasks.

Information processing which takes place outside the diagonal in Figure 7 will not serve the organization well. In those cases where the organizations use rich media to resolve unequivocal issues, the organizing process will be inefficient. Face-to-face discussions to process routine and well-understood events will confound rather than clarify. Participants will feel uninvolved because the equivocality that triggers discussion is not present. Face-to-face meetings will not serve a purpose or help resolve problems. On the other hand, when the organization inadvertently uses media low in richness to process equivocal information, the organization's interpretation will be ineffective. This would be the case when equivocal events are arbitrarily quantified and fed into computers for reports to top management. The equivocality reduction will not reflect the consensus among management, and will not be the outcome of diverse perspectives forged into a common grammar. This is analogous to what happened in the business school example at the beginning of this chapter. A number was assigned to the complex research record of professors. The numbers were assigned prematurely because department heads had not developed a common perspective and evaluation criteria thorough discussion. The richness reduction process was short circuited, and the resulting information was inaccurate.

The implication for organization design is that information media should fit the vertical information task. Environments change. They can be hard to analyze. Organizations should stay open to the environment. They do that by using rich media at the top. Senior managers should maintain personal contacts in key external domains and use personal observation. Within the organization, top management should undertake informal discussions on unclear events. Executives can pool perspectives and build a common interpretation that will guide organizational activities.

As shared interpretations develop, the outcomes can be transmitted downward through less rich media. This creates certainty for lower level participants. Top management absorbs uncertainty through rich media, thereby enabling other employees to concentrate on production efficiency. To have everyone involved in equivocality reduction would be inefficient. Likewise, reliance on paper media by top management would close off the organization from the environment. Media of low richness do not transmit adequate cues to interpret the environment and do not permit managers to establish a common view and grammar.

HORIZONTAL INFORMATION MODEL

Galbraith's (1973, 1977) model of organization design specified structural devices to handle internal information processing. Computers, assistants-to, and information systems can be used to process data within organizations. Galbraith also specified structural devices for horizontal communications, including direct contact among managers, liaison roles, teams, task forces, and full time integraters. Any of these devices might be implemented depending upon amount of information needed within the organization.

We propose that one horizontal information task within organizations is to reduce equivocality, which Galbraith's model did not incorporate. A department in an organization is a system within a system. Each department develops its own functional specialization, time horizon, goals, (Lawrence & Lorsch, 1967), language, and frame of reference. Bridging wide differences across departments is a complex and equivocal problem. The perspectives of marketing and R&D departments, for example, are more divergent than between industrial engineering and mechanical engineering. Coordination devices in the organization must not only match requirements for information amount, but must enable managers to overcome differences in values, goals, and frames of reference.

Information processing between departments has two purposes: reducing equivocality and providing a sufficient amount of information for task performance. Equivocality reduction is required by different frames of reference, which is similar to what Lawrence and Lorsch (1967) called differentiation. The amount of information needed between departments is determined by interdependence. The greater the interdependence between departments, the greater the coordination required. When frames of reference differ, coordination activities also involve equivocality reduction.

Rich information is needed when information is processed to overcome different frames of reference across departments. Managers must meet face-to-face, discuss their assumptions, goals, and needs, and develop a common language and framework with which to solve problems. In the initial stages of a new product, managers from research, marketing, and production would have to resolve their differences and reach agreement through task forces or committee meetings. Once these differences are resolved, less rich media can satisfy information requirements. Progress toward a common goal could be plotted on a pert chart, or data could be communicated with reports or other documents.

The decision process in the business college to give super raises across departments was an example of diverse frames of references. Each department had a different view on research quality. Rich media were needed to resolve these differences and achieve a common perspective for allocating raises. When the business college used face-to-face discussion to achieve a common grammer and perspective, the decision outcome was satisfactory to participants. However, when department heads used media low in richness (written description, numeric ratings) to resolve differences and make recommendations, coordination was not successful. Differences across departments were not integrated into a common grammar. Equivocality had not been resolved to the point where less rich media could be used. Only after a common perspective is established will paperwork and numerical ratings be accurate.

Interdependence determines the amount of information that must be processed between departments. As information amount increases, devices will be utilized that enable large amounts of data to be transmitted. An occasional telephone discussion between managers may be sufficient in the case of low interdependence. A daily meeting of a task force may be required when interdependence is great.

The ideas for horizontal information processing are summarized in Figure 8. Two problems must be faced—frames of reference and interdependence. The need to reduce equivocality is caused by divergent frames of reference that require rich media to resolve. Once a common language and perspective have been established between departments, less rich media such as memos, paperwork, and reports can be used for coordination. As the interdependence between departments increases, devices must be in place to allow sufficient volume of information to be processed, otherwise organizational performance may suffer.

Devices such as full time integraters, integrating departments, and the matrix organization provide both rich media and large amounts of information (cell 2). These structural devices are required when organizational

	INTERDEPENDENCE BETWEEN DEPARTMENTS	
	Low	**High**
High DIFFERENCE BETWEEN DEPARTMENTS (frames of reference)	*1. High Difference, Low Interdependence* a. Media high in richness to reduce equivocality. b. Small amount of information. *Examples*: Occasional face-to-face or telephone meetings, personal memos, planning.	*2. High Difference, High Interdependence* a. Media high in richness to reduce equivocality. b. Large amount of information to handle interdependence. *Examples*: Full time integrators, task force, project team.
Low	*3. Low Difference, Low Interdependence* a. Media low in richnes. b. Small amount of information. *Examples*: Rules, standard operating procedures.	*4. Low Difference, High Interdependence* a. Media low in richness. b. Large amount of information to handle interdependence. *Examples*: Plans, reports, update data bases, MIS's, clerical help, pert charts, budgets.

Figure 8. Relationship between interdepartmental characteristics and coordination devices.

216

departments are highly interdependent, yet highly specialized with distinct technologies and frames of reference. When interdependence is high but differences are small (cell 4), information can be processed with less rich media. Written reports, data bases, formal information systems, letters and memos will provide sufficient information for coordination. Clerical staff could be used to process more information through the paperwork system of the organization.

In the case of divergent frames of reference and low interdependence (cell 1), direct contact between departments can be used as needed. Face-to-face meetings would resolve differences, but would only be needed occasionally. Only a small amount of time and data would be processed in this situation. Finally, when differences and interdependence are both low (cell 3), coordination is a minor problem. Standing rules and procedures will be sufficient to accommodate any differences and information needs that exist.

The implication for organization design is that horizontal coordination devices should accommodate the dual needs of equivocality reduction and information amount. Different departmental frames of reference increase equivocality, hence the organization should design devices to process rich information and reduce equivocality in order to facilitate coordination. High interdependence between departments requires a large amount of information, so devices should be designed for sufficient volume of information to facilitate coordination. An organization design that achieves the correct amount of both equivocality reduction and information amount between departments will experience effective coordination, and hence high performance.

RESEARCH EVIDENCE ON VERTICAL AND HORIZONTAL INFORMATION MODELS

In this section we will briefly review research evidence on information processing by organizations. Research pertaining to interpretation of the environment (vertical model) is considered first, then evidence concerning internal coordination (horizontal model) will be discussed.

Vertical Model

One surprise in the literature on interpretation of the environment is that so few studies have been reported. Virtually all writers agree that organizations are open systems that must monitor the external environment. Yet studies of this process are notably sparse (Pfeffer & Salancik, 1978). The specific evidence sought for this section is whether organizations use rich media to interpret the environment, and whether interpretations are then translated through less rich media to provide greater certainty at lower organization levels. The task of equivocality reduction is expected to diminish at lower hierarchical levels.

Hierarchical Level.   Parsons (1960) proposed three levels of decision making in the organizational hierarchy: institutional, managerial and operational. These three levels were illustrated in Figure 6. The institutional level is the top of the organization, where the primary task is to set broad goals, and to decide the organization's products, technology, policy, strategy, and relationship with the external environment. The managerial level is the middle level in the organization. The requirement here is to plan and direct the activities of the organization and coordinate tasks laterally. This level is concerned with day-to-day management of organizational affairs. The technical level is at the bottom of the organizational hierarchy. At this level the operational work of the organization is accomplished.

Preliminary evidence indicates that the problems confronting the organization differ by level. Brightman (1978) argued that problems differ in uncertainty, complexity, and political nature. Problems at the top tend to be less programmed than decisions at the bottom. Stimuli at the top are less well structured (Leifer, 1979; Brightman, 1978). While there may be a few routine elements, managers at the top have to deal with economic, legal, political, and social factors that are hard to analyze and define. They also must anticipate the impact of these factors on the organization and consider possible responses. Problems within the organization, although they are sometimes ill-structured, generally reflect a greater proportion of routine and well understood stimuli (Leifer, 1979).

Is the difference in organizational levels associated with information richness? Leifer (1979) argued that inputs at the top of the organization tend to be informational while inputs used at the lower levels are data. Data tend to be more quantitative, objective, and less rich than the personal, subjective information used by top managers. Kefalas and Schoderbeck (1973) found that upper level executives spent more time gathering information about the environment than those at the lower levels. Gorry and Scott (1971) also proposed that information characteristics at the upper level tend to be broad and less accurate. These data are richer than the detailed, well defined, narrow data used at lower levels. Finally, the literature on management information systems reviewed earlier concerning manager information behavior (Dickson, Senn, Cheway, 1977; Tushman & Nadler, 1977; Higgins & Finn, 1977) suggested that the formal systems were not used by top managers. MIS's are a low rich medium, and are more useful for well defined activities at lower hierarchical levels.

Scanning.   Scanning pertains to the organization's intelligence–gathering mechanisms. Most environmental scanning takes place at the upper levels of the organization (Aiken & Hage, 1972). The few studies which have actually observed scanning behavior indicated that most scanning utilizes rich media. Aguilar (1967) compared personal to impersonal sources about the environment. He found that personal sources were of much greater importance to executives than impersonal material. Keegan (1967) compared human to documentary sources of information used by headquarters' executives in multinational companies. He found that two-thirds of information episodes were with human sources. The businessmen he studied used a network of human contacts in a variety of organizations to interpret the international environment. Documentary sources, such as the *Wall Street Journal* and the *New York Times*, were read regularly by the executives, but were less influential sources of information.

Bauer, Pool, and Dexter (1964) concluded that to a large degree American business communication is oral or by personal memorandum. Allen (1966) studied information sources for engineering decisions, and found that customers and vendors were the most used information source. Engineers had personal contact with these people to provide information on such things as new product needs. The formal literature, by contrast, was the least used source for this information.

The Keegan (1976) and Allen (1966) studies also indicated that information media reflect the nature of the underlying task. Keegan found that financial executives were more likely to use documentary sources, which is consistent with the well understood nature of accounting systems. General management and marketing, which experienced greater change and uncertainty, made greater use of human sources. Allen found that scientists who were working on well specified research problems made greater use of literature sources than did engineers who were involved in new product development.

Another source of information for top executives is personal observation. This is a very rich medium. It is not unusual for executives to take special tours, which involve face-to-face meetings with subordinates and the observation of facilities (Mintzberg, 1973). Rich media provide greater insight into the organizational needs and problems than would be obtained by relying on letters or formal documentation (Keegan, 1976).

Kefalas (1975) reported a survey of scanning activities by managers in farm-equipment and meat packing companies. He found that upper-level executives devoted more time to scanning the external environment than did lower level managers. The source of scanning information was primarily face-to-face meetings with other people. Moreover, executives spent more time scanning the environment when it was dynamic rather than stable. The dynamic environment represented greater uncertainty and complexity, which was associated with greater use of rich media.

Conclusions reached independently by Keegan (1976) and Kefalas

(1975) revealed the small role played by formal paperwork for senior managers. Keegan's study included fifty executives who each reported three communication incidents. Computer-based or quantitative reports were not reported in a single case as the source of external information. In much the same fashion, Kefalas found tht formal surveillance received very little emphasis in organizations. Many businesses support organized technological and market research activities, but this data is not widely used within the organization. These systems are sometimes haphazardly designed so that information is not always available to the right people. These systems also fail to capture the novel and unstructured aspects of the external environment.

Summary. There has not been a great deal of research on the relationship between media richness and hierarchical level, but a reasonable inference is that the relationship proposed in Figure 6 receives modest support. Upper level management activities differ systematically from lower level activities, and upper level managers make extensive use of rich media to interpret and understand the external environment. Personal contacts appear to be essential for interpreting the external environment and reducing equivocality. Organizations undergo a process of richness reduction from the top to the lower levels of the organization. Rules, procedure, job descriptions, technical reports, and other forms of less rich media are more widely used at lower organizational levels. Rich information media are used for interpretation and decision making at the top, and sequentially less rich media are implemented at lower levels. Variation in media richness helps explain how equivocality reduction necessary for survival and efficient internal performance takes place.

Horizontal Model

A number of studies have examined communication and information processing inside organizations. Research relevant to the information richness models in Figures 7 and 8 are in the categories of technology, interdependence and internal culture.

Technology. Technology is a source of uncertainty for employees within the organization and thus, it influences information processing. Empirical studies have indicated that complex, nonroutine tasks require more information processing than simple, routine tasks. This relationship has been observed in small groups (Bavelas, 1950), simulated organizations (Becker and Baloff, 1969), research and development groups (Tushman, 1978, 1979), and other organizational departments (Van de Ven and Ferry, 1979; Randolph, 1978; Daft & MacIntosh, 1980).

Relevant to the theory presented in this chapter is evidence that media usage is associated with technological uncertainty. Woodward's (1965) seminal study of organizational technology found that communication media changed according to complexity of the task. People in highly routinized mass production organizations tended to rely on written communication and to have extensive formal procedures. Organizations that had less clear technology, such as continuous process or small batch, relied more on verbal media. The complexity of the task was associated with information media richness.

Studies by Van de Ven, et al. (1976) and Daft and MacIntosh (1980) support this general relationship. Van de Ven, et al. found that when task uncertainty was high, managers made more frequent use of unscheduled meetings and other forms of horizontal communications. When task uncertainty was low, rules and plans were the primary means of communicating. Daft and Macintosh reported that when tasks were less analyzable, participants preferred less precise information. Information had greater equivocality and required personal experience to interpret and actual use to solve the unanalyzable problems.

Meissner (1969) found that as technology varied from uncertain to certain, the media used by employees shifted from verbal to objective signs and written communications. Randolph (1978) observed that verbal media were used more frequently as technology increased in uncertainty. He also observed a shift from verbal to horizontal communication. Finally, Gaston (1972) found that nonstandardized tasks were associated with more face-to-face information transfer than were standardized tasks.

The communication patterns associated with technological uncertainty are consistent with our proposed models of information processing. The forms of communication observed by Woodward (1965), Van de Ven, et al. (1976), Daft and Macintosh (1980), Meissner (1969), Randolph (1978) and Gaston (1972) can be interpreted to reflect differences in the continuum of information media. Media high in richness (face-to-face, personal contact) were used when tasks were complex and uncertain. Media low in richness (rules, regulations, written) were used when tasks were simple and certain.

Interdependence. There have been fewer studies of interdependence, but the general direction of findings seems to be similar (Tushman & Nadler, 1978). As interdependence increases, the need for communication between groups increases, so the amount of information processed to achieve coordination increases (Van de Ven, Delbecq, & Koenig, 1976).

Interdependence is also related to media richness. Thompson (1967) argued that when interdependence increased from pooled to sequential to reciprocal, techniques of coordination should change from rules to standardization to mutual adjustment. These coordination techniques are changes in media. Rules do not convey rich information, but mutual adjustment (face-to-face) is very rich. Van de Ven, et al. (1976) also found that communication shifted from rules to meetings as interdependence among employees increased. This finding also fits the richness model in Figure 8.

We theorized that differences in frames of reference across departments would require highly rich media to resolve. This idea receives modest support from the research of Lawrence and Lorsch (1967), who found that personal modes of coordination were used when differentiation within organizations was high. However, their study did not compare personal to impersonal media. The lateral information processing they found was face-to-face, which suggests the need for highly rich media to accomodate divergent frames of reference and perspectives.

Internal Culture. Organizational culture and climate may also be associated with information media. There is intriguing evidence to suggest that myths, stories, and metaphors are effective means of preserving social and emotional aspects of organization (Boje & Rowland, 1977; Clark, 1972; Meyer & Rowan, 1977; Mitroff & Kilman, 1976). Myths, legends; sagas, and stories are prevalent in most organizations. These stories usually pertain to the socio-emotional side of the organization and provide employees with history, background, and meaning for their role within the organization.

Myths and sagas are not written down, and if they were, their usefulness might be lost. A similar finding is true for gossip and the use of the grapevine (Davis, 1953). Information processed along the grapevine generally is of a personal nature and is communicated through rich media. The reason is that stories, myths and gossip pertain to the ill-defined, emotional aspects of organization that are best transfered through informal, personal media. Transmitting myths or gossip through informal, impersonal media would transform the stories into rational facts, and they would no longer pertain to the deeper, emotional needs of participants.

Summary. Once again, evidence from the research literature provides tentative support for the theoretical ideas expressed in this chapter. The findings suggest that rich media tend to be used when tasks are complex, and when differences between departments are great. Task complexity and interdependence are also related to information amount.

Taken together, these findings may mean there is a positive relationship between media richness and amount of information processed, since both seem to increase with task complexity and interdependence. The face-to-face medium, for example, enables managers to process rich information cues. Cues convey more insight, so managers actually acquire more information for understanding a complex issue or developing a new cognitive map. Amount of information may be increased by spending more time communicating or by shifting to richer media. The general conclusion is that requirements for horizontal information processing influence both richness and amount of information. Organizational design should enable the appropriate amount of information to be processed, and should provide managers with appropriate media richness depending on task uncertainty and interdependence.

DISCUSSION AND IMPLICATIONS

Early in this chapter, we proposed that organizational success is related to the organization's ability to manage information richness. Information richness was defined, and three models were proposed. The major points contained in this chapter are as follows.

1. Information is a core construct for understanding organizational form and process.

2. Human organizations, unlike lower level systems, must use information to reduce equivocality.

3. Organizations have two information related tasks, which are to interpret the external environment and to coordinate internal activities. Each of these tasks requires the reduction of equivocality and the processing of a sufficient amount of information.

4. Information richness is an important concept for explaining how organizations perform the task of reducing equivocality to an acceptable level for internal efficiency. Rich media utilize multiple cues, feedback, and high variety language. Rich media enable people to interpret and reach agreement about difficult, unanalyzable, emotional, and conflict-laden issues. Face-to-face discussions lead to a shared language and interpretation. Media of low richness are appropriate for communicating about routine activities within the organization. Paperwork, rules, and computer printouts are accurate and efficient for the transmission of unequivocal messages.

5. Media richness is the basis for the model of manager information processing behavior. For difficult, equivocal topics, managers use face-to-face discussion for interpretation and equivocality reduction. Memos, bulletins, reports and other media of lower richness are used when the topic is specific and better understood. In a sense, there are two sides to managerial communication. Managers use informal, personal, direct contact when problems are ambiguous and unclear. They use formal, paperwork communications for routine matters. Effective managers should have skills with all media and be able to select among them depending on the nature of the problem.

6. Media richness also explains how organizations interpret the external environment, as described in the vertical information model. Media selection enables the organization to learn about an uncertain environment, yet provide a sense of certainty and direction for participants within. Face-to-face and other rich media are used to receive cues about the environment and to define a common grammar for use within the organization (Weick, 1979). The organization reduces media richness as information moves down the organizational hierarchy. Media of low richness can be used to specify goals, policies, procedures, and technology at lower levels, thereby providing clarity and certainty for the efficient performance of routine activities. The key to vertical information processing is to incorporate a balance of media. When the environment is uncertain and equivocal, rich media are called for. Organization design should encourage face-to-face discussion to reduce equivocality and provide certainty within the organization. When activities are stable and analyzable, less rich media should be used.

7. Media richness is also the basis for the horizontal information model that explains how organizations coordinate internal activities. When departments are highly differentiated and interdependent, equivocality is high. When equivocality is high organizations will use rich information media to resolve departmental differences and to reach a common language and perspective. Once differences are resolved and agreement is reached, less rich forms of communication, such as memos and formal reports, will be sufficient for coordination. Media selection within the organization is related to the extent of differentiation and interdependence among departments.

Relationship To Other Frameworks

One outcome of the ideas described in this chapter is that they are consistent with other frameworks in the literature. Current perspectives can be reinterpreted in terms of media richness. Three frameworks—organic versus mechanistic organizations, bureaucracy, and politics—are considered here.

Organic Versus Mechanistic Organizations. The environment is a major source of uncertainty for organizations. Complexity, variability, and rate of change in the environment create additional uncertainty for managers in the organizations. Participants must spend more time finding out about the environment and adapting to changes in the environment.

Perhaps the most widely accepted relationship between organization and environment is that organic structures tend to evolve in uncertain environments, and mechanistic structures are suited to certain environments (Burns & Stalker, 1961). In an organic organization, people are continually redefining and renegotiating tasks. There is widespread discussion about activities. Rules and responsibilities are ill-defined or nonexistent. In a mechanistic organization, activities are more rigidly defined. Rules, regulations and job descriptions are available to control behavior. Task redefinition is nonexistent. Communication tends to be vertical rather than lateral.

We suggest that the principle difference between organic and mechanistic organizations is media richness. The organic structure facilitates communication through rich media. The organization is constantly learning. Changes in the external environment are being interpreted and translated into new roles and internal tasks. Widespread face-to-face discussion enables continuous interpretation and adaptation to take place. The process of richness reduction is minimized in the organic structure because the entire organization is involved in interpretation, discussion and change.

The mechanistic structure makes greater use of media low in richness. Rules, procedures, and job descriptions contain the information necessary for successful task accomplishment within the organization. An extensive reduction in richness from the top to the bottom of the organization is accomplished. A small percentage of people are involved in environmental interpretation. Rules and regulations enable the organization to respond from habit and previous experience rather than through new interpretations. Formal media are appropriate in organizations that have well understood, predictable environments. Of course organic organizations would still utilize some low rich media and mechanistic organizations some high rich media. But rich media are used more extensively in organic organizations where the environment is changing and complex. Media low in richness are used more extensively in mechanistic organizations within stable environments.

Bureaucracy. Research on bureaucratic organizations has indicated that bureaucracy is similar to the mechanistic organizations studied by Burns and Stalker (1961). The literature suggests that as organizations increase in size, bureaucratic traits increase (Kimberly, 1976). Weberian characteristics such as division of labor, rules, and paperwork, are more extensive in large organizations (Blau & Schoenherr, 1971; Dewar & Hage, 1978).

These findings support the idea that richness reduction takes place. In a large organization, communication can be standardized, and relevant information is contained within the formal documentation of the organization. Large organizations develop a niche within the environment so that external conditions are relatively stable. Large organizations learn to take advantage of internal efficiencies by responding through habit or by buffering the technical core when external changes do occur.

Studies that show increased formalization and large clerical ratios with organization size support the idea of reliance on information of lower richness (Daft, 1978; Kasarda, 1974). Formalization is a measure of the amount of documentary data in the organization. Large clerical ratios provide people to process large amounts of paperwork. Small administrative ratios in large organizations means the organization is run with less personal observation (rich media) and more by rules and regulations that act as substitutes for supervision. Media of low richness are substituted for media of high richness during bureaucratization. Even the increasing complexity in large organizations reflects information processing to some extent. An increasing number of departments and specialties is a way to divide the total information base needed for effective performance. Each department can develop a common language and frame of reference that will enable the use of less rich media for task accomplishment.

Politics.   Politics is defined as those activities used to obtain one's preferred outcome in organizations when there is uncertainty or disagreement about choices (Pfeffer, 1981). Recent surveys of organizational politics (Gantz & Murray, 1980; Madison, Allen, Porter, Ranwick, & Mayes, 1980) indicate that political behavior occurs most often at the upper levels of organizations and for decisions high in uncertainty.

We propose that political behavior involves the utilization of rich media (face-to-face) to reach agreement when diverse goals and reference frames are brought to bear on uncertain problems. Disagreement is the result of diverse perspectives and goals across departments. Uncertainty is the result of the ill-defined nature of political issues. Politics is a device to encourage face-to-face discussion among a broad group of executives until a coalition is formed that reflects a common grammar and understanding. Media low in richness cannot be used to resolve political issues because paperwork and reports cannot convey the subtleties of power, obligations, and other intangibles. Politics is one vehicle through which rich media are used to reduce equivocality. Politics occurs both at upper levels and across departments when events are uncertain and reference frames diverge.

By contrast, rational models of decision making reflect the use of low rich media to process information and make decisions. The rational model is effective when factors are certain, and when participants agree on desired goals and cause–effect relationships (Pfeffer, 1981). The rational model makes use of documentary sources of information, such as statistics and quantitative analysis. This approach to information and decision making is used more often for operational and technical decisions at lower levels in the organization.

Future Research Directions

The models in this chapter not only relate to the established frameworks above, they also can be the basis for a lengthly agenda of new empirical research. Very little research has been reported on topics such as the selection of media by managers, how organizations interpret the external environment, or the mechanisms used to process information horizontally between departments. A study by Lengel (1983) supports the underlying concept of a media richness and the relationship between media richness and the nature of communication topics. Additionl studies based upon the models presented in this paper and beyond are suggested below.

Media Selection and Usage. The model of manager information processing in Figure 3 might be tested in a number of ways. A large sample of communications typically sent and received via each medium could be obtained and analyzed for systematic differences in content. Managers might be asked to describe critical communication incidents and to describe the medium used. Another approach would be to systematically test the relationship between task complexity and media selection. A sample of communication episodes could be developed according to complexity, ambiguity, conflict, emotional content, and accessability. Then managers could be surveyed to determine their media choice for each episode. Analysis of these data would indicate the extent to which task complexity influences media selection. These data could also be analyzed by manager effectivenss and manager hierarchical level to see if media selection is associated with manager differences. A study could also test these relationships in the laboratory. Specific topics would be communicated through various media, such as telephone, face-to-face, and written. This research would indicate how media influence trust, understanding, and agreement among managers.

Boundary Spanning. Pfeffer and Salancik (1978) proposed that organizations face two problems in their relationship to the environment: (1) how to register needed information about the environment, and (2) how to act upon that information. The first problem is one of boundary spanning. Exploratory case type studies have been conducted by Aguilar (1967) and Keegan (1974), but systematic analyses of external information sources have not been published. An appropriate study would be to interview boundary spanning managers about information topics important to their functions. After two or three critical topics are identified, sources of information on these issues could be determined. External sources such as magazines, personal contacts, and opinion surveys can be identified. The transmission of information into the organizational decision center could also be traced. This study could begin with in-depth interviews of boundary spanning personnel, with a follow up questionnaire survey of information sources for specific topics. The outcome of this study would begin to shed new light on the intelligence gathering activities of formal organizations.

Interpretation and Effectiveness. Weick and Daft (1982) proposed that organizations systematically differ with respect to interpretation style. Interpretation style is an outgrowth of boundary spanning activity, and includes the development of shared perception, goals, and strategies among top managers. In a study of interpretation style, senior managers could be interviewed to identify how they learn about the environment. The role of organization design, such as the existence of a formal department to scan and analyze the environment, could also be examined. The effectiveness of interpretation systems could be evaluated by direct comparison of several organizations in a similar environment. Organizations in the same industry that have differing levels of profit, innovation, or other outcomes can be evaluated for interpretation differences.

Interdepartmental Coordination. Interdepartmental coordination pertains to horizontal information processing in organizations. Van de Ven, Delbecq and Koenig (1976) studied mechanisms used to coordinate members within a department. No studies have been conducted of coordination between departments or between major divisions of a large corporation. Galbraith's (1973, 1977) framework argues that coordination mechanisms reflect differences in information processing needs. A valuable study would examine these coordination processes in more detail. Specific coordination issues could be followed through the organization to learn how coordination was achieved. The model in Figure 7 could be tested by observing the extent to which media richness is related to frames of reference or to the amount of interdependence between departments.

Equivocality Reduction. The theme that underlies this entire chapter is equivocality reduction. Organizations must be able to translate uncertainty to certainty in order to achieve internal efficiency and stability (Skivington, 1982). Equivocality may originate in the external environment or through internal disagreements. Despite the importance of equivocality reduction to organizational interpretation and coordination, we know virtually nothing about it from an empirical perspective. The process of perceiving an equivocal stimuli, evaluating it, discussing it, and coming to a resolution could be the focus of new research. This type of study might be conducted in either the laboratory or in the field. Groups or simulated organizations could be presented with an equivocal stimuli to observe how it is resolved. Specific environmental events might be traced into and through real organizations to learn how an acceptable level of understanding and certainty is reached. Almost any study of equivocality reduction, however exploratory and tentative, would discover significant new knowledge about organizations.

Symbolic Value of Media. Feldman and March (1981) proposed that information in organizations serves as signal and symbol. More information is gathered than organizations use, yet managers may request even more. Formal reports may not influence the rational decision process, but be used to support a course of action previously agreed upon. Feldman and March argued that the use of information is highly symbolic, and that information processing cannot be fully understood by considering only rational communication exchanges and decision making. The selection of media also may have strong symbolic overtones. Face-to-face discussion may be used when a manager wishes to communicate personal interest or to show others that he cares about them. Formal reports might be used to signal that extensive study lies behind a supposedly rational decision. Letters and memoranda convey a sense of the official and symbolize the legitimate role of the organization. The symbolic aspect of media could be assessed by identifying communication episodes and asking managers why they selected a specific medium. The deeper reasons for using media might be elicited through open-ended interviews. Similar interviews might be conducted with people who receive communications through various media. The deeper significance of media in the interpretation of messages could suggest new insights into the types of signals communicated within organizations.

CONCLUSION

This chapter has introduced the concept of information richness and proposed models of managerial information processing, organizational interpretation, and internal coordination processes. The models in this chapter have attempted to integrate ideas and topics from the literature on organizations. These topics include manager preference for personal contact and informal information, sources of information used by managers in various tasks, the observation that organizations must reduce equivocality about the environment (Weick, 1979), and Galbraith's (1973) description of organization structure as a means of directing communication flows. The notion of information richness shed light on all these activities. When the task is complex and difficult, rich media enable successful information sharing. The information richness model provides a way to understand the behavior of individual managers as well as to integrate the notions of equivocality reduction and internal coordination.

Any model involves tradeoffs and unavoidable weaknesses. Probably the greatest weakness in the models presented in this chapter is reflected in Thorngate's (1976) postulate of commensurate complexity. Thorngate states that a theory of social behavior cannot be simultaneously general, accurate, and simple. Two of the three are possible, but only at a loss to the third. The models in this paper are general and simple, and hence are not very precise at predicting details. The models represent frameworks that apply to organizations in general. More specific elaboration of the models can only be developed after additional study and research.

The major conclusion from the paper is the need for organizations to manage information richness. Richness has to reflect the organization's need to interpret an uncertain environment and to achieve coordination within. Organizations are complex social systems that have information needs unlike lower level machine and biological systems. Rich information will have to be processed because environments will never be certain and internal conditions will never be characterized by complete agreement and understanding. Without some level of rich information, organizations would become rigid and brittle. They could not adapt to the environment or resolve internal disagreements in a satisfactory way. The process and outcomes of information processing are a good deal less tidy than would be the case in simpler, machine models of organizations. The ideas proposed in this chapter suggest a new view—perhaps a starting point of sorts—from which to interpret the richness of organizational activity.

NOTES

1. The names in these examples are ficticious, but the examples are based on actual events.

REFERENCES

Ackoff, R. L. Management misinformation systems. *Management Science,* 1967, *14,* 147–156.

Aguilar, F. J. *Scanning the business environment.* New York: Macmillian, 1967.

Aiken, M., and Hage J. *Organizational permeability, boundaries spanners, and organization structure.* Paper presented at the American Sociological Association, New Orleans, Louisiana, 1972.

Allen, T. J. The differential performance of information channels in the transfer of technology. In W. H. Gruber and D. G. Marquis (Eds.), *Factors in the transfer of technology.* Cambridge, MA: MIT Press, 1969.

Arrow, K. J. *The limits of organization.* New York: Norton, 1974.

Azien, I. Intuitive theories of events and the effects of base-rate information on prediction. *Journal of Personality and Social Psychology,* 1977, *35,* 303–314.

Bauer, R. A., Pool, I. S. & Dexter, L. A. *American business and public policy.* New York: Atherton Press, 1964.

Bavelas, A. Communication patterns in task-oriented groups. *Journal of Acoustical Society of America,* 1950, *22,* 725–730.

Becker, S. W., & Baloff, N. Organization structure and complex problem solving. *Administrative Science Quarterly*, 1969, *14*, 260–271.

Blandin, J. S. and Brown, W. B. Uncertainty and management's search for information. *IEEE Transactions on Engineering Management*, 1977, *4*, 114–119. (EM-24)

Blau, P. M., & Schoenherr, R. A. *The structure of organizations*. New York: Basic Books, 1971.

Bodensteiner, W. D. *Information channel utilization under varying research and development project conditions: An aspect of inter-organizational communication channel usages*. PhD Dissertation, The University of Texas, 1970.

Boje, D. M., & Rowland, R. M. *A dialectical approach to reification in mythmaking and other social reality constructions: The P-A-C-E model and OD*. Unpublished manuscript, University of Illinois, 1977.

Borgada, E., & Nisbett, R. The differential impact of abstract versus concrete information. *Journal of Applied Social Psychology*, 1977, *7*, 258–271.

Boulding, K. E. General systems theory: The skeleton of a science. *Management Science*, 1956, *2*, 197–207.

Brightman, H. J. Differences in ill-structured problem solving along the organizational hierarchy. *Decision Sciences*, 1978, *9*, 1–18.

Brown, W. Systems, boundaries and information flows. *Academy of Management Journal*, 1966, *9*, 318–327.

Burns, T. & Stalker, G. *The management of innovation*. London: Tavistock Press, 1966.

Clark, B. R. The occupational saga in higher education. *Administrative Science Quarterly*, 1972, *17*, 178–184.

Daft, R. L. System influence on organizational decision making: The case of resource allocation. *Academy of Management Journal*, 1978, *21*, 6–22.

Daft, R. L., & Macintosh, N. B. A tentative exploration into amount and equivocality of information processing in organizational work units. *Administrative Science Quarterly*, 1981, *26*, 207–224.

Daft, R. L., & Wiginton, J. C. Language and organization. *Academy of Management Review*, 1979, *4*, 179–191.

Davis, K. Management communication and the grapevine. *Harvard Business Review*, September–October 1953, pp. 43–49.

Dearden, J. "MIS is a mirage." *Harvard Business Review*, January–February 1972, pp. 90–99.

Dewar, R., & Hage J. Size, technology, complexity, and structural differentiation: Toward a theoretical synthesis. *Administrative Science Quarterly*, 1978, *23*, 111–136.

Dickson, G. W., Senn, J. A., & Chervany, N. L. Research in management information systems: The Minnesota experiments. *Management Science*, 1977, *23*, 913–923.

Feldman, M. S., & March J. G. Information in organization as signal and symbol. *Administrative Science Quarterly*, 1981, *26*, 171–186.

Feldman, N. S., Higgins, E. T., Karlovac, M., & Ruble, D. N. Use of consensus information in causal attribution as a function of temporal presentation and availability of direct information. *Journal of Personality and Social Psychology*, 1976, *34*, 694–698.

Galbraith, J. *Strategies of organization design*. Reading, MA: Addison-Wesley, 1973.

———. *Organizational design*. Reading, MA: Addison-Wesley, 1977.

Gaston, J. Communication and the reward system of science: A study of national invisible colleges. *The Sociological Review Monograph*, 1972, *18*, 25–41.

Gorry, G. A., & Scott Morton, M. S. A framework for management information systems. *Sloan Management Review*, 1971, *13*, 55–70.

Grayson, C. J., Jr. Management science and business practice. *Harvard Business Review*, July–August 1973, 41–48.

Hansen, R. D., & Donoghue, J. The power of consensus: Information derived from one's and other's behavior. *Journal of Personality and Social Psychology*, 1977, *35*, 294–302.

Higgins, J. C., & Finn, R. The chief executive and his information system. *Omega*, 1977, 5, 557–566.

Holland, W. E., Stead, B. A., & Leibrock, R. C. Information channel/source selection as a correlate of technical uncertainty in a research and development organization. *IEEE Transactions on Engineering Management*, 1976, 23, 163–167.

Kasarda, J. D. The structural implications of social system size: A three level analysis. *American Sociological Review*, 1974, 39, 19–28.

Keegan, W. J. Multinational scanning: A study of the information sources utilized by headquarters executives in multinational companies. *Administrative Science Quarterly*, 1974, 19, 411–421.

Kefalas, A. G. Environmental management information systems (ENVMIS): A reconceptualization. *Journal of Business Research*, 1975, 3, 253–266.

Kefalas, A. G., & Schoderbek, P. P. Scanning the business environment—some empirical results. *Decision Sciences*, 4, 63–74.

Kimberly, J. R. Organizational size and the structuralist perspective. *Administrative Science Quarterly*, 1976, 21, 571–597.

Ladendorf, J. M. Information flow in science, technology, and commerce. *Special Libraries*, May–June   , 61,

Larson, H. P. EDP - A twenty-year ripoff. *Infosystems*, November 1974, 21, pp. 26–30.

Lawrence, P. R., & Lorsch, J. W. Differentiation and integration in complex organizations. *Administrative Science Quarterly*, 1967, 12, 1–47.

Leavitt, H. J. Beyond the analytic manager: I. *California Management Review*, 1975, 17, 3; 5–12.

Leifer, R. *"Designing organizations for information/data processing capability."* Paper presented at the National Academy of Management Meetings, Atlanta, GA, 1979.

Lengel, R. H. *Managerial information processing and communication-media source selection behavior.* Unpublished PhD Dissertation, Texas A&M University, 1983.

Madison, D. L., Allen, R. W., Porter, L. W., Renwick, P. A., & Mayes, B. T. Organizational politics: An exploration of managers' perception. *Human Relations*, 1980, 33, 79–100.

Manis, M., Dovalina, I., Avis, N., & Cardoze, S. Base rates can affect individual predictions. *Journal of Personality and Social Psychology*, 1980, 38, 231–248.

Martin, J., & Powers, M. E. *If case examples provide no proof, why underutilize statistical information.* Paper presented at the American Psychological Association, New York, 1979.

———. Truth or corporate propaganda: The value of a good war story. In L. Pondy, P. Frost, G. Morgan, and T. Dandrige (Eds.), *Organizational Symbolism.* Greenwich, CT: JAI Press, 1983.

———. *Skepticism and the true believer: The effects of case and/or baserate information on belief and committment.* Paper presented at the Western Psychological Association Meetings, Honolulu, HI, 1980.

Mason, R. O., & Mitroff I. I. A program for research on management information systems. *Management Science*, 1973, 19, 475–485.

McArthur, L. C. The how and what of why: Some determinants and consequences of causal attribution. *Journal of Personality and Social Psychology*, 1972, 22, 171–193.

———. The lesser influence of consensus than distinctiveness information on causal attributions: A test of the person-thing hypothesis. *Journal of Personality and Social Psychology*, 1976, 33, 733–742.

Meherabian, A. *Silent messages.* Belmont, CA: Wadsworth, 1971.

Meissner, M. *Technology and the worker.* San Francisco: Chandler, date.

Meyer, J., & Rowan, B. Institutionalized organizations: Formal structure as myth and ceremony. *American Journal of Sociology*, 1977, 30, 434–450.

Mintzberg, H. The myths of MIS. *California Management Review*, 1972, *15*, (1), 92–97.
———. *The nature of managerial work*. New York: Harper and Row, 1973.
Mitroff, I. I., & Kilmann, R. H. Stories managers tell: A new tool for organizational problem solving. *Management Review*, July 1975, pp. 18–29.
Nisbett, R., & Ross, L. *Human inference: Strategies and short-comings of social judgment.* Inglewood Cliffs, NJ: Prentice-Hall, 1980.
O'Reilly, C. A. III Individual and information overload in organization: Is more necessarily better? *Academy of Management Journal*, 1980, *23*, 684–696.
———. Variations in decisionmakers' use of information sources: The impact of quality and accessibility of information. *Academy of Management Journal*, 1982, *25*, 756–771.
O'Reilly, C. A. III, & Anderson, J. C. Organizational communication and decision making: Laboratory results versus actual organizational settings. *Management Science*, in press.
Parsons, T. *Structure and process in modern societies*. New York: Free Press,
Perrow, C. A framework for the comparative analysis of organizations. *American Sociological Review*, 1967, *32*, 194–208.
Pfeffer, J. *Power in organizations*. Marshfield, MA: Pitman Publishing, 1981.
———. Management as symbolic action: The creation and maintenance of organizational paradigms. In L. L. Cummings and B. M. Staw (Eds.), *Research in organizational behavior* (Vol. 3). Greenwich, CT: JAI Press, in press.
Pfeffer, J., & Salancik, G. R. *The external control of organizations: A resource dependent perspective*. New York: Harper and Row, 1978.
Pondy, L. R. & Mitroff, I. I. Beyond open systems models of organization. In B. M. Staw (Eds.), *Research in organizational behavior* (Vol. 1). Greenwich, CT: JAI Press, 1979.
Poole, M. S. An information-task approach to organizational communication. *Academy of Management Review*, 1978, *3*, 493–504.
Porter, L. W., & Roberts, K. H. Communication in organizations. In M. P. Dunnette (Ed.), *Handbook of industrial and organizational psychology*. Chicago: Rand-McNally, 1976.
Randolph, W. A. Organization technology and the media and purpose dimensions of organization communication. *Journal of Business Research*, 1978, *6*, 237–259.
Skivington, J. *Strategic planning and organizational stability*. Unpublished manuscript, Texas A&M University, College Station, 1982.
Thompson, J. *Organizations in action*. New York: McGraw-Hill, 1967.
Thorngate, W. 'In general' vs. 'It depends': Some comments on the Gergen-Schlenker debate. *Personality and Social Psychology Bulletin*, 1976, *2*, 404–410.
Tushman, M. L. Technical communication in research and development laboratory: The impact of task characteristics. *Academy of Management Journal*, 1978, *21*, 624–645.
———. Work characteristics and subunit communications structure: A contingency analysis. *Administrative Science Quarterly*, 1979,*24*, 82–98.
Tushman, M. L., & Nadler, D. A. Information processing as an integrating concept in organizational design. *Academy of Management Review*, 1978, *3*, 613–624.
VandeVen, A., Delbecq, A. L., & Koenig, R., Jr. Determinants of coordination modes within organizations. *American Sociological Review*, 1976, *41*, 322–338.
VandeVen, A. H., & Ferry, D. L. *Measuring and assessing organizations*. New York: Wiley-Interscience, 1979.
Weick, K. E. *The social psychology of organizing* (2nd ed.). Reading, MA: Addison-Wesley,

Weick, K. E., & Daft, R. L. The effectiveness of interpretation systems. In K. S. Cameron and D. A. Whetten (Eds.), *Organizational effectiveness: A comparison of multiple models*. New York: Academic Press, 1983.
Woodward, J. *Industrial organization: Theory and practice*. New York: Oxford University Press, 1965.

THE EFFECTIVENESS OF
INEFFECTIVENESS

Kim S. Cameron

ABSTRACT

This essay introduces a new approach to assessing and improving organizational effectiveness. It focuses on the factors that inhibit successful organizational performance rather than on factors that contribute to or indicate successful organizational performance. Its basic assumption is that it is easier, more accurate, more consensual, and more beneficial for individuals and organizations to identify ineffectiveness (problems or faults) than it is to identify criteria of effectiveness (competencies). Under this approach, effectiveness is viewed as a continuum ranging from ineffectiveness to high effectiveness. An organization is defined as having achieved basic effectiveness when it is free from characteristics of ineffectiveness. A technique for assessing and improving organizational ineffectiveness, called Fault Tree Analysis, is explained and illustrated. Advantages and disadvantages of this technique are discussed relative to research in organizational behavior.

Research in Organizational Behavior, vol. 6, pages 235–285
Copyright © 1984 by JAI Press Inc.
All rights of reproduction in any form reserved.
ISBN: 0-89232-351-5

There are two major problems that cause confusion and frustration in understanding and investigating organizational effectiveness. One is the enigmatic nature of the construct (Cameron & Whetten, 1983). The other is the disparity in the use of organizational effectiveness by practicing managers versus organizational theorists. Each of these problems is described in the first section of this essay in order to set the stage for a new approach to defining and assessing effectiveness. The second section introduces an alternative way of conceptualizing effectiveness and explains a methodology for assessing the construct. The essay concludes with comparisons of this new approach to several major approaches to effectiveness, and suggestions are made as to research settings in which each approach is most appropriate.

THE ENIGMA OF EFFECTIVENESS

Conceptually, organizational effectiveness is an enigma. On the one hand, it is probably the most central construct in organizational behavior. On the other hand, its definition and meaning are ambiguous, and there has never been agreement on how to measure it. Effectiveness is both apex and abyss in organization behavior research. It is an apex in the sense that all conceptualizations and theories of organizations are aimed, ultimately, at identifying effective performance. It is the fundamental dependent variable in organizational investigations, and judgments of effectiveness and ineffectiveness are an inherent part of the activities of theoreticians, researchers, and practitioners in organizations. It is an abyss in the sense that no valid theories of organizational effectiveness exist in organizational behavior, and no list of criteria has ever been formulated that is either necessary or sufficient for evaluating the construct. Moreover, the judgments of effectiveness made by individuals frequently are based on an unidentifiable set of preferences and assumptions.

There are two primary reasons for this engima—one is conceptual, the other is empirical. In this section, the conceptual reasons are discussed first followed by the empirical reasons.

Multiple Conceptualizations of Organizations

The construct of organizational effectiveness is closely associated with conceptualizations of organizations. That is, distinctions between effective and ineffective designs, performance, processes, and so forth, are an inherent part of any view of what an organization is. Variety in conceptualizations of organizations, therefore, leads to variety in models and approaches to organizational effectiveness.

Organizations have been conceptualized in numerous ways in the literature of organizational behavior. For example, they are called networks of objects (Tichy & Fombrun, 1979), rational entities in pursuit of goals (Perrow, 1970), coalitions of powerful constituencies (Pfeffer & Salancik, 1978), individual need-meeting cooperatives (Cummings, 1977), meaning-producing systems (Pondy & Mitroff, 1979), information-processing units (Galbraith, 1977), open systems (Thompson, 1967), collegiums (Millett, 1962), garbage cans (March & Olsen, 1976), language games (Wittgenstein, 1968), psychic prisons (Morgan, 1980), machines (Taylor, 1911), social contracts (Keeley, 1980), and so on. Each of these conceptualizations highlights, even uncovers, organizational phenomena that were missed or ignored by the others. Research conducted under these different conceptualizations focuses on different phenomena, proposes different relationships among variables, and judges effectiveness differently.

This is not to argue, of course, that there *should be* only one conceptualization of organizations and therefore only one model of organizational effectiveness. In fact, there are important reasons for perpetuating multiple conceptualizations and multiple models of effectiveness. Variety in conceptualizations of organizations serves a useful purpose. Davis (1971) pointed out that what is interesting about organizations can only be uncovered by contradicting commonly held propositions. Rothenburg (1979) argued that Janusian thinking (i.e., holding contradictory thoughts simultaneously in the mind) is the most productive means for scholarly progress. Weick (1977) illustrated a contradictory approach to effectiveness by pointing out examples of criteria that are opposite to those commonly held as indicative of smooth functioning organizations. Though organizations are efficient and controlled, for example, they also are clumsy and wandering. Morgan (1980) pointed out that increased insight can be achieved by using a variety of metaphors to describe organizations, not just one.

> Viewing organizations systematically as cybernetic systems, loosely coupled systems, ecological systems, theaters, cultures, political systems, language games, texts, accomplishments, enactments, psychic prisons, instruments of domination, schismatic systems, catastrophes, etc., it is possible to add rich and creative dimensions to organization theory [p. 615].

Daft and Wiginton (1979) suggested that not only is a single conceptualization impossible because of the limitations of language, or of the symbols used to make sense of organizations, but multiple symbols, models, and metaphors have utility in organizational behavior in capturing the complexity inherent in organizational phenomena.

Some writers on organizational effectiveness have continued to advocate the replacement of other models of effectiveness with their own models (Bluedorn, 1980; Connolly, Conlon, & Deutsch, 1980; Kilmann & Herden, 1976; Price, 1972; Stasser & Denniston, 1979). These arguments have not proven fruitful, however, because the different models are based on different conceptualizations of what an organization is. The differences among the models relate to disparate emphases, not to superiority of one over the other. An effective organization-as-social-contract (Keeley, 1980), for example, is not the same as, and may even be contradictory to, an effective organization-as-rational-goal-pursuer (Scott, 1977). The first conceptualization emphasizes an absence of organizational goals and purposes where participant needs are supreme. The second emphasizes the presence of organizational goals and purposes where participant needs are subordinate to organizational accomplishment. Multiple constituency models of effectiveness (Connolly et al., 1980; Miles, 1980; Pfeffer & Salancik, 1978) are consistent with the first case, while the goal model (Bluedorn, 1980; Campbell, 1977; Price, 1972; Scott, 1977) follows from the second.

Construct Space

Variety in definitions and approaches to organizational effectiveness results not only from association with different conceptualizations of organizations, but also from its nature as a *construct*. Constructs in the social sciences are abstractions that give meaning to ideas or mental images, but they have no objective reality. They exist in the minds of individuals, and they are only inferred from observable phenomena. Other examples of constructs are leadership, intelligence, satisfaction, and motivation.[1] It is inherent in the definition of a construct that the total meaning of the phenomenon can never be completely circumscribed. That is, the necessary and sufficient evidence for identifying the presence of a construct cannot be explicated because the meaning of constructs is, ultimately, a product of mental imagery. Indicators of constructs may not be the same across individuals, and there is no comprehensive list that must be used by everyone.

Compare the construct of organizational effectiveness with the construct of insanity, for example. In both cases, individuals may observe similar phenomena but make disparate judgments about whether the phenomena indicate the presence of the construct. When asked to identify indicators of these constructs, widely differing lists may be produced, even by experts. And, as evidenced by the case of John Hinkley Jr.'s insanity verdict in 1982, when judgments are made about the presence or absence of these constructs, contradictory opinions about the accuracy of those judgments are probable.

The construct of organizational effectiveness is enigmatic, then, because the "construct space" of organizational effectiveness cannot be totally mapped. And when advocates of various approaches to effectiveness adopt one exclusionary stance—that is, when their model is presented as the necessary and sufficient one[2]—motivation to map more of the construct space is inhibited. Effectiveness, then, should be treated as representing an unmapped terrain where different approaches and models add to the *completeness* of the map, and debates about the *accuracy* of one viewpoint versus another are put aside.

Preference-Based Criteria

This construct characteristic of organizational effectiveness leads to the second major reason for its being enigmatic: the importance of *measuring* effectiveness in organizations but the inability to identify criteria precisely. It is to be expected that when the construct space of effectiveness is unclear, its measurement also will be unclear. But, empirically, the reason that consensual criteria for assessing effectiveness have not been produced is that organizational effectiveness is inherently subjective—that is, it is based on the personal values and preferences of individuals. There are several difficulties with attempting to assess individual preferences and values in research on effectiveness. One problem is that individuals have difficulty explicating their preferences. Nisbet and Wilson (1977) and Slovic and Lichtenstein (1971) reviewed a large number of empirical studies and drew the conclusion that individuals are not good at specifying their preferences. Individual's behavior or judgments and the criteria upon which those behaviors and judgments are based are not always consistent (see, also, Argyris and Schon, 1978, for a discussion of the distinction between theories-in-action and theories-in-use). Another problem with assessing preferences is that preferences are not stable. They frequently change. For example, research in social psychology has demonstrated that preference changes often follow from behavior changes (see Brehm & Cohen, 1962, and Sherwood, Barron, & Fitch, 1969, for reviews). Cameron and Whetten (1981), Miles and Cameron (1982), and Quinn and Cameron (1982) found evidence that changes occurred in preferences related to effectiveness as organizations progressed through their life cycles. MacDonald (1975), Miles and Cameron (1982) and Zammuto (1982) discovered examples of changes in preferences as a result of different constituencies in organizations obtaining more (or less) power. Changing preferences can complicate the assessment of organizational effectiveness, therefore, because depending upon *when* the assessment is made, the relevant criteria of effectiveness may differ markedly. The relationships among criteria at two different points in time often are not clear, so that effectiveness in the past may not be a good predictor of effectiveness in the present or the future.

A third problem with preferences that inhibits consensual criteria in assessing effectiveness is that individuals, and organizations, may hold contradictory preferences simultaneously. That is, they may pursue two mutually exclusive, desirable end states (e.g., to increase adaptability and therefore slack resources in the organization and, at the same time, to improve efficiency and therefore to decrease slack resources). Cameron's (1981) research on colleges and universities, and Miles and Cameron's (1982) investigation of the U.S. tobacco industry illustrate how organizations pursue criteria of effectiveness that conflict with one another. In these organizations, contradictory preferences for effectiveness in organizations led to "incrementalism" (i.e., trading off one set of preferences against another; Lindblom, 1959), "satisficing" (i.e., fulfilling all preferences to only a limited extent; Simon, 1947), or "sequencing" (i.e., alternating emphasis among preferences; Cyert & March, 1963). Identifying accurate criteria of effectiveness under these conditions is difficult, however, because it is not clear which preferences are being advanced.

In addition, several studies have found that different constituencies hold preferences that are negatively related to one another (Dubin, 1976; Friedlander & Pickle, 1968; Rohrbaugh, 1981; Whetten, 1978). This incompatibility of constituency preferences makes it difficult to identify which individuals should specify criteria of effectiveness. Since all possible constituencies can never be tapped, and since the preferences both within and between constituencies frequently conflict, it often becomes an arbitrary choice of the researcher to select preferences that are easily accessible or that have been used in other investigations.

On the other hand, multiple and contradictory preferences may serve a useful purpose because they allow organizations to be judged effective— and consequently to acquire needed resources from various constituencies—even though widely different types and levels of performance are displayed. Variety in preferences contributes to discretion and freedom of action for organizations because they are bound to "satisfy some of the people some of the time" no matter what they do. In addition, they are provided with the freedom to manage the image or impressions of effectiveness, regardless of levels of objective performances (Pfeffer, 1981). It is this variety in performance, in the population ecology view, that enhances the probability of organizational survival (Hannan & Freeman, 1977).

Empirically, organizational effectiveness is enigmatic, therefore, because it is based on individuals' subjective preferences. Because these preferences are unstable, contradictory, and multiple, it is difficult to precisely measure effectiveness in organizations. But this unstability, contradiction, and multiplicity may actually enhance the effectiveness and survival of the organizations themselves.

DISPARITY IN THE USE OF EFFECTIVENESS

The second major problem with effectiveness, and the one that is rarely acknowledged in the literature, is the disparity in the uses of organizational effectiveness between theorists and researchers versus managers and practitioners. Most of the scholarly writing on organizational effectiveness has little practical utility (Steers, 1978), and it finds its audience almost exclusively among other organizational scholars. Managers faced with day-to-day decisions largely ignore the debates about goal versus system resource models, which strategic constituency approach is most appropriate, and the other theoretical issues that are typical of current effectiveness literature.

Similarly, the effectiveness writing done by managers on the basis of their practical experience is almost always rejected by the scholars and researchers. Prescriptions for managerial action, and recordings of how one organization improved, are seldom judged to be generalizable or valid for more than a single organization at one point in time. Generalizable criteria of effectiveness are generally given little serious thought by these writer/practitioners. One group, therefore, is accused of being in an ivory tower, and out of touch with the real world. The other group is accused of being over-simplistic and non-rigorous. The problem is that progress in understanding, predicting, and improving effectiveness is inhibited because of the gap between these two groups.

This disparity between managers and researchers results from the different use that each group makes of organizational effectiveness. This difference may be illustrated by comparing organizational effectiveness to the physical health of a human being. Physical health lies on a continuum. At one end of the continuum is excellent physical health. Indicators of this condition may be a slow heart rate, high lung capacity, cardiovascular fitness, superior muscle tone, low percentage of body fat, 20/20 vision, no cavities in the teeth, and so on. On the other end of the continuum is illness, as indicated by the inability of the body to function properly, and by the presence of abnormal symptoms such as congestion, infection, bleeding, and so on. In between these two extremes is a condition of basic health, or equilibrium. The body has an absence of illness, but it may not possess the characteristics of excellent health. An individual may be overweight, out of shape, a high relative percentage of body fat, and require glasses, but physical health would still generally be considered acceptable. It is doubtful, for example, that a life insurance company would turn down such a person for a policy because of poor health. Physical health, then, is generally defined as an absence of characteristics of illness. But in order to be judged in excellent health, additional characteristics have to be taken into account.

Effectiveness for organizations can be considered as being similar to health for physical bodies. Effectiveness also lies on a continuum. On one end is high effectiveness, on the other end is ineffectiveness. In the middle lies basic effectiveness, or equilibrium. The characteristics that indicate high effectiveness are different than the characteristics that indicate ineffectiveness. That is, both the absence of characteristics of ineffectiveness and the absence of characteristics of high effectiveness indicate basic effectiveness or equilibrium. But to assess one end of the continuum versus the other, qualitatively different characteristics must be considered.

This is also similar to Herzberg's (1959) model of individual motivation. He found that the factors that individuals identified as increasing their satisfaction with their work (i.e., achievement, recognition, responsibility) were different from the factors identified as decreasing their satisfaction (i.e., security, pay, supervision). Measuring satisfaction versus dissatisfaction requires attention to different sets of phenomena. Figure 1 illustrates this comparison in graphic form.

The figure suggests that on the individual health continuum, medical doctors are, by and large, concerned with criteria of illness; that is, they are concerned with eliminating disease. Physical fitness specialists (e.g., health clubs) are mainly concerned with the excellent health end of the continuum, that is, with improving basic health levels. On the organizational level, managers and practitioners are mainly concerned with the ineffectiveness end of the continuum, while researchers and theorists have focused almost exclusively on the high effectiveness end of the continuum. That is, managers are faced with the problem of making organizations operate smoothly. The elimination of organizational dysfunctions and weaknesses is a major focus of managerial behavior. As Sayles (1979) put it:

> The organizational setting within which managers must manage is more recalcitrant than one first imagines. While we live in a world of organizations and could not survive without them, these institutions impose extraordinary constraints on managerial effectiveness. . . . Management, in large measure, is dealing with the unexpected that interferes with expectations and routines, with unanticipated crises, and petty little problems that require much more time than they're worth [p. 3, 15].

If the organization is running smoothly (i.e., in equilibrium), there is little motivation for managers to do things differently. The luxury of pursuing

ORGANIZATIONAL LEVEL

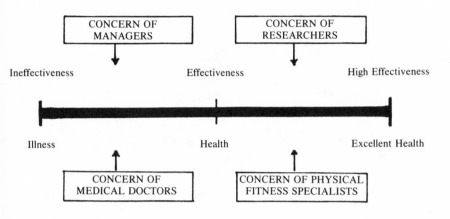

INDIVIDUAL LEVEL

Figure 1. A Compairson of Continua of Individual Health and
Organizational Effectiveness

a more excellent way is largely beyond the scope of managerial concerns.
For most managers, then, the major concern is with overcoming obstacles
to basic organizational effectiveness.

On the other hand, researchers and theorists have been much more
concerned with criteria that indicate high levels of organizational performance (Cameron, 1981). They have proposed models that focus on
high performing systems (Vaill, 1978), that is, those that are more effective
than the average. For example, Vaill (1981) indicated that high performing
systems are those that perform excellently against a known standard,
perform excellently relative to their potential, perform excellently relative
to their past, performing excellently relative to other similar organizations, and so on. This is typical of the perspective taken by most models
of organizational effectiveness: that is, that effective organizations perform excellently. What this orientation implies, however, is that research
results and models of effectiveness in the organizational behavior literature may not be very helpful to managers who are concerned with qualitatively different phenomena. Thus far, the effectiveness models "in-
use" frequently have focused on different criteria than the effectiveness
models "in-theory" (Argyris & Schon, 1978). Because of this difference

in focus, researchers have had little influence on the effectiveness of the organizations that they study. As Steers (1978) pointed out in reviewing scholarly contributions on effectiveness:

> They have few answers and we already know the problems. . . . One could even hope that someone might have taken the trouble to suggest what all this means to the poor beleaguered manager but, alas, this is not to be found [p. 515].

These two problems of organizational effectiveness—i.e., its conceptually enigmatic nature, and the disparity in its use—have led to severe criticism of the research conducted on the subject and to an ignoring of the scholarly literature by those who try to improve organizational effectiveness. In the past two decades, at least eight books have been produced on the subject of organizational effectiveness (Cameron & Whetten, 1983; Ghorpade, 1970; Goodman & Pennings, 1977; Mott, 1972; Price, 1968; Spray, 1976; Steers, 1977; Zammuto, 1982). Without exception, each has begun by pointing out the conceptual disarray and methodological ambiguity surrounding this construct. None, however, has focused specifically on the management end of the effectiveness continuum, consequently, none is required reading for those who strive to improve organizational performance. Several hundred articles and book chapters also have been written in the last 20 years (see Cameron, 1982, for a bibliography), and almost all acknowledge that little agreement exists regarding what organizational effectiveness means, how to properly assess it, or how to improve it. The writing has been fragmented, noncumulative, and frequently downright confusing. Some writers have become so discouraged by the literature on effectiveness that they have advocated abandoning the construct altogether in scholarly activity (Hannan & Freeman, 1977b). Goodman, (1979a) for example, asserted that "there should be a moratorium on all studies of organizational effectiveness, books on organizational effectiveness, and chapters on organizational effectiveness (p. 4)."

This abandonment of organizational effectiveness, of course, is both impossible (i.e., it is a construct that is firmly embedded in both scholarly and managerial language) and unwise (i.e., it serves as an important variable in research and as an important construct in interpreting organizational phenomena). However, some suggestions for improving research on organizational effectiveness are needed given the confused state of the literature and its irrelevancy for managers.

In the following section of this essay, a new approach to assessing effectiveness is introduced and an alternative working definition of the construct is proposed. This suggestion is not to be construed as a replacement for other approaches and definitions, rather it is an alternative that helps address some of the problems faced by past researchers, and it provides practical guidelines for those faced with evaluating and improving effectiveness. Its major focus is on the managerial end of the effectiveness continuum; therefore, it holds certain advantages over many of the approaches to assessing effectiveness currently being used.

ORGANIZATIONAL EFFECTIVENESS AS AN ABSENCE OF INEFFECTIVENESS

This alternative approach to organizational effectiveness focuses on the factors that *inhibit* successful organizational performance rather than on the factors that contribute to or indicate successful organizational performance. It is based on the notion that not only is it more relevant to managers, but also it is easier and more accurate for individuals to identify criteria of ineffectiveness—that is, faults or weaknesses—than it is to identify criteria of effectiveness—that is, competencies or desirable outcomes. This alternative approach merges the "critical questions" in assessing effectiveness advanced by Cameron and Whetten (1983) with "fault tree analysis" (Haasl, 1965): a procedure developed to analyze systems in the field of safety engineering.

The explanation of this alternative approach to organizational effectiveness first considers the advantages of focusing on *ineffectiveness* as opposed to effectiveness in assessments of organizations. Second, the history and development of fault tree analysis is briefly explained, and an explanation is provided on how to construct and analyze fault trees in assessing organizational ineffectiveness. Third, the advantages and disadvantages of this approach are discussed in relation to research on effectiveness. Finally, an example of the acutal use of fault tree analysis in analyzing an organization is provided for illustrative purposes.

Advantages of Ineffectiveness

The difficulty of identifying appropriate criteria stands as the single most important problem in organizational effectiveness research (Brewer, 1982; Cameron, 1978; Campbell, Brownas, Peterson, & Dunette, 1974; Nord, 1982). Most of the criticism of the literature has focused on the reliability, validity, and generalizability of the criteria used in assessments. One reason for this difficulty in identifying criteria is, as discussed above, the nature of the construct itself. Another important reason pointed out earlier is the difficulty individuals encounter in trying to identify indicators of success. Van de Ven and Ferry (1980) found, in attempting to generate criteria of effectiveness among constituencies in the Wisconsin Job Service and in some Texas child-care organizations, for example, that individuals had great difficulty producing effectiveness criteria "because

users had not operationalized their value judgments in their own minds
. . . [and] as might be expected, users found it impossible to formulate
criteria they would use to measure intangible goals [p. 46]." Van de Ven
and Ferry concluded that "users could not break out of their reactive role
and proact by generating new effectiveness measures, even when asked
to do so but not provided with a process for doing so. . . . [p. 47]."

Shulz, Greenley, and Peterson (1982) discovered, in their study of hospital effectiveness, that respondents found it much easier to identify weaknesses (or indicators of ineffectiveness) than strengths of their organization (or indicators of effectiveness). Generating criteria indicating
success was a major obstacle for respondents.

It also has been discovered that organizational change and improvement
is motivated more by knowledge of problems than by knowledge of successes. Negative feedback is more conducive to advancement than is
positive feedback. For example, Hirschman and Lindblom (1962) studied
decision making in public administration, international economic development agencies, and research and engineering programs and concluded
that the stress produced by negative performance feedback was the necessary precondition for organizational learning. Cangelosi and Dill (1965),
in an investigation of simulated business firm performance concluded:
"Failure, we agree, leads to change. The consequences of success, we
argue, are less clear [p. 196]." Miles and Randolph (1980) found similar
associations between organizational learning, organizational effectiveness, and negative feedback about performance. Individuals took more
responsibility for organizational outcomes when negative information was
received instead of positive information, coordination of tasks became
more advanced in organizations receiving negative information than
among those receiving positive information, and faster and greater quan-
tities of organizational learning were present in organizations receiving
negative performance feedback compared to those receiving positive performance feedback. DeNisi, Randolph, and Blencoe (1982) concluded
after a study of the effects of feedback on individual and group performance:

> It is noteworthy that . . . objective performance actually improved significantly fol-
> lowing negative individual level feedback from peers, and negative group level feed-
> back from a superior [p. 178].

These empirical results are consistent with common experience which
indicates that individuals have an easier time identifying faults than positive traits in others, as well as in themselves, they are motivated to improve their own behavior more readily when weaknesses rather than
strengths are point out, and negative feedback is given much more at-

tention than is positive feedback when received from significant others. Stephens (1976) concluded that individuals also are prone to reach agreement more easily on characteristics of failure than on characteristics of success.

> Analysis in terms of success, however, is much more problematic than analysis in terms of failure. Not only is it difficult to achieve consensus as to those design characteristics and functions, the channels and interactions, which lead to system success, but experience has shown that in complex systems, it is much easier to describe and achieve consensus as to what constitutes failure. When a system is functioning smoothly, it is not at all easy to specify precisely what combinations of events contribute to this state. But when breakdowns occur, they are immediately apparent, although their causes and their "downstream" effects may be more obscure [p. 3].

This point of view is consistent with the writings of many philosophers who propose that whereas people vary considerably in what they seek to achieve (i.e., their desired outcomes), they are very much alike in what they seek to avoid (i.e., failures) (see Baier, 1958; Watkins, 1963; Popper, 1966).

All this is to say that the construct space of *ineffectiveness* appears to be more narrow and more easily mapped than is the construct space of *effectiveness*. Preferences are more easily identified and more consensual. Moreover, there is evidence to suggest that organizational improvement is more likely when knowledge of faults is present than when knowledge of successes is present.[3] It seems reasonable to suggest, then, that an approach to assessing organizational ineffectiveness instead of effectiveness may help expand our understanding of the construct of organizational effectiveness, permit potentially more accurate assessments, and prove useful to managers by focusing on criteria that they find most relevant. Under this approach, organizational effectiveness takes on the following definition: *An organization has achieved basic effectiveness to the extent that it is free of characteristics of ineffectiveness.*[4] A particular technique for analyzing organizational ineffectiveness has been developed in the field of safety engineering, but it has not been applied widely in the organizational sciences. This technique, called fault tree analysis, is explained in some detail in the paragraphs below.

An Explanation of Fault Tree Analysis

Fault tree analysis provides a well-developed procedure for systematically identifying indicators of ineffectiveness. The criteria of ineffectiveness are the faults, weaknesses, or major problems existing in an organization. The analysis focuses on these faults, therefore, instead of on indicators of organizational success. Fault tree analysis is generally thought of as a procedure for increasing the likelihood of success in any system by analyzing the most likely causes of failure (Stephens, 1972). It is a technique of reliability analysis used to diagnose potential or real problems in systems. Unlike conventional forms of reliability analysis in systems engineering, fault tree analysis relies on deductive processes rather than inductive processes. That is, conventional reliability analysis techniques are concerned with assuring that all discrete parts of a system will reliably accomplish their assigned functions (e.g., do all elements in a light bulb work properly?). Fault tree analysis is concerned with relating a single fault or failure to the various parts of a system that may be casually connected (e.g., what factors are related to the light not turning on?).

Fault tree analysis was developed by H. A. Watson at Bell Laboratories in 1961 (Fussell, Powers, & Bennetts, 1974). Its original purpose was to evaluate the safety of the Minuteman Launch Control System in order to prevent the accidental launching of a missile. The applicability of fault tree analysis to the aerospace industry was recognized by individuals at North American Aviation (Hiltz, 1963) and at Boeing Company, so that in 1965 a symposium was held to introduce the technique to a wider audience and to acquaint others with refinements and modifications (Mearns, 1965; Haasl, 1965; Michels, 1965; Nagel, 1965; Feutz & Waldeck, 1965). Fault tree analysis became an accepted technique of reliability analysis in safety engineering over the next ten years, but its application stayed mostly in the area of non-human systems. Most of the literature produced on the technique was discussions of quantification advancements and computer program refinements. Until the mid-1970s, there were almost no applications of fault tree analysis to systems involving human behavior, mainly because of the unreliability of predicting failures in that behavior.

However, beginning with the first application of fault tree analysis outside the field of safety engineering by Witkin and Stephens (1968) in the Alameda County vocational education program in California, a number of doctoral dissertations in the field of educational administration were written using fault tree analysis. These were written largely under the tutelage of Kent Stephens, a former member of the Boeing aerospace group. No research related to behavioral systems other than those dissertations has been published to date, however. Furthermore, none of those applications were concerned explicitly with evaluating organizational ineffectiveness. Instead, most focused on more narrow phenomena such as teacher turnover, student self-confidence, management behavior, and so on. The use of fault tree analysis in effectiveness research, therefore, is largely virgin territory.

In order to understand this technique and its applicability to the assessment of ineffectiveness, the components of fault tree analysis and the procedures used to construct fault trees are explained below.[5] (For a more detailed discussion on this technique see references to fault tree analysis at the end of this essay.)

Critical Questions in Assessing Ineffectiveness

Prior to constructing a fault tree—that is, prior to identifying faults or problems in an organization—analysts should consider seven critical questions that both define and circumscribe the scope of the analysis. No study of effectiveness or ineffectiveness can include all possible criteria from all possible points of view, so some way must be found to specify precisely what the study does and does not include. Seven critical questions discussed in Cameron and Whetten (1983) serve as guidelines for circumscribing assessments, and they have particular relevance when constructing fault trees. The critical questions are as follows.

Question 1: From whose perspective is ineffectiveness being judged?

Ineffectiveness must be defined and assessed from someone's viewpoint, and it is important that the viewpoint be made explicit. The criteria used by different constituencies to define ineffectiveness may differ markedly, and there are no agreed upon decision rules available to identify one constituency's criteria as being more important than another constituency's criteria. Organizations never satisfy all their constituencies, and what appears to be high effectiveness from one point of view may be interpreted as being mediocre or low effectiveness from another point of view. The specific point of view being accepted, therefore, must be made explicit.

Question 2: On what domain of activity is the analysis focused?

Domains arise from the activities or primary tasks that are emphasized in the organization, from the competencies of the organization, and from the demands placed upon the organization by external forces (Cameron, 1981; Meyer, 1975). A variety of domains can be identified for almost all organizations, but no organization is maximally effective in all its domains. Moreover, the relevant criteria to be considered often differ markedly in one domain versus another. It is important, therefore, that the particular domain(s) to be assessed be clearly specified.

Question 3: What level of analysis is being used?

Judgments of ineffectiveness can be made at the individual level of analysis, at the subunit level, at the organization level, at the population or industry level, or at the societal level. Although ineffectiveness on each of these different levels of analysis may be interrelated, often it is not, and ineffectiveness on one level may be independent of ineffectiveness on another level. Without attention being paid to which level of analysis is most appropriate, meaningful judgments of ineffectiveness cannot be made.

Question 4: What is the purpose for assessing ineffectiveness?

The purpose(s) for judging ineffectiveness almost always affects the judgment itself. For example, Brewer (1982) pointed out that changing the purposes of the evaluation creates different consequences both for the evaluator and for the unit being evaluated. Different data will be made available, different sources will be appropriate, different amounts of co-operation or resistance will be encountered, and different types of assessment strategies will be required, all as a result of differences in purpose (also see Argyris, 1970). Sometimes the analyst can determine his or her own purposes, but frequently the purposes for judging ineffectiveness will be prescribed a priori by the client, the participants in the evaluation, or the external environment. Whatever the case, a clear conception of purpose is critical.

Question 5: What time frame is being employed?

Selecting an appropriate time frame is important because long-term ineffectiveness may be incompatible with short-term ineffectiveness. Some organizations, for example, may tolerate short-term ineffectiveness in order to obtain long-term effectiveness, or vice versa, so that not being clear about what time frame is being employed could severely handicap an assessment. Judgments of ineffectiveness are always made with some time frame in mind, so it is important that the time frame be made explicit.

Question 6: What type of data are being used for judgments of ineffectiveness?

This involves a choice between using information collected by individuals outside the organization with that collected by individuals inside the organization itself. In addition, it involves a choice between objective data (e.g., organizational records) or subjective, perceptual data (e.g., interviews or questionnaire responses). Data collected inside the organization has the advantage of being more fine-grained, detailed, and potentially more accurate than data collected outside the organization, but it also may be more biased and partial, especially regarding areas of weakness. Data collected from individuals outside the organization has the advantage of assessing the public image and effects of organizational action, but it also may miss important phenomena without an insider's view.

Objective data have the advantage of being quantifiable, potentially less biased than individual perceptions, and representative of the official organization position, but often they are unavailable. The advantage of the subjective or perceptual data is that a broader set of criteria of ineffectiveness can be assessed from a wider variety of perspectives. In addition, operative criteria or theories-in-use (Argyris & Schon, 1978) can more easily be tapped. The disadvantages, however, are that bias, dishonesty, or lack of information on the part of respondents may hinder the reliability and validity of the data. The selection of data by which to judge ineffectiveness is important because perceptions may generate one set of criteria of ineffectiveness while objective data may indicate a totally different set (see Hall & Clark, 1970, for an example).

Question 7: What is the referent against which ineffectiveness is judged?

There are a variety of referents or standards against which to judge organizational performance. For example, one alternative is to compare the performance of two different organizations against the same set of indicators (comparative judgment). Another alternative is to select a standard or an ideal performance level and then compare the organization's performance against the standard (normative judgment). A third alternative is to compare organization performance on the indicators against the stated goals of the organization (goal-centered judgment). Still another alternative is to compare an organization's performance on the indicators against its own past performance on the same indicators (improvement judgment). A fifth alternative is to evaluate an organization on the basis of the static characteristics it possesses, independent of its performance on certain indicators (trait judgment). Effective organizations are those that possess these characteristics. Because judgments of ineffectiveness can differ markedly depending on which referent is used, it is important to be clear about the referent that serves as the basis for those judgments.

As a result of answering these seven questions at the outset of an assessment, the analyst can determine how detailed the fault tree analysis should be, for whom the fault tree analysis will be most useful, and the types of procedures to be used in gathering information for the construction of a fault tree. Once those answers are specified, formal fault tree analysis can proceed.

Identification of Criteria of Ineffectiveness

The first step in constructing a fault tree involves the identification of "top faults" (also called undesired events or critical failures). A top fault is a summary statement of the most crucial problem in the organization. The top fault may be a compilation of several related, but more minor problems, or it may stand alone. It is essentially the answer to the question: "What is it that keeps this organization from being what it could be?'' or "What is the major indicator of organizational ineffectiveness?'' The top fault should be a problem that *directly* inhibits the organization from being more effective (i.e., it keeps the organization from acquiring needed resources, from satisfying constituencies, from attaining goals, or in other ways inhibited from being judged as effective). In any organization, there may be several top faults, but the number of top faults considered should be limited in an analysis since a separate fault tree must be drawn for each top fault.

A top fault should be identified through the use of a consensus building technique such as nominal group or delphi, where a variety of individuals identify what they consider to be the top fault(s), and then a consensus is reached, or a critical incident methodology (Tarrant, 1963) may be used where individuals are asked to agree on a critical failure event or problem in the organization's past that led to ineffectiveness. The top fault may identify a problem that *could* exist to make the organization ineffective, but doesn't exist at present. This is the general approach in safety engineering (e.g., the radar system *could* fail). It may identify a past problem that is no longer directly present (e.g., there was a black-out power failure in New York in 1975). Or it may identify a current problem that inhibits the organization from being effective (e.g., profitability is declining). Once the top event has been determined, it is placed at the top of the fault tree, and analysis proceeds deductively.

After identifying the single most important top fault, the next step in the analysis is to identify "primary faults,'' or factors that contribute to the occurrence or presence of the top fault. These should be factors that are *directly* related to the top fault in time, in space, or in other ways. This step is a critical one because it is the primary faults that compose the branches of the fault tree. Therefore, selecting the appropriate data sources (see critical questions 1 and 6) is an important consideration. Fault tree analysis is designed not to analyze all possible contributing factors to the top fault, just those that are major and directly related.

One way to generate valid and reliable primary faults is to ask a group of experts—those who know well the domain being assessed—to identify the factors contributing to the top fault. Another is to analyze critical incidents as a way to discover primary faults. Other sources may be organizational records or theoretical relationships among factors shown by past research to be significant in contributing to the problem. Factors outside the organization, as well as those inside, should be considered. Because the primary faults must be directly related to the top fault, it is important that individuals who identify them be familiar with the processes present in the organization. A broad representation of viewpoints is generally desirable, although it is not a prerequisite (Stephens, 1976).

Van de Ven and Ferry (1980) pointed out that it is frequently easier for individuals to identify the factors that *cause* or predict effectiveness than to identify the factors that *indicate* effectiveness themselves. They suggested that people generally carry around with them a model of *why* their organization is or isn't effective. In terms of fault tree analysis, this suggests that primary faults may be readily recoverable from the minds of experts without having to go through a rigorous system analysis. The application of fault tree analysis in a limited number of educational settings confirms this notion (see references). Whereas identifying the primary faults for a complete fault tree is generally time consuming, it is by no means an unreasonable task (see, for example, Barker, 1976, and Driessen, 1971).

The primary faults that directly contribute to the top fault are listed directly below it in the tree, and they constitute the second level of the fault tree. Each of the second level primary faults is then analyzed separately, so that the factors that contribute to their presence or occurrence in the organization are identified. That is, the analysis takes this form: the failure of A is due to B1, B2, B3, . . . BN; the failure of B1 is due to C1, C2, C3, . . . CN; the failure of C1 is due to D1, D2, D3, . . . DN; and so forth.

Faults on lower levels of the tree are more specific and precise than are faults on higher levels of the tree. The accuracy of fault tree analysis is generally enhanced if all primary faults on one level are identified before going on to the next level. The number of primary faults that are analyzed as contributing causes, and the level of detail pursued, are determined by the answers to the seven critical questions discussed above (e.g., the purpose of the assessment, the domain of analysis being considered, and so on), by the amount of information available regarding the primary faults, and by the amount of information needed to overcome or solve the top fault. Analysis can stop when specific change targets have been identified. Elementary fault trees may have only three or four levels of primary faults, complex trees may have as many as 16.[6] Each primary event need not be developed to the same level of specificity as others, however, so that a fault tree may have some branches with few levels and other branches with many.

Relationships Among Criteria of Ineffectiveness

The key to fault tree analysis, and what makes it unique among other reliability analysis techniques, is the connections made among faults on lower levels of the tree with faults on higher levels. These connections occur through "logic gates" derived from Boolean algebraic expressions. The Boolean logic gates most frequently used are the AND and OR expressions. The AND logic gate is used when two or more faults coexist in order to produce a more general fault. It is symbolized by the following figure: ⌂ . This gate is used only if all the faults are present simultaneously in order to produce a more general fault. Its use is illustrated in Figure 2. In this illustration, fault A is present only if faults B and C coexist.

The OR gate is much more common in behavioral systems, and it refers to the condition where any one fault on a lower level could produce the more general fault above it in the fault tree. The graphic symbol for the OR gate is ⌂. Figure 3 illustrates its use. In this illustration, fault A is produced by either fault B *or* fault C. An *inclusive* OR gate indicates a situation where B or C or *both* could produce A (i.e., faults are non-mutually exclusive). An *exclusive* OR gate indicates a situation where B or C but *not both* could produce A (i.e., faults are mutually exclusive).

In addition to logic gates, the other types of symbols used in fault tree analysis identify the nature of the actual faults themselves. These symbols are derived from system safety engineering and are used to show the kind of primary faults that compose the fault tree analysis. There are five common types of symbols.

A rectangle (▭) is the most common symbol, and it signifies a fault that results from a combination of less general faults through a logic gate. A circle (○) signifies a fault that is at the lowest (most specific) level of

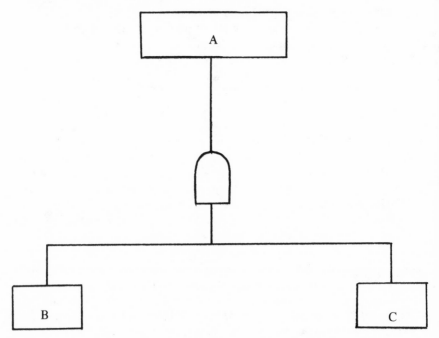

Figure 2. Illustration of the *and* logic gate

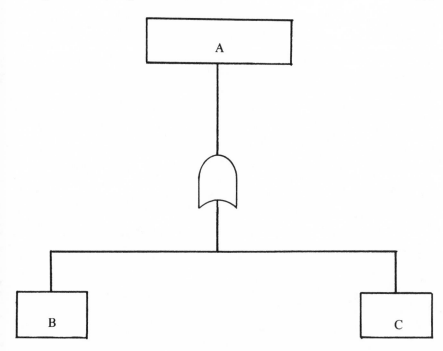

Figure 3. Illustration of the *or* logic gate

analysis on the fault tree. It is a "bottom" fault. A rhombus (◇) signifies a fault that cannot be developed further because of lack of information, a remote possibility of occurrence, or some other constraint. It also is a "bottom" event, but not because it is sufficiently developed. A house (⌂) signifies a fault that is not normally a fault. It is a factor that is present in the organization, but it does not usually indicate ineffectiveness. When combined with other faults in the tree, however, it contributes to the occurrence of a more general fault. A triangle (△) is used to indicate that a particular fault is developed further at another place in the fault tree diagram. For example, a fault may contribute to more than one general fault and so is listed more than once in the tree.

Figure 4 illustrates the use of each of these symbols in a fault tree. The tree in the figure has three branches and three levels, and it is interpreted as follows: Fault A is produced by either faults B, C, D, or any combination of the three. Fault B is produced by faults E and F. Fault C is produced by faults G or H or both. Fault D is developed further at another place in the tree (not shown). Faults E and G are developed as specifically as is needed in the three. Fault F is not analyzed further because of some constraint in the analysis. Fault H is not normally an indicator of ineffectiveness, but it does contribute to the presence of fault C.

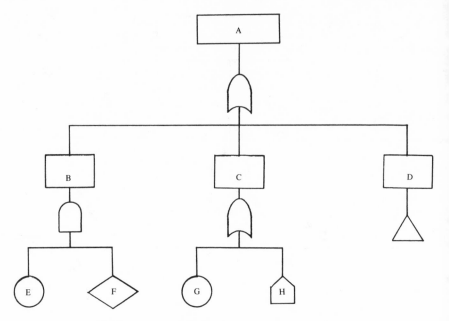

Figure 4.   An elementary fault tree diagram

After constructing a fault tree, an additional procedure is desirable to help assure that the tree is accurate and as complete as possible. Experts should be asked to answer the following questions about each of the faults:

1.   Is this an indicator of ineffectiveness in the organization? Is it a problem that stands in the way of successful performance?
2.   Are all its major contributing factors (primary faults) listed below it?
3.   Do the connecting logic gates accurately characterize the relationship of the primary faults to the more general fault above them?

The advantage of conducting a fault tree analysis in assessing ineffectiveness is that relationships among problems within the organization are identified, and insights not normally apparent often emerge. Because a variety of alternative "causes" are generated, the risk of inaccurately judging a single cause–and–effect relationship is minimized. Moreover, because faults (or evidence of ineffectiveness) are being considered and not successes (or evidence of effectiveness), more specificity can generally be achieved. Stephens (1976) suggested additional advantages of this process.

Recent work with FTA [fault tree analysis] of complex systems, however, has shown that failure analysis gives perspectives on a system which go beyond the simple logical inversion of success analysis to failure analysis and back again. In fact, the FTA methodology itself appears to have a heuristic value, both for those participating in the analysis and the managers and other decision makers to whom the results and recommendations are communicated. It generates questions about the system which do not occur under the usual conditions of success analysis. Additionally, the methodology, by facilitating consensus formation processes of groups, promotes team building activities which, in turn, lead to greater productivity.

Quantifying Fault Tree Analysis

Once a fault tree has been constructed, the analysis turns to a determination of a *strategic path*. A strategic path is a route from a bottom fault to the top fault that identifies the faults that are the most important to overcome in order to improve organizational effectiveness. A strategic path is determined by computing weights for the various faults. The goal is to identify which faults are the most critical in causing organizational ineffectiveness. Because organizational effectiveness is increased as important indicators of ineffectiveness are resolved or eliminated, computing a strategic path through the fault tree allows the analyst to identify the most important problems or faults in the system that inhibit successful performance. Change efforts can thereby be focused in the most critical areas of the organization.

The weights assigned to faults represent *probabilities*. In systems safety engineering, these probabilities are a product of one or two major approaches: (1) calculation, or (2) simulation. That is, when working with hardware systems (e.g., a nuclear reactor), there are definite probabilities associated with the occurrence of a fault or a failure. The life span of a component part, for example, can be calculated based on past experience with the part, or its life span can be determined by computer simulation (see, for example, Henley & Lynn, 1976). With both of these procedures, however, it is assumed that an objective probability actually exists for each fault, and the analysts' job is to estimate that probability as accurately as possible. In behavioral systems (e.g., organizations), however, objective probabilities are not associated with specific faults, and they cannot be determined by calculating past event probabilities or by simulation. Therefore different methods are required in order to assign weights.

The best procedure for determining a strategic path in behavioral systems was introduced by Stephens (1972). It involves the use of consensual expert ratings to estimate (1) the relative contribution or *importance* of the fault, and (2) the *frequency* of fault occurrence (i.e., urgency). The rating of the importance of faults is done via a consensus building approach such as nominal group or through delphi techniques according to their relative contributions to a more general fault. A percentage contribution is assigned to the faults on each level of the tree. That is, the weightings of all the contributing faults on one level of one branch of the tree should sum to 1.00. If fault A is caused by faults B and C, for example, the rating of the importance of faults B and C must sum to 1.0 (i.e., fault B = .6, fault C = .4). Asking individuals to assign quantified values to their ratings is consistent with the advice of Kotler (1970).

> Executives and experts who are asked to put their judgments in the form of numbers tend to give harder thought to the problem, especially if the numbers are a matter of record.
>
> Quantification helps pinpoint the extent and importance of differences among executives with respect to the decision problem. Numbers permit the analyst to perform a sensitivity analysis to determine how much a decision depends on particular differences in judgment (p. 80).

Judgments regarding the *frequency* of occurrence of the fault are made only for bottom faults. This is because the frequency of occurrence for more general faults (or the urgency with which they must be addressed) is a result of the frequency of the faults on lower levels.[7] Estimates of frequency are produced by having experts assign probabilities to faults based on a scale of how often they occur. For example, two possible scales are illustrated in Figure 5. Each fault is rated independently—

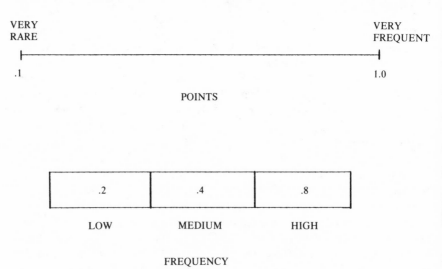

Figure 5.   Illustration of two frequency scales

unlike the ratings of relative contribution which are set in relation to one another—so weights need not sum to 1.0 for each set of contributing faults. The scale used for the ratings depends largely on researcher preference, as long as it makes sense relative to the faults being analyzed.

Figure 6 contains an illustration of a fault tree with numerical estimates assigned to each fault. The importance ratings are circled, the frequency ratings are in parentheses, and the overall fault weight is in a box in the figure. The weighting assigned to the bottom faults is a product of expert estimates of importance and frequency. It signifies the relative contribution of that particular fault to the occurrence of the fault on the next highest level of the tree. In Figure 6, fault B is the most important contributor to fault A when compared to faults C and D. Fault E is a more

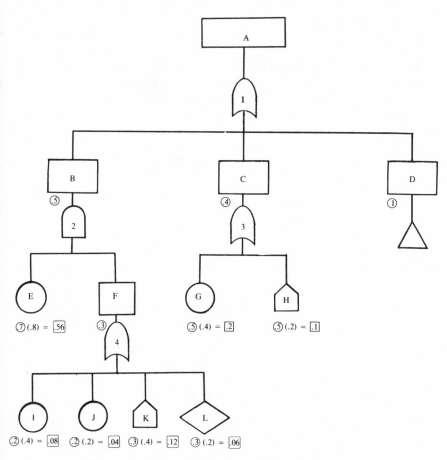

Figure 6. Illustration of a weighted fault tree

important contributor to fault B than is fault F. Fault G contributes more to the occurrence of fault C than does fault H. And fault K contributes more to fault F than do faults I, J, or L.

Having weights assigned to each primary fault in the tree now permits the computation of the "strategic path." In safety engineering, the strategic path represents the weakest links in the system, or the areas in which failure is most probable. In organizations, it identifies the interactions among the most important problems in the organization that inhibit organizational effectiveness. Computing the strategic path helps to identify guidelines for implementing future organizational change that eliminate or overcome faults.

Strategic paths are identified by using Boolean algebraic formulas (the algebra of events) to compute weights for each *logic gate* in the tree, beginning at the lowest levels in the tree. The weights of the individual events are used as the basis for the computations. The algebraic formulas applicable to each of the three different types of logic gates are given in Table 1.

To illustrate the computation of a strategic path for the elementary fault tree in Figure 6, the following computations should be made, assuming that faults G and H and faults I, J, K, and L are nonmutually exclusive— that is, that logic gates 3 and 4 are *inclusive OR* gates. Beginning at the

Table 1. Algebraic Formulas for Computing Strategic Path Values for Three Types of Logic Gates

Formula Number	Type of Gate	Formula
1	Exclusive OR	$SPW^* = P^{**}(Fault_1) + P(Fault_2) + \ldots P(Fault_N) \cdot$ (<u>importance</u> weight of the more general fault)
2	Inclusive OR	$SPW = P(Fault_1 \cup Fault_2 \cup \ldots Fault_N) \cdot$ (importance weight of the more general fault) SPW (for a gate with 3 faults) $= \{P(Fault_1) + P(Fault_2) + P(Fault_3) - P(Fault_1 \cap Fault_2) - P(Fault_1 \cap Fault_3) - P(Fault_2 \cap Fault_3) + P(Fault_1 \cap Fault_2 \cap Fault_3)\} \cdot \{$importance weight of the more general fault$\}$ where $P(Fault_1 \cap Fault_2 \cap Fault_3)$ $P(Fault_1) \cdot P(Fault_2) \cdot P(Fault_3)$
3	AND	$SPW = P(Fault_1 \cap Fault_2 \cap \ldots Fault_N) \cdot$ (importance weight of the more general fault) $SPW = \{P(Fault_1) \cdot P(Fault_2) \cdot \ldots P(Fault_N)\} \cdot \{$importance weight of the more general fault$\}$

* SPW = Strategic Path Weight
** P = *Probability* of fault in non-behavioral systems; *weight* calculated for the fault in behavioral systems.

bottom of the tree, the following computation is done for logic gate 4:

SPW = [(.08 + (.04) + (.12) + (.06) − (.08) (.04) − (.08) (.12) − (.08)
(.06) − (.04) (.12) − (.04) (.06) − (.12) (.06) + (.08) (.04) (.12)
(.06) + (.08) (.04) (.06) + (.04) (.12) (.06) − (.08) (.04) (.12) (.06)]
[.3] = [.267] [.3] = .0801

For logic gate 2:

SPW = [(.56) (.3)] [.2] = [.168] [.2] = .0336
For logic gate 3:
SPW = [(.2) + (.1) − (.2) (.1)] [.08] = [.28] [.08] = .0224

Figure 7 illustrates the primary strategic path and a secondary path (the next most important path) for this elementary fault tree. The advantage of quantifying the strategic paths rather than simply estimating them a priori is that more precise and more accurate analyses result (Kotler, 1970;

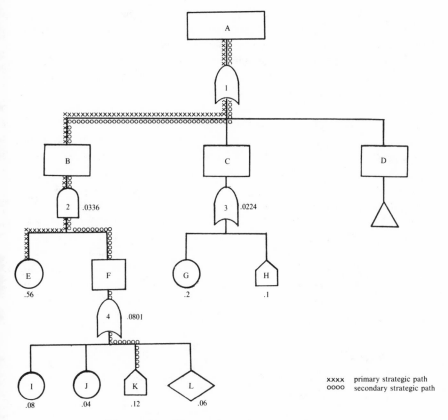

Figure 7. Illustration of a strategic path

Wood, Stephens, & Barker, 1979) and a clear strategy for change is specified. In complex fault trees, an awareness of where to begin organizational change is not always obvious because of the sheer number of contributing faults in the tree. Whereas in Figure 7 it is relatively easy to
map out a strategy of changes without going through the strategic path
calculations, this is not generally possible in real organizational assessments. The formulas derived from Boolean algebra, therefore, are designed to make precise the couplings among the faults in the tree and to
identify which faults should be overcome first. Therefore if the fault tree
has been properly constructed, and the bottom faults are precise enough
to be alterable, the strategic path maps a way to improve organizational
effectiveness by eliminating ineffectiveness.[8]

An Example of an Elementary Fault Tree Analysis

Most fault trees constructed in behavioral systems are composed of
several hundred faults that have taken hundreds of person-hours to construct (see Wood, Stephens, & Barker, 1979, for a summary of the size
and time involved in producing several different fault tree analyses). Fault
trees constructed for hardware systems, however, frequently are much
more time consuming. For example, Powers (1974) reported a fault tree
constructed for a nuclear power plant requiring over 25 person-years to
complete.

The following example presented is an abbreviated one with relatively
few faults, and it is presented only for the purpose of illustrating the
potential usefulness of fault tree analysis in assessing organizational ineffectiveness. The data were derived from an actual investigation of organizations, but many of the faults identified are aggregated among organizations, so this tree does not necessarily identify any one organization
in that study. The example assumes that the faults listed are a product
of the consensual judgments of experts in the organization. It is intended
to provide a simplified prototype of an alternative approach to research
on organizational effectiveness.

This exercise analyzes a private, liberal art college in terms of its indicators of ineffectiveness. It assumes that the following answers have
been derived for the seven critical questions:

QUESTION	*ANSWER*
1. From whose perspective is ineffectiveness being judged?	Members of the dominant coalition inside the organization comprise the relevant constituency.

QUESTION	ANSWER (continued)
2. On what domain of activity is the analysis focused?	The overall financial condition of the organization is of concern.
3. What level of analysis is being used?	The organization level of analysis is the focus.
4. What is the purpose for assessing ineffectiveness?	Discovering ways to improve the financial health of the organization and to enhance survival potential is the goal of the strategic constituency.
5. What time frame is being employed?	Analyses are based on present circumstances but with consideration given to contributing factors up to 15 years ago.
6. What type of data are being used in assessing ineffectiveness?	Perceptions of dominant coalition members provide the relevant data for the fault tree.
7. What is the referent against which ineffectiveness is judged?	An objective (ability to meet expenses) referent is appropriate in assessing financial health.

The fault tree identifies "the declining ability of the institution to meet its fiscal obligations" as the priority indicator of ineffectiveness. The assumption is made that if that top fault could be overcome, the organization would be judged to be effective, given the constraints imposed by the seven critical questions. The fault tree analysis reproduced in Figure 8 identifies four major contributing faults on level 2 of the fault tree. These four faults are, in turn, analyzed in terms of their primary or contributing faults, and so on through level 4 of the tree. Many of the faults are drawn as rhombuses not because they could not be analyzed further, but because additional analysis would make the tree too complex for illustrative purposes.

The tree suggests that the four major faults directly contributing to the top fault are: (A2) inadequate fiscal controls, (B2) nonsupportive alumni, (C2) declining enrollments, and (D2) over-expansion in a past growth era. These four faults are connected to the top fault by an inclusive OR gate which signifies that the four faults are not mutually exclusive. Any one of the faults singly or in combination could contribute to the occurrence of the top fault. For example, over-expansion (fault D2) may be a major

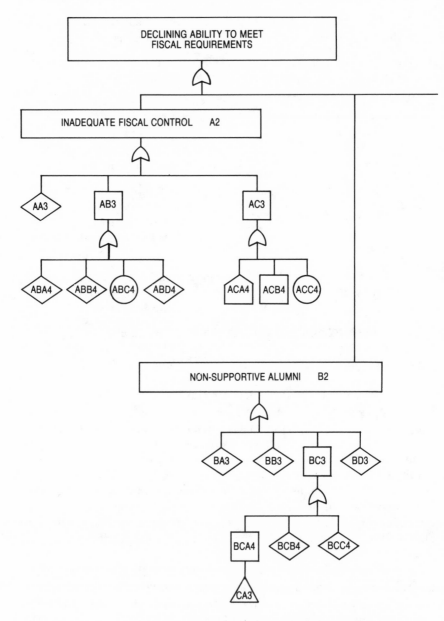

Figure 8. A prototype fault tree analysis for organizational ineffectiveness

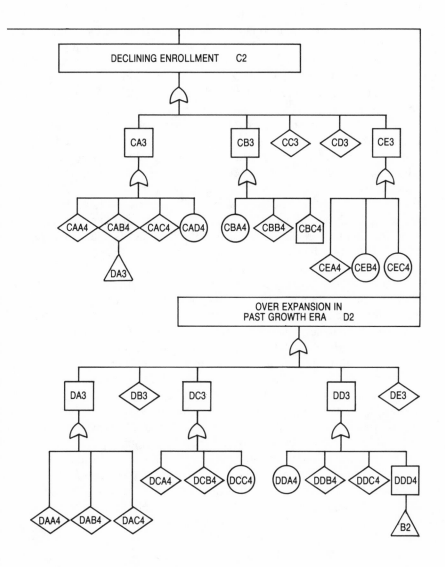

indicator of ineffectiveness, but it is especially so when accompanied by declining enrollments (fault C2). These four faults constitute level 2 of the fault tree, and they divide the tree into four major branches. The interpretation of the fault tree can be illustrated by examining the faults in branch A.

Branch A. Three primary faults contribute to inadequate fiscal controls—(AA3) no long-range financial planning, (AB3) outdated accounting procedures, and (AC3) an informal reporting structure. They are connected to fault (A2) by means of an inclusive OR gate. The first of these faults (AAE) is not analyzed further in this illustration, so it is diagrammed as a rhombus. The other two faults are analyzed to the fourth level, so they are diagrammed as rectangles. An untrained business manager (ABA4), no investment in micro-computer technology (ABB4), no trained accountants in the administration (ABC4), and no perceived need for tight monetary control (ABD4) are the fourth level faults contributing to fault (AB3)—outdated accounting procedures. That is, fault AB3 is an indicator of ineffectiveness because of these four major contributing factors, which could occur singly or in combination. The circled fault, no trained accountants in the administration, indicates a bottom fault that needs no more analysis in order to solve. The other three faults could be analyzed further in the tree but are not for the sake of parsimony.

Three fourth level faults contribute to the presence of the other third level fault (AC3), a loose reporting structure. They are: informal, collegial relations among administrators (ACA4), a tradition of not discussing fiscal operations with the board of trustees (ACB4), and the personal style of the business manager to keep others out of his area (ACC4). Fault (ACA4), an informal, collegial relationship among administrators, is not normally an indicator of ineffectiveness in an organization. However, in this case, it does contribute to the presence of a more general fault in the organization—a loose reporting structure relative to fiscal matters (AC3)—therefore it is diagrammed as a house. The other two contributing faults on level four are not analyzed further: fault (ACC4) because it is a bottom fault and fault (ACB4) because of the need for parsimony in the example.

Explanations of the other branches of the fault tree in Figure 8 should not be necessary here in order to make the example clear. However, in an actual assessment of organizational ineffectiveness, the fault tree would be explained in detail to the dominant coalition members in order for them to rate its accuracy and completeness (i.e., to analyze its validity).

This simplified example points out that fault trees can become extremely large and complex relatively quickly, so computation of primary and secondary strategic paths becomes a necessity. Just analyzing this example partially through only four levels produced 51 primary faults with a variety of relationships existing among them (i.e., some primary faults jointly contribute to more than one general fault, some primary faults coexist with other faults on the same level of the tree, some primary faults independently contribute to organizational ineffectiveness, and so on). These relationships frequently are not evident without a deliberate fault tree analysis. For example, it may not be obvious that the cost of on-campus housing (fault DCB4) is a contributing factor to the ineffectiveness of the organization unless a fault tree is constructed. Furthermore, by addressing some of the more specific faults on level 4, more general faults on the upper levels can be overcome, whereas there may not have been an obvious way to approach them otherwise. By forming joint or coordinated academic programs with the state college in the area (fault CEB4), for example, the institution in this example may overcome the more general fault of declining enrollments (fault C2).

Strategic Paths. To determine the most productive course of action to take in overcoming or eliminating these major faults, and thereby increase organizational effectiveness, strategic paths were computed. All bottom faults cannot be addressed at once, and a strategic path indicates which faults should be overcome first in order to have the greatest impact on the top fault. Figure 9 shows the prototype fault tree drawn with the hypothetical primary and secondary strategic paths computed. The weightings for each fault used to compute the strategic paths are also provided.

If the incomplete analysis present in the fault tree in Figure 9 is ignored for the sake of the example, the strategic paths provide valuable information concerning the most productive ways to overcome organizational ineffectiveness. The primary strategic path suggests that by cultivating state or federal government support (through student loans, subsidized programs or tax benefits) and by reducing organization expenses (such as energy costs and maintenance), declining enrollments (CA3) can be reversed (e.g., more students can be attracted by offering them financial assistance) which in turn can lead to the elimination of the top fault: the inability to meet financial obligations. These two faults, in other words, are the most important primary faults that contribute to organizational ineffectiveness, and by overcoming them, organizational effectiveness can be significantly improved.

The secondary strategic path in Figure 9 specifies the second most important set of contributing faults. It indicates that the second priority for overcoming ineffectiveness is to address high mortgage and energy expenses. As it turns out, this is the same fault that was identified by the primary strategic path. That is because the fault, high expenses, contributes to two different more general faults. In the fault tree, it is located at

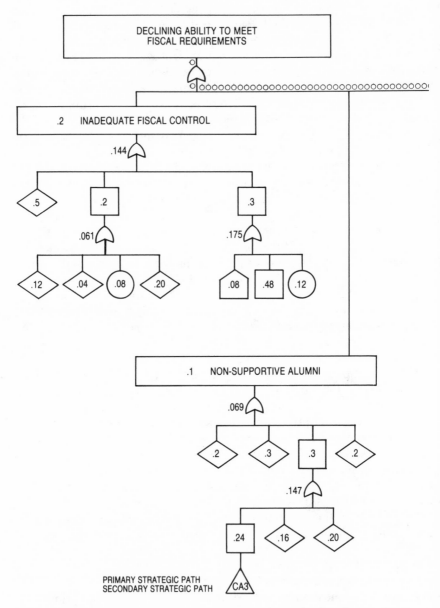

Figure 9.   Primary and secondary strategic paths for the prototype
fault tree

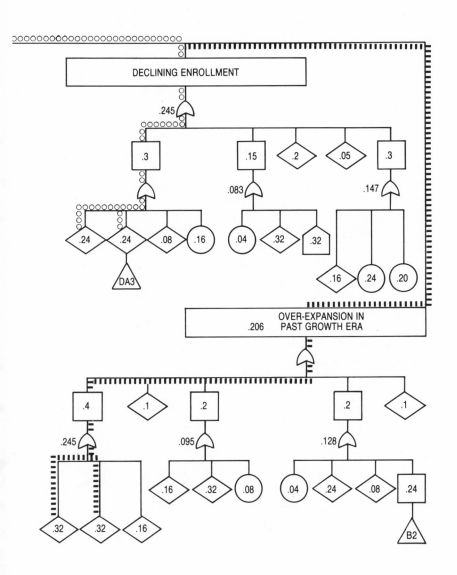

CAB4 and at DA3. The triangle below CAB4 indicates that this fault is analyzed in more detail at another place in the fault tree (i.e., at DA3). Consequently, in this example, the prescription for overcoming ineffectiveness and improving organizational performance is clear from both the primary and secondary strategic paths—*reduce expenses*. This prescription is the first priority and the one with the most potential effect for overcoming organizational ineffectiveness. However, it is not the only fault that should be considered in organizational improvement. Other strategies that focus on other bottom faults also can be considered, but they are not expected to be as powerful in overcoming the top faults as are those along the strategic paths.

The validity of the prescriptions for improving effectiveness rests, of course, on the completeness of the tree and the accuracy of the weights given to the primary faults by the dominant coalition members. The decision as to which constituency(s) to include in assessments of ineffectiveness is an important consideration because the weightings of the faults that lead to the strategic paths must result from an understanding of the system being assessed. Expert judgments of the domain being considered, therefore, are likely to be the most valid. Care also should be taken to include a validity check after the fault tree is constructed so that the appropriate constituency can assure that the fault tree is complete. Finally, agreement must be reached within this constituency as to their weightings of the faults in order to increase the probability that the weightings are accurate.

If proper procedures are used in constructing the fault tree, and if consensus is reached regarding ratings, there is evidence to suggest that judgments regarding faults will be correct. For example, in a classic study of the accuracy of prediction by groups, Kaplan, Skogstad, and Grishick (1950) found that a group decision produced 67% accuracy in predicting social and technological events as opposed to independent judgments and to discussion followed by separate judgments by individuals, which produced only 52% accuracy (also see, Dalkey & Helmer, 1963; and Winkler, 1968). No research has been conducted directly on the accuracy or efficacy of fault tree judgments, but it is reasonable to assume, based on past social psychological research, that some confidence in the judgments is warranted given the use of proper procedures.

Summary. In summarizing the procedures used in fault tree analysis when assessing organizational ineffectiveness, the following are the steps that should be followed in sequence.

1. Answer the seven critical questions to limit the scope of the assessment.

2. Determine the top fault by specifying the major (priority) indicator of ineffectiveness in the organization.
3. Identify the primary faults or problems that contribute to the occurrence of that top fault using consensus building methods.
4. Continue the analysis on more specific levels of the tree until a level of specificity is reached that identifies a specific change strategy.
5. Determine weights for the faults in the tree through subjective judgments of importance and frequency.
6. Compute primary and secondary strategic paths through the logic gates.
7. Identify prioritized change strategies for improving organizational effectiveness based on the strategic paths.

Advantages and Disadvantages of Fault Tree Analysis

Defining organizational effectiveness as the absence of indicators of ineffectiveness and then assessing ineffectiveness through means of fault tree analysis presents several advantages over many of the past approaches to effectiveness, but it also may present some disadvantages. Several of the more prominent advantages and disadvantages of this approach are outlined below.

Advantages. One of the most obvious advantages of this approach to organizational effectiveness is that it is easier to generate and to agree on faults, problems, and weaknesses in organizations than on strengths or successes. Particularly in complex organizations where goals are difficult to identify and where there are various preferences among constituencies regarding what the organization should be pursuing, agreement about what the organization should *avoid* is much more easily specified. Faults are nearer the cognitive surface than are strengths. Just as it is easier to identify what is wrong with a machine than to identify what is right—because faults are aberrations from the expected performance pattern and their occurrence motivates efforts to re-establish equilibrium, so ineffectiveness is easier to assess than is effectiveness. Because consensus circumscribes constructs, this approach to assessment helps narrow and make more specific the construct space being investigated.

A second advantage is that a focus on criteria of ineffectiveness is congruent with managerial concerns. It helps fill the void that has existed in much of the literature on effectiveness regarding managerial problems. Since overcoming organizational problems and faults constitutes a large part of managerial behavior, this approach helps tie together researcher analysis with managerial interest. Scholarly writing on effectiveness can therefore be of as much value to those with operational interests as to those with conceptual interests.

Yet another advantage is that by including broad participation of organizational members both in the diagnosis and assessment as well as in the identification of strategies for improved effectiveness, the dysfunctional consequences of rigorous research are avoided (see Argyris, 1968). In traditional assessments that rely on questionnaire responses or structured interviews, misinformation or inadequate information, rejecting or ignoring the findings, second-guessing the study design, and other forms of resistance are common occurrences. In this approach, both analysts and organizational participants learn collaboratively about the criteria under investigation. As Argyris (1968) suggested:

> In our experience the more subjects are involved directly (or through representatives) in planning and designing the research, the more we learn about the best ways to ask questions, the critical questions from the employees' views, the kinds of resistance each research method could generate, and the best way to gain genuine and long-range commitment to the research (p. 194).

Van de Ven and Ferry's (1980) approach to organizational assessment is similar to fault tree analysis in also placing a high value on organizational member participation. Both approaches suggest that the *process* of generating the analysis may be more beneficial than the results of the analysis itself.

A fourth advantage is that an understanding of the organization and the inter-relationships among subparts is enhanced by this approach. The interrelationships among factors in the organization that contribute to weakness and ineffectiveness are made clearer by engaging in fault tree analysis. The approach is similar to that advocated by Karmiloff-Smith and Inhelder (1975), Hedberg, Nystrom, and Starbuck, (1976), and others when they suggested that if a problem is difficult to solve (i.e., if organizational effectiveness is difficult to assess) the solution is to reformulate the problem, not to reformulate the solution alternatives (i.e., redefine effectiveness and the approach to its assessment). This approach helps overcome some past obstacles in the assessment of effectiveness by reformulating the conceptualization of the problem.

A fifth advantage of this approach is that it combines description with prescription. Most past attempts to assess organizational effectiveness have focused on identifying a point on a scale that characterizes an organization's performance. This fault tree approach not only serves descriptive purposes (i.e., it describes the current state of organizational performance), but it also serves a prescriptive or normative purpose as well in that it generates strategies for improvement. Therefore, improving effectiveness and assessing effectiveness are products of the same analysis. Starbuck and Nystrom (1983) pointed out that, "Organizational effectiveness affords another instance of the general proposition that prescription has to come before understanding. The notion that one should understand organizations before one tries to improve them is backwards [p. 155]." Combining description and prescription in the fault tree analysis of ineffectiveness enhances the understanding of organizations by suggesting strategies for changing them. At the same time, it does not ignore the need for systematic, a priori analysis as well.

The sixth advantage is that this approach can be used for multiple purposes besides assessing current organizational ineffectiveness. For example, identifying strategic paths and determining strategies for change can provide the political justification needed in organizations for real location of resources. Taking resources from one area in order to improve another area that is weak is always a sensitive political issue in organizations, especially under conditions where little organizational slack is present. A fault tree analysis can provide a rational justification for implementing such change. Another example is that this approach can be used to assess organizational potentialities as well as current levels of functioning. Brewer (1983), Mohr (1983), and Nord (1983) implied that evaluations of organizational effectiveness not only should focus on what organizations *do* produce, but consideration also should be given to what they *could* produce. A fault tree analysis can be constructed in the future tense and analyzed in terms of what the major indicators of ineffectiveness are that *could* occur in the organization. Strategies are then recommended to prevent organizational ineffectiveness from occurring. As an illustration of this use, Zarzycki (1971) suggested:

> . . . fault tree analysis has value . . . in making an analyst aware of the possible occurrences which might lead to production losses. The awareness gained from a fault tree is a major step toward future loss control [p. 11].

Disadvantages. Of course, focusing on organizational ineffectiveness through fault tree analysis may have drawbacks. It is not an approach that resolves all of the problems surrounding past research on organizational effectiveness. Six potential disadvantages are pointed out in the paragraphs below.

First, ineffectiveness, like effectiveness, is a construct that is a product of individual values and preferences. The enigmatic problems that characterize effectiveness, therefore, are completely resolved merely by focusing on the left end of the effectiveness continuum. Changing, contradictory, and multiple preferences are still present in assessing ineffectiveness, and the construct space is still unbounded. However, these problems appear to be less severe for ineffectiveness than for effectiveness because of the relative ease and consensus in identifying faults and weaknesses in organizations.

Second, information may not exist regarding all the organization's major faults. Contributing faults on lower levels of a fault tree may be difficult to uncover, and underlying causes of problems may not be apparent or may be inaccurately assumed. Identifying some faults may even be the result of political processes, so that different fault trees may be produced depending on which group is asked. For example, constituencies may identify only those faults that place blame on other groups or on uncontrollable factors so as to relieve themselves of responsibility for weaknesses in the organization or of a need for change. Disowning responsibility for failure by projecting it externally is a common occurrence in the attribution process. Because of these potential biases, differences existing in individual and constituency perspectives must be considered in all assessments.

Third, constructing accurate fault trees may take a large number of hours and the involvement of many people. It is certainly not as easy as sending out a questionnaire to managers in a sample of organizations and tabulating the results. Moreover, fault tree analysis, as currently developed, is limited to one unit of analysis, and comparisons among organizations require separate fault trees for each organization. The purpose of fault tree analysis focuses more on improving a single unit than on making comparisons among multiple units. Comparison among units is difficult unless similar faults are identified in the trees. The amount of time and effort required to analyze and compare the ineffectiveness of multiple units of analysis may be prohibitive.

Fourth, there is no guarantee that solving a problem on a lower level of the fault tree will automatically solve the problem to which it contributes on an upper level of the tree. Whereas fault tree analysis can identify the faults that are most tightly coupled in the tree, and that contribute most to ineffectiveness, it does not guarantee that a domino effect will result from solving one bottom fault. Moreover, no empirical work has been published to date demonstrating that the faults identified along the strategic path are, in fact, the most powerful in overcoming the top fault. Anecdotal evidence has appeared in several articles, but it is not certain that intuitive judgments or a random selection of solutions would not be just as efficacious as rigorous fault tree analysis for overcoming or eliminating the top fault. This is an area where further research is needed.

Fifth, this approach does not pay attention to organizational strengths; instead, it pays attention to organizational weakness. Some policy analysts suggest that organizations are better off focusing resources and organizational energies on what the organization does well. That focus advocates capitalizing on what is successful already. Resources should not be plowed into problem areas, according to that view. On the other hand, this approach takes the opposite stance by defining effectiveness as the absence of ineffectiveness. It advocates concentrating on organizational weaknesses in order to overcome them, which implies a reallocation of resources into problematic areas. The relative efficacy of overcoming weaknesses versus magnifying strengths is another fruitful area for future research.

Sixth, some kinds of organizations function well because they are *not* understood very well. These organizations have loose coupling, non-existent or fuzzy goals, fluid structures, etc. The advantage of this kind of design is that organizational discretion is maximized and multiple demands can be addressed at once. Two problems may occur in these organizations, however, because of fault tree analysis. First, relationships among faults that are identified by fault tree analysis may be too loosely coupled and dynamic for a reliable analysis. Second, fault tree analysis, because of its relatively fine-grained analysis, may destroy some of the mystique of these organizations. Enarson (1981) illustrated the problem of this phenomenon with this statement: "The enchantment with the university is at a low ebb when the number of graduates is at an all-time high. *We are known too well.*" Just as the popularity of politicians usually wanes when they become well known by the public—when the mystique wears off—so some organizations may resist fault tree analysis because it exposes them in too much detail.

Despite these potential disadvantages, however, the analysis of organizational ineffectiveness through a fault tree presents a potentially useful alternative to the assessment of organizational performance. In the section below, this approach to effectiveness is compared to other well-known approaches and suggestions are made regarding the usefulness of each.

A COMPARISON OF MODELS OF EFFECTIVENESS

This alternative approach to organizational effectiveness does not aspire to replace other major approaches used in the past. Instead it should be viewed as a useful addition to the repertoire of models. Assessing organizational ineffectiveness provides some advantages that are not present in other approaches, and it helps address some of the major problems with past organizational effectiveness literature. Crucial for the analyst to be aware of in selecting an approach to effectiveness, however, is when one model is more appropriate than another; or in the present case, the conditions which make fault tree analysis the most appropriate alternative for assessing ineffectiveness. Table 2 summarizes seven major models of organizational effectiveness that have received attention in the literature

Table 2. A Comparison Among Major Models of Organizational
Effectiveness

Model	Definition	When Useful
	An organization is effective to the extent that . . .	*The model is preferred when . . .*
Goal Model	it accomplishes its stated goals.	goals are clear, time-bound, and measurable.
System-Resource Model	it acquires needed resources.	a clear connection exists between inputs and outputs.
Internal Process Model	it has an absence of internal strain, with smooth internal functioning.	a clear connection exists between organizational processes and the primary task.
Strategic-Constituencies Model	all strategic constituencies are at least minimally satisfied.	constituencies have powerful influence on the organization (as in times of little organizational slack), and it must respond to demands.
Competing Values Model	the emphasis of the organization in four major areas matches constituent preferences.	the organization is unclear about its own emphases, or changes in criteria over time are of interest.
Legitimacy Model	it survives as a result of engaging in legitimate activities.	the survival or decline and demise among organizations must be assessed.
Ineffectiveness Model	there is an absence of characteristics of ineffectiveness.	criteria of effectiveness are unclear, or strategies for organizational improvement are needed.

(see Cameron & Whetten, 1983, for other models of effectiveness that are based on a variety of academic disciplines). The table also suggests when each model is appropriate for use in assessments. A basic point of that table, and of this essay, is that multiple models of effectiveness not only are necessary, but that different perspectives are very useful under different conditions.

The *goal model* has received wider attention than any other approach to effectiveness, and more writers have argued that it represents *the* universal model of effectiveness than any other model (see Bluedorn, 1980; Campbell, 1977; Scott, 1977). Its usefulness is limited, however, by its reliance on measurable, time-bound goals. Because many organizations cannot be characterized by such goals, analysts should select this model only when it is clear what the end result should be, when it should occur, and who says so.

The *system resource model* was developed in the realy 1960s in reaction to what was perceived as an over-reliance on goals (see Georgopolous & Tannenbaum, 1957; and Yuchtman & Seashore, 1967). This model emphasizes the interchange between the organization and its environment, whereas the goal model largely considers organizational goals irrespective of environmental context. Particular attention is given in the system resource model to the acquisition of needed resources. This model is appropriate when there is a clear connection between resources received by the organization and the primary task of the organization. An organization that simply gathers resources and stores them, for example, or that increases organizational fat by obtaining irrelevant resources would not be judged to be effective. Resource acquisition, therefore, must be clearly connected to organizational outcomes.

The *internal process model* emerged largely from the human resource development (HRD) and organization development (OD) perspectives. The focus is on the interaction of individuals within the organization in terms of its participativeness, humanitarianism, absence of strain, and so forth. This model is based on a normative set of principles describing how an organization should function to provide maximum potential for human growth and development (see Likert, 1967; and Argyris, 1962 for examples). It is most appropriate when the organizational processes under consideration are closely associated with the primary production task of the organization (Rice, 1965). An extremely smooth, but subversive communication system in an organization, for example, would indicate good process but an absence of organizational effectiveness.

The *strategic constituencies model* arose in the 1970s as a result of more sophisticated analyses of the external environments of organizations. Several different versions of this model have been introduced (Connelly, Conlon, & Deutsch, 1980; Keeley, 1978; Miles, 1980; Pennings & Goodman, 1977; Zammuto, 1982), but each places the satisfaction of the demands of various constituencies of the organization as the primary concern. This model is most appropriate when constituencies have powerful influence on what the organization does or when an organization's actions are largely reactive to strategic constituency demands. The mission or the domain of some organizations is mandated by external special interest groups; by contrast, other organizations are more proactive and autonomous in their activities. Similarly, some organizations exist in an environment where certain constituencies clearly are more powerful than others, whereas other organizations have no clear powerful constituency. In the former, the strategic-constituencies model would be a useful approach. In the latter, the model would not be as appropriate.

The *competing values model* is based on the notion that individuals who judge organizational effectiveness do so by making trade-offs on two general value dimensions. These dimensions are assumed to represent core values that are at the center of human judgment. One is a trade-off between flexibility (freedom, fluidity) and control (constraint, determinism). The other is a trade-off between emphasizing people concerns over organizational concerns, or vice versa. Making those trade-offs in judging effectiveness results in four major emphases on criteria of effectiveness. Organizations have been found to differ substantially on which criteria they emphasize (see Quinn & Rohrbaugh, 1981, 1982, for a more complete explanation). Because of its emphasis on trade-offs in criteria and the shifts that occur in organizations' profiles, this model is most appropriate when determining what changes occur in relevant criteria of effectiveness over time, and when there is a need to help the organization itself understand its major areas of emphasis.

The recently introduced *legitimacy model* is frequently associated with the population ecology perspective in that organizational survival is the ultimate aim. Organizations strive for legitimacy with the external public in order to enhance their longevity and to avoid being selected out of the environment (i.e., to suffer demise). Since doing the right thing is far more important than doing things right in this perspective, the model is most appropriate on macro levels of analysis when determining which organizations survive and which decline or die.

The *model of ineffectiveness* introduced in this essay is most appropriate when criteria of effectiveness either cannot be identified or cannot be agreed upon, and when there is a need to systematically develop strategies for organizational improvement. A major advantage of this model is that it provides managers with practical guidelines for organizational diagnosis and improvement. None of the other models in Table 2 serve these functions.

CONCLUSION

There have been few areas of agreement in the literature of organizational effectiveness thus far. Some authors have attributed this condition to the fact that effectiveness is a political concept (Kanter & Brinkerhoff, 1981), that organizations have many effectivenesses (Cameron, 1980; Hrebiniak, 1978), that effectiveness has been inadequately measured (Steers, 1977), and even that effectiveness is largely a nonsensical term (Goodman, Atkin, & Schoorman, 1979). Despite these obstacles, however, this essay has indicated some points in which consensus is possible regarding the construct of effectiveness. The following statements of conclusion represent some of these major points.

1. Organizational effectiveness is a construct with unspecified boundaries. It is impossible, therefore, to produce one model of effectiveness that encompasses all relevant criteria.
2. Different conceptualizations of organizations produce different models of organizational effectiveness. Because organizational conceptualizations are interested in completeness more than in accuracy, multiple conceptualizations are both possible and desirable.
3. Criteria for judging organizational effectiveness are founded in the preferences and values of individuals. Individual differences preclude consensus regarding one universal set of criteria.
4. Criteria of effectiveness are time constrained, so that depending on when effectiveness is assessed, or depending on whether a long-term view or a short-term view is taken, criteria differ in their relevance.
5. It is easier for individuals to identify and agree on criteria of ineffectiveness than criteria of effectiveness. Problems and faults in organizations serve to circumscribe the construct space of ineffectiveness more narrowly than successes and desirable outcomes circumscribe effectiveness.
6. Different models of organizational effectivenesses are useful in different circumstances. None of the major models of effectiveness supercedes all others, so that each model possesses some legitimacy in organizational assessments.
7. Researchers can make fruitful additions to the literature of organizational effectiveness by selecting a model of effectiveness that is congruent with the specific circumstances being considered. Limiting the scope of any investigation by means of the seven critical questions permits a comparable and cumulative literature to emerge.
8. Organizational effectiveness lies on a continuum ranging from ineffectiveness to high effectiveness. Criteria indicating each end of this continuum are qualitatively different.
9. Identifying strategies for improving organizational effectiveness is more precisely done by analyzing organizational ineffectiveness as opposed to organizational effectiveness.

ACKNOWLEDGMENTS

Preparation of this research was sponsored by the National Institute of Education, contract number 400-80-0109. I appreciate the helpful comments and suggestions of Ellen Chaffee, Ray Zammuto, Dave Whetten, and the editors of this volume during the preparation of this essay.

NOTES

1. For these constructs, however, researchers have narrowed the construct space by agreeing on a common set of indicators or criteria. Consensus circumscribes construct space. For effectiveness, no such consensus of criteria exists, and therefore, little narrowing has occurred.

2. Advocates of the goal model (Bluedorn, 1980; Price, 1972), the system resource model (Seashore & Yuchtman, 1967), the internal processes or maintenance model (Bennis, 1966; Nadler & Tushman, 1980), the strategic constituencies model (Connolly, et. al., 1980; Kelley, 1978; Pfeffer & Salancik, 1978), the legitimacy model (Miles & Cameron, 1982; Zammuto, 1982), and the competing values model (Quinn & Rohrbaugh, 1982) as the single best approach to effectiveness all are correct in some circumstances. But none of these models captures the total construct space of the total meaning of effectiveness. Whereas each is valuable in its own right because it includes distinctions absent in the others, none has enough explanatory power to supercede other approaches.

3. There may be several reasons why faults in organizations are easier to identify and to reach consensus on than strengths. For example, the effects of faults are generally more obvious than are the effects of strengths in an organization. When things go wrong, it is more obvious than when things are smooth-running. Individuals are more uncomfortable in the presence of organizational faults and mistakes than they are comfortable when things are right. That is, faults produce dissatisfaction and effort on the part of individuals to reestablish equilibrium (effectiveness). An absence of faults, on the other hand, does not necessarily produce high satisfaction. The presence of criteria of effectiveness produce satisfaction, but these criteria are qualitatively different from criteria of ineffectiveness. (See note 4.) Theories of cognitive dissonance suggest that individuals are motivated to perform cognitive work only when they experience dissonance or discrepancy. Hence faults, which produce discrepancies, are more readily evident in the environment than are strengths.

4. Defining organizational effectiveness as the absence of characteristics of ineffectiveness suggests that the middle of the continuum on Figure 1 is the focus of attention. As pointed out above, qualitatively different criteria are required to assess effectiveness under this definition than to assess effectiveness under more traditional definitions which focus on the high effectiveness end of the continuum. Therefore, this definition represents a qualitatively different approach to the construct than most definitions take up to now, not just a flipside of the same approach.

5. It is important to keep in mind that fault tree analysis is a *tool* for analyzing organizational effectiveness. It is not a model of organizations in and out of itself.

6. A computer program has been designed to handle up to 16 levels of fault tree inputs in behaviorally oriented systems. (Developed by Kent Stephens at Brigham Young University.)

7. It may be the case that not all frequently occurring small faults contribute to the occurrence of a larger fault, but if the fault tree is constructed properly—where the faults on the lower levels of the tree are identified as having a causal relationship to the faults immediately above them—the logic of this computational formula holds.

8. The power of fault tree analysis may be enhanced if it is used as an iterative process. That is, when procedures have been employed to eliminate faults along the strategic path, the relative weightings of other faults in the tree may change. A new analysis may uncover

a new strategic path that was not identified in the earlier fault tree. Continuous self-analysis in an organization, then, could enhance the self-design and self-renewal process.

REFERENCES

Argyris, C. *Intervention theory and method.* Reading, MA: Addison-Wesley, 1970.

Argyris, C. Some unintended consequences of rigorous research. *Psychological Bulletin,* 1968, *70,* 185–197.

Argyris, C. *Interpersonal competence and organizational effectiveness.* Homewood, IL: Irwin, 1962.

Argyris, C., & Schon, D. *Organizational learning: A theory of action perspective.* Reading, MA: Addison-Wesley, 1978.

Baier, K. *The moral point of view.* Ithaca, NY: Cornell University Press, 1958.

Baker, B. O. *Fault tree analysis: Its implications for use in education.* Unpublished masters thesis, Department of Instructional Media, Utah State University, 1976.

Bennis, W. G. The concept of organizational health. In W. G. Bennis (Ed.), *Changing organizations.* New York: McGraw-Hill, 1966.

Bluedorn, A. C. Cutting the gordian knot: A critique of the effectiveness tradition in organization research. *Sociology and Social Research,* 1980, *64,* 477–496.

Brehm, J. W., & Cohen, A. R. *Explorations in cognitive dissonance.* New York: Wiley, 1962.

Brewer, G. D. Assessing outcomes and effects. In K. S. Cameron and D. A. Whetten (Eds.), *Organizing effectiveness: A comparison of multiple models.* New York: Academic Press, 1983.

Cameron, K. S. Measuring organizational effectiveness in institutions of higher education. *Administrative Science Quarterly,* 1978, *23,* 604–632.

Cameron, K. S. Critical questions in assessing organizational effectiveness. *Organizational Dynamics,* 1980, *9,* 66–80.

Cameron, K. S. Domains of organizational effectiveness in colleges and universities. *Academy of Management Journal,* 1981, *24,* 25–47.

Cameron, K. S. *A comprehensive bibliography of organizational effectiveness.* Boulder, CO: National Center for Higher Education Management Systems, 1982.

Cameron, K. S., and Whetten, D. A. Perceptions of organization effectiveness across organizational life cycles. *Administrative Science Quarterly,* 1981, *26,* 525–544.

Cameron, K. S., & Whetten, D. A. *Organizational effectiveness: A comparison of multiple models.* New York: Academic Press, 1983.

Campbell, J. P. On the nature of organizational effectiveness. In P. S. Goodman and J. M. Pennings (Eds.), *New perspectives on organizational effectiveness.* San Francisco: Jossey-Bass, 1977.

Campbell, J. P., Brownas, E. A., Peterson, N. G., & Dunnette, M. D. *The measurement of organizational effectiveness: A review of relevant research and opinion.* Minneapolis: Final report, Navy Personnel Research and Development Center, Personnel Decisions, 1974.

Cangelosi, V. E., & Dill, W. R. Organizational learning: Observations toward a theory. *Administrative Science Quarterly,* 1965, *10,* 175–203.

Connolly, T., Colon, E. M., & Deutch, S. J. Organizational effectiveness: A multiple constituency approach. *Academy of Management Review,* 1980, *5,* 211–218.

Cummings, L. L. Emergence of the instrumental organization. In P. S. Goodman and J. M.

Pennings (Eds.), *New perspectives on organizational effectiveness.* San Francisco: Jossey-Bass, 1977.

Cyert, R. M., & March, J. G. *A behavioral theory of the firm.* Englewood Cliffs, NJ: Prentice-Hall, 1963.

Daft, R., & Wiginton, J. C. Language and organizations. *Academy of Management Review,* 1979, *4,* 179–192.

Dalkey, N., & Helmer, O. An experimental application of the Delphi method to the use of experts. *Management Science,* 1963, *8,* 458–467.

Davis, M. S. That's interesting: Towards a phenomenology of sociology and a sociology of phenomenology. *Philosophy of Social Science,* 1971, *1,* 309–344.

DeNisi, A. S., Randolph, W. A., & Blencoe, A. G. Level and score of feedback as determinants of feedback effectiveness. *Academy of Management Proceedings,* 1982, 175–179.

Driessen, G. J. *Cause tree analysis: Measuring how accidents happen and the probabilities of their causes.* Paper presented at the 78th Annual Meeting of the American Psychological Association, September 1970.

Dubin, R. Organizational effectiveness: Some dilemmas of perspective. *Organization and Administrative Sciences,* 1976, *7,* 7–14.

Feutz, R. J., & Waldeck, T. A. *The application of fault tree analysis to dynamic systems.* Paper presented at the Systems Safety Symposium, Seattle, Washington, June 1965.

Flanagan, J. C. The critical incident technique. *Psychological Bulletin,* 1954, *51,* 327–358.

Friedlander, F., & Pickle, H. Components of effectiveness in small organizations. *Administrative Science Quarterly,* 1968, *13,* 289–304.

Fussell, J. B., Powers, G. J., & Bennetts, R. Fault tree: A state of the art discussion. *IEEE Transactions on Reliability,* R-23, April 1974, 51–55.

Galbraith, J. *Organizational design: An information processing view.* Reading, MA: Addision-Wesley, 1977.

Georgopolous, B. S., & Tannenbaum, A. S. The study of organizational effectiveness. *American Sociological Review,* 1957, *22,* 534–540.

Ghorpade, J. *Assessment of organization effectiveness.* Santa Monica, CA: Goodyear, 1970.

Goodman, P. S. *Organizational effectiveness as a decision making process.* Paper presented at the 39th Annual meeting of the Academy of Management, Atlanta, Georgia, 1979.

Goodman, P. S., & Pennings, J. M. *New perspectives on organizational effectiveness.* San Francisco: Jossey-Bass, 1977.

Haasl, D. F. *Advanced concepts in fault tree analysis.* Paper presented at the Systems Safety Symposium, Seattle, Washington, June 1965.

Hannan, M. T., & Freeman, J. The population ecology of organizations. *American Journal of Sociology,* 1977, *82,* 929–964.

Hedberg, B. L. T., Nystrom, P. C., & Starbuck, W. H. Camping on seesaws: Prescriptions for a self designing organization. *Administrative Science Quarterly,* 1976, *21,* 41–65.

Henley, E. J., & Lynn, J. W. *Generic techniques in systems reliability assessment.* Leyden, Netherlands: Noordhoff, 1976.

Herzberg, F., Mausner, B., & Synderman, B. *The motivation to work.* New York: Wiley, 1959.

Hiltz, P. A. *The fundamentals of fault tree analysis.* Downey, CA: North American Aviation, Inc., November 1965.

Hirschman, A. O., & Lindblom, C. E. Economic development, research and development, policy making: Some converging views. *Behavioral Science,* 1962, *8,* 211–222.

Hrebiniak, L. G. *Complex organizations.* St. Paul, MN: West Publishing, 1978.

Kanter, R. M., & Brinkerhoff, D. Organizational performance: Recent developments in measurement. *Annual Review of Sociology,* 1981, *7,* 321–349.

Kaplan, A., Skogstad, A. L., & Grishick, M. A. The prediction of social and technological events. *Public Opinion Quarterly*, Spring 1950.

Karmiloff-Smith, A., & Inhelder, B. If you want to get ahead, get a theory. *Cognition*, 1974–75, *3*, 195–212.

Keeley, M. Organizational analysis: A comparison of organismic and social contract models. *Administrative Science Quarterly*, 1980, *25*, 337–362.

Keeley, M. A social justice approach to organizational evaluation. *Administrative Science Quarterly*, 1978, *22*, 272–292.

Kilman, R. H., & Herden, R. P. Toward a systematic methodology for evaluating the impact of interventions on organizational effectiveness. *Academy of Management Review*, 1976, *1*, 87–98.

Kotler, P. A guide to gathering expert estimates. *Business Horizons*, 1970, *13*, 79–87.

Kuhn, T. S. *The structure of scientific revolution*. Chicago: University of Chicago Press, 1962.

Likert, R. *The human organization*. New York: McGraw-Hill, 1967.

Lindblom, C. E. The science of muddling through. *Public Administration Review*, 1959, *20*, 79–88.

MacDonald, J. *The game of business*. Garden City, NJ: Anchor Press, 1975.

March, J. G., & Olsen, J. P. *Ambiguity and choice in organizations*. Oslo, Norway: Universitetsforlaget, 1976.

Mearns, A. B. *Fault tree analysis: The study of unlikely events in complex systems*. Paper presented at the Systems Safety Symposium, Seattle, Washington, June 1965.

Meyer, M. W. Organizational domains. *American Sociological Review*, 1975, *40*, 599–615.

Michaels, J. M. *Computer evaluation of the safety fault tree model*. Paper presented at the Systems Safety Symposium, Seattle, Washington, June 1965.

Miles, R. H. *Macro organizational behavior*. Santa Monica, CA: Goodyear, 1980.

Miles, R. H., & Cameron, K. S. *Coffin nails and corporate strategies*. Englewood Cliffs, NJ: Prentice-Hall, 1982.

Miles, R. H., & Randolph, A. Influence of organizational learning styles on early development. In J. R. Kimberly and R. H. Miles (Eds.), *The organizational life cycle*. San Francisco: Jossey-Bass, 1980.

Millett, J. *The academic community*. New York: McGraw-Hill, 1962.

Mohr, L. R. The implications of effectiveness theory for managerial practice in the public sector. In K. S. Cameron and D. A. Whetten (Eds.), *Organizational effectiveness: A comparison of multiple models*. New York: Academic Press, 1983.

Molnar, J. J., & Rogers, D. C. Organizational effectiveness: On empirical comparison of the goal and system resource approach. *Sociological Quarterly*, 1976, *17*, 401–413.

Morgan, G. Paradigms, metaphors, and puzzle solving in organizational theory. *Administrative Science Quarterly*, 1980, *25*, 605–622.

Mott, P. E. *The characteristics of effective organizations*. New York: Harper and Row, 1972.

Nadler, D. A., & Tushman, M. L. A congruence model for organizational assessment. In E. E. Lawler, D. A. Nadler, and P. Cammann (Eds.), *Organizational assessment: Perspectives on the measurement of organizational behavior and the quality of working life*. New York: Wiley, 1980.

Nagel, P. M. *A Monte Carlo method to compute fault tree probabilities*. Paper presented at the Systems Satefy Symposium, Seattle, Washington, June 1965.

Nisbet, R. E., & Wilson, T. Telling more than we can know: Verbal reports on mental processes. *Psychological Review*, 1977, *134*, 231–259.

Nord, W. R. A political-economic perspective on organizational effectiveness. In K. S.

Cameron and D. A. Whetten (Eds.), *Organizational effectiveness: A comparison of multiple models*. New York: Academic Press, 1983.

Pennings, J. M., & Goodman, P. S. Toward a workable framework. In P. S. Goodman and J. M. Pennings (Eds.), *New perspectives on organizational effectiveness*. San Francisco: Jossey-Bass, 1977.

Perrow, C. *Organizational analysis: A sociological view*. Belmont, CA: Wadsworth, 1970.

Pfeffer, J. Management as symbolic action: The creation and maintenance of organizational paradigms. In L. L. Cummings and B. M. Staw (Eds.), *Research in organizational behavior* (Vol. 3). Greenwich, CT: JAI Press, 1981.

Pfeffer, J., & Salancik, G. R. *The external control of organizations*. New York: Harper and Row, 1978.

Pondy, L. R., & Mitroff, I. Beyond open systems models of organization. In B. Staw (Ed.), *Research in organizational behavior*. Greenich, CT: JAI Press, 1979.

Popper, K. R. *The open society and its enemies* (5th ed.). Princeton, NJ: Princeton University Press, 1966.

Powers, G. J. Fault tree synthesis for chemical process. *AICHE Journal*, 1974, *20*, 376–387.

Price, J. L. The study of organizational effectiveness. *Sociological Quarterly*, 1972, *13*, 3–15.

Price, J. L. *Organizational effectiveness: An inventory of propositions*. Homewood, IL: Irwin, 1968.

Quinn, R. E., & Cameron, K. S. Life cycles and shifting criteria of effectiveness: Some preliminary evidence. *Management Science*, 1983, *29*, 33–51.

Quinn, R. E., & Rohrbaugh, J. A competing values approach to organizational effectiveness. *Public Productivity Review*, 1981, *5*, 122–140.

Quinn, R. E., & Rohrbaugh, J. A spatial model of effectiveness criteria: Towards a competing values approach to organizational effectiveness. *Management Science*, forthcoming.

Rice, A. K. *Learning for leadership: Interpersonal and intergroup relations*. London: Tavistock, 1965.

Rohrbaugh, J. Operationalizing the competing values approach. *Public Productivity Review*, 1981, *5*, 141–159.

Rottenburg, A. *The emerging goddess*. Chicago: University of Chicago Press, 1979.

Sayles, L. R. *Leadership: What effective managers really do, and how they do it*. New York: McGraw-Hill, 1979.

Scott, W. R. Effectiveness of organizational effectiveness studies. In P. S. Goodman and J. M. Pennings (Eds.), *New perspectives on organizational effectiveness*. San Francisco: Jossey-Bass, 1977.

Seashore, S. E., and Yuchtman, E. Factorial analysis of organizational performance. *Administrative Science Quarterly*, 1967, *12*, 377–395.

Sherwood, J. J., Barron, J. W., & Fitch, H. G. Cognitive dissonance: Theory and research. In R. V. Wagner and J. J. Sherwood (Eds.), *The study of attitude change*. Belmont, CA: Brooks/Cole, 1969.

Schultz, R., Greenley, J., and Peterson, R. *Why do some health services provide higher quality care and/or private care at lower costs than others?* Working paper, Department of Preventive Medicine, University of Wisconsin-Madison, 1982.

Simon, H. A. *Administrative behavior*. New York: Free Press, 1947.

Slovic, P., & Lichtenstein, S. Comparison of Bayesian and regression approaches to the study of information processing in judgment. *Organizational Behavior and Human Performance*, 1971, *6*, 649–744.

Starbuck, W. H., & Nystrom, P. C. Pursuing organizational effectiveness that is ambiguously specified. In K. S. Cameron and D. A. Whetten (Eds.), *Organizational effectiveness: A comparison of multiple models.* New York: Academic Press, 1983.

Stasser, S., & Deniston, L. O. A comparative analysis of goal and systems models designed to evaluate health organization effectiveness. *Proceedings of the Academy of Management,* 1979, 342–347.

Steers, R. M. *Organizational effectiveness: A behavioral view.* Santa Monica, CA: Goodyear, 1977.

Steers, R. M. Review of S. L. Spray (Ed.), *Organizational effectiveness: Theory, research, and application.* Kent, Ohio: Kent State University Press, 1976, and P. S. Goodman and J. M. Pennings (Eds.), *New perspectives on organizational effectiveness.* San Francisco: Jossey-Bass, 1977. In *Administrative Science Quarterly,* 1978, *23,* 512–515.

Stephens, K. G. *A fault tree approach to needs assessment—An overview.* Paper presented at the Needs Assessment Conference, Oakland, CA, April 1976.

Stephens, K. G. *A fault tree approach to analysis of systems as demonstrated in vocational education.* Unpublished doctoral dissertation, University of Washington, 1972.

Thompson, J. D. *Organization in action.* McGraw-Hill, 1967.

Tichy, N., & Fombrun, C. Network analysis in social settings. *Human Relations,* 1979, *32,* 923–965.

Vaill, P. B. *The purposing of high performing systems.* Paper presented at a conference on Administrative Leadership: New Perspectives on Theory and Practice, University of Illinois, Urbana, July 1981.

Vaill, P. B. Toward a behavioral description of high performing systems. In M. McCall and M. Lombardo (Eds.), *Leadership: Where else can we go?* Durham, NC: Duke University Press, 1978.

Van de Ven, A. H., & Ferry, D. *Measuring and assessing organizations.* New York: Wiley, 1980.

Watkins, J. W. N. *Negative utilitarianism.* Proceedings of the Aristotelian Society, *37,* 95–114.

Weick, K. E. Re-punctuating the problem. In P. S. Goodman and J. M. Pennings (Eds.), *New perspectives on organizational effectiveness.* San Francisco: Jossey-Bass, 1977.

Whetten, D. A. Coping with incompatible expectations: An integrated view of role conflict. *Administrative Science Quarterly,* 1978, *23,* 254–271.

Winkler, R. L. The concensus of subjective probability distributions. *Management Science,* 1968, *13,* 61–75.

Witkin, B. R., & Stephens, K. G. *Fault tree analysis. A research tool for educational planning* (Technical Report No. 1) Hayward, CA: Alameda County PACE Center, 1968.

Wittgenstein, L. [*Philisophical investigations*] (GEM Anscombe, trans.) Oxford: Blackwell, 1968.

Wood, R. K., Stephens, K. G., & Barker, B. O. Fault tree analysis: An emerging methodology for instructional science. *Instructional Science,* 1979, *8,* 1–22.

Yuchtman, E., & Seashore, S. E. A system resource approach to organizational effectiveness. *American Sociological Review,* 1967, *32,* 891–903.

Zammuto, R. F. *Assessing organizational effectiveness: Systems change, adaptation, and strategy.* Albany, NY: SUNY Albany Press, 1982.

Zarzycki, J. H. *Fault tree analysis as a managerial tool for production loss control* (USAMC-ITC Report No. 2-71-14) Texarkana, TX: U. S. Army Logistics Management Center, Red River Army Depot, 1971.

OCCUPATIONAL COMMUNITIES:
CULTURE AND CONTROL IN
ORGANIZATIONS

John Van Maanen and Stephen R. Barley

ABSTRACT

One of the more persistent themes in sociology has been the presumed dichotomy between communal or colleagual and rational or administrative forms of work organization. While theories of organizations adopt the latter perspective, a conception of work organized in terms of occupational communities approximates the former. To this end, we define an occupational community as a group of people who consider themselves to be engaged in the same sort of work; whose identity is drawn from the work; who share with one another a set of values, norms and perspectives that apply to but extend beyond work related matters; and whose social relationships meld work and leisure.

The diverse origins of occupational communities are next discussed in relation to how physical and social conditions surrounding particular lines of work promote any or all of the definitional characteristics. Occupational communities are seen to create and sustain relatively unique work cultures consisting of, among other things, task rituals, standards for proper and improper behavior, work codes surrounding relatively routine practices and, for the membership at least, compelling accounts attesting to the logic and value of these rituals, standards and codes. We suggest that the quest for occupational self control provides the special motive for the development of occupational communities.

State support, an elaborate and advancing theoretical and procedural base to inform and mystify practice, and a relatively unorganized market in dire need of an occupational community's talents lend structural support to a community's quest for self control. We also suggest that the professions, when appropriately unpacked by speciality and interest, are best viewed as occupational communities and that they differ from other lines of work (and each other) only by virtue of the relative autonomy each is able to sustain within the political economy of a given society. Finally, the implications of occupational communities are explored in four domains of organizational research: careers, complexity, loyalty, and innovation.

Research in Organizational Behavior, vol. 6, pages 287–365
Copyright © 1984 by JAI Press Inc.
All rights of reproduction in any form reserved.
ISBN: 0-89232-351-5

To the study of human behavior in organizations, a field already choking on assorted paradigms, hypotheses, methods, variables, and other objects of intellectual passion, we offer in this essay even more conceptual paraphernalia. Specifically, we shall argue the utility of viewing behavior in organizations through an occupational rather than organizational lens. Considerable lip service has been paid to such a perspective by organizational theorists but, for a variety of reasons, focused and conceptually-driven research based on such a perspective has been notably absent in the organization behavior literature. This neglect has consequence, not the least of which is that organization researchers largely disregard the phenomenological boundaries recognized by members of particular work worlds. Descriptions of these intersubjective boundaries and the shared activities, social interactions, and common understandings established by those who fall within these boundaries are found, however, in the growing ethnographic records of contemporary work worlds. Such empirical materials represent lively, rich accounts of occupational ways of life; accounts we believe must be reckoned with if organizational theories are to locate and explain more of the behavioral variability of the workplace than has been the case to date.[1]

Consider, for example, the contrast between ethnographic writings about a person's work and career and the writings on the same topics found in the organization behavior literature.[2] The ethnographic versions feature closely detailed narratives of everyday work activities, first-hand accounts of observed events (routine and otherwise), free-flowing, lengthy descriptions of the various belief systems that appear to inform a person's selection of career and, perhaps all too frequently, precious little attempt to generalize across occupations or careers. The particular and occasionally unique things people do for a living are matters uncovered by ethnographers along with the meanings such activities hold for the people who do them. In the equally stylized organization behavior literature, the specifics of work and careers are glossed over while the aggregate and occasionally general ways people believe and behave in occupational settings are emphasized.

Such divergence is, of course, hardly surprising since the two genres differ in purpose, audience, format, and language. Yet, the dissimilarities between the two approaches are not simply matters of contrasting form or style, nor should the discrepancies be dismissed with the claim that variable-based research is somehow more objective or analytic than the context-sensitive ethnographic research and, therefore, less passionate, idiosyncratic, or biased. In our view, it remains noteworthy that "Charlie, the automobile repairman down at Joe's Garage" is, in the ethnographic writings, a "mechanic" and, in the organization behavior writings, an "employee."

We hold these genre disparities to be substantive, reflecting alternative and potentially conflicting models of how work is organized and interpreted. One perspective views a person's work from an organizational frame of reference and thus accentuates the meaning that such work has for others. The other approach employs an occupational perspective and concentrates upon the meaning of work for those who do it (Berger, 1964). Both perspectives operate as templates to select, mold, and present the subject in ways which transcend the obvious conceits of the genres. Several contrasting assumptions are at work when either framework is utilized.

From an organizational standpoint, most people are seen to regard their work careers largely in terms of movement (or lack thereof) within a set sequence of hierarchically ascending positions, each position offering more or less prestige, power, money, and other rewards. Observers employing an occupational perspective imply that persons weave their perspectives on work and career from the existing social, moral, physical, and intellectual character of the work itself. Individual assessments of work and career are cast in terms of one's getting better (or worse) at what one does, getting support (or interference) from others, exerting more (or less) influence over the nature of one's work, and so on. The two perspectives also differ on the importance of "work" as a concept for explaining social order. From the organizational perspective, a person's work is but a small part of the larger problems of coordination, authority, workflow, production method, or service design. Work is a concept subsidiary to the more abstract (but logically intertwined) relationships that are thought to engender the economic and social order of an organization or the society at large. From the occupational perspective, work and the groups that are inspired or flattened by it are themselves focal concepts for explaining social structure because they provide the basis of an occupationally stratified organization or society.

Contrasts such as these arise from placing differential emphasis on what Weber (1968:40) called the rational (associational or organizational) and traditional (communal or occupational) aspects of modern economy and society. For the most part, rational aspects have dominated organizational research and interest has been persistently directed toward the brisk correlates of organizational performance rather than the substantive nature of the work people perform during their working lives. Similarly, conflicts of interest in organizational settings have been examined almost exclusively by reference to vertical cleavages of authority or friction between functional units rather than by reference to clashes between organizational authorities and occupational interest groups.[3]

In this paper, we develop the notion of an occupational community as an alternative to an organizational frame of reference for understanding why it is that people behave as they do in the workplace. In essence, we want to develop a perspective that will prove valuable when regarding our hypothetical auto repairman as a "mechanic" rather than an "employee." Several analytic aims are served by this approach.

First, a focus on occupations preserves some of the existential, everyday reality of the firsthand experience of work. The fact that one works the swing shift in a cattle slaughterhouse as a hind-toe-remover is a rather straightforward descriptive statement. But, it is a statement that we belive conveys considerably more information than that conveyed by organizationally designed job descriptions of the sort seized upon by organizational researchers in their search for generality, such as unskilled laborer, machine operator, or assembly line worker. Social worlds coalesce around the objects produced and the services rendered by people at work. To focus on occupation, as the semantic tag tying together the bundle of tasks which constitute a given line of work, brings such social worlds and their many meanings to light.

Second, by examining the social worlds that coalesce around occupations, we broaden our understanding of social control in organizations. We take as axiomatic that the fundamental problem of organization—or, more properly, the management of organizations—is the control of the labor process. Occupational matters are undeniably central to this problem since all positions have histories marking their rise (and fall) in terms of the amount of self-control occupational members possess over the fruits and methods of their labors. The ongoing struggle of stable and shifting, formal and informal, large and small groups to develop and occupy some niche in the occupational structure of society is played out every day in organizations where rational or administrative principles of control (e.g., codification, standardization, hierarchical discipline, etc.) compete with traditional or communal principles of control (e.g., peer pressures, work ideologies, valued symbols, etc.).

Third, a focus upon work and occupation casts new light on problems of diversity and conflict in the workplace. From an administrative standpoint, "deviance" among organizational members is defined in terms of exceptions to managerial expectations. The sources of such deviance are typically ignored or muted since administrative solutions are sought in terms of correcting the "system" so that expectations can be met. That deviance is willful is a point often made in organizational studies, but seldom elaborated upon beyond bland reference to the ubiquitous "informal" groups contained within organizations. Even when deviance is treated seriously and in some depth by organizational theorists concerned with the individual orientations of organizational members toward their work, it is often treated as merely the result of non-work factors such as universal human needs ignored by the designers of work systems (Roethlisberger & Dickson, 1939); too rigorous, tight, punitive, or otherwise unenlightened management practices (McGregor, 1960; Argyris, 1964); narrow, standardized, efficiency-focused, mass production technologies (Blauner, 1964; Hackman & Oldman, 1979); subcultural, class-based norms imported into the workplace from outside (Katz, 1965; Dubin, 1956); situational opportunities seized upon by employees to improve earnings, thwart boredom, advance careers, or reduce risk (Dalton, 1969; Roy, 1960); and so on.

While these sources of informal adjustments or member deviance are undoubtedly present in all organizations, willful violation of managerial expectations may also correspond to a pervasive logic embedded within the historically developed practices of occupational members doing what they feel they must. Rather than a reflection of class interests or a knee-jerk response to flawed managerial schemes, organizational deviance may be proactive, not reactive. More important, it may also reflect the way a given line of work has come to be defined and practiced relatively independent of technology, managerial mistakes, or organization structure (Silverman, 1970). What is deviant organizationally may be occupationally correct (and vice-versa).[4] Aside from some of the early work conducted in the Tavistock sociotechnical traditions, organization theory rarely concerns itself with such contradictions (Trist & Bamforth, 1951; Rice, 1958).

Fourth, a focus on the common tasks, work schedules, job training, peer relations, career patterns, shared symbols, or any and all of the elements that comprise an occupation brings forth a concern regarding how a given line of work can be said to influence one's social conduct and identity, both in and out of the workplace. Goffman (1961a:87–88) makes this point nicely when he suggests: "A self (then) virtually awaits the individual entering a position; he needs only to conform to the pressures on him and he will find a 'me' ready-made for him. . . . being is doing." Although a position is organizationally created and sanctioned, the work that comprises such a position often has a history of its own and, therefore, a context that is not organizationally limited. Even rigidly defined positions are almost always more than most organization designers, authorities and, alas, researchers make them out to be (e.g., Roy, 1960). Some of these positions may offer an occupant far more than a job. Indeed, some may offer a rewarding and valued "me." The identity-bestowing characteristics of positions are, in short, frequently matters which are occupationally specific.

To develop an occupational perspective on concerns often considered organizational, we first identify and expand upon the notion of an "occupational community." Next, we suggest that occupational communities of all types are marked by distinctive work cultures promoting self control and collective autonomy for the membership. As a result, we take issue with the stance of many organization theorists who regard professional work as an occupational category clearly separable from other lines of work by describing, in comparative terms, some of the structural or external conditions that appear to foster self control. Following this discussion, we note how each of several long standing research domains within organizational studies—careers, conflict, loyalty, and innovation—can be enriched empirically and advanced conceptually by paying serious attention to the role occupational communities play within organizations.

ON THE NATURE OF OCCUPATIONAL COMMUNITIES

To know what dentistry, firefighting, accounting, or photography consists of and means to those who pursue it is to know the cognitive, social, and moral contours of the occupation. Of course, not all occupations can be said to possess decipherable contours, since the degree to which knowledge, practices, and values are shared among practitioners varies across occupations, across time, and across settings. However, some occupations display a rather remarkable stability in social space and time and, hence, can be decoded. It is for them that the idea of an occupational community is most relevant since it draws attention to those occupations that transmit a shared culture from generation to generation of participants.

The notion of an occupational community derives from two classical sociological premises. First is the contention that people bound together by common values, interests, and a sense of tradition, share bonds of solidarity or mutual regard and partake of a communal way of life that contrasts in idyllic ways with the competition, individualism, and rational calculation of self-interest associated with persons organized on utilitarian principles. The distinction between communal and utilitarian forms of human association and the consequences of the transformation of the former into the latter are issues that preoccupied social theorists of the late 19th and early 20th centuries. Comte, Weber, Durkheim, Tonñies, and Marx each sensed that Western civilization was undergoing a social upheaval brought about by industrialization of the economy and bureaucratization of the state. While disagreeing over the meaning of the transformation, all concurred that a shift from "gemeinshaft" to "gesellshaft" was irrevocable.[5]

The central dilemma spawned by such a transformation lies in the nature of the social contract: How can human relationships remain socially integrated and rewarding in and of themselves when they are based on principles of utilitarianism and rational calculation of self-interest? One answer claims that rational associations are themselves meritorious. Thus, Weber, while acutely aware that rational organization generates its own problems (notably, rigidity and narrowness of scope), put forth more persuasively than any of his contemporaries the special virtues of rational organization in his depiction of ideal state bureaucracies. The attributes of Weberian bureaucracy are well known: division of labor by specialization, qualification by examination, coordination by impersonal rules, and authority legitimated by hierarchical office. In comparison to other forms of state organization, Weber thought bureaucracy superior insofar as it sought, through rationalization, to eliminate advancement by patrimony or special interest, to eradicate encrusted traditions, and to promise collective achievement through the use of member expertise.

Durkheim (1933) was also relatively optimistic about the potential benefits of rational organization (particularly in his early writings). He claimed that gesellshaft relationships engender their own peculiar devices for moral integration since rational contracts presume trust and negotiated reciprocity. However, Durkheim, much like Weber, tempered his optimism with the proposition than only gemeinshaft-like relationships could ameliorate the anomic side effects of rational organization and the division of labor. Durkheim's prescription for maintaining the social fabric of community amplified the very cleavages born of the division of labor: The formation of occupational groups to serve as political entities as well as reference groups. We trace to Durkheim the second premise upon which the notion of occupational community rests: the idea that the work we do shapes the totality of our lives and, to a great extent, determines who we think we are.

> Besides the society of faith, of family, and of politics, there is one other . . . that of all workers of the same sort, in association, all who cooperate in the same function; that is, the occupational group or corporation. Identity of origin, culture, and occupation makes occupational activity the richest sort of material for a common life.
>
> Durkheim (1951:578)

> . . . this character of corporative organization comes from very general causes . . . When a certain number of individuals in the midst of a political society are found to have ideas, interests, sentiments, and occupations not shared by the rest of the population, it is inevitable that they will be attracted toward each other under the influence of these likenesses. They will seek each other out, enter into relations, associate, and thus little by little a restricted group, having its special characteristics, will be formed in the midst of the general society. But once the group is formed, a moral life appears naturally carrying the mark of the particular conditions in which it has developed. For it is impossible for men to live together, associating in industry, without acquiring a sentiment of the whole formed by their union, without attaching themselves to that whole, preoccupying themselves with its interests, and taking account of it in their conduct.
>
> Durkheim (1933:14)

The implication of Durkheim's remarks is that modern society is not only structured vertically by the rationality of industrial and state organization, but that it is also structured horizontally by occupational groupings. Although Durkheim proposed that occupations might provide the moral fabric for society, the so-called Chicago school of sociology showed empirically the diversity of this moral fabric.[6] For instance, the writings of Park and Burgess (1924), Hughes (1958, 1971), Becker (1963) and (especially) Becker et al. (1968), display the many moral, aesthetic, and social parameters of occupational groupings from the high status to low. In particular, Chicago School sociologists stress that the meaning of a line of work is socially constructed and validated in practice by members of an occupation; that an occupational career is decipherable only by reference to occupationally specific meanings; that occupations foster particular categorization schemes which structure work worlds as well as the larger social environment; and that work roles provide incumbents with a social identity and a code for conduct, both within and without the workplace.

The fusion of the community ideal, with the notion that one's work shapes one's life, finds expression in the vision of the artisan whose very being is inseparable from his means of livelihood and whose work suffuses every relationship with meaning. C. Wright Mills (1956:223) provides the example with his lyrical description of the craftsman.

> The craftsman's work is the mainspring of the only world he knows; he does not flee from work into a separate sphere of leisure . . . he brings to his non-working hours the values and qualities developed and employed in his working time. His idle conversation is shop talk; his friends follow the same line of work as he, and share a kinship of feeling and thought.

This blurring of the distinction between work and leisure, and the idea that certain kinds of work bind people together and help shape the course of their existence lies at the core of research ventures into occupational communities. For instance, working with high status occupations, Gertzl (1961:38) used the phrase "occupational community" to reflect the "pervasiveness of occupational identification and the convergence of informal friendship patterns and colleague relationships." Salaman (1974) elaborated upon the same theme when characterizing the work worlds of architects and railroaders. The term has also been used in the labor relations literature to describe relationships among union members or residents in towns where employment can be found in, or tightly bound to, only one line of work (Glaser, 1977; Hill, 1981).

The conception of occupational community developed here seeks to draw together much of this previous work. Our definition of an occupational community contains four elements. Each is separate analytically but interconnected empirically. By occupational community, we mean a group of people who consider themselves to be engaged in the same sort of work; who identify (more or less positively) with their work; who share a set of values, norms, and perspectives that apply to, but extend beyond, work related matters; and whose social relationships meld the realms of work and leisure.

Boundaries

In his critique of the concept of community, Gusfield (1975:31–32) cautions against operationally identifying communities on the basis of obvious or ascribed attributes of a group of individuals.[7] Two popular criteria for defining communities, inhabitance of common territory and possession of similar backgrounds, are especially misleading. Not only may the inhabitants of a small village be decisively divided into smaller groups that compete among themselves for resources, but persons with very diverse histories and traditions can attain a sense of solidarity (as did Jews of German and Russian origin who emigrated to the United States). Moreover, since human groups and relationships are multi-faceted, any number of attributes can be invented or discovered along which members can be compared and contrasted. Consequently, even if members are alike in some respect, there is no guarantee that the respect is relevant. More crucial parameters for identifying communities are the social dimensions used by members themselves for recognizing one another, the social limits of such bonds, and situational factors which amplify or diminish the perceived common identity. Gusfield (1975:33) writes that "the concept of community is part of a system of accounts used by members and observers as a way of explaining or justifying the member's behavior. It is the criteria of action . . . rather than the physical arena within which action occurs . . . it is the behavior governed by criteria of common belonging rather than mutual interest."

Following Gusfield's idea that "consciousness of kind" is the fundamental basis for a community, we submit that the relevant boundaries of an occupational community are those set by the members themselves. Hence, the first attribute of an occupational community is that it is composed of people who consider themselves "to be" members of the same occupation rather than people who "are" members of the same occupation. This distinction relies solely upon internal rather than external accounts and is of theoretical and methodological significance.[8]

The social organization of an occupation as seen by insiders is typically quite different from that seen by outsiders. Insiders may group themselves along connotative dimensions that escape the uninitiated and these connotative dimensions may lead some members to separate themselves from others who do denotatively similar work. This point, well established in cognitive anthropology (Goodenough, 1970; Spradley, 1979), is crucial when empirical work turns toward intensive occupational study because official occupational titles provide only a dim suggestion of where community boundaries may lie. Occupational studies that rely on Census Bureau classifications are obviously well outside our definitional limits. "Professional, technical and kindred" covers authors, draftsmen, strip tease artists and accountants; "managers, officials and proprietors" embraces political appointees, bank officials, taco vendors and chief executive officers.

Nor are commonsensical and conventionally applied occupational labels particularly helpful. Conventional labels typically represent the theoretical limit of an occupational community. Within this boundary, socially significant types (i.e., of dentists, of firefighters, of accountants, etc.) are sure to exist which are, for all practical purposes, mutually exclusive and quite distinct in the minds of the insiders. When studying occupational communities, it is to the ethnographic record a researcher must go.

Commerical fishing provides a useful example because within its boundaries are found several rather distinct occupational communities. "Traditional fishermen" recognize differences between themselves and "nontraditional fishermen" such as "educated fishermen," "part-timers," and "outlaw fishermen" (Miller & Van Maanen, 1982). Even more important are distinctions made within types. Thus, in the port of Gloucester, Massachusetts, traditional fishermen divide themselves into two groups, Guineas and Greasers.[9] Each group represents an identifiable and self-referential occupational community. Though members of both groups call themselves fishermen and exemplify the traditional approach to the trade, the two groups neither work together nor associate with one another outside of work. Both the social idealization and the practical realization of a fishing career are quite different within each group.

More familiar examples are easily located within academic settings. Consider the sub-worlds to be discovered within scholarly disciplines as catalogued by Crane's (1971) insightful mapping of "invisible colleges." Consider also the two sociologies so elegantly portrayed by Dawe (1980). In the United States, social theorists of both symbolic interactionist and structural-functional bent certainly consider themselves sociologists. Yet, the members of each theory group rarely cite work done by members of the other group (except as targets for attack), almost never collaborate on joint research projects, and interact professionally only with some difficulty. When one considers the research programs advocated in each camp, the inescapable conclusion is that whatever a symbolic interactionist is, a structural functionist is not.

The failure of well-known occupational labels to identify the bounds of an occupational community is also aggravated by the fact that many occupations are effectively hidden from public view. Given the indefinite number of jobs that exist and their respective distance from social researchers, superficial occupational descriptions are the norm in work studies, not the exception. Abstractions such as "unskilled labor," "semi-skilled labor," "manager," and even "engineer," are merely linguistic proxies for an uncharted population of distinct occupational pursuits. Few of us would guess that petroleum landmen share a particularly strong occupational community because few of us would even know that petroleum landmen exist, and we certainly would not know what they do (Bryant, 1972a).

Obscurity is not the only blinder. A greater myopia is the presumption that our categories are actually descriptive. The muddle of research on cosmopolitan and local orientations of so-called professionals is, in part, the outcome of inadequately specified occupational boundaries or limits. Not only have researchers in this domain confused "industrial scientist" with "industrial engineer" (Glaser, 1964; Ritti, 1968), they have also failed to recognize that worlds of engineering are differentiated by specialties as well as by differences in the scope, type, and intent of the work that passes as engineering in industry (Allen, 1977; Bailyn, 1980). Engineers themselves are often unable to say what engineers do except within the well defined setting of some company (Becker & Carper, 1956).

Abstract aggregation serves as ideology. It allows stereotypes to masquerade as knowledgeable descriptions. A classic example is the uncritical acceptance of the proposition that workers in "unskilled" and "semi-skilled" occupations lack careers or career ladders. Since some research has shown that some "unskilled" workers (in some occupations, in some periods, in some industries) are unlikely to follow or hope for an orderly progression of jobs (Chinoy, 1955; Wilensky, 1961; Beynon & Blackburn, 1972), researchers extend the attribute of "career-less-ness" to an undifferentiated mass of nominally unskilled workers. This uncritical generalizing of results proceeds by reducing a heterogeneous population to homogeneity and by discounting the probability that occupational life is shaped by specific contexts of work. More insidiously, generalizing across aggregates discourages particularistic research which might surface conditions under which the generalizations do not hold. Thus, so-called anomalies, such as the existence of career paths for laborers on pipeline construction crews (Graves, 1958), for janitors in urban communities (Gold, 1964), for steelworkers in South Chicago (Kornblum, 1974), or for poker players in California gambling establishments (Hayano, 1982) are unlikely to be discovered, or, when discovered, discounted as mere exceptions to the general rule.

Adequate delineation of the boundaries of occupational communities requires research strategies open to the discovery of socially meaningful work groups and methodologies that resonate to the inner cleavages of work worlds. In lieu of sufficiently detailed and phenomenologically sensitive taxonomies of occupational groupings, researchers face a dual task: the actual discovery of existing occupational communities and the depiction of the dimensions along which they are formed. The two tasks must proceed simultaneously since delimiting boundaries entails knowing the social criteria that generate them.[10]

One final point regarding boundaries concerns the territorial or geographic dispersion of the membership of an occupational community. Geographic proximity or common territory are, to many, natural indicators of community and, indeed, propinquity undergirds the use of the term "occupational community" by those researchers who employ it as a label for occupationally homogeneous towns or villages (Hill, 1981). Our use of the phrase, however, does not presume that members of an occupational community necessarily live or work near one another. Propinquity is then an attribute along which occupational communities vary. Certainly, propinquity may hasten and otherwise contribute to the development and maintenance of an occupational community, but it is not itself a definitional matter. Whether a particular community is geographically dispersed or clustered is an empirical question to be answered as communities are identified and analyzed.

Social Identity

The second definitional feature of an occupational community is that members derive valued identities or self-images directly from their occupational roles. In brief, individuals, from our perspective, carry social selves, each constructed and reconstructed in daily interaction with others as people learn to view themselves from the point of view of others (Mead, 1930; Blumer, 1969; Van Maanen, 1979). To be sure, these social selves are contextually tied, but, as they are refined and confirmed as more or less impressive and serviceable across recurrent situations, they typically enable a person to present a reasonably comfortable, consistent, and, with occasional lapses, socially acceptable image to others (Goffman, 1959).

Some social selves are, of course, more central to one's sense of identity than others. The more central the social self, the less easily modified and the more omnipresent it is in everyday interaction (Schein, 1971). In occupational communities, the social identities assumed by most members include, in a prominent position, one based upon the kind of work they do and, as such, it is often quite central in their presentations of self to others (particularly to those outside the community) in everyday life. In this sense, a person may be, among other things, a guinea fisherman, a

Catholic, and an employee for Peter Pan. Another may be a street cop, a jogger, and a mother. Individuals do not necessarily order the importance and value of such presentations (they are all important and valuable). Without question, social identities are sensitive to and reflective of the social situations to which an individual is party. But, for members of occupational communities at least, occupational identities are typically presented to others with some pride and are not identities easily discarded for they are central to an individual's self-image (Van Maanen, 1979).

Indirect evidence of identification with an occupation is demonstrated by distinctive accouterments, costumes, and jargon. Members of fishing communities wear particular types of baseball caps to tell other fishermen what port they are from and what their involvement with fishing is likely to be (Miller & Van Maanen, 1982). Police officers carry courtesy cards, off-duty revolvers, and wallet badges. The unique properties of each convey significant clues to other officers as to where the owner stands in the community (Van Maanen, 1974; Rubinstein, 1973). Bawdy urban procurers are known to drive automobiles of distinctive style and color called "pimpmobiles" (James, 1972). Electricians recognize other electricians by the color of their overalls and by the shoes they wear (Reimer, 1977). And, one needs only to catch snippets of conversation among members of an occupational community to appreciate the role special language plays (e.g., "We apprehended that dirtbag on a stand-up just next to my duck pond on 3rd and Main").

These visible identification devices serve as "tie-signs" that establish cognitive and socially verified links between person and occupation (Goffman, 1971: 194–5). More fundamentally, they represent only the most obvious of a multitude of signs that comprise a complex system of codes which enable the members of an occupation to communicate to one another an occupationally specific view of their work world. Although languages are the most versatile of all codes and may call attention to themselves when they take the form of jargon and argot, any object, event, or phenomenon becomes a part of a code, a sign, when it signifies something to someone (Pierce, 1958; Barthes, 1964). Since signs and codes are established by the conventions of a particular group and are imparted by socialization practices, any given entity can potentially carry many connotations and denotations (Hawkes, 1977; Eco, 1976). The loose and arbitrary coupling between vehicle and content implies that a particular word, object, or event can signify different meanings for people who employ different codes.

We typically assume that specialists know more than laymen because of the knowledge presumably gained by extensive training. But, differences in understanding are qualitative as well as quantitative. Expertise arises, in part, because experts and laymen employ different codes for interpreting events. Where a frustrated parent sees only an incorrigible child, the psychotherapist sees vestiges of an unresolved Oedipal conflict. Where a puzzled automobile owner hears but a strange puttering, the mechanic recognizes a missing cylinder or worn points. Becoming a member of an occupation always entails learning a set of codes that can be used to construct meaningful interpretations of persons, events, and objects commonly encountered in the occupational world.

The more pervasive, esoteric and numerous the codes employed by members of an occupation, the more likely the occupation engenders identity because the confluence of codes overdetermines a perspective on reality and overrides the plausibility of naive interpretations of the same matter (Barley, 1983). Even when on vacation, police officers see cues of wrongdoing and danger in everyday settings. Funeral directors, when out on the town, continue to monitor their demeanor (Habenstein, 1962). Psychiatrists in training practice their trade by staying diagnostically alert to the emotional and mental states of their friends and acquaintances (Light, 1980). When codes of an occupation generate such an all-bracing orientation, an occupational community is likely to be found.

The possession and use of pervasive and peculiar codes is but one factor that encourages positive identification with an occupation. Occupational identities are also fostered by high involvement in the work itself. In a study of the work worlds of graduate engineers, Lynch and Bailyn (1980) note that involvement in work implies something quite different than simply seeking or drawing satisfaction from work. Involvement implies, among other things, absorption in the symbolic nature of work so that work takes on a special significance and sets the involved apart from others who do not pursue the same livelihood in the same fashion. The sense of being apart and different underlies the development of a shared identity. Discussing the concept of community, Weber (1968: 42–43) insisted that "consciousness of kind" arises structurally and only in conjunction with "consciousness of difference."

> "A common language, which arises from a similarity of tradition through the family and surrounding the social environment, facilitates mutual understanding. . . . but, taken by itself, it is not sufficient to constitute a communal relationship. . . . it is only with the emergence of a consciousness of difference from third persons who speak a different language that the fact that two persons speak the same language and, in that respect, share a common situation, can lead them to a feeling of community and to modes of social organization consciously based on the sharing of the common language."

Ethnographically detailed research on occupations describe several factors that appear to compel special involvement with work as well as a sense of commonality and uniqueness among the members of an occupation. Danger ranks high on this list. For example, Haas (1977) documents the cameraderie, mutual regard, and intense involvement among high-steel ironworkers and attributes much of this to the constant, eminent peril that comes with working on open girders hundreds of feet above the ground. Danger also invites work involvement and a sense of fraternity among police officers and fishermen where the consequences of one simple mistake may be severe (Van Maanen, 1980b). Recognition that one's work entails danger heightens the contrast between one's own work and the safer work of others, and encourages comparison of self with those who share one's work situation. Attitudes, behavior, and self-images for coping physically and psychologically with threat become part of an occupational role appreciated best, it is thought, only by one's fellow workers. Danger spawns an insider-outsider dichotomy characteristic of communal identities (Becker, 1963; Gusfield, 1975).

A second factor encouraging involvement and identification with one's occupation occurs when members of an occupation possess (or, more properly, believe they possess) certain esoteric, scarce, socially valued, and unique abilities. Skilled tradesmen occupy separate subworlds in the construction industry because mastery of their craft licenses them (as does the state and the occupational association) to make autonomous, specialized, minute-by-minute decisions (Stinchcombe, 1959). Thus carpenters raise roofbeams and plumbers attend sinks and toilets in rather splendid isolation, despite the often frantic coordinating attempts of contractors.

The crafts and trades are often held forth as the last vestiges of occupations that encourage a sense of identity and community. But, according to the deskilling argument, technological innovations such as the numerical machine tool (Braverman, 1974; Noble, 1977) and bureaucratic controls (Johnson, 1972; Edwards, 1979) increasingly promote and permit the encoding of the craftsman's expertise and the subsequent partitioning and rationalization of trade work. A careful and detailed look at the systematic and disturbingly unilateral dismantling of several occupational communities of craftsmen in the steel industry by cost-conscious managers is provided by Stone (1979) and given theoretical meaning by Marglin (1974).

While managerially-sponsored technology may deskill some occupations, technological innovation in other settings may generate occupational communities whose members possess new forms of esoteric skill. Pettigrew's (1973) study of the installation of computers into a Scottish firm underscores the power computer programmers and systems analysts derive from their knowledge of the machine and its language. For a number of years, the programmers in Pettigrew's firm were allowed to develop work identities, a community, and customs that clashed with the managerial, staff, and production cultures in the organization simply because the programmers controlled scarce and impenetrable knowledge. Similarly, new radiological technologies, such as ultrasound, create a community of radiologists and radiological technicians who are the only individuals in the hospital capable of interpreting the meanings of images that appear to be just noise to consulting physicians. Command of such expertise has led some radiologists to assert with more than a little enthusiasm that radiology has become a crucial link in the hospital's delivery of services (Barley, forthcoming).

Rather than claim progressive deskilling and the general demise of all occupational identities and communities, a theory of occupational change modeled after the notion of speciation provides a more plausible view. As the technical expertise of some occupations becomes codified, disseminated, partitioned, grasped by outsiders, normalized and demystified, the occupational community wanes. But, at the same time, new forms of technical expertise and new occupations may arise in the wake of the old, thus creating new occupational communities. A population of occupations in a state of ebb and flow may more accurately depict historical experience. As the knowledge of computer programming becomes more widespread and uncoupled from knowledge of mathematics, programming becomes far less esoteric. At the same time, however, a new occupational identity arises to deal with the remaining indeterminacies programming entails, the systems analyst (Pettigrew, 1973). Consequently, to the degree that those pursuing a line of work manage to maintain control over a scarce set of abilities or to develop an expanded knowledge base which only they can apply, occupational identities are likely to be sustained over time, if not enhanced. These are topics we will return to in following sections for they bear directly on the definitional questions surrounding the nature of what is (and what is not) usually called professional work.

Claimed responsibility for others is a third factor promoting identification with and involvement in a line of work. The "hogsheads" (locomotive engineers) studied by Gamst (1980) believe they perform especially important work which sets them apart from other workers because the safety of the train, its passengers, and its cargo depend on their performance. Air traffic controllers, police officers, taxi drivers, nurses, and emergency medical technicians, all extoll the virtues of service as an occupational creed. In some cases, there accrues a certain reverence, awe, and prestige for those in occupations granted life-and-death responsibilities over others. Even when responsibilities are not so weighty or visible in the public eye, members of the occupation may still attempt to manufacture and maintain a sense of occupational honor through doing the public good (Hughes, 1958). Garbage collectors develop an ideology around the public health functions of their work which, in turn, may (but usually does not) provide a respectable basis for adopting the identity of sanitation worker (Lasson, 1971). When one believes that one holds a symbolic trust, identification with an occupation is facilitated.

In essence, the confrontation of danger in one's work, the possession of esoteric skills, and the belief that one does special and socially significant work provide conditions which encourage the perception that oneself and one's colleagues are somehow different from the rest of the working population. Common skills, common risks, and common adventures form the basis for a communal identity by promoting interaction with those others who "know the score" and thereby increase the probability that members of such occupations will consider themselves to be unique.

Reference Group

To maintain a social identity, support and confirmation from others is required (Mead, 1930; Goffman, 1959). The third defining feature of an occupational community is that members take other members as their primary reference group such that the membership comes to share a distinct pattern of values, beliefs, norms, and interpretations for judging the appropriateness of one another's actions and reactions.[11] This would include moral standards surrounding what work is to be considered good and bad, what work is "real work" and, therefore, in contrast to "shit work," what formal and contextual rules of conduct are to be enforced, what linguistic categories are to be used in partitioning the world, and so forth. To say an occupational community provides members with a value system is to say that members make use of a collective perspective in everyday matters, that they evaluate themselves in its light, and that such a perspective carries over to matters falling outside the realm of work itself.

Several conditions appear to foster the adoption of shared occupational values. First, when an occupation is stigmatized or viewed by outsiders as marginal in society, members will turn to one another for aid and comfort and, through such interaction, sustain a view of the world that justifies and vindicates itself as a defense against outsiders. Street sweepers in India are avoided by members of higher castes because the work they do is considered polluting. Yet, sweepers who live together in closed communities in Benares share a value system that partially compensates for the low social status of their work by positing that the very attributes feared by higher castes are, in fact, qualities to be appreciated (Searle-Chaterjee, 1979). Sweepers are likely to flaunt their untouchable status and wield it as a collective political and social weapon for securing autonomy and other occupational rewards incommensurate with their caste's status.

The solidarity of marginal or stigmatized occupations is by no means confined to societies with rigid caste systems. Becker's (1951) jazz musicians come to respect only the judgements, tastes, and perspectives of like-minded musicians. These values are predicated upon, and, at the same time create, the musicians' view of themselves as different from the "square" majority. Such aloofness and self-sealing interaction loops are also found in the high status occupations whose members are celebrated rather than stigmatized. In some cases, outsiders may even consider the occupation to be inspirational as seems to be the case with medicine and the clergy. However, we must note that the celebrated status of such occupations is contingent upon more than the presumed social problems addressed or socially valued work performed by occupational members since the celebration is both cultivated and protected by occupational members. Physicians have long sought, for example, to build and maintain a view of themselves as knights in the battle against pestilence. The current attack upon medical prestige and practice takes shape through the attempted destruction of the "myth of the healer" as promulgated by medical interest groups (e.g., Illich, 1976).

Occupations that penetrate multiple aspects of a person's life also create conditions favorable to taking members of the occupation as one's primary reference group. To maintain a career in some occupations requires adopting a particular style of life. For example, funeral directors with neighborhood-based practices understand that their work dictates the modeling of certain community and religious standards. Since advertising is considered inappropriate by local funeral directors, they rely upon their community involvement and reputation to attract clientele. Under the theory that certain kinds of behavior might offend potential clients, funeral directors present themselves with heightened personal reserve and the sort of social conservatism respectful of local traditions (Habenstein, 1962). Consequently, certain forms of public behavior, for instance, drunkenness, boisterousness, or even the relative luxury of not attending religious services regularly, are taboo not only for the funeral director but often also for his family. Moreover, the practices of providing twenty-four hour availability and living in the funeral home are widespread across the membership of the occupation. These features act as common denominators that foster a shared world view for interpreting the occupational experience (Barley, 1980). Such social conditions suggest funeral directing's similarity to other occupations whose members are required to be constantly "on" (e.g., entertainers, priests, presidents, and, arguably, college professors in small towns). Only others who face the same demands can constitute a reference group able to bolster performances and sustain the centrality of the role to the membership (Messinger et al., 1962).

Rigorous socialization is a third condition that influences members to adopt the standards of the occupational group. The ordeal-like atmosphere of the police academy draws individuals together for mutual support and creates a recruit culture within which novice police officers can interpret their experiences in ways shared by others (Van Maanen, 1973). Various occupations utilize different socialization practices, but, in general, the more harsh, formal, lengthy, and isolated the process, the more uncertain the outcome, and, the more controlled the aspirant by the social pressure of peers, the more similar the values adopted by those who pass into the occupation (Van Maanen & Schein, 1979). Elite professional schools are obvious exemplars in this regard.

Social Relations

The fourth and final attribute of an occupational community to be singled out is the blurring of the distinction between work and leisure activities within occupational communities. The melding of work and leisure may come about when leisure activities are connected to one's work or when there is extensive overlap between work and social relationships. In some occupational communities, specific leisure pursuits themselves are linked to the occupation. The connection may either be simple and intuitively obvious, or unexpected, but nonetheless regular. Both Salaman (1974) and Gamst (1980) provide examples of unsurprising links when they note that many railroaders include among their hobbies the building of model trains which are displayed to one another during recreational hours. An unexpected link is found in the case of early nineteenth century loom-weavers in London who were also widely known as botanists and entomologists, and who established a number of floricultural, historical, and mathematical societies (Braverman, 1974).

The point here lies not in the substantive nature of the tie between work and leisure, but rather in the tight network of social relations created when members of an occupation seek, for whatever reasons (e.g., pleasure, anxiety reduction, opportunistic advantage, etc.), close relationships with one another outside the workplace. As with the other defining characteristics, several conditions appear to favor the overlapping of work and social relations.

First is the degree to which members of an occupation are geographically or organizationally clustered. While physical proximity is neither a necessary nor sufficient condition for the formation of an occupational community, proximity nevertheless promotes and eases social interaction. Fishermen, police officers, prison guards and lumberjacks, for example, must work closely together and temporal considerations require them to live relatively near where they work. Neiderhoffer and Neiderhoffer (1968) report that the residences of members of some police departments are so geographically congregated that certain neighborhoods gain reputations for attracting only the police as homeowners. When the materials and resources with which an occupation operates are localized or when the majority of the residents of a vicinity are employed in the same line of work, overlap between work and social relationships becomes almost inevitable as is the case for coal miners in West Virginia or dockers in Hull, England (Hill, 1981). A similar phenomenon is apparently found among computer engineers in California's Silicon Valley and in the Boston suburbs along Route 128 (*Los Angeles Times*, July 12, 1982).

The melding of work and social relationships is also encouraged by occupations whose characteristics restrict their members' social relations. Shift work, night work, extensive travel, isolated postings, long periods of work-induced isolation followed by extended periods of leisure, all tend to mitigate opportunities for establishing friendships outside of work. Such restrictions alter time schedules so that members of the occupation are out of sync with the rhythm of a "normal" work week and must structure leisure time in ways that are at odds with the repose times of the majority of other employed persons. Cottrell (1938) and Salaman (1974) document how the enslavement of railroaders to precise time schedules, federal regulations on work hours, and variable shift work precludes the possibility of their participation in typical community and family activities. Another example of how work shapes social relations is found among New York City firefighters, many of whom frequently spend large portions of their off-duty time at station houses chatting with on-duty colleagues (Smith, 1972).

Third, occupations that are kin-based and entered by virtue of birth lead to an extensive overlap among social and work relations. Commercial fishing is an occupation where sons typically follow fathers into the line of work and all family members are, to a large degree, caught in its net (Miller & Van Maanen, 1982). One New England fisherman, when asked how he decided to enter the occupation, replied quite succinctly (and with some bemusement), "I'm a fisherman until I prove that I'm not." Funeral directing is another occupation sharing this kin-based recruitment pattern (Barley, 1980).

A final condition favorable to an overlap between work and social relationships arises through a sort of occupational intrusion into all aspects of a person's life. To paraphrase Goffman (1961), some occupations are "total work institutions." The lives of fighter pilots, submariners, intelligence officers, as well as most military personnel and their spouses come immediately to mind. Stationed on bases and encouraged to socialize only with other colleagues (of similar rank and function), occupational communities are created almost by fiat (Janowitz, 1960). But, the military is not the only example of the total work institution. Bryant (1972b) notes that carnival personnel are likely to work, eat, sleep, relax, fight, and travel with one another. Carnival people are also quite likely to intermarry and to provide collectively for on-the-road education of their children. Less exotic examples are trained counselors who hold full time, live-in positions in college residence halls. In situations where the college provides the counselors with room, board, and recreation as well as work, the counselors are most likely to establish social relations mainly with fellow counselors (Barley, 1979). In short, those who live within an occupational embrace find their work and leisure pursuits mixed in many ways and mixed so that where one ends and the other begins is a matter of some ambiguity (Kanter, 1977).

OCCUPATIONAL COMMUNITIES AS WORK CULTURES

Any outsider who observes naturally occurring conversation among self-defined members of an occupational community would quickly discover that members who have not previously met and who are of different ages, geographic regions, sexes, ethnic origins, or educational backgrounds are able to converse over a wide range of topics indecipherable by outsiders. Such is the manifestation of a shared culture. When, for example, a police officer remarks to another officer, "We didn't do any police work tonight, wrote a couple of movers and watched Stripes jump another one of our fucking calls," that officer makes substantial use of cultural materials which a listener who is familiar with such materials must make use of when assigning meaning to the remark. A description of the knowledge necessary to understand such an interaction would represent, then, a partial description of the culture. Such knowledge can never be fully explicated, in part, because it is inextricably tied to the context which gives rise to its use and, in part, because even the most astute of cultural members know that such knowledge is continually in flux and thus more than an occasional problem for cultural members themselves. From this standpoint, culture is as much a dynamic, evolving way of thinking and doing as it is a stable set of thoughts and actions.

This is not to say, however, that culture is just another variable. Culture is not something a group possesses more or less of at any given time; it is something it is. When cultures are described, meanings are central, not

frequencies.[12] This is a cognitive, ideational view of culture that emphasizes, by definition, "the things a person must know to be a member of
a given group" (Goodenough, 1970; 41). In occupational communities
these "things" include decoding schemes for assigning meaning to the
various practical routines which members engage in during the workday,
as well as the typical objects, persons, places, times, and relations members encounter at work (and, often, beyond). At a deeper, interpretive
level, these surface manifestations of culture reflect integrative themes
or ordering assumptions held by the membership which provide for some
commonality and connection across specific domains of thought and action (Geertz, 1973). In the police world, for example, an "asshole" is a
technical term used by officers to signify those citizens believed to be out
to provoke and embarrass the police in routine social interaction (Van
Maanen, 1978). The use of such a term (and others of like ilk) is premised
upon the police officers' taken-for-granted assumptions regarding just
what is and is not proper and orderly social interaction with members of
the public (i.e., an interaction initiated, directed, and terminated by the
police, not the citizen). Cultures vary, therefore, on the basis of differing
meaning systems. To compare cultures is to compare codes and assumptions which give rise to behavioral and cognitive diversity.

Occupational communities, as we have suggested, transmit to new
members shared occupational practices, values, vocabularies, and identities. More to the point, such cultural transmission transcends specific
organizational settings since members who are widely dispersed and unfamiliar with one another display similar understandings and attitudes
toward the work they do. Although, as we will discuss, occupational
communities penetrate and are certainly penetrated in various ways by
employing organizations, they are to be sharply distinguished from other
work cultures—such as the much discussed organizational ones—on several grounds.[13]

Members of occupational communities are favorably oriented toward
their jobs and careers. To them, work is more than merely "making a
living;' it is a source of meaning and value. The secretaries and office
workers studied by Benet (1972) certainly possess both an identity and a
distinct work culture within the confines of their employing organization,
but neither do they value the identity nor is the culture much more than
a set of responses to specific managerial practices of the office. It is a
"culture of resistance" based upon opposition to subordinate position
and status within a given organization. Our hypothetical "hind-toe-re-
movers" presumably check their social identities and cultures of reference at the gate when entering the slaughterhouse in the morning and
pick them up again when leaving in the evening. While they may partake
of a work or organization culture while on the job, the centrality of that

culture to their life outside the workplace is minimal. There are social identities (held at a distance) involved here, but the flow of identities and interests is from outside into the workplace. For those in occupational communities, the flow is reversed.[14]

Individual status within occupational communities is, in the abstract, based on displayed skill and performance of those tasks most members consider essential to the occupation. Member judgements on such matters are based on historically developed standards which represent definitions of proper (and, by implication, improper) occupational practice. In this sense, a "culture of achievement" exists in occupational communities, not a "culture of advancement" so often reported in studies of organizations and their managers (e.g., Dalton, 1959). Segmentation and specialization are, to be sure, found in occupational communities, as are hierarchies, but whatever segmentation, specialization, or hierarchical distinctions are to be found have origins within, not without, the community and, therefore, reflect the performance standards of the membership. In the ideal, only the members dictate how their labor is to be organized.

To the extent that the occupation and the bundle of tasks and interactions it involves are matters held in high regard by members of occupational communities, one would expect the membership to lay claim to control the work they do. In essence, occupational communities are premised upon the belief that only the membership possesses the proper knowledge, skills, and orientations necessary to make decisions as to how the work is to be performed and evaluated. Here lies the core of the matter, for it is obvious some occupational communities (notably the so-called free professions and, to a lesser extent, the established trade associations and unions) have been more successful than others in creating, maintaining, and protecting a distinctive and relatively autonomous culture. Self-control of occupational matters is then the key variable upon which distinctions among occupational communities are to be made. Self-control refers to the occupational community's ability to dictate who will and will not be a member, as well as how the content and conduct of a member's work will be assessed. The grounds upon which such self-control is based are numerous, complicated, and constantly problematic for the membership. Four particularly crucial (yet relatively general) obstacles to occupational self-control are evident.[15]

Service to Management

If service to organizational officials who are not occupational community members is a condition of employment, occupational self control decreases. Self-employment or employment within an occupationally-based organization such as is found in certain legal practices, trade unions, public service agencies, and medical groups increases occupational self-control. The matter is not, however, quite so straightforward. For example, many studies have noted that management goals are not necessarily exclusive of those rooted in an occupation (e.g., Montagna, 1973; Schreisheim, et al., 1977). To wit, certain kinds of engineers often discover that their collective aims and identities can be satisfied only within large, heteronomous organizations where sufficient resources to pursue occupationally-valued ends are to be found (Scott, 1965; Harlow, 1973; Brown, 1981). Many public service organizations, such as hospitals, maintain separate administrative and occupational hierarchies thus allowing occupational values to be served alongside organizational ones (Freidson, 1970). In both cases, members of the respective occupational communities retain substantial self control over their work, even though many of them are located well down the formal chain of command in the organization.

From this perspective, self control is problematic to members of an occupational community only when organizational officials seek to impose certain "outsider" standards, goals, work tasks, evaluative schemes, and so forth upon the membership. In and of itself, hierarchy is not an issue. It is the use of hierarchical authority to direct member activities in ways the membership considers untoward that presents the problem and threat to self control. Such a threat and its realization may vary, of course, by the organizational position held by an occupational community member. For example, there is apparently substantial autonomy for many senior accountants in business corporations. For these highly placed accountants, occupational values and standards play a large role in their everyday activities (and may influence even the direction of the firm itself). But, much less autonomy exists for accountants at the junior and lower levels of the same corporations who may, to their chagrin, find themselves performing organizationally dictated, highly regimented bookkeeping functions which provide little opportunity to exercise valued occupational skills (Montagna, 1973). Such tasks are held in low regard, perhaps contempt, by community members, even though, within an administrative frame of reference, the performance of such tasks provides an important service to management.

More generally, self control for employees within any organization varies by employment opportunities elsewhere (Hirschman, 1970). For members of occupational communities, opportunities to engage in solo practice or in highly specializaed organizations promoting occupational interests are no doubt important conditions that help sustain the very norms and identities which constitute the community. Such opportunities provide an exit option to members who are displeased with the way their skills are being utilized by an organization. The more limited such opportunities, the more community members must bend their occupational standards to organizational interests and whims.

Finally, we must note that loyalty and tenure considerations may dampen the value of self control for members of organizational communities who remain in a given organization for long periods of time. External labor value typically decreases with age (e.g., Bloch & Kuskin, 1978). Thus occupational mobility of the sort requiring organizational shifts may be restricted to younger, more recently trained, and (perhaps most crucially) cheaper members of the community (Pfeffer, 1983). The so-called "golden handcuffs" associated with many long tenure organizational careers represent telling examples in this regard. The point here is that such handcuffs signify ties to an organization and its managerially-designed reward systems rather than ties to an occupation and its member-designed reward systems. To the degree that service to management provides unique and valued rewards that are believed to surpass those obtainable through service to the occupation, the importance of self control to occupational members will undoubtedly lessen.

Theory and Procedure in Occupational Practice

If an occupational community is able to maintain a relative monopoly over its theory and procedures, self control will be maintained. If other groups secure access to such knowledge, self control is reduced (Child & Fulk, 1982). Both theory and procedure have explicit (i.e., cognitive) and implicit (i.e., skill) components. These components and their interaction are vital elements when accounting for the mandate occupational communities are able to manufacture and sustain within a society as well as within an organization.

The cognitive base of an occupation represents declarative sorts of knowledge such as facts, descriptions, and technologies. Since declarative knowledge is rule-based, it can be transmitted by word of mouth or by print. Although it may be complex, scientific in origin, and take years to master, it is, in principles, subject to codification. In contrast, skill is fluid and, to outsiders at least, mysterious. Skill is akin to what is called "know-how" and is represented by what acknowledged experts in all fields are demonstrably able to do but are often unable or unwilling to precisely describe (Roberts et al., 1966). For example, cab drivers in Boston know that direct traffic has the right of way over vehicles making left-hand turns in an intersection. This is a cognitive or declarative matter. But, these cab drivers also know when there is just enough time for them to "safely" make left-hand turns before the next approaching car enter the collision zone. That cab drivers skirt collisions in most instances is a result of perceptual understanding, aggressive motor behaviors, and probably sheer nerve, all of which are learned by experience. Such skill defies description by general rule. To build on Polanyi's (1966:4) much quoted line, cab drivers "know more than they can (or will) tell."[16]

This distinction is helpful when considering how occupational self-control is amplified or reduced. On one hand, the larger the cognitive component and the more rapid the rate at which it grows, the more likely occupational self-control will be sustained. On the other hand, the cognitive component is, in the ideal, available to others since it can be codified (Child & Fulk, 1982). The recent spate of books on do-it-yourself divorce, the at-home pregnancy test, the design-your-own home handbook, or complete-idiot's-guide to television repair are all mundane examples of domains in which occupational communities have potentially lost a degree of self-control. Perhaps more seriously, Oppenheimer (1973) and Haug (1975, 1977) have claimed that computer technology is hastening the "proletarianization of the professions" since it enables non-experts to utilize expert techniques by virtue of electronic storage and retrieval of professional routines. Hence, the central question in terms of self-control over the cognitive component of occupational practice concerns the pace at which new knowledge is being acquired and monopolized by community members relative to the rate at which old knowledge is being standardized and dispersed.

Regarding the procedural knowledge contained within an occupational community, self-control can be threatened by damaging public disclosures which reveal practices most members would prefer to keep private. Boston taxi drivers notwithstanding, demystification of certain occupational practices is always possible and various forms of muckraking can be of serious consequence. The threat is even more serious when an occupation is shown to have claimed skill when, in fact, little skill has been exercised (or, perhaps, even needed). For example, proposals for Civilian Review Boards seem to follow police scandals, and political intrusions into welfare agencies are apparently generated whenever documented claims reveal a large number of "welfare cheats." To the degree an occupational community is able to conduct its business in private, train and license its members relatively free from the scrutiny of audiences not of its choosing, and maintain the strong loyalties of its members so that even the disenchanted are unlikely to speak publicly, its sacred procedural knowledge is relatively secure. But, like Toto pulling on the Wizard of Oz's curtain, when "know-how" is made public, the show may be damaged. All occupational communities rely on ill-defined procedures and techniques as the sort of mystical heart of the practice, a heart that, to keep beating, must remain protected.

The two knowledge forms of an occupational community are linked together in intriguing ways. Typically, the greater the cognitive base, the more skill required to put such cognitive matters into practice and the more distant both become to lay actors outside the community. Thus, even if non-members become users of well developed occupational practices, they may still turn to a community member at some point, if only for simple assurance that their use has been proper and in accord with community standards. Thus, even when not legally required to do so, some highly skilled do-it-yourself home builders turn to professional contractors to inspect the results of their work (Glaser, 1972). In this sense, the demand for cognitive or technical knowledge may decrease, but the occupational community remains unaffected because the demand for skill and the judgemental prerogatives associated with recognized procedural knowledge remain fixed. Transactions in such instances are based on the provision of sanctioning evaluations rather than the provision of direct labor. In this manner, the uncertainty and indeterminacy surrounding "know-how" protects occupational self-control.

Market Structure

All else being equal (certainly the exception in social life), the more visible, organized, and homogeneous the market to which an occupational community is linked, the less self-control will be held by that community. The more isolated, individualized, and heterogeneous the market, the greater the self-control. Submissiveness of client or consumer groups is a central characteristic of many occupational communities which have developed strong self-control mandates. The patient vis-à-vis the doctor (Freidson, 1970), the accused vis-à-vis the public defender (Sudnow, 1965), the bereaved vis-à-vis the funeral director (Mitford, 1969) all stand as good examples. Far less self-control is found among commercial fishermen operating within monopsonistic markets comprised of a few large fish buyers (Van Maanen, et al., 1982). Teachers possess relatively less self-control when employed by homogeneous rather than heterogeneous school districts (Lortie, 1974).

There are, of course, some ironies involved with this relationship. One concerns the asymmetry of authority between an occupation and its marketplace. The more direct and transparent the occupational community's effect on consumers or clients, the more likely those consumer or clients will themselves organize as a means of mediating such effects (Child & Fulk, 1982). The growing movement toward socialized medicine and legislation establishing health service organizations represent good examples in this regard, for both developments attempt to limit the autonomy of physicians and hospitals. The dialectic is also amplified because as client submissiveness declines. members of an occupational community may further solidify behind a common front. A sort of "us-versus-them" stance is one result and a struggle for control ensues. Again, medicine provides the case in point. Where consumers or clients have no alternatives to highly valued products or services, the struggle is likely to be lengthy and highly charged.

State Control

Occupational self-control varies directly with the degree to which the state sanctions such control. Self-control of an occupation is sought in part because members deem it just, and in part because it serves the cause of upward social mobility for the occupational community as a whole. Occupational communities lobby directly and indirectly to gain control of relevant market segments via state intervention. The state intervenes in matters of vital interest to an occupation. Consider the funding of training programs, the limitations set upon the size of an occupational community, work and safety standards, the providing of direct employment in the public sector, the setting (or not setting) of cost and price guidelines for products and services, the provision of payments for occupational work, and numerous other interventions as examples of state-directed activities that significantly influence the amount of self-control available to members of an occupational community. Mystique may erode, clients may revolt, cognitive dimensions of practice may be codified and widely distributed, and organizational managers and owners may be the prime beneficiaries of occupationally-produced goods or services, but if the state chooses to protect an occupational community by granting it, in effect, a legal monopoly on practice, self-control will stubbornly persist. The traditional professions of law and medicine are reminders of just how crucial a role the state plays in providing for occupational self-control (Johnson, 1972). In effect, the distinction of having an occupation rather than having a job or position is that those with an occupation potentially can call on sources of legitimacy for their work performances other than those offered by the employing organization. When these sources are backed up and certified by the state, legitimacy and self-control are virtually synonymous.

CAREERS OF OCCUPATIONAL COMMUNITIES

We have argued thus far that occupational communities represent bounded work cultures populated by people who share similar identities and values that transcend specific organizational settings. Moreover, self-control is a prominent cultural theme in all occupational communities, although its realization is highly problematic. Occupational communities vary with respect to how much self-control they have been able to carve out. The more self-control possessed by an occupational community, the more distinct and self-perpetuating its culture. Although occupational communities hermetically sealed off from a society would be impossible to find, occupational communities can be arrayed on a continuum of self-control. The differing values, practices, ideologies, and selected identities associated with each represent strategic choices exercised within a community as to how best to present itself and exert occupational control.

Much historical and sociological work documents the rise and fall of occupations, the sources of prestige and status among occupations, and changes in the occupational structure within a society.[17] This work highlights how occupations have gained varying degrees of self-control. Unionization and professionalization are prominent strategies in this regard since each presumably promotes the interests of the collective over time. They are bootstrapping tactics used by some occupational communities (sometimes simultaneously, sometimes separately) to enhance the collective career of the membership (Van Maanen, 1976).

Unionization is a means of modifying and reducing the degree to which members of an occupation employed in organizational contexts are directed and controlled by the non-occupational members of an organization. Although unionization is frequently associated with an ideology stressing occupational control over the work its members perform, this ideology must not be accepted uncritically. Unions are hardly identical in either form or function. For example, in the United States at least, unionization trends has been toward consolidated unions, such as the United Auto Workers, which claim to speak for a diversity of occupational groups. Such diversity may well interfere with the interests of distinct occupational communities contained within umbrella-like unions.

On the other hand, some unions, such as the International Typographical Union or the United Mine Workers, appear to be organized as occupational associations whose members share similar occupational interests. Thus, the more similar the tasks performed by union members, the more likely the union itself promotes the special concerns of an occupational community, including self-control. To paraphrase Hirschman's (1971) catchy terms, such unions offer to members of occupational communities "voice" rather than "exit" as a way of influencing where, when, how, for whom, and for what rewards their work is to be provided. Once unionization is itself achieved, it may become the means by which the community can monopolize and protect areas of expertise, control its labor market, and attain upward social mobility. This is, at least, the promise, if not the reality, of most single-occupation unionization campaigns.

More generally, the primary mission of unions concerns the well-being of its membership. As institutionalized through collective bargaining in the United States, unions are involved in determining the terms and conditions of employment which bear on job satisfaction (Dunlop, 1958). When these terms are defined to include policies governing the content and quality of products and services provided by the members of an occupational community as well as the more traditional bread-and-butter issues, then the union is essentially involved in promoting the occupational norms and mission within the society. When successful, the career of the community is itself furthered. Consider, for example, the potential status and position of American auto workers were they able to bargain with management over the poor quality of American cars. Hence, we are suggesting, along with Haug and Sussman (1973), that the presumed antithesis between normative commitments to service or quality and the so-called bread-and-butter functions of labor unions are largely a fiction (even though, in practice, the bread-and-butter concerns are often traded off against normative concerns).

Professionalization is a process serving goals similar to those of unionization. The traditional, and what Turner and Hodge (1970) have called the "formal organization" approach to the study of the professions, holds that professions are somehow quite different from other occupations.[18] Typically, advocates of this approach propose a set of attributes or traits which define the difference (Carr-Sanders & Wilson, 1933; Greenwood, 1957; Vollmer & Mills, 1966). Though the trait lists vary by author, four attributes found on all lists are: (1) possession of a substantive body of knowledge imparted to novices through systematic training; (2) formation of an occupational association which certifies practitioners; (3) societal recognition of the occupation's authority and (4) a service orientation articulated by a code of ethics.

The critique of a separate sociology of the professions has been intensified of late and it is one of some strength (Johnson, 1972; Roth, 1974; Larson, 1977; Klegon, 1979). In essence, the trait approach to the professions has been examined closely and comes up wanting. From the vantage point of the critique, professions are not distinct because of the sterling personal qualities of their membership or the attributes of the work their members perform, but because of the success those self-defined professionals have had in claiming occupational self-control. For example, Johnson (1972) holds that the professions represent a peculiar form of social control in which the producers define the needs of the consumers. Larson (1977) argues that a profession is merely the end state in a process of upward social mobility for a collective wherein the producers eventually come to monopolize the market for their expertise. Freidson (1970) bluntly suggests that a profession contrasts to other occupations only in that it has been given the right by the state to control its own work. Moreover, the critics note that trait approaches to the professions must take for granted the separate and distinct status of a particular line of work since, by definition, such approaches seek to uncover features of the work (or its membership) which will justify the ascribed, yet unquestioned, status. Wittingly or unwittingly, such approaches and the self-referential tropes they employ provide symbolic support for professional uniqueness, an argument which clearly furthers the self-interest of any line of work called professional (Roth, 1974; Whittington, 1982).

Even more crucially, the list of traits which comprise the ideal type of profession have been shown to be empirically suspect. For example, even in the most revered of professions, medicine, recent research questions the effectiveness and even existence of colleagual control (Millman, 1979; Bosk, 1979). Other studies suggest that the attributed characteristics of the clientele are at least as significant in terms of treatment as any universalistic or scientific methods of diagnosis and therapy (Freidson, 1970; Bucher & Strauss, 1961). Altruistic norms of public service have also been severely questioned when examinations of pay schedules, geographical distribution of licensed physicians, or medical review practices dealing with surgical mistakes have been undertaken (Glaser, 1970; Garfield, 1970; Millman, 1979). At best, trait theories such as those surrounding the definition of medicine as a profession suggest not what the profession is, but what it pretends to be (Hughes, 1951).

When researchers examine what professionals actually do in everyday life to negotiate and sustain their special positions, a rather different perspective emerges. We find that the normative attributes are important to professional practice and practitioners, but they are important because they are used (with more or less success) as arguments and accounts to legitimize professional self-control.[19] Like members of many other occupations, those considered professionals have sought to free themselves from administrative control, to secure the sanctity of their theory and procedures, and to control the market structure they face so as to secure occupational autonomy. If the professions can be set apart from other occupational groups it is because their vaunted autonomy is ultimately secured by the grace of the state, a grace which requires massive and continual nurturing and monitoring through legal and political processes. From this standpoint, professions exercise self-control largely because of their state-protected monopoly on conditions of practice, the knowledge upon which such practice rests, and the right to control entrance to and exit from the profession.

Even with state support, the maintenance of market control is not to be blindly assumed. For example, demand itself must be generated and sustained. Further challenges may arise when the consumers of the service attempt to counterbalance monopolistic authority over the delivery of services. Moreover, when a profession's performance no longer meets the values and needs of the society that suffers it, the demise of that profession is but a matter of time (Bledstein, 1976). This is merely to say that social change has numerous implications, some of them of enormous impact, upon professional status and practice within a society. Successful revolutionaries who initiate their regimes by exporting (or worse) the lawyers of the old order provide a pointed reminder of just how dependent the professions are upon the good will and tolerance of the society of which they are a part.

Even within the professions, challenges to occupational self-control will appear as new specialties are created alongside the old. As Freidson (1970) points out, there is a continuous process of occupational differentiation within all professions. At any given time, wide discrepancies of status and rewards exist such that any one profession (even with its institutional support systems, its self-administered code of ethics, and its professional schools and associations) is a mix of many occupations and occupational communities. As new technologies and approaches evolve, new groups of practitioners who understand and promote the innovations arise to challenge the authority and control of the communities within whose domain the service previously lay. Again, medicine provides an example with its enormous number of specialties and keen competition among them for clients and intra-professional status. Bucher and Strauss (1961) provide the key words: "Professions are loose amalgamations of diverse segments pursuing different manners, and more or less held together under a common name in a particular period of history."

Three points are to be drawn from our discussion thus far. First, a profession is not an occupational community per se, although some of its subdivisional units or specialties may be. Second, and far more important, the professions are not to be considered as a class apart from other occupations. The notion of a profession is one of those seemingly natural concepts fraught with unexamined ideological baggage that has penetrated much organizational and occupational research. Too often researchers simply accept a profession's own definition and image of itself without examining what uses are to be found behind such definitions and images. Third and finally, the process of professionalization must be understood as but one path by which occupational communities may gain self-control. There are no fundamental distinctions to be found between a profession and an occupation which are inherent in the work itself.

These points suggest that both professionalization and unionization can be considered strategies for advancing the collective career of an occupational community (or a collection of related communities). The difference between unionization and professionalization is, therefore, one of means, not ends. The distinction between the two strategies hinges, first, upon the degree to which an occupation attempts to trade on its special knowledge and, second, the degree to which an occupation faces organized opposition when attempting to assert its independence and establish the legitimacy of self-control. The values and ideologies supporting each process reflect choices about how occupational self-control can best be gained and guarded rather than any deep discontinuities of purpose.

An example of the similarities and the differences between these two processes is provided by the so-called "New Unionism" or "Professional Unions" (Jessup, 1978). Such hybrid associations have developed in the wake of what Mechanic (1976) calls the "bureaucratization of the professional." Particularly in public services, members of relatively high-status occupational communities have tried to unionize as a way of confronting managerial decrees seen to violate member standards of proper conduct (Fielding & Portman, 1980). While relatively narrow economic self interest are most certainly relevant, control over the work itself is nonetheless also a prominent objective for members of professional unions. For example, after citing the slogan "social work, not paperwork," one nationally prominent arbitrator observed in a somewhat shocked, if not outraged fashion: "What is really happening in public service is that the sovereignty argument has now been transferred to the scope of bargaining questions" (Rock, 1968, quoted in Mendes, 1982).[20]

Unionization or professionalization are, of course, not always achieved. As the bloody history of organized labor in the United States makes clear, the processes are political and full of uncertainty and strife. Professionalization, when realized, is perhaps the more powerful and convincing form of self-control in this country since groups opposing professionalization tend (historically) to be relatively unorganized and of lesser status than those comprising the occupational community seeking the professional label and its symbolic protection. Professionalization may also be a somewhat cleaner, less visible struggle, fought mainly by mannered proxies on the floors of courtrooms and government agencies rather than by angry members of an occupation on the docks or in the mines. Moreover, conventional use of the professional label in the United States usually connotes "sacred" attributes such as rationality, public service, and disinterest rather than "profane" attributes such as economic expediency, corruption, and self-interest often associated with the term "union" in this society (Hill, 1981).[21]

In this regard, it is interesting to examine strategies utilized by some occupational communities currently attempting to convince relevant audiences that its members should be accorded professional status. As we have previously argued, the so-called traits of a profession provide resources for such purposes. However, it appears that new traits are also being added to the old list. One new trait, stress, is worth considering in some detail since it currently seems to be achieving some notoriety as a mark of occupational status and, therefore, serves nicely as an example of how any given trait can be used to further occupational ends.

The notion of job stress, particularly when used in the context of public service jobs, is a perfect vehicle to convey the symbolic virtues of an occupation not yet recognized as professional. Good examples of occupations that have strategically embraced stress include: police service, nursing, air traffic controlling, public school teaching, firefighting, and social work. While Merton's (1949) notion of "sociological ambivalence" and Goode's (1960) idea of "role strain" are of some merit in understanding the sociological sources of stress, they are less valuable in understanding the occupational practice of making stress claims. Terry (1981b), in an examination of selected occupational literatures, found nearly ten times the number of articles dealing with job stress in police and nursing periodicals than in comparative periodicals of law and medicine.[22] Since stress in all these occupations is said to arise largely from the responsibility occupational members carry for alleviating other people's misery, the question must be raised as to why the nurses and the police are claiming stress and the doctors and lawyers are not. Both occupational pairs work in similar domains with similar clients. If anything, doctors and lawyers carry more of a burden for the fate of their clients than do nurses or police officers. Were stress keyed only to the work performed by occupational members, a reversal of such claims would be expected. It appears then, that stress is relatively more important (and useful) to the bootstrapping occupations than to those occupations already established at the top of the reward and recognition ladder.

Empirical investigations of claims of occupational stress lend credence to its largely symbolic nature for one finds little systematic evidence to document the alleged consequences of stress. For example, in the police world, the results of stress are thought to be job dissatisfaction, chronic alcoholism, high divorce rates, suicide, and a veritable laundry list of mild to serious physiological ailments. But, as Terry (1981a) shows, these claims have been highly exaggerated. Turnover in police agencies is quite low and police officers do not display high levels of job dissatisfaction; cardiovascular disease is high, but lower than the incidence rate among music teachers, transportation workers, cooks, and firefighters; divorce is lower than the national average, as is (in most cities) police suicide; alcoholism does not seem to be out of line with other occupational groups of comparable economic and social standing. Most important perhaps is the fact that any and all stress claims made by the police are notoriously difficult to document.

Whether or not stress (and its consequences) is an objective condition of the work in these ambitious occupational communities is, for our purposes, less important than its presence or absence in public discourse and its conscious employment as a means of achieving occupational goals including greater self-control. We are not suggesting, however, that by emphasizing stress an occupation will magically be granted greater reward, recognition, and self-control. Stress may, in fact, be more important internally as a way of sharing common problems and increasing the sense of fellowship among members. Externally, stress stands as an indicator of a larger family of occupational claims (e.g., service goals, responsibility for other people's problems, personal sacrifice, bureaucratic interference or indifference) residing under the sacred canopy of "being called to a set of higher ideals." Such a canopy cannot be conjured up on claims alone. As Hughes (1958) and many others have pointed out, there also needs to be widespread agreement among the public regarding the importance of the occupational service, some consensus surrounding the validity of the occupation's claim to be able to provide such a service, and, perhaps most importantly, no real or perceived alternative sources for the performance of the service. These are indeed powerful constraints and, as the police and other public servants—such as those who once served in the now-defunct Association of Air Traffic Controllers—have discovered, they are not easily bypassed.

CAREERS IN OCCUPATIONAL COMMUNITIES

Although the careers of individual members of occupational communities are clearly affected by the fortunes of the community within the larger occupational structure of society, individual careers are also based upon processes of attainment existing within the communities themselves. In this section, we are concerned with individual careers as they are played out within specific occupational boundaries, holding at bay, for the moment, the question of just how occupational communities themselves fare within organizational marketplaces.

The idea of a career necessarily imputes coherence and order to a sequence of experiences, roles, statuses, or jobs. Attributions of coherence underlie every formal definition of a career that makes of it something more than a job history (e.g., Becker & Strauss, 1956:253; Glaser, 1968:1; Wilensky, 1961:251; Goffman, 1961b:128, Slocum, 1966:5; Hall, 1976:3). But, since work careers are constructed from contextual and historical particulars, the particulars attain coherence only when viewed against some backdrop or setting. Beyond the conspicuous setting of an organization, careers can be played out against such backdrops as an occupation (Hughes, 1958), a family life cycle (Schein, 1978), a social category or label (Goffman, 1961; Becker, 1963), an internal standard such as a "career anchor" (Schein, 1978), and so forth. These backdrops not only direct and constrain the visible path of a person's "external" career, they also provide tasks, colleagues, symbols, and ideologies that influence the individual's subjective construction of an "internal" career—the meaning a person attributes to the sequence of work-related experiences that comprise the career.[23]

The indispensability of understanding the context within which a person's career is played out is underscored by two frequently-made academic points (academic in the sense that they are points alarmingly overlooked when career research is undertaken). First, the career setting noticed by the observer may not be the one used by the person in the career. It is not, for example, readily apparent that all who work in an organization consider their careers in organizational terms. Industrial scientists are certainly employed in organizational contexts, but they may well measure their careers against the backdrop of their specialties (Marcson, 1960; Kornhauser, 1962; Ritti, 1968). Academics, too, belong to organizations, but evidence suggests that some see themselves in the context of their scholarly fields (Caplow & McGee, 1958; Gouldner, 1957). Second, when constructing careers, people may make use of several backdrops, sometimes simultaneously and sometimes sequentially (Van Maanen, 1980a; Kanter, 1979).

Recent career research and theory is tied to the experiences of people occupying a relatively small set of organizationally-defined positions (Sonnenfeld & Kotter, 1982). In particular, managers and administrators receive most of the attention. These positions carry career lines defined largely in terms of hierarchical advancement. In fact, many current terms and descriptive cliches found in discussions of careers only make sense when the relevance of an organization's hierarchy is presumed. "Plateauing," "up or out," "demotion," "lateral move," "fast track," and "career ladder" are understandable only when juxtaposed to the vertical dimension of organizations. But, if one is to regard U.S. Department of Labor Statistics (1980) as an authoritative source, only 12 percent of the labor force is counted as currently occupying managerial or administrative posts.

What is troubling about considering vertical mobility within an organization to be the centerpiece of career research is the accompanying tendency to deny careers to be a substantial portion of the working population. Consider the following examples:

> With reference to occupational careers in organizations, the theoretical model involves entry into a position that requires the performance of occupational duties at the lowest rung of the occupational ladder. This is followed by a sequence of promotions into higher-level positions within an organization, leading eventually to the pinnacle, and finally to retirement. Although this generalized model calls for upward

progression from the bottom to the top, we know that not every entrant moves through all these steps. There are thus varying degrees of conformity to the model . . .

(Slocum, 1966:5)

Occupational careers that conform reasonably well to the model are restricted to professionals, managers, skilled craftsmen and a few others . . . this does not mean the concept of career has no relevance for the study of other occupations. However, it has little utility for the study of unskilled occupations or others that do not provide differentiated steps or grades.

(Slocum, 1966:226)

Individuals may work at a series of activities during their lives, but with no perception that they follow a career path. We might speak of the career of a dentist or an accountant, but we would hardly speak of the career of a dishwasher or a hospital orderly. Unless the person and the containing social structure see some relation between the activities, there is no career.

(Braude, 1975:112)

One wonders if it would not be more appropriate for Slocum and Braude to question their models than to default an unknown but obviously large percentage of the working population from the universe of career holders.[24] A key to how career theorists circumscribe career's domain of reference lies in what Braude calls the "containing social structure." We suppose what is meant by this term is something akin to an organization or a set of reasonably high(er) status actors (managers) who are deemed fit to "see some relation between the activities" and "the career." If we accept an upwardly mobile, white collar, organizational model of the career, then it is true that few people will have careers simply because most people work at the base of organizational pyramids. Given that positions decrease as one ascends a pyramid, even if we are willing to grant the liberal assumption that promotions are handed out randomly, the probability of a person being promoted decreases rapidly the closer that person is to the pyramid's base. Rosenbaum (1979) estimates the probability that non-management personnel will be promoted in a large utility company peaks at age 35 at one in five. Afterwards, the probability of promotion decreases exponentially.

An organizational model of career may simply be inappropriate for the majority of the labor force. An alternative model would be to consider the "containing social structure" of a career to be the social context which the worker considers most proximal. Hence, a career's backdrop is the standard by which the career holder measures the career, not the standard of the observer. Although potential contexts for constructing a career are probably numerous and certainly particularistic, consider how careers might be constructed within the context of an occupational community.

One striking feature associated with the work-specific illustrations we have thus far emphasized as more or less meeting the definitional requirements of an occupational community is that for many of them there are few hierarchical levels or offices of authority to which members might aspire. Although crew members may specialize in particular tasks, traditional fishermen are, with the exception of the captain of a boat and perhaps his eldest son, of essentially equal status (Miller & Van Maanen, 1982).[26] Musicians in orchestras may change chairs or join a major symphony, but their movement is across lines of skill and prestige and does not entail the formal accrual of power and authority over others in the occupational line (Faulkner, 1974). The careers of police officers are relatively flat. Only a very few patrol officers reach the rank of sergeant during their police careers, and those who do find themselves distrusted and considered outside the occupational community comprised of their former colleagues (Van Maanen, forthcoming). The tag "steady state" career used by Driver (1981:9–10) nicely captures some key elements of work careers in occupational communities:

> The steady state concept refers to a view of careers in which one makes an early commitment to a field and holds it for life. There may be minor changes . . . and inner growth of competence in one's field leading to some upward movement, but the essential thing is a fixed identity within a field.

Schein's (1971, 1978) model of an organization provides a dimension of particular interest when careers in occupational communities are examined. Though originally applied to the task of describing organizational careers, the model is applicable to many social settings (Van Maanen & Schein, 1979). The model uses three dimensions to describe a person's location in an organization. The three dimensions are hierarchy, function, and inclusion.[25] When considering occupational communities, of most interest is the third dimension, inclusion.[26]

Persons who move toward greater inclusion gain centrality within the network of community members. They may attain special privileges, increased rewards, become privy to secrets about "how things really work," and gain heightened respect from community members. Individuals who have achieved visible centrality in the community are often identified by the labels or folk types used by members to note occupational wisdom. The "sage," "pro," "guru," "old hand," and legendary "old timer" are stereotypes in this regard. As these social types suggest, centrality can carry prestige, honor, knowledge, and power.

Penetration toward a more central position in an occupation involves one or more of what Glaser and Strauss (1971) call "status passages." All occupations provide for a period of training and testing during which neophytes are taught (and usually learn) the "rules of the game" while their willingness to play by these rules is scrutinized by their more experienced workmates (Van Maanen, 1980a). For example, newcomers may be assigned "dirty work" as a way of having their mettle tested to reveal any character flaws, or as a way of testing their commitment to the occupation or work group. The period of testing and training may be informal and unplanned or highly structured and formalized. Both can be rigorous. Haas (1977) offers a witty account of how high-steel workers are informally taught to maintain a front of fearlessness while remaining keenly aware of the danger of the work. The testing process includes "binging," a barrage of barbed and crude insults slung at recruits by veteran ironworkers as a way of ascertaining the emotional calm and physical dexterity of novices on high steel.

Psychiatrists, during the early phases of training, are assigned the so-called hopeless cases as a way of "socializing them to failure", according to Light (1980). Other apprenticeship periods may compel the green recruit to do distasteful service as the butt of community pranks or as the unwitting scapegoat for mistakses made by others. Whenever special skills and complex role behaviors are central components of occupational responsibility, relatively intense induction programs are likely to be present (whether by design or accident). It makes little difference how special and complex such role behaviors are relative to others or how central such behaviors are in the actual occupational scheme of things; what is crucial is that members consider them to be special, complex, and central.

Beyond the status passages that occur during the early periods of occupational learning, we find ourselves in poorly charted domains.[27] Precisely what steps lead to more or less centrality in occupational communities are unclear. Some occupational communities such as certain medical specialties, legal practices, and craft associations, have well formulated boundaries through which members pass as they move toward the inner circles. Some occupational communities are premised on a sort of downward slide where members enter (or achieve at a very early phase) centerstage, obtaining a more central position in the occupation than they will every again occupy. Modeling, prostitution, and professional athletics provide worhty examples in this regard. In other occupational communities, the transitions in or out may be smooth, occurring in nearly invisible ways.

Since any of these alternatives are feasible, the pattern holding for a given occupational community is an empirical matter on which data are scarce. It is possible, however, to extract from the literature on work and occupations at least three domains of involvement through which members of an occupational community conceivably attain centrality as seniority and work experience accumulate. The three domains are: the work itself; the setting(s) in which the work is performed; and the network of social relations which surround the work. Consider each in turn.

The Work Itself.   Members of some occupational communities attain centrality by acquiring reputations for expertise. Such recognition may accompany the invention or mastery of more advanced technique, knowledge, and skill; the accumulation of experience with a variety of work situations and the acquisition of a repository of occupational wisdom; or, the development of finesse, flair, or style in one's work. Renowned craftsmen are known for their subtlety and refinement of technique. Police detectives acquire centrality among fellow sleuths as they build widespread informant networks, develop interrogation tactics and theories, and, to a much smaller degree, master fingerprinting and ballistics testing (Saunders, 1977). Academics gain recognition by accumulating lists of publications and achieve acclaim when they are seen to advance technique or pose new paths of inquiry (Crane, 1972). Senior electricians carry devices and tools which signify their ability to handle jobs seldom entrusted to more inexperienced colleagues (Reimer, 1977).

The Work Setting.   Within some occupational communities, centrality may be attached to working in particular settings. Gold (1964) notes that janitors gain recognition from peers by becoming custodians in upper-middle class apartment buildings where the pay is only slightly higher, but the probability of servicing "good tenants" is greater. Hockey players move to the center of their occupation when they move from the minors to the majors (Faulkner, 1974) and jazz musicians have made it when they find gigs before more appreciative audiences (Becker, 1951). The notion of the "big leagues" underlies this sort of movement, as when a newspaper reporter working on a small, insignificant, local paper yearns to become a reporter for the *New York Times.* Deep sea fishermen, like bears that go over mountains, long to work better waters where more lucrative fishing holes are though to be found (Zulaida, 1981). One should note that in each case the work remains essentially the same, but the characteristics of the setting change.

The Social Network.   Finally, centrality may be gained by strategic expansion or revision in one's network of acquaintances. With whom one works and who one knows become dimensions upon which careers may rest. Any doctoral student will verify that the reputation of the faculty represents a special catapult for launching a career in academia. To be allowed to stand on the bridge with the captain during a fishing trip taps a fisherman for initiation into the intricate and well-guarded secrets of captain's work and signals to the crew the fisherman's probable succession to the helm. Faulkner (1982) provides a most useful example of an occupational career highly dependent upon one's position in a given social network. The context is the movie business and Faulkner's analysis shows that film composers move to the inner core of their occupation (where work is plentiful and prestigious) only as they become connected to certain film producers, directors, and agents. The network that counts in Hollywood is the one linking high status members across occupational communities since only a few members of each community handle most of the industry's work. The vast majority of members in a given community compete among themselves for the little work that remains. The career rule is simple: Central and successful producers work only with central and successful film composers. Career opportunities in other occupational communities may be similar if they are constructed on the sort of project-by-project (or job-by-job) basis as typified by film composers. Unlike organizational careers based on promotions which create opportunities for others in the organization, an "opening" for a film composer has little effect on other film composers outside the charmed circle. Only by entering the circle can skill and talent be displayed.

In occupational communities where the work is spread more evenly across the membership, the opportunity to move toward a more central position is enhanced. Of importance always is the chance to exhibit skills highly valued by colleagues and these chances may have their own distribution of occurrence, little affected by the membership. For example, to maintain one's calm and mannered indifference while handling the wheel of a prowl car in a high speed chase serves to increase a street cop's prestige among his colleagues, many of whom are listening intently to the communication stream occurring between dispatch and the involved officer. Any hint of terror or the losing of one's cool are sure to be noted by others. The killing of the proverbial "fleeing felon" can also enhance the patrol officer's reputation (Van Maanen, 1980b). Among tradesmen and construction workers, those with quick situational wit are often at the hub of the work group (Riemer, 1977). Such displays of situational talent and the stories that become associated with them can ennoble (or embarrass) occupational members, moving them toward the center (or periphery) of their fellow workers.

The observation that occupational careers may be tied to colleagual relations, settings, or the work itself is primarily an analytic convenience. The three spheres are closely interconnected and relative success in one usually brings success in the others. But, by considering each spere in turn, we have tried to emphasize the importance of performance when considering career movement in occupational communities. Whereas orgnizational careers of the sort premised on what White (1970) calls "vacancy chains" (openings move down as people move up) shuffle people continually across varied work roles, occupational careers contain less role variability across moves. Moreover, individual moves by a member within the community may have little or no effect on other members except to the extent that such moves increase or diminish the status of the collective as a whole, vis-a-vis outsiders.

Role Performance

In essence, careers in occupational communities are based upon what any given member's activities say to other members. Role performances (in both the theatrical and accomplishment senses) in occupational communities have strong communicative powers by which members, through their daily actions, carve out and display a central or peripheral (but unique) position within the membership. Three domains of role performance in occupational communities deserve comment for they reflect directly upon the knowledge base of the occupation discussed previously in the context of occupational self-control.

Knowledge. First, for a would-be member contemplating membership in an occupational community, knowledge must be acquired. Learning, socialization, practicing, training, feedback, testing, memorizing, and so forth are all involved, but the nature of these acquisition and transmission mechanisms varies across communities. What doesn't vary is the fact that recruits must master the substantive core of the occupation. Police officers must learn the laws they are charged with enforcing, dentists must learn the procedures they will use, pilots must learn how to read instrument panels and communicate with control towers. Such learning constitutes the dues to be paid before one earns the right to claim membership in an occupational community. By and large, such learning serves only to distinguish the initiated from the uninitiated.

Application. The second crucial aspect of role performance is the application of basic knowledge and skill to the continuously varying work members must, in an everyday sense, perform. To know the law is not to know when its use will be considered appropriate or inappropriate by other members. Situational features of the work become important and the initiated must begin learning routine and contextual applications. Skill and knowledge acquisition give way to the learning of task rituals where particular practices for getting the job done become taken for granted. Members of occupational communities utilize conventionalized, practical methods to accomplish much of what they do, and it is on the use of such rituals that members can assess one another in terms of proper role performance. Police officers have practical methods to issue tickets and make departmentally-defined quotas (Van Maanen, 1974). Welfare workers possess informal techniques for satisfying formal record-keeping demands

(Zimmerman, 1969). Public defenders have collective rules of thumb to guide their handling of individual cases (Sudnow, 1965). The point here is that these learned rituals are applied to tasks viewed as important because in the work world they are unavoidable and frequent. Such activity can be and is organized routinely with a purpose and significance for occupational members that transcends externally imposed standards such as managerial notions of efficiency or productivity and internally valued claims such as quality service or humane treatment. The routine properties of the gynecological exam by which doctors and nurses defuse their potentially embarassing probes into the body of a patient by use of strategically placed garments, ritualized humor, speedy procedures, and a most restricted sociability with the probed provide another superb exhibit of such task rituals (Emerson, 1969).[28]

Innovation. The third role performance feature of concern to occupational members involves the discarding of set skills and practical routines. Testing or breaking rules may secure a central position in the community for members who can accomplish valued occupational goals in new and untried ways. Schein (1971) uses the phrase "content innovations" to distinguish such actions. Working at the margin on different, perhaps difficult ventures, using resources in innovative ways, dealing smoothly with crises, pushing performance successfully to the limits of personal safety are the matters by which reputations are made. Members who work by design or accident at these margins, and who avoid failure where neither traditional occupational skills nor task rituals offer any predictable formulas for success, are quite likely to be the heroes of the occupation (Klapp, 1962). Such performances become displays of the "right stuff" of which stories are told and legends are made. The potential for stylish, episodic rule-breaking available to the membership transforms mundane, typically uneventful occupational life into a source of passion and drive. Simply to listen to carpenters talking about the successful completion of tough jobs, to cops on the raw details of how they handled a family fight, or to fishermen on the nature of storms endured, is to hear vivid testimony on what is, and what is not, central in their respective communities.

Individual careers in occupational communities are matters measured by centrality and work performance. Centrality may be achieved in a variety of ways, of course, but the more spectacular careers will almost invariably entail the violation of social conventions, accepted knowledge, or the received wisdoms of the trade. Such violations also have the potential to transform the occupational community itself in certain ways through the vivid demonstrations of new ways of seeing and doing things.

When such transformations occur, "role innovation" is achieved and occupational goals themselves are altered (Schein, 1971). In such a fashion,
an occupational community itself may gain (or lose) status.

It is true, too, that in other occupational communities the technical,
social, or moral innovators may never achieve centrality. The central
positions may be reserved only for those members who best exhibit and
articulate the community's traditional values, norms, and perspectives.
Innovators may be widely recognized and perhaps consulted by core
members, but they may not be accorded great honor, respect, or position.
Nor is centrality, when ahieved, necessarily enduring or obvious. There
are no doubt many members who are, in fact, central in occupational
communities but who do not feel special, rewarded, or even successful
within their individual lines of work. Caplow and McGee (1956) report
on a number of academics who, even though widely cited within their
disciplines, consider their work and careers to be "trivial," "unrecognized;" "stalled," "cannibalized," and so forth. This seems indeed to
be a major problem for those seeking careers in occupational communities
generally since the basis upon which one can assess the "success" of
one's career is multidimensional, shifting, uncertain, and, more often than
not, tied to the career of the occupation itself.

Finally, we must again note that individual careers in occupational communities are premised on the existence of some niche carved out in the
occupational structure of society that is more or less controlled by fellow
occupational members. Clearly, such a niche is not always to be found,
nor is such a niche always secure since there are other social processes
at work in occupational settings which attempt to deny or strip away such
self-control. Organization, technological change, bureaucratization,
standardization, formalization, are all processes of concern to those who
seek to follow an occupational career. These processes potentially subject
members to authority and discipline coming from outside the community
boundaries. Braverman's (1974) analysis of deskilling is useful in this
regard for it provides considerable insight into the demise of some occupational communities (and, perhaps, some not-too-subtle indicators as
to why some occupational communities never emerge). In brief, Braverman shows how occupational members lose control of the labor process
as job skills and knowledge become codified and standardized. By gathering, formulating, and systematizing the skills and traditions of certain
crafts, managers of organizations are able to separate the conception and
execution of work projects under their authority. No longer in sole possession of technique, occupational communities subjected to substantial
rationalization lose their basis for market control and power (Giddens,
1973).[29] Such processes potentially affect the careers of all members of
occupational communities, particularly those whose skills are employed

exclusively in organizational contexts. It is to selected aspects of these organizational matters that we now turn.

OCCUPATIONAL COMMUNITIES AND ORGANIZATION

Three generic types of interlocking relationships between occupational communities and organizations are possible. First, an occupational community may itself be organized to promote member interests and self-control. Typically, such organizations do not employ but rather enroll practitioners of a given occupation. Occupations organize in voluntary or compulsory associations in order to secure more favorable conditions for the membership (e.g., to secure useful legislation, to control entrance to the occupation, to set standards of work, etc.). Of course, forms of occupational organization vary across a broad range, from unions to professional societies, from informal coalitions to formal interest groups employing many lobbyists, and so on. Forms of association within an occupation differ also. For example, fishermen in several New England ports have organized cooperatives to obtain supplies more cheaply and market fish more effectively than they were previously able to do. Fishermen in other ports have organized unions in an effort to mediate the influence of large, powerful fishbuyers (Van Maanen, Miller & Johnson, 1982). While the formation of an association of some type is usually the first step toward legal control of work through professionalization of unionization (Caplow, 1954; Bledstein, 1976), the motive for formation need not always be economic. As many academic specialties have done, geographically dispersed occupational communities may develop societies simply to foster communication among members. Although the formation of an association entails the creation of positions to which members may aspire, these offices are sometimes best construed as structured paths for attaining centrality or for bestowing prestige on central members within the community since they may not provide much in the way of material rewards or grant much power (other than symbolic) to direct, supervise or dictate members' occupational endeavors. In other cases, these offices carry considerable authority and provide rewards that go well beyond the purely symbolic. Careers for aspiring or designated leaders in these occupational communities are then available (although they are usually few in number).

Second, an organization may employ only members of a given occupational community so that the organiztion itself provides a locale for the activities of an occupation. Some medical research laboratories, law firms, consulting firms, fire departments, and academic departments exemplify such confluence of organizational and occupational interests. Glaser (1964) notes that within research and development laboratories where recognition for scientific achievement is the primary means of career advancement, the achievements and perspectives that lead scientists to greater centrality in their occupational communities also lead to vertically-ascending organizational careers. Bailyn (1982) has recently commented upon the ironies and contradictions of such careers since considerable personal ambivalence and role strain seem to be associated with hierarchically-graded occupational careers. Research-centered universities encourage professors' deep involvement in occupational communities, but such involvement does not preclude organizational advancement and, in fact, may encourage it, to the possible distress of the professors who no longer profess (Schein, 1978). For many people in these settings, the organization may be of only secondary importance, but, nonetheless, its value (and its demands) cannot be ignored because it provides scarce resources necessary for pursuing occupational interests; resources which may not be available elsewhere.

Bureaucratic growth, in particular, seems to create problems for occupationally-based organizations. Administrative concerns such as efficiency, quality control, specialization, and productivity tend to increase in salience, thus potentially driving out occupationally-based traditions and interests. Displacement of goals is the classic phrase used to describe situations where fundamental occupational objectives appear thwarted by administrative demands (Merton, 1949; Blau, 1955). In welfare agencies, for instance, occupational members at the bottom of the organization often believe that members at the top prohibit or at least divert them from accomplishing their "real work," the work which presumably led all of them into the occupation in the first place. From the caseworker's perspective, managerial demands for "people processing" and properly documenting the eligibility of welfare clients eliminate any opportunity to really help people in need (Lipsky, 1979). Even though most administrators began their careers as welfare workers and may well continue to consider themselves members of the occupational community, the practical demands of general administration eclipse occupationally-relevant goals. Thus, even in single service organizations, where all members at least nominally share membership in the same occupational community, across-rank conflict is seldom absent.

Third and finally are those settings where organizations employ members of existing occupational communities, (or, through employment, create an occupational community) but where the membership in the community and the organization is not co-extensive. Incomplete overlap between an occupational community and an employing organization is, without question, the most frequent form of relationship between the two and represents the critical intersection of potentially competing work systems. As we noted earlier, when occupational communities are nested within heteronomous organizations, it is generally more difficult for the local membership to maintain occupational standards of work and also more difficult for the membership to prevent non-occupational members from performing work which lies within the occupation's traditional domain. From this perspective, understanding organizations very much involves understanding how members of occupational communities cope with, negotiate, and otherwise deal with organizational demands (i.e., Schein, 1972). How organizations are, in part, shaped by virtue of the occupational communities employed within them is the subject of the following discussion as we examine some rather familiar streams of organization theory in light of the occupational community framework presented in this paper.

Organizational Complexity and Managerial Control

Organization theory offers two complementary structural explanations for the complexity of organizations and for conflict within them. On one hand, an organization grows complex as tiers of subordination multiply, lengthening the chain of command. The greater the number of levels in a hierarchy, the more likely it is that messages will be distorted as they pass from stratum to stratum. To the degree that each level evolves its own peculiar tasks and sets of problems, the probability of conflicts of interest between levels increases since each may project different objectives for the organization. On the other hand, organizational complexity also increases as the number of departments and divisions within the organization multiply. Since each functional area tends to develop its own language, norms, time-horizons, and perspectives on the organization's mission, when forced to compete for resources or to cooperate on joint ventures, departments are likely to vie for the privilege of defining the situation (e.g., Lawrence & Lorsch, 1967; Thompson, 1967).

The problem with using horizontal and vertical differentiation to describe complexity is not that they are inaccurate, but rather that they do not go far enough. Ironically, their limitations arise from their virtues. Hierarchical and functional lines of demarcation are both theoretically parsimonious and methodologically elegant and they both correspond to the ways organizations formally depict themselves (Bittner, 1965). Consequently, researchers can identify presumably conflicting groups and perspectives by quick reference to the table of organization. They can construct simple empirical indices of structural complexity by counting hierarchical levels or functionally distinct groups, measuring spans of supervisory control, calculating staff-to-line ratios, and so forth, but as descriptions of an organization's social structure, hierarchy and function, as detailed by the official table, underestimate the extent and ambiguity of an organization's complexity along several lines.

First, departmental or divisional demarcations entail a level of analysis that hides potential interest groups and unrealistically homogenizes functional areas. Departments are often composed of smaller groups which may or may not be formally designated, but whose interests nevertheless clash. Divisions of student affairs in universities are typically composed of several departments such as counseling services, student unions, and housing or residence life. On some issues (budgeting for example) each department acts as a unified interest group. On other issues, segmentation within departments is quite visible. Housing departments, for instance, employ some personnel who are oriented primarily toward maintenance of the physical plant and others who view themselves as student personnel workers. While the two are grouped together in an administrative unit, those concerned with the physical plant are often at odds with their student personnel colleagues on specific issues such as how to handle students who damage university property, or over what constitutes an adequate room painting policy (Barley, 1979). Functional areas often contain a plurality of interest groups who coalesce as a unified entity only on rare occasions.

Second, relevant groupings in organizations crosscut both divisional and hierarchical lines. To again take Barley's (1979) example, because student personnel workers are trained as counselors, they often align themselves with counseling service personnel, thereby forming a coalition of peers that blurs, if not erases, functional boundaries. Nor are hierarchical lines of demarcation sacrosanct. Even in the quasi-military context of police agencies, supervisory personnel frequently side with the supervised rather than with each other or with higher officials in the agency on matters such as work pacing, scheduling, discipline, and productivity (Van Maanen, 1983).[30]

Finally, as our lengthy discussion of occupational communities suggests, some members of an organization align themselves with groups external to the organization and thereby possess a potentially useful resource to both support and oppose specific organizational policies and practices. Organizational development personnel, for example, marshall forth the wisdom of their occupational peers when recommending particular actions to decision makers of the firms for which they work (Klein, 1976). More familiar perhaps is the potential conflict existing when organizations employ individuals with even stronger occupational identities. Clinicians in university medical clinics emphasize the confidential nature of therapist-client relations as do therapists in other settings. Although the clinical value system generally coexists peacefully with the interests of other groups in the university, on occasion the clinician's vow of confidentiality conflicts with the demands of administrative personnel. For example, when a client has been referred for disruptive behavior, the clinician may become privy to information of interest to administrators who might prefer to take punitive or legal action against the student. In such cases, administrators and clinicians are thrown into conflict because the latter's insistence upon inviolate confidentiality thwarts speedy disciplinary action on the part of the former (Barley, 1979).

Such altogether transparent observations bring us back to the view that organizations are most accurately viewed as complicated sets of sometimes issue-specific coalitions, each exhibiting varying degrees of stability and overlapping memberships (March & Simon, 1962; Bacharach & Lawler, 1980). Formal indices of potential coalitions, such as hierarchical and functional differentiation, may provide clues to the relevant lines of conflict, but from an insider's point of view they portray only the tip of the iceberg. A more veridical approach would be to identify groups based upon the distinctions organizational members make among themselves. Member-relevant distinctions would be based upon dimensions of perceived commonality as well as upon the particular circumstances that make perceived commonality salient by setting one group against another. Since specific members of an organization can draw upon numerous social statuses and roles for referencing and identifying themselves, a plurality of overlapping groups is possible. Within organizations, potential bases for forming coalitions include proximity of work station, shift, perceived career potential, gender, education, friendship, and similarity of work. When this last factor—similarity of work—is descriptively relevant and the observed coalition formed in its shadow demonstrates a unity of purpose and structural stability over time and across a wide range of potentially divisive organizational controversies, the coalition represents a local manifestation of an occupational community. Such coalitions will be tenacious and, as we have suggested, not easily managed by those who fall outside its membershi boundaries.

Occupational communities promote self-serving interpretations of the nature and relevance of their work in the organization as a means of generating control over that work. Moreover, occupational communities represent relatively well integrated social systems. To the extent occupational communities succeed in convincing themselves and other that they solely command the expertise necessary to execute and evaluate their work, they gain autonomy and discretion. Hence, internally, occupational communities are tightly coupled systems but may be only loosely coupled to the larger organization (Weick, 1976, 1979).[31]

From this standpoint, many organizations more closely resemble tribal federations or fiefdoms than they do computing machines. Such organization has value even though the links between any two subsystems are highly problematic. Weick (1979) in particular has been persuasive when pointing to the virtues of increased complexity (caused, in part, by loose-coupling) such as a reduced responsiveness to external pressures or uncertainties and the greater variability of an organization's output. Several conditions relevant to our concern with occupational communities appear to foster loose-coupling in organizations.

First, geographically dispersed occupational communities that enjoy social and legal recognition and whose skills are in high demand can, with some impunity, resist managerial requests. The occupational community need not be a large component of the organization nor be seen as particularly crucial to the organization's mandate to secure and protect its relative autonomy. In some cases, such communities exercise considerable influence over the direction of the organization itself as its members assume high positions in the organization. Second, the numerical strength of an occupational community in an organization may promote loose-coupling since relative numerical superiority provides a political base in the organization for resisting administrative control. Third, an occupational community located at a critical juncture in the flow of an organization's work may foster loose-coupling. The mechanics studied by Crozier (1964) countered both managerial and production worker appeals to alter their occupational habits largely because their ever-reluctant services were considered by management and worker alike to be too vital to organizational functioning to risk confrontations. Fourth, scarcity of expertise, maintained in part by an occupational community through its monopoly of technique and knowledge, promotes loose-coupling in organizations. Since alternative sources of expertise are not readily available, management must take care not to offend the source it has, and thus may grant them relatively high amounts of autonomy. Organizations highly dependent upon new knowledge and proprietary technologies may find they are more successful buying such knowledge and granting its holders liberty than by trying to develop it internally under managerial direction.

These sources of complexity and loose-coupling are, by and large, structural matters. Complexity, however, also arises and is sustained by the very practices that make an occupational community distinct no matter what structural supports are to be located within the organization. Consider the role that codes and languages play in an organizational life. When occupational members employ community-based codes for interpreting and communicating the meaning of work-related events, it is difficult for outsiders to penetrate the codes in order to know what is really going on. Since codes allow their users to segment a flow of events, they provide members of an occupational community with more than a degree of freedom to reconstruct the meaning of events. Such transformations loosen the theoretical bonds between stimulus and response and allow members of occupational communities to perform their work relatively free from the influence of outsider demands (Manning, 1979). Moreover, since occupational codes appear mysterious, esoteric, and vaguely intimidating to those not well versed and practiced in their use, the understanding of certain phenomena may appear to be impenetrable to those outside the occupation. Certainly in the past and, to a lesser extent, currently, computer programmers and systems analysts have been able to secure a certain amount of occupational autonomy within some organizations because, in part, their languages are indecipherable by those not introduced to the mysteries of the occupational community and because, in further part, the codes blind members to the realities of other work groups (Haug, 1973).

All of this is not to say that complexity and conflicting sources of authority are welcomed by organizational managers. Loose-coupling is hardly embranced enthusiastically by administrators and others who must worry about coordination and control across their organization. The image and its referents are in high contrast to the ideal managerial organization whose well-lubricated parts are interdependent and mutually responsive. From this standpoint, it is easy to understand why so many organizational intervention techniques (e.g., participatory management, team building, goal setting, management-by-objectives, project and matrix supervision, etc.) aim to bolster the lagging integration and responsiveness among groups within an organization. More to the point, however, the decline of many occupational communities suggests that organizational principles of control are hardly on the defensive although, as we have tried to point out by emphasizing the diverse orientations of organizational members toward their work, the use of such principles is far more problematic than commonly conveyed. Two very general strategies for tightening organizations merit discussion. Each directly influences the very existence of an occupational community.

Fragmentation of work through its subdivision into component parts represents the most powerful method of increasing managerial control of the labor process and, by implication, of occupational communities. The celebrated robot is, of course, the perfect employee for it entails no mystery, possesses no loyalties, and seeks no exclusiveness. It is the ideal command-based work system. The application of tacit skill and judgement in the performance of work tasks is obviously ruled out. But the tasks that are programmed will be accomplished without ritual or exception. In the absence of robots, highly rationalized, minutely designed and carefully monitored work processes serve the same goals. Since control by fragmentation and standardization has been a centerpiece of organizational writings after Frederick Taylor established his devilish pact with Schmidt, the pig-iron loader, we will not comment further except to note the occasional irony presented by control systems that become so complex themselves that they increase the very problems they were designed to prevent. Gouldner's (1954) justly famous "vicious cycle of rules" is a case in point.[32]

Hierarchical control is the second managerial strategy of relevance to this discussion. To the degree that coercive authority and the application of discipline in the workplace is required, hierarchical control can quickly get out of hand since strong cultures of resistance can be expected to develop (Etzioni, 1964). Authority, in all its guises, is most effective when those to whom it is directed are favorably disposed to obey. When the orientation of organizational members is to the organization as represented by higher authorities in the workplace rather than to the occupation as represented by skillful practitioners who may or may not be higher authorities in the organization, control and direction of the labor process is eased. The Weberian solution to this problem is to provide careers for employees in such a way that their loyalty and effort become tied to organizational matters, not occupational ones. Edwards (1979:134) offers some thought-provoking evidence regarding the degree to which such a strategy has been employed in some organizations.

> With eighteen different job families, three hundred job titles and fourteen different pay grades, not to mention the dichotomy between salaried and hourly workers, it might appear that Polaroid had gone far enough in dividing and redividing its workers. Not so. Each job is now further positioned along the pay scale so that for any given job . . . seven distinct pay steps are possible, from entry level through 5 percent increments to top pay for the job . . . taking just the job titles and pay steps and ignoring the job families classification, Polaroid has created roughly 2,100 (300 times 7) individual slots for its 6,397 hourly workers.

One must pause for a moment at such categorization. Finely graded job structures represent the stuff of which organizational careers are made. The differences in positional characteristics hardly noticeable to the outsider often provide enormous incentive value to employees eager for advancement (Kanter, 1979). An "Assistant Professor, Step Two" may not appear different than an "Associate Professor, Step Three" to the outsider, but, to insiders, the differences are sure to be noticed and felt. Such tightening creates internally contrived images of mobility and, at times, prevents organizational participants from seeing the similarity of their position to others both inside and outside the organization (Jermier, 1982). Organizational careers, when used by employees as the measure of vocational success, serve to break up occupational communities and, in general, to increase compliance with managerial directives. One study suggests that in the higher circles of management the fundamental criteria used in the promotion of subordinates is their "orientation to advancement" as read by superiors (Sofer, 1970).[33]

In sum, complexity can be seen to be furthered both by the presence of occupational communities in organizations and by the efforts of management to drive them out or, at least, reduce their influence. Managerial control, however, is always problematic. Its effectiveness waxes and wanes over historical periods and varies across organizational and occupational contexts. We do not propose any general formula by which complexity can be predicted or control fully understood. These are highly uncertain issues. But we can say that to examine complexity and control in organizations as if the orientations of the membership to their work and occupation were unimportant would be folly. It is to these orientations we now move.

Organizational Loyalty and Work Careers

For members of occupational communities, employment in heteronomous organizations involves concomitant membership in two social systems of work. Such dual membership may generate an ever-present tension as an employee attempts to pursue simultaneously both an organizational and an occupational career, each of which may proceed in quite different directions and demand different loyalties. The issue for the person, the occupational community, and the organization as well, is which of the two social systems (if either) will achieve relative ascendancy in the person's vocational scheme of things.

Loyalty splits between an occupation and an organization and the dilemma of choosing between an occupational or organizational career resemble issues addressed by research on the "local" and "cosmopolitan" orientations of organizational members. Despite the fact that the local-cosmopolitan literature intends to illuminate the sources and consequences of the conflict between occupational and organizational loyalty, this literature has historically lacked coherence, displayed a rather shoddy methodology, failed to clarify its concepts, and, over the years, generated a muddle of contradictions (Grimes & Berger, 1970).[34] A good part of the problem is that the concept of "professional" undergirds research conceptualizations of the occupations thus far studied. By framing the debate in terms of an individual's orientation to occupational communities and to employing organizations, some of the pitfalls may be avoided while retaining the basic insights of the original theory.

Gouldner (1957, 1958) adopted the terms "local" and "cosmopolitan" from Merton (1949) who originally used them to differentiate between community leaders whose influence arises from contacts and accomplishments within the community (locals) and those whose influence arises from contacts and accomplishments beyond the community (cosmopolitans). Gouldner's intent was to distinguish between individuals whose loyalty and careers were tied to their employing organization and those whose careers and loyalty were focused on their occupational groups (Gouldner, 1957:288–89). Since Gouldner studied college faculty and administrators, the correspondence between local and organizational orientations and between cosmopolitan and occupational (or disciplinary) orientations was more or less acceptable, at least for academics in disciplines given to publication and research. Yet, once the concepts were extended beyond the academic setting to other occupational groups, discrepancies between predictions and results began to accumulate.

Consider several telling examples. In the Bennis et al. (1958) study of an outpatient clinic, "cosmopolitan nurses" were defined as those who sought professional careers by remaining tied to nursing work and "local nurses" were defined as those who sought administrative careers within the hospital by rising in the ranks of the nursing hierarchy. The researchers found, to their apparent surprise, that cosmopolitan nurses were more loyal to their work groups then local nurses. The results were contrary to the predictions flowing from the theory that guided the research. Similarly, studies of engineers employed in heteronomous organizations suggest that most engineers are local in orientation, yet local engineers, like their cosmopolitan colleagues, personify the values of technical excellence. Research on engineering occupations has yet to demonstrate any consistent differences between the two orientations in terms of work values, technical knowledge, commitment to keeping abreast of the field, conference attendance, or even journals that (presumably) are read (Kornhauser, 1962; Ritti, 1968; Goldberg, 1976).

Currently there are no general results to be found in the empirical literature devoted to exploring the local-cosmopolitan distinction (as defined operationally by the administrative-professional career orientations of organizational participants). The research indicates only that conflict is not always indicated by the findings and there is high variability in the types of relationships that exist between different occupational groups and the organizations in which they are employed (e.g., Hall & Lawler, 1970; Satow, 1975; Tuma & Grimes, 1981). Yet, since these studies are not comparative, the systematic basis for such variability has not been pursued and what is being "discovered" (and rediscovered) is that in specific circumstances members of this-or-that occupational group will adapt to organizational life and not experience the presumed inevitable conflict. The conceptual underpinnings of the theory are then left in place while, paradoxically, empirical work raises fundamental questions about the usefulness of the theory.

One problem with using the local-cosmopolitan or administrative-professional distinctions to differentiate the occupationally and the organizationally loyal is the assumption that an occupational orientation is based on a reference group external to the employing organization.[35] Although external reference groups may exist for members of some occupations such as tradesmen, academics, or industrial scientists, people in many lines of work do not know people who do denotatively similar work in other settings. Police officers, teachers, and fishermen know there are other police officers, teachers, and fishermen in other work settings, but they may not personally know them or interact with them on more than a sporadic or episodic basis. In many lines of work there are no annual meetings to attend, trade journals to read, or frequent opportunities available to meet colleagues outside the workplace who are not also members of one's employing organization.

What is crucial for the development of an occupational community is not, however, the presence of an extended work group, but rather that, through socialization, an occupation's value system comes to shape a person's work perspectives and self concepts—work perspectives and self–concepts that are supported over time in a person's daily interactions. Hence, one may be occupationally oriented but local. The concept of an occupational community does not assume that the occupational group of reference necessarily extends beyond an organization. Since the concept is defined phenomenologically, the researcher must first assess the community's interactive borders as they are perceived by members. Only when such an analysis reveals that an occupational community is organizationally extended in the experience of the membership will occupational loyalty be congruent with a cosmopolitan orientation. When the occupational community is clustered within the organization, people may choose an occupational over an organizational orientation and yet, like nurses and perhaps engineers, be local in their orientation.

When occupational communities do not extend beyond the organization, several conditions appear to influence personal loyalties. Promotion opportunities seem to be particularly salient (Sykes, 1965; Kanter, 1979). If the occupational community is small and the chance for promotion within the organization reasonably good, then organizational careers are likely to prove seductive, particularly if the occupational community lacks power by virtue of its peripheral position in the workflow or by its inability to provide scarce resources in high organizational demand. Social scientists in technically-driven universities provide a convenient (if biased) example in this regard. However, if the organization does not itself offer much opportunity for advancement, or if the occupational community comprises a large proportion or powerful segment of the organization's membership, then individuals may be more inclined to choose careers in the occupational community. Such a choice might appear as a "plateau" from the perspective of an organizationally grounded theory of career. But, from the perspective of the membership within an occupational community, the choice carries no negative connotations. It is, of course, sometimes the case that to be called "a real pro" implies that one will never be anything else.

Often the loyalty issues are not apparent until organization or occupational shifts have been undertaken (Lieberman, 1956; Schein, 1978). Thus, when individuals are shifted from one functional area to another or when hierarchical movement occurs within an organization, exit from the occupational community may be forced upon persons more or less against their will. Becker and Strauss (1956) have suggested that many, if not most, passages in the workplace induce problems of loyalty for the person undergoing the transition. When a member of an occupational community accepts a supervisory position or shifts to another department, members left behind may feel the person is "no longer one of us." A new organizational role may also demand the development of new skills because different problems are faced and, in learning these skills, an entirely new set of colleagues is encountered. In cases where major shifts of perspective are to be expected when moving up and away from one's occupational community, strong prohibitions may exist among the membership to discourage such movement, even when some members are favorably disposed toward an organizational career.

For example, Manning (1977) documents how an occupational community of police officers protected its members from the scrutiny of organizational authorities. Among members of this police community, to become a sergeant was to betray the very trust upon which the community rested. Promotion-seeking itself may estrange individuals from colleagues by requiring the promotion seeker to act in ways regarded as inappropriate by members. Van Maanen (1983) observed in another police community that even to talk about one's desire for upward mobility in the organization was to invite the ridicule of one's colleagues. Not only were such aspirations seen as foolishly optimistic, higher rank itself was seen by patrol officers to offer only the paperwork headaches that come with virulent forms of memo madness. The power of such shaming tactics should not be disregarded by students of organizational careers, Shaming may be directed at the most central and skilled members of the community, leaving only the most peripheral members free from its influence. The pool of those available for administrative or organizational careers may then be comprised largely of the least respected and least skilled members of an occupational community. Deans who are not thought by the professoriate to be "real scholars" come to mind in this regard, as are doctors-turned-hospital-administrators who, when evaluated by the medical staff, are held in low regard for "never having really practiced."

It appears that a paradox occurs when particularly strong occupational communities are enclosed within an organization. In such cases, organizational loyalty is negatively correlated with occupational loyalty. But, since the community is bounded by the organization itself, committed members will be reluctant to leave. Leaving would demand exiting the occupational community. Hence, occupational loyalty would be negatively correlated with turnover. Considering these relationships together, organizational loyalty appears positively associated with turnover insofar as the relation is premised upon the existence of an occupational community within the organization. Just such a situation seems to exist in police agencies where patrol officers most desirous of a managerial career and most committed to the organization are typically the least satisfied and most estranged from the patrol officer community (Van Maanen, 1975). Such members are also the most likely to "turnover" since promotion is both quite slow and (seemingly) capricious in police agencies. Occupational communities profit by this paradox since those least attracted and attractive to the membership are also the most likely to depart.

Although dual membership in an occupational community and an organization engenders conflicts of loyalty, researchers must not assume that the issue of loyalty is always in the foreground or that the choice of an organizational career automatically alienates a member from others who continue to follow the occupation. Conflicts of loyalty are typically contextual and issue-specific. While many patrol officers do not desire the sergeant rank, many engineers do aspire to supervisory positions. Patrol officers often feel making rank reduces their ability to control what they do while engineers often believe making rank will help them achieve such control (Van Maanen, 1983; Goldner & Ritti, 1967). Clearly, to study occupational-organizational tensions and differentiate in any meaningful way between the occupationally and organizationally loyal is also to study the moral, social, and cognitive contours of occupational communities. As several decades of research suggest, much variability is sure to be found.

Innovation, Technology, and Managerial Control

The fertility of occupational communities for the creation and introduction of work-oriented innovations is equivocal. On one hand, to the degree that an occupational community represents a traditional social system that claims sole propriety over the jurisdiction of its work, resistance may be expected to any form of organizational or technological change which would threaten the community's sovereignty in its work domain. Certainly organizational interventions designed to increase the community's responsiveness and integration within the organization will be dismissed as attempts to destroy the autonomy of the occupational community. Technological innovations which are interpreted as potentially deskilling or which might disrupt the social structure and prestige of the community as it is currently organized will be resisted and, if possible, sabotaged.[35] For example, spotters in the Israeli artillery have traditionally prided themselves on their ability to relay accurate and timely coordinates over a field radio to soldiers in the batteries. However, since the radio is a public medium, many spotters gain notoriety for their airwave antics and personae as well as for their military acumen. After the last war with Egypt, the Israeli command installed computerized radio transmitters in spotters' halftracks. The computers were intended to enhance the spotter's efficiency since a spotter could now enter the coordinates directly into the computer and relay them into another computer attached to a fieldpiece by the mere push of a button. Needless to say, faced with the loss of potential status, many spotters gutted or otherwise disengaged the electronic equipment and continued to broadcast live. Of course, housings were discreetly left mounted and intact in case officers happened to inspect the operation. (Kunda, 1982).

On the other hand, since members of an occupational community identify with their work and with their skill and expertise, innovations which come from within the community may very well be encouraged and embraced. Skilled craftsmen and machinists who design new tools that allow easier, more precise, and perhaps speedier, work as well as computer programmers who constantly seek more elegant algorithms provide examples of innovations that serve to advance one's standing in the occupation by providing benefits to all members. Perhaps the best indicator of a community's response to innovation is whether or not the innovation comes from within the community and whether or not it will remain under the community's control.

It is worth noting too, that some occupational communities are apparently quick to adopt technological innovations, even those characterized by the membership as "not invented here." Yet, the evidence does not suggest that the adopted innovations necessarily improve the community's ability to conduct its work effectively or efficiently. There is no functional imperative that works in this domain. Police agencies are notorious consumers of new technology and police officers of all ranks take pride in sporting the newest electronic gadgets, the latest model cars, the most powerful weapons, and so forth. But, despite the rising sophistication of crime–fighting technology, there is absolutely no evidence that the ability of the police to detect and deter crime has improved (Wilson & Kelling, 1982). There is even a hint that this rising sophistication has impaired their ability (Manning, 1979).

Of course, some technological innovations have not been adopted so enthusiastically by the police. Electronic scanners that make possible continuous monitoring of patrol car activities are one such innovation that has stirred up considerable controversy within police agencies. Consider also that when two-way radios were first being installed in patrol cars, replacing the fixed-post telephone systems of communication, many radios were reported lost, stolen, broken, jammed, or otherwise tampered with by "unknown persons" (Rubinstein, 1973). Similar reports are heard today with even the most foolproof communication systems wherein dispatchers are unable to establish the whereabouts of errant squad cars due to [claimed] static, low-flying objects, or black holes in the airwaves.[37]

As a general rule, the more technologically or methodologically sophisticated an occupational community becomes, the more splintered and fragmented its membership—becoming, at times, many little occupational communities rather than one. Social scientists developed statistical routines to aid in the interpretation of collected data. Over the years, small pockets of statisticians have penetrated each of the social sciences. The more refined and powerful the analytic techniques, the fewer the number of occupational community members familiar and comfortable with their use (Daft, 1980). Such splintering heightens the possibilities for organizational control since managers may argue that only occupational members with particular (rather than general) skills are to be employed. Some members benefit, others may vanish and a wedge is driven into the community. In occupational communities where the knowledge base and technical skills are rapidly advancing, cohort splintering may be prominent. New members possess more recent knowledge and hence may be of more value to organizations (and perhaps to the occupational community as well) than the older members. The wedge is driven further because there are usually economic incentives to be found when purchasing young talent rather than buying, retaining, or upgrading old talent.

The ambivalence of some occupational communities toward innovation is hardly surprising given that their own demise may be forthcoming. Nor is the glee and eager pursuit of innovation among managerial bodies difficult to understand since innovation may be as valuable in terms of controlling the membership of an organization as it is for whatever reputed gains in productivity or efficiency are to be claimed for its implementation. Office automation and the computerization of newspaper printing are good examples in this regard (Champion, 1967; Wallace & Kallenberg, 1982). In both spheres, technological innovation has central-relevant implications since it has enlarged the prerogatives of management and diminished craft practices and judgemental tasks required of both secretaries and newspaper printers.

Where the knowledge base and skill levels contained within an occupational community remain relatively stable, danger to the community from lack of innovation may develop. Accounting provides an interesting case for it appears that the mystique and exclusivity once associated with the black (and white) arts of accounting have significantly eroded as knowledge of accounting principles and financial management techniques have become less arcane and more dispersed throughout an organization. The new technology surrounding computer programming, making the use of computing machines far more accessible to those untrained in information processing, represents another erosion of a formerly glamorous occupational community (Kraft, 1979).

This is not to say that increases in information or new technologies always disrupt and reorder the status and power of occupational communities. Certainly knowing the technology does not allow an analyst to predict what forms of social organization will develop to surround it as the comparative industrial experience of Britain and Japan all too pointedly testify (Dore, 1973). The claim that new technologies inevitably fragment work and deskill people will not hold across the board. Some technologies, as we have suggested, conceivably create occupational communities where none existed before, or empower existing communities. New diagnostic devices such as head and body scanners (CATscans) now used in some radiology departments of large hospitals seem to bolster the technicians' sense of work community and give them occupational clout because, within a given hospital, they are among the only skilled and practiced interpreters of the output created by the new machines (Barley, forthcoming).

In sum, occupational communities are bound to rise and fall with social and technological innovation, but the precise path such a rise and fall may take and the ripple effects it will have on organizational matters are quite difficult to reckon with in the abstract. We do not share the Marxist gloom that craft skills and communal occupational ties are always destroyed by the advance of technology in capitalistic societies. Nor are we convinced by the more sanguine predictions made by those enamored with technology of the new freedoms and work communities to be encouraged. Historical, longitudinal, comparative studies are required and there are precious few such studies currently available in the organizational literature to be able to say much about what theories will or will not be generally useful in this area.

SOME CLOSING COMMENTS

We had two purposes in mind while constructing this essay. First, we wanted to convey a set of ideas for understanding work and work organizations that might complement those ideas currently in fashion within organization theory. In particular, we have tried to show how the concept of an occupational community might provide greater insight into the way careers are understood by people, the way complexity is managed and magnified, the way occupational loyalty is played out in organizations, and so forth. Our first intent then was to complicate organizational theorizing by suggesting how some of the "blooming, buzzing, confusion" of phenomenological approaches to the study of work worlds can be captured by our theories.

Our second purpose was more rhetorical and informed by some structural observations. Here we wanted to convey a sense of disenchantment with handed-down organization theory emphasizing harmony and cooperation in the workplace. Too often organizational research represents a sort of effete innocence which speaks of attitudes, values, supervision, structure, goals, rules, ethos, culture, and communication, but not of conflict and power. To this end, we have tried in our essay to dismantle some of the seeming neutrality surrounding organization studies by emphasizing the political and economic roots of occupational self-control, by questioning the assumed traits of service and knowledge so often considered definitional when professions are studied and, in general, by presenting alternative sources of workplace authority. Our second intent then was to open up organizational theorizing in a manner that would allow some of these broader and ideologically sensitive matters to be addressed.

Whether or not such purposes have been served well or poorly is not ours to say. What we can do in these few remaining pages, however, is to briefly review our main points and then make a few suggestions as to why and where we think these points are particularly relevant.

We began by noting that a persistent theme in the sociological literature is the presumed dichotomy between communal or colleagual and rational or administrative forms of work organization. Occupational communities, we argued, approximate the former and must be defined in terms of member-perceived boundaries. Within such boundaries, members of occupational communities claim a distinctive and valued social identity, share a common perspective toward the mission and practices of the occupation, and take part in a sort of interactive fellowship that transcends the workplace.

The diverse origins of occupational communities were discussed in terms of how certain physical and social conditions surrounding particular lines of work might promote any or all of these definitional characteristics. Occupational communities were seen to create and sustain relatively unique work cultures consisting of, among other things, task rituals, standards for proper and improper behavior, work codes which surround relatively routine practices and, for the membership at least, compelling accounts attesting to the logic and value of these rituals, standards and codes. The difficult but persistent quest for occupational self-control represented the single universal in our scheme. Although this quest has a Sysiphus-like character for all occupational communities, some have developed and maintain considerable structural advantages such as state support, an elaborate and advancing theoretical and procedural base to inform (and mystify) practice, and a relatively unorganized market in dire need of an occupational community's talents. We then suggested that the professions, when appropriately unpacked by specialty and interest, were best viewed as occupational communities, and that they differ from other lines of work (and each other) only by virtue of the relative autonomy each is able to sustain within the political economy of a given society. Finally, we catalogued a few of the implications the study of occupational communities posed for certain domains of organization research. Careers (individual and collective), complexity, loyalty, and innovation were areas given special attention.

By and large, throughout this paper we have taken organization behavior researchers to task for paying inordinate attention to the way managers attempt to control the labor process in organizations, and not enough attention to the ways those who are managed also attempt to control their labor. Along with Kerr (1977), we think theories of organization behavior exaggerate the role formal leadership plays as a control device in organizations by too often failing to consider the nature and source of employee work orientations. Diversity is masked and only the most visible tip of the control structure is apparent when the research focus is upon hierarchy and workflow. One (and we emphasize one) way to redirect attention is through the study of occupational communities. The standards of evaluation, grounds for respect, and sources of ambition vary across occupational communities, yet we currently know very little about the conditions under which such variance is to be expected. A fruitful and ongoing research rask, then, is to add to the ethnographic record of occupational communities, particularly those that appear to be located in organizational contexts.

Longitudinal studies of selected occupations are also needed. Communities rise and fall with social and economic change. The organizational implications of such shifts are more or less unknown. There may be some urgency to this task since many occupations are changing rapidly in the face of new technologies designed to alter work practices. The increased codification of occupational knowledge carries with it the distinct potential for allowing persons outside an occupational community to perform tasks previously reserved for the membership. Computer-based diagnostic routines, for example, make it possible for technicians to perform certain medical examinations without a doctor's presence. While some of these tasks may seem trivial and unrelated to the "real work" of a given occupation, over time the inroads made by outsiders may well loosen occupational monopolies, demystify practice, and increase the amount of administrative control exercised over occupational members. Such a theme is becoming prominent in sociological circles where, within a decade, the happy concern for the "professionalization of everyone" (Wilensky, 1964) has become a sour concern for the "deprofessionalization of everyone" (Haug, 1975).

A focus on occupational communities offers new directions for research on organizational careers and socialization practices. Interorganizational career studies is one area to be developed (Faulkner, 1982). Skill acquisition and the learning of specific work routines and practices is another. While new entrants are socialized into the mores of a company, for example, they are also absorbing from colleagues and others the accumulated wisdom of an occupation, say, management. Such enculturation often transcends the organization's learning requirements and provides continuity (or lack thereof) with the lessons learned during anticipatory socialization undergone in educational institutions. To focus on occupational careers may also become less a matter of choice than a requirement. The sluggish economy with no surge in sight and the apparently common situation of declining opportunity in many, if not most, Western industries suggests a need to place more emphasis upon how to generate increases in both the quantity and, perhaps more importantly, the quality of goods and services produced by our major work institutions. This must be done without appeal for massive infusions of additional capital which, in all probability, will be in short supply. We believe members of occupational communities have much to tell us in this regard.

Dedication to high standards of work performance and craft excellence are not matters easily promoted from outside an occupational community. Ways must be found, therefore, to preserve and encourage such dedication. At the same time, we need to more carefully examine the social (and ideological) mechanisms of accommodation to stable, "plateaued" organizational careers. A concern for how people draw meaning and value from what to some are "stalled" or "flattened" careers will have considerable practical importance. Bailyn (1982) makes this same point more forcefully in the context of how different career paths influence men and women in their relations outside the workplace. Ways which protect and expand the influence of occupational communities within organizations may become as interesting to researchers (and managers) as the ways that destroy them are now.

All this is not to suggest that the study of those whose work histories are punctuated by disorderly and rapid shifts among jobs and occupations is to be foregone. An occupational community can be understood only by knowing what it is not. Discretion over the methods, pace, schedule, and outcome of one's work is the ambition of occupational communities but it is an ambition not often achieved and, even when achieved, it can be grasped only tentatively. Historical studies promise to untangle some of the knots which presently restrict understanding occupational communities by depicting the origins of such communities within the larger society (e.g., Larson, 1977; Edwards, 1979). An important feature of this work is that it also reveals organizational control principles. Occupational communities are, by and large, those work domains where member identities and work practices have not been fragmented into organizationally-defined positions by highly detailed job descriptions, where work performance is not ultimately judged by a management cadre, and where entrance to and exit from the occupation is not controlled by any one heteronomous organization. These are, of course, matters of degree but, as principles of occupational authority and control, they contrast to those prevalent in management textbooks. An historical study awakens us to some fundamental constraints on management influence that go far beyond the much-discussed limitations of improper spans of control, poor supervisory style, insensitive task design, or inadequate goal setting procedures.

One final caveat. We think the study of occupational communities vital to a concern for what people at work do all day (or would like to do). Organization theory has had relatively little to say about the things people actually do at work (although much to say about what others think they should be doing). We are just now learning, for instance, that middle and high level executives do not spend much time thinking or planning about what strategic options are available to their firms or departments. Evidence suggests they may not think or plan much at all, since they are busily rushing about answering phones, attending meetings, and engaging in brief encounters of the short kind (Stewart, 1968; Mintzberg, 1973; Feldman, 1982). Strategic decisions, then, are more or less backed into, and justified retrospectively with little, if any, foresight. Many organizations seem to move more from drift than design based on, in Weick's (1982) marvelous phrase, "the presumption of managerial logic." Certainly at lower levels of organizations the disparity between depictions and predictions (both manager and researcher) of what people do all day and descriptions and accounts (both member and researcher) of what people, in fact, do all day is equally disturbing and upsetting of received theories of organizational behavior (Van Maanen, 1981). Studies of occupational communities, by forcing the analyst to move inside them to discover member understandings of the work they do, give license to explore the practical and moral contours of work worlds against which organization theories can be assessed. With this remark, we are back to where we began and can wonder again in print whether it makes more or less sense to view Charlie, our hypothetical auto repairman down at Joe's Garage, as a "mechanic" or as an "employee." We suspect that for Charlie the former matters and not the latter, although that answer must not be assumed.

ACKNOWLEDGMENTS

A dim and most abbreviated version of this paper was first presented at the ORSA/TIMS National Meetings, Colorado Springs, November 11, 1980, under the title "Careers in occupational communities: On being what you do." We have extensively revised that paper (several times), sometimes deleting, but mostly adding, materials we felt appropriate. Critical readers of note include Lotte Bailyn, L. L. Cummings, Deborah Kolb, Peter K. Manning, Edgar H. Schein, and Barry Staw. They are not to be blamed for whatever substantive or judgemental errors are contained in this paper. They tried to warn us. Partial support for the writing was provided by: Chief of Naval Research, Psychological Services Division (Code 453), Organizational Effectiveness Research Programs, Office of Naval Research, Arlington, Virginia, 22217; under Contract Number N00014-80-C-0905; NR 170-911.

NOTES

1. A sociology of knowledge perspective informs the way we handle the various work ethnographies (Berger and Luckman, 1966; Schutz and Luckman, 1973). Such an approach emphasizes the many ways people make sense of their lives and find meaning in work. A sociology of knowledge perspective also encourages the enlargement of our field of study by suggesting that people draw meaning and worth from endeavors beyond those traditionally studied by organizational researchers. Streetcorner hustlers, carnival workers, organic farmers, dishwashers, drug dealers, gamblers, fishermen, street sweepers, and housewives all work and, for the most part, define what they do as work. Such activities are rarely part of the popular conception of "real work" in this society, yet, for those involved, such activities are, indisputably, work. We follow Polanyi (1958) in this regard and take the view that any activity used to make a living is to be treated as work and, as such, treated as an occupation. Miller (1981) provides an excellent introduction to this approach.

2. For examples of the best in the genres, we would suggest, in the ethnographic writings: Millman's (1977) examination of the wonderful world of surgery, Willis's (1977) care-

fully detailed analysis of how working class youngsters get working class jobs, and much of the qualitative materials appearing in the journal *Urban Life*. In the organization behavior writings, Pfeffer's (1981) analysis of the sources and uses of power in organizations comes to mind as does Weick's (1979) highly charged writings on social systems and virtually all that appears in *Administrative Science Quarterly*. To bring these two literatures to bear on one another is an important task.

3.   An exception to this general rule is found in studies of labor-management relations. Historically, the so-called institutional school emphasized participant-observation studies of work life and suggested that the roots of labor-management conflict are found in the expropriation of labor value by management (Hill, 1981). More recently, however, the institutional approach has lost ground (at least in the United States), replaced by the more sanguine view of work organization as a "system" by which divergent interests are brought into line through such mechanisms as collective bargaining, strikes, grievance procedures, and so on (Dunlop, 1958). Studies in this newer tradition take a variable approach, emphasizing large samples and sophisticated, quasi-experimental, statistical research designs in the apparent hope of uncovering the correlates of various dispute settlement patterns. As a result, the industrial relations literature and the organization behavior literature have begun to very much resemble one another (e.g., Kochan, 1980; Bacharach and Lawler, 1980). When labor-management clashes are unavoidable, such impasse is seen in terms of the divergent interest of unions (composed of a federation of occupations) and organizations (composed of managers representing de facto ownership). Rarely, then, do the thwarted but specified occupational interests of workers (or managers) enter into the analysis of union-management relations. Braverman's (1974) work represents a break from U.S. traditions, but such work has yet to become the research norm. A good review of these traditions and an overview of what, in England, has become the "New Industrial Relations" is provided by Hill (1981).

4.   This conceptual situation is, in part, an artifact of viewing work organizations as systems for the achievement of goals (Bernard, 1938). Such a view emphasizes cooperation and anything seen to disrupt goal achievement is, by definition, dysfunctional and deviant. Behavior is viewed according to plan and is of note only when it is out of line. Key figures in the control scheme are supervisors who keep the enterprise "on track" by providing "negative feedback" to correct deviations. The so-called natural or taken-for-granted condition is the existing set of organizational relations and goals to which organizational members are to attach themselves. When they do not, moral or ethical questions are entertained, thus making any demonstrated lack of attachment deviant. The failure of researchers to appreciate value diversity, particularly in regard to worker resistance to dissatisfying work roles and goals, is a failure we would like very much to correct. This point has been a key notion in the so-called Critical Theory approach to organizational theorizing and is made powerfully by Clegg and Dunkerley (1980). A brief discussion of the role critical theory might play within an interpretive and phenomenological framework is provided by Van Maanen (1981).

5.   The two forms of social organization were given different names by various theorists. Weber (1968) wrote of the "communal" and the "associative." Durkheim (1933) contrasted "mechanistic" with "organic" solidarity. Tonñies (1957) used "gemeinshaft" and "gesselshaft" which, according to Gusfield (1975) are the terms most frequently adopted by sociologists.

6.   On the Chicago School's contribution to an understanding of modern life, see both Faris's (1979) social history and Rock's (1979) intellectual history. The theoretical perspective most frequently associated with Chicago School sociology is symbolic interactionism of which Blumer's (1969) description is authoritative.

7.   Gusfield's caution and preference for phenomenologically sensitive depictions of the boundaries of a community echo those of Weber (1968:42):

"It is by no means true that the existence of common qualities, a common situation, or common modes of behavior imply the existence of a communal social relationship. Thus, for instance, the possession of a common biological inheritance by virtue of which persons are classified as belonging to the same 'race,' naturally implies no sort of communal social relationship between them. By restrictions on social intercourse and on marriage, persons may find themselves in a similar situation, a situation of isolation from the environment that imposes these distinctions. But, even if they all react to this situation in the same way, this does not constitute a communal relationship. The latter does not even exist if they have a common 'feeling' about this situation and its consequences. It is only when this feeling leads to a mutual orientation of their behavior to each other that a social relationship arises between them rather than of each to the environment. Furthermore, it is only so far as this relationship involves feelings of belonging together that it is a 'communal' relationship."

8. The distinction used by Harris (1968, 1975) between "emic" and "etic" modes of analysis is useful in this regard. Emic study attempts to understand and describe the world from the perspective of those who are studied. Etic study attempts to understand and describe the world scientifically, using variables which pattern behavior in ways typically hidden from those who are studied. Though we perhaps err in the direction of run-on emics when depicting work worlds (in part, a reaction to the abstract and rather dull organizational theorizing currently in vogue), the interplay between the two is very much our concern in this paper.

9. "Guinea" is a term used by fishermen in Gloucester to identify Italian fishermen, typically Sicilian, who have more or less adopted American customs and mores. "Greaser" is a term used by Guineas to refer to recent immigrants, also typically Sicilians, who have not yet become acculturated to the larger American scene. Greasers are thought to cling stubbornly to their native language and the ways of the old country (Miller and Van Maanen, 1979).

10. Joining network analysis with interview or ethnographic techniques offers a promising methodological strategy in this regard. Network models operate on observed or self-reported connections (e.g., exchanges, communications, acquaintances, etc.) among members of a given population. The meaning of such networks to members, as well as the grounds upon which such networks are built and change are, however, matters not so easily mapped since they require sensible qualitative study. Usually, one method or the other is employed in social research, but rarely both. The result is an elegant network model whose meaning to those modelled is quite unclear; . . . or, a rich account of the meanings members provide to their world whose empirical references (and connections) are left largely unchecked. A recent exception to this rule is Faulkner's (1982) inventive melding of the two approaches. Granovetter (1974) provides an early example.

11. By reference groups, we follow Shibutani's (1962:132) lead: "[The] group whose presumed perspective is used by an actor as the frame of reference in the organization of his perceptual field. . . . A reference group is an audience consisting of real or imaginary personifications, to whom certain values are imputed. It is an audience before whom a person tries to maintain or enhance his standing." It is hard to improve on this definition.

12. Culture, from this standpoint, is not strong or weak any more than it is good or bad. It simply is. Any two cultures will, of course, contrast but it takes an outsider to provide the dimensions of contrast and, as we suggest in this paper, such dimensions may or may not be of relevance to cultural members. On alternative perspectives on culture, Sanday's (1979) review of ethnographic paradigms has direct relevance to organizational and occupational research.

13. Occupational cultures may, of course, reside more or less peacefully within (and as part of) organizational cultures, may exist alongside and in opposition to them, may be

buried by them, or may even contain them. Within organizations, occupational cultures are subcultures harboring segments of relative diversity within a generally approved organization plan; alongside organizations, occupational cultures compete with the plan, offering to its membership alternative goals; when buried by organizations, occupational cultures cease to exist; and, when containing organizations, the occupational and organization cultures are one and the same. This crude taxonomy, discussed in more depth later in the paper, only begins to suggest the kinds of interactions possible. The main point is, however, the need to explain each rather than assume the priority of one over the other. Schein's (forthcoming) analysis of organizational culture is sensitive to these issues, unlike other ventures into this domain where culture is treated too often as an undifferentiated organizational variable subject to varying degrees of managerial control (Schwartz and Davis, 1981; Deal and Kennedy, 1982). In such a fashion, culture becomes merely another roadside attraction in the study of organizations, something to be attended to or not, based on an analyst's preference.

14. Goffman's (1961a) version of role distance is of obvious relevance here as are some of the empirical materials on the role working class cultures play inside some organizations, such as Katz (1965), Shostack (1969), Ferree (1976), and Foner (1976). Much of this material suggests that the less control people have over the pace, methods, outputs of work, the more likely they are to smuggle in interests and identities relevant outside the workplace. As noted in the text, in occupational communities the flow of interests and identities goes the other way.

15. The materials in this section draw on work highly critical of research treating the professions as homogeneous social groups whose members are united by common expertise and a calling to service (e.g., Johnson, 1972; Roth, 1974; Larson, 1977; Bledstein, 1976). As noted later in the text, professions are best regarded as loose federations of multiple groups, some of which may be occupational communities, forming around special interests, ideologies, and skills (Bucher and Strauss, 1961). The structural conditions allowing an occupational group self-control more or less are derived from Child and Fulk's (1982) first-rate comparative analysis of the professions' control of occupations. We think these dimensions have a more general worth and thus have followed their lead in this section.

16. We turn back to this topic later in the paper when discussing occupational careers. There we will argue that the cognitive learning associated with an occupational role precedes the learning of skills and that the difference is reflected in the popular conceptions of "knowing" and "know-how." The latter, in terms of establishing an occupational niche, is far more important than the former.

17. Caplow (1954) still provides the sociological primer on these matters; the examples may be dated, but the ideas are not. Bensman and Lilienfeld (1973) provide a useful reading of the historical sources of meaning in work. Recent writings tend toward the more specific and, hence, occupationally unique histories such as Noble's (1979) look at engineers in America or Miller's (1977) comparative treatment of cops and bobbies.

18. Turner and Hodge (1970) also point to a second approach to the professions which they call the "community approach." This approach emphasizes social characteristics, in particular the attitudes and values of those certified to practice the profession (Goode, 1957). We fall closer to the community approach but do not feel it is useful, as discussed in the following section, to sharply distinguish the professions as unique occupational communities.

19. Lyman and Scott (1970) on "accounts" and Hewitt and Stokes (1975) on "disclaimers" are mandatory reading on this matter. Both owe debts to Mills (1940) "vocabulary of motives" idea. Bringing this line of thought to organizational theorizing is Starbuck (1982) in his examination of organizational ideologies.

20. The classic case of occupational control via union activity is, of course, the now woefully out-of-date Lipset et al. (1956) study of the typographical union. Currently, the battle of occupational self-control through unionization seems most visible in the public

services—particularly in teaching (e.g., Cole, 1969) and policing (e.g., Long and Fenulli, 1974). Freidson's (1973) reader is good on the issues raised by occupational communities in public organizations as is a recent article by Ponak (1981).

21.   Bledstein (1976) is good on this point, taking care to note the special and elite connotations the term "professional" holds for Americans in contrast to the equally special but low connotations carried by the union-member tag. Larry Cummings (personal communication) suggests that unionization of an occupational group may actually lower the occupation's social status. For example, faculty unionization may lower the status of an institution's faculty in the eyes of the general public. While data are scarce on these matters, similar propositions seem not to hold in Western Europe where union membership neither symbolizes the vulgar pursuit of filthy lucre, nor conveys relatively low social standing. Unlike Europe, in the United States union membership as a proportion of the workforce has been on a downward slide for some time (Edwards, 1979:202). Certainly this suggests the diminished appeal of unions in the U.S., but the reasons underlying such trends are no doubt far more complicated than by what can be slipped in under the social status argument.

22.   Representative writings on occupation stress (and its popular semantic referent, "burnout") in the human service industry include Paine (ed.) (1982), and Cherniss (1980). Perhaps one reason behind the disproportionate attention given to stress in the bootstrapping versus elite occupations is that the elite are well compensated for their efforts and are relatively more distant from the carriers and substance of "other people's misery." Were the elite trades such as law and medicine to claim "burnout," the public might well begin to question the practical premises upon which these occupations are based (i.e., that they do what they claim to do and the practitioners are well qualified and screened to do it). Aside from more money, one solution to stress, infrequently mentioned in the literature of course, is for an occupational community to somehow generate a "better class" of clients which, empirical evidence suggests, also leads to heightened professional standing (Freidson, 1970).

23.   The terms "external" and "internal" career are found in Van Maanen, Schein, and Bailyn (1977). The phrase "external career" refers to the path and sequence of positions and roles that constitute a career in an organization or occupation. "Internal career" connotes the meaning career related roles and experiences have for an individual. See Van Maanen (1977) for an elaboration of how internal careers are constructed.

24.   The use of "career" to refer to advancement within a sequence of hierarchically arranged positions no doubt reflects the use of the term in everyday language. We are suggesting, however, that popular discourse may not be the best guide for the definition of a concept thought to have theoretical value. Indeed, we are arguing that, as an analytic construct, the term "career" needs to be broadened beyond its colloquial connotation. Lotte Bailyn (personal communication) argues that to achieve such aims we may need to invent a new term devoid of an implied escalator clause. We tentatively agree, but are waiting for inspiration.

25.   Although the least studied of Schein's (1971) three dimensions, some recent work has been devoted to formalizing the inclusionary or centrality dimension. Van Maanen (1980a) notes that movement along this dimension can be seen in terms of rule learning, rule use, rule breaking, rules about rule breaking, and so on. Gregory (1980) provides a taxonomy of organizational inclusion that is sensitive to cross-cultural contexts.

26.   The rigid separation between captain and crew seems, in the United States at least, to be less prominent than sea stories would have us believe. In particular, the increasing geographic mobility of fishermen, along with the diminishing (regulated) lengths of fishing seasons, has created a situation where many fishermen jump from port to port throughout the year. These so-called flying fishermen not only fish different species in different ports in different seasons of the year, they often do so in different occupational roles. Thus, a

skipper on a salmon vessel may also be an engineer on a tuna boat and a deckhand on a groundfish dragger. With such movement has come greater egalitarianism among fishermen. For a descriptive treatment of the causes and consequences of this relatively recent phenomena, see Van Maanen, Miller, and Johnson (1982).

27.   We must note that the phrase "early periods of occupational learning" is a relative one. Some occupations require apprenticeships that extend over very long periods of time. Trades such as masonry are excellent examples where one passes from laborer or helper, to apprentice, to journeyman, and, finally to craftsman. The trek takes many years. Consider, also, psychiatrists, who may be well into their mid- to late-thirties before fully shedding the student role. Greer (1972) provides a nice set of examples of varying forms of apprenticeship.

28.   On the matters of practical reasoning and task rituals, ethnomethodologists have much to say as Garfinkel's (1967) classic analysis of "good reasons for bad organizational records" demonstrates. From this perspective, Kolb (forthcoming) provides a marvelous example of how the members of one relatively tight occupational community (federal mediators) routinely orchestrate work matters in ways that dramatically contrast to those rituals adopted by another, relatively similar, occupational community (state mediators).

29.   This process is, at least according to Marxist scholars, in no way a natural or evolutionary one. Deskilling proceeds through the conscious design of management rather than being merely a technical requirement of the production of particular goods and services (Braverman, 1974). We tend to agree but hasten to add, as does Giddens (1973), that class determinism is as equally full of dogma and unsupported contention as the technological determinism it seeks to replace.

30.   Our discussion of coalitions parallels Dalton's (1959:57–65) more refined consideration of clique-formation in management circles. In Dalton's scheme, three general types of cliques can be identified: vertical, horizontal, and random. Vertical cliques subdivide into the symbiotic varieties where exchanges between higher level and lower level members of the organization are more or less balanced and the parasitic varieties where lower level members receive more than they give. Horizontal cliques are distinguished by their defensive or aggressive stance vis-a-vis general organizational policies. Random cliques are those based strictly on friendship and social satisfaction without conscious consideration of organizational policy or work goals. Occupational communities, if viewed as cliques inside an organization, would typically fall into Dalton's horizontal-aggressive classification when not faced with immediate threat. But, occupational communities, in our view, are much more than cliques since: (1) their formation rests on matters not organizationally specific; (2) the ties binding the membership are long lasting, potentially binding across the working lives of the members; and (3) though they may perform some of the same functions cliques in organizations do, such as bridging the official and unofficial goals of organizational members, their substantive concern for occupational self-control will invariably transcend issue-specific organizational concerns.

31.   The essence of loose-coupling, as used in the organization literature, is that the stimulus-response links between any two subsystems are unpredictable (Glassman, 1973; Weick, 1976). A very nice, highly detailed illustration of equivocal and tentative links is provided in Manning's (forthcoming) analysis of police communication systems where the subsystems of dispatch and patrol are shown to be loosely-coupled for a variety of structural and phenomenological reasons. Attempts to tighten the links between the two by police administrators have repeatedly met with failure.

32.   Gouldner's (1954) "vicious cycle" emerged from a study of underground miners who, prior to a personnel switch in management, possessed considerable work autonomy. When new management moved to call in some of this autonomy by formulating a set of new work rules, the miners reacted by claiming new ares of autonomy which brought forth more rules from management, and so on. A related point, well made by Douglas (1970), is that formal rules indicate deviance: the more rules, typically, the more rules, typically, the more

and more widespread the deviance. That the two play off each other is Gouldner's (1954) original point.

33. The irony should not be lost. What Sofer's (1970) work suggests is that promotion is based, in part, on one's "desire for promotion." A self-sealing cycle may be created in which ambition is valued for ambition's sake, driving out even the most sincere efforts to pin promotions upon demonstrated performance at a given level. Part of the problem is, no doubt, the ambiguity surrounding the assessment of managerial work so the search for promotional criteria leads back to such personal attributions as ambition, desire, drive, strength, will, and so forth Apparently, the situation in many American firms is that, in the absence of performance indicators, striving will do. Sennett (1977) provides interesting commentary on these matters, updating the master work in the field of organization men by Whyte (1956).

34. Despite this list of four deadly sins, research in the area is by no means dead. Recent work is still attempting to clarify the meaning of "local" and "cosmopolitan." Several studies proceed by factor analysis of items drawn from Gouldner's original questionnaire or from a questionnaire developed by Goldberg, *et al.* (1965). For example, Berger and Grimes (1973), Flago and Brumbaugh (1974), and Tuma and Grimes (1981) all show that localism and cosmopolitanism are independent dimensions rather than bi-polar, and that each are aggregate concepts "tapping" any number of underlying concepts. Whether or not such studies, in fact, clarify the meaning of local and cosmopolitan is, in our view, most uncertain.

35. This assumption derives directly from Gouldner's (1957:290) original paper where he notes "cosmopolitans are oriented to outer reference groups whereas locals use an inner reference group."

36. Lest we be accused of being Luddites in this regard, we must specify our context. In some areas, notably communication systems through which stolen cars and property can be traced, technology has increased the police's ability to at least detect, if not deter, crime. In other areas, such as the use of automobile patrol units in high population density neighborhoods, technology has impaired police functioning since they have lost touch with their clientele whose cooperation is essential for detecting some crimes, particularly street crimes. The ambiguity of technology in the context of police work is a point well covered by Manning (1981; forthcoming).

37. Again, Manning (1981) provides the empirical materials in his police communication work. The point not made explicitly in the text is that the presence of static, low flying objects, and black holes serves a purpose for patrol officers who are busy at times with matters from which they do not wish to be distracted. Not wanting to be bothered by intrusive dispatchers who may try to whisk them away on other, less desirable, missions of mercy such as locating barking dogs or calming belligerent drunks, patrol officers simply fail to respond to dispatch, claiming later, if the matter arises, that they never heard the command or request. While sophisticated equipment allows dispatchers to efficiently send a message with very little noise, they must still rely on human contact to discover that their message has been received. This stands almost as a textbook example of a loosely-coupled system masquerading as a tightly-coupled one.

REFERENCES

Allen, T. *Managing the flow of technology.* Cambridge, MA: MIT Press, 1977.

Argyris, C. *Integrating the individual and the organization.* New York: Wiley, 1964.

Bacharach, S. B., and Lawler, E. J. *Power and politics in organizations.* San Francisco: Jossey Bass, 1980.

Bailyn, L. *Living with technology.* Cambridge, MA: MIT Press, 1980.

Bailyn, L. *Work and family: Testing the assumptions.* Paper presented at the Academy of Management Annual Meetings, New York, 1982.

Barley, S. *The student life office: A case study.* Unpublished manuscript, Cornell University, 1979.

Barley, S. *Taking the burdens: The strategic role of the funeral director.* Working paper No. 1129-80, Sloan School of Management, MIT, 1980.

Barley, S. The semiotics of funeral work. *Urban Life*, 1983, *12*, 3–33.

Barley, S. The professional, the semi-professional, and the machine: A study of the introduction of new imaging modalities into three radiology departments, (PhD dissertation) MIT, forthcoming.

Barthes, R. *Elements of semiology.* Boston: Beacon Press, 1967.

Becker, H. S. The professional dance musician and His audience. *American Journal of Sociology*, 1951, *57*, 136–144.

Becker, H. S. *Outsiders: studies in the sociology of deviance.* New York: Free Press, 1963.

Becker, H. S. and Carper, J. The elements of identification with an occupation. *American Sociological Review*, 1956, *21*, 341–48.

Becker, H. S. and Strauss, A. Career, personality, and adult socialization. *American Journal of Sociology*, 1956, *62*, 253–263.

Becker, H. S., Geer, B., Riesman, D. & R. Weiss. *Institutions and the person.* Chicago: Aldine, 1968.

Benet, M. K. *The secretarial ghetto.* New York: McGraw-Hill, 1972.

Bennis, W. G., Berkowitz, N., Affinito, M., & M. Malone. Reference groups and loyalties in the outpatient department. *Administrative Science Quarterly*, 1958, *2*, 481–500.

Bensman, J. & Lilienfeld R. *Craft and consciousness.* New York: Harper and Row, 1973.

Bernard, C. I. *The functions of the executive.* Cambridge, MA: Harvard University Press, 1938.

Berger, P. L. *The human shape of work.* South Bend, IN: Gateway, 1964.

Berger, P. L. & Luckman, T. *The social construction of reality.* New York: Doubleday, 1966.

Berger, R. R. & Grimes, A. J. Cosmopolitan and local: A factor analysis of the construct. *Administrative Science Quarterly*, 1973, *18*, 223–235.

Beynon, H. 1973, & Blackburn, R. M. *Perceptions of work: variations within a factory.* Cambridge: Cambridge University Press, 1972.

Bittner, E. The concept of organization. *Social Research*, 1965, *32*, 239–255.

Blau, P. K. *The dynamics of bureaucracy.* Chicago: University of Chicago Press, 1955.

Blauner, R. *Alienation and freedom.* Chicago: University of Chicago Press, 1964.

Bledstein, B. J. *The culture of professionalism.* New York: Norton, 1976.

Bloch, F. E. & Kuskin, M. S. Wage determination in the union and non-union sectors. *Industrial and Labor Relations Review*, 1978, *31*, 183–192. (no. 28)

Blumer, H. 1978, *Symbolic interactionism.* Englewood Cliffs, NJ: Prentice-Hall, 1969.

Bosk, C. L. *Forgive and remember: managing medical failure.* Chicago: University of Chicago Press, 1979.

Braude, L. *Work and workers: A sociological analysis.* New York: Praeger Publishers, 1975.

Braverman, H. *Labor and monopoly capital.* New York: Monthly Review Press, 1974.

Brown, A. J. *The structure of career opportunities in organizations* (General Series Discussion Paper #95). Coventry, England: Centre for Industrial Economic and Business Research, University of Warwick, 1981.

Bryant, C. D. Petroleum Landmen: Brothers in the 'Oil Fraternity'. In C. D. Bryant (Ed.), *The Social Dimensions of Work.* Englewood Cliffs, NJ: Prentice-Hall, 1972a.

Bryant, C. D. Sawdust in their shoes: The carnival as a neglected complex organization and work culture. In C. D. Bryant (Ed.), *The Social Dimensions of Work.* Englewood Cliffs, N.J.: Prentice-Hall, 1972b.

Bucher, R. & Strauss, A. Professions in Process. *American Journal of Sociology*, 1961, *66*, 325–334.

Caplow, T. *The Sociology of Work*. New York: McGraw Hill, 1954.

Caplow, T. & McGee, R. J. *The academic marketplace*. New York: Basic, 1958.

Carr-Sanders, A. M. & Wilson, P. A. *The professions*. Oxford: Clarendon, 1933.

Cherniss, C. *Staff burnout: Job stress in the human services* (Volume 2.). Beverly Hills, CA: Sage, 1980.

Child, J. & Fulk, J. Maintenance of occupational control: The case of professions. *Work and Occupations*, 1982, *9*, 155–192.

Chinoy, E. *Automobile workers and the american dream*. New York: Doubleday, 1955.

Clegg, S. & Dunkerly, D. *Organization, class, and control*. London: Routledge and Kegan-Paul, 1980.

Cole, S. *The unionization of teachers: A case study of the UFT*. New York: Praeger, 1980.

Cottrell, W. F. Of time and the railroader. *American Sociological Review*, 1934, *4*, 190–198.

Crane, D. *Invisible colleges: diffusion of knowledge in scientific communities*. Chicago: University of Chicao Press, 1972.

Crozier, M. *The bureaucratic phenomenon*. London: Tavistock, 1964.

Daft, R. L. The evolution of organizational analysis in ASQ: 1959–1979. *Administrative Science Quarterly*, 1980, *25*, 623–636.

Dalton, M. *Men who manage*. New York: Wiley, 1959.

Dawe, A. *The two sociologists*. London: Longmans, 1980.

Deal, T. and A. Kennedy (1982) *Corporate Cultures: The Rites and Rituals of Corporate Life*, Reading, MA: Addison-Wesley.

Dore, R. P. *British factory—Japanese factory*. Berkeley: University of California Press, 1973.

Douglas, J. D. (Ed.). *Understanding everyday life*. Chicago: Aldine, 1970.

Driver, M. J. Career concepts and organizational change. In C. B. Derr (Ed.), *Work family and career: New frontiers in theory and research*. New York: Praeger, 1980.

Dubin, R. Industrial workers' worlds. *Social Problems*, 1956, *3*, 131–142.

Dunlop, J. *Industrial relations systems*. Carbondale, IL: Southern Illinois University Press, 1958.

Durkheim, E. [*The division of labor in society*] (G. Simpson, trans.) New York: Free Press, 1933. (Originally published, 1893.)

Durkheim, E. [*Suicide*] (J. A. Spaulding and G. Simpson trans.) Glencoe, IL: Free Press, 1951. (Originally published, 1897.)

Eco. *A theory of semiotics*. Bloomington: Indiana, 1976.

Edwards, R. *Contested terrain*. New York: Basic, 1979.

Emerson, J. Behavior in public places: sustaining definitions of reality in gynecological examinations. In H. P. Dreitzel (Ed.), *Recent sociology*. New York: Macmillan, 1970.

Faris, R. E. L. *Chicago sociology, 1920–1932*. Chicago: University of Chicago Press, 1979.

Faulkner, R. R. Coming of age in organizations: A comparative study of career contingencies and adult socialization. *Sociology of Work and Occupations*, 1974, *1*, 131–173.

Faulkner, R. R. *Music on demand*. Philadelphia: Trans-action Books, 1982.

Feldman, S. P. *The culture of monopoly management: An interpretive study in an american utility*. Unpublished Ph.D. Dissertation, University of Pennsylvania, 1982.

Ferree, M. M. Working-class jobs: Housework and paid work as sources of satisfaction. *Social Problems*, 1976, *23*, 431–441.

Fielding, A. G. & Portwood, D. Professions and the state: Towards a typology of bureaucratic professions. *Sociological Review*, 1980, *28*, 1, 23–53.

Flango, V. E. & Brumbaugh, R. B. The dimensionality of the cosmopolitan-local construct. *Administrative Science Quarterly*, 1974, *19*, 198–210.

Foner, P. S. *Factory girls*. Urbana, IL: University of Illinois Press, 1977.

Freidson, E. *Professional dominance: The social structure of medical care*. New York: Atherton Press, 1970.

Freidson, E. (Ed.). *The professions and their prospects*. Beverly Hills, CA: Sage, 1973.

Gamst, F. C. *The hogshead*. New York: Holt, Rinehart, and Winston, 1980.

Garfield, S. R. The delivery of medical care. *Scientific American*, 1970, *222*, 15–23.

Garfinkel, H. *Studies in ethnomethodology*. Englewood Cliffs, NJ: Prentice-Hall, 1967.

Geertz, C. *The Interpretation of Culture*. New York: Basic, 1973.

Gertzl, B. G. Determinants of occupational community in high status occupations. *Sociological Quarterly*, 1961, *2*, 37–40.

Giddens, A. *The class structure of the advanced societies*. London: Hutchinson, 1973.

Glaser, B. G. *Organizational scientists*. Indianapolis: Bobbs-Merrill, 1964.

Glaser, B. G. (Ed.). *Organizational careers: A sourcebook for theory*. Chicago: Aldine, 1968.

Glaser, B. G. & Strauss, A. *Status passages*. Chicago: Aldine, 1971.

Glaser, B. G. *Expert versus laymen: A study of the patsy and the subcontractor*. Mill Valley California: The Sociology Press, 1972.

Glaser, W. A. *Paying the doctor: systems of remuneration and their effects*. Baltimore: Johns Hopkins Press, 1970.

Goffman, E. *The presentation of self in everyday life*. Garden City, NY: Anchor, 1959.

Goffman, E. *Encounters*. Indianapolis: Bobbs-Merrill, 1961a.

Goffman, E. The moral career of a mental patient. *Asylums*. New York: Anchor, 1961b.

Goffman, E. *Frame analysis*. New York: Harper and Row, 1974.

Gold, R. L. In the basement: The apartment building janitor. In P. L. Berger (Ed.), *The Human Shape of Work*. South Bend IN: Gateway, 1964.

Goldberg, L. C., Baker, E. & Rubenstein, A. H. Local-cosmopolitan: Unidimensional or multidimensional. *American Journal of Sociology*, 1965, *2*, 704–710.

Goldner, F. H. & Ritti, R. R. Professionalization as career immobility. *American Journal of Sociology*, 1967, *72*, 489–502.

Goode, W. J. A theory of role-strain. *American Sociological Review*, 1960, *25*, 483–496.

Goode, W. Community within a community. *American Sociological Review*, 1957, *22*, 194–200.

Goodenough, W. *Description and comparison in cultural anthropology*. Chicago: Aldine, 1970.

Gouldner, A. Cosmopolitans and locals: toward an analysis of latent social roles. *Administrative Science Quarterly*, 1957, *2*, 281–306.

Granovetter, M. S. *Getting a job: A study of contacts and careers*. Cambridge, MA: Harvard University Press, 1974.

Graves, B. Breaking out: An apprenticeship system among pipeline construction workers. *Human Organization*, 1958, *17*, 9–13.

Greenwood, E. Attributes of a Profession. *Social Work*, 1957, *2*, 45–55.

Greer, B. (Ed.). *Learning to work*. Beverly Hills, CA: Sage, 1972.

Gregory, K. L. Work organizations and careers: A theoretical framework for anthropologists and three cross-cultural applications. Unpublished paper, Department of Anthropology, Northwestern University, 1980.

Grimes, A. J. & Berger, P. K. Cosmopolitan-local: evaluation of the construct. *Administrative Science Quarterly*, 1970, *15*, 407–416.

Gusfield, J. R. *Community: A critical response*. New York: Harper and Row, 1975.

Haas, J. Learning real feelings: A study of high steel ironworkers reactions to fear and danger. *Sociology of Work and Occupations*, 1977, *4*, 147–171.

Habenstein, R. W. Sociology of occupations: The case of the american funeral director. In A. Rose (Ed.), *Human Behavior and Social Processes*. Boston: Houghton Mifflin, 1962.

Hackman, J. R. & Oldham, G. R. *Work redesign*. Reading, MA: Addison-Wesley, 1979.

Hall, D. T. *Careers in organizations*. Pacific Palisades, CA: Goodyear, 1976.

Hall, D. J. & Lawler, E. E. Job characteristics and pressures and the organizational integration of professionals. *Administration Science Quarterly*, 1970, *57* (3), 271–281.

Harlow, D. Professional employees' preference for upward mobility. *Journal of Applied Psychology*, 1973, *57* (2), 137–141.

Harris, M. *The rise of anthropological theory*. New York: T. Y. Crowell, 1968.

Harris, M. Why a perfect knowledge of all the rules that one must know in order to act like a native cannot lead to a knowledge of how natives act. *Journal of Anthropological Research*, 1975, *30*, 5–22.

Haug, M. The deprofessionalization of everyone. *Social Focus*, 1975, *8*, 197–213.

Haug, M. Computer technology and the obsolescence of the concept of profession. In M. R. Haug and J. Dofny (Eds.), *Work and Technology*. Beverly Hills: Sage, 1977.

Haug, M. R. & Sussman, M. B. Professionalization and unionism: A jurisdictional dispute? In E. Freidson (Ed.), *The Professions and their Prospects*. Beverly Hills, CA: Sage, 1973.

Hawkes, T. *Structuralism and semiotics*. Berkeley: University of California Press, 1977.

Hayano, D. *Poker faces: The life and work of professional card players*. Berkeley: University of California Press, 1982.

Hewitt, J. W. & Stokes, R. Disclaimers. *American Sociological Review*, 1975, *40* (1), 1–11.

Hill, S. *Competition and control at work: The new industrial sociology*. Cambridge, MA: MIT Press, 1981.

Hirschman, A. O. *Exit, voice and loyalty: Responses to decline in firms, organizations, and states*. Cambridge, MA: Harvard University Press, 1970.

Hughes, E. C. Work and self. In J. Rohrer and M. Sherif (Eds.), *Social Psychology at the Crossroads*. New York: Harper and Row, 1951.

Hughes, E. C. *Men and their work*. Glencoe, IL: Free Press, 1958.

Hughes, E. C. *The sociological eye: Selected papers on work, self, and the study of society*. Chicago: Aldine, 1971.

Illich, I. *Medical nemesis*. New York: Pantheon, 1976.

James, J. On the block. *Urban Anthropology*, 1972, *4*, 125–140.

Janowitz, M. *The professional soldier*. Glencoe, IL: Free Press, 1960.

Jermier, J. J. Labor process control in modern organizations. Unpublished paper, Department of Management and Administrative Sciences, University of Florida, 1982.

Jessup, D. K. Teacher unionization: A reassessment of rank and file motivation. *Sociology of Education*, 1978, *51*, 41–55.

Johnson, T. J. *Professions and power*. London: Macmillan, 1972.

Kanter, R. M. *Men and women of the corporation*. New York. Basic, 1979.

Katz, F. Explaining autonomy in formal work groups in complex organizations. *Administrative Science Quarterly*, 1965, *10*, 204–223.

Kerr, S. Substitutes for leadership: Some implications for organizational design. *Organization and Administrative Sciences*, 1977, *8*, 135–146.

Klapp, O. E. *Heroes, villains, and fools*. Englewood Cliffs, NJ: Prentice-Hall, 1962.

Klegon, D. The sociology of the professions: An emerging Perspective. *Sociology of Work and Occupations*, 1979, *5* (3), 276–292.

Klein, L. *A social scientist in industry*. London: Gower Press, 1976.

Kochan, T. A. *Collective bargaining and industrial relations*. Homewood, IL: Richard D. Irwin, 1980.

Kolb, D. *The Mediators*. Cambridge, MA: MIT Press, forthcoming.

Kornblum, W. *Blue collar community*. Chicago: University of Chicago Press, 1974.

Kornhauser, W. *Scientists in industry: Conflict and accommodation.* Berkeley: University of California Press, 1962.

Kraft, P. The routinization of computer programming. *Sociology of Work and Occupations,* 1979, *6* (2), 139–155.

Kunda, Gideon. Personal communication. MIT, 1982.

Larson, M. S. *The rise of professionalism.* Berkeley: University of California Press, 1977.

Lasson, K. *The workers: Portraits of nine american jobholders.* New York: Grossman, 1971.

Lawrence, P. R. & Lorsch, J. W. *Organization and environment.* Cambridge, MA: Harvard University Press, 1967.

Lieberman, S. The effects of changes in role on the attitudes of role occupants. *Human Relations,* 1956, *9,* 385–402.

Light, D. *Becoming psychiatrists.* New York: Norton, 1980.

Lipset, S. M., Trow, M. & Coleman, J. *Union democracy.* New York: Free Press, 1956.

Lipsky, M. *Street level bureaucracy.* New York: Sage, 1980.

Long, G. & Feuille, P. Final offer arbitration: Sudden death in eugene. *Industrial and Labor Relations Review,* 1974, *27,* 186–203.

Lortie, D. C. *Schoolteacher.* Chicago: University of Chicago Press, 1975.

Lyman, S. & Scott, M. *A Sociology of the absurd.* New York: Meredith, 1970.

Lynch, J. T. & Bailyn, L. *Engineering as a lifelong career.* Unpublished paper, Sloan School of Management, MIT, 1980.

Manning, P. K. *Police work: The social organization of policing.* Cambridge, MA: MIT Press, 1977.

Manning, P. K. *Crime and technology: The role of scientic research and technology in crime control.* Paper prepared for the National Science Foundation Science and Technology Project, Washington, D. C., 1979.

Manning, P. K. *Producing drama: Symbolic communication and the police.* Unpublished paper, Wolfson College, Oxford University, 1981.

Manning, P. K. Organization control and semiotics. In M. Punch (Ed.), *Control in Police Organization.* Cambridge, MA: MIT Press, 1983.

March, J. G. & Simon, H. A. *Organizations.* New York: Wiley, 1958.

Marcson, S. *The scientist in american industry.* New York: Harper and Row, 1960.

Marglin, S. A. What do bosses do: The origins and functions of hierarchy in capitalist production. *Review of Radical Political Economics,* 1974 *6,* 60–112.

McGregor, D. *The human side of enterprise.* New York: McGraw-Hill, 1960.

Mead, G. H. *Mind, self, and society.* Chicago: University of Chicago Press, 1930.

Mechanic, D. *The growth of bureaucratic medicine.* New York: Wiley, 1976.

Mendes, R. H. P. *Sociological ambivalence, role strain, and the professional union.* Unpublished paper, Department of Sociology, Brooklyn College, 1982.

Merton, R. K. Patterns of influence: A study of interpersonal influence and of communications behavior in a local community. In P. F. Lazarsfeld and F. Stanton (Eds.), *Communications Research 1948–49.* New York: Harper, 1949.

Messinger, S. L., Sampson, H. & Towne, P. D. Life as theatre: Some notes on the dramaturgic approach to social reality. *Sociometry,* 1962, *25,* 98–110.

Midford, J. *The American way of death.* New York: Simon & Shuster, 1963.

Miller, G. *It's a living: Work in modern society.* New York: St. Martin's Press, 1981.

Miller, M. & Van Maanen, J. Boats don't fish, people do: Some ethnographic notes on federal management of fisheries. *Human Organizations,* 1979, *38,* 377–385.

Miller, M. & Van Maanen, J. Getting into fishing: Social identities of fishermen. *Urban Life,* 1982, *11,* (1), 27–54.

Miller, W. *Cops and bobbies.* Chicago: University of Chicago Press, 1977.

Millman, M. *The unkindest cut: Life in the backrooms of medicine.* New York: Morrow Quill, 1977.

Mills, C. W. Situated actions and vocabularies of motive. *American Sociological Review*, 1940, *5*, 904–913.

Mills, C. W. *White Collar*. New York: Oxford University Press, 1956.

Mintzberg, H. *The nature of managerial work*. Englewood Cliffs, NJ: Prentice-Hall, 1973

Montagna, P. D. The public accounting profession: Organization ideology and social power. In E. Freidson (Ed.), *The Professions and Their Prospects*. Beverly Hills, CA: Sage, 1973.

Niederhoffer, A. & Niederhoffer, E. *The police family*. Lexington, MA: D.C. Heath, 1978.

Noble, D. F. *America by design*. New York: Oxford University Press, 1977.

Oppenheimer, M. The proletarianization of the professional. *Sociological Review Monograph*, 1973, *20*, 213–227.

Paine, W. S. (Ed.). *Job stress and burnout*. Beverly Hills, CA: Sage, 1982.

Park, R. E. & Burgess, E. W. *Introduction to the science of sociology*. Chicago: University of Chicago Press, 1924.

Peirce, C. S. *Collected Papers of Charles Sanders Peirce*. Cambridge, MA: Harvard University Press, 1931–1958.

Pettigrew, A. M. *The politics of organizational decision making*. London: Tavistock, 1973.

Pfeffer, J. Organizational demography. In L. L. Cummings and Barry M. Staw (Eds.), *Research in Organizational Behavior*, Vol. 5. Greenwich, CT: JAI Press, 1983.

Polanyi, M. *Personal knowledge: Towards a post-critical philosophy*. Chicago: University of Chicago, 1958.

Polanyi, M. *The tacit dimension*. Garden City, NJ: Doubleday, 1966.

Ponok, A. M. Unionized professionals and the scope of bargaining. *Industrial and Labor Relations Review*, 1981, *34*, 396–407.

Reimer, J. Becoming a journeyman electrician. *Sociology of Work and Occupations* 1977, *4*, 87–98.

Rice, A. K. *Productivity and social organization: The ahmedabad experiment*. London: Tavistock, 1958.

Roberts, J. M., Thompson, W. E. & Sutton-Smith B. Expressive self-testing in driving. *Human Organization*, *25*, 54–63.

Rock, P. *The Making of Symbolic Interactionism*, Totona, NJ: Rowman and Littlefield.

Ritti, R. Work goals of scientists and engineers. *Industrial Relations*, 1968, *7*, 118–131.

Roethlisberger, F. J. & Dickson, W. J. *Management and the worker*. Cambridge MA: Harvard University Press, 1939.

Rosenbaum, J. E. Organizational career mobility: promotion chances in a corporation during periods of growth and contraction. *American Journal of Sociology*, 1979, *85*, 21–48.

Roth, J. A. Professionalism: The socilogist's decoy. *Sociology of Work and Occupations*, 1974, *1*, 6–23.

Roy, D. Banana time: Job satisfaction and informal interaction. *Human Organization*, 1960, *18*, 158–168.

Rubinstein, J. *City Police*. New York: Farrar, Straus & Jeroux, 1973.

Salaman, G. *Community and occupation*. London: Cambridge university press, 1974.

Sanday, P. R. The ethnographic paradigm(s). *Administrative Science Quarterly*, 1979, *24*, 527–538.

Sanders, W. B. *Detective work*. New York: Free Press, 1977.

Satow, R. L. Value-rational authority and professional organizations. *Administrative Science Quarterly*, 1975, *20* (4), 526–531.

Schein, E. H. The individual, the organization, and the career: A conceptual scheme. *Journal of Applied Behavioral Science*, 1971, *7*, 401–426.

Schein, E. H. *Professional education: Some new directions*. New York: McGraw-Hill, 1972.

Schein, E. H. *Career dynamics: Matching individual and organizational needs*. Reading, MA: Addison-Wesley, 1978.

Schriesheim, J. M., Von Glinow, A. Kerr, S. Professionals in bureaucracies: A structural alternative. In P. Nystrom and W. Starbuck (Eds.), *Prescriptive Models of Organizations*. New York: North-Holland, 1977.

Schutz, A. & Luckmann, T. [*The Structure of the Life-World*] (R. M. Zaner and H. T. Engelhardt, Jr. trans.) Evanston, IL: Northwestern University Press, 1973.

Schwartz, H. & Davis, S. M. Matching corporate culture and business strategy. *Organizational Dynamics*, 1981, pp. 30–48.

Scott, W. R. Reactions to supervision in a heteronomous professional organization. *Administrative Science Quarterly*, 1965, *10*, 65–81.

Searle-Chatterjee, M. The polluted identity of work: A study of benares sweepers. In S. Waldman (Ed.), *Social Anthropology of Work*. New York: Academic Press, 1979.

Sennett, R. *The Fall of Public Man*. New York: Knopf, 1977.

Shibutani, T. Reference groups and social control. In A. Rose (Ed.), *Human Behavior and Social Processes, An Interactionist Approach*. Boston: Houghton Mifflin, 1962.

Shostak, A. B. *Blue collar life*. New York: Random House, 1969.

Silverman, D. *The theory of organizations*. New York: Basic, 1970.

Slocum, W. L. *Occupational careers: A sociological perspective*. Chicago: Aldine, 1966.

Smith, D. *Report from engine company eight two*. New York: Dutton, 1972.

Sofer, C. *Men at mid-career*. Cambridge: Cambridge University Press, 1970.

Sonnenfeld, J. & Kotter, J. P. The maturation of career theory. *Human Relations*, 1982, *35* (1), 19–46.

Spradley, J. *The ethnographic interview*. New York: Holt, Rinehart, and Winston, 1979.

Starbuck, W. J. Congealing oil: Ideologies to justify acting ideologies out. *Journal of Management Studies*, 1982, *19*, (1), 3–28.

Stewart, R. The manager's job: Discretion vs. demand. *Organizational Dynamics: Managers and Their Jobs*. London: Macmillan, 1968.

Stinchcombe, A. Bureaucratic and craft administration of production: A comparative study. *Administrative Science Quarterly*, *1959*, *4*, 168–187.

Stone, K. The origins of job structures in the steel industry. *Review of Radical Political Economics*, 1974, *6*, 61–97.

Strauss, G. Union government in the U.S.: Research past and future. *Industrial Relations*, 1977, *16*, 215–242.

Sudnow, D. Normal crimes: Sociological features of the penal code in a public defender office. *Social Forces*, 1965, *12*, 25–76.

Sykes, A. J. M. Some differences in the attitudes of clerical and manual workers. *Sociological Review*, 1965, *13*, 297–310.

Terry, W. C. Police stress: The empirical evidence. *The Journal of Police Science and Administration*, 1981a, *9*, (1), 61–75.

Terry, W. C. *Police Stress as a professional self-image*. Unpublished paper, Department of Sociology, University of Florida, 1981b.

Thompson, J. D. *Organizations in action*. New York: McGraw Hill, 1967.

Tonñies, F. [*Community and Society*] (C. P. Loomis, trans.) East Lansing, MI: Michigan State University Press, 1957. (Originally published, 1887.)

Trist, E. L. & Bamforth, L. K. Some social and psychological consequences of the longwall method of coal getting. *Human Relations*, 1951, *4*, 1–38.

Tuma, N. B. & Grimes, A. J. A comparison of models of role orientations of professionals in a research-oriented university. *Administrative Science Quarterly*, 1981, *26*, 187–206.

Turner, C. & Hodge, M. N. Occupations and professions. In J. A. Jackson (Ed.), *Professions and Professionalization*. Cambridge: Cambridge University Press, 1970.

Valentine, C. A. *Culture and poverty*. Chicago: University of Chicago Press, 1968.

Van Maanen, J. Observations on the making of policemen. *Human Organization*, 1973, *32*, 407–418.

Van Maanen, J. Working the street: A developmental view of police behavior. In H. Jacob (Ed.), *The Potential for Reform of Criminal Justice*. Beverly Hills, CA: Sage, 1974.

Van Maanen, J. Police Socialization. *Administraive Science Quarterly*, 1975, *20* (3), 207–228.

Van Maanen, J. Breaking-in: Socialization to work. In R. Dubin (Ed.), *Handbook of Work, Organization and Society*. Chicago: Rand McNally, 1976.

Van Maanen, J. Experiencing organizations: Notes on the meaning of careers and socialization. In J. Van Maanen (Ed.), *Organizational Careers: Some New Perspectives*. New York: Wiley, 1977.

Van Maanen, J. The Self, the situation, and the rules of interpersonal relations. In W. Bennis, J. Van Maanen, E. H. Schein, and F. G. Steel, *Essays in Interpersonal Dynamics*. Homewood, IL: Dorsey Press, 1979.

Van Maanen, J. Career Games. In C. B. Derr, (Ed.), *Work, Family, and the Career*. New York: Praeger, 1980a.

Van Maanen, J. Beyond account: The personal impact of police shootings. *The Annals of the American Academy of Political and Social Science*, 1980b, *451* (3), 145–156.

Van Maanen, J. *Some thoughts (and afterthoughts) on context, interpretation, and organization theory*. Paper presented at Academy of Mangement Annual Meetings, San Diego, CA, 1981.

Van Maanen, J. The boss: A portrait of the american police sergeant at work. In M. Punch (Ed.), *Control in Police Organization*. Cambridge, MA: MIT Press, 1983.

Van Maanen, J. & Schein, E. H. Toward a theory of organizational socialization. In B. Staw (Ed.), *Research in Organizational Behavior*. Greenwich, CT: JAI Press, 1979.

Van Maanen, Miller, J. M. & Johnson, J. C. An occupation in transition: traditional and modern forms of commercial fishing. *Work and Occupations*, 1982, *9*, 193–216.

Van Maanen, J., Schein, E. H. & Bailyn, L. The shape of things to come. In L. W. Porter et al. (Eds.), *Perspectives on Behavior in Organizations*. New York: McGraw Hill, 1977.

Vollmer, H. M. & Mills, D. L. *Professionalization*. Englewood Cliffs, NJ: Prentice Hall, 1966.

Weber, M. [*Economy and society*] (G. Ruth and C. Wittich, Eds.) Berkeley, CA: University of California Press, 1968. (Originally published, 1922.)

Weick, K. *The Social Psychology of Organizing*. Reading, MA: Addison Wesley, 1979.

Weick, K. *The presumption of managerial logic*. Unpublished paper, Department of Business Administration, Cornell University, 1982.

White, H. C. *Chains of opportunity*. Cambridge, MA: Harvard University Press, 1970.

Whittington, B. *The Fall and Rise of Trait Theories of the Professions*. Unpublished paper, Graduate School of Management, University of California at Irvine, CA, 1981.

Willis, P. *Learning to labor*. New York: Columbia University Press, 1977.

Wilson, J. Q. Kelling, G. L. Broken windows: The police and neighborhood safety. *The Atlantic Monthly*, March 1982, pp. 29–38.

Whyte, W. H. *The Organization Man*. New York: Simon and Schuster, 1956.

Wilensky, H. L. Orderly careers and social participation: The impact of work history on social integration in the middle mass. *American Sociological Review*, 1961, *26*, 251–539.

Wilensky, H. L. The professionalization of everyone? *American Journal of Sociology*, 1964, *70*, 137–158.

Zimmerman, D. H. Record keeping and the intake process in a public welfare organization. In S. Wheeler (Ed.), *On Record*. New York: Russell Sage Foundation, 1969.

Zulaida, J. *Terranova: The ethos and luck of deep sea fishermen*. Philadelphia: Institute for the Study of Human Issues, 1981.

TRANSORGANIZATIONAL DEVELOPMENT

Thomas G. Cummings

ABSTRACT

This paper explicates and develops an emerging field of planned change having to do with multi-organization systems. Referred to as transorganizational development, this form of planned change is concerned with creating and improving the effectiveness of transorganizational systems: groups comprised of organizations that have joined together for a common purpose. Based on two streams of relevant research, interorganizational relations and social problem solving, the paper first presents a conceptual framework for understanding transorganizational systems and then addresses the practical implications of applying that knowledge to developing them. It is argued that because transorganizational systems constitute a distinct logical type higher than that of single organizations, they require a theory and practice of planned change commensurate with that higher level. After discussing what that higher level of planned change comprises, the paper concludes with several directions for advancing transorganizational development as a scientific and practical strategy for developing transorganizational systems.

Research in Organizational Behavior, vol. 6, pages 367–422
Copyright © 1984 by JAI Press Inc.
All rights of reproduction in any form reserved.
ISBN: 0-89232-351-5

The past two decades have witnessed a growing interest in aggregates or groups of organizations as a unit of analysis. Organizational researchers have expanded their focus from organization and environment relations to networks and populations of organizations (see, for example, Hannan & Freeman, 1977; Aldrich &Whetten, 1981). Similarly, practitioners of planned change have gone beyond single organizations to the collective performances of sets of organizations (see, for example, Trist, 1979). Movement in this macro direction has resulted in identification of different forms of collectives of organizations, and in clearer understanding of their structures and processes. This paper is concerned with a major type of multi-organization group referred to as transorganizational systems (TS), and with explication and preliminary development of a new field of planned change having to do with those systems, called transorganizational development (TD).

Transorganizational systems are comprised of organizations that have joined together for a common purpose. They have been variously referred to as "action-sets" (Aldrich & Whetten, 1981), "social action systems" (Van de Ven, 1976), "interorganizational domains" (Trist, 1979), "consortiums" (Brown, et al., 1974), "joint ventures" (Aiken & Hage, 1968), "directed interorganizational systems" (Lawless, 1982), "community decision organizations" (Warren, 1967), and "network organizations" (Metcalf, 1976). TSs' have a number of distinct characteristics differentiating them from other kinds of organizational collectives, such as networks and mergers. In terms of inclusive decision making (Warren, 1967), TSs are federative or coalitional structures whose member organizations maintain their separate identities and disparate goals, yet employ either some formal organization or informal collaboration for joint decision making. TS's have a corporate identity (Aldrich & Whetten, 1981), and in the case of federations, a "referent organization" (Trist, 1979) which can undertake purposive action on behalf of the collective.

As functional social systems, TS's comprise a level of social systems intermediately between single organizations and societal systems. They are embedded in a larger environment which itself can be considered a network or field of organizations (Aldrich & Whetten, 1981; Warren, 1967) whose parts are causally related (Emery & Trist, 1965; Mannheim, 1951). TS's constitute a logical type (Whitehead & Russell, 1910) higher than that of single organizations, and consequently, they require a figure/ground reversal of the traditional organization and environment relationship (Trist, 1976)—a shift from the egocentric focus on single organizations to the network–centric study of systems of organizations (Aldrich & Whetten, 1981).

Transorganizational development is concerned with improving the effectiveness of TS. It has evolved mainly from conceptual work on the causal texture of organizational environments (Emery & Trist, 1965) and from attempts to help organizations cope with environmental complexity and change (Trist, 1967; Emery & Trist, 1973). The initial literature in this area was devoted largely to making the case for extending planned change beyond single organizations to sets of organizations (Culbert et al., 1972); more recent writings have described TD projects (see, for example, Trist, 1978; Taber et al., 1979; McCann, 1980) and methods of TD application (Trist, 1979; Gricar, 1981a; McCann, 1981; Boje, 1982).

Despite this growing body of literature, TD is still in a formative state of development. It covers a loose set of concepts and methods, and has yet to achieve a coherent direction or thrust. At least two factors impede TD progress. The first problem concerns the lack of a comprehensive theory for understanding TS's. All applied disciplines require conceptual understanding of the phenomenon in question. To date, TD has tended to rely on a limited set of concepts for explaining TS behavior. These derive mainly from a social ecological perspective of social problem solving among organizations (Emery & Trist, 1973) and are normatively oriented towards collaborative relationships. Although the extensive research on interorganizational relations has considerable relevance to TS, it has been relatively neglected in TD. The second impediment to progress in TD involves the lack of a systematic methodology for developing TS. Most of the tools and methods for practicing TD have derived from case studies and similar reports of TD projects. This material tends to be anecdotal and specific to the circumstances at hand, making it difficult to draw valid and generalizable conclusions. The few serious attempts to integrate these methods into an overall change strategy have focused mainly on social problem–solving relationships, and have failed to account for other forms of TS linkage. Also, lack of an adequate conceptual base makes it difficult to tie these methods to specific features and properties of TS.

The primary intent of this paper is to help resolve these problems, and to advance the field of TD as a scientific and practical approach to developing TS. The paper is organized into four sections. Section I introduces two major streams of research which are relevant to understanding and developing TS, interorganizational relations and social problem solving. It is argued that the two perspectives offer distinct yet complementary contributions to TD. In Section II, the two research streams are integrated into a comprehensive framework for understanding TS. The integrative model provides the necessary conceptual knowledge for subsequently developing TS. Section III applies the model to TD practice. Here it is argued that TS's are generally underorganized systems and require a form of planned change distinctly different from that traditionally occurring in organization development. Finally, Section IV draws conclusions and sets out clear directions for further advancement of the TD field.

I. TWO STREAMS OF RELEVANT RESEARCH

Transorganizational systems are social collectives composed of organizations which have joined together for a common purpose. Although knowledge about TS's is in a formative stage, at least two distinct streams of research provide preliminary insight into their structures and processes: interorganizational relations (IR) and social problem solving (SPS). Historically, the two fields have converged on the study of TS from almost opposite directions. IR started primarily from a concern with single organizations and their relations with the wider task environment, including other organizations. Gradually, this focus widened to interorganizational relationships within networks of organizations, and to aggregates of organizations taken as social collectives. SPS, on the other hand, originated mainly from consideration of the wider contextual environment itself considered as a system, and to how the dynamics of that macro environment pose complex and uncertain problems for organizations. This focus eventually narrowed to concern over how organizations could join together to resolve macro problems which could not be solved by organizations acting alone.

The IR and SPS fields provide relatively unique yet complementary approaches to understanding TS. This section presents an introductory overview of the two perspectives and compares them on several pertinent dimensions. A more comprehensive account of the streams of research appears in the next section, where the two are integrated into a framework for understanding TS.

A. Interorganizational Relations

The underlying rationale for the study of interorganizational relations derives from the open-systems premise that organizations are dependent upon their task environment for inputs which are essential to their functioning, such as raw materials, information, clients, and legitimacy (see, for example, Thompson, 1967; Terreberry, 1968; Aldrich & Pfeffer, 1976; Katz & Kahn, 1978). Typically referred to as the "resource dependence model" (Aldrich, 1976; Cook, 1977; Pfeffer & Salancik, 1978), this perspective proposes that organizations enter into relationships with other organizations in order to obtain needed resources. Moreover, because such resources are generally scarce, organizations tend to compete with one another, attempting to gain power and control over essential resources while trying to minimize dependencies threatening organizational autonomy (Benson, 1975; Schmidt & Kochan, 1975, 1977).

Starting from this resource dependence framework, IR researchers have examined voluntary exchange relationships between organizations

(Levine & White, 1961), relationships mandated externally (Turk, 1973; Aldrich, 1976; Hall, et al., 1977), and power/dependency relationships where one organization is coerced into interaction by a more powerful other (Schmidt & Kochan, 1975, 1977). Much of this research has taken place in the public sector, where a predominate concern has been coordinating activities, resources, and information between agencies delivering related services (Aldrich & Whetten, 1981). Although coordination of services has received some criticism in contrast to a more free market, competitive model (Waren, 1970; Baker & O'Brien, 1971), a key research issue has been to discover those mechanisms ensuring organizations their individual autonomy in areas of conflict, while permitting unified effort in areas of agreement (Litwack & Hylton, 1962).

Interorganizational coordination or conflict studies have focused on comparative properties of the relevant organizations, including domains, goals, and membership; on the relational properties of the exchange itself, such as formalization, intensity, and standardization; and on how features of the larger context affect interorganizational relations, including the density of organizations, availability of resources, and complexity and change rate of the environment (see Marrett, 1971, Van de Ven, et al., 1975, and Whetten, 1981 for reviews of this literature). Generally, this research has been oriented to describing existing, natural interorganizational relationships, with little attention to changing them or creating new kinds of relations. Major attention has been directed at classifying and measuring appropriate variables, borrowing heavily from organization theory, and cross-sectional analysis of relationships among them.

The predominate focus of IR has been on relationships between organizations taken mainly from the perspective of a single, focal organization. For example, Evan's (1966) popular concept of the organization-set references the interorganizational environment to a focal organization; it deals with the transactional environment of the focal organization and examines pairwise relations between that unit and relevant organizations in the environment. IR researchers have argued, however, that many activities of IR cannot be explained by analyzing relationships between pairs of organizations; the behavior of aggregates or collectives of organizations requires network analysis of relationships among organizations (Aldrich, 1972; Levine & White, 1972; Rieker, et al., 1974; Zeitz, 1975; Warren, et al., 1975; Stern, 1979).

This shift to collectives of organizations is evident in the conceptual work on "interorganizational fields" (Warren, 1967), "interorganizational collectives" (Van den Ven, et al., 1976; Van de Ven, 1976) and "action-sets" (Aldrich & Whetten, 1981), and in the growing number of network interorganizational studies (see, for example, Turk, 1970, 1973; Galaskiewicz, 1979; Stern, 1979; Van de Ven, et al., 1979; Boje & Whetten,

1981). Major contributions of this network perspective of IR have been conceptualizing the systematic properties of aggregates of organizations and developing methods for decomposing networks of organizations into identifiable sets of interacting organizations and techniques for analyzing the properties of those networks (see Aldrich & Whetten, 1981, for a review and synthesis of this research).

B. Social Problem Solving

The SPS field also starts from the premise that organizations are open systems, dependent on their task environment for necessary resources and information. Its major focus, however, is on helping organizations to cope with environmental complexity and change by forming multi-organization collectives. Briefly, it is argued that as the causal texture of organizational environments becomes more turbulent—i.e., the organizational population of the environment becomes more dense and richly joined—organizational actions produce unanticipated and dissonant consequences throughout the field (Emery & Trist, 1965). Because this turbulence is reflected in complex "metaproblems" (Chevalier, 1966, 1967) or "messes" (Ackoff, 1975) which are too extensive and many-sided for single organizations to resolve, requisite responses to turbulence rest on inter- and multi-organizational action among those organizations sharing the environment. Such collective action is hypothesized to provide the initial conditions for a negotiated order to emerge among the organizations, hence reducing environmental turbulence to more manageable levels (Emery & Trist, 1973; Trist, 1967, 1976, 1979; Gricar, 1981a; McCann, 1980, 1981; Boje, 1982).

In many ways, the SPS area is an evolving perspective without a preplanned direction or focus. In discussing its early roots at the Tavistock Institute of Human Relations, Trist (1967) pointed out that concern for multi-organization collectives grew out of action-research studies with single organizations which were facing increasing environmental complexity and change. Attempts to cope with such environments using traditional methods of planned change were relatively ineffective because environmental problems derived from complex interactions among organizations comprising the environment. Trist and his colleagues were forced to develop approaches to planned change which went beyond the boundaries of single organizations to include establishing collaborative relations among organizations as a means of reducing environmental turbulence. Research projects were more future oriented, longer in time scale, and involved a larger inter-disciplinary mix than the earlier, single organization studies. Moreover, because the action researchers were committed both to helping organizations and to advancing scientific knowledge, they had to simultaneously develop methods for multi-organization problem solving and approaches for action research in this area.

Emery and Trist (1973) described the method of inquiry emerging from these studies as "domain-based problem-oriented research," a convergence of science and policy. They suggested that such inquiry is neither fundamental research where scientific interests dominate, nor applied research where client interests predominate, but a collaborative mixture of both. If scientists, professionals, administrators, and political representatives are to achieve common commitment to a problem, they must recognize their complementary contributions and pluristically surrender power on behalf of joint problem solving and research. Given the inherent difficulty of reconciling these different interests and values, Emery & Trist (1973) argued that researchers will have to engage in institution-building at high enough levels to encompass the conflicting interests and to sanction problem solving and research efforts. In an SPS study of industrial democracy in Norwegian industry, for example, institution building occurred at the national level, where government, labor, and management formed a joint research committee to sanction and guide the national project; researchers were members *pro tem.* of that committee (Emery & Thorsrud, 1969).

Most of the SPS studies have been action-research projects where researchers have attempted to generate applied knowledge by engaging in multi-organizational problem solving. Among these studies have been attempts to revitalize local industries and communities in the United States, Canada, and Great Britain (Trist, 1978); projects concerned with social change in housing (Gricar, 1981a), herbicides (Motamedi, 1981), and nuclear energy (Gricar, 1981b); efforts to improve communications in the British building industry (Higgin & Jessop, 1963), industrial democracy in Norway (Emery & Thorsrud, 1969), the criminal corrections system of Minnesota (McCann, 1980), and the environmental response of members of the National Union of Farmers in England (Trist, 1967). The major contributions of this research have been rich case descriptions of the structures and dynamics of SPS, identification of important action levers for changing such processes, and conceptual understanding of how to develop and conduct research on this form of organization collective. Equally significant has been the preliminary identification of socio-ecological principles, as distinct from bureaucratic principles, for designing transorganizational systems.

In comparing the IR and SPS approaches to understanding transorganizational systems, several pertinent differences emerge. In terms of unit of analysis, the IR field has tended to have an ego-centric focus on the single organization, typically examining interorganizational relations in respect to a focal organization; the resource dependence model reinforces this "rugged individualism," depicting the organization as maneuvering to maintain autonomy and manage power/dependence. Coversely, the SPS area has concentrated almost exclusively on sets or groups of organizations as the unit of analysis, arguing for collaboration and surrender of power as the path towards managing environmental turbulence. In terms of environmental relationships, IR has attended mainly to the transactional environment directly affecting the focal organization, and to pairwise relationships between organizations.

SPS, on the other hand, has focused largely on the contextual environment itself taken as a system, and to multiple relationships among organizations. The nature of inquiry within the two fields also differs. IR has primarily been discipline-based/research oriented. Dominated by organization theorists mainly from sociology, IR research has aimed mainly at describing and explaining interorganizational phenomena, and only secondarily at changing and developing them. Major concern has been classifying and measuring relevant interorganizational variables and examining relationships between them. SPS inquiry can be characterized as domain-based/problem oriented, as researchers from multiple disciplines and backgrounds have focused on understanding and developing collectives of organizations to resolve complex problems. Research outcomes have tended to be case-study descriptions of the problem solving process and normative prescriptions for improving it.

The differences between the IR and SPS fields are somewhat exaggerated and intended mainly to distinguish the two streams of research from each other. Indeed, there has been considerable convergence between them, with the IR area moving towards collectives of organizations and network analysis of relationships among organizations, and the SPS field tending towards classification and measurement of variables and relationships. More importantly, the comparison between the two areas suggests that the two approaches complement one another. The IR field provides knowledge about existing transorganizational systems, while SPS furnishes information for changing and improving them. Moreover, IR emphasizes the organizational autonomy and power/dependence side of TS, while SPS stresses their collaborative nature. The next section of the paper integrates IR and SPS research into a comprehensive framework for understanding and developing transorganizational systems.

II. INTEGRATIVE FRAMEWORK

Following Lewin's (1946) dictum that there is nothing so useful as a good theory, transorganizational development must proceed from knowledge of transorganizational systems. Moreover, if such knowledge is to be useful for developing such systems, it must not only describe existing TS's, but provide alternatives to the status quo and information about how to create and implement them. Although such knowledge is still in a formative state, the IR and SPS fields provide fundamentally different yet necessary kinds of information for understanding and developing TS. IR research is predominately descriptive, and is oriented to describing the status quo. Such knowledge is useful for understanding how existing TS's operate and maintain their basic forms. SPS, on the other hand, is largely normative, and is oriented to creating TS alternatives to those currently existing and to understanding how to transform the status quo.

Although such normative research has traditionally been considered outside of the bounds of normal science, it can have significant knowledge-generation possibilities as suggested by Argyris (1980), Gergen (1978), and others. By generating new forms of social organization that do not exist naturally, action research can furnish new alternatives for social action as well as uncover significant phenomena which may not appear naturally in social systems. Similarly, by engaging with organizations in system design and implementation, action research can gain understanding about how to change or implement social systems within action contexts. Such on-line knowledge is necessary for knowing how to change the status quo. We believe that both descriptive and normative approaches are necessary for understanding and developing TS; the former provides a base of explaining how existing TS's function, while the latter points out alternative TS forms and how to implement them.

The intergrative framework presented here derives from the related work of Hackman and Morris (1975) and Cummings (1981) on group task effectiveness, and extends the authors' general paradigm for explaining group effectiveness to groups of organizations or TS's. This cross-level extension provides a scheme for categorizing and relating the diversity of relevant TS literature; it explains how certain features of TS can be expected to interact with environmental and task variables to impact TS performances.

A general outline of the framework is shown in Figure 1, and represents an input-process-output model of TS functioning. A key premise of the model is the role of interaction processes in mediating input-outcome relationships. Specifically, it is proposed that certain interaction processes occurring among member organizations, such as the level and coordination of effort expended on interaction, proximately impact TS outcomes, such as organizations' collective performances. The interaction processes in turn are affected by various TS inputs, such as organizations' motivation to interact and organizations' assessments of each other. Thus, for example, organizations' motivation to interact can be expected to affect the level of effort expended on interacting, and that level of effort impacts the collective performances of TS members.

Moreover, because we are concerned with organizations which have joined together for a common purpose, the model proposes that the nature of that task/problem will affect how interaction processes are translated into TS outcomes. TS tasks which are relatively structured for example, might require high levels of joint effort for effective performance; less structured tasks might depend more on the utilization of organizations' skills than on efforts for effective performance. The framework also proposes that the larger environment within which the TS is embedded can impact TS inputs, interaction processes, and tasks/problems. The amount of resource scarcity within the environment, for instance, can be expected to affect organizations' motivation to interact; the amount of environmental stability can impact the structuredness of TS tasks/problems. Finally, the model proposes that TS outcomes feed back to affect subsequent interaction processes, inputs, and environments. Satisfactory TS performances, for example, might promote higher levels of organizations' motivation to interact as well as environmental stability.

The remainder of this section fills in the general framework shown in Figure 1 with the relevant IR and SPS literature. First, the input-interaction process relationship is examined, and specific TS inputs are proposed to have significant impacts on certain interactions processes. The presentation is organized around four key interaction processes: (a) the level of effort member organizations expend on interacting with each other; (b) the coordination of those efforts; (c) the performance strategies used by member organizations in carrying out the shared task/problem; and (d) the level and utilization of organizations' knowledge, skills, and resources applied to the task. These interaction processes derive from Hackman and Morris' (1975) and Cummings' (1981) group models, and they provide a logical starting point for understanding how interaction process operates in TS's. The second part of this section examines the environment, task/problem, and feedback relationships shown in Figure 1.

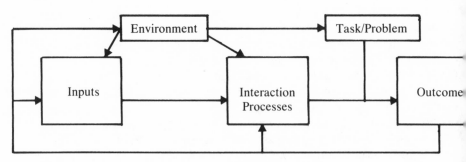

Figure 1.   Framework Outline

A. Level of Effort

We propose that the level of effort that member organizations expend in relating to one another is affected mainly by organizations' motivation to interact. Typically, relevant research has examined the relationships between various motives to interact and the intensity of interorganizational relations; the latter being measured by the size of the resource investment required by the exchange and/or the frequency of interaction between organizations (Marrett, 1971). Intensity of interaction can be used as a measure of the level of effort organizations expend on interrelating, and three major motivational bases affecting intensity are discussed below: (a) resource dependency; (b) commitment to problem solving; and, (c) mandate.

1. Resource Dependency. As discussed previously, the dominant perspective on interorganizational relations is the resource dependence or exchange model (Cook, 1977). It suggests that organizations cannot internally generate all needed resources, and must relate with elements in the environment, such as other organizations, in order to obtain those resources. Moreover, environmental resources are in short supply because of interorganizational competition and consequently, organizations attempt to outmaneuver one another in gaining scarce resources (Aldrich, 1976; Aldrich & Pfeffer, 1976; Pfeffer & Salancik, 1978). Schmidt and Kochan (1977) suggested that resource dependency can result in two types of interorganizational relations, symmetrical exchanges where both organizations are motivated to interact to maximize their joint benefits, and asymmetrical or power/dependency interactions where one party is motivated but the other is not; interaction occurs when the motivated organization is powerful enough to induce the other to relate.

Symmetrical exchanges occur when two or more organizations perceive mutual benefits from interacting (Levine & White, 1961). Based on extensive reviews of the relevant research, Van de Ven (1976) and Whetten (1977) identified at least four variables relating to the intensity of interactions: (a) the extent to which the relevant organizations are aware of each other's potential resources; (b) the extent to which there is consensus among the parties regarding their respective domains; (c) the extent to which the organizations are assured that their overall autonomy will not be threatened by the exchange, and that whatever autonomy is surrendered will be equitably compensated; and, (d) the extent to which there is moderate, as opposed to extremely low or high, goal similarity among the relevant organizations.

Asymmetrical linkages are based on power/dependency and for at least one of the organizations, exchange is not voluntary but externally in-

duced. In studying 23 employment service districts and the primary organizations interacting with them, Schmidt and Kochan (1977) found that
the intensity of asymmetrical relationships was positively related to the
extent to which the less motivated party saw the other as powerful—i.e.,
as being important, influential, and aggressive in pursuing its interests.

2. Commitment to Problem Solving. A second motivational force for
engaging in TS is organizations' commitment to jointly solving problems
that are too extensive and multi-faceted for single organizations to resolve
(Emery & Trist, 1973; Trist, 1967, 1976, 1979; Van de Ven, 1976). As
discussed earlier, the underlying impetus for such commitment derives
from the larger social field within which the relevant organizations are
embedded (Lewin, 1951; Warren, 1967) as the causal texture (Emery &
Trist, 1965) of that field becomes more complex and changing or turbulent,
organizations encounter problems and areas of uncertainty that they cannot cope with alone. By joining together to resolve field-related problems,
organizations can negotiate a more stable order and reduce turbulence to
more tolerable levels (Emery & Trist, 1965, 1973; Trist, 1967, 1976, 1979).

Although the research linking commitment to problem solving to intensity of interaction is mainly case study and anecdotal, several factors
have been identified as potentially affecting such interaction. Van de Ven
(1976) proposed that the greater the frequency of communication among
relevant organizations, the greater the awareness of and commitment to
joint problem solving. In an action-research study of a temporary TS
designed to deal with problems caused by sudden, large-scale unemployment in a community, Taber et al. (1979) found that channels of communication among the service organizations were necessary so that the
parties could learn about the extent of their shared problem and identify
available resources for resolving it. They also discovered that protecting
organizations from threats to their boundaries was an important prerequisite to interaction. Consistent with these findings, other related studies
have found that recognition of the scale and complexity of shared problems and awareness of organizations' common interests and interdependence are precursors to engagement in joint problem solving (Aram
& Stratton, 1974; Evan & Klemm, 1980; Gricar, 1981a & b). In a study
of six TS's in the public sector, Lawless (1982) confirmed these findings,
and also showed that financial incentives and the prestige of belonging
to the TS are important motives for transorganizational problem solving.

Because motivation to engage in problem solving depends in large part
on organizations perceiving a common problem and recognizing the need
to resolve it jointly, considerable effort has gone into understanding how
organizations recognize and define shared problem domains, and how that
process can be improved. McCann (1980, 1981) referred to this preliminary
stage of TS problem solving as "problem-setting," and proposed that it

was primarily concerned with defining the problem domain and bounding it apart from the larger environment. Trist (1979) and Gricar (1981a) suggested that the interorganizational communications and shared appreciations (Vickers, 1965) necessary to define a problem domain are likely to occur through existing networks of organizations. Because networks are loosely organized structures which can provide relatively fluid and rapid channels for interorganizational communication, they permit shared problem domains to develop—a view consistent with Aldrich and Whetten's (1981) conclusion that TS's or action-sets form along existing networks and become relatively stable subsystems of those networks.

Boje (1982) proposed that such networking could be facilitated through a process of "network mobilization." Briefly, this method seeks to create appropriate networking around a common problem by making organizations aware of their interdependence, and motivating them to engage in joint problem solving. This is accomplished by first defining a transcendent issue of sufficient magnitude to draw relevant "stakeholders" or those organizations which are affected by the problem and claim a right to influence its outcome (Gricar, 1981a). Then mapping and negotiating inducements/contributions bargains necessary to engage them in shared problem solving is conducted. Network mobilization also entails forming a temporary core nucleus of participating organizations which can articulate and channel the energies of the loosely organized set of stakeholders. Trist (1979) and Gricar (1981a) suggested that network mobilization is frequently carried out by proactive people who seek to create linkages among people with related interests; such "reticulists" tend to be boundary spanners and novelty detectors.

M. Emery (1976), F. Emery (1977), and Williams (1980) developed an experiential learning method for helping organizations identify common environmental problems and devise integrative strategies for resolving them. Referred to as the "search conference," this process brings together representatives from organizations located in a common problem domain and helps them assess their environment and discover alternatives for pursuing interdependent ends. The search conference is highly participative and task-oriented and occurs in a relatively short time period under protected conditions. It employs small-group problem-solving and experiential learning methods, and typically progresses from assessing the current environment and how it evolved, to sharing values and specifying desirable aims and futures, and, finally, to devising appropriate transorganizational strategies for moving in the desired direction.

Search conferences generally produce written reports of the proceedings, clearer understandings of the extent to which the participating organizations constitute a network capable of integrated action, and specific proposals for future interaction. Because such proposals invariably require further negotiating with a wider set of organizational constituents and stakeholders in the problem domain, search conferences are only an initial step in motivating organizations to interact around a common problem.

3. Mandate. A third motivation for organizations to relate with each other is when some higher authority, law or regulation mandates it. Mandated relationships are generally governed by rules, and as suggested by Warren's (1970) critique of human service coordination, they represent a form of social planning where services are controlled through central planning and avoidance of domain overlap. The research in this area suggests that mandates can motivate organizations to interact with each other. In a study of local employment service offices and social service organizations, Aldrich (1976) showed that mandated interactions tended to be more intense than other types of exchange. Whetten (1977) argued that hierarchically-mandated exchanges can overcome interaction problems caused by lack of domain consensus, but that such motivating potential can be offset to the extent that the proposed interactions are seen as threatening to the organizations.

Other research on mandated exchanges suggests that although mandates can impact effort to relate, whether that effort is subsequently coordinated is dependent on other factors. We will review that research here as a prelude to the second interaction process variable: coordination of efforts. Molnar and Rogers (1979) suggested that mandates may increase interorganizational conflict if they push organizations into areas in which they lack resources and expertise. Hall et al. (1977) studied relationships among members of an action set concerned with problem youth, and found that under conditions of mandated exchange, intensity of interactions was positively related to coordination among the organizations. They also found, however, that positive interorganizational assessments, quality of communications, and lack of conflict related to coordination in the mandated situation, suggesting that intensity of interaction alone may not be sufficient for coordination in mandated situations.

B. Coordination of Efforts

The second interaction process variable affecting TS outcomes is the coordination of organizations' efforts around the shared task or problem. We propose that coordination of efforts is impacted mainly by TS integrating mechanisms. Considerable research and conceptualization have gone into identifying variables related to coordination between and among organizations, and those are discussed below in terms of five integrating devices: (a) leadership; (b) structure; (c) compatible features; (d) communication processes; and, (e) positive assessments.

1. Leadership. TS leadership is typically discussed in terms of "co-ordinating agencies" (Litwak & Hylton, 1962), "referent organizations" (Trist, 1979), or "linking-pin organizations" (Aldrich & Whetten, 1981; Stern 1979) which serve a leadership function for the participating organizations. Such organizations can emerge naturally from within the network of existing organizations, usually by occupying a dominant or centralized position, or they can be created anew to perform a leadership role on behalf of the constituent organizations. In the latter case, TS leadership organizations can be created by the interacting organizations themselves, or they can derive from external sources such as government mandates, funding agencies, and the like.

TS leaders can promote coordination of efforts among the parties by serving a number of distinct functions. In discussing the role of coordinating agencies in the public sector, Litwak and Hylton (1962) suggested that these organizations can perform the complementary roles of managing cooperation between organizations and of preserving members' autonomy in the face of conflict by communicating pertinent information, adjudicating disputes, providing standards of behavior, and promoting areas of common interest. Aldrich and Whetten (1981) argued that linking-pin organizations can play a key role in integrating a population of organizations by serving as communication channels between the organizations, by linking third parties to one another, by serving as role models, and by actively directing the behaviors of TS. Trist (1979) proposed that referent organizations are critical to the development of shared problem domains because they provide the centering necessary to take purposeful action in the name of the domain. He suggested that such leadership organizations perform a regulative as distinct from an operational function; they manage interactions, orient the organizations to future trends and issues, mobilize resources, establish external relations with relevant outsiders, and facilitate interactive planning among the stakeholders.

Several case studies shed further light on the role of leadership in TS coordination. Lawless' (1982) study of six public service TS's showed that considerable leadership time was spent on three integrating activities: building exchange relationships, resolving interagency conflicts, and managing the interface among agencies. He also found that serving as a retainer of the mission of the TS was a major leadership function, especially in the face of intermittant involvement among the participating organizations. Aram and Stratton (1974) showed that although official coordinating agencies had little impact on initiating interaction among 20 agencies servicing the aged in a public housing project, such leadership did provide clear support for subsequent interaction. In an insightful analysis of the development of the National Collegiate Athletic Association, Stern (1979) showed that the administrative leadership gradually tightened control of the network through supplying valuable resources for which members had no suitable substitutes. In this case, the leadership controlled access to television contracts, recruitment of athletes, and championship competition. In Taber's et al. (1979) study of a community-based TS involved with sudden unemployment, the researchers found that the leadership organization, the Community Services Council, provided a forum for face-to-face meetings and personal linkages among representatives from participating organizations. This personalized interaction facilitated coordination of members' actions. Metcalfe (1976) showed how Great Britain's National Economic Development Council facilitated cooperation between government, management, and unions in promoting economic development. Serving as a TS leader, the Council enhanced cultural integration among the parties by developing an ideology linking economic growth to tripartite cooperation. It improved communicative and normative integration by establishing an identity and legitimacy with important outside groups, by seeking recognition of mutual interests among the parties, and by devising solutions incorporating their diverse interests.

   2. Structure.   TS's, like organizations, can implement structural arrangements to facilitate coordination of members' efforts. Van de Ven (1977) suggested that as the intensity of interactions among organizaions increases, informal personal contacts and meetings become inefficient mechanisms for coordinating activities; under norms of rationality, organizations attempt to formalize exchanges through rules, policies, and standard procedures. Moreover, he argued that this increased formalization will be accompanied by increased centralization of decision making by the representative committee or board managing TS decision making. Van de Ven reasoned that this group, in deciding to formalize exchanges, makes binding decisions on behalf of the TS, hence increasing its centralized control. Marrett (1971), in conceptualizing about the dimensions of interorganizational exchange, also proposed that intensity, standardization, and formalization of interaction are positively related. She argued, however, that only the size-of-resource-investment measure of intensity is related to standardization and formalization of exchange. If substantial resources are to be committed to the exchange, organizations are likely to seek formal agreements and established procedures. Based on Reid's (1964) conceptualization of standardization of interorganizational exchange, Lawless (1982) found that in all six TS's studied, increased intensity of exchange in terms of frequency and units of exchange was related to increased standardization of exchange.
   Based on Durkheim's (1964) study of anomie, Warren (1967) suggested that organizations delivering interdependent services in a community can adapt their behavior to each other in more deliberate ways by more clearly defining norms and rules governing their interaction. Consistent with this

need for role clarity, McCann (1980, 1981) argued that structuring interactions is a necessary stage in the development of shared problem domains
among organizations. He suggested that in order to institutionalize this
problem-solving process, stakeholders need to negotiate functional roles
and responsibilities and create regulative processes to promote coordination. Taber et al. (1979) suggested that such structuring may itself need
to undergo change as new TS goals evolve; they made structural interventions in order to move the community-based TS from a resource-
gathering to a resource-providing organization. Moreover, they warned
that the structural changes made the TS particularly vulnerable to dis-
integration because the agreements and arrangements initially holding it
together were left behind.

3. *Compatible Features.* The extent to which participating organizations' features, needs, and values are compatible across organizations can
facilitate coordination of efforts (Whetten, 1979). Hall's et al. (1977) interorganizational study of agencies dealing with problem youth showed
that compatible operating philosophies related positively to coordination
under conditions of voluntary exchange, but not in the legally mandated
situation. These findings suggest that compatibility of philosophy may
only be salient when organizations have a choice about interacting. Gillespie and Miletti (1979) proposed that complementary technologies can
facilitate interaction among organizations, and Metcalfe (1976) suggested
that this can form the basis for functional integration in TS's if organizations have the entrepreneurial skills to recognize technical complementarity and the political skills to exploit it. Both Reid (1964) and Whetten (1977) proposed that complementarity of resource needs is a powerful
force for coordination of efforts because symbiotic organizations have a
stake in each other. Phillips (1960) and Metcalfe (1976) identified similarity
or compatibility of values and attitudes among organizations as positively
impacting coordination of efforts. Reid (1964) proposed that shared goals
can promote TS coordination, especially if they are shared at both official
and operational levels. Taber et al. (1979) found that developing domain
consensus was an initial task in achieving coordination in the TS studied.

4. *Communication Processes.* Communication among participating organizations is vital to coordination of efforts. It serves to maintain and
integrate resource flows between organizations, and is necessary both for
initiating interactions and managing recurrent exchanges (Van de Ven,
1976; Metcalf, 1976). Relevant research has tended to focus on two aspects of interorganizational communication: its quality and type, such as
person-to-person, group meetings, and written reports. Hall et al. (1977)
found that quality of communications and person-to-person contact were
positively related to coordination for the entire sample of organizations
studied. However, only person-to-person contact related significantly to

coordination in the voluntary situation, while only quality of communication related in the legally mandated condition. Interestingly, neither quality of communication nor person-to-person contact related significantly to coordination when exchange was voluntary yet governed by a formal agreement. Perhaps such formal contracts either preclude the need for communication or render it inappropriate for coordination.

Van de Ven et al. (1979) examined interactions among three different clusters of organizations which were members of a larger regional council for children and youth: a resource transaction cluster, a planning and coordination cluster, and a direct services group. They found that the type of communication varied depending on the primary reason for interacting. The resource transactions cluster had the highest formalized agreements and contracts and reported the highest frequency of written reports and letters, and the lowest frequency of face-to-face contacts, telephone calls, and meetings—results consistent with those of Hall et al. (1977). On the other hand, the direct service cluster had the least formalized interactions and reported the highest frequency of face-to-face contacts and telephone calls, and the least frequency of written reports and letters. The planning and coordination cluster fell intermediately between the other two clusters in terms of types of communication, except for meetings, where it scored the highest. Both studies suggest that communication is important for coordinating efforts among organizations, but that the type of necessary communication varies depending on the basis or reason for interacting: the more formalized and legally contractual the exchange, the more formalized the type of communication.

5. *Positive Assessments.* The final variable impacting TS coordination is the assessment organizations make of each other's performances and competence of personnel. Hall et al. (1977) found that such positive assessments were the strongest predictors of coordination in the mandated and voluntary/informal situations studied, but were unrelated to coordination in the voluntary/formal agreement case. They surmised that issues of competence and performance were likely resolved prior to entering into a formal agreement and were no longer salient. Benson (1975) argued that interorganizational evaluation is likely to be balanced with three other equilibrium components: domain consensus, ideological consensus, and work coordination. These components can be balanced at various equilibrium levels, and coordination can intensify negative evaluations if underlying interest conflicts among the organizations are not resolved.

C. *Performance Strategies*

The third interaction process variable affecting TS outcomes is the performance strategies participating organizations use to perform tasks or solve problems. Such strategies include choices members make both about desirable outcomes and about how to go about achieving them. We propose that TS performance strategies are affected primarily by performance norms governing the task and problem-solving behaviors of participants. Organizations can bring to TS similar performance norms because of common experience and learning. In this situation, TS interaction process serves primarily to implement existing strategies, and to the extent that those strategies are task or problem relevant, the major issue facing TS is coordinating members' efforts in the enactment of those norms. On the other hand, if organizations do not already share norms or if existing performance norms are task inappropriate, TS's need to develop shared performance norms anew or reformulate those shared norms that are task inappropriate. Relevant research has identified at least four methods for helping TS's develop or change performance norms: (a) direction setting; (b) diagnosis; (c) frame breaking collective definitions; and, (d) changing networks.

1. Direction Setting. McCann (1981) proposed that a critical stage in developing shared problem domains among organizations is direction setting: establishing valued ends and clarifying shared directions for action. He suggested that direction setting is mainly concerned with domain legitimacy and involves two related issues. First, stakeholders must reach consensus on ends which reflect directions for action that are responsive to the given problem domain. Such responsiveness helps to legitimate the ends as realistic directions for resolving the problem. Second, organizations must devise specific action plans or performance strategies that are seen as accurate and feasible operationalizations of the desired direction for action. This increases the probability that expectations for problem solving will be realized.

In an action-research study of organizations trying to decentralize Minnesota's criminal corrections system, McCann (1980) found that direction-setting interventions needed to occur at three levels simultaneously: (a) an appreciative level where awareness of desired ends is sought; (b) a planning level where ends and directions for action are articulated into action plans; and, (c) an operational level where specific action steps and implementation issues are identified. He showed that work at the three levels was often interactive, with appreciations of ends and of beliefs about reaching them leading to better articulated action plans and specific flow charts for implementing them. The direction-setting interventions described by McCann included workshops along the lines of search conferences, domain-wide survey feedback, and small group and one-on-one interactions among limited members of the larger problem domain. Although it is beyond the scope of this paper to discuss these more fully, such interventions, when focused around direction setting, seem particularly appropriate for developing initial performance norms and strategies for a newly-created TS.

2. *Diagnosis.* Diagnosis refers to the systematic collection and dissemination of data about a system for purposes of learning about it and possibly changing it. Typically, diagnosis is conducted by someone outside the system and involves three steps: (a) entry where an agreement about the diagnosis process is negotiated between the outsider and relevant system members; (b) data collection through various methods such as questionnaires, interviews, and observations; and, (c) feedback where data is shared with system members and interpreted by them. Although diagnosis is usually considered a prelude to system change, there is evidence to suggest that the very process of engaging people in diagnosing their system can produce significant changes in that system (Brown, 1972; Alderfer & Brown, 1975).

Considered an integral part of organization development, diagnosis has been applied to helping TS members understand their existing performance norms and reformulate them, if necessary. Schermerhorn (1979) and Cummings (1980), in extending organization development to interorganizational relations, argued for the need to develop diagnostic methods at this level of analysis. Based on existing research, they identified several diagnostic issues related to motivation to interact and coordination of efforts. Most of these are included among the variables discussed previously under these topics. Gricar (1981a) also proposed that diagnosis can help TS's formulate needed changes, and suggested that change is more complex and protracted when groups of organizations are considered as opposed to single organizations. Kaplan (1980) confirmed this premise in a diagnosis of a community mental health board and 11 agencies receiving funding from it. He found that gaining entry into the TS took almost one year. Kaplan attributed this longevity to the instability of Board membership which slowed the decision making and funding process, and to the problems of convening 11 organizations, the Board, and other relevant stakeholders, a first-time-ever occurence. He also found that disclosure of feedback data among the agencies and between the agencies and the Board was relatively limited, making joint decision making and changes difficult. Kaplan attributed this limitation to weak relationships among the members of the TS; he suggested that such loosely organized or underorganized systems require some tightening up before any form of intervention such as diagnosis can take place. Indeed, much of Kaplan's year-long entry process was devoted to bringing enough integration to the TS so that diagnosis was feasible.

3. *Frame Breaking of Collective Definitions.* Boje (1982) suggested that

interactions among organizations are controlled as much by social construction and ideological persuasion as by resource exchange patterns. He argued that "collective definitions" give legitimacy and meaning to actions, and that once constructed, such definitions are highly resistant to change. For example, Warren et al. (1974) showed that Model Cities organizations had little success in urban reform because they were unable to change the prevailing inter–organizational paradigm which was inappropriate to that task. Similarly, it can be expected that TS performance norms are highly influenced by social construction processes, particularly because norms represent organizations' collective definitions about what ends are desirable and how they should be achieved. To the extent that TS members share and enforce performance norms, it is likely to require relatively powerful interventions to change them, a process that Boje called "frame breaking of collective definitions".

Boje (1982) proposed three methods for breaking organizations' collective definitions: (a) new language; (b) new history and, (c) myth making. He suggested that alternative languages can be introduced to give new meaning to existing problem domains. This can help participating organizations appreciate the shared domain in novel ways and discover new approaches to problem solving. Boje argued that because tradition constrains current actions and alternatives, a promising way to change the present is to change recollections of the past. He proposed, for example, that TS members could be encouraged to reconstruct how the TS started and evolved to its present state; those recollections that provide relevant learning and values for current conditions could be accented and embellished, while those that suggest outdated ends and strategies could be downplayed or ignored. Finally, Boje proposed that a potentially powerful approach to changing TS goals and performance norms is myth making. He argued that revolutionaries have successfully used myths to change social orders, and that such myth-making approaches as charismatic leadership, propaganda, and symbolic targeting of enemies could be applied to TS change.

Boje warned that the above mentioned frame-breaking methods require skilled interventionists and highly activist, system-wide change efforts. Both of these requirements may be difficult to fulfill given the paucity of knowledge and training in TS intervention currently available, and the underorganized nature of many TS's as suggested by Kaplan (1980). Although Boje presented relatively little direction and evidence for how frame breaking actually works in TS's, changing organizations' collective definitions may be a necessary prelude to developing and reformulating performance strategies. Indeed, Watzlawick's et al. (1967, 1974) pioneering work on communications and problem solving suggests that frame breaking may be the only effective way to change deeply-entrenched patterns of interaction and problem solving. Clearly, Boje's proposals for TS frame breaking are innovative and deserve further systematic inquiry and practical development.

4. Changing Networks. The final method for helping TS's develop or change performance norms involves changing the network of relationships among the participating organizations. We are concerned here with two key issues. First, the extent to which the network is loosely or tightly coupled can be considered a measure of TS cohesion or the degree to which member organizations share and enforce performance norms. Networks which are too loosely coupled may preclude development of shared norms, while those which are too tightly coupled may have norms which are difficult to change. A second issue concerned with changing performance norms is the direction of those norms. Whereas network coupling relates to the degree of norm sharing and enforcement, direction is concerned with whether those norms promote development and change of performance strategies or conservatism and stability. In order to develop new performance strategies, it is necessary to assure first that there is requisite network coupling so that norms are shared and enforced, and second that the direction of those norms promotes innovation in performance strategies.

The research related to network coupling provides some clues for how the degree of coupling can be changed, hence modifying the extent to which member organizations are likely to share performance norms. Aldrich and Whetten (1981) suggested that dominant organizations can manipulate network coupling through encouraging or discouraging interactions with other organizations. Similarly, Boje (1982) proposed that modifying the power structure can change strategic couplings in a network. Brown (1980) discussed change strategies that can be used to alter system coupling, and suggested that planned change is fundamentally different depending on whether lower or higher coupling is sought. In situations where coupling is too tight and norms are too entrenched, change is directed at decreasing leadership control, relaxing conformity to norms, providing for more flexible structures and behaviors, and revising technology to promote member discretion. When coupling is too loose and norms are unlikely to be shared, change is aimed in the opposite directions on those variables just mentioned. Like Boje (1982), Brown argued that interventions aimed at changing system coupling pose difficult challenges to interventionists, especially around the subjects of whose values are being enhanced or thwarted and how power relations are created or changed.

The research concerning the direction of performance norms suggests that whether norms promote innovation or stability depends heavily on the view of those organizations having power in the network. Aldrich and Whetten (1981) suggested that in community networks, powerful organizations frequently share a paradigm which defines the nature of community problems and how best to solve them. To the extent that the dominant paradigm emphasizes conservatism, existing performance strategies are unlikely to be questioned and reformulated, unless those changes are compatible with the interests of powerful network members.

Boje (1982) argued that powerful network leaders impact the direction of performance norms, and if those norms are too conservative and need to be changed to promote development of performance strategies, power-oriented change strategies may be needed. He suggested that those advocating change in norms may have to change power relationships through such methods as campaigns, pressure tatics, coercion, and willful violation of norms. It is open to question to what extent those kinds of change strategies would destroy the TS or constructively refocus its performance norms. In a study of General Motors' relationships with its dealers, for example, Assael (1969) showed that constructive conflict led to effective adjustments in power relationships among the organizations only under certain conditions. These related mainly to the organizations' willingness to reappraise and change resource exchanges, and to show self-restraint, especially among the more powerful organizations.

D. Level and Utilization of Organizations' Knowledge, Skills, and Resources

The fourth interaction process variable impacting TS outcomes involves the level and utilization of participating organizations' knowledge, skills, and resources applied to the shared task or problem. We propose that this variable is affected mainly by the composition of the TS. Put simply, a TS composed of organizations with high levels of task-relevant knowledge, skills, and resources is more likely to have high performances than one that does not. The relevant transorganizational literature has identified at least two related approaches for affecting TS composition: (a) the expanding network model; and, (b) stakeholder analysis.

1. Expanding Network Model. This model derives from the action-research of Taber et al. (1979) on forming a TS to resolve community unemployment problems. It involves starting from a smaller core group of organizations and expanding membership as additional stakeholders and resource groups are identified and recruited. In the TS studied, one of the initial tasks of the leadership group, the Council, was to expand membership in the TS so that relevant organizations and resources could be brought to bear on the community problem. This was accomplished by inviting acknowledged leaders in fields related to unemployment to attend a Council meeting. They were asked to be committee chairpersons, and charged with the task of identifying and recruiting additional resources and persons needed for problem solving. Taber et al. showed that this process resulted in identification and recruitment of five resource groups, each composed of organizations with expertise and knowledge relevant to unemployment. The health group, for example, included representatives from four area hospitals and the County Health Department. The researchers concluded that the expanding network model was ideally suited to identifying and recruiting needed resource organizations. Its success appears to depend heavily on gaining the support of acknowledged experts and leaders in problem-relevant fields, and assuring that they have the requisite skills and influence to act as linking-pins relating available resource organizations to the shared problem domain.

    2. Stakeholder Analysis. This process involves identifying and selectively recruiting organizations and groups that are affected by the problem domain and have a stake in its solution. Mason and Mitroff (1981) suggested several practical methods for generating a comprehensive list of stakeholders. The imperative approach lists imperatives, slogans, catchwords, and acts of defiance that have emerged in relation to the organizations' shared issue or problem. The sources of those imperatives and acts are then considered as potential stakeholders in the TS. The positional method identifies those occupying formal positions in organizations potentially connected to the TS task/problem, and elicits them as potential stakeholders. The reputational approach is similar to the expanding network model in that it entails asking knowledgeable or important persons to nominate those whom they believe should be TS stakeholders. The social-participation method identifies stakeholders in terms of their previous and current participation in helping to resolve the TS task/problem. The opinion-leadership method identifies stakeholders on the basis of their leverage or influence in relation to the TS task/problem. The demographic method selects stakeholders on various demographic characteristics that can affect problem resolution. For example, TS's involved with providing services to the elderly might consider certain organized groups of elders as stakeholders in the TS. The final method suggested by Mason and Mitroff involves selecting a core group of organizations or a referent organization, and having it map out the wider environment in order to locate stakeholders. Whatever the method chosen, Mason (1978) and Williams (1979) warned that identifying stakeholders not only involves judgements about resources and problem interests, but political assessments as well. Failure to identify and possibly include powerful stakeholders can weaken the TSs' legitimacy and problem-solving capability.

    Boje (1982) suggested that TS's may need external help in stakeholder analysis, especially in including important but uninfluential stakeholders. Based on the work of Goodman and Huff (1978), he listed several reasons why such stakeholders might be excluded from the TS: they may be unfamiliar with this type of policy making and group problem solving; their impact might be considered peripheral; TS members might feel that if uninfluentials become involved in problem solving, they might demand more control over the process; they might speak different languages and jargon and exhibit different behaviors than TS members. Also, the sheer number of possible stakeholders might dissuade TS members from identifying and including relevant organizations in the problem solving process. Emery (1976) proposed an innovative method for overcoming this size problem. He suggested that the leadership group or governing board of the TS could be chosen from a random sample of stakeholder organizations. Those selected would serve a fixed term and then new representatives would be chosen and so on, similar to selecting people for jury service. Emery argued that this would allow for equitable representation in the leadership function of the TS, and decrease the chances that the TS would be dominated by the more powerful organizations and special interest groups. Over time, it also allows for a larger number of stakeholders to be more directly included in shared problem solving.

Although the expanding network model and stakeholder analysis can help to assure that TS's are composed of organizations with task-relevant skills, knowledge, and resources, the subsequent utilization of that knowledge in the service of the shared task or problem may still be toublesome. Members may not combine their expertise effectively or weigh organizations' contributions appropriately, thus wasting appropriate talent and resources. Some of the previously discussed TS inputs applicable to coordination of efforts and performance strategies seem relevant to assessing and possibly improving how TS members utilize available knowledge and skills. For example, communication processes and diagnosis could be directed at how members apply, combine, and weigh their separate talents and how that process could be improved. Moreover, to the extent that such communication and diagnosis are themselves the subject of learning, the available pool of TS expertise and knowledge can be increased, as suggested by the work of Argyris and Schon (1978) on organizational learning.

E. TS Environment, Task/Problem, and Feedback

The general framework in Figure 1 proposes that the TS larger environment impacts inputs, interaction processes, and task/problem characteristics; that the TS task/problem influences the extent to which the interaction process variables are salient for TS performances; and that TS outcomes feed back and affect subsequent inputs, interaction processes and environment. Relevant research has focused largely on how various features of the task environment affect relationships between organizations; relatively little attention has been directed at how tasks interact with interaction processes to affect TS outcomes, or how those outcomes feed back to affect the TS. Because it is premature to predict precisely how these environmental, task and feedback components of the framework are likely to affect the TS, the discussion below is speculative and raises several issues for further conceptualization and research.

1. Environment. Like organizations, TS's are embedded in environments which influence the system directly through resource and information transactions and indirectly through an extended field of interwoven relations among environmental parts. Aldrich and Whetten (1981) suggested that this larger context can be considered a network and that TS's are relatively stable subsystems of loosely joined, interorganizational networks.

As a prelude to describing how specific features of the environment can impact TS's, it is informative to assess the long-term environmental conditions giving rise to these forms of social organization. Using a population ecology model of organizations, Hannan and Freeman (1977) suggested that federative forms of organizations like the TS described in this paper have a competitive advantage and thus are favored or selected for under the following environmental conditions: when there is uncertainty as to the future states of the environment; when the demands of different environmental states differ, and when the typical duration of environmental states is long relative to the life of the organization. Hannan and Freemen argued that under these conditions, specialist organizations will not fare well because the duration of environmental states differing in demands is long, and the consequences of having an inappropriate specialist strategy are great. Interestingly, although generalist organizations do better in these situations, they still do not achieve high levels of effectiveness because variation of enduring environmental states is uncertain. Hannan and Freeman suggested that polymorphic or federative forms of organizations consisting of heterogeneous collections of specialist organizations who pool resources have a competitive advantage in these environments. The costs of maintaining a federative structure are offset by the fact that regardless of the state of the environment, at least a part of the federation will do well. They identified universities and general contractors in the construction industry as examples of federative organizations; both face uncertainty over environmental states of relatively long duration, and hence both use their more fortunate subunits to subsidize those units facing lean environments. In effect, such federative organizations sacrifice specialized efficiency for flexibility; they hedge their bets by seeking a wider variety of resource bases.

While Hannan and Freeman's (1977) ecological analysis accounts for the longer-term environmental processes favoring federative forms of organizations, the environment also has shorter-term consequences for TS's. Environmental stability and heterogeneity can affect TSs' integrating mechanisms. Aldrich (1975) proposed that stability increases opportunities for formalized interorganizational relations, but that the combination of instability and heterogeneity reduce the ability to standardize exchanges. Concentration and abundance of resources in the environment can impact motivation to interact. Aldrich (1975) suggested that concentration of resources can attract organizations to seek relations with those having resources. Whetten (1979) argued that both extremes of resources—scarcity and abundance—can thwart motivations to interact. Organizations faced with scarcity may be extremely cautious about entering into relationships that might drain their limited resources, while those facing abundant conditions may have little incentive to engage with the environment. Gillespie and Perry (1975) in a case study of interactions between a new social-service organization and existing welfare agencies found that resource scarcity led to interactions only to the extent that the new organization was formalized; they argued that in the absence of such formality, existing organizations, being better equipped to achieve goals, are likely to absorb the personnel of the new organization leaving it without a resource base. Based on Emery and Trist's (1965) conceptualization of the causal texture of organizational environments, several authors have argued that increasing levels of environmental complexity and change contribute to the turbulence chacterizing meta-problems and messes. Because organizations cannot resolve these problems by acting alone, there is motivation to join together to reduce the turbulence to more manageable levels (Trist, 1967; Gricar, 1981a; McCann, 1981; Boje, 1982; Lawless, 1982). Aldrich (1976) argued that environmental turbulence heightens problems of resource scarcity, and organizations seek to keep uncertainty to tolerable levels by routinizing and standardizing as much of their interorganizational exchange as possible.

In addition to impacting inputs and interaction processes, TS environments can affect the nature of TS task/problems. Based on the work of MacCrimmon and Taylor (1976), task/problems can be characterized as falling along a continuum from structured to ill-structured, depending on the extent to which participating organizations feel familiar with the current state of the task/problem, its desired terminal state, and how to resolve the gap between the two. MacCrimmon and Taylor reviewed the extensive problem-solving literature and identified three environmental conditions contributing to degree of structuredness: certainty, complexity, and conflict. They argued that to the degree the environment is uncertain, complex, and conflictual in respect to shared problem solvers' goals or preferred resource allocations, problems will be experienced as ill-structured. Clearly, many TS task/problems occur under uncertain, complex, and conflictual conditions, and consequently are relatively ill-structured.

2. Task/Problem. The integrative model proposes that the nature of TS tasks/problems affects which of the different interaction processes, or combinations of them, are important for effective TS performances. The task moderates the relationship between interaction processes and outcomes by determining the types of behaviors which contribute to success for that task. This critical interaction between tasks and interaction processes is central to Hackman and Morris' (1975) and Cummings' (1981) group models, and we propose that a similar relationship operates in a TS. The key issue is to identify significant task/problem contingencies that are likely to determine the types of TS interaction processes necessary for successful TS performances. Although little, if any, attention has been directed at this issue in the literature reviewed here, related research on problem solving (MacCrimmon & Taylor, 1976) and group task design (Susman, 1976; Cummings, 1978, 1981; Slocum & Simms, 1980) suggests two task/problem contingencies potentially applicable to TS's.

The first contingency derives from MacCrimmon and Taylor's (1976) review of the problem solving research, and involves the degree to which TS task/problems are structured. It seems reasonable to expect that problem structuredness would impact the type of interaction processes required for effective TS performances. When task/problems are relatively structured, TS performances are likely to depend more on the level and coordination of organizations' efforts applied to the task than on innovative performance strategies or high levels of skills and knowledge. Conversely, ill-structured tasks are likely to place higher demands on TS performance strategies and members' skills and knowledge than on level and coordination of efforts. Because the environmental conditions surrounding ill-structured tasks are uncertain, complex, and conflictual, TS members are likely to face difficult challenges defining the initial state of the task/problem, arriving at a consensus about the desired state, and discovering how to reach it.

The second contingency impacting TS interaction processes derives from Susman's (1976), Cummings' (1978,1981) and Slocum and Simms' (1980) work on the relation between technological interdependence and group task design. They proposed that as technical interdependence becomes higher—i.e., moving from pooled to sequential to reciprocal (Thompson, 1967)—group task effectiveness becomes increasingly dependent on coordination of members' efforts, skills, and information. At lower levels of interdependence, coordination rests largely on rules and schedules and at higher levels, on the self-regulation of members within the group. Because task/problem interdependence is a major rationale for forming a TS, it seems logical that the degree of interdependence should affect the kinds of interaction processes required for effective performances. When TS task interdependence is low such as pooled interdependence, performance is likely to depend on the level of effort organizations expend individually on the task. Conversely, as interdependence becomes higher, effective performances would depend increasingly on coordination of efforts.

Although highly speculative, the two contingencies discussed above—problem structuredness and task interdependence—suggest a rudimentary typology for understanding how TS tasks/problems interact with interaction processes to affect TS performances. The typology is shown in Figure 2, and comprises low and high values on the structuredness and interdependence dimensions of TS tasks. Under cell 1, conditions of low interdependence and high structuredness, TS performances are likely to depend on the level of effort organizations expend individually on the task. Here the need for coordination of efforts is low, and the demand on performance strategies and organizations' skills and knowledge is negligible. When task interdependence is low but problems are ill-structured, cell 2, the critical interaction processes affecting performances would involve performance strategies and members' skills and information. Because there is little need for coordination and because problem solving requires judgment and innovation, the level and coordination of organizations' efforts should play a minor role in TS performances. In cell 3 where interdependence and structuredness are both high, task perform-

		Problem Structuredness	
		High	Low
Task Interdependence	Low	Level of Effort	Performance Strategies Level and Utilization of Knowledge, Skills, and Resources
	High	Level of Effort Coordination of Effort	Coordination of Effort Performance Strategies Level and Utilization of Knowledge, Skills, and Resources

Figure 2. Interaction of TS Task/Problem and Interaction Processes

ance is likely to depend on the level and coordination of efforts, with little demand on performance strategies or members' skills and knowledge. Finally, in cell 4 where task interdependence is high and structuredness is low, TS performances are likely to depend on organizations being able to coordinate their efforts around inventing appropriate performance strategies and integrating members' skills and information. Here the need for high levels of effort is questionable.

3. *Feedback.*   Finally, the integrative framework proposes that TS outcomes feed back to affect subsequent inputs, interaction processes, and environments. Citing research by O'Toole (1972) on the Cleveland Rehabilitation Complex, Van de Ven (1976) suggested that a TS evolves slowly with small initial success encouraging further interaction and so on. Similarly, Warren (1972), Akinbode and Clark (1976), and Evan and Klemm (1980) have argued that interorganizational performances and experiences with joint programs can impact subsequent interactions. Hall et al. (1977) showed that positive evaluations relate strongly to interorganizational coordination, suggesting that member perceptions of successful TS performances are likely to encourage further coordinative efforts. Aldrich (1976) found that perceived cooperation can impact subsequent interorganizational interactions.

Although TS success appears to lead to further positive inputs and interaction processes, failure on TS tasks/problems may not necessarily lead to reduced interaction and commitment of resources. Staw's (1981) research on escalation of commitment shows that under certain conditions, decision makers commit increasing amounts of resources to failed courses of action. Although it is beyond the scope of this paper to discuss this research more fully, unsuccessful TS outcomes may lead to increasing interactions and commitments of resources, particularly if such interactions are undertaken voluntarily by organizations and involve large investments in time and effort.

F. Summary

This section of the paper presented an integrated framework for understanding TS's; the fully-elaborated framework appears in Figure 3. It shows that TS outcomes are proximately affected by four interaction process variables: (a) the level of effort participating organizations expend on interacting around the shared task or problem; (b) the coordination of those efforts; (c) the performance strategies organizations use in carrying out the task; and, (d) the level and utilization of members' knowledge, skills, and resources applied to the task/problem. Although any number of possible inputs can impact any one of these process variables, the model

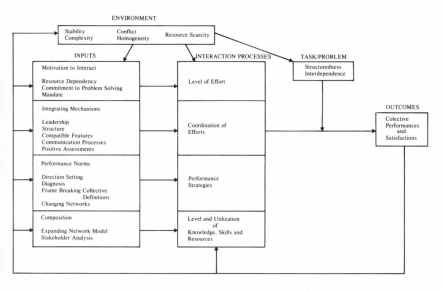

Figure 3. Integrative Framework

suggests that certain input factors are more useful than others. Specifically, the level of organizations' efforts is affected mainly by motivations to interact, and three motivational bases seem relevant: (a) resource dependency; (b) commitment to problem solving; and, (c) mandate. Coordination of efforts is impacted largely by TS integrating mechanisms, including leadership, structure, compatible features, communication processes, and positive assessments. Performance strategies are affected mainly by norms governing the task and problem-solving behaviors of participants. Four methods for helping TS's develop or modify these norms include: (a) direction setting; (b) diagnosis; (c) frame breaking collective definitions; and, (d) changing networks. Level and utilization of organizations' knowledge, skills, and resources are affected primarily by the composition of the TS, and two approaches for impacting composition are the expanding network model and stakeholder analysis.

It is important to emphasize that because the inputs were culled from both descriptive and normative kinds of research, they include descriptive correlates of interaction processes as well as action levers for changing process. The descriptive correlates appear mainly in the input categories having to do with motivation to interact and integrating mechanisms, and it is open to question how manipulable they may be in an actual TS setting. The inputs appearing in the performance norms and composition categories derive largely from normative change studies, and although we can have some confidence that they can be manipulated, considerable research is needed to assess whether they actually produce intended effects and precisely under what conditions those effects can be expected.

The integrative framework also suggests that certain features of the TS larger environment impact inputs, interaction processes, and tasks/problems. These environmental characteristics include stability, complexity, conflict, homogeneity, and resource scarcity. The model proposes that two TS task/problem contingencies determine which of the interaction processes is salient for successful performances—problem structuredness and task interdependence. Finally, the framework suggests that TS outcomes feed back to affect subsequent inputs, interaction processes, and environments. Although TS success seems to lead to positive inputs and processes, the feedback effects of failure are more questionable, leading either to reduced inputs and interactions or escalation of TS commitments.

III. TRANSORGANIZATIONAL DEVELOPMENT PRACTICE

Like organization development (OD), transorganizational development is concerned with improving system effectiveness related to task performances, wider environmental relationships, and member satisfactions. It aims to accomplish these objectives through application of relevant scientific knowledge to planned change and development, typically with the help of professional practitioners. While OD has evolved relatively comprehensive concepts and methods for improving organizations, TD is just starting to formulate requisite theory and practice for developing TS's. Unfortunately, the nature of a TS precludes a straightforward extension of OD knowledge to TD. Rather, TS's constitute a distinct logical type (Whitehead & Russell, 1910) higher than that of single organizations and as suggested by Trist (1976), TS require theory and practice commensurate with that higher level of social collective.

The preceeding section of this paper presented an integrative framework for conceptualizing about TS's and developing them. The model contained both descriptive and normative research and thus presents a mixture of how existing TS's function and of how key parts of them can be changed to produce a TS alternative to the status quo. This section addresses the practical implications of applying that knowledge to improving and developing TS's. First, an introductory overview of the nature of planned change in TS is presented, and then three fundamental stages of TD are discussed: identification, convention, and organization.

A. The Nature of Planned Change in TS

The integrative framework suggests that in contrast with most organizations, TS's are relatively "underbounded" (Alderfer, 1977, 1981) or "underorganized" (Brown, 1980). Generally, relationships among member organizations are loosely coupled and indirect (Aldrich & Whetten, 1981); leadership and power are dispersed among autonomous organizations rather than hierarchically centralized and commitment to joint task performance is sporadic as membership in the TS changes (Lawless, 1982). These typical features of a TS make it difficult to identify the system or separate it from the wider environment, and make regulation of member organizations' behaviors tenuous.

Brown (1980) proposed that planned change in underorganized systems differs from the more traditional OD approach, which has tended to derive from overorganized systems. He suggested that in underorganized systems, change strategies should be aimed at increasing shared norms and values, and designing structures, roles, and technologies to create predictability and regularity. Brown argued that the typical phases of planned change in OD—entry, diagnosis, intervention, and evaluation—assume the existence of an identifiable, tightly coupled system which needs to be entered and opened up. The phases of change in underorganized systems, on the other hand, assume the need to create a system and involve: identification of the relevant system and its members; convention of those members to start the linkage process; organization of the system to regularize behaviors, and evaluation of that organization in terms of intended effects. In essence, these phases of planned change are tended to mobilize and bring order to the TS. Brown concluded that the nature of the relationship between clients and change agents in underorganized systems should model the change process, with high degrees of clarity and regulation governing that interface.

Brown's (1980) conception of planned change in underorganized systems has considerable support from the TS field. The action-oriented field search of SPS (Trist, 1978, 1979; Kaplan, 1979; Taber, et al., 1979; Gricar, 1981a&b; McCann, 1981; Boje, 1982) suggests a similar progression of developmental steps, from identifying relevant stakeholders, to convening the members, and to organizing appropriate structures and processes for joint task performance. Similarly, Schermerhorn's (1979) and Cummings' (1980) applications of interorganizational research to planned change underscore the need first to identify and motivate relevant organizations to interrelate, and then to design coordinative mechanisms and structures. Because of the relative scarcity of knowledge about this type of planned change and because many TS's are underorganized, the following pages are devoted primarily to explicating the identification, convention, and organization phases of change. Although the integrative model is in a formative state, we explore how it might guide those steps. It is recognized, of course, that some TS's are relatively organized and in those cases, application of the more traditional phases of OD is likely to suffice. Because there is considerable knowledge about that form of planned change and because of space limitations, planned change in a highly organized TS is not discussed.

B. Identification

This initial phase of transorganizational development involves identifying organizations potentially comprising the TS. It serves to specify the relevant participants for the convening and organizing stages of TD and to bound them apart from the wider environment. In an underorganized transorganizational system, identifying members can be difficult because linkages among them are loosely coupled or nonexistent. Moreover, criteria for membership in such systems may be so ambiguous and difficult to assess that precise setting of boundaries is impossible. Although the identification of relevant TS members is inherently arbitrary, that process can be made explicit and practically meaningful, hence increasing the likelihood that appropriate membership boundaries will be drawn. This is especially critical at the initial stages of TD, where failure to include relevant organizations can undermine subsequent development of the TS. Also, as suggested by the integrative model, membership composition is important to the extent that the TS task/problem is ill-structured and demands high levels of organizations' knowledge, skills, and resources.

Because transorganizational systems are intended to achieve specific purposes, a practical criterion for identifying members is how much organizations can contribute to those purposes. Assessment of such contribution involves both technical/rational and political judgements. Technically, evaluations of the TS task/problem can reveal those organizations that are needed for effective task performances. Such task analysis can show the levels and types of required knowledge, skills, and resources; this information can then guide the TS inputs related to composition, such as the expanding network model and stakeholder analysis. For example, Taber et al. (1979) used experts in community unemployment first to assess the skills and resources needed to resolve that problem, and second, to identify and recruit organizations meeting those requirements. Politically, it is necessary to study the wider context of the TS task/problem in order to identify organizations controlling resource flows, information, and legitimacy related to task performance. Aldrich and Whetten (1981) argued that examination of the TS' broader context is likely to involve indirect, as opposed to direct, ties among organizations; failure to account for indirect linkages influencing the TS can affect the subsequent viability and legitimacy of the system. Similarly, Boje (1982), Gricar (1981b), and Williams (1980) warned that excluding legitimate and important stakeholders may not only bias the directions and outcomes of the TS, but can foster opposition and resistance from the wider political context.

While the above mentioned technical and political judgements can identify the population of organizations potentially relevant for TS membership, additional analyses can help to assess which of those organizations should be directly included in the TS. A promising approach to this boundary problem involves decomposing the larger network or population of organizations into more tightly coupled subsets. Aldrich and Whetten (1981), Gricar (1981a), and Trist (1979) have argued that TS's often form along previous networks of organizations, and are relatively indentifiable subsystems of those loosely joined networks.

Application of network analytic techniques to the population of organizations identified above can help to locate such subsystems, thus providing an empirically-based method for assessing membership in the TS. For example, Van de Ven et al. (1979) used questionnaire data and block modeling analysis to empirically derive three tightly-coupled clusters of agencies from a larger population of 26 organizations having to do with youth services in an urban region of Texas. They found that each cluster appeared to exist for a predominant reason, and in terms of TS membership, the findings could be used to identify organizations comprising three distinct TS's. Galaskiewicz (1979) used questionnaire data and smallest space analysis to describe networks of 73 community-based organizations along three dimensions of linkage: money, information, and support. He showed that the organizations clustered into discrete groupings according to the type of linkage studied. Again, this form of analysis could be used to assess which organizations, from a larger population of potentially relevant organizations, should be included in the TS.

Although network analytic methods can empirically help to derive TS membership, at least three practical problems need to be resolved in applying them to TD. First, all statistical operations on graphs or matrices of relationships among organizations assume that the population is meaningful. If the initial population of potentially relevant organizations excludes important organizations or includes inconsequential ones, the resulting clusters will have little practical significance for identifying TS members. Careful attention to generating a complete and exhaustive list of relevant organizations can reduce this problem. Second, because many of the clustering techniques are based on relationship measures among organizations, only organizations with relatively tightly-coupled ties are identified as belonging together. While this helps to identify members of already existing subsets of TS, it fails to account for those situations where linkages are just emerging or not yet established. This suggests that the statistical techniques may need to be supplemented with more qualitative assessment of TS membership, including weak but potentially important linkages and indirect ties. Third, the size of the population of potentially relevant organizations can be quite large. This places severe demands on data gathering, particularly because thorough assessment of linkages requires measures of each organization's relations with all others. Specific sampling methods can help to resolve this size problem (see, for example, Warren et al., 1974), and organizations' reluctance to supply relevant data can be reduced with interesting and relevant interviews and questionnaires, and unobtrusive measures of linkage (Aldrich & Whetten, 1981).

So far the identification phase of TD has been discussed apart from those actually doing it. In underorganized TS, it is frequently difficult to know who should be making membership decisions. Because such systems tend to be polycentric with multiple and often competing sources of influence and legitimacy (Benson, 1975; Gerlach & Palmer, 1981), leadership groups that can perform the identification task usually do not exist or are not recognized as legitimate by potential TS members. In these situations, outside interventionists may need to help organizations achieve sufficient agreement on TS membership, so that the convening and organizing stages are viable. For example, Taber et al. (1979) and Trist (1967, 1979) suggested that practitioners can aid in establishing a referent organization which in turn can identify appropriate TS members; such institution building needs to occur at high enough levels to encompass conflicting perspectives and to achieve legitimate scantion for TD. Gricar (1981b) proposed that third parties can help competing organizations negotiate about TS membership if the outsiders are seen as neutral and credible by those involved. Conversely, Boje (1982) and Gricar and Brown (1981) argued that interventionists may need to take more activist roles in helping important, yet uninfluential organizations achieve membership in the TS. Such advocacy is value-laden and political (Laue, 1978), and is typically aimed at redressing perceived inequities in power among the relevant stakeholders. Finally, Aldrich and Whetten (1981) suggested that linking-pin organizations are likely to have high status and extensive ties within networks of organizations. Practitioners could seek to elicit the support of such key organizations in identifying relevant TS members.

C. Convention

Once the initial members of the TS are identified, the convention phase of TD brings them together in order to assess whether creating a TS is plausible and desirable. This stage explores organizations' motivations to interact and perceptions of the task/problem, and seeks to establish sufficient levels of motivation and of task/problem consensus to form the TS.

In terms of motivation to interact, the integrative model identifies three sources of motivation—resource dependency, commitment to problem solving, and mandate—and lists those variables promoting each source. This information can be used to help organizations assess their motivation for joining the TS, and those factors facilitating or blocking it. Each organization could evaluate the costs and benefits of interacting in respect of its own goals. This would provide an initial assessment of whether it is beneficial to join the TS, and which of the motivational bases is most salient for that system. Then, evaluation of factors promoting that source of motivation would point to potential motivational problems. For example, if organizations perceive mutual benefits from interacting and judge resource/dependency as the major motivational source, four facilitating factors have been identified: (a) mutual resource awareness; (b) domain consensus; (c) protection of autonomy; and, (d) moderate degrees of goal similarity. Evaluating the extent to which these dimensions are present provides a measure of the overall difficulty of interacting, and identifies potential motivational problems. Such information furnishes a systematic basis for deciding whether TS membership is worthwhile, and if so, what motivational issues, if any, need to be resolved.

In addition to motivations for interaction, the convention phase concerns organizations' perceptions of the TS task/problem. Because TS task performances involve collective efforts among organizations, it is necessary to reach consensus on the nature of the joint task. This agreement anchors organizations' motivations to specific task behaviors, and orients subsequent decisions about coordination of efforts, performance strategies, and level and utilization of organizations' knowledge, skills and resources. Typically, assessment of the task/problem occurs simultaneously with evaluations of the motivational base of commitment to problem solving, and follows the motivational analysis for resource/dependency and mandated exchanges. The integrative model directs attention to problem structuredness and task interdependence as key task/problem characteristics, and points to environmental conditions contributing to them, such as complexity and stability. Organizations could share perceptions of the TS task/problem and environment. This would provide understanding of the overall structuredness and interdependence of the task, as well as key environmental conditions impacting it. Such analyses would also reveal if there is sufficient agreement on task definition to form the TS.

Apart from the motivational, task/problem, and environmental analyses, the convening phase of TD poses practical problems for intervenors. The first issue concerns who should convene the participating organizations. In underorganized TS, a legitimate authority may not exist to perform the convening function, and attempts to fill that role by regular stakeholders may meet with apathy or resistance. Gricar (1981b) suggested that in such situations, a third party can serve as convenor if that person is seen as a legitimate and credible authority by the relevant organizations. In many of the SPS studies discussed previously, for example, the convenors belonged to universities or research institutes with reputations for neutrality and expertise in TS. Brown et al. (1974) and Gricar (1981b) warned, however, that such neutrality can be difficult to maintain as powerful adversaries attempt to co-opt convenors to favored positions.

A second problem with convening involves who should represent the participating organizations at the convening event. Interorganizational researchers have typically used organizational boundary spanners as respondents because they have the most relevant knowledge about relationships with other organizations (Van de Ven, 1976). Aldrich and Whetten (1981) argued that organizational members in different functional areas and at different hierarchical levels tend to have different frames of reference, and are likely to focus on different aspects of interorganizational linkage. Van de Ven (1976) suggested that one approach to choosing from among pertinent, yet diverse boundary spanners is to ask the top leaders of the organizations to nominate those individuals most directly responsible for relating with other TS members. Such persons can be expected to have relevant task/problem knowledge as well as the interest and motivation to engage actively in the convening process. In discussing the search conference as a convening method, Williams (1980) proposed that ideally the conference should bring together 30 to 35 people representing the range of interests of the potential TS members. When there is a large number of possible members, the convenor could identify groups of organizations having common interests, and select a member of each group to participate in the conference. Although this would protract the convening process as representatives periodically caucus with constituent organizations, it accounts for diverse stakeholder interests in the initial formation of the TS.

A third issue related to the convening phase concerns the kinds of interventions for helping organizations explore motivations and perceptions of the task/problem. Underorganized TS's are likely to require considerable structure and direction during this initial stage of TD (Brown, 1980); participating organizations tend to have diverse motives and views, weak ties, and limited means for resolving differences. In most studies of the convening process, outside practitioners organized and managed it. Their interventions were aimed at generating relevant motivational and task/problem data, and helping organizations arrive at a sufficiently agreed upon view of reality to permit joint action. For example, Brown et al. (1974) and Kaplan (1979) collected interview and questionnaire data from each potential TS member, and fed back that information to organizational representatives at a convening workshop. Williams (1980) described search conferences as having an explicit task focus; social scientists designed discrete tasks, usually in the form of sets of questions, requiring participants to analyze and share perceptions of the task/problem and its environment and to devise action steps for joint problem solving. Taber, et al. (1979) facilitated the convening of the community-based TS by acting as communication channels between organizations, making group-process interventions during convening meetings, gathering and feeding back relevant task data, and giving advice to TS leaders about organizational design.

Because the convening process is likely to be conflictual as organizations seek to work through differences and to reconcile their own self interests with those of the larger TS, interventions need to account for both the convening tasks and the underlying social processes through which they are accomplished. Kaplan (1979) found that organizations were often reluctant to share feedback data with each other, particularly if relationships among them were weak. Williams (1980) argued that organizations are likely to feel that the convening process is confusing and unproductive unless they experience it as making progress on meaningful tasks. Because outsiders typically design and manage those tasks, they must be careful not to usurp participants' ownership of and responsibility for task outcomes.

D. Organization

Assuming that the convention phase of TD results in a decision to create a TS, the organization stage provides the necessary structures and mechanisms to regulate organizations' task behaviors. This step involves determining appropriate kinds of organization for the task/problem and environment at hand, and implementing them. Because underorganized TS's require creation of organization where little or none exists, the discussion is oriented to designing new, rather than existing TS's. Much of the material could be easily adapted to redesigning a TS, however.

The integrative framework provides a general guide for generating appropriate kinds of organization for a TS. Starting from the outcomes shown in Figure 3 and working backward through the model to inputs, the diagnosis could proceed as follows. First, TS members would determine the outcomes desired from joint actions; these would provide standards for assessing the effects of organization. Second, the task/problem and its environment would be assessed. This information would specify critical task contingencies and point to those interaction processes that are most salient for meeting those requirements. Third, the inputs affecting relevant interaction processes could be identified and these would be used to generate appropriate kinds of organization.

In practice, the inputs identified in Figure 3 can serve as TS design variables. For example, if the task analysis reveals the need for high levels of coordination of efforts, the inputs having to do with integrative mechanisms would be most appropriate: (a) leadership; (b) structure; (c) compatible features; (d) communication processes and, (e) positive assessments. These dimensions can be used as general guides to generate more specific structures and mechanisms for coordinating efforts. Using leadership as a design guide, for instance, TS members may decide to create a referent organization to manage interactions among themselves, like the Council described in Taber's et al. (1979) study of a community-based TS or using structure to coordinate efforts, TS members may choose to formalize exchanges by creating rules, policies and standard operating procedures. Similar use could be made of the other kinds of inputs in Figure 3, especially performance norms which affect how organizations go about performing TS tasks/problems. Because of the preliminary state of the integrative model, however, it seems prudent to apply the inputs as a design checklist, pointing to general classes of variables that can affect specific TS interaction processes.

After identifying appropriate inputs for regulating organizations' behaviors, the organization phase of TD involves implementing those design variables. So far, there has been little systematic knowledge about how to manipulate or change the inputs in order to achieve requisite degrees of TS organization. The relevant literature either ignores implementation or presents anecdotal data and advice. Although that information is limited scientifically, it points to several practical implementation issues. The first topic concerns the extent to which TS members should be involved in the implementation process. Based on the extensive participative management literature (see, for example, Lowin, 1968; Delbecq, 1974) Gricar (1981b) argued that organizations should participate in TS changes because it increases acceptance of and commitment to implementing them. Trist (1979) suggested that when TS's are organized according to socio-ecological principles, such as centrality of interdependence, diffusion of power, and shared understanding of issues, high member involvement is necessary for implementing those principles.

In general, the choice about organizations' involvement in the implementation process seems to depend on how much organizational change is required to implement the inputs. To the extent that inputs involve major changes in how organizations customarily relate to each other, TS members should be involved in determining and implementing those changes. Thus, for example, structures intended to standardize existing information exchanges among organizations could likely be implemented by outsiders, such as higher authorities or management consultants, while new methods for joint decision making are likely to require higher member involvement for implementation.

A second, yet related issue is how to include organizations in the implementation process in those cases requiring moderate to high levels of participation. Conceptually, the relevant unit of analysis is the TS and its constituent organizations, and ideally, all of them should be included in implementing organizing inputs when participation in needed. Practically, however, it may not be feasible to work directly with the entire membership, usually because of size, interest, and resource constraints. Trist (1978, 1979) and Taber et al. (1979) overcame this problem by creating referent organizations and having them carry out the organization phase of TD on behalf of the TS. Similarly, McCann (1980) worked with selected subsets of transorganizational system members, and accomplished TS organizing tasks in group settings where interaction could be intense and free from external disruptions.

Although referent organizations and subgroups of TS members can provide participation in implementing the organizing inputs, both may have problems of generalizing their efforts to the larger TS and of getting other TS members to support those outcomes. Trist (1979) suggested that referent organizations are likely to represent TS members effectively to the extent that they perform a regulative as opposed to an operational function and are controlled by TS members rather than by outsiders. McCann (1981) argued that the transfer of subgroup plans and actions to the larger TS can be facilitated by making subgroup products understandable and usable to average TS members, and by confronting wider implementation issues within the subgroup itself.

A third implementation issue involves levels of change. Trist (1979) and McCann (1981) suggested that TD occurs simultaneously at two levels: an appreciative level concerned with organizations' perceptions and understandings and a task level involved with plans and operations. They argued that because the two levels are inextricably linked, it is necessary to account for them both in implementing TS structures. In helping to create a community-based corrections TS in Minnesota, for instance, McCann (1980) worked on appreciative and task changes. The former included expanding organizations' perceptions of the options and choices for organizing the TS, and the latter involved negotiation of members' roles and responsibilities and monitoring whether they were actually being enacted. McCann reported that appreciative–level learnings often occurred while working on structuring tasks; by considering the tasks in relation to the three phases of TD—identification, convention, and organization—organizations gained a fuller appreciation of the TS developmental context. Similarly, Taber, et al. (1979) attended both to organizations' perceptions and to specific organizing tasks in implementing TS structures. Moreover, they found it necessary to refocus on some of the earlier appreciative and task issues when reorganizing the TS from a resource-gathering to a resource-providing system.

A fourth implementation topic concerns the use of data to guide the implementation process. Researchers in organizational design have argued that implementing new organizations involves a tailoring process by which general design prescriptions are fitted to the specific situation (see, for example, Starbuck & Dutton, 1973; Cummings, 1981; Mohrman & Cummings, 1982). This tailoring process is guided by data feedback about whether the various aspects of the organization are being implemented and whether they are having their intended effects. Data-guided implementation seems especially applicable to TS, where the organizing inputs are general and must be made situation-specific during implementation.

Both Taber et al. (1979) and McCann (1980) collected and fed back data to TS members during implementation; this information helped organizations make appropriate adjustments in the TS organization. For example, Taber et al. made copious process observations of the meetings of the leadership Council, and used that data to help Council members focus their TS leadership role in relevant directions. Key points in providing implementation data are that it include measures of the organizing inputs themselves and of their expected effects, and that it be collected repeatedly at short intervals, so that it can be used to make gradual modifications in the TS organization. Clearly, these requirements place severe demands on the measurement process, both in operationalizing the input and outcome variables and in providing reliable and relatively nonreactive measures of them.

E. Summary

This section discussed the practice of TD. It argued that TS's constitute a distinct logical type higher than that of single organizations and thus require a form of planned change commensurate with that level. Moreover, because TS's are typically underorganized, planned development occurs differently from that in OD which has tended to derive from work with overorganized systems. Specifically, TD involves three developmental phases: identification, convention, and organization. Table 1 lists those phases and exemplifies the major kinds of issues appearing at each stage; it also shows those TS inputs which seem most relevant for resolving each set of issues. It should be emphasized that this represents only a preliminary list of potential TD issues, and that the mapping of inputs onto issues is speculative and only meant to be suggestive of the ways TS inputs might contribute to TD.

Briefly summarizing from Table 1, the identification phase of TD is concerned with specifying the potential members of the TS. Here issues concern the nature of the TS task/problem and the kinds of skills, knowledge, and resources required to perform it effectively. This provides a base for identifying potential task contributors as well as other organizations which can impact the task more indirectly The TS input having to do with composition of the TS seems most relevant to this phase of TD, and both the expanding network model and stakeholder analysis can help to identify appropriate TS members. The convention phase brings potential members together to assess whether forming a TS is desirable and feasible. Issues here concern gaining the necessary motivation to interact, and arriving at a sufficient consensus of the TS task/problem to permit joint task performances. The motivation-to-interact input appears most applicable to resolving these issues, particularly by identifying different bases for interaction and potential roadblocks thwarting such motivations. The organization phase of TS provides the necessary structures and mechanisms to regulate organizations' task/problem behaviors. Here issues are concerned with identifying salient interaction processes for effective task performances, and designing and implementing appropriate organizing schemes for supporting those processes. The TS inputs having to do with integrating mechanisms and performance norms seem most relevant for organizing the TS. They provide the leadership, structure, communication processes, and interaction strategies for accomplishing the TS task/problem.

IV. CONCLUSIONS AND DIRECTIONS

There has been growing interest in aggregates or groups of organizations as a unit of analysis. Research in interorganizational relations has gradually extended from organization and environment relations to networks of organizations. Similarly, the more applied research of social problem solving has increasingly engaged with groups of organizations in order to improve organizations' joint performances. While interorganizational research has added greatly to knowledge of TS's, it has generally neglected the practical side of how to develop or improve them. Conversely, while social problem–solving research has provided considerable practical knowledge about TS's, it has frequently been lax in conceptualizing and systematically studying them. Clearly, better integration and cross-fertilization of these so far separate streams of research is needed to create a more coherent conceptual understanding of TS, and an applied methodology for developing them.

Table 1. Phases of TD: Issues and TS Inputs

TS Inputs	Phases of TD
	IDENTIFICATION
Composition	1. What is the nature of the TS task/problem?
1. Expanding network model	2. What knowledge, skills, and resources are needed for task performance?
2. Stakeholder analysis	3. What organizations can provide those skills and resources?
	4. What organizations control resources, information, and legitimacy related to the TS task/problem?
	5. Who should provide leadership for identifying potential TS members?
	6. How can such leadership be enacted?
	CONVENTION
Motivation to interact	1. What are the cost/benefits of interacting?
1. Resource dependency	2. What is the motivational base of interaction?
2. Commitment to problem solving	3. What are the motivational problems of interaction?
3. Mandate	4. What is the nature of the TS task/problem, and how does the TS environment impact the task?
	5. Who should convene potential TS members?
	6. Who should represent the organizations at the convening event?
	7. How should the convening event be managed?

Integrating Mechanisms

1. Leadership
2. Structure
3. Compatible features
4. Communication processes
5. Positive assessments

Performance Norms

1. Direction setting
2. Diagnosis
3. Frame breaking collective definitions
4. Changing networks

1. What are the desired outcomes of the TS?
2. What is the nature of the TS task/problem and environment?
3. What interaction processes are salient for the TS task/problem?
4. What inputs impact those salient interaction processes?
5. How involved should TS members be in implementing the TS organization?
6. How to include all TS members when high participation is needed for implementation?
7. Are both appreciative and task levels being attended to during implementation?
8. What data should/can we collect to guide the implementation process?

The primary intent of this paper has been to provide a preliminary synthesis of this relevant research as an initial step towards developing the emerging field of transorganizational development. The paper has attempted to provide a theoretical model for understanding TS, and an outline of how that knowledge can be applied to TD. In particular, the paper briefly reviewed the two streams of relevant research, and then merged them into an integrative model of TS. Because the research included both descriptive and normative studies, the model explains existing TS, and provides knowledge of alternative TS and how they might be created. The paper applied the integrative framework to three phases of TD—identification, convention, and organization—and discussed key practical issues having to do with this form of planned change.

The material presented in the paper provides clearer understanding of TD and preliminary boundaries within which further work in this area might proceed. The integrative model and applied methodology suggest several directions for advancing transorganizational development as a scientific and practical approach to developing TS.

The first path concerns the integrative model itself both as a conceptual framework and as a diagnostic tool for assessing TS. Conceptually, the model categorizes relevant TS variables and proposes certain relationships among them. It attempts to explain TS outcomes as being proximately controlled by specific interaction processes, which in turn are impacted by selected inputs. This input-process-output model derives from conceptualizations of the small group literature (Hackman & Morris, 1975; Cummings, 1981), and when applied to TS, provides a meaningful integration of relevant research findings. Considerable research is needed, however, to assess directly whether the causal relationships proposed in the framework are operative in TS. The research summarized in Figure 3 has been mostly cross-sectional or case study, and has focused on limited aspects of the variables and relationships in the framework. What is needed are more longitudinal studies which examine a wider range of those variables and relationships. Specifically, it is necessary to discover whether the four interaction processes are powerful proximate causes of TS performances, and whether the particular inputs impact the interaction processes as predicted. Moreover, it is necessary to find out how TS tasks/problems interact with interaction processes to affect performances, and how environmental variables and TS outcomes impact the other parts of the framework.

At least two types of field research can help to assess the causal linkages proposed in the model, and to refine and extend knowledge in this area. The first kind involves long-term examination of a large number of naturally-occurring TS across a diversity of task contexts. This should provide the necessary time scale to observe temporal effects across the sets of input, process, and outcome variables; it should also provide the necessary task variance to examine interaction effects between process and task variables. One research possibility might be to track through time, with questionnaires, selected interviews, and archival data, TS occurring within industries facing different levels of environmental complexity and change. Presumably, TS in relatively stable industries would have more structured tasks than those in unstable industries, and comparative analysis of TS across industries might provide sufficient task variance for examining some of the relationships proposed here.

The second type of research involves attempting to create effective transorganizational systems by manipulating the TS inputs. This would provide clearer understanding of the malleability of the inputs, and would likely allow the interaction processes to vary more widely than that generally occuring in natural TS's. In contrast to many current TS case studies, this applied research would need to measure each set of variables contained in the framework, and employ stronger quasi-experimental research designs in order to increase the validity of the findings. One relatively simple research design would be to compare TS's which are undergoing planned input changes with those which are not. This nonequivalent control group design would add greatly to the strength of action research in this area, especially if time-series data were collected. The logistics of obtaining comparable data in both experimental and control TS's could be accomplished by having action researchers and descriptive researchers coordinate their measurements. Each could continue to divide their labor and interests—the action researchers studying TS's undergoing change and the descriptive researchers examining naturally-occurring TS's. So long as they measured some variables in common, the necessary control group data so often missing in action research would be available.

Both types of research mentioned above will likely discover that a single general model cannot feasibly include the complexity of factors affecting TS performances; rather, several mid-level frameworks, each accounting for TS outcomes under certain conditions, will likely emerge. For example, as more becomes known about the properties of TS tasks/problems, there will likely be development of specific task-contingent models of TS performance. Each model will focus on only those subsets of the interaction processes and inputs shown in Figure 3 which are salient for a particular task situation. This will allow more precise and accurate specification of variables and casual linkages than is currently permitted. The general framework presented here provides an initial base for eventual development of more refined theories of TS effectiveness.

Diagnostically, there is still considerable research which needs to be accomplished before the integrative framework can reliably be used to assess the developmental needs of TS. It is necessary to operationalize the TS variables and to devise methods for measuring them validly and reliably. To date, several parts of the model have been operationalized and measured mainly by researchers in the IR field: the interaction processes having to do with level and coordination of efforts, the inputs related to motivation to interact and to integrating mechanisms, the environmental features of stability, complexity, conflict, resource scarcity, and homogeneity, and task/problem structuredness. These measures provide a useful starting point for devising diagnostic instruments. Improvement is needed, however, in establishing the psychometric properties of many of the questionnaires currently in use, and in creating unobstructive measures of the variables. These latter measures are especially needed in TD because they are nonreactive and are unlikely to interact strongly with interventions and because they alleviate much of the problem of asking respondents to answer an exhaustive lists of questions. Similar measurement development is also needed for the remaining variables in the model which have yet to be operationalized and measured.

A second direction for advancing TD concerns the developmental phases through which TS's become organized and functional systems. It was proposed that TS's are generally underorganized, and, consequently, require three stages of planned change which are aimed at developing requisite degrees of organization for the task/problem at hand: identification, convention, and organization. Although these proposals are consistent with the applied literature on TS, it remains open to question to what extent TS's are actually underorganized and require that particular sequence of planned changes to become functionally operational. It can be argued, for example, that the applied literature is biased towards reporting about underorganized TS, because such systems are probably more in need of professional help and are likely to receive it than organized or overorganized TS's. At this stage, it seems prudent to treat the degree of organization of TS's as an empirical question, and to accumulate data on this dimension across a large and diverse population of TS's.

In terms of the three developmental phases, it is necessary to discover whether underorganized TS's gain necessary organization along these stages or others. Based on the extensive literature on small group development (see, for example, Heinen & Jacobson, 1976), it can be expected that research in this area would produce a considerably more refined view of TS development process than the one presented in this paper. Such understanding is needed to extend and refine the applied methods for developing TS's described previously. For example, in applying the integrative model to the three phases of TD as shown in Table 1, we suggested that the TS inputs may vary in importance depending on the developmental stage. Specifically, the input having to do with TS composition was discussed as relevant for the identification phase; motivation to interact was presented as appropriate for the convention stage; and integrating mechanisms and performance norms were included in the organization phase. Although speculative at present, research linking TS inputs to phases of TS development would reveal the specific kinds of changes or interventions that are needed at each stage of development. Such practical knowledge is fundamental to TD.

The final direction discussed here concerns the practice of TD. Although there has been little systematic research in this area, the material presented earlier suggests several practical issues needing conceptual and empirical clarity. The first topic involves the values underlying TD. Laue (1978) has argued that all social science intervention is value-laden; it requires choice among alternatives, and affects the power configuration of the target system. So far, TD practitioners have tended to borrow heavily from OD values and change orientations, often without questioning their applicability to TS. These include values promoting collaboration among organizations and change strategies aimed at maintaining the viability of the existing system. For example, Trist (1979) proposed that social problem solving requires diffusion of power and collaboration among organizations; Aldrich (1976) argued that a collaboration paradigm underlies most interorganizational research in the public sector.

Cummings (1980), Gricar and Brown (1981) and Boje (1982) have questioned whether interventions promoting collaborative values and system maintenance are powerful enough to change TS, especially where there are power and dominance relations among organizations, competition for scarce resources, and disputes over task/problem definition. In these loosely coupled, political systems, they suggested that TD practitioners may need to use more power-oriented change strategies in order to mobilize TS members and induce new forms of linkage. These kinds of change strategies derive mainly from the community change literature (see, for example, Warren, 1965; Slavin, 1969; Litwak, et al., 1979; Reid, 1975), and include such coercive and power tactics as campaigns, contests, and strikes. Here, practitioners cannot take a neutral stance, but must take sides and commit to some specific values at the expense of others.

The aforementioned discussion suggests that at this stage of development, uncritical acceptance of one set of values to guide TD is unwise. Indeed, it is questionable whether there is currently enough knowledge in this area to effectively carry out a particular value orientation. Without sufficient understanding of the dynamics underlying TS functioning, it is difficult, if not impossible, to assure that any specific intervention will promote particular kinds of values. For example, interventions aimed at enhancing collaboration among organizations may unwittingly damage some participants in situations frought with power/dependence. Similarly, changes intended to gain power over others may inadvertantly ignore opportunities for mutual gain in situations with underlying interdependencies among organizations. Until sufficient knowledge about TD becomes available, it seems prudent and ethical to openly question the value premises underlying different intervention choices, including the behaviors of interventionists.

A second practical issue concerns the kinds of skills and competencies needed to practice TD effectively. To date, TD practitioners have come from a diversity of disciplines and applied backgrounds, and have generally shown strong competence in systems approaches to change and in process-oriented interventions. Indeed, many practitioners were initially trained and gained experience in OD, and have extended that skill upward to TS's. Although such competence seems especially relevant to collaborative TD interventions, it is questionable whether it is sufficient for the more power-oriented strategies. Brown (1980) has argued, for example, that while interpersonal competence is required for planned change in overorganized system, political competence is needed in underorganized systems. Here, the practitioner must understand the distribution of power, conflicts of interests, and value dilemmas inherent in such systems, and be able to manage his/her own role and values in respect to those dynamics. Boje (1982), Gricar and Brown (1981), and Cummings (1980) have argued similarly that OD competence is likely unsuited to dealing with the political side of a TS, and that more political saavy and skills are needed. Clearly, more attention to what these skills comprise and how they can be acquired is needed for advancing TD practice.

The final practical issue concerns the type of applied strategy that is needed at this formative stage of TD. The material presented in this paper suggests strongly that TD is a large-scale and long-term effort at planned change. In almost all case studies of TD reviewed here, the projects involved multiple, simultaneous interventions aimed at both the TS itself and its constituent organizations. The developmental phases were protracted; requiring considerable time to identify relevant organizations, to convene them, and to organize for joint performances. The practitioners comprised a team with each member performing different yet related intervention tasks. Because of the heavy resource and time commitments required for TD, and because of the high need for empirical knowledge in this area, full advantage should be taken of the research and learning opportunities available in TD projects. This will require joint committment to practice and research on behalf of both the intervention team and the participating organizations; sanction which legitimizes both types of activities. Moreover, it will require multi-skilled and probably multi-disciplinary teams of practitioners/researchers performing different yet related functions. Emery and Trist's (1973) model of domain-based problem-oriented research and Lawler's (1977), Goodman's (1979) and Mohrman et al.'s (in press) strategies for combining practice and research in the quality–of–work–life area seem promising approaches for applying and advancing TD, and further development along those lines is sorely needed.

Perhaps the greatest challenge to developing a combined practice and research thrust in TD is changing the attitudes and behaviors of those working in this area. People who are mainly interested in descriptive research will have to gain a greater practical experience with TS's, and show a willingness to engage with practitioners and organizations in joint learning processes. Those who are largely practice oriented will have to gain a greater appreciation for the empirical and conceptual issues in TD, and open their activities to scientific inquiry. Hopefully, this paper makes these challenges a bit less formidable.

ACKNOWLEDGMENTS

I would like to thank Warren Bennis, Dave Brown, Barbara Gricar, and Dave Whetten for helpful comments on an earlier draft of this paper, and especially Kurt Motamedi who provided materials and encouragement necessary to undertake the task of writing this paper.

REFERENCES

Ackoff, R. *Redesigning the future*. New York: John Wiley & Sons, 1975.

Aiken, M. & Hage, J. Organizational interdependence and intra-organizational structure. *American Sociological Review*, 1968, *33*, 912–930.

Akinbode, I. A. & Clark R. A Framework for analyzing interorganizational relationships. *Human Relations*, 1976, *29*, 101–114.

Alderfer, C. & Brown, L. D. *Learning from changing*. Beverly Hills, CA: Sage, 1975.

Aldrich, H. An organization-environment perspective on cooperation and conflict between organizations in the manpower training system. In A. Negandhi (Ed.), *Interorganization theory*. Kent, OH: Kent State University Press, 1975.

Aldrich, H. Resource dependence and interorganizational relations. *Administration and Society*, 1976, *7*, 419–454.

Aldrich, H. & Pfeffer, J. Environments and organizations. In A. Inkeles (Ed.), *Annual review of sociology* (Vol. 2). Palo Alto, CA: Annual Reviews, 1976.

Aldrich, H. & Whetten D. A. Organization-sets, action-sets, and networks: Making the most of simplicity. In P. Nystrom and W. Starbuck (Eds.), *Handbook of organizational design* (Vol. 1). London: Oxford University Press, 1981.

Aram, J. & Stratton, W. The development of interagency cooperation. *Social Science Review*, 1974, *3*, 412–421.

Argyris, C. *Inner contraditions of rigorous research*. New York: Academic Press, 1980.

Argyris, C. & Schon, D. *Organizational learning: A theory of action perspective*. Reading, MA: Addison-Wesley, 1978.

Assael, H. Constructive role of interorganizational conflict. *Administrative Science Quarterly*, 1969, *14*, 573–582.

Baker, F. & O'Brien, G. Intersystem relations and coordination of human service organizations. *American Journal of Public Health*, 1971, *61*, 130–137.

Benson, K. The interorganizational network as a political economy. *Administrative Science Quarterly*, 1975, *20*, 229–249.

Boje, D. *Towards a theory and praxis of transorganizational development: Stakeholder networks and their habitats* (Working Paper 79-6). Behavioral and Organizational Science Study Center, Graduate School of Management, University of California at Los Angeles, February, 1982.

Boje, D. & Whetten, D. Effects of organizational strategies and contextual constraints on centrality and attributions of influence in interorganizational networks. *Administrative Science Quarterly*, 1981, *26*, 378–395.

Brown, L. D. Research action: organizational feedback, understanding, and change. *The Journal of Applied Behavioral Science*, 1972, *8*, 697–711.

Brown, L. D. Planned change in underorganized systems. In T. Cummings (Ed.), *Systems theory for organization development*. Chichester, England: John Wiley & Sons, 1980.

Brown, L. D., Aram, J. & Bachner, D. Interorganizational information sharing: A successful intervention that failed. *The Journal of Applied Behavioral Science*, 1974, *10*, 533–554.

Chevalier, M. *A wider range of perspectives in the bureaucratic structure.* Working paper. Ottawa, Canada: Commission on Bi-Lingualism and Bi-Culturalism, 1966.

Chevalier, M. *Stimulation of needed social science research for canadian water resource problems.* Working paper. Ottawa, Canada: Privy Council Science Secretariat, 1967.

Cook, K. Exchange and power in networks of interorganizational Relations. In J. K. Benson (Ed.), *Organizational analysis: Critique and innovation*. Beverly Hills, CA: Sage, 1977.

Culbert, S., Elden, J., McWhinney, W., Schmidt, W., & Tannenbaum, R. Trans-organizational praxis: A search beyond organization development. *International Associations*, 1972, *XXIV*, 98–104.

Cummings, T. Interorganization theory and organization development. In T. Cummings (Ed.), *Systems theory for organization development*. Chichester,: John Wiley & Sons, 1980.

Cummings, T. Designing effective work groups. In P. Nystrom and W. Starbuck (Eds.), *Handbook of organizational design* (Vol. 2). Oxford: Oxford University Press, 1981.

Cummings, T. Self-regulating work groups: A socio-technical synthesis. *Academy of Management Review*, 1978, *3*, 625–634.

Delbecq, A. Contextual variables affecting decision making in program planning. *The Journal for the American Institute for Decision Sciences*, 1974, *5*, 28–38.

Durkheim, E. *The division of labor in society*. New York: The Free Press, 1964.

Emery, F. Adaptive systems for our future governance. *National labour institute bulletin*, New Delhi, 1976. (No. 4, 14–21)

Emery, F. *Futures we are in*. Leiden, The Netherlands: Nijhoff, 1977.

Emery, F., & Thorsrud, E. *Form and content in industrial democracy*. London: Tavistock Publications, 1969.

Emery, F., & Trist, E. The causal texture of organizational environments. *Human Relations*, 1965, *18*, 21–32.

Emery, F., & Trist, E. *Towards a social ecology*. London: Plenum, 1973.

Emery, M. *Searching*. Occasional Paper in Continuing Education No. 12. Canberra: Australian National University, Center for Continuing Education, 1976.

Evan, W. The organization-set: Toward a theory of interorganizational relations. In J. D. Thompson (Ed.), *Approaches to organizational design*. Pittsburg: University of Pittsburg Press, 1966.

Evan, W., & Klemm, R. C. Interorganizational relations among hospitals: A strategy, structure and performance model. *Human Relations*, 1980, *33*, 315–337.

Galaskiewicz, J. The structure of community organizational networks. *Social Forces*, 1979, *57*, 1346–1364.

Gergen, K. Toward generative theory. *Journal of Personality and Social Psychology*, 1978, *36*, 1344–1360.

Gerlach, L., & Palmer, G. Adaptation through evolving interdependence. In P. Nystrom and W. Starbuck (Eds.), *Handbook of organizational design* (Vol. 1). Oxford: Oxford University Press, 1981.

Gillespie, D., & Mileti, David. *Technostructures and interorganizational relations*. Lexington, MA: Heath, 1979.

Gillespie, D., & Perry, R. The influences of an organizational environment in interorganizational relations. *American Journal of Economics and Sociology*, 1975, *34*, 29–42.

Goodman, P. *Assessing organizational change*. New York: Wiley-Interscience, 1979.

Goodman, R., & Huff, A. Enriching policy premises for an ambiguous world. In J. Sutherland (Ed.), *Management handbook for public administrators*. New York: Van Nostrand Reinhold, 1978.

Gricar, B. Fostering collaboration among organization. In H. Meltzer and W. Nord (Eds.), *Making organizations humane and productive*. New York: John Wiley & Sons, 1981.(a)

Gricar, B. *The legitimacy of consultants and stakeholders in interorganizational problems*. Paper presented at Annual Meetings of Academy of Management, San Diego, August, 1981.(b)

Gricar, B., & Brown, L. D. Conflict, power and organization in a changing community. *Human Relations*, 1981, *34*, 877–893.

Hackman, J. R., & Morris, C. Group tasks, group interaction process, and performance effectiveness: A review and proposed integration. In L. Berkowitz (Ed.), *Advances in experimental social psychology* (Vol. 8). New York: Academic Press, 1975.

Hackman, J. R., & Oldham, G. *Work redesign*. Reading, MA: Addison-Wesley, 1980.

Hall, R., Clark, J., Giordano, P., Johnson, P., & Van Roekel, M. Patterns of interorganizational relations. *Administrative Science Quarterly*, 1977, *22*, 457–474.

Hannan, M. T., & Freeman, J. The population ecology of organizations. *American Journal of Sociology*, 1977, *82*, 929–964.

Heinen, J. S., & Jacobson, E. A model of task group development in complex organizations and a strategy for implementation. *Academy of Management Review*, 1976, *1*, 98–111.

Higgin, G., & Jessop, N. *Communications in the building industry*. London: Tavistock Publications, 1963.

Kaplan, R. *Diagnosis in a stratified interorganizational setting*. Paper presented at the 39th Annual Meeting of the Academy of Management, Atlanta, Georgia, August, 1979.

Katz, D., & Kahn, R. *The social psychology of organizations* (2nd Ed.). New York: John Wiley & Sons, 1978.

Laue, J. Advocacy and sociology. In G. Weber and J. McCall (Eds.), *Social scientists as advocates: Views from applied disciplines*. Beverly Hills, CA: Sage, 1978.

Lawler, E. Adaptive experiments. *Academy of Management Review*, 1977, *2*, 576–585.

Lawless, M. *Directed interorganizational systems: Network strategy making in public service delivery*. Unpublished paper, 1982. Available from Department of Management, California State University, Northridge.

Levine, S., & White, P. Exchange as a conceptual framework for the study of interorganizational relations. *Administrative Science Quarterly*, 1961, *5*, 583–601.

Lewin, K. Action research and minority problems. *Journal of Social Issues*, 1946, *2*, 34–46.

Lewin, K. *Field Theory in Social Science*. New York: Harper, 1951.

Litwak, E., & Hylton, L. Interorganizational analysis: A hypothesis on coordinating agencies. *Administrative Science Quarterly*, 1962, *6*, 395–420.

420   THOMAS G. CUMMINGS

Litwak, E., Shiroi, E., Zimmerman, L., & Bernstein, J. Community participation in bu-
reaucratic organizations: Principles and strategies. *Interchange*, 1970, *1*, 44–70.
Lowin, A. Participative decision making: A model, literature critique, and prescriptions for
research. *Organizational Behavior and Human Performance*, 1968, *3*, 68–106.
MacCrimmon, K., & Taylor, D. Decision making and problem solving. In M. Dunnette
(Ed.), *Handbook of industrial and organizational psychology*. Chicago: Rand McNally,
1976.
Mannheim, K. *Man and society in an age of reconstruction: Studies in modern social struc-
ture*. New York: Harcourt, Brace, 1951.
Mason, R. *Management by multiple advocacy* (Working Paper No. 4). Study Center in Public
Services Management and Policy, Graduate School of Management, University of Cal-
ifornia at Los Angeles, 1978.
Mason, R., & Mitroff, I. *Challenging strategic planning assumptions*. New York: John Wiley
& Sons, 1981.
Marrett, C. On the specification of interorganizational dimensions. *Sociology and Social
Review*, 1971, *56*, 83–89.
McCann, J. *Developing interorganizational domains: Concepts and practice*. Unpublished
Doctoral Dissertation, The Wharton School, University of Pennsylvania, Philadelphia,
1980.
McCann, J. Design parameters for problem solving interventions. Unpublished paper, The
Wharton School, University of Pennsylvania, 1981.
Metcalfe, J. L. Organizational strategies and interorganizational networks. *Human Rela-
tions*, 1976, *29*, 327–343.
Mohrman, S., & Cummings, T. Implementing quality of work life projects. In R. Ritvo and
A. Sargent (Eds.), *NTL managers' handbook*. Washington, D.C.: National Training
Laboratories Institute of Applied Behavioral Science, in press.
Mohrman, S., Cummings, T., & Lawler, E. Creating useful knowledge: Content and process
issues. In R. Kilmann and K. Thomas (Eds.), *Producing Useful Knowledge for Or-
ganizations*. New York: Praeger, in press.
Molnar, J., & Rogers, D. A comparative model of interorganizational conflict. *Administra-
tive Science Quarterly*, 1979, *24*, 405–425.
Motamedi, K. Transorganizational relations and the herbicide movement. Working paper,
Graduate Business School, Pepperdine University, Los Angeles, 1982.
O'Toole, R. *The cleveland rehabilitation complex: A study of inter-agency coordination*.
Cleveland: Vocational Guidance and Rehabilitation Services, 1972.
Pfeffer, J., & Salancik, G. *The external control of organizations*. New York: Harper & Row,
1978.
Phillips, A. A theory of interfirm organization. *Quarterly Journal of Economics*, 1960, *74*,
602–613.
Reid, W. Interagency coordination in delinquency prevention and control. *Social Service
Review*, 1964, *38*, 418–428.
Reid, W. Inter-organizational coordination in social welfare: A theoretical approach to anal-
ysis and intervention. In R. Kramer and H. Specht (Eds.), *Readings in community
organization practice*. Englewood Cliffs, NJ: Prentice Hall, 1975.
Reiker, P., Morrissey, J., & Horan, P. *Interorganizational relations: A critique of theory
and method*. Prepared for an Organizations Day Round Table Presentation at the American Sociological Association Annual Meeting, Montreal, August, 1974.
Schermerhorn, J. Interorganizational development. *Journal of Management*, 1979, *5*, 21–
38.
Schmidt, S., & Kochan, T. An application of a 'political economy' approach to effectiveness:
Employment service—employer exchanges. *Administration and Society*, 1975, *7*, 455–
473.

Schmidt, S., & Kochan, T. Interorganizational relationships: Patterns and motivations. *Administrative Science Quarterly*, 1977, *22*, 220–234.

Slavin, S. Concepts of social conflict: Use in social work curriculum. *Journal of Education for Social Work*, 1969, *5*, 47–60.

Slocum, J., & Simms, H. A typology of technology and job redesign. *Human Relations*, 1980, *33*, 193–212.

Susman, G. *Autonomy at work*. New York: Praeger, 1976.

Staw, B. The escalation of commitment to a course of action. *Academy of Management Review*, 1981, *6*, 577–587.

Stern, R. The development of an interorganizational control network: The case of intercollegiate athletics. *Administrative Science Quarterly*, 1979, *24*, 242–266.

Starbuck, W., & Dutton, J. Designing adaptive organizations. *Journal of Business Policy*, 1973, *3*, 21–28.

Taber, T., Walsh, J., & Cooke, R. Developing a community-based program for reducing the social impact of a plant closing. *The Journal of Applied Behavioral Science*, 1979, *15*, 133–155.

Terreberry, S. The evolution of organizational environments. *Administrative Science Quarterly*, 1968, *12*, 590–613.

Thompson, J. D. *Organizations in action*. New York: McGraw-Hill, 1967.

Trist, E. *Engaging with large-scale systems*. Paper delivered at McGregor Conference on Organization Development, Endicott House, 1967.

Trist, E. *A concept of organizational ecology*. Invited address to Department of Psychology, University of Melbourne, Australia, July, 1976.

Trist, E. *New directions of hope*. The John Madge Memorial Lecture, Glascow University, November, 1978.

Trist, E. *Referent organizations and the development of interorganizational domains*. Paper delivered at the Academy of Management 39th Annual Meetings, Atlanta, Georgia, August, 1979.

Turk, H. Interorganizational networks in urban society: Initial perspectives and comparative research. *American Sociological Review*, 1970, *35*, 1–19.

Turk, H. *Interorganizational activation in urban communities*. Rose Monograph, American Sociological Association, 1973.

Van de Ven, A. On the nature, formation and maintenance of relations among organizations. *Academy of Management Review*, 1976, *4*, 24–36.

Van de Ven, A., Emmett, D., & Koenig, R. Frameworks for interorganizational analysis. *Organization and Administrative Sciences*, 1974, *5*, 113–129.

Van de Ven, A., Walker, G., & Liston, J. Coordination patterns within an interorganizational network. *Human Relations*, 1979, *32*, 19–36.

Vickers, G. *The art of judgement*. New York: Basic Books, 1966.

Warren, R. Types of purposive social change at the community level (Brandeis University Papers in Social Welfare, No. 11). Brandeis University, 1965.

Warren, R. The interorganizational field as a focus for investigation. *Administrative Science Quarterly*, 1967, *12*, 396–419.

Warren, R. Alternative strategies of inter-agency planning. In P. White (Ed.), *Inter-organizational research in health: conference proceedings*. The Johns Hopkins University, 1970.

Warren, R. The concerting of decision as a variable in organizational interaction. In M. Tuite, et al. (Eds.), *Interorganizational decision making*. Chicago: Aldine, 1972.

Warren, R., Burgunder, A., Newton, J. W., Rose, S. The interaction of community decision organizations: Some conceptual considerations and empirical findings. In A. Negandhi (Ed.), *Interorganization theory*. Kent, OH: Kent State University Press, 1975.

Warren, R., Rose, S., & Bergunder, A. *The structure of urban reform*. Lexington, MA: Heath, 1974.

Watzlawick, P., Beavin, J., & Jackson, D. *Pragmatics of human communication*. New York: Norton, 1967.

Watzlawick, P., Weakland, J., & Fisch, R. *Change*. New York: Norton, 1974.

Whetten, D. Toward a contingency model for designing interorganizational service delivery systems. *Organization and Administrative Sciences*, 1977, *8*, 77–96.

Whetten, D. Interoganizational relations: A review of the field. *Journal of Higher Education*, 1981, *52*, 1–28.

Whitehead, A. N., & Russell, B. *Principia mathematica* (Vol. 3). Cambridge: Cambridge University Press, 1910.

Williams, T. The search conference in active adaptive planning. *The Journal of Applied Behavioral Science*, 1980, *16*, 470–483.

Zeitz, G. Interorganizational relationships and social structure: A critique of some aspects of the literature. In A. Negandhi (Ed.), *Interorganization theory*. Kent, OH: Kent State University Press, 1975.

CROSS-NATIONAL ORGANIZATIONAL RESEARCH:
THE GRASP OF THE BLIND MEN

Karlene H. Roberts and Nakiye A. Boyacigiller

ABSTRACT

This paper advances a set of eight criteria that would recharacterize a good paradigm of cross-national organizational research. It then examines five large scale cross-national organizational research efforts against these criteria, noting the most severe problems in those studies. Finally, emerging from this examination, three issues are discussed in detail because they are issues felt to afford the greatest possibility of immediate payoff if attended to in cross-national organizational research. These issues are concerned with focusing on environments in which organizations operate, the necessity of dealing with serious time problems generated in this kind of research, and problems emanating from the fact that most studies in this area are static in nature.

Research in Organizational Behavior, vol. 6, pages 423–475
Copyright © 1984 by JAI Press Inc.
All rights of reproduction in any form reserved.
ISBN: 0-89232-351-5

One glance at contemporary world developments leads to the conclusion that it is imperative for the social science of organizations to mature. Science is the game of describing and predicting phenomena in the natural and socially constructed worlds and without predictive power we are likely to build organizations that will help, if not fully determine, mankind's undoing.

As part of the recent national dialogue in the United States concerning ways to control and reduce the awesome and frightening nuclear arsenals of the superpowers, Jonathan Schell (1982) provides an impassioned argument that nuclear weapons make war obsolete and world government imperative. Any world government will be necessarily composed of interlocked organizations. If mankind is to survive, we must design and operate those organizations in an effective manner. To do that requires knowing what kinds of organizations are or can be effective in various settings.

The continuous development of high-speed information technology will lead to a proliferation of yet more modern complex organizations and further differentiation among those already in existence. The availability of such technology fosters the conditions under which new organizations can develop, using resources of the old and old organizations can move into new domains without certain overextension. Additionally, this technology will allow contact among or even integration across organizations in widely distant locations. It will be possible, as never before, to tie together organizations with vastly different histories, operating in situations with vastly different constraints and acceptable norms, and seeking vastly different goals.

Finally, while we have not yet seen, as was once predicted (Galbraith, 1967), multinational corporations replacing some political organizational forms, or reducing the place of the nation state in the world, the multinationals are powerful. By 1974 their combined sales exceeded the gross national product of every country except the United States and the Soviet Union (Barnet & Müller, 1974). Multinationals will continue to grow and must be designed and operated to reduce risks of failure which result in negative consequences for the social and economic good of mankind. Their efficiency must be improved so inputs are not wasted in a world of diminishing resources.

With such pressing problems at hand, all of them crossing national boundaries, one wonders what tools the cross-national study of organizations does or can provide. More important, one wonders what promise there is in developing a mature science that necessarily underlies engineering applications. So that the limitations of cross-national organizational research can be viewed in their proper light we must keep in mind the extreme youth of systematic research in this area.

Until the 1950s systematic research and theorizing about organizations was confined to Great Britain and the United States (Glaser, 1975). Despite Udy's (1961) and Crozier's (1964) early forays into cross-national work there was virtually no follow-up. Hydebrand's 1973 edited compilation of thirty organizational studies, considered by many as an excellent representation of the work at that time, contained only one cross-national investigation. Harbison and Myers (1959) first studied cross-national management, and Haire, Ghiselli, and Porter (1966) did the first systematic large-scale survey of managers cross-nationally. Early cross-national forays were limited primarily to Western Europe and the United States, and this trend continues. All of this is understandable against the following backdrop:

> Today between fifteen and thirty of the 120 countries of the world with less than one-third of its population, possess practically all of its science [von Alleman, 1974].

If all science is practiced in fewer than thirty of the world's nations, then all social science is practiced in still fewer, and all organizational science in still fewer yet. Against that record it seems unlikely solutions will be found for the severe social and political problems that are increasing worldwide at a geometric rate.

It is not our purpose here to provide a comprehensive review of the cross-national organizational literature. A number of those exist (Bhagat & McQuaid, 1982; Child, 1981; Ferrari, 1974; Negandhi, 1974). Rather, our purpose is to go back to a recommendation made earlier by one of the authors of this paper (Roberts, 1970) that until some fundamental issues are dealt with, a retrenchment should occur in cross-national organizational research. That statement was made within the framework of the parable of the blind men and the elephant, each man "seeing" only a part of the elephant. Here we address some basic questions regarding criteria that should be met by a body of cross-national organizational research, examine the assets and liabilities of some existing large-scale studies, and offer some suggestions about the kind of research and theory building we think will be most fruitful in the near future. This essay begins by taking seriously the following comment:

> We can continue along the present lines by conducting largely eclectic studies that may have very different theoretical, methodological domain and intent bases, and hope that individually and collectively they are sufficient and sufficiently additive to make a science of organizations. There are many virtues and many proponents of such an approach. Conversely, a sufficient number of scholars and researchers could decide that the field is essentially floundering and needs integrative model building and conceptualizing before research can become meaningful and additive. This would imply that many of our best minds should focus on the search for and development of such integrative models which would hopefully move us to another level of re-

search. . . . The extent to which these proponents can and will do the job is certainly
problematical [England, Negandhi, & Wilpert, 1979, p. 13].

Kuhn (1970) describes scientific paradigms as "universally recognized
scientific achievements that for a time provide model problems and solutions to a community of practitioners" (p. viii). "Men whose research
is based on shared paradigms are committed to the same rules and standards for scientific practice. That commitment and the apparent consensus it produces are prerequisites for normal science . . ." (p. 11). That
the area of cross-national research is pre-paradigmatic, floundering, and
fragmented is obvious. There is little agreement about the issues that
should be examined or about the conduct of those examinations.

First, what does cross-national research seek to do? Based on existing
research, it appears its raison d'etre is to extend variance on setting characteristics to understand their impacts on organizations, on organizational
members, on a variety of relationships within organizations. These relationships can be among individual characteristics, organizational characteristics, or relations between the two. The purpose of this approach
to organizational research is to find universalism or divergence in these
various kinds of relationships across settings. This is represented in Figure
1. Figure 1 diagrams virtually all the kinds of relations we have seen
studied in cross-national organizational research.

Cross-national organizational research is no different from any other
organizational research in which setting characteristics are attended—
with one exception. Some single nation researchers are beginning to examine the impact of organizations on limited parts of their environments.
For example, researchers have looked at such things as conditions that
foster the takeover of one firm by another (Demsetz, 1982; Pfeffer, 1972).
Most cross-national researchers, to the contrary, focus on outside-in
causal linkages and that is exactly what they should do because the field
is, as yet, too underdeveloped and fragmented to warrant spreading the
research effort any thinner.

When one compares the quality of single national organizational research which examines setting to most cross-national organizational research which examines setting, single nation work generally wins. The
reasons are clear. In cross-national organizational research, all the problems of single nation studies are exacerbated by two conditions. The first
is extension on the independent variable. Setting characteristics are difficult to conceptualize and even more difficult to measure. The usual
external organizational variables seen in cross-national organizational research are either undefined entirely or their definitions are sufficiently
amorphous so that they are unclear. This is particularly true in moving
from explication to operation. The second condition is the Tower of Babel

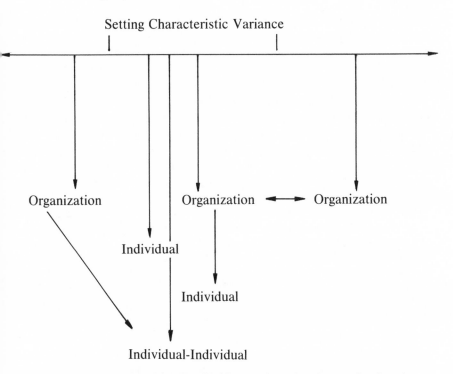

Figure 1. Relationships studied in cross-national organizational research

created when researchers attempt to investigate settings in which there are different values and heritages, and often use research teams whose members also differ from one another on these dimensions. Such differences require compromise and often the end result seeks the lowest common denominator of research standards.

IF A FIELD IS TO BE A FIELD: SUGGESTED CRITERIA FOR CROSS-NATIONAL ORGANIZATIONAL RESEARCH

For progress to be made in cross-national organizational research, all efforts should be devoted to paradigm development and a complete moratorium should be called on small studies that seek answers to limited and often unimportant questions. That is not to say that researchers will agree on a correct approach to paradigm development. Rather, progress can only be made with the development of vocal camps of researchers and their followers willing to argue the merits of a few major avenues. Currently the field is not defined by the existence of well-developed camps but rather by as many research notions as their are scholars to implement them.

Here we discuss some criteria that would characterize a good paradigm in cross-national organizational research as an area of study. All of these criteria cannot be met in each and every study. Rather, the mosaic of the field should acknowledge the importance of each criterion and studies should overlap one another in terms of standards of excellence, much as in the fish scale model proposed by Campbell (1969). Many issues discussed here are as true for single nation as for cross-national organizational research; the two are inextricably linked. Here we focus on those points we feel are more crucial to cross-national than to single nation research, indicate something about why we feel the situation is as it is, and recommend some strategies for moving on. The criteria and their discussion follows.

1. *A good paradigm will either specify a definition of culture or replace it with a set of measurable variables that might together reflect potentially important setting impacts on organizations.*

Most criticisms of cross-national organizational research, of all cultural anthropological research, and cross-national psychological research, begin with the problem of lack of definition of the term culture (Beres & Portwood, 1981; Dachler, 1979; Evan, 1975; Kroeber & Kluckhohn, 1952). Some of these criticisms end with the suggestion that we eliminate the term entirely because it lacks heuristic value (see, for example, Bhagat & McQuaid, 1982; Dixon, 1977; Heller & Wilpert, et al., 1981; Negandhi, 1974). Obviously this problem is at the heart of all cross-national organizational research, but is irrelevant to some kinds of single nation studies in which investigators can be impervious to anything outside the skin of the organization.

The definitional problem comes about because of our almost slavish reliance on definitions provided by cultural anthropologists who typically focus on man-made constructions that distinguish one community from others that belong to different traditions (see, for example, Benedict, 1934; Kroeber & Klockhohn, 1952). However, the modern complex organizations in which most of us are interested are influenced by setting characteristics in addition to the institutions and norms focused on by anthropologists. For example, they are influenced by market structures, political alliances, legal systems, environmental uncertainties, and organizational interdependencies.

Progress might be made by thinking simultaneously about institutional, market, and normative setting characteristics that fall in the bailiwick of many social science disciplines. Attention might also be given to historical constructs external to organizations and to the simple impact of time on organizational development and operation. In some respects, this kind of extension to a larger set of environmental characteristics boggles the mind in terms of our ability to understand their impact on organizational life. However, we are struck with pursuing this needed extension because it is now clear that a small number of relatively amorphous variables, derived from an examination of man-made constructs that typically focus on values and norms, is insufficient for explaining variance in organizations.

At the onset this is a theoretical not an empirical issue. Researchers should look for the setting characteristics that are most likely to influence organizations and then *think about* the relation of those characteristics to one another and their probable impact on organizations. That the Tower of Babel may grow is a possibility. Strategies for ameliorating against this are discussed later.

2. *An adequate paradigm will integrate multidisciplinary views of organizations in any single research project and/or in reviews of existing research.*

The second most frequent criticism we hear is that cross-national organizational research is provincial because each researcher applies the constructs and methodologies typical to the academic domain in which he or she was trained or works. Clearly fragmentation came about as knowledge accumulated in the various social sciences. As more information is obtained, social forces for differentiation and fragmentation grow in the scientific community. Yet, if cross-national research is as depicted in Figure 1, by its very nature, it must draw at least from anthropology, economics, political science, sociology, and various brands of psychology. It is simply too much of an elephant not to. While it cannot be expected that any single study will draw from all the social sciences, it should show a recognition of how the problem under investigation might be viewed from different perspectives. Surely integrative reviews should go even farther. This issue is clearly not true for some kinds of single nation investigations. Examples are studies of human resource issues that draw legitimately and heavily on paradigms offered by industrial psychologists.

What can be done to make progress toward integration and counter forces of differentiation? If, by definition, good cross-national organizational research includes ideas of many people, who speak different disciplinary languages and have different blinders, implementation of social psychological prescriptions about good group problem solving and decision making is needed. The application of good management practices might work toward integrating ideas and honing research projects likely to produce quality results. Who is better qualified to do this across scientific communities than management researchers?

> 3. *Good research in this area will reflect agreement about sets of variables that should be studied.*

The kinds of activities discussed thus far provide suggestions on how to meet this criterion. At least camps of workers would agree among themselves about sets of variables that would most profit from empirical study. These camps could then set out to do the kind of strong inference research discussed by Platt (1964), developing studies in which competing hypotheses are tested within investigations. In the hard sciences, for example, there is at least a pattern of agreement within each discipline about what it is legitimate to study. In cross-national organizational research today, everything is up for grabs because there is no agreement. While this may be more true of cross-national research than of single nation organizational research or of research in disciplines contributing to both of these areas, cross-national reasearchers cannot shoulder the blame alone for this lack of focus.

> 4. *An adequate paradigm will reflect agreement about appropriate strategies or methodologies for conducting research.*

Historically, cross-national organizational research has borrowed heavily from the structuralist and static approaches developed in economics, psychology, and sociology and to a lesser extent, from the more fluid process approaches of anthropology and some aspects of sociology. Particularly because there is no agreement among the contributing disciplines about the appropriateness of one approach over another, there probably can be no agreement about this in cross-national organizational research.

One might hope for technological breakthrough to resolve conflict about research strategies. That is not a far-flung hope in an age of increasingly flexible high-speed computers that can be used for both data collection and analysis. Computers can be programmed to collect both process and static data or any other kind of information researchers think is interesting. We need mechanisms to analyze and integrate several kinds of data.

In the absence of a technological breakthrough, we must accept the fact that process and structural approaches usually seem best suited to different kinds of problems. However, for some problems we might take both approaches simultaneously (see, for example, Heller & Wilpert, et al., 1981) in an effort to see if one informs better than the other. The alternative is what currently happens. Warring parties face off, credibility of each side is discounted by the other, and arguments made by one side to the other go unheard. Static structural studies dominate, possibly because thay are easier to do and are more consistent with existing reward systems than are process studies. Because of what has just been said, this should be true, at least in the near future. Research strategy in cross-national organizational work is simply too onesided, and should be evened out by the presence of more process studies.

Agreement about methodology poses greater problems in cross-national than in single nation organizational research. This may be because there is greater variance in philosophies and research approaches among cross-national than single nation researchers. Single nation United States-dominated organizational research is typically done by people trained in more homogeneous values than people from different nations who do cross-national organizational research. Perhaps we are fortunate that social science research is conducted in few countries of the world. Imagine the vast heterogeneity of philosophies and approaches one would have to consider if the nature of modern scientific research were not determined by Western tradition.

The next three criteria have more to do with content than with building a general edifice of cross-national research that is something other than a house of cards.

5. *All organizational research needs to reduce reliance on rationalistic views of organizations.*

This criterion is certainly not limited to cross-national organizational research. In fact it is particularly applicable to United States-based single nation research. Rationalistic models, drawn primarily from economics, are so pervasive that their influence on cross-national work needs to be stressed. Attempts by some sociologists and political scientists to counter this influence may one day provide a more balanced set of models in organizational research in general. Perhaps infusion of this kind will be a smaller problem for cross-national researchers than for United States single nation researchers because some cross-national researchers embrace neo-Marxist positions to a greater extent than do the single nation researchers who are usually United States bred and trained.

6. *Adequately designed cross-national organizational research will include the role of history.*

Thinking about historical impacts on organizations, institutional, political, or religious changes that influence organizations and are influenced by them, is important to both single nation and cross-national organizational research. It is all the more important in cross-national organizational research because it might uncover clues about the gamut of external organizational variables likely to influence organizational activity. As an example, we know but rarely document the fact that an organization's

form is, in great part, determined by the social technologies available at
the time of its birth (Stinchcombe, 1965). Obviously, to the extent we
heed this criterion, we also include process in our work and heed the
following criterion.

7. *Time must be increasingly accounted for in all organizational research.*

We fail to include theories of time in our research, which results in the
measurement of "things" at one's convenience or when one is allowed
into organizations. With the advent of time series studies, the situation
has worsened in that the time intervals used appear, for the most part,
to be random. Often there are natural benchmarks to guide theoretical
development with regard to introducing time into our research: semester
and grade report intervals in schools, seasons in resorts, etc. In cross-
national organizational research the role of time is possibly more important than in single nation studies because time is thought about and perceived differently in different nations (Hall, 1973; McGrath & Rotchford,
1983).

8. *Studies should build upon one another so that a world view of organizations emerges.*

If cross-national research met both the first four criteria concerned with
research strategy, and the next three criteria concerned with content, this
last criterion would also be met. As stated previously, it is not expected
that all criteria discussed here will be met in any single research effort.
It is hoped, though, that a more coherent field can emerge that generally
meets these criteria.

By definition, cross-national research seeks a world view and without
it, such research cannot address the very real problems of survival faced
by organizations and their members. It appears to use that cross-national
researchers have been studying in Petri dishes problems that simply do
not fit into Petri dishes. The scope of the problems of interest in cross-
national organizational research is simply larger and more complex and
must be studied in different arenas with tools that reflect its size and
complexity. Obviously, single nation researchers should not be under
mandate to provide a world view to the degree that their cross-national
colleagues are.

Summary

It is a tragedy that, for the most part, those of us trained in management
skills have not applied them well to ourselves. One reason is that we
infrequently have the resources to do real multidisciplinary large-scale

work in which coordination and control problems are so crucial. Alternatively, even when we have the intellectual resources of good teams, we fail to take seriously in our everyday research activities that would encourage the emergence and discussion of different ideas, reduce posturing behavior, encourage creative problem solving, create team structures that encourage novel solutions, etc. If we could better grapple with the overlay of interpersonal social issues in research team activities, at least camps of researchers might reach greater integration about definitions of specific setting characteristics and appropriateness of materials contributed from a number of disciplines. Cross-national organizational research might then reflect the obvious fact that organizations are composed as much of people as they are of roles and role interactions, structures, etc. Both psychologists and sociologists would have equal time in identifying internal organizational relations and a responsibility to merge their thinking.

None of this can be accomplished without attention to changing reinforcement contingencies that operate in many research shops (perhaps more in the United States and Canada than in other parts of the world). Developmental efforts such as those recommended require considerable time. Many academicians are on a publish-or-perish clock to tenure and cannot afford to engage in such activities. Additionally, the entire social science research community operates under a norm in which everyone must answer correctly the question, "How much did you publish last year?" It is difficult to publish a great deal when one must not only think through a problem, collect, analyze, and interpret data, but learn the languages of colleagues in other fields, and from other nations, as well.

A SET OF MAJOR CROSS-NATIONAL
ORGANIZATIONAL STUDIES

One mechanism for assessing progress is to examine existing investigations across the gamut of comparative organizational research from micro to macro and to ask whether they meet these criteria. However, it is impossible to examine all existing research or even that completed in the last few years in this regard because of the sheer volume of research activity in this area.

Our perusal of the literature indicated that, as is true of single nation organizational research, cross-nation investigations fall into two categories. There are surveys and interviews that provide cursory snapshots of organizational life and there are ethnomethodological studies that provide thick description (Geertz, 1973) and questionable generalization. It is difficult, if not impossible, to integrate these two kinds of investigations.

The kinds of nets they cast and the kinds of fish these nets are likely to trap are as different as sharks and bluegills. While both are fish, we have as yet found no recipe for an adequate stew composed of the two. Again, as is true in single nation organizational research, the majority of the comparative investigations fall into the snapshot category. Consequently, a set of these investigations are examined in some depth.

Among the structural systematic comparative studies, we selected five for in-depth examination which by no means exhausts the population of such studies. They were selected for two reasons: they received widest "press" among such investigations and they represent research efforts conducted over rather long periods of time and usually by teams of researchers. That is, they are the "Big Macs" (Multi-Attribute Cultural Studies) in the area. Table 1 lists the selected investigations, the countries investigated, and sources of data. It then summarizes the questions asked in each study, underlying theoretical guidance, how culture or nation state is handled, the variables assessed, how they are assessed, and the findings.

Prior to discussing what might be learned from examining the investigations together, we offer brief summaries of what was done and indicate some inherent problems in each of the studies. In our summary of the studies taken together we will attempt to differentiate those problems particularly crucial to cross-national organizational research from those common also to single nation studies. At the outset it is important to keep in mind that although each study is flawed, they all represent Herculean efforts at conceptualizing and implementing large-scale comprehensive research programs.

England (1975): The Manager and His Values

England's five-nation, ten-year study is the most micro of the investigations here. It is an investigation of managerial values. England's value construct is derived from and builds on existing theory about values (for example, Allport & Vernon, 1969; Rokeach, 1968). One wonders why England chose to go cross-national, and this issue is never adequately answered. The author does not discuss how organizational, industrial, national, or cultural aspects might be expected to influence values and in fact, makes it clear that he is not studying organizations, industries, nations, or cultures (p. 4). If the domain of purposes for doing cross-national organizational research is covered in Figure 1, why does England go cross national when it appears in his initial chapters he is interested in none of the relationships in that domain?

England developed a scale (the Personal Values Questionnaire—PVQ) to measure value importance and value orientation along three dimensions (pragmatic, ethical, and affective). PVQ development is based entirely on United States-based research, building ethnocentrism into the study at its outset. It is entirely possible that this set of values is incomplete for managers from any nation and irrelevant for some. While England considers the issue of relevance in his conceptualization, the instrument itself is of such a nature that it probably cannot uncover irrelevance. Values are judged as high-medium-low importance, but any respondent would probably feel compelled to report that at least some of the sixty-six stated values are important.

The major theoretical notion underlying this investigation is that to the extent that individual behavior is a function of values, it is a joint function of the concepts important to that individual and his/her personal orientation. Concepts making up a person's operative values have the greatest impact on behavior. Intended and adopted values are less central and have less impact on behavior. Value profiles can be constructed for individual managers by listing concepts in the PVQ that are operative, intended, adopted, and weak (irrelevant) for that individual. Conditional probabilities are used to obtain individual value profiles. This rather complex scoring procedure may mask true similarities and differences within individual cognitions.

Individual responses can be aggregated for any group. Aggregation shows for each of the sixty-six concepts the number of individuals as a proportion of the group for which the concept is operative, intended, adopted, and weak. High proportion implies high behavioral relevance. A concept is viewed as operative if it fits his primary orientation (pragmatic, ethical, or affective); as intended if it is important but does not fit the primary orientation; as adopted if it fits the primary orientation but is average or low in importance; and as weak if it is neither important nor fits a primary orientation. Sixty-six scores derived this way are a bit difficult to compare across groups.

One behavioral relevance summary score for a group is generated by using a weighting scheme for all sixty-six concepts that weights the four value categories in descending order from operative to weak values. Behavioral relevance scores derived this way range from 0 to 100. Thus:

$$\text{Behavioral relevance of a construct for a group} = \frac{3(\text{operating value score}) + 2(\text{intended value score}) + 1(\text{adopted value score})}{3}$$

A second summary behavioral relevance score is simply the percentage of the total group for whom the concept is operative. This score varies from 0 to 100. The two summary scores correlate .97 to .99 across constructs.

Text continues on page 444

Table 1. A Set of Major Cross National Organizational Studies

Authors	Countries Studied	Questions	Theoretical Derivations	How Nation/Culture Treated
England (1975)	US, Japan, Korea, India, Australia (N = 5). Length of study: 10 yrs beginning 1966.	"Our starting point is the individual manager in a work organization; our interest is in his personal values and what they tell us about his work behavior and outcomes of this work behavior (p. 4)." B → f(IΩPO)c Behavior insofar as it is a function of values is a joint function of concepts important to him which also fit his personal orientation.	Consistent with Allport-Vernon-Lindzey and Rokeach approaches. Values are general, permanent, perceptual frameworks. They vary in terms of behavioral relevance. Values are concerned with goals of business, personal goals, group and institutional goals, ideas associated with people and ideas about general topics. Derived from American research. Values differ in behavioral relevance from nonrelevant to adopted, to intended, to operative.	Categorically
Hofstede (1980)	Argentina, Australia, Austria, Bahamas, Belgium, Bolivia, Brazil, Canada, Chile, Columbia, Costa Rica, Denmark, Dominican Republic, Egypt, Equador, Finland, France, Great Britain, Germany, Ghana, Greece, Guatamala, Hong Kong, Honduras, Indonesia, India, Iran, Ireland, Iraq, Israel, Italy, Jamaica, Japan, Kenya, South Korea, Kuwait, Lebanon, Libya, Malaysia, Mexico, Neth. Antibes, Netherlands, Nicaragua, Nigeria, Norway, New Zealand, Pakistan, Panama, Peru, Philippines, Portugal, South Africa, El Salvadore, Singapore, Spain, Sweden, Switzerland, Taiwan, Thailand, Trinidad, Turkey, Urguay, U.S.A., Venezuela, South Vietnam, Zambia, Yugoslavia (N = 40). Length of study: 5 yrs surveyed around 1968 and around 1972.	Argues people "carry 'mental' programs" which are developed in the family in early childhood and reinforced in schools and organizations, and that these mental programs contain a component of national culture (p. 11)." There are 3 levels of uniqueness in human mental programing; universal, collective, and individual. Values are mental programs that are relatively unspecific, having intensity and direction. Power distance and uncertainty avoidance derived from Aston work.	"'Culture's Consequences' aims at being specific about the elements of which culture is composed. It identifies four main dimensions along which dominant value systems in the 40 countries can be ordered and which affect human thinking, organizations, and institutions, in predictable ways (p. 11)."	Based on Kluckholn's (1951) and Kroeber and Parsons (1958) definitions. "In this book I treat culture as the collective programming of the mind which distinquishes members of the human group from another (p. 25)." "Power distance, uncertainty avoidance, individualism and masculinity satisfy Kluckhohn's criteria for "universal categories of culture (p. 313)."

Table 1. (Continued)

Variables Assessed	How Variables Assessed	Findings	% Variance Attributable to Nation/Culture Versus Other Variables	Number/Kind Respondents
Primary value mode of importance and three secondary modes; pragmatic, moralistic, affective and mixed. Decision making behavior Managerial success Job satisfaction Respondent age Organizational characteristics.	66 constructs culled from 200 by experts. Questionnaire (PVQ) formulated in English, translated and back translated. 5 perceptual incidents 4 Hoppock satisfaction scale questions: Age Organizational size Level of respondent Industry (mfg/non-mfg) Pay/age.	Values related to decision making, managerial success, and organizational context: (1) Some managers have pragmatic orientation, some ethical-moral. Few affect or feeling. (2) Values stable over time. (3) Values related to way managers behave on job. (4) Managers in different contexts (i.e. labor unions vs other) have different values. (5) Differences and similarities in values across countries.	Value patterns of country pairs significantly and positively related (r = 44 − .95). For relationship success and values, more similarities then differences across countries.	2556 managers: sampled from corporate executive directories, no public management, Av. age = 45, Av. yrs. mgr = 15.
Power distance Uncertainty avoidance Individualism Masculinity Demographics Country Data Underutilization Individual Differences	Questionnaire conceived and constructed in English. Translated and back translated. Selected 60 core and 66 recommended questions for questionnaire: ·Age ·Sex ·Years education ·Years with company ·Latitude ·Population ·Income inequality ·GNP ·Population growth ·Political systems ·Religion ·Ideologies ·Theories of power ·Educational systems ·Perception ·Control for level ·Functional responsibility ·Age.	(1) Main finding is that orgs are culture bound (p. 372). Refutes McClelland & Maslow by showing societal norms for uncertainty absorption and masculinity affect what will motivate people in different cultures. Colder countries are less masculine. Individualism is the culture dimension most clearly linked to the state of geographic-economic system. (2) Finds country clusters: Over time no sign of convergency. (3) Negative & positive shifts in power distance over time. (4) Shifts upward in uncertainty avoidance, individuality, and masculinity over time.	Much, according to author.	116,000 mgrs from one multinational. 50 occupations, some students from IMEDE.

Table 1. (Continued)

Authors	Countries Studied	Questions	Theoretical Derivations	How Nation/Culture Treated
Heller Wilpert Docherty Fourcade Fokking Mays Roig Weinshall t'Hooft (1981)	U.S.A., Britain, Germany, France, Netherlands, Spain, Sweden, Israel (N = 8). Length of study: 4 years.	Three objectives: to throw light on decision making processes, participation and power sharing; to link up with other research; to link up with current controversial debate about employee participation and industrial democracy. Tested assumption that successful mgrs in successful companies do not use same method of decision making in all circumstances. Develop notion that outcome of using power sharing methods is better use of human resource. Test proposition that circumstances that operate in close psychological proximity to decision maker influence decision choices more than more distal circumstances.	From Miles (1965) human relations/human resources model, influence of Glacier Metal experience (Brown & Jaques, 1965). Studies of organizational uncertainty. Transitory contingency perspective that focuses on critical circumstances that influence outcomes. "Research was guided by a set of hypotheses which were developed on the basis of ongoing theorizing and relevant research findings in the field of organization behavior, leadership and decision making (p. 61)" (American Style).	Categorically "Our research is not in a position to assess . . . specifical cultural factors."

Table 1. (Continued)

Variables Assessed	How Variables Assessed	Findings	% Variance Attributable to Nation/Culture Versus Other Variables	Number/Kind Respondents
degrees of decision participation. ills needed for job learning time needed to develop skill level necessary for L₁ job. ills used on job. o constraints. vironmental turbulence. ture changes. ork satisfaction. onsequences of participation. dustrial sector/technology. yad age.	Questionnaire (influence power continuum-IPC) assessed 12 specific decisions, decisions in general, extent participation relative to colleagues. Questionnaire Group feedback analysis (GFA) Objective data on skills, experience, educational level, company training, external training work related journals, and professional & scientific assns. Perceptions of time pressure, lack of role authority, organizational constraints, change (technical, customer requirements). Perceptions re: government and money constraints and general uncertainty. Perceptions 4 questions in 7 nations. Questions re: quality and speed of decision and satisfaction & morale of subordinates & bosses. Controlled across countries Length time L₁ − L₂ mgr work together. Example of scoring: PD1 = 3 questions. Score = 135 − 25 (question 1) + (% question 3 for time 1). Similar scoring other values.	(1) Subordinates describe more decision making than their superiors allow for. (2) Across all cultures high average participation. (3) Participation used less with colleagues than with subordinates. (4) Culture cluster thesis (Haire, et al. 1966, Lammers & Hickson, 1979) not supported. (5) Contradiction of widely held opinions of national stereotypes: rejects managerial gap thesis that claims that higher productivity of US firms compared to European due to greater participation and delegation. (6) Low skill differences. (7) L₁ − L₂ best prediction of decision style. (8) Most frequently used methods are prior consultation and joint decision making. (9) Successful managers vary decision making methods to suit the situation. (10) Participation increases with environmental uncertainty. (11) More participation in larger work groups. (12) The younger the manager the more variance in methods used. (13) The more skilled the manager the more participation used. (14) Managers judge own and other level skills as underutilized.	"The country factor accounts for 10–15 percent of the variance in decision making patterns (p. 101)." Corroborates culture bound thesis "Behavior of managers will be more strongly influenced by micro level variables close to the decision maker and less strongly by meso and macro level variables (p. 138)."	1600 level 1 and level 2 managers from 129 companies.

Table 1. *(Continued)*

Authors	Countries Studied	Questions	Theoretical Derivations	How Nation/Culture Treated
Heller Wilpert Docherty Fourcade Fokking Mays Roig Weinshall t'Hooft (1981)				
Hickson, McMillan & Associates (1981)	U.S.A., Britain, Canada, West Germany, Sweden, Poland, India, Jordan, Egypt and Japan. Length of study: Data collected in late 60's and early to mid 70's. The studies collected in this book were not part of a single coordinated research effort although all derive their foundations from the original Aston programme.	Basic question: "Are societal differences overwhelming, or are there stable relationships between such contextual factors and the structures of work organizations, relationships which hold good whatever the society in which the organizations are situated?" (p. 4). General hypothesis: Relationships between the structural characteristics of work organizations and variables of organization context will be stable across societies (p. 8). Some of the studies did consider alternative hypotheses such as the "late-development effect" (Dore, 1973) and the influence of political/economic systems.	The Aston Studies	Categorically

Table 1. *(Continued)*

Variables Assessed	How Variables Assessed	Findings	% Variance Attributable to Nation/Culture Versus Other Variables	Number/Kind Respondents
		(15) No homogeneous manager culture found. (16) Managers in different sectors use similar styles. (17) Superiors and subordinates use similar styles. (18) Decision task better determinant of style, than personal characteristics.		
Dependent variables: ·Formalization: the extent to which rules, procedures, communications and instructions are written in the organization. ·Functional specialization: degree to which activities of the organization are divided into mutually exclusive sets. ·Centralization: the locus of decision making authority. *Independent variables*: ·Organizational size. ·Organizational dependency: degree to which an organization is tied to others in its environment. Organizational technology: automaticity of the bulk of the equipment used by the organization (p. 203).	Standard schedules via structured interviews. *Dependent variables*: Formalization: the scoring (0/1) of existence of certain documents. Possible range: 0–41. Functional specialization: scoring (0/1) of whether specialists do certain activities. Possible range: 0–18. Centralization: Scored (0–5) on 37 recurrent decisions to assess "the lowest level in the hierarchy where assent must be obtained before legitimate action is taken" (p. 200). Possible range: 0–185. *Independent variables*: Organization size: logarithm of number of employees. Organization dependence: scored by 4 additive scales assessing dependence. Possible range: 0–11. a) status of organization unit b) size relative to owning group c) public accountability of the group. d) organizational representation on policy making body. Organizational technology: Scored according to the yardstick of automation of Amber and Amber (1962). Possible range: 0–5. (0 = hand tools; 5 = computer control).	(1) Overall product moment correlations showed constancy of the a) direction of the relations and b) the magnitude of relations as indicated below. Size positively correlated with formalization and specialization, negatively correlated with centralization. Size of parent organization positively correlated with formalization and specialization. Dependence positively correlated with centralization and usually positively correlated with formalization. (2) Still leaves room for cultural explanations.	Although the dominant theme is that of convergence, many of the studies did focus upon cultural or nation state variables (economic/political system) to explain some of the discrepancies that were found between countries. See Child and Kieser (chapter 4); Kuc, Hickson & McMillan (chapter 5); Badran & Hinings (chapter 7), Shenoy (chapter 8) and Azumi & McMillan (chapter 9).	Respondent: chief executive, officers. Sampled organizations from the very small (30 employees) to the very large (23,000 employees).

441

Table 1. *(Continued)*

Authors	Countries Studied	Questions	Theoretical Derivations	How Nation/Culture Treated
Tannenbaum Kavcic Rosner Vianello Wieser (1974)	Marxist/Socialist: Yugoslavia Israel Kibbutz systems. Free enterprise: U.S. Austria Italy. Israel Kibbutz: ideology of equality & formalized procedures to ensure it. Yugoslav plants in Slovenia (culturally close to Austria). Italian, Austrian orgs. traditional, non-participative bureaucratic pattern. Length of study: Cross-sectional study. The years the study was conducted are not clear.	"We explore in *Hierarchy in Orgs,* the general proposition that these conditions (private ownership abolished, a high degree of formal participativeness & equalitarianism) reduce if not eliminate the unintended dysfunctional effects of hierarchy (p. xix)."	Social-Psychological Approach "Hierarchy, an organizational characteristic, has profound psychological implications for members (p. 8)." Previous work: *Control in Organizations.*	Categorically. Basis for selecting socialist-Marxist vs free enterprise countries. In chapter 6 attempt to hold culture constant by looking at within country variances. Actually the independent variable differences in societal conditions (see 2nd col) are hypothesized to lead to differences in gradient of distribution of control, which in turn leads to differences in reaction and adjustment of members. Ideology of participation key factor here.

Table 1. (Continued)

Variables Assessed	How Variables Assessed	Findings	% Variance Attributable to Nation/Culture Versus Other Variables	Number/Kind Respondents
Decision making & control: ·Participation (formal) ·Interpersonal participation (informal) ·Distribution of control ·Bases of Power ·Rewards & Sanction ·Peer & Superior Control. Hierarchy: ·Attitude toward advancement ·Benefits/Requirements of hierarchy ·Authority Influence ·Opportunities on the job ·Physical Qualities of the job ·Salary ·Demographic characteristics. Gradients of reaction & adjustment: ·Satisfaction w/job ·Satisfaction w/knowledge ·Attitude toward leadership ·Satisfaction w/pay ·Sense of responsibility ·Initiative ·Motivation ·Psychological Adjustment ·Alienation ·Peptic ulcer ·Perceptions ·Ideals ·Ideals-actual.	*Questionnaire*: ·Back translated (items from earlier research). ·Administered to 35 in each plant. ·Preinterview & data on official position. *Hierarchical position*: ·distance from top & from bottom (may be 2 different measures). ·define length of "chain" individual is in; may be in multiple chains.	(1) Did separate analysis for large vs small firms; found many of the findings muted in larger firms. Suggests Kerr's logic of industrialism argument may be supported. (2) Interpersonal participation (informal) in following order: Kibbutz, U.S., Yugoslavia, Austria, Italy. (3) Kibbutz in Israel plants, while "power equalized," have a moderately high amount of control. (4) Counterintuitive: Yugoslavia high on participation yet respondents didn't have favorable attitudes or open communication. (5) *All* the countries had distribution of sex-hierarchical. Even egalitarian organizations are sexist! (6) Tannenbaum suggests that Kibbutz defy Michel's Iron Law of Oligarchy; benefits of being high in hierarchy don't offset the perceived costs. (7) All societies show hierarchy although Kibbutz & Yugoslav significantly less than US, Austria & Italy. (8) Formal participation: Kibbutz, Yugoslav, US, Austria, Italy. (9) Participative systems (Yugoslav & Kibbutz) show less steep gradients in influence/hierarchy but authority & influence increase with hierarchy regardless of country.	High with respect to participation.	10 plants in each country. Attempted to 'match' along lines of numbers of employees. All moderate size industries: plastics, nonferous foundry, food canning, metal works, furniture. Respondents: n = 35 in each org. (maximized the number of uninterrupted chains). Oversampled upper levels.

Table 1.   (Continued)

Variables Assessed	How Variables Assessed	Findings	% Variance Attributable to Nation/Culture Versus Other Variables	Number/Kind Respondents
Tannenbaum Kavcic Rosner Vianello Wieser (1974)		(10) Reaction and adjustment: Italy steepest gradient then Austria, US, Yugoslavia, Kibbutz. (11) Overall gradients relatively steep with respect to satisfaction with job and salary, sense of responsibility, motivation & initiative. Gradients less steep with respect to psychological adjustment, alienation, perceptions and ideals of members. Quality of adjustment: Kibbutz, US: high; Yugoslavia, Austria: medium; Italy: low. (12) Yugoslavia and Kibbutz: power equalized, managers less control compared with other countries, workers more.		

Text continued from page 435

While the data can generate a large number of comparisons across groups, it would be foolhardy to think any group of people can be described adequately with a minimal set of concepts, even only within the value domain. Yet, even this large number of comparable concepts is derived from a set of only three value orientations, suggesting the model itself may yet be too simplistic.

England investigates within-country variance among the concepts and cross-nation similarities and differences. Both similarities and differences are found within and between nations. As we might expect, possibly due to cultural homogeneity and nation size, Japanese managers have the most homogeneous values. Considerable variation exists among primary orientation of managers within the five countries. Again, it is difficult to know what this means if the PVQ does not tap a relatively full set of managerial values, or if some managerial groups the set tapped is largely irrelevant. The basic argument for these two criticisms has to do with constraints due to the way the instrument was developed. However, England's results are largely consistent with those of other studies of values, which supports this approach (see, for example, Cummings, Harnett, & Stevens, 1971; Hayashi, Harnett, & Cummings, 1973; Whitely, 1979).

England next examines relationships of values of "behavior." Behavior, however, is assessed in only two countries by providing managers with critical incidents requiring decisions about budgeting, a morally questionable procedure with regard to research and development funds, selection of an assistant, and delegation of authority. Managers are asked what they would do with regard to each incident. This strategy offers a strong possibility for obtaining correlated response error.

Managerial values are also related to success, age, job satisfaction, organizational size, organizational level, and organizational type (manufacturing versus nonmanufacturing). An interesting measure of success is used—pay relative to age. The age categories are decade intervals. There is some question as to whether managerial age is appropriately chopped at decades. Might one expect to see managers spurt to success somewhere in their thirties or somewhere between twenty-five and thirty-five? In addition, if time is handled differently in different nations, would a spurt toward managerial excellence in one age group in one country be at all relevant for managers in another country?

Many similarities emerged across the four countries used in relating values to success, leading England to suggest the use of the PVQ in making selection and placement decisions. More successful, as opposed to less successful, managers had values "seated in High Productivity, Profit Maximization, Managers, My Subordinates, Labor Unions, Ability, Aggressiveness, Prejudice, Achievement, Creativity, Success, Change, Competition, and Liberalism" (p. 69).

Job satisfaction is assessed using four items from the Hoppock Job Satisfaction scale. Managers in all five countries are fairly well satisfied. PVQ scores and job satisfaction are moderately and similarly related across the five countries. Interestingly, a different set of values is related to job satisfaction than to managerial success. Value profiles of different age managers show many significant differences and no consistent patterns across nations.

Relationships among values and organizational characteristics are highly country-specific, and form no overall international pattern or convergence. Job level is used as one organizational characteristic. We question, however, whether it is truly an organizational or an individual difference characteristic. It is important that researchers provide the theoretical rationale for categorizing their variables.

In regard to studies such as this, it is difficult not to slip into causal language. Do values cause job success? Does job success cause values? What else might a relation between values and success mean? If the measurement problems contribute to correlated response error, one might obtain results found here—except those concerning relationships of values to success. That is, values are highly and similarly related across nations to variables measured similarly to the way values are measured. Values are less similarly and consistently related across nations to variables measured differently than the values are measured. At the very least it is difficult to know what the relationships mean because the summary value scores tend to entangle whatever the primary measures contributing to them mean. Then, too, managers may feel compelled to call relevant what is not and wonder why they are not confronted with the value most relevant to them.

More optimistically, one might say that managerial values appear most highly related to more proximal variables (other cognitions like job satisfaction, their own success, etc.) and not as related to more distal stimuli (organizational size, etc.) and that these relations are consistent across nations, suggesting managers are managers are managers. This argues for looking for micro cultural factors (such as norms about various things, individual religious orientations, etc.) to explain individual differences and macro cultural aspects (for example, political or legal systems) in relation to more macro organizational aspects (size, differentiation, etc.).

Hofstede (1980): Culture's Consequences

Hofstede, in a five-year, forty-nation study also investigated values. His survey was conducted twice, once around 1968 and again around 1972, and includes 116,000 respondents in one multinational (HERMES) firm. By controlling for organizational characteristics, this study restricts generalizability. Various kinds of multinationals probably attract personnel somewhat different from one another on critical personality characteristics.

Hofstede begins with a detailed discussion of culture, appropriate approaches to cross-cultural research, and the relationship of values to culture. He presents several multidimensional classifications of culture, drawn from various academic disciplines. Ultimately, however, he uses Kluckhohn's (1951) consensus of anthropological definitions:

> Culture consists in patterned ways of thinking, feeling, and reading, acquired and transmitted mainly by symbols, constituting the distinctive achievements of human groups, including their embodiments in artifacts, the essential core of culture consists of traditional . . . ideas and especially their attached values [Kluckhohn, 1951: p. 25].

Values, then, are attributes of individuals and collectivities. According to Hofstede, values are broad tendencies to prefer certain states of affairs over others. This, says Hofstede, is a simplification of Kluckhohn's position. Thus, conceptually for Hofstede, values and culture are interlocked and inseparable. Values are nonrational mental programs that are relatively unspecific and are programmed early in a person's life. They have both intensity and direction.

> *Culture's Consequences* aims at being specific about the elements of which culture is composed. It identifies four main dimensions along which dominant value systems . . . can be ordered and which affect human thinking, organizations and institutions in predictable ways. . . . In this book I treat culture as "the collective programming of the mind" which distinguishes the members of one human group from another [pp. 11, 25].

Hofstede's theoretical reasoning resulted in two of his value dimensions, and statistical analyses yielded the other two. For his first two dimensions, power distance and uncertainty avoidance, he offers indepth theoretical reasoning. In the first case, the basic issue involved is inequality, an issue for which different societies have found different solutions. Hofstede follows Mulder (1976), who notes in his power distance reduction theory that subordinates will try to reduce the power distance between themselves and their bosses, and bosses will try to maintain or enlarge it. Hofstede contends that the level at which both these tendencies will find their equilibrium is societally determined. Does this mean they are culturally determined?

Hofstede next states that uncertainty about the future is a basic fact of human life. People use the domains of technology, law, and religion to cope with uncertainty. "In organizations these take the form of technology, rules, and rituals" (p. 153). Hofstede notes that nonrational means of dealing with uncertainty in organizations are rarely recognized in organizational theory and that only March and his colleagues' (Cohen, March, & Olsen, 1972; Cyert & March, 1963; March & Simon, 1958; March & Olsen, 1976) theories make room for them. Actually, Hofstede misses writers like Meyer and Rowan (1977) and Zucker (1977), who have discussed such phenomena for a long time. The author notes that power distance is related to concentration of authority while uncertainty avoidance has shared meaning with structuring activities, which are variables in the Aston studies.

The remaining two dimensions were basically derived through factor analyses of the data base. Individualism describes the relation between the individual and the collectivity prevailing in a given society. It reflects the way people live together, and whether emphasis is on individual pursuit or group productivity. Masculinity reflects the duality of the sexes as a fundamental fact with which societies cope in different ways.

To this point Hofstede handles the conceptualization of his variables and their derivation from culture better than any of the other authors mentioned here. In several instances he burrows deep into the fabric of a society for examples, as when in his discussion of power distance he cites Alpert's summary of societies in which "filial piety, associated with rigidly hierarchical ordering of all social relations, draws together in a single formation masses of verbal and behavioral data" (cited in Hofstede, 1981, p. 99). His arguments for selecting the values he focuses on are more complete and convincing than are England's. One comes away with the sense that Hofstede has tapped at least four major issues that must be contended with in all societies. Finally, Hofstede relates his own thinking to other dominant conceptualizations in organizational research.

The major problem in Hofstede's work begins with the way he renders variables operational. Here we examine the assessment of power distance as an example. The central question in Hofstede's three–item power distance index (pdi) is "How frequently, in your experience, does the following problem occur: employees being afraid to express disagreement with their managers?" That kind of indirect questioning makes assumptions about respondents' frames of reference when answering such questions. This question is answered on a five-point scale. Four types of managerial decision making are described and the two other pdi questions ask respondents to indicate their preferred type and their perceptions of their bosses' type. Actual computation of country pdi scores uses mean scores for the five-point scale question and percentages for the other two questions. The mean for the five-point scale question is multiplied by twenty-five to make its range and contribution to the pdi relatively equal to that of the other questions. In the case of the actual manager question, 1968 and 1972 data are combined, but for the preferred manager question only data from the first time period are used. The formula for combining the questions is:

PDI = 135 − 25 (mean score of the five-point scale question)
         + (% perceived manager) − (% preferred manager).

A constant of 135 is added to give country index values a range between 0 and 100. The questions are conceptualized in English, translated into numerous other languages, and back translated. the pdi score is a subsidiary or country or ecological score, not an individual score.

To compose country scores, mean scores of respondents in seven occupational categories are used. Controlling for occupational category also controls for age and sex, because few occupations have women in them and age is correlated with job title. Each occupational category contributed equally to country scores regardless of actual numbers of respondents in the occupational category. Data for missing occupational categories were extrapolated. If data for one time period but not for the other were available, data for the missing period were derived by correcting for the mean shift that occurred in the country's other occupational categories between the two surveys. If data for a category were missing for both time periods, "they were derived from the other categories' data correcting for the occupational differences found in the total world data" (p. 73). Stability correlation coefficients were computed for countries between the first and second surveys. These vary from .12 to .95 and Hofstede considers scores stable if the coefficient exceeds .50. Questions with stability coefficients of less than .39 were excluded from further analyses.

The most serious problems with Hofstede's work have to do with measurement. He criticizes other authors for their ethnocentrism in using United States-developed measures in other countries, but apparently does the same thing. There is no evidence this research is informed by theory developed from different cultural perspectives. Another serious difficulty is that the meanings of at least the power distance and uncertainty indices are completely entangled. The uncertainty index is developed similarly to the pdi. Combining data from differently formatted questions in the way it is done for these indices makes it impossible to tell what the indices really measure. The individualism and masculinity indices were developed through more straightforward factor analyses of five-point scale questions; the handling of missing data through creating data compounds problems of interpretation. Developing scales using the same data base on which hypotheses will later be tested introduces further problems. Finally, the time period for each data collection is sufficiently long to create potential problems of synchrony (Kenny, 1975).

Hofstede compares survey results over the two time periods included, but offers no theory of time to justify his selected interval. The questions comprising the power distance and uncertainty avoidance indices do not shift together over the four-year period. The individualism and masculinity indices increase over time. There is no sign of convergence between extreme countries; rather, divergence seems to occur.

The four value dimensions were related to country and occupational level data. In addition, when employee categories included sufficient numbers of both males and females, the four dimensions were associated with sex. They are also looked at in relation to country economic growth, latitude, population size, population growth, population density, and organizational size.

The patterns of each of the four values correlated with country data are different in each case. In the case of power distance Hofstede suggests, based on correlational analyses, a causal choice that includes these other variables. For example, in low pdi countries parents put less value on children's obedience, there is more need for education of lower strata people, there is technological momentum for change, less centralization of power, etc., than in high pdi countries. There are strong differences in correlations with national geographic, economic, and demographic indicators for wealthy and poor nations. Individualism and masculinity are correlated with large numbers of country-level indicators, and the author states that these correlations provide pictures of the individualism-collectivism, and masculine-feminine dimensions of societal norms.

The HERMES data are related to similar survey data obtained from IMEDE students and then looked at in relation to other survey studies of small numbers of firms, including the Tannenbaum work to be discussed here. Hofstede carefully integrates his data with what is known from other investigations and for each of the four value dimensions examines possible impacts of such factors as history, legislation, religion, political systems, etc.

In the case of each of the four value dimensions, Hofstede discusses origins and consequences of high and low national scores on the value. To do this he uses vast literatures, drawing implications from other studies as well as his own. This is a truly formidable job, but one wonders how much we really know from it. The author tries to integrate results of very different kinds of studies that produced data that are definitely not synchronous across studies. For example, national data from one year are compared with attitudinal data generated at a completely different time. In the case of the pdi a causal chain of origins is developed using, at best, correlational data.

Hofstede intends to study different nations and maintains that level of analysis throughout, relying as he does on aggregate value scores. However, in his policy chapter he discusses implications of his findings and other theories for policies meant to control the behavior of individuals. He does so without disentangling various theories meant to apply to different aggregate levels, for example Herzberg's and Maslow's theories developed to discuss individual differences and his own findings that cannot be disaggregated to the individual level.

Finally, while Hofstede's initial treatment of culture is commendable, he ultimately looks at the four values in relation to a garbage can of societal variables. While he tells us values are cultural variables, derived as they are from one's upbringing, are such societal factors as legislation, religion, etc., also indicators of culture? If so, culture in this study is correlated with culture.

Heller and Wilpert with Docherty, Fourcade, Fokking, Mays, Roig, Weinshall, and t'Hooft (1981): Competence and Power in Managerial Decision Making

Heller and Wilpert and their colleagues report a four-year, eight-nation investigation of organizational decision making designed by a multinational team of researchers. The research had three purposes. First it "throws light on the process of decision making, participation, and power sharing in 129 successful companies as seen from the policy making senior two levels of the organization" (p. xiii). A second objective was to link up with other research, and a third objective was to link with current controversial debate about employee participation and industrial democracy.

These authors avoid dealing with culture at all.

> We avoid [the term] culture for two reasons. First, it has strong emotional implications and secondly any reasonable definition of "culture" refers to deep set characteristics of personality, habit and value patterns, tradition, and the social heritage of a community transferred from generation to generation [p. 41].

Heller and his colleagues examine five methods of managerial decision making (making own decision without explanation, own decision with explanation, prior consultation, joint decision making, and delegation). They call the range of choices across these methods the influence power continuum (IPC).

The model on which the research is based is derived from the American-made human resources approach (Miles, 1965). These authors argue that they are in search of relative truths, of relationships between two or more variables that are assumed to exist only under certain circumstances. Thus, they indirectly indicate their interest in extending variance on some independent setting characteristics and examining the impact of those on decision making.

They predict that successful managers in successful companies do not use the same decision making methods in all or most situations. Successful managers are predicted to use relatively autocratic strategies when decisions affect their organizations broadly and are immediately important to subordinates. When an issue is of great immediate importance to a subordinate but is not critical organizationwide, it tends to be shared between boss and subordinate. A second aspect of the model is that the outcome of power sharing is better use of human resources. The third aspect is that circumstances influence choice, particularly those in closest psychological proximity to the decision maker.

In each of the eight countries in the sample, organizations were selected to match for products, technologies, and managerial level. Thus, 129 organizations contributed 1600 managers to the study. Managers were assembled in groups, the research was explained, and fourteen short questionnaires were administered. The research team then compiled questionnaire results and fed them back to the managers. The discussions that followed were tape recorded, resulting in a second round of data collection (group feedback analysis).

In addition to asking how decisions are made generally, the questionnaires included items about job satisfaction, similarities and differences in level-one and level-two jobs, the time and skills a subordinate would need to learn the incumbent's job, job constraints, environmental turbulence, skill utilization, skill qualifications, and education. Thus, the majority of the data discussed were obtained by paper and pencil techniques, and the study suffers all the problems of these techniques. An interesting measure of managerial success takes into account managerial age relative to the mean managerial age in an industrial sector at a particular level and the variability of age within that sector. This measure is favorably compared to England's measure of success.

A decision centralization score was obtained by multiplying by another number the percentage of time managers responded to each of the five IPC dimensions with regard to a particular decision, adding the five resulting numbers together, and dividing by 100. As in work previously discussed, convoluted methods of arriving at scores mask the meaning of these scores. Factor and cluster analyses were used to assess internal consistency of the forms. Correlational, analysis of variance, and regression analyses procedures were used along with nonparametric techniques to analyze relationships posited.

Heller and Wilpert et al. are strong advocates of group feedback analysis as both a potential data collection device and as a tool for organizational development. Their book, however, focuses much more on statistical analyses than on process data. This may illustrate the severe difficulties involved in combining structural and process approaches to studying a problem. While these authors did not develop a process approach as extreme as ethnomethodology, it is still difficult to think about how to analyze appropriately and interpret group feedback analysis data. One might have expected at least some content analyses that could have been compared to the more rigid statistical data.

The results of the study showed managers used more than one decision-making method, depending on the circumstances. Managers bring subordinates into the process considerably more frequently than they do colleagues at the same level. Participation is apparently used to improve the quality of decision making and to improve communication. However, group feedback analysis showed that managers had serious reservations about engaging in group decision making. Participation increases with perceived environmental uncertainty, size of the work group, the age of the manager-subordinator dyad, and managerial skill. There were more similarities across nations than differences in managerial decision making, one form of convergence. In some industries (representing different technologies), there is considerably more participation than in others. A number of other findings, many of which are not directly relevant to decision making, are discussed. The authors discuss implications of their findings for managers; the level of analysis at which their theory is discussed.

The major problem with this study, other than failure to diverge as much as it appears they had promised from a paper-and-pencil approach, is in the level of sophistication of theory. The authors feel they provide theoretical advancement. We feel many of the findings are common sensical. One suspects that a good review of American managerial decision-making research would show many of the same kinds of findings produced by these authors, and in addition, the weaving together of a more theoretically tight set of variables.

Hickson, McMillan, and Associates (1981): Organization and Nation

This book is a collection of cross-national extensions of the original Aston studies (Pugh, Hickson, Hinings & Turner, 1968, 1969a, 1969b). The papers are about organizations in such diverse societies as Poland, the United States, West Germany, Jordan, Egypt, Britain, Canada, Japan, Sweden, and India. The specific hypotheses addressed differ somewhat from chapter to chapter, but the overwhelming concern is to enlighten the fundamental question first posed by Hickson, Hinings, McMillan, and Schwitter (1974): "Are societal differences overwhelming or are there stable relationships between such contextual factors and structures of work organizations, relationships which hold whatever the society in which the organizations are situated" (p. 66). This question is a microanalytic approach to the convergence hypothesis. All the studies utilize the methodology and measures of the Aston group (Pugh, et al., 1969a, 1969b; Hickson, Pugh, & Pheysey, 1969; Inkson, Pugh, & Hickson, 1970; McMillan, Hickson, Hinings, & Schneck, 1973).

Sampling strategies differed in the various studies, but because the Aston works are interested in the influence of organizational size on the structure of bureaucracies, the organizations sampled are primarily large ones. Even in countries in which firms tend to be small, the authors preferred to focus on the largest organizations. (Ayoubi states that in Jordan only 55 firms out of 589 have more than thirty employees, yet these are the ones he sampled.) Still, compared to the original Aston samples with a mean size of 3,379 employees per organization (Pugh et al., 1968) and 1,542 employees per organization (Child, 1972), much more variation in firm size is achieved here. The organizations range in size from very small (30 employees) to very large (23,000 employees). The status of the organizations, measured by the dependence score, varies from independent organizations to branches or subsidiaries of larger organizations.

It is difficult to assess the veracity of these studies without voluminous debate over the measures and methodology of the original Aston work. These debates already exist (Aldrich, 1972; Crozier & Friedberg, 1980;

Pugh & Hickson, 1972; Scott, 1981; Starbuck, 1981). Our particular concern is with problems conceptualizing and measuring size, technology, and dependence that seems evident in this research.

Kimberly (1976) reviewed eighty comparative studies of size and organizational structure, and detailed the theoretical and methodological problems with the construct of size. He cites Child's study showing a range of intercorrelations of various measures of size (e.g., physical capacity, personnel, organizational inputs) which suggests that different ways of conceptualizing size have different implications for structuring organizations. Another oft-cited problem with size is that it is not independent of other aspects of organizing; operations can and are divided at managerial discretion.

As a technology measure, the authors use the yardstick for automation developed by Amber and Amber, "an estimate of the automaticity of the bulk of the equipment used by the organization in its workflow activities— 'bulk' meaning the modal or most frequently occurring piece of equipment" (Hickson, McMillan & assoc., 1981: p. 203). As Hickson et al. (1974) explain, due to problems of inconsistency in the interrelationships among scales of technology used in the original Aston studies, they focused on the single automaticity mode (p. 69). Theoretical justification for focusing on automaticity is not given. The authors simply indicate that "its inclusion in this paper is due to its being common to all the studies analyzed and does not imply that it alone is an adequate measure of technology" (Hickson et al., 1974, p. 69). This represents the strength and the weakness of building on previous research; the research begins to take on a reality of its own.

The original Aston studies have been criticized for taking a too narrow view of technology (Fry, 1982; Gerwin, 1979; Kmetz, 1978; Scott, 1975) by focusing only on operations rather than materials or knowledge, two other aspects of technology. Further, there is a level of analysis problem with technology. It may mean different things and have vastly different repercussions depending on the unit of focus. In most of the Aston studies, the chief executive provides all information. It is questionable whether top management has the same perspective of technology as someone working on the line.

The final independent variable, organizational dependence, measures the degree to which an organization is tied to others in its environment. Hickson et al. (1974) use three of the original seven scales assessing dependence. They justify this by noting the high intercorrelations among scales (Inkson et al., 1970). Thus, they obtain data on origin (foundation), status (independent principal unit or branch), and relative size of the unit. Other studies in the book also measure organizational representation on the policy makeup body and public accountability of the group as aspects of dependence.

The data were collected via structured interviews with chief executives. For the most part, confirmatory data were not collected. Thus the major source of information in all the studies were the perceptions of one or two individuals. As questions are asked on nonpersonal aspects of the organization, the use of perceptual measures is not too detrimental. Yet evaluating an organization's key attributes with the input of so few individuals is a definite weakness. Organizations may look decidedly different depending on whether one's vantage point is that of a chief executive officer or a foreman.

Scales are constructed for dependence, automaticity, functional specialization, formalization, and centralization. The authors state that the unidimensionality of the scales was established by Pugh et al. (1968, 1969) and Inkson et al. (1970). "Organizations are scored either 1 or 0 depending on whether a firm possesses each item, and the scores are added without differential weighting" (p. 69). Each organization gets an overall score for each scale which is then used to determine country level scores, the mean of all the organization level scores in a country. These studies are superior to the earlier Aston work in one important aspect. By handling structural measures separately, the authors avoid the theoretically vacuous construct "structuring of activities," which was arrived at through factor analysis and which lost the theoretical veracity of the original measures.

A problem that surfaces throughout the book is that of explaining differences which were found between countries. The better studies in the volume couple the Aston measures with a sufficiently well-versed interpretation of the cultural, economic, and sociopolitical milieu of the country. For example, although Child and Kieser (chapter 4), in their study of German and English organizations, find the magnitude and direction of the relationships between context and structure to be in line with the contingency thesis, they did find that German firms tend toward greater centralization. They explained this difference by examining German culture and analyzing the differences in managerial roles between German and English managers.

Alternative hypotheses posited are the late development effect (Dore, 1973) which states that countries which industrialize late will have more developed bureaucracies from the start or that the particular political economic regime will have an effect on organizational characteristics. An example of the latter is given in Badran and Hining's study of Egyptian organization's (chapter 7). The authors state that Egypt's planned economy requires "considerable information for producing plans, targets, monitoring and evaluation" which influences the level of specialization and formalization (p. 131).

Kuc, Hickson and McMillan (chapter 5), in their comparative study of Poland, Britain, Japan and Sweden, find an especially high level of centralization in Poland that they associate with the role of the state in organizational decision making and the influence of central planning. They also find Poland has a higher level of specialization (focusing on the mean and range of scores). This, they suggest, may be a reflection of the late development effect.

One problem alluded to by the editors stems from changing the scales to fit the research aims in a particular country. This prevents comparison with results from other countries. Yet a researcher must make his/her own choices within a given study; and the Aston scales are not perfect. This is an issue warranting debate among the "Aston" scholars. There are certain problems with the constructs (automaticity not being a complete technology score; dependence being relatively narrowly defined) and with the method of data collection. Yet a vast data base of relatively comparable measures has been developed in ten countries. Given the paucity of comparable data to date, this in itself is no mean achievement.

As for results, what is the relationship between context and structure and is it stable across societies? Although product moment correlations for the most part show constancy of direction and magnitude, there are enough discrepancies for Hickson and McMillan to be cautious in their concluding chapter. Use of nonequal interval scales limits the comparisons of the numerical scores that can be made. As a result, both researchers and readers are left asking, "How close is similar enough?" It is necessary to eyeball correlations between certain factors to try to discern where there are significant differences. Although several of the authors allude to these problems and to the fact that causality cannot be inferred from correlations, there is an overwhelming suggestion that size as a "contextual variable" has an inordinate effect on the structuring of organizations.

Size is viewed as having a much greater impact than operations technology, which is viewed as being "little, if at all, related to structural features beyond those directly linked with the workflow itself" (p. 16). We believe this to be an overstatement.

First, technology was measured in a much less encompassing manner than was size. That is, the conceptual "size" of the two variables as measured is not the same and consequently comparisons of their correlations with other variables are suspect. While most of the work in the Aston tradition points to the ubiquity of size as having an important effect on structure, technology too has been found to have significant effects in other studies (see Fry 1982 for a comprehensive review). Pfeffer and Le-

Table 2. Relationships between Organizational Structure and
Organizational Context

	Formalization	*Specialization*	*Centralization*
Size	+	+	−
Size of parent organization	+	+	
Dependence	+ usually		+

Source: Hickson, McMillan, et al., 1981, Chapter 12, p. 193.

blebici (1973) found the relationship between technology and structure to
vary, given the level of competition in the environment. Unfortunately
no assessment is made of this aspect of the environment. In the final
analysis, the relationships among technology, size, and environment are
interactive. Overall, Hickson and McMillan (chapter 12) suggest that the
following conclusions in Table 2 be taken "with a pinch of salt" (p. 193).

While most of the studies did corroborate the relations indicated by
Hickson and McMillan, the tone of their book suggests that cultural and
nation-state variables are important. The "bold hypothesis" of the early
cross-national Aston studies (Hickson, et al., 1974) that states that con-
text-structure relations are stable across societies is somewhat muted. In
their concluding chapter Hickson and McMillan are content to say, and
rightly so, that similarities in work organization across societies seem to
outweigh differences. But why?

*Tannenbaum, Bogdan, Rosner, Vianello, and Wieser (1974): Hierarchy in
Organization*

Tannenbaum and his colleagues explore the general proposition that
certain conditions, the abolition of private ownership, a high degree of
formal participation and egalitarianism, reduce, if not eliminate, the unintended and dysfunctional effects of hierarchy. This work is a cross-
national extension of *Control in Organizations* (Tannenbaum, 1968),
which presented a research agenda for the study of control. Its approach
is a social psychological one, in the tradition of Likert, based on the
underlying tenet that hierarchy and organizational characteristics have
profound psychological implications for organizational members (1974).

The study was conducted in five countries: Israel, Yugoslavia, Austria,
Italy, and the United States. The countries were chosen for differentiation
along the dimensions of private ownership, degree of formal participation,
and egalitarianism. The kibbutz in Israel and the plants in Yugoslavia
were organized ostensibly in a Marxist socialist manner, whereas the

plants in the United States, Austria, and Italy, in free enterprise countries, presumably were organized in the traditional nonparticipative bureaucratic pattern. The underlying theoretical argument is that these differences in conditions of society lead to differences in the gradient of distribution of control, which in turn lead to differences in the reactions and adjustments of organizational members.

The authors begin by presenting short discussions of the management systems in the five countries. These provide excellent introductions for the uninitiated and a common starting point for all readers. More important, they clarify the justifications for the various hypotheses presented. All cross-national work would benefit from similar exposition.

Ten plants are sampled in each country and matched on size (number of employees) and type of industry (five industries: plastics, nonferrous foundry, food canning, metal works, and furniture). Tannenbaum et al. collect their data with survey instruments (translated and back translated) administered to thirty-five people in each plant. They oversample the upper levels of the organization to maximize the uninterrupted chains of authority that are selected. One should note that Tannenbaum and his colleagues are careful to distinguish between large and small plants. They indicate that while their hypotheses are valid in the smaller plants, the larger plants may more closely support the Kerr et al. (1960) "logic of industrialism" argument.

The researchers ask questions grouped into three categories: decision making and control, hierarchy, and gradients of reaction and adjustment. Several of the decision making control items are on participation; in fact, this book may tell us more about participation than it does control. Data are also collected on the official hierarchical position each person holds (two measures of distance from the top and bottom of the organization), as well as information about the length of the reporting chain the respondent is in.

Through their analysis of control graphs, Tannenbaum et al. state that hierarchy exists in all societies, although the kibbutz and Yugoslavian plants have flatter gradients than the plants in the other nations. This is substantiated by the fact that kibbutz and Yugoslav plants have less steep gradients of control than do plants in the other nations. Authority and influence increase with hierarchy regardless of nation. In the power-equalized plants of Yugoslavia and the kibbutz, managers have less control compared to other countries. There is also a moderately high amount of control in these plants.

While the Yugoslav plants were high on formal participation, members did not have favorable attitudes or open communication. Satisfaction with one's job and salary, a sense of responsibility, motivation, and initiative, tend to increase with hierarchy while psychological adjustment and alienation do not. In all countries, organizations have distributions of sex that were hierarchical; even the egalitarian organizations were sexist! The interaction between superior and subordinate is characterized by informal participation in the American and kibbutz plants but not in the Yugoslav, Italian, or Austrian ones. Thus, "differences between the two systems [Marxist and Capitalist] are not consistent on all criteria; differences occur within the two systems as well as between them" (1974, p. 211).

While most of these findings make sense, we have problems with methodology used by Tannenbaum et al. that render our acceptance of them problematic. The conceptualization of power and control which they use is quite narrow, especially given current developments. Even if evaluated in terms of the level of theoretical theory development in 1974, they would have been better off with some structural measures of power and control. In order to accept these results, one must accept reputational perceptual measures of control, influence, and power. The authors feel their large sample sizes insure their measures are valid. We do not consider this sufficient.

Tannenbaum et al. use the mean average of all respondents, managers, workers and executives, to determine control and participation. Surely managers and workers view distribution of control differently; difference scores would have been useful. Means of individual responses are plotted for control graphs and country-level inferences are made from these aggregated, individual-level scores. The concept "total amount of control" is difficult to understand. If the question on control had been divided into substantive areas, it might be easier to make sense of it. A better measure might be to ask who makes decisions about budgets, vacations, schedules, hiring, adjustment of machines, and so forth.

Finally, we question the use of control graph methodology which is not a graph in the mathematical sense. And while a picture is said to be worth a thousand words, in this case it appears to lend more veracity to the measures than is warranted. A few more statistical measures, especially measures of dispersion around means, would have been helpful.

Summary

Many of our criticisms of the studies reviewed here are true of single-nation as well as cross-national research. Frequently, however, these faults are writ large when research goes cross-national. For example, the world is filled with criticisms of the original Aston work (see, for example, Aldrich, 1972; Crozier & Friedberg, 1980; Scott, 1981; Starbuck, 1981) and when these same issues and methods are taken abroad, further problems abound. We can, though, limit our view solely to the cross-national arena and evaluate these studies in two ways.

First, we can ask whether they meet their own stated goals (see Table 1). Generally they fail to do so for two primary reasons. The first is that linkages between construct and operation are weak and/or the aggregations and analyses are so convulted that the meanings of the inputs to them are lost. Second, in one form or another, these studies stack the cards in favor of desired outcomes.

Alternatively, we can look more intensely at the problems identified that may be more important to cross-national organizational research than to single-nation studies. The most severe problems in these investigations are weak conceptualization and poor linkage from concept to operation. When one varies setting characteristics, which is the entire reason for cross-national research, the weakness of setting concepts influences the inferences that can be drawn, and the weakness of other constructs is highlighted to a greater degree than in single-nation work. All of the studies reviewed are subject to this criticism. Also falling into this domain are issues concerning ethnocentrism, treating environments too narrowly, questioning the relevance of certain variables in certain settings, the correlation of culture with aspects very similar to culture, lack of clear conceptualization and justification of constructs, and the use of indirect questioning that makes assumptions about respondents' frames of reference.

The second most severe problem in these studies is the way measures are obtained, aggregated, and analyzed. This problem is surely more severe in cross-nation than single-nation studies because problems of meaning are inherently more difficult in the former than the latter. When one weights survey data in complex ways, assumes responses from people at different organizational levels are equivalent, derives scores in complex ways, and analyzes data using complex techniques, inferences become problematic.

Level of analysis problems are also inherent in a number of these studies. As one illustration, technology may mean different things at different levels of the organization. Another example is the use of country-level data to inform policy relevant to individuals in organizations. By definition, in cross-national research one adds a level of construct (environment) in addition to what is usually seen in single-nation work. Greater care must be taken with regard to consistency across theory, measurement, analysis, interpretation, and application of results than in investigations involving few levels of concern (Roberts, Hulin, & Rousseau, 1978).

Related to levels of analyses are problems concerning time. We see several here, including lack of justification for time intervals over which data in any one investigation are collected, attempts to integrate studies in which data are collected over considerable ranges of time (lacking in synchrony) or are collected using very different "envelopes" of time, and lack of attention to time at all.

This set of investigations, as is true of the gamut of cross-national investigations, is not inclusive of organizational life. For example, the Aston studies fail to think about the role of people in organizations though their respondents are all people. In studies such as Tannenbaum's and Hofstede's, important dimensions of organizational life are ignored and severe problems in aggregation are exposed.

There is, also, a slavish adherence to paper-and-pencil measures, resulting in static pictures of organizational life. Even in the one situation in which some process data were collected, little use was made of them. Similarly, to all contingency approaches these investigations

> cast organizational life in rigid deterministic terms. In an extreme form variables like technology, organizational structure, task, or turbulence may be introduced as straightjackets allowing little freedom of choice and strategy. People . . . emerge as puppets in a network of contingency relations. [Crozier and Friedberg cited in Heller and Wilpert, 1981, p. 57]

Given these circumstances, it is not surprising that we have not developed a cumulative research base or any overarching world view of organizational life. We made no attempt here to fully review cross-national organizational research and the issue of cumulation cannot be addressed on the basis of a few studies. However, our review of cross-national work published in major academic journals during the last ten years (Roberts & Boyacigiller, in press) comes to the same conclusion. That the studies looked at here are almost nonintegratable is a more serious problem in terms of pushing forward future research.

Finally, as a set these studies are representative of most cross-national organizational research in that they fail to take advantage of the strengths of the basic social science disciplines from which they emerge. For example, Heller and Wilpert and their colleagues do not really provide a thick description as would an anthropological ethnomethodologist, though they flirt around it. England and Hofstede derive their respective work from a dominant psychological approach to attitudes. Because attitude research is one of the oldest aspects of social psychology, sufficient time has passed for it to be brought into the mainstream of cross-national research. However, current social psychology attitude research is considerably more sophisticated than is this work. In the more macro areas that should be informed by the sociological literature, as for example participation, we do not see much borrowed from that literature in either the work of Heller and Wilpert and their colleagues or in the research of Tannenbaum and his colleagues.

Generally, then, we do not see the strengths of anthropology contributing either to cultural identification (Hofstede's is the only investigation that takes anthropology seriously) or methodology in this kind of research. Neither the important organizational constraints generated by political science and economics nor the theories developed in sociology and psychology are incorporated into this research. All in all, the studies reviewed here do not sufficiently meet the criteria set out for an adequate paradigm of cross-national organizational research. Is the elephant too large or the researcher too blind?

THREE MAJOR ISSUES

Short of calling for a moratorium on cross-national organizational research, what can be done? Progress will be slow until (a) underlying contributing disciplines are better developed, (b) researchers borrow more carefully from those disciplines, and (c) they develop theory and avoid the pitfalls in translation of concepts to data gathering and interpretation. The rest of this paper addresses these issues.

Rather than focusing on all eight criteria for good scientific cross-national organizational research simultaneously, a seemingly impossible task, we discuss three issues we feel should be tackled first. These issues are chosen because they emerge in both criterion development and in our review of the Big Macs. Obviously, other important issues are ignored. For example, while it is important to find ways to develop a truly multidisciplinary approach to the area and avoid aggregation problems, this is not discussed in this paper. Instead we address those issues which we think have the greatest possibility of immediate payoff. They are also selected because, while we agree that each is important in single-nation organizational research, we think they are vastly more important in cross-national research for reasons stated previously. The issues are:

1. The tendency of the game in cross-national organizational research to focus more specifically on environments in which organizations exist. This is often not true of single-nation organizational research.
2. The introduction of serious time problems. Time is used differently in different cultures. Researchers usually compound this problem by failing to specify theories of time underlying their work, gathering data over randomly selected intervals, and measuring and relating variables that reflect different time intervals.
3. Static studies that cannot assess the permeability of organizations by their environments.

Culture

As we stated previously, definitions of culture inherited from anthropologists often are not heuristically valuable to organizational researchers. Often this is because they cannot be made operationally independent of the very organizational constructs in which we are interested. Second, they tend to cast a qualitatively different net than the one cast by issues in which cross-national organizational researchers are usually interested. When cross-national organizational researchers borrow definitions of culture from anthropologists or develop their own, they typically do not worry about correspondence rules between those external organizational constructs and internal constructs of interest to them.

Then too, when systems are organized according to different principles, their treatment as a single system of environed and environing events is problematic (Klausner, 1971). Thus, for example, the notion of man/machine systems is imprecise because the two, man and machines, are organized around different principles. If one system is the environment for another, it must naturally influence it and boundary interaction mechanisms must be specified. Physical facts, says Klausner, have physical environments, but physical and chemical facts may have social interpretation and share boundaries with social and psychological facts.

Klausner states that "social organization is borrowed from the British anthropologists as a generic term referring to the whole complex of relations which connect members of a society" (1971, p. 37). If man and nature are related as parts of an organic system, independent definitions of them are not feasible. One must look at one in relation to the other. A problem with all organizational research is that it fails to do this. The cross-national organizational researcher is in an ideal position to remind his or her single-nation research brethren of this necessity.

If we are to pursue cross-national organizational research, we cannot wait for the wish of true interdisciplinariness to come true. As a stopgap measure, we offer here a simple set of specifications one might follow. These specifications emerge from examining several frequently invoked definitions of culture, which include the following: "Culture is best seen not as complexes of concrete behavior patterns—customs, usages, traditions, habit clusters . . . but as a set of control mechanisms, plans, recipes, rules, instructions for the governing of behavior" (Geertz, 1973, p. 44). " 'Culture' refers to the learned repertory of thoughts and actions exhibited by members of social groups—repertories transmissible independently of genetic heredity from one culture to the next" (Harris, 1979, p. 47). "Most cultures and the institutions they engender are the result of having to evolve highly specialized solutions to rather specific problems" (Hall, 1981, p. 5).

The common element in these definitions is that they impose constraints on human behavior. Thus, it is difficult to differentiate those constraints discussed by anthropologists from those discussed by organizational/environmental researchers. We might say, then, that from an organization's perspective, culture is the sum of a set of external constraints that permeate it and influence its micro and macro responses. But because of its breadth, this definition of culture is heuristically useless.

How can one narrow this broad definition to give it heuristic value? A general rule is to select an organizational problem of interest and then borrow or develop a theoretical argument relating this problem to a set of relatively proximal external constructs. Proximal setting characteristics should be focused on first because their links with organizational characteristics are less likely to be interfered with by other unknown constructs than are linkages of distal setting and internal organizational characteristics. Once those constructs are identified, the search for boundary interchange mechanisms can begin.

In the long run, as organizational science develops an agreed-upon set of substantive issues for examination and requisite methodologies, the field will provide real building blocks for cross-national research. Alternately, a paradigm shift will occur and most of what we have said will fall by the wayside. In the short run, pockets of researchers will define pockets of organizational constructs and into these pockets cross-national researchers can place external environmental constructs. Not only should they look to previous cross-national research for identification of these constructs but to the organizational-environmental literature, as underdeveloped as it is. Existing large-scale economic and political data banks can be pursued to enhance theoretical development since it is unlikely even pockets of researchers have resources to collect large-scale national data.

The Role of Time in Organizations and Organizational Theories

"Only when time is a part of our research designs is it possible to move from a static to a process view of organizations" (Roberts, Hulin, & Rousseau, 1978, p. 92). These authors go further and warn us that time series studies can generate misinterpreted results if the wrong time interval is chosen. Here we face two problems relevant to incorporating time into our thinking and research. The first has to do with how time is conceptualized in organizations and nations and the second has to do with time issues to which we, as cross-national researchers, are particularly susceptible in our research.

McGrath and Rotchford (1983) provide a philosophical review of the nature of time in organizations. They note that each culture develops a dominant conception of time. "The general culture underlying recent and current western, industrialized societies is a context . . . within which we . . . are embedded. That culture generally views time as: homogeneous, divisible, linear, measurable, singular, objective, and abstract" (p. 7). It is thought that these conceptualizations about time were set down and constrained by the cultural and organizational constraints existing at the time of the industrial revolution.

It is not clear to us that this particular view of time is correct in all organizational life even within a single culture, much less across cultures. While the form and function of manufacturing organizations of the industrial revolution may have molded our view of time, the current cultural forces in nations into which those organizations have expanded may have modified this view. On the cross-national organizational researcher's agenda should be the issue of whether or not this is true, and if true, to what extent. Here is an area in which cross-national research can feed back into mainstream single-nation organizational knowledge. Cross-national organizational researchers should be best equipped to ask questions about the degree to which various conceptualizations of time and time usage in organizations are a function of factors external to the organization or characteristics of the organization itself. Exciting research possibilities abound now because organizations are shifting from a manufacturing/industrialized production mode to service and high technology modes, and at the same time are spreading to parts of the world grossly out of synchronization with both older and newer forms of modern organizations.

We caution against researchers and theoreticians in our area engaging in finely articulated existential discussions of time. The mesh of that kind of philosophical net is woven more finely than needed to catch the typical organizational fish. Rather, researchers should examine carefully how organizational participants think about and use time and weave the results of these examinations into their cross-national theorizing (see, for example, Graham, 1981). McGrath and Rotchford (1983) indicated that organizations attempt to resolve time problems through scheduling, synchronizing, or coordinating segregated parts and activities and by allocating time across different sets of activities. A starting point for cross-national organizational researchers might be to examine the differential degrees to which these three activities may be focused on or given attention to at all in organizations of different national settings.

In terms of their own use of time and inclusion of it in their research, cross-national organizational researchers must attend a quite different set of issues. First, it may be that incorporating time into our theories will clarify whether our science is a mere reflection of history designed to perpetuate current Western values (Gergen, 1973; Ekehammar, 1974).

Then, in thinking about problems to be examined in any investigation, researchers must ask themselves if the problem itself or the organizational form in which it is stuck have any natural time benchmarks. Such natural benchmarks should be explicated and worked into theory and empirical exploration. For example, if one were interested in the impact of pay and benefit packages on employee behavior, it might be advisable to tie empirical data collection to periods of change with regard to these variables, perhaps based on renegotiation of union contracts. Alternatively, one might have theoretical reason to tie data collection to periods of stability. In addition, too often we see data on one set of variables collected at one time and under one set of conditions correlated either directly in a single study or indirectly in discussions across studies with data on another set of variables collected at a different time and under a different set of conditions (see, for example, Hofstede, 1980).

Researchers should examine the socio-technical forms of organization available at the period of a particular organization's birth and ask whether these forms make some different predictions about the use of time than did organizational and social forms available to early builders of modern production organizations. This needs to be done since we know that organizations, once established, are difficult to change.

As Roberts, Hulin, and Rousseau (1978) state, at least three problems emerge in research when we fail to consider time in our theorizing. First, data collected for samples at different points in time are often combined— with little attention given to whether supposedly similar conditions for all samples are, in fact, similar. This easily occurs more in cross-nation than single-nation organizational research for a number of reasons. When multidisciplinary teams work to design research they tend to control for factors such as industry type, organizational size, etc., but fail to control for factors heavily associated with time like the business cycle (see, for example, Heller and Wilpert, 1981). When they go cross-national, researchers are likely to extend data collections over lengthy time intervals in which virtually anything can happen in one setting and not in another (for example, see England, 1975).

A second problem is that there is considerable research comparing measurements of the same variables across arbitrary intervals (see, for example, Hofstede, 1980). This problem relates back to the issues of time and theory previously discussed. A theoretically specified causal interval is never mentioned. This is particularly important in cross-national research if one thinks that environmentally determined cycles, like annual representation of some culturally important phenomenon, influence organizational life. Some sort of interactionist perspective laid atop structural views, as mentioned before, may help here.

The third problem discussed by Roberts, Hulin, and Rousseau is more directly related to the nature of measurement itself. Data points related to one another may reflect vastly different time frames. For example, when one correlates job satisfaction and productivity, the satisfaction measures may stretch over a much longer period of remembered time than the two weeks in which productivity data were obtained. The Aston measures of organizational size and technology, as another example, may relate variables enveloping different units of time. Lack of synchronization among measures is likely to result. It is our hope that future research will bring into synchrony issues relating time to organizational life through focus on the envelopes of time associated with both environmental and organizational variables.

The Static Nature of Static Studies

More than any other kind of organizational research, cross-national organizational research is concerned with the permeability of organizations to their settings and to the values and issues people in those organizations bring with them. Thus, studies in this area should take on a relational character. Few of them do; most are of the rigid statistical nature we have seen. Again, that Heller and Wilpert and their colleagues did not convincingly lay on their structural data the rich process data they must have collected attests to the potential impossibility of merging the two. But try we must if we are ever to obtain a more complete picture of organizational life. Typically, relational theorizing has been of a higher quality than the data generated by such theorizing. The cross-national researcher then has the double problem of trying to integrate with existing structural data a more fluid theoretical perspective and deriving from that perspective strong observations.

One suggestion might be to impose on cross-national studies a multiple level of analysis framework and see if progress can be made in the design and conduct of future research. For example, if participation continues to be a ''hot topic'' in cross-national research, one might impose a social information processing model on the issues of interest to Heller and Wilpert, perhaps a la Weick (1979), at the individual managerial level. This would focus attention in different ways on aspects of participation, such as information availability, that are of interest to researchers like Heller and Wilpert and their colleagues. It would also focus attention on different issues, one of which might be how managerial values (England, 1975) in various nations condition acceptability of information to a manager receiver.

At the organizational level, a symbolic interactionist overlay a la Glaser and Strauss (1968), or a relational interactionist perspective a la Crozier and Freidberg (1980), would draw attention to different correlates of participation than, for example, the hierarchies that interest Tannenbaum et al. As Crozier reminds us, "once we have accepted diversity we must then go on to investigate why certain rules, relational arrangements and game constructs are in force rather than others. Cultural analysis is an answer to this question" (1980, p. 101). Unfortunately these authors fail to deal further with culture. Crozier provides one metatheory that might be paralleled by the clever cross-national researcher to our structural data bases in order to provide richer data sets. For example, following Crozier we would look at the power games that indirectly structure the strategies actors can devise and perhaps gain a better understanding of the relation of hierarchy and control, adding to what Tannenbaum et al. have to say.

At the national or societal level, a thick description approach (Geertz, 1973) might help us better understand the permeability of organizational boundaries. At the very least it would caution us against the error of viewing environments as one-way causal influences on organizations and direct our attention more specifically to reciprocal relations between organizations and their environments.

An Example

As an example of how one might proceed, we use the issue of participation which not only manifests itself in different ways and at different levels of organizations but was the subject of two of our Big Macs. Participation seems particularly alive and well in cross-national organizational research.

Our first task is to think about ways participation manifests itself throughout organizations. One might come up with a list of macro organizational manifestations that includes such factors as representation on committees, centralization of decision making, job titles of participants in critical decision making, representation on boards of directors, etc. Consistent with our earlier caution in thinking about including time in our theorizing, one might work into a theory of participation notions such as lengthening time for decision processes as a corollary to shortening time for decision implementation. At the micro level of organizational analysis, participation could manifest itself in perceptions that job incumbents have about the degree to which they participate, the broadness or narrowness of individuals' views of organizations that may be corollaries of their own participation beyond the scope of a single job, the degree to which individuals are active in work activities, etc.

The appropriateness of this or some other list of manifestations of participation depends on the list maker's theoretical orientation and his or her reliance on findings from past studies. One might begin with such a list and think about probable importance of the various entries on it, honing and pruning to develop a tight conceptual network. The variables we selected are easily translated into measures. Researchers will have to think about how to make translations such that both static and process methodologies can be evoked. Some aspects of participation (and anything else) lend themselves more to one approach than the other but effort should be given to blending the two.

The next task is to think about external factors that potentially influence participation. Again, it is important to keep separate the micro and macro aspects of participation so that variables proximal to each will be thought about and so that dimensionally similar variables are examined together. For example, it makes intuitively better sense to examine the relation of something like regional rather than national employment levels to something like job scope. Job scope in any organization may be influenced by the available local labor pool. It is less likely influenced by more aggregate national data. Again, the list of constructs generated is dependent on the theoretical bent of the researcher and on contributions from past research. These characteristics categorized as macro might be societal and institutional variables while proximal characteristics might include industry factors.

With regard to the macro organizational participation characteristics discussed here, it appears to us that one reasonable societal institutional factor to look at initially is the impact of legislative systems. Thus, one should examine relationships of legislation across settings to the macro manifestations of participation in organizations in those settings. Legislation may also have an historical consequence for organizations. For example, one might hypothesize that it would be difficult to find high participation in organizations which are not in democratic settings. This would lead to developing an external organizational network of variables that somehow consider isms, (capitalism, socialism, communism, etc.) and borrow from comparative economics. As we saw in our review, in part this is done when one looks at a variable like abolition of private ownership (Tannenbaum, et al., 1974).

In examining societal relations to organizations, one cannot ignore the convergence-divergence argument so often seen in the literature (Meyer, 1970; Meyer, Boli-Bennet, & Chase-Dunn, 1975; Kerr (1983). Kerr (1983) provides the most well-developed version of convergence and some of his nine dimensions along which convergence should be assessed might well be examined in relation to organizational participation. The dimensions are content of knowledge, mobilization of resources of production, organization of production, patterns of work, patterns of living, economic structure, political structure, and patterns of belief. Kerr states that worldwide convergence is occurring on the first six and divergence on the last three dimensions. While we do not agree with Kerr's assessment, the dimensions he offers and the data bases he cites might be considered in developing a theoretical position with regard to environmental influences on participation. As indicated above, it appears to us that economic and political structures influence organizational participation. That such macro characteristics are difficult to measure and enormously subject to error (see Morgenstern, 1963) almost goes without saying. Perhaps this is why economists have been unsuccessful in their attempts to solve worldwide economic difficulties. Until we merge constructs drawn from diverse bodies of thought, we really will not maximally benefit from what various social science disciplines have to contribute to cross-national organizational research.

More proximal to organizations, one might think the existence of institutional precedents for sharing power would influence organizational participation. Industry level analyses could be used to flesh out such potential influences. Additionally, one could abstract from the organizational environmental literature, as we have seen done in previous studies, a notion like industry turbulence or uncertainty. Conceptualization should not forget the role of time which may be reflected in market changes, such as concentration, that are surrogates for uncertainty (Pfeffer & Leblebici, 1973).

In conceptualizing micro aspects of organizational life (the things people do in organizations), one must focus on a different set of inputs. It makes intuitive sense to include values and beliefs (drawn from society) about such matters as authority relations or the salience and importance of work in one's conceptualization. Level of individual education, or the content of knowledge available, following Kerr, are variables potentially related to individual manifestations of organizational participation. One could, too, draw from Triandis' (1981) seventeen dimensions of culture a set of those factors that appear most relevant for understanding participation. The most likely candidates appear to us to be past-present-future orientation, the degree to which human nature is perceived as changeable, whether human nature is perceived as good, bad, or neither, and finally three dimensions Hofstede also uses: power distance, inequality, and uncertainty avoidance.

As with other sets of variables we have discussed, some of these lend themselves better to process and some better to static appraisal. Process appraisal forces a concern for time. It is probably easier to develop some sort of relational interactionist perspective at this level of concern than it would be in thinking about societal macro organizational relationships. This appears to us a good place to start.

Here we have offered a set of outcroppings of participation that seem both important and fairly easily translated into measurement. Our perusal of past cross-national organizational research, recent organizational environmental work, and some work in political economy and comparative economics suggests a set of potential external influences on participation. It seems possible to us to take a limited set of variables such as this and develop well-reasoned theory and hypotheses about them and translate these into measurement, thus meeting some of the criteria elaborated previously. A danger is in ending up with a plethora of variables (see, for example, Farmer and Richman's (1970) seventy-six by twenty-nine matrix of economic and political country indices). This can be avoided by careful attention to theory construction.

CONCLUSION

Our perusal of major issues in cross-national organizational research and of a set of "Big Macs" in the area suggests both the negative and positive aspects of this kind of research. On the negative side, researchers from various disciplines have not yet been pushed into jointly developed theoretical systems with agreed upon exemplars, styles of inquiry, and major substantive issues. They are still confusing science and engineering and are generally conducting static and largely eclectic studies that have "different theoretical, methodological, domain, and intent bases" (England, Negandhi, & Wilpert, 1979, p. 13), and typically carry a made-in-the-USA label. One has the feeling that mud is still being flung at a wall in hopes that some of it will stick. As a result, an adequate feel has yet to be obtained for what constitutes appropriate internal organizational and external environmental constructs of interest, much less boundary interaction mechanisms between them. The roles of society, culture, nation state, time, and history are neglected. By no means is all of this to be blamed on cross-national researchers. They are victims of constraints imposed by the more basic contributing social science disciplines.

On the more positive side, we do not feel cross-national organizational research is as heavily dominated by elite managerial concerns as is single-nation United States organizational research. Following Doob (1980) the investigations generally do reach a little higher than they might have if the author's gaze had been fixed on only one society. There is always the problem of team research seeking the lowest common denominator, and most cross-national organizational research will have to be of the team variety. Compared to ten years ago, current research is more ambitious and pays more attention to theory. More interesting questions are posed and greater attention is given interrelated sets of issues. Some decentering is occurring.

What does all of this say about the elephant? First, the six blind men are now sixty-six and the elephant is larger. More attention has been given to the whole of the elephant, possibly because researchers are beginning to examine contiguous parts, possibly because they are less blind. On the other hand, not much is known about characteristics that comprise the elephant and we are totally deficient when it comes to predicting his behavior.

With regard to addressing and solving pressing societal problems, we are making all the speed of a glacier in a world that requires much more. In addition to the more specific suggestions offered here, we close by suggesting renewed effort in developing a true science that can address these problems.

REFERENCES

Aldrich, H. Technology and organization structure: A reexamination of the findings of the Aston group. *Administrative Science Quarterly*, 1972, *17*, 26–43.

Allport, G. W., & Vernon, P. T. *A study of values*. Boston: Houghton Mifflin, 1931.

Barnet, R. J., & Müller, R. *Global reach*. New York: Simon & Schuster, 1974.

Benedict, R. *Patterns of culture*. New York: Houghton Mifflin, 1934.

Beres, M. E. & Portwood, J. D. Sociological influences on organizations: an analysis of recent research. In A. R. Negandhi & B. Wilpert (Eds.) *The functioning of complex organizations*. Cambridge, MA: Oelgeschlager, Gunn & Hain, 1981.

Bhagat, R. S., & McQuaid, S. J. Role of subjective culture in organizations: A review and directions. *Journal of Applied Psychology*, 1982, *67*, (5), 653–685.

Brown, W., & Jaques, E. *Glacier project papers*. London: Heinemann, 1975.

Campbell, D. T. Ethnocentrism of disciplines and the fish-scale model of omniscience. In M. Sherif & C. W. Sherif (Eds.), *Interdisciplinary relationships in the social sciences*. Chicago: Aldine, 1969.

Child, J. Organization structure and strategies of control: A replication of the Aston study. *Administrative Science Quarterly*, 1972, *17*, 163–176.

———. Culture, contingency, and capitalism in the cross-national study of organizations. In L. L. Cummings & B. M. Staw (Eds.), *Research in Organizational Behavior* (Vol. 3). Greenwich, CT: JAI Press, 1981.

Child, J. & Kieser, A. Organization and managerial roles in British and West German companies: An examination of the culture-free thesis. In C. J. Lammers & D. J. Hickson (Eds.), *Organizations alike and unlike*. London: Routledge & Kepan Paul, 1979.

Cohen, M. D., March, J. G., & Olsen, J. P. A garbage can model of organizational choice. *Administrative Science Quarterly*, 1972, *17*, 1–25.

Crozier, M. *The bureaucratic phenomenon*. Chicago: University of Chicago Press, 1964.

Crozier, M., & Friedberg, E. *Actors and systems: The politics of collective action*. Chicago: University of Chicago Press, 1980.

Cummings, L. L., Harnett, D. L., & Stevens, O. V. Risk, fate, conciliation and trust: An international study of attitudinal differences among executives. *Academy of Management Journal*, 1971, *14*, 285–304.

Cyert, R. M., & March, J. G. *A behavioral theory of the firm*. Englewood Cliffs, NJ: Prentice-Hall, 1963.

Dachler, H. P. *Constraints on current perspectives for the cross-cultural study of organizations*. Presented at 39th annual meeting of the Academy of Management, Atlanta, 1979.

Demsetz, H. Antitrust: Problems and proposals. In J. F. Weston & M. E. Granfield (Eds.), *Corporate enterprise in a new environment.* New York: K.C.G. Productions, 1982.

Dixon, K. Is cultural relativism self-refuting? *British Journal of Sociology,* 1977, *28,* 75–88.

Doob, L. W. The inconclusive struggles of cross-cultural psychology. *Journal of Cross-Cultural Psychology,* 1980, *11,* 59–73.

Dore, R. *British factory—Japanese factory: The origins of national diversity in industrial relations.* Berkeley, CA: University of California Press, 1973.

Ekehammar, B. Interaction in personality from a historical perspective. *Psychological Bulletin,* 1974, *81,* 1026–1048.

England, G. W. *The manager and his values: An international perspective from the United States, Japan, Korea, India, and Australia.* Cambridge, MA: Ballinger, 1975.

England, G. W., Negandhi, A. R., & Wilpert, B. *Organizational functioning in a cross-cultural perspective.* Kent, OH: Kent State University Press, 1979.

Evan, W. M. Measuring the impact of culture on organizations. *International Studies of Management and Organization,* Spring 1975, *5,* 91–113.

Farmer, R. N., & Richman, B. M. *Comparative management and economic progress.* (2nd ed.). Bloomington, IN: Cedarwood Press, 1970.

Ferrari, S. Cross-cultural management literature in France, Italy and Spain. *Management International Review,* 1974, *14*(4–5), 17–23.

Fry, L. W. Technology-structure research: Three critical issues. *Academy of Management Journal,* 1982, *25,* 532–552.

Galbraith, J. K. *The new industrial state.* Boston: Houghton Mifflin, 1967.

Geertz, C. *The interpretation of cultures.* New York: Basic Books, 1973.

Gergen, K. J. Social psychology as history. *Journal of Personality and Social Psychology,* 1973, *26,* 309–320.

Gerwin, D. The comparative analysis of structure and technology: A critical appraisal. *Academy of Management Review,* 1979, *4,* 41–51.

Glaser, B. G., & Strauss, A. L. *The discovery of grounded theory.* London: Weidenfeld and Nicolson, 1968.

Graham, R. J. The role of perception of time in consumer research. *Journal of Consumer Research,* 1981, *7,* 335–342.

Haire, M., Ghiselli, E., & Porter, L. W. *Managerial thinking: An international study.* New York: Wiley, 1966.

Hall, E. T. *The silent language.* New York: Anchor Press/Doubleday, 1973.

————. *Beyond culture.* Garden City, New York: Anchor Press, Doubleday, 1981.

Harbison, F., & Myers, C. A. *Management in the industrial world: On international analysis.* New York: McGraw-Hill, 1959.

Harris, M. *Cultural materialism: The struggle for a science of culture.* New York: Random House, 1979.

Hayashi, K., Harnett, D. L., & Cummings, L. L. *Personality and behavior in negotiations: An American-Japanese empirical comparison.* Working paper, Institute for International Studies and Training, Fujinomuya, Japan, 1973.

Heller, F. A., Wilpert, B., Docherty, P., Fourcade, J. M., Fokking, P., Mays, R., Roig, B., Weinshall, T., & t'Hooft, W. *Competence and power in managerial decision-making: A study of senior levels of organization in eight countries.* New York: Wiley, 1981.

Hickson, D. J., & McMillan, C. J. *Organization and nation: the Aston programme IV.* Westmead, England: Gower Publishing Company Limited, 1981.

Hickson, D. J., Pugh, D. S., & Pheysey, D. C. Operations technology and organization structure: An empirical reappraisal. *Administrative Science Quarterly,* 1969, *14,* 378–397.

Hickson, D. J., Hinings, C. R., McMillan, C. J., & Schwitter, J. P. The culture-free context of organization structure. *Sociology*, 1974, *8*, 59–80.

Hofstede, G. *Culture's consequences: International differences in work-related values.* Beverly Hills: Sage Publications, 1980.

Hydebrand, W. V. *Comparative organizations: The results of empirical research.* Englewood Cliffs, NJ: Prentice Hall, 1973.

Inkson, J. H. K., Pugh, D. S., & Hickson, D. J. Organization context and structure: An abbreviated replication. *Administrative Science Quarterly*, 1970, *15*, 318–329.

Kenny, D. A. Cross-lagged panel correlation: a test for spuriousness. *Psychological Bulletin*, 1975, *82*, 887–903.

Kerr, C. *The future of industrial societies: Convergence or continuing diversity?* Cambridge, MA: Harvard University Press, 1983.

Kerr, C., Dunlop, J. T., Harbison, F. H., & Myers, C. A. *Industrialism and industrial man: The problems of labor and management in economic growth. Cambridge, MA: Harvard University Press, 1960.*

Kimberly, J. *Organizational size and the structuralist perspective: A review, critique, and proposal. Administrative Science Quarterly*, 1976, *21*, 571–597.

Klausner, S. Z. *On man in his environment.* San Francisco: Jossey-Bass, 1971.

Kluckhohn, C. The study of culture. In D. Lerner & H. D. Lasswell (Eds.), *The policy sciences.* Stanford, CA: Stanford University Press, 1951.

Kmetz, J. A critique of the Aston studies and results with a new measure of technology. *Organization and Administrative Sciences*, 1977/1978, *8*, 123–144.

Kroeber, A. & Kluckhohn, C. *Culture: a critical review of concepts and definitions.* Cambridge, MA: Peabody Museum, 1952.

Kuhn, T. S. *The structure of scientific revolutions* (2nd ed.). Chicago: University of Chicago Press, 1970.

March, J. G., & Olsen, J. P. *Ambiguity and choice in organizations.* Bergen: Universitelsforlaget, 1976.

March, J. G., & Simon, H. A. *Organizations.* New York: Wiley, 1958.

McGrath, J. E., & Rotchford, N. L. Time and behavior in organizations. In B. Staw & L. Cummings (Eds.), *Research in Organizational Behavior* (Vol. 5). Greenwich, CT: JAI Press, 1983.

McMillan, C. J., Hickson, D. J., Hinings, C. K., & Schneck, R. E. The structure of work organizations across societies. *Academy of Management Journal*, 1973, *16*, 555–569.

Meyer, A. G. Theories of convergence. In C. Johnson (Ed.), *Change in communist systems.* Stanford, CA: Stanford University Press, 1970.

Meyer, J. W., Boli-Bennett, J., & Chase-Dunn, C. Convergence and divergence in development. *Annual Review of Sociology*, 1975, *1*, 223–246.

Meyer, J. W., & Rowan, B. Institutionalized organizations: Formal structure as myth and ceremony. *American Journal of Sociology*, 1977, *83*, 340–363.

Miles, R. E. Human relations or human resources? *Harvard Business Review*, 1965, *43*, 148–163.

Morgenstern, O. *On the accuracy of economic observations.* Princeton. NJ: Princeton University Press, 1973.

Mulder, M. Reduction of power differences in practice: The power distance reduction theory and its applications. In G. Hofstede and M. S. Kassem (Eds.) *European contributions to organization theory.* Assen, Neth.: Van Gorcum, 1976.

Negandhi, A. R. Cross cultural management studies: Too many conclusions, not enough conceptualization. *Management International Review*, 1974, *14*(6), 59–67.

Pfeffer, J. Merger as a response to organizational interdependence. *Administrative Science Quarterly*, 1972, *17*, 382–394.

Pfeffer, J., & Leblebici, H. The effect of competition on some dimensions of organizational structure. *Social Forces*, 1973, *52*, 268–279.

Platt, J. R. Strong inference. *Science*, 1964, *46*, 347–353.

Pugh, D. S., & Hickson, D. J. Causal inference and the Aston studies. *Administrative Science Quarterly*, 1972, *17*, 273–276.

Pugh, D. S., Hickson, D. J., Hinings, C. R., & Turner, C. An approach to the study of bureaucracy. *Sociology*, 1968, *1*, 61–72.

———. Dimensions of organizational structure. *Administrative Science Quarterly*, 1969a, *13*, 121–134.

———. The context of organization structures. *Administrative Science Quarterly*, 1969b, *14*, 91–114.

Roberts, K. On looking at an elephant: An evaluation of cross-cultural research related to organizations. *Psychological Bulletin*, 1970, *74*, 327–350.

Roberts, K. H., & Boyacigiller, F. N. A survey of cross-national organizational researchers: their views and opinions. *Organization Studies*, in press.

Roberts, K. H., Hulin, C. L., & Rousseau, D. M. *Developing an interdisciplinary science of organizations*. San Francisco: Jossey-Bass, 1978.

Rokeach, M. *Beliefs, attitudes and values*. San Francisco: Jossey-Bass, 1968.

Schell, J. *The fate of the earth*. New York: Knopf, 1982.

Scott, W. R. Organizational structure. *Annual Review of Sociology*, 1975, *1*, 1–20.

———. *Organizations: Rational, natural and open systems*. Englewood Cliffs, NJ: Prentice-Hall, 1981.

Starbuck, W. H. A trip to view the elephants and rattlesnakes in the garden of Aston. In A. H. Vondevan and W. F. Joyce (Eds.), *Perspectives on organizational design and behavior*. New York: Wiley, 1981.

Stinchcomb, A. L. Social structure in organizations. In James G. March (Ed.), *Handbook of organizations*. Chicago: Rand-McNally, 1965.

Tannenbaum, A. S. *Control in organizations*. New York: Basic Books, 1968.

Tannenbaum, A. S., Kavcic, B., Rosner, M., Vianello, M., & Wieser, G. *Hierarchy in organizations*. San Francisco: Jossey-Bass, 1974.

Triandis, H. *Some dimensions of intercultural variation and their implications for interpersonal behavior*. Technical report. Department of Psychology, University of Illinois at Urbana-Champaign, 1981.

Udy, S. H. Technical and institutional factors in production organization: a preliminary model. *American Journal of Sociology*, 1961, *67*, 247–254.

von Alemann, H. International contacts of university staff members: Some problems in the internationality of science. *International Social Science Journal*, 1974, *26*, 445–457.

Weick, K. *The social psychology of organizing* (2nd ed.), Reading, MA: Addison-Wesley, 1979.

Whiteley, W. A cross-national test of England's model of managers' value systems and their relationship to behavior. In G. W. England, A. R. Negandhi, & B. Wilpert (Eds.), *Organizational functioning in a cross-cultural perspective*. Kent, OH: Kent State University Press, 1979.

Zucker, L. G. The role of institutionalization in cultural persistence. *American Sociological Review*, 1977, *42*, 726–743.

Research in
Organizational Behavior

An Annual Series of Analytical Essays and Critical Reviews

Edited by **Barry M. Staw**
School of Business Administration, University of California, Berkeley
and **L.L. Cummings**
J.L. Kellogg Graduate School of Management, Northwestern University

REVIEWS: . . . "A new approach for the area of organizational behavior. . . The nine intermediate length essays presented here provide a valuable new facet. . . quality is variable — in this case from good to excellent. . . The text is highly recommended for acquisition but with the caveat that series acquisition will be required to maximize utility. . ." — *Choice*

". . . this collection is a well-written, scholarly contribution to other texts because of its integration of new theoretical considerations and critical literature review. It is very well organized and may be consulted frequently by those of us teaching management and administration in schools of social work." — *Administration in Social Work*

". . . a number of think pieces that accurately portray the complexities involved in understanding and explaining some aspect of organizational behavior. As could be expected, many of the chapters, primarily because they reflect the long-term research interests of the writers, are quite informative and challenging. Social scientists interested in interdisciplinary and/or applied organizational issues will find the book particularly informative." — *Contemporary Sociology*

Volume 1, 1979, 478 pp.
ISBN 0-89232-045-1

Edited by **Barry M. Staw,** *Graduate School of Management, Northwestern University*

CONTENTS: Editorial Statement, *Barry M. Staw.* **Beyond Open System Models of Organization,** *Louis R. Pondy, University of Illinois and Ian I. Mitroff, University of Pittsburgh.* **Cognitive Processes in Organizations,** *Karl E. Weick, Cornell University.* **Organizational Learning: Implications for Organizational Design,** *Robert Duncan and Andrew Weiss, Northwestern University.* **Organizational Design and Adult Learning,** *Douglas T. Hall and Cynthia V. Fukami, Northwestern University.* **Organizational Structure, Attitudes and Behaviors,** *Chris J. Berger, Purdue University and L. L. Cummings, University of Wisconsin - Madison.* **Toward a Theory of Organizational Socialization,** *John Van Maanen and Edgar H. Schein, Massachusetts Institute of Technology.* **Participation in Decision-Making: One More Look,** *Edwin A. Locke and David M. Schweiger, University of Maryland.* **Leadership: Some Empirical Generalizations and New Research Directions,** *Robert J. House and Mary L. Baetz, University of Toronto.* **Performance Appraisal Effectiveness: Its Assessment and Determinants,** *Jeffery S. Kane, Advanced Research Resources Organization and Edward E. Lawler, III, University of Michigan.* **Bibliography. Index.**

Volume 2, 1980, 368 pp.
ISBN 0-89232-099-0

Edited by **Barry M. Staw,** *Graduate School of Management, Northwestern University* and **L.L. Cummings,** *Graduate School of Business, University of Wisconsin*

CONTENTS: Editorial Statement, *Barry M. Staw, and L.L. Cummings.* **Construct Validity in Organizational Behavior,** *Donald P. Schwab, University of Wisconsin.* **Rationality and Justification in Organizational Life,** *Barry M. Staw, Northwestern University.* **Time and Work: Towards an Integrative Perspective,** *Ralph Katz, Massachusetts Institute of Technology.* **Collective Bargaining and Organizational Behavior Research,** *Thomas A. Kochan, Cornell University.* **Behavioral Research on Unions and Union Management,** *Jeanne Brett, Northern University.* **Institutionalization of Planned Organizational Change,** *Paul S. Goodman and Max Bazerman, Carnegie-Mellon University and Edward Conlon, Georgia Institute of Technology.* **Work Design in the Organizational Context,** *Greg R. Oldham, University of Illinois and J. Richard Hackman, Yale University.* **Organizational Growth Types: Lessons from Small Institutions,** *A. C. Filley and R. J. Aldag, University of Wisconsin.* **Interorganizational Processes and Organizational Boundary Activities,** *J. Stacy Adams, University of North Carolina.*

Volume 3, 1981, 356 pp.
ISBN 0-89232-151-2

Edited by **L.L. Cummings,** *Graduate School of Business, University of Wisconsin* and **Barry M. Staw,** *School of Business Administration, University of California, Berkeley*

CONTENTS: Editorial Statement, *L.L. Cummings and Barry M. Staw.* **Management as Symbolic Action: The Creation and Maintenance of Organizational Paradigms,** *Jeffrey Pfeffer, Stanford University.* **Relative Deprivation: A Theory of Distributive Injustice for an Era of Shrinking Resources,** *Joanne Martin, Stanford University.* **The Politics of Upward Influence in Organizations,** *Lyman Porter, University of California, Irvine, Robert W. Allen, University of California, Irvine, and Harold L. Angle, University of Minnesota.* **Organization as Power,** *David J. Hickson, University of Bradford, England, W. Graham Astley, University of Pennsylvania, Richard J. Bulter, University of Bradford, England, and David C. Wilson, University of Bradford, England.* **An Attributional Model of Leadership and the Poor Performing Subordinate,** *Terrence R. Mitchell, University of Washington, Stephen G. Green, University of Washington, and Robert Wood, University of Washington.* **Employee Turnover and Post-Decision Accommodation Processes,** *Richard M. Steers, University of Oregon, and Richard T. Mowday, University of Oregon.* **Attitudinal Processes in Organizations,** *Bobby J. Calder, Northwestern University, and Paul H. Schurr, University of North Carolina.* **Cultural Contingency and Capitalism in the Cross-National Study of Organizations,** *John Child, University of Aston, England.*

Volume 4, 1982, 364 pp.
ISBN 0-89232-147-4

Edited by **Barry M. Staw,** *Graduate School of Business Administration, University of California, Berkeley* and **L.L. Cummings,** *J.L. Kellogg Graduate School of Management, Northwestern University*

CONTENTS: Editorial Statement, *Barry M. Staw and L.L. Cummings.* **Organizational Life Cycles and Natural Selection Processes,** *John Freeman, University of California, Berkeley.* **The Evolution of Organizational Forms: Technology, Coordination and Control,** *Howard Aldrich and Susan Mueller, Cornell University.* **Bureaucratic Versus Profit Organization,** *Marshal W. Meyer, University of California, Riverside.* **The Meanings of Absence: New Strategies for Theory and Research,** *Gary Johns, Concordia University and Nigel Nicholson, University of Sheffield.* **Workers Participation in Management: An International Perspective,** *George Strauss, University of California, Berkeley.* **Unidimensional Measurement, Second Order Factor Analysis, and Causal Models,** *John E. Hunter, Michigan State University and David W. Gerbing, Baylor University.* **A Matrix Approach to Literature Reviews,** *Paul Salipante, Case Western Reserve University, William Notz, University of Manitoba and John Bigelow, Oregon State University.*

Volume 5, 1983, 350 pp.
ISBN 0-89232-271-3

Edited by **L.L. Cummings,** *J.L. Kellog Graduate School of Management, Northwestern University* and **Barry M. Staw,** *Graduate School of Business Administration, University of California, Berkeley*

CONTENTS: Editorial Statement, *L.L. Cummings and Barry M. Staw.* **Interactional Psychology and Organizational Behavior,** *Benjamin Schneider, University of Maryland.* **Paradigm and Praxis in Organizational Analysis,** *J. Kenneth Benson, University of Missouri.* **Time and Behavior in Organizations,** *Joseph E. McGrath and Nancy L. Rotchford, University of Illinois.* **The Use of Information in Organizational Decision Making: A Model and Some Propositions,** *Charles A. O'Reilly, University of California, Berkeley.* **Performance Appraisal: A Process Focus,** *Daniel R. Ilgen, Purdue University and Jack M. Feldman, University of Florida.* **Social Comparison Processes and Dynamic Conservatism,** *Ken K. Smith, Univeristy of Maryland.* **Employee Owned Companies,** *Arnold S. Tannenbaum, University of Michigan.* **Sex Bias in Work Settings: The Lack of Fit Model,** *Madeline E. Heilman, New York University.* **Organizational Drmography,** *Jeffrey Pfeffer, Stanford University.*

 **JAI PRESS INC., 36 Sherwood Place, P.O. Box 1678
Greenwich, Connecticut 06836**
Telephone: 203-661-7602   Cable Address: JAIPUBL

Research Annuals in
ECONOMICS

JAI PRESS INC.